THE COMPENSATION HANDBOOK

THE COMPENSATION HANDBOOK

A State-of-the-Art Guide to Compensation Strategy and Design

Lance A. Berger and
Dorothy R. Berger, Editors

Fourth Edition

McGraw-Hill

New York   San Francisco   Washington, D.C.   Auckland   Bogotá
Caracas   Lisbon   London   Madrid   Mexico City   Milan
Montreal   New Delhi   San Juan   Singapore
Sydney   Tokyo   Toronto

Library of Congress Cataloging-in-Publication Data

The compensation handbook: a state-of-the-art guide to compensation strategy and design / Lance A. Berger and Dorothy R. Berger, editors.—4th ed.
    p.   cm.
    Includes bibliographical references and index.
    ISBN 0-07-134309-1
    1. Compensation management—Handbooks, manuals, etc. I. Berger, Lance A II. Berger, Dorothy R.

    HF5549.5.C67H36   1999
    658.3'22—dc21   99-047477

McGraw-Hill

*A Division of The **McGraw·Hill** Companies*

1 2 3 4 5 6 7 8 9 0 DOC/DOC 9 0 9 8 7 6 5 4 3 2 1 0 9

ISBN 0-07-134309-1

The sponsoring editor for this book was Richard Narramore, the editing supervisor was Paul R. Sobel, and the production supervisor was Modestine Cameron. It was set in Times New Roman per the NM3 design by Deirdre Sheean of McGraw-Hill's Professional Book Group composition unit.

Printed and bound by R. R. Donnelley & Sons Company.

This publication is designed to provide accurate and authoritative information in regard to the subject matter covered. It is sold with the understanding that neither the author nor the publisher is engaged in rendering legal, accounting, or other professional service. If legal advice or other expert assistance is required, the services of a competent professional person should be sought.
—From a declaration of Principles jointly adopted by a Committee of the American Bar Association and a Committee of Publishers.

McGraw-Hill books are available at special quantity discounts to use as premiums and sales promotions, or for use in corporate training programs. For more information, please write to the Director of Special Sales, Professional Publishing, McGraw-Hill, Two Penn Plaza, New York, NY 10121-2298. Or contact your local bookstore.

 This book is printed on recycled, acid-free paper containing a minimum of 50% recycled de-inked fiber.

Contents

Part 3   Variable Compensation

Part 4   Executive Compensation

Part 7 International Compensation

Preface

TWENTY-SEVEN YEARS AGO, Milton L. Rock realized the need of compensation professionals to have an authoritative, practical, comprehensive reference book that would provide an all-inclusive guide for establishing and maintaining an effective wage and salary program for every employee over the vast range of industries. Milt assembled a corporate and academic advisory board to develop the format for this groundbreaking venture. The winning formula they created has brought the original *Handbook of Wage and Salary Administration* through two previous revisions to this fourth edition. All four editions provide timely and useful codified compensation methodologies and conceptual frameworks presented by recognized experts. Although the world has undergone enormous technological changes, companies have appeared or disappeared, companies have merged or downsized, job markets have evolved or dissolved, and workforce issues have increasingly come to include work environment, learning opportunities, and work-life benefits, the original handbook format remains a viable means for covering all compensation issues.

Thanks to the efforts of 56 compensation specialists, the fourth edition addresses current and future compensation issues with a similar hands-on, how-to-approach that was developed for the initial book. Chapters on computer technology, work-life issues, and global compensation have been added to address emerging themes. Many of the original chapter headings, although the chapters were revised to reflect changing conditions, are pertinent today.

We dedicate the fourth edition of *The Compensation Handbook* with appreciation and affection to Milton L. Rock, business guru and visionary.

Dorothy R. Berger

Lance A. Berger

Contributors

H. N. (Rug) Altmansberger   Goal Sharing Consultant, Overland Resource Group, Overland, Kansas (*Chapter 16*)

Hilary Belanger   Consultant, Aon Consulting, Philadelphia, Pennsylvania (*Chapter 10*)

John G. Belcher, Jr.   President, J. G. Belcher Associates, Houston, Texas (*Chapter 17*)

Dorothy R. Berger   Managing Director, Haverford Business Press, Haverford, Pennsylvania (*Chapter 2*)

Lance A. Berger   Chief Executive Officer, Lance A. Berger & Associates, Ltd., Bryn Mawr, Pennsylvania (*Chapters 1 and 3*)

Debra K. Besch   Principal, William M. Mercer, Inc., Philadelphia, Pennsylvania (*Chapter 40*)

Duncan Brown   Principal, Towers Perrin, London, England (*Chapter 12*)

Peter Chingos   National Director, Executive Compensation Consulting Practice, William M. Mercer, Inc., New York, New York (*Chapter 27*)

Bruce E. Clouser   Director Global Human Resource Solutions, PricewaterhouseCoopers LLP, Philadelphia, Pennsylvania (*Chapter 30*)

Neil K. Coleman   Vice President, Organization Resources Counselors, Inc., New York, New York (*Chapter 46*)

Jerome A. Colletti   Colletti-Fiss, LLC, Scottsdale, Arizona (*Chapter 23*)

Frederic W. Cook   Frederic W. Cook, & Co., Inc., New York, New York (*Chapter 38*)

Eugenie S. Dieck   Principal, William M. Mercer, Inc., Philadelphia, Pennsylvania (*Chapter 40*)

Jack Dolmat-Connell   Vice President and Managing Director, Wilson Group, Inc., Concord, Massachusetts (*Chapter 35*)

Mitchell Fein   President, Mitchell Fein, Inc., Hillsdale, New Jersey (*Chapter 18*)

Mary S. Fiss   Colletti-Fiss, LLC, Scottsdale, Arizona (*Chapter 23*)

Louise R. Fitzgerald   Principal, William M. Mercer, Inc., New York, New York (*Chapter 39*)

Luis R. Gomez-Meijia   Ph.D., Professor, Management Department, College of Business, Arizona State University, Tempe, Arizona (*Chapter 22*)

Deborah A. Grigson Consultant, Aon Consulting, Philadelphia, Pennsylvania (*Chapter 5*)

Steven E. Gross Principal, William M. Mercer, Inc., Philadelphia, Pennsylvania (*Chapter 21*)

Robert L. Heneman Ph.D., Director of Graduate Programs in Labor and Human Resources, and Associate Professor of Management and Human Resources in the Max M. Fisher College of Business, Ohio State University, Columbus, Ohio (*Chapter 11*)

Jim Holden Founder and Chief Executive Officer, Holden Corporation, Hoffman Estates, Illinois (*Chapter 24*)

Jeffrey S. Hyman Principal, Hewitt Associates LLC, Rowayton, Connecticut (*Chapter 28*)

Anne C. Ilsemann Partner, Arthur Andersen & Co., S.C., Philadelphia, Pennsylvania (*Chapter 15*)

Bernard Ingster Ph.D., Consultant, Human Resources Management, Philadelphia, Pennsylvania (*Chapters 6 and 13*)

Jay Jacobsen Performance Practice Manager, Holden Corporation, Hoffman Estates, Illinois (*Chapter 24*)

Alan M. Johnson Managing Director, Johnson Associates, New York, New York (*Chapter 26*)

James F. Kisela Chief Executive Officer, Work-Life Productions, Inc., Wayne, Pennsylvania, Faculty member, University of Phoenix (Philadelphia Campus) (*Chapter 43*)

Eric C. Larre Vice President, Aon Consulting, San Francisco, California (*Chapter 25*)

Geoffrey W. Latta Executive Vice President, Organization Resources Counselors, Inc., New York, New York (*Chapter 45*)

Peter V. LeBlanc CCP, Principal and Business Leader, Return on Human Capital Division, Sibson & Company, Raleigh, North Carolina (*Chapter 42*)

Gerald E. Ledford, Jr. Ph.D., Senior Consultant and Practice Leader, Employee Effectiveness and Rewards, Sibson & Company, Los Angeles, California (*Chapter 11*)

D. Terence Lichty Senior Corporate Compensation Consultant, The Raytheon Company, Lexington, Massachusetts (*Chapter 7*)

Michael Lockwood Vice President, Maritz, Inc., Fenton, Missouri (*Chapter 20*)

Marvin A. Mazer Vice President, Aon Consulting, Atlanta, Georgia (*Chapter 25*)

Jerry L. McAdams National Practice Leader, Reward and Recognition Systems, Watson Wyatt Worldwide, St. Louis, Missouri (*Chapter 20*)

Pearl Meyer Pearl Meyer & Partners, Inc., New York, New York (*Chapter 31*)

Gloria A. Nofsinger Senior Manager, Arthur Andersen & Company, S.C., Philadelphia, Pennsylvania (*Chapter 32*)

Johannes M. Pennings   Ph.D., Department of Management, The Wharton School, University of Pennsylvania, Philadelphia, Pennsylvania (*Chapter 29*)

Sydney R. Robertson   Executive Vice President, Organization Resources Counselors, Inc., New York, New York (*Chapter 44*)

Andrew S. Rosen   Vice President, Aon Consulting, Philadelphia, Pennsylvania (*Chapter 10*)

Ruth Ann Ross   Codirector, Ross Gainsharing Institute, Chapel Hill, North Carolina (*Chapter 19*)

Timothy L. Ross   Codirector, Ross Gainsharing Institute, Chapel Hill, North Carolina (*Chapter 19*)

Craig Eric Schneier   Ph.D., President, Craig Eric Schneier Associates, Princeton, New Jersey (*Chapter 37*)

Douglas G. Shaw   Principal, Craig Eric Schneier Associates, Princeton, New Jersey (*Chapter 37*)

Mark Simms   Manager, Arthur Andersen & Co., S. C., Philadelphia, Pennsylvania (*Chapter 15*)

Trista Slobodzian   Consultant, Aon Consulting, Philadelphia, Pennsylvania (*Chapter 9*)

Bruce I. Spiegel   Senior Vice President, Aon Consulting, Philadelphia, Pennsylvania (*Chapter 9*)

Gerald W. Stoffel   Vice President, Aon Consulting, Philadelphia, Pennsylvania (*Chapter 5*)

Rodger Stotz   Vice President, Maritz, Inc., Fenton, Missouri (*Chapter 20*)

Tracey B. Weiss   Ph.D., Tracey Weiss Associates, Philadelphia, Pennsylvania (*Chapter 33*)

Theresa Welbourne   Ph.D., Associate Professor of Organizational Behavior and Human Resource Management, University of Michigan Business School, Ann Arbor, Michigan (*Chapter 22*)

Thomas B. Wilson   President, Wilson Group, Inc., Concord, Massachusetts (*Chapter 36*)

Martin G. Wolf   Ph.D., President, Management Advisory Services, Inc., Jalisco, Mexico (*Chapters 4 and 14*)

Diane Yellin   Director Reward Information, Hay Group, Philadelphia, Pennsylvania (*Chapter 8*)

John Yurkutat   Director HIS Product Management, Hay Group, Philadelphia, Pennsylvania (*Chapter 8*)

Jack Zigon   President, Zigon Performance Group, Media, Pennsylvania (*Chapter 34*)

Patricia K. Zingheim   Ph.D., Partner, Schuster-Zingheim and Associates, Inc., Los Angeles, California (*Chapter 41*)

THE COMPENSATION HANDBOOK

PART

1

Introduction

THE ROLE OF COMPENSATION IN CORPORATE TRANSFORMATION

Lance A. Berger, Chief Executive Officer

Lance A. Berger & Associates, Ltd.

ALDOUS HUXLEY IN *BRAVE NEW WORLD* suggests that we could become a society so flooded with trivia that our citizens could no longer distinguish between fact and factoid. In today's highly competitive, media-driven environment, this obfuscation is enhanced by the super-hype created by sophisticated self-promoters emphasizing slick marketing approaches over meaningful research. These glib marketeers claim that their fad *du jour* is the holy grail that will solve all our problems. Sometimes the promoted fad is old wine in a new bottle, sometimes it is poisoned water packaged as expensive champagne, and sometimes it is really champagne.

Every new craze has some useful element of truth that shines through the haze of free-floating factoids and becomes a permanent part of our collective wisdom. Compensation professionals have to look for that wisdom and incorporate it into their collective body of knowledge. The collective body of truthful knowledge is critical because it is the basis upon which we make important decisions that support the continual, sometimes rapid transformation of organizations.

This chapter provides a conceptual framework, or decision-making tool, that incorporates the experience my colleagues and I have had, as well as our research, focus groups, and interviews and information we have learned from existing compensation literature, including this book. It is not a magic bullet, but with appropriate modifications, the framework can be a productive point of departure in the creation of a compensation program.

WORKFORCE MANAGEMENT

In my experience, compensation programs are complex financial distribution systems serving a multitude of overlapping, conflicting, and frequently unclear purposes. Chapters in this book describe how compensation programs are used to attract, retain, motivate, and reward employees. Certainly these goals are worthy and justifiably have remained part of our psyche for decades. I have found, however, that the real purpose and use of compensation programs, under which the previous rubrics are subsumed, is workforce management. This goal is not effectively met because companies are frequently clumsy and sometimes disingenuous in their application of both selective pay distribution and the support systems necessary to affect this activity.

My definition of *workforce management* is the *planned, selective* attraction and retention of specific individuals and classes of employees, derived from a human resources strategy, based on a business blueprint or success model. A pay premium is assigned to an individual, or group of individuals, because of their performance, potential future organizational contribution, special talent group, or some other value-differentiating characteristic. A workforce assessment process must be conducted to determine premium individual and talent classes in order to effectively implement a viable compensation system. Such an assessment system clearly identifies high-potential and high-performing employees as well as critical replacements and "hot" talent markets.

When "the rules of pay engagement" are ambiguous, inconsistent, or arbitrary, or perceived as such by employees, dysfunctional performance, unwanted turnover, and/or morale problems are triggered. Historically, company compensation programs sought internally to minimize differences in external pay markets, choosing to establish a small number of salary structures favoring internal equity over market conditions. Typically, companies selected the strongest pay markets as their reference points, or benchmarks. This approach, according to Martin Wolf (Chapter 4), resulted in overpaying some employee classes and individuals while underpaying others. My experience indicates that in these situations more employees were overpaid than underpaid, and this overpayment was a major contributor to unaffordable payrolls in the seventies and eighties. The overpay practices coupled with higher unemployment rates concealed the emerging pay gaps in certain talent markets and increased the likelihood of losing top talent and retaining mediocre performers.

The "peanut butter" approach of spreading dollars evenly over the workforce was destined for obsolescence as all sizes and types of U.S. businesses began to realign their strategies, operations, and human resources to effectively compete on a global basis. This natural alignment process, combined with a growing economy and changing workforce demography, led us to reaffirm what we already knew: There is no single approach to employee pay that works in all situations, and whichever approach is used will most likely require adaptation as a company's business situation changes in a rapidly evolving business environment. Additionally, it is likely that one pay system will not work for all employee groups, let alone premium subclasses of these groups. What fits best today may be history tomorrow. The time, cost, and long-range credibility of an implementation plan must be carefully considered because it could become obsolete before it is completed and it may not be applicable to all covered employees.

Companies are always transforming themselves. Most of the transformational changes are small but have large cumulative effects over time. Some transformations are major, and these are becoming more frequent. Given the transformational nature of companies, and specifically the continual need for managing workforce transformation, the question of how to structure transformational compensation systems must be addressed. My experience and research confirms that the answer is found in the reconciliation of business phases (stage of growth), multiple external talent (pay) market demands, and pay techniques. Successfully reconciling these forces requires not only a high level of technical expertise but also a certain boldness and willingness to embrace change.

What is *transformation?* It is a situation that is created when a company anticipates and responds to changes in its customer base, competitive environment, or internal capacity to deliver a service or product. Based both on external forces and internal capacity for adaptability, the magnitude and speed of change will vary within companies. Internal change readiness is related to the alignment of a company's strategy, operations, culture, and reward systems. Any perceptible change in one or more of the first three elements in any business unit should trigger a reassessment of compensation systems. When a change trigger destabilizes an organization, a snapshot of the company's alignment of compensation with its existing strategy, operations, and culture should be taken and its targeted alignment or blueprint must be developed. The gap between current and future compensation becomes the basis for developing a transformational plan.

Both the snapshot and blueprint should contain the following elements of pay strategy: identification of pay aspects of *each* talent market based on sources of recruitment and turnover activities; mix of compensation (base salary, annual and long-term incentives, benefits, and work-life factors); and competitive level. Within its total level of affordability, a company will manage a portfolio of pay strategies that will allocate compensation to individuals and classes of employees based on their premium value to the company. The goal is not to lose anyone that the company can't afford to lose, while encouraging turnover among individuals and employee groups that are not as essential to the long-range business and human resources plan.

Transformational compensation activities involve realigning one or more of the pay components that include external pay market, competitive level, mix, or pay technique (delivery system). Transformational compensation necessitates a willingness to alter programs when change occurs and to focus on greater customization of pay packages. To this end, this chapter presents a series of tools that may help practitioners better formulate their options for compensation decisions.

THE ALIGNMENT MODEL

The Change Management Handbook[1] describes a process for establishing a pay strategy and illustrates how pay is aligned with phases of the business cycle. Figure 1.1 illustrates an alignment model. This model should be customized to the industry of each business unit within a corporation.

The most difficult transformations occur when a business unit rapidly shifts to a different phase of growth and its internal alignment is no longer appropriate. This is evident in the radical adaptations made by companies through downsizing, mergers, and acquisitions. It is also true when smaller companies experience a deceleration in their growth rate and companies of all sizes experience sudden growth. The alignment model suggests that radical and sudden change requires a different culture and, in turn, a different reward system. Regrettably, an existing culture may not support the new business scenario. Additionally, a company may not be able to adjust its pay packages in accordance with the implications of customization in Fig. 1.2. The success of the realignment of internal change elements (strategy, operations, human resources, and compensation) will determine the survival and effectiveness of the business.

The following tools were developed to assist in making an informed choice when change triggers affect internal alignment. The tools are intended to be illustrative and not exhaustive. For details of the various discussed techniques, see chapters throughout the book. The reader should refer to the appendix to find additional information that expands upon the tabular data in this chapter.

---

[1]L. A. Berger, M. J. Sikora, and D. R. Berger, *The Change Management Handbook: A Road Map to Corporate Transformation* (New York: McGraw-Hill, 1994).

FIGURE 1.1 **Alignment model.** *(Copyright © 1999 Lance A. Berger & Associates, Ltd.)*

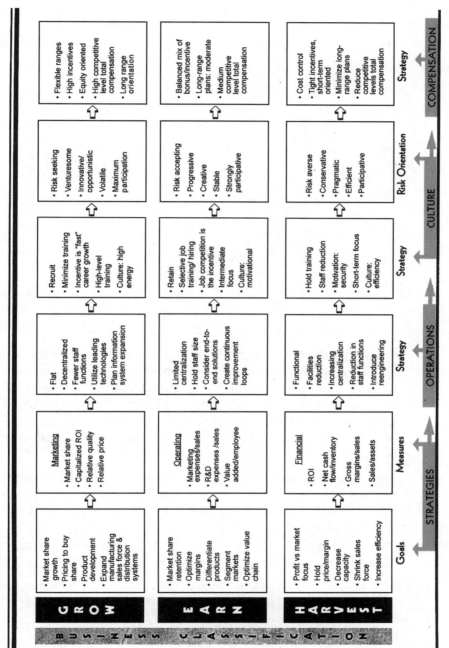

FIGURE 1.2   Customizing a compensation system.

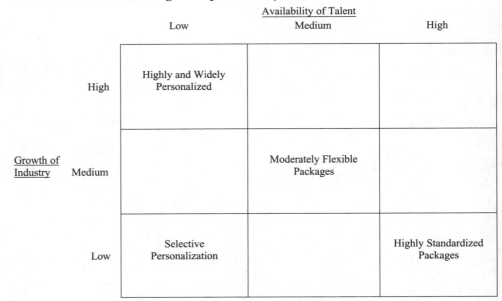

The tools are organized into three sections. The sections are as follows:

- *Business situations and pay techniques (Figure 1.3):* This chart relates 9 different business situations to 16 separate pay techniques. Each cell contains X's reflecting the effectiveness of the technique associated with the business situation. For example, group, team, and opportunity sharing incentives are very effective in times of financial difficulty, and broadbanding is effective when there are current or expected frequent changes in job content.

- *Pay techniques, descriptive matrix (Figure 1.4):* This chart summarizes four important characteristics associated with the pay techniques identified in Figure 1.3. For example, key contributor programs must be supported by a credible process for identifying must-keep employees, and profit sharing requires a communication process focusing on a common fate for all employees.

- *Culture and pay techniques (Figure 1.5):* These charts summarize eight culture considerations involved in pay techniques. For example, profit sharing could add to employee dissatisfaction if trust in management were low.

Under the most successful scenario, a business should plan a compensation transformation before it is destabilized by market, competitive, or internal change triggers. A company's potential for survival is increased by fast response and quick

FIGURE 1.3 Business situations and pay techniques.

Business Situation/ Pay Techniques	High Cyclicality	Emerging Business	Financial Difficulty	Inflated Wages	Controlling Turnover	Down-sizing	Culture Change	Simulate Entrepreneurship	Frequent Job Content Shifts
Profit Sharing	XXXXX	XX	XXX				XXXXX	XX	
Subjective Perf. Bonus	XXXXX	XXX			XX				
Opportunity/ Gain Sharing	XXXXX		XXXXX				XXXXX		XXX
Group/Team Incentive			XXXXX				XXXXX		XXX
Individual Incentive	XXX		XXX				XXXXX	XXXXX	
Key Contributor Programs	XX	XXXXX			XXXXX		XXXXX	XX	XXX
Competency, Knowledge or Skill-Based Pay			XXXXX				XXX		XXXXX
Broadbanding	XXX		XXX		XXXX		XXXXX		XXXX
Long-Term Plans	XX	XXXXX			XXXXX		XXXXX	XXXXX	
Pay Cuts			XXXXX	XXXXX		XXX			
Pay Freeze			XXXXX	XXXXX		XXXXX			
Two-Tiered Pay System *				XXXXX		XXXXX			
Lump Sum in Lieu of Increase			XXXXX	XXXXX					
Extended Pay Review Intervals			XXXXX	XXXXX					
Work-Life		XXXXX			XXXXX		XXXXX		
Non-Monetary	XXX	XXX		XXX	XXXX		XXXXX		XXXX

Xs indicate the effectiveness of the technique
* New employee at lower rate than current employees

adaptation. The following simplified steps can be helpful during the transformation process:

1. *Determine the direction of the transformation, that is, the acceleration or deceleration of growth.* In general, the amount of *leverage* (percentage variable pay) will increase or decrease with the projected rate of business growth with the specific amount varying by individual, organization level, and work unit. There may be problems with employee cultures that are risk averse or risk oriented and that may not therefore fit a business shift. Poor culture fit may delay the complete and timely introduction of a new pay plan.

FIGURE 1.4 Pay techniques: Descriptive matrix.

Pay Technique	How does this technique work?	What business situations lead companies to consider this technique?	What conditions are important for this technique to succeed?	What are the risks of using this technique?

Profit Sharing	• Share the profit once-a-year.
	• Profit can be taken as:
	  - Cash/stock
	  - Deferred for retirement
	  - Split between options above
	• Promotes employee involvement in improving profits.
		• Underachieving financial performance.
		• Need to lower relative labor costs.
		• Desire to create sense of common fate.
		• Shift from entitlement mentality to performance.
		• Quality orientation.
			• Sense of common fate.
			• Management credibility/trust.
			• Employee involvement/ participation.
			• Open communications.
			• "Accurate" financial statements.
				• Profitable years are rare.
				• Employees view plan as a benefit.
				• Link between individual payout and organization performance is weak.
				• Expectations are not met.
				• Management uses the plan as a low pay supplement.
				• Application is forced.
				• Employees focus on short-term results.
				• Uncontrollable factors exist (adversely impact profits).

Subjective Performance Bonus	• Unexpected bonuses. • Intent is to "present" behavioral models AXZto the organization.	• Rapid change. • Trust, support, and commitment on everyone's part. • Good communications • Use of reinforcement in addition to other alternative rewards.	• Credible performance. • Credible management judges. • Sound communication system.	• Weak selection. • Poor communications. • Inequity of awards. • Does not inspire most employees.
Opportunity/Gain Sharing (Small Group, Rucker, Scanlon, Improshare, Team)	• A group of highly interdependent workers is selected. • Piece rate or measured day, standard hours, sales, R&D, technical milestones or unit measures can be used.	• Need to work in groups. • Highly interdependent employees. • Group can influence its own work.	• Group must be able to collaborate and work together. • Measures must be group not individual. • All awards paid on group results. • Employees trust management. • Group identity.	• Group unable to influence end result. • Payouts may not relate to corporate performance. • Groups sometimes act to destroy another group. • Manipulation of standards.
Group/Team Incentive	• Rewards quality, production, project milestones or other financial or operational objectives. • "Shares" profit according to pre-determined formula. • Targeted incentive awards vary based on organization level, total targeted compensation.	• Need to improve productivity and quality. • Shrinking margins. • Focus on information sharing, employee commitment/ involvement and teamwork.	• Management credibility/trust. • Employee opportunity to impact/ improve. • Sufficient demand/market potential. • Workforce interdependence. • Adequate support systems. • Management acceptance of employee work. • Commitment to change. • Strong measures.	• People can't work together. • Lack of top management commitment. • Use as a "Band-Aid". • Inadequate information sharing/ employee involvement. • Inadequate design, administration, and follow-through. • Lack of understanding of risks. • Payouts for gains are not a result of employee efforts. • Weak measures.

FIGURE 1.4   Pay techniques: Descriptive matrix. (*Continued*)

Pay Technique	How does this technique work?	What business situations lead companies to consider this technique?	What conditions are important for this technique to succeed?	What are the risks of using this technique?

Targeted Individual Incentives	• Once a year:
	  – Develop a pool or fund based on affordability, performance, and pay.
	  – Distribute to employees.
	• There is a threshold before a payout can be made.
	• Typical focus on financial measures resulting from cascading goals.
	• Formula for payout ties to corporate goals and measures.
	• Total value of pool ties to total compensation levels.
	• Allocate funds on the basis of individuals or groups.
		• Performance focus.
		• Affordability
		• Goals/measures focus.
			• Risk accepting or entrepreneurial culture.
			• Measurable results and good follow-up.
			• Attainable goals.
			• Individuals influence results.
				• Organization doesn't define performance measures.
				• Entitlement culture resists risk based pay.
				• Decisions are not under executive control.
				• Organization unable to objectively judge performance.

Targeted Individual Incentives – Piece Rate	• Pay individuals for each unit produced with predetermined amounts of money for each unit (typically sole performance measure). • Differentiate base rate on levels of production. • Create a clear link between pay and performance.	• Need to motivate employees in de-skilled environment.	• Simple, repetitive manufacturing process. • Results of the work are easy to measure. • Minimum amount of interdependence. • Minimum need for cooperation. • Trust • Job security.	• Employees create counter - productive behavior trying to "beat the system". • High costs to maintain the incentive system because every time a technological change is made or a new product is introduced, new rates need to be considered.
Targeted Individual Incentives – Measured Day	• Fixed pay assuming employees maintain specified level of performance. • Guaranteed incentive payment in advance. • Pay does not fluctuate in the short-term.	• Inappropriate condition for piece rate. • Long job cycles.	• Total commitment of management/employees. • Effective work measurement/ control system. • Logical pay structure.	• Worker ingenuity has lowered the standard (used to create measured day work rate). • Relieves pressure to perform. • Escalates labor cost (additions to staff).
Key Contributor Programs	• Individuals with historical high performance are priced in plan (usually in technical or R&D). • Special compensation in addition to traditional pay is given (stock/cash). • There is usually a waiting period to receive the award.	• Strong need for innovation culture. • Retention is imperative for certain employees. • Business is in growth stage. • Special pay market conditions.	• Able to clearly identify "must keep" employees. • Environment must provide for individual contribution. • Employee has resources and can influence resources.	• Selection of recipients not credible. • Non-recipients may be discouraged.
Competency, Knowledge or Skill-Based Pay	• Determine pay progression based on competencies (skills, behaviors, knowledge) associated with superior performance.	• Large skilled, technical or professional workforce and/or presence of career ladders. • Focus on work teams and need for workforce flexibility. • Slower growth rates/fewer opportunities. • Linkage to broadbanding.	• Well-defined position competencies. • Value person, not job. • Well-developed training and assessment programs. • Willingness to pay for unused capacity.	• Weaken the pay-for-performance link. • Majority of employees with limited growth opportunities. • Unaffordable labor cost. • Investment on faith.

FIGURE 1.4 Pay techniques: Descriptive matrix. (*Continued*)

Pay Technique	How does this technique work?	What business situations lead companies to consider this technique?	What conditions are important for this technique to succeed?	What are the risks of using this technique?
Broadbanding	• Pay structures which consolidate large numbers of grades and ranges into a smaller number of "bands" (ranges) with wide salary spreads between minimum and maximum.	• Reengineering. • Downsizing. • Organization restructuring. • Fewer upward job prospects. • Need for multi-skilled employees. • Focus on career development.	• Current program is not credible. • Company has commitment, money, and time for major change. • High level of trust between management and supervisors/managers. • Viable/credible performance and career development systems are in place. • Workforce is change ready and a crisis is perceived.	• Lack of trust in management. • Poor understanding of broadbanding. • Poor implementation. • Loss of control over compensation. • Cultural resistance. • "Old wine in a new bottle." • Inadequate support systems (performance/management). • Low sense of urgency by management/employees.
Long-Term Plans	• Employees are provided with special forms of pay based on results over a 3 to 5 year period. • Stock options give employees the right to purchase shares at a fixed price over a time period, creating a long-term financial interest; alternative stock plans can be used. • Some long-term plans use cash instead of stock.	• Need to focus on strategic issues and measures. • Attraction of key talent. • Retention of key talent. • Need to create sense of common fate. • Need to align more closely with shareholders. • Encourage entrepreneurship, particularly in start-ups.	• Measures must be correctly established. • Employees must be willing to take risks. • Management/employee trust.	• Options "under water". • Limited participation in plan. • Windfalls can produce exaggerated payouts. • Poor measures of competitiveness. • Overly complex stock and surrogate programs.
Work-Life	• Package of benefits designed to help balance conflicting demands of family, personal life, and work. • Provide childcare, paid time off, family services, flexible work arrangements, eldercare, convenience services.	• Recruiting in tight market. • Meet specific needs of workforce. • Strategy is to become "employer of choice." • Employees wanting to make culture statement.	• Accurate determination of workforce needs (survey). • High levels of communication. • Cost/benefit analysis. • Employee/management trust. • Ongoing monitoring. • Pay at or above market.	• Inability of supervisors and managers to implement program. • Pay levels not competitive. • Low employee perception of value of benefits. • Insufficient management commitment.
Non-Monetary Awards	• Recognition of outstanding performance using non-cash awards. • Focuses on creating awareness of successful behaviors exhibited by recognized employees (role models). • Awards include: merchandise, travel, time-off, symbolic (trophy), praise. • Awards can be individual, group or team.	• Supplement to sound cash programs. • Retention of key people in tough market. • Helpful when goals change frequently. • Can apply across most employee populations.	• Recognized employee behaviors must be credible to organization. • Award "judges" must be credible. • Communications system explaining program before and after awards must be in place.	• Rewarding wrong behaviors. • Rewarding weak or wrong results. • Using non-cash in place of cash program.

FIGURE 1.5 Culture and pay techniques.

Pay Technique	Role of Employee /Management Trust	Achievement Orientation	Capacity to Measure Performance	Current Compensation Issues
Profit Sharing	Could add to dissatisfaction if trust is low.	Culture must be performance oriented.	Can be used where accounting data is all that is available.	Consider total compensation effect.
Subjective Performance Bonus	Trust level varies with individual's relationship with management.	May be counter-productive in risk adverse organization.	Successful plans have good measurement.	
Opportunity/ Gain Sharing	Most need neutral to positive level. Standards are an issue.		Requires good cost of goods and labor data.	
Group Incentive	Should be positive. Standards are an issue.		Varies with degree and focus desired.	An additive built on sound base salary, not a substitute.
Targeted Individual Incentive	Perceived attainability of goal is critical.	Works best with high achievement individuals. Largely dependent on culture.	Objectives must be measurable.	Consider total compensation effect.
Key Contributor Programs	If negative, participant backlash could be a problem.		Able to identify key contributors.	An additive built on sound base salary, not a substitute.
Competency, Knowledge or Skill-Based Pay			Must be able to assess level of knowledge or skill.	Can be expensive. Must be justified by impact on productivity.
Broadbanding	Aspects of application requires high levels of trust at all organization levels or could be perceived as arbitrary.	Lack of quality performance management system and performance culture will negate approach.	Must have solid linkages between corporate strategy and performance measures down to individual and/or team level.	Can disrupt and distract organization or improve morale, performance, and organization strength when compared to existing system
Long-Term Plans	Trust in equitable assignment and appropriateness of measures is critical.	Achievement orientation must be focused over a longer term.	Must be able to select appropriate measures which satisfy all stakeholders.	Predicting long-term stock payouts can be a source of conflict.
Work-Life Benefits	Employees must believe management is sincere and supportive.			Compensation levels must at least equal and preferably exceed pay market.
Non-Cash	Potential for arbitrary decisions makes it important to make basis of reward explicit.	Does not require organization wide achievement orientation.	There should be clear measures of behaviors and results.	Compensation levels should approximate pay markets. Awards are taxable.

FIGURE 1.5 Culture and pay techniques. (*Continued*)

Pay Technique	Power of the Technique	Potential Impact on Employee Compensation	Organizational Issues	Culture Characteristics	Organizational Pressure For Performance
Profit Sharing	Diffuse unless backed by culture.	Can be demoralizing if no profit to share.	A good option where measurement capability is limited.	Most compatible with a group-oriented culture.	Can reinforce and help raise level of demand.
Subjective Performance Bonus	Arouses desire to do well, but does not focus employee in advance.	Unpredictable.	Often found where direction is unclear.	Focuses on individual accountability.	Can be successful if clearly defined.
Opportunity/ Gain Sharing	Powerful if done right. Effective at focusing efforts.	Upside 5% - 15%. Downside varies by plan type.		Fits a group-oriented culture best.	Supports emphasis on performance. Adds peer pressure.
Group Incentive	Strongest with small cohesive group.	Upside potential controlled by group output.	Clear goal-setting needed.	Requires a group-oriented culture.	Fits medium to high demand.
Targeted Individual Incentive	Strongest if achievable cash award.	Opportunity must be at least 10 % – 15% to have an impact.	Clear goal-setting needed.	Totally focused on individual accountability.	Good for high demand situations.
Key Contributor Programs	Powerful for retention. Recognition can be motivational.	Must be sizable and not very variable.	Must be limited to "truly key" contributors.	Will culture accept "individual deals?"	Aimed at retaining proven performers.
Competency, Knowledge or Skill-Based Pay	Objective is workforce flexibility, not incentive.	Should be large enough to make acquiring skills worthwhile.			Most useful as part of a broader productivity effort.
Broadbanding	Relieves employee frustration over perceived loss of career opportunities and pay growth. Focuses on performance when support systems are in place.	Some redistribution of pay based on perceived individual actual/potential contribution. Need for adequate assessment tools.	Organization commitment to implement and support. Strong rationale is rapid organizational change.	Tolerance of ambiguity necessary or bands will be structured similar to grades. High commitment to communications.	Better for medium demand. Unproven in creating high performance demand.
Long-Term Plans	Driven by significant capital accumulation.	Maximize or minimize competitiveness of total compensation.		Executives must be able to collaborate and sacrifice unit for company performance.	High performance pressures optimize success.
Work-Life Benefits	Works best as loyalty and morale builder. Helps recruitment and retention.	Reduces employee out-of-pocket expenses.	Communications, supporting policies and procedures, orientation of supervisors is key.	Works best in IT, R&D and related cultures and in younger workforce.	Fits all situations.
Non-Cash	Role modeling and public recognition can be an incentive for future behavior.	Should make no impact.	Good option when goals are unclear or changing frequently.	Highly collaborative cultures might resist individual or group recognition.	Fits all situations (individual, group, or team).

2. *Determine the amount affordable by the business unit over a 2- to 3-year period.* Annual increases must be distributed selectively to critical employees or classes of employees to avoid a crippling turnover.

3. *Identify the characteristics of each discrete pay market in which the company competes for talent.* Remember that these competitors may not be business competitors. The list can be found in recruitment sources, turnover analyses, and internal promotion data. Initially each pay market should be discretely segmented, although they may converge or remain separate and then change over time.

4. *Within each pay market and within the company as a whole, assess the competitive level of total human resources cost (include base salary, variable pay, benefits, training, education, work-life, and other relevant programs) of the workforce.* This will help further set the limits of affordability and the allocation of pay since the costs of some employee groups may be too high or low in relationship to their value creating contribution.

5. *With each pay market, determine the difficulty of recruitment, time to recruit, turnover rate, skill levels required, and training necessary.* Difficulties in recruitment when combined with long recruitment times, high turnover rates, strong skill requirements, and high internal training costs will require a greater allocation of pay than is required for talent groups and individuals scoring low on these dimensions.

6. *Assess affordability based on the feasibility of basing more pay on incremental profits.* A company can afford to pay a higher competitive level if variable pay is funded by incremental profit. However, the risk factor of greater leverage may not suit the business culture, and its introduction might further destabilize a workforce in transition.

7. *Assess change readiness.* If the culture won't support the requirements of business, organization, and human resources alignment, then the compensation transformation might have to be geared to the rate of actual culture transformation, or perhaps slightly leading it, to communicate a new business paradigm.

8. *Identify pay techniques relevant to each pay market.* Once preliminary competitive levels and degree of leverage are established for each market, consideration for specific pay techniques can follow. The outlined approach is as follows:
   - Identify pay techniques associated with your particular business situation (Figure 1.3).
   - Assess the nature of business techniques using Figure 1.4.
   - Refine the assessment of pay techniques using the culture factors described in Figure 1.5.

- Use the final list of options to develop a more detailed understanding of implementation mechanisms using chapters in this book and other literature as appropriate.

9. *Utilize succession and workforce assessment to customize compensation programs for must-keep employees.*

10. *Develop customized pay strategies, administrative processes, performance management, and career management processes for each talent pay market by combining those with similar characteristics and segmenting others that do not fit together.*

11. *Communicate new programs.* Describe the basis of each employee's compensation clearly and honestly to your workforce.

This chapter's purpose is to summarize some key compensation elements that have become part of our collective wisdom. The goal is to provide a prototypical framework and set of tools to help overcome some of the trivia and hype in order to distinguish fact from factoid. The empirical basis is my experience and my colleagues' experiences, a study of 350 companies of various sizes representing different industries and stages of development, focus groups, literature, and interviews. The only conclusion that can be drawn from our review is that different approaches will work under different circumstances, in different times, and in different places.

Compensation practitioners involved in company transformation should be mindful of the words of Machiavelli, the great human resources professional, *"It must be considered that there is nothing more difficult to carry out, nor more doubtful of success, nor more dangerous to handle than to initiate a new order of things."*

C H A P T E R

2

MILLENNIUM COMPENSATION TRENDS

Dorothy R. Berger, Managing Director

Haverford Business Press

A s we enter the **2000s, compensation practices** are being shaped by supply and demand influences within the labor market, as well as by an enlightened employee pool whose issues include work environment and learning opportunities as well as salary and benefits. Many workers are willing to gamble on themselves, and often on their employers, by opting for equity in their companies over larger base salaries. Workers are increasingly viewing themselves as self-employed as they build competencies and demand challenges whether within a large corporation, small company, or as an outsourcer.

SELF-EMPLOYMENT TRENDS

Mindsets are changing as quickly as technology, and more and more people are opting for self-employment. In 1999, 20 percent of the labor force was self-employed, and that percentage was growing daily. Moreover, both large and small companies are increasingly eager to give people work without giving them a job. In these cases, a mutually beneficial arrangement between outsourcer and company is developed. The company engages a skilled worker at a fixed project or hourly rate without making a long-term commitment or paying benefits. The worker is paid premium dollars for his or her skills and is given personal flexibility. Outsourcers use corporate jobs to garner the transferable skills and experiences needed to sell themselves again and again to companies. Many outsourcers emerge from downsized companies. They possess highly marketable skills developed within a corporation, and they may eventually even work as consultants for their former employers.

JOBS AS PERSONAL DEVELOPMENT OPPORTUNITIES

Talent migrates quickly as individuals are enticed to move on to bigger challenges. More and more workers are living a nomadic kind of existence. As soon as they land a job, they begin hunting for their next challenge. A chance to develop their skills is usually more appealing than immediate monetary payoffs. These individuals choose to build their skills and résumés in a variety of companies that may even be in the same industry. "Companies will try to buy experience rather than grow it organically"—a growing trend that has been observed by Michael Snipes of Allstate Insurance Company. Ambitious workers, recognizing this trend, will seek training and development while they are with a company and will move on if learning opportunities present themselves elsewhere.

Even those remaining within the confines of one company seek various positions in order to gain knowledge and develop skills. Increasing numbers of workers view their careers as skill building rather than ladder climbing. They take an entrepreneurial approach by viewing themselves as in house free-lancers. Companies can call upon these versatile individuals to wear many hats and tackle projects on a demand basis. These workers are assets to their companies for the length of their tenure and are very marketable commodities when they choose or are forced to move on.

THE RAPID RISE OF THE SMALL COMPANY

As we enter the new millennium, most people work in small companies. All real job creation over the past 20 years has been in small companies. The mergers and acquisitions trend has been escalating, and the result has been that the combined, larger companies have been shedding overlapping departments and employees. Many of the released employees have been moving into smaller companies where pay packages are competitive with the former, larger employers. Small companies do not employ human resources professionals, but they have the capacity to customize reward systems based on the specific talent markets in which they recruit. They offer high levels of opportunities for personal growth, equity in the company, and flexible work-life styles. Companies marketing technology innovation are especially productive for those seeking new challenges and enormous opportunity.

As Wally Nichols, executive director of the American Compensation Association (ACA), points out, "Companies with fewer than 100 people pay for competencies. If workers can do several jobs, they are paid for it. Large companies are trying to re-create environments found in small entrepreneurial workplaces." Big companies will study and survey small companies since their reward practices will make them the employer-of-choice in critical talent markets.

JOBS AS SUPPORTING PERSONAL LIFESTYLES

Workers, having personally experienced or watched their parents or fellow workers undergo downsizing, feel little loyalty toward their employers. Their personal needs are their first and often only priority. Furthermore, many workers are attempting "to gain control of their lives," and to do so, they are willing to make career concessions or work for companies that grant desired work-life benefits. Some workers are seeking flexible work schedules so that they can balance family obligations and avocational pursuits, while others are seeking a certain lifestyle while at work. Work-life issues, such as job sharing, maternity leave, family emergency leave, family nonemergency leave, on-site child care, and on-site medical care, are growing in importance when workers choose among potential employers. Alan Ritchie, vice president for compensation benefits and health services at Lucent Technologies, iterates, "Workers are willing to trade a lot of noneconomic lifestyle factors for money."

THE GLOBAL WORK COMMUNITY

In 1999 about 3.3 million Americans lived and worked outside the United States. According to the State Department, this number quadrupled over the preceding 30 years and is still growing. Workers are willing to gamble on a fixed-term expatriate situation in order to gain valuable experiences and adventure in working for a foreign company on foreign soil. On the other hand, more and more foreign nationals work for American companies or international conglomerates on their native soil or other locations.

The Internet has made it possible for companies to recruit worldwide. Many companies have already discovered the advantages of placing their help-wanted ads on the worldwide net. This trend will certainly escalate as Internet access reaches more segments of the global community. Worldwide recruiting will necessitate that compensation philosophies become global. A benefit to soliciting résumés on a global scale is gaining knowledge of worldwide pay requirements for listed jobs. According to Michael Snipes of Allstate Insurance Company, "There is a growing need to design compensation schemes to enforce business objectives on a global basis." International compensation practices will be a major issue as global mergers continue to rise and companies continue to spread their wings beyond home borders.

A SEGMENTED SELLER'S MARKET

"Work environments are being driven by a seller's market," indicates Wally Nichols of the ACA. Although the seller's market does not reach into all positions or industries, there is still a growing tolerance for different behaviors in key areas where demand is greater than the talent supply. Employers are willing to make concessions in dress, work habits, and so on, in order to fill job vacancies. Recognition of talent market differences by corporations has generally been benign and unsystematic. As time goes on, corporations will take a more disciplined and visible approach to tracking these issues.

The increased variation in talent markets is forcing employers to recognize that reward packages are defined differently by different groups. Reward systems developed by employers in "in-demand" talent markets have created enormous pressure on corporations to manage talent market diversity in a fair and equitable manner.

"This seller's market will be further exacerbated by an aging baby-boomer population," points out Larry Acorn of United Technologies. "In 5 to 10 years there will be a major exodus from the workforce, and the competition for highly skilled, highly educated individuals will increase accordingly." Yet many people will retire much later in life due to an older social security age and attractive retention programs put in place by companies reluctant to lose valuable talent.

Job growth combined with shortages of talent in selected employee markets, further exacerbated by high levels of competition, have forced and will continue to force organizations to favor market factors over broad-based internal equity as the basis for reward strategies. As Barbara D'Ulisse Morrow, compensation professional at Sunoco, indicates, "There is a shift from considering the *job* as a major pay determinant to considering a hybrid of the *job, person, and the market.*" Different employee supply and demand characteristics in different talent markets will force a segmented approach to reward strategies since there is a growing differential in pay in these markets. Segmentation will continue to escalate due to the ongoing and rapid restructuring of companies and industries resulting from global competition, mergers and acquisitions, industry restructuring, and technology changes. The future may bring an increased pay gap between low-skilled and technically skilled workers as the supply and demand curve escalates in favor of technical skills. Alan Ritchie of Lucent Technologies sees the spread between the low end and high end of the pay spectrum increasing.

Companies not addressing the talent market segmentation issue quickly and efficiently run the risk of being unable to attract or retain employees while overpaying or underpaying all or part of their workforce. Human resources staffs will increasingly turn to traditional market research tools and business strategy technology to address the talent market segmentation issue in a way similar to sales and marketing departments. Market research, marketing, and product management terminology will become incorporated into the human resources jargon. Compensation surveys will deal with supply and demand forecasts in addition to compensation statistics.

THE VISIBLE AND INVISIBLE PAYCHECKS

The *new compensation model* includes both a *visible paycheck,* which reflects base salary, incentives, and benefits, and an *invisible paycheck,* which includes work-life and personal growth incentives. Each of these compensation components has a value to different talent segments and a cost to the company. Talent markets composed of workers with similar competencies will be cross generational with regional and cultural differences as well. The employer-of-choice will recruit individuals within a talent pool with the "ideal" package to meet both employee and business requirements.

Wally Nichols calls the next 10 to 20 years the "age of the employee." He foresees four areas as the bargaining points for employees when looking at total rewards in a job: base salary, benefits, work environment, and learning and training. He sees learning and training as gaining in importance when employees make the decision to go with one employer over another. "Companies will be compelled to allow people to expand opportunities and marketability."

Therese Voevodsky, president of Compensation Data Source, terms customized pay packages "cafeteria-style compensation." She too sees increased collaboration between employer and employee in designing the total package. The rules of the cafeteria approach will likely be based on traditional approaches to product-service design and delivery concepts. A shell containing all components of reward, the competitive level targeted for a specific market for all components, and the mix of the components will be the working model.

Alan Ritchie of Lucent Technologies foresees a "customization of compensation." He sees technology allowing companies to move away from pay programs for groups of employees to programs for individual employees. He believes that "the trend is away from internal equity." He, like Nichols, looks ahead to contracts, and he sees contracts as renewable on a project basis. "The company will establish the economic value of a specific job with the parameters of the job determined by the strategic needs of the company. When company requirements mesh with an employee's needs, a contract will be written for specific goals and time spans." Ritchie foresees the day when severance packages will disappear. If employers utilize customized compensation correctly, only motivated, directed, highly skilled individuals will be hired for a specified project.

This type of customization will inevitably affect the compensation professional, and the impact will filter into all levels of management. Nichols warns that "old-line managers will have a hard time adapting." HR departments will construct talent market strategies in the same way that marketing and sales departments handle competitive service or product strategies. They will use internal employee surveys in a more targeted fashion to define and understand the reward system strategies valued by different talent market segments. Practitioners, using a cafeteria compensation approach, will design individual reward packages within total-cost parameters and make them available to line management for their use.

The method of valuing employee contributions within the company will shift from job, accountability, and dollar dimensions to the person, current competencies, and projected résumé value. Internal equity will become more focused on market value of employee competencies, personal achievement, and future potential.

Barry Bingham of Monsanto summarizes the need for company management to "throw away the crutches" and focus on "pay market, a person's qualifications within that pay market, and performance" when developing compensation strategies. "The bureaucratic processes such as grades, ranges, and point systems represent too much energy in the cost-benefit equation."

EQUITY AND VARIABLE PAY

The primary purpose of any pay scheme or incentive structure is to *focus* behavior. As observed by Michael Snipes of Allstate Insurance Company, "Companies need to deal with a *line of sight*. People need to feel that their efforts are driving business, and they need to feel that compensation is part of this effort." Companies are grappling with turning their employees' attention to how individual performance is linked to shareholder interest. Companies are spreading stock options further and further down into the organization with the hope that stock options will focus the employee on his or her role in influencing the stock price. Stock options vested over a period of years also act as an effective retention device. Companies, such as Eastman Kodak, also use options as special rewards to recognize significant contributions. Global companies are utilizing worldwide broad-based stock grants deep into the organization in order to reinforce globally that every employee affects the larger company.

As long as the stock market maintains an upward curve, the stock option form of incentive will gain in popularity among employees. Larry Acorn of United Technologies foresees a movement back to performance plans if the stock market stagnates while Jerry Francis of Eastman Kodak iterates that an emphasis on long-term incentives will weather a stock market downturn.

John Belcher in his chapter on variable pay (Chapter 17) points out that two-thirds of large and medium-sized companies have some form of variable pay. This phenomenon is being driven by international competition. "American management has come to realize that it cannot survive the rigors of international competition without the commitment and involvement of employees at all levels." With the ongoing cultural change from autocratic to team-based participative management systems, a compensation system is needed that communicates business priorities and reinforces behaviors such as continuous improvement and teamwork that are critical to success in a highly competitive environment.

The entrepreneurial employee with an appetite for risk taking is becoming more and more the norm. These types of workers generally are willing to forgo some base pay in return for the opportunity to earn much higher levels of equity compensation delivered if the company is financially successful. These pay preferences coincide with the employer's desire to leverage their own risk and preserve cash for investment in business development. Thus variable pay is being driven further and further down into the organization.

Variable pay creates pressure to define measurements and fund allocation. Many companies are opting for payouts based on a balanced scorecard that takes into account the interests of shareholders, customers, and employees. Measures including productivity, market share, time to market, and customer and employee satisfaction are factored into the bonus pool along with the profitability of the company.

The trend is toward team-based measures, but many compensation specialists iterate that individual reward must continue to have its place. According to Rolf Naku of Sunoco, "If you want top-caliber people, you must give performance-driven incentives." In individual rewards, more and more pressure will be placed on line managers to rank their subordinates and to master job appraisal and communication skills.

COMPENSATION AND COMMUNICATION

In her chapter on culture and compensation (Chapter 39), Louise Fitzgerald points out, "A compensation plan, no matter how brilliantly designed, will not accomplish its objectives without a communication strategy that is just as brilliantly designed as the plan itself." Michael Snipes at Allstate Insurance Company points out that it is the CEO and president of his company who run Allstate's town meetings in order to communicate earnings per share: "You must connect the dots for employees as to how they play in the larger corporate picture. Employees must understand their role in earnings per share in order for them to understand the last piece in the puzzle—what's in it for me and how can I benefit."

At Sunoco, Barbara D'Ulisse Morrow points out that their *Employee Brochure on Total Compensation* was developed in order to explain variable pay design changes and to meet "the need to improve employees' understanding of the value of their compensation at Sunoco and how these programs are aligned with business strategy." Although this is a costly option due to frequent changes in the brochure, D'Ulisse Morrow stresses the positive effect on employees. She also foresees a trend toward communicating compensation matters via Web sites, which is cost effective and allows for speedier transfer of information. Charlene Parsons at Unisys indicates that managers at her company are being trained in how to have performance and pay discussions with subordinates. The discussions will include compensation information and backup data so that employees can have a clear picture of how their pay package matches up both internally and externally with those of other individuals in comparable positions.

NO-INFLATION ECONOMY

Today, and perhaps into the future, businesses, consumers, bankers, and investors nearly everywhere in the developed world confront an economy with hardly any inflation. This means that workers must get used to raises that look small but are worth more than the bigger raises awarded when inflation controlled the purse strings. Inflation-adjusted salaries will serve as another challenge for compensation professionals and human relations departments who must communicate compensation information.

THE CHANGING ROLE OF HUMAN RESOURCES AND
COMPENSATION PRACTITIONERS

Reengineering of human resources and compensation staffs has led to smaller departments, greater reliance on technology for administrative support, and greater access to compensation systems by line management. This trend has changed the role of the compensation professional. Compensation specialists will be forced to articulate, rationalize, and systematize the rules of customized target market compensation, cafeteria reward systems, and performance management, and they will have to train line management in their application. They will have to establish and monitor success in application and be prepared to assist when conditions force a change in approach.

In addition to the human resources reengineering trend, line managers have openly challenged the command-and-control orientation of human resources and compensation departments and have sought more authority over rewarding their staffs. A collaborative approach has emerged in which human resources and compensation professionals, as subject matter experts, coaches, and strategists providing the framework, processes, and data, advise line management manipulating their own reward systems.

OUTSIDE CONSULTANTS AND ACADEMICS
WITHIN COMPANIES

Smaller staffs, less expertise, and outsourcing—the conditions that both caused, and were the result of, human resources reengineering—are increasing the influence of both outside consultants and academics within the business community. As a result of this trend, companies must exercise sound professional judgment when adopting touted compensation practices. Often companies get on a "fad bandwagon" in their search for painless cures. Charlene Parsons of Unisys warns, "Adopting another company's best practices, if they have a different strategy, might not work in your company."

For the most part, there is little credible objective research upon which companies base many of their important reward system decisions. Decision making, therefore, must be intuitive and demand the development and application of better diagnostic approaches. Due to the complexity, cost, and time factor involved, there will not be available an abundance of objective research on compensation techniques upon which compensation professionals may draw. There will, however, be an increased awareness of the need for better anecdotal reporting with emphasis on diagnostics and case analysis.

The rate of globalization, industry transformation, technology innovation, and workforce segmentation will increase beyond today's fast pace. This evolution will translate into a need to apply change management techniques to reward systems. To accomplish this, companies will require ongoing talent market assessment devices and systems, as well as networks in which to share and deploy new information quickly with line management.

We would like to thank the following individuals for their contributions in developing the preceding chapter:

R. Larry Acorn, Director, Compensation, United Technologies Corporation

Wendy Ahearne, Compensation and Benefits Manager, Johnson Controls, Inc.

Peter Au-Yang, Corporate Compensation, Cigna

Charles V. Bell, Director, Global Compensation and Benefits, The Dow Chemical Company

Barry Bingham, Director, Compensation and Benefits Strategy, Executive Compensation, Monsanto

Barbara D'Ulisse Morrow, Senior Compensation Consultant, Human Resources, Sun Company, Inc.

Dennis H. Eade, Vice President, Human Resources, American Seating Company

Gillian Ebeling, Senior Employee Relations Consultant, Kellogg Company

Jerry D. Francis, Director of Executive Compensation, Eastman Kodak Company

Joseph A. Frick, Senior Vice President, Human Resources and Administration, Independence Blue Cross

Gerry M. Gust, PECO Energy Power Team

Gloria Herney, Compensation Administrator, BF Goodrich Aerospace

Terri M. Koway, Manager, Compensation Programs, Rohm and Haas Company

Rolf D. Naku, Director, Compensation and Benefits, Human Resources, Sun Company, Inc.

Wallace J. Nichols, Executive Director, American Compensation Association

Charlene Parsons, Staff Vice President, Strategic and Executive Compensation, Unisys Corporation

Robert F. Pelliciari, Vice President, Human Resources, Elf Atochem North America, Inc.

Anabel I. Pichler, Manager, Compensation, Human Resources Department, Hercules, Inc.

Michael L. Postuma, Senior Compensation Administrator, Amway Corporation

Thomas Powell, Vice President, Human Resources, Attwood Corporation

Alan J. Ritchie, Vice President, Compensation, Benefits and Health Services, Lucent Technologies, Inc.

Michael A. Snipes, Assistant Vice President, Executive Compensation, Allstate Insurance Company

Arnold A. Trillet, Vice President, Human Resources, Information Services, Johnson & Johnson

Therese Voevodsky, President, Compensation Data Source, LLC

Dana A. Walters, Vice President, Human Resources, Hastings Mutual Insurance Company

3

THE EVOLUTION OF COMPENSATION PRACTICES

Lance A. Berger, Chief Executive Officer

Lance A. Berger & Associates, Ltd.

"Those who cannot remember the past are
condemned to repeat it."

GEORGE SANTAYANA

A LOOK BACKWARD

This chapter originated in a conversation between Arnie Trillet, vice president, human resources for information services at Johnson & Johnson, and me during the formative stages of this book. When asked if he thought that there were any new trends in compensation, Trillet replied, "No, only the context." He suggested that we trace the 27-year history of *The Compensation Handbook* to illustrate his point. We thought that it might be both constructive and interesting to follow this suggestion. What mistakes have we made in the past? Have we repeated them? What lessons have we learned? This chapter may answer some of these questions.

This publication is the fourth edition of *The Handbook of Wage and Salary Administration,* the original title. It was published in 1972 and again in 1984 by the McGraw-Hill Book Company. The first two editions were developed by the legendary Milton L. Rock, managing partner of Edward N. Hay & Associates. I was Rock's partner, in charge of Hay's worldwide compensation practice, in the late 1980s and was witness to the events that would shape our compensation practices today. In 1988, following our "Hay Days," I was delighted when Rock asked me to develop with him the third edition of this book. We realized that compensation practices had changed dramatically since 1984, and we retitled the book *The Compensation Handbook: A State-of-the-Art Guide to Compensation Strategy and Design.*

In 1984, the perspective, management, and authorship of the book began to shift to the children of Tom Brokaw's "greatest generation,"—the baby-boomers. In 1999, another shift is under way. The children of the baby-boomers are an important influence on the fourth edition.

THE FIRST EDITION: 1972

The context for the first edition was late 1960s and early 1970s. This period saw one of the largest sustained economic growth periods in the history of the United States. Between 1960 and 1970, largely fueled by the Vietnam War and the Great Society programs, the gross national product (GNP) doubled. It was an era of war protest and social upheaval. This era was framed by Woodstock, *The Feminine Mystique,* war protests, a presidential resignation and *Hair,* the Broadway musical. We were still fighting the Cold War, but over 500,000 troops were in a hot war. Men landed on the moon in 1969 but never returned to the moon after 1972. In 1972, the GNP exceeded $1 trillion. Nixon's treasury secretary was George Shultz, and wage and price controls were instituted to slow down inflation that was approaching 9 percent. People were still engrossed in the Kennedy assassination, and medicare, the Higher Education Act, and the Clean Water Act were enacted. In 1972, the Dow-Jones Industrial Average (DJIA) was 1,036, unemployment was 5.6 percent (having increased from the 3.5 percent averages of the 1960s), people worked an average of 37 hours per week, the consumer price index (CPI) was 42.1 (meaning that the average price level was 42.1 percent higher than the average price level during the 1983 through 1984 period). The minimum wage was $1.60 an hour, and nonfarm productivity had risen to 3.4 percent. Cost-of-living pay increases were becoming more prevalent.

In 1972, there were no PCs, Internet, or cellular phones. *The Godfather* won the Oscar, the Dallas Cowboys won the Super Bowl, and the Oakland Athletics won the World Series. Life expectancy was 71 years, and IBM was the largest company in market capitalization. Intel, Microsoft, and Amazon.com didn't exist. Management used the term *reduction in force,* or RIF, to explain organization cutbacks. *Downsizing* had not found its way into popular speech, *reengineering* was important in product enhancement, and a *Hammer* was still a tool for pounding nails—not people. The worldwide approach to business was becoming more multinational.

Milt Rock developed the first edition "to help managers create a compensation process to meet their needs,…a practical reference work to improve their effectiveness." All succeeding editions strive to achieve this goal. While the first edition clearly was a reflection of the times, viewed through the eyes of "the greatest generation," it was also prophetic. So much of what the early authors wrote is still pertinent that I am led to believe that those of us who do not learn from the lessons of the past are condemned to plagiarize it.

The growing, yet inflationary, economy was reflected in continued emphasis on structuring and controlling the principal component of compensation base pay. At the same time, the book contributors were mindful of the growing importance of benefits, particularly in view of their nontaxable nature, in a period of higher taxes and tax surcharges. Compensation was continuing to emerge as a discipline, and practitioners were seeking ways to professionalize their discipline. When this force combined with pressures to better manage pay in the fast-growing, inflationary economy, compensation professionals were compelled to develop highly codified approaches to facilitate compensation management. Revisionist thinkers in the 1990s put a negative spin on this approach, calling it "command and control."

The first edition, driven by base pay management, emphasized job description, analysis and measurement, salary surveys, formal pay structure, and performance appraisal linked clearly to compensation structure. A variety of performance appraisal models, ranging from management by objectives to trait-based assessment, were suggested. One important point to note is that the contributors began to identify the conditions under which different appraisal formats would work. This contingency approach, although widely understood by professionals, did not become fully recognized. The next quarter of a century saw rampant use of fads influencing the practice of human resources management.

The 1972 edition dealt marginally with incentive programs although it did recognize their potential contribution to corporate performance. Executive compensation, sales incentives, and other forms of incentives were seen as "special"—not mainstream elements of the compensation professional's job. While this first work can be viewed as "The Nuts-and-Bolts Compensation Handbook," it was also highly prophetic. For example, Milt Rock believed that compensation professionals must take into consideration the employees' needs to self-actualize and to understand clearly their contributions to the company. Additionally, he believed that the nature of work and the organizational environment needed to be factored into the compensation equation. This sounds as though Rock was talking about "work-life" years before the term was coined. Bernard Ingster, a contributor to the first book and a contributor to this edition, spoke about utilization of the *critical incidents method* of performance appraisal, which was based on observing good and bad behaviors in the workplace. He also suggested tying specific behaviors and traits to performance measurement criteria. This concept is eerily related to behaviorally anchored rating scales and competency-based pay. Ray Hollerbach proposed, in the first edition, that we might have to eliminate salary ranges and that special pay packages might have to be developed for workers in skill shortage areas. Other contributors were already dealing with multiple pay market structures and "wide-range spreads." This sounds a lot like *differential market-based pay* and *broadbanding*.

In 1972, Milt Rock reported that there would be changes in thinking by the workforce "on how it wants to be paid." He perceived that "cafeteria-style pay" would address this issue by giving individuals a choice of payment. Rock was the Nostradamus of compensation.

Perhaps the most prophetic chapter in the first edition was written by Charles Hughes of Texas Instruments. Charles Hughes predicted: There would be a shift from jobs to roles and a phasing out of the traditional superior-subordinate relationship; teams and work groups would replace individual assignment; the traditional organization chart would come to resemble a flowchart of project teams and individuals interconnected for maximum effectiveness; and work would be organized around business objectives rather than function. Michael Hammer said these same ideas came to him 10 years before he published *Reengineering the Corporation* in 1993. Mr. Hughes published his version 11 years before Hammer began to think about the subject.

"Many younger workers view companies and jobs in the broad context of society's needs. Moreover, having grown up in relative affluence, they tend to be less concerned with money and security than their elders, and more concerned with self-expression." These words were not expressed in the 1990s. They were written 27 years ago by Milt Rock in the first edition.

SECOND EDITION: 1984

The 1970s and early 1980s shaped the second edition. During this period, Nixon resigned from the presidency and was succeeded by Ford, Carter replaced Ford, and Reagan replaced Carter. Presidential turnover destabilized both domestic and foreign policy. The Vietnam War ended, and the economy was lethargic with rampant inflation. This period is remembered for long gas lines and natural resources shortages. Given this scenario, the public, not surprisingly, had a lingering suspicion of government as evidenced by frequent protests. China was in chaos after the death of Mao, and socialist-oriented regimes dominated many governments, including Great Britain. There was social turmoil in Ireland, Latin America, and Africa and diminishing prospects for stable economic growth in a large portion of the world.

By 1984, the Reagan era had begun, and inflation had declined to about 5.5 percent. The Dow-Jones Industrial Average rose to 1,287 (an increase of 24 percent in 12 years), but the unemployment rate increased to 7.5 percent (about 34 percent over the rate in 1972), and the CPI increased to 103.3, or 145 percent over 1972. The average workweek dropped to 35.2 hours (down about 5 percent), the nonfarm output rate dropped from 3.4 percent in 1972 to 1.7 percent in 1984 (a decline of about 50 percent), and the minimum wage stood at $3.35 an hour (a 109 percent increase). Increases in the minimum wage did not keep up with increases in the consumer price index, resulting in a real loss in spendable income. Corporations and governments began to base compensation and benefits increases on cost-of-living changes. Large-scale government deficit spending was under way, presided over by Donald Regan, Secretary of the Treasury. In 1984, *Amadeus* won the Oscar, the Detroit Tigers won the World Series, and the Los Angeles Raiders won the Super Bowl. Personal computers were being used widely by businesses and individuals, fax machines were speeding document flow, cellular phones were creeping into public consciousness, and the Internet was still a sleeping giant. Japan was flexing its economic muscles with strong increases in its GNP, productivity, worldwide market penetration, and low unemployment. The multinational companies continued to grow.

Although inflation had begun to decline at the time the second edition was published, the focus of the revision's contents was still driven by controlling its influence. The advice of Milt Rock and his contributors reflected continued high unemployment rates and declining productivity—about 36 percent of the contributors were holdovers from the first book and were battle-tough inflation warriors. Reconciling internal equity, external competitiveness, and individual performance was the ongoing effort of practitioners. Of the three, internal equity consideration influenced by a buyer's market was the dominant focus. However, it was clear that Rock and the contributors were now becoming wary of the growing segmentation of pay markets. In response, they expanded the sections on salary surveys and special compensation programs to reflect the need to measure external pay markets more precisely. While the content of the book still overwhelmingly focused on the control of fixed payroll expenses, such as base salary and benefits, through the traditional salary administration approaches outlined in the first and second editions, contributors began to recognize the importance of variable pay packages in keeping employee costs down. Additionally, Rock reinforced the notion, expressed 12 years earlier, that the "job content approach by itself is not sufficient" in determining employee pay. Indeed, he reiterated Charles Hughes's prophesy that people will have roles, rather than jobs, in an integrated process aimed at specific end results.

Perhaps the most striking change in the second edition was the addition of three chapters devoted to handling the compensation factors implicated in equal opportunity and equal pay. Today, we have categorized, repackaged, and promoted such advice under the rubric of "diversity and comparable worth." Another contextual change that occurred in the second edition was the recognition of cultural influences on pay determination and the necessity to implement sound communications programs to help employees both understand and support compensation programs.

The second edition, like the first, was replete with prophesies of change. These included the relationship between business cycle and mix of pay, differential compensation treatment of multi-business unit companies, and personalized compensation packages that integrated both pay market and individual employee compensation requirements. The growing use of the computer to effectively analyze compensation data pervaded chapters on surveys and salary administration.

According to Milt Rock in 1984, "Wage earners are going to demand that the modern techniques developed for salary administration be applied to determining their pay structures." He was right, but the full impact of the employees' compensation revolution would wait until the late 1990s when the economy forced a shift from a buyer's to a seller's market.

THIRD EDITION: 1991

Capitalism flourished anew in the late 1980s and early 1990s. This was the Reagan-Bush era. Socialistic governments began to be replaced by more conservative ones, exemplified by that of Margaret Thatcher in the United Kingdom. Gorbachev promoted *Glasnost* and *Perestroika,* the Berlin Wall finally toppled, and the Soviet Union disintegrated into multiple nations. This period saw an economic boom fueled by tax cuts, deregulation, and deficit spending. We will remember this era for its hostile takeovers, junk bonds, leveraged buyouts, stock market crash and subsequent revival, and Michael Douglas's quote in the movie *Wall Street,* "Greed is good." The unending turmoil in the Middle East exploded into the short-lived Persian Gulf War of 1991. The seeds of the new Europe began to grow in the form of the European Economic Community—a common market with over 300,000 people. Public consciousness was raised to the aging of the baby-boomers and other changing demographics, which included higher participation rates of women and minorities in the workforce.

In 1991, Nicholas Brady was the secretary of the treasury, the Dow-Jones Industrial Average stood at 3,169 (a 146 percent increase in 7 years), inflation had declined to 3 percent, and the consumer price index increased to 134.4 (about 30 percent in 7 years, which is an annual rate far lower than the previous period). The unemployment rate decreased to 6.9 percent (from 7.5 percent in 1984), the minimum wage rose to $4.25 per hour (about 27 percent more than 1984), the average workweek declined another 0.5 hours per week, as did the rate of nonfarm output (0.7 percent versus 1.7 percent in 1984). In 1991, *Silence of the Lambs* won the

Oscar, the Minnesota Twins won the World Series, and the New York Giants won the Super Bowl. *Windows* software and the PC were helping to make individuals and businesses more efficient, while fax machines and cellular phones were becoming prevalent. Over 1 million people were using the Internet. A strong Japan was touted as a model of an economic engine. U.S. companies were talking about "globalism" rather than "multinationalism." The metaphor *glocal*—"think global and act local"—was coined.

I joined Milt Rock in 1991 as an editor-in-chief. We changed the name of the publication to *The Compensation Handbook* to encompass shifts in our perception of our readers' needs. Specifically, we transferred our focus from base salary administration to contingent or variable reward programs to reflect reward packages that were more performance driven and cost effective, and we expanded our section on performance management to support the chapter on variable pay. Additionally, we increased our coverage of executive compensation to deal with the growing complexity of this discipline and involvement by compensation professionals. We also introduced a comprehensive section on the computer in compensation, now more user friendly and pervasive. To more fully address the growing need to link employees and business requirements to compensation, we added a new section on culture and compensation. Only 14 percent of the book's contributors were authors who had written chapters for the preceding book, reflecting both a change in content and the need to add new perspectives.

In 1991, we predicted that compensation practices in the United States would be affected by slow economic growth through the year 2000, which would reduce the rate of growth of employee pay; increased corporate globalism driven by the interconnectedness of the world economy and international competition; technological advances reshaping the structure of the work environment including fewer job levels and the increased use of teams; corporate restructuring leading to a reduction in the numbers and changes in the types of jobs; the growth in the number of small businesses (in part created by corporate restructuring, mergers, and acquisitions); shifts in the value structure of the workforce with increasing emphasis on personal lifestyle issues; segmentation of pay markets based on selective shortages of workers; and the growing diversity of the workforce by age, gender, ethnic background, and race. We were right on point in all predictions except that of economic growth. Our linear extrapolations failed to consider that the economic impact of many of the forces listed above would be rapid economic growth, low inflation, an elevated stock market, and low unemployment.

Ike Greenspan, in Chapter 19 of the third edition, described a situation in which GTE Corporation introduced team incentives in order to break down "certain historical management processes that were deemed to impede rapid improvements in performance. One of the chief villains was the tradition-bound departmentalized organizations." Lyle Spencer describes, in Chapter 23 of that edition, the need to develop new pay programs to reward "knowledge workers" who continually work on "developmental assignments" with the organization benefiting more from their unique competencies than past performance. Judging from the content of the third edition, it is clear that the future was upon us.

THE PERIOD BETWEEN THE THIRD AND FOURTH EDITIONS

The 7 years following the third edition was one of the most economically volatile and exciting periods in the nation's history. The post–Cold War era heralded in the acceleration of globalism as both small and large businesses recognized that markets were indeed worldwide and that they must be prepared to deal with competitors from all over the world.

Industries that had been destabilized by mergers and acquisitions in the previous period began to reshape themselves, going beyond the bottom-line orientation of reengineering to the top-line perspective of market growth. Corporate development shifted from the hostile takeover to the strategic acquisition. Economic growth accelerated in the middle of the decade and continued on, with corporate profit exceeding 6 percent for the decade. The North America Free Trade Act (NAFTA) was enacted after a long struggle conducted over three presidential terms. This decade will be remembered for White House scandals, presidential impeachment, quantum technology advances, globalization of corporations, budget surpluses, outsourcing, the return of Hong Kong to China, diversity, the rise and fall of reengineering, the Asian economic meltdown, the end of welfare, work-life issues, and the public's awakening to the threat to social security. The minimum wage rose to $5.15 per hour (a 21 percent increase over 1991) while the consumer price index increased to 159.7 (an increase of 19 percent over 1991), and spendable income for entry-level workers increased—although slightly. The average workweek continued its decline, arriving at 34.6 hours (0.1 hour less than 1991), and productivity (nonfarm output per hour) jumped 2.2 percent—a rate that was more than three times that of 1991. In 1998, the unemployment rate dramatically declined to 4.5 percent (about 35 percent lower than 1991), and talent-labor market shortages were widely occurring. The workforce was also becoming increasingly diverse with women and minority workforce participation rates increasing beyond those of white males.

While large businesses were merging and laying off workers, small businesses were emerging and growing astronomically to absorb not only terminated workers but new workforce participants. From 1992 through 1996, businesses with under 500 employees created all of the net new jobs, with companies of over 500 employees showing a decrease of 600,000 workers. Based on 1995 data, the United States had over 5 million businesses with employees; of those businesses, 99.7 percent had fewer than 500 employees. There were over 100 million nongovernment employees in the workforce in 1995. About 80 percent of these employees were located in businesses with fewer than 500 people, and 87 percent worked in companies with fewer than 1,000 people. All of the growth in employment in companies over 1,000 employees occurred in companies like Microsoft that were not on anyone's screen in 1980. The 1990s were not only the era of globalism but also the era of the small business.

In the 1992 through 1996 period, manufacturing jobs in the category of 500+ workers declined by over 1 million workers, and retail jobs decreased by over 400,000 workers. Concurrently, the service sector created over 1 million jobs. About 900,000 jobs were created in the manufacturing sector in companies with fewer than 500 employees, and over 6 million jobs were created in service companies with fewer than 500 workers.

At the end of 1998, the Dow-Jones Industrial Average stood at 9,338 (having risen 195 percent since 1991), and the gross national product exceeded $8 trillion (eight times the level in 1972, while the CPI increased less than three times during the same period). After declining between 1960 and 1990, corporate profits rose dramatically between 1990 and 1998 to over 6 percent. President Clinton must share his era with Robert Rubin, Treasury Secretary, and Alan Greenspan, Chairman of the Federal Reserve System, who are being called the "architects of prosperity."

Between 1972 and the year 2000, life expectancy increased to 76.5 years, or 8.1 percent. Life expectancy is expected to continue to increase due to technology with an enormous market opportunity created for services and products for aging baby-boomers. Additionally, the growing workforce shortage in critical skill areas will likely induce employers to attempt to hire and retain retirement-oriented baby-boomers.

In 1998, the Denver Broncos won the Super Bowl, the New York Yankees won the World Series, and the best motion picture was *Shakespeare in Love*. Over 100 million people are now using the Internet, and over a billion will log on by 2005. The computer is omnipresent, and fax machines are being phased out by e-mail. Cellular phones have gone from analog to digital, and the country is adding area codes to deal with the telecom explosion. Table 3.1 illustrates the changes in the top company ranking worldwide in market capitalization (stock price times number of shares) between 1972 and July 1998. Only 2 of the top 10 companies in 1972 remain on the list in 1998—General Electric and Exxon. Five of the top 10 have fallen below the top 100. In 1972, 2 companies on the 1998 list did not exist—Microsoft and Intel—and Wal-Mart was just 10 years old.

While Japan's economic engine was touted in 1991, by 1998 it was in a recession, and its economy was shrinking. Between 1992 and 1997, the U.S. gross domestic product grew at 3.1 percent while Japan's grew at only 1.5 percent with

TABLE 3.1 Top Company Rankings Worldwide in Market Capitalization Between 1972 and July 1998

Top 10 Companies in 1972	1972 Company Rank in 1972	1972 Company Rank in 1998	Top 10 Companies in 1998
IBM	1	15	General Electric
AT&T	2	23	Microsoft
Eastman Kodak	3	Below top 100	Coca-Cola
General Motors	4	79	Royal Dutch/Shell
Exxon	5	5	Exxon
Sears Roebuck	6	Below top 100	Merck
General Electric	7	1	Pfizer
Xerox	8	Below top 100	Wal-Mart Stores
Texaco	9	Below top 100	Nippon Telephone & Telegraph
Minnesota Mining & Mfg.	10	Below top 100	Intel

current estimates for 1998 pointing to a decline of between 2.5 and 3 percent. For the first time in decades, the U.S. unemployment rate was below that of Japan. The "fadmeisters" of the late 1990s were now looking at the United States as the source of business excellence rather than Japan. The 1990s in many ways resembled the 1950s in that it was the "American Business Decade." Our prosperity is clearly reflected in the following:

- Growth in productivity
- Low inflation
- Low unemployment and selected labor shortages
- Profit growth
- Workforce diversity
- Technology explosion
- Small-business explosion
- Globalism
- Quantum stock market growth
- The resurgence of the New York Yankees in the World Series

THE FOURTH EDITION: THE FUTURE IS NOW

When one considers the information presented in past editions and the hype surrounding every fad of the past 10 years, what becomes glaringly apparent is that we have become experts at disassembling, reassembling, repackaging, renaming, promoting, and marketing the concepts, systems, and methodologies of our parents and grandparents. The principal focus of the sales effort has been toward convincing about 1 percent of all companies, which house fewer than 15 percent of the U.S. employee base, that much of what we are saying is really new and innovative. A more honest, and less cynical, view would recognize our ancestors' contributions and build on their efforts. In the first edition, Milt Rock suggested simply that the book be written as a practical reference work for managers who want to improve their effectiveness. The best way to do this, he believed, was to address their needs. This means that each edition should recognize the context in which our approaches operate. Thus, we focused this book on the following:

1. Identifying real issues and solutions that managers in any size company must deal with

2. Identifying what aspects of the compensation discipline work under what conditions and why

3. Refining what we know

To sharpen our perspective, we conducted extensive focus groups and individual interviews with compensation professionals in companies of different sizes and industries. We again recruited chapter contributors with recognized expertise in their subject areas. Contributors were asked to present their perspectives while avoiding irrational exuberance of specific approaches. We believe the contributors satisfied this requirement. About 34 percent of our chapter writers were contributors to the last book, which helped create a sense of informational continuity.

Our research on compensation issues and trends is captured in Chapter 4. We expanded the sections on variable pay, executive compensation, performance management, and culture. We added a section on international compensation. It is likely that the last-named subject, as in the case of benefits, will have its own handbook. We have also reduced the size of the section dealing with base compensation.

What have we learned from the past? To recognize, respect, refine, adapt, and build upon its lessons.

Base Compensation

4

COMPENSATION: AN OVERVIEW

Martin G. Wolf, Ph.D., President

Management Advisory Services, Inc.

TRADITIONALLY, COMPENSATION PROGRAMS have had three primary design criteria: They must be internally equitable (i.e., they must pay people in proportion to the relative value of their job), externally competitive (i.e., they must pay people in proportion to the market price for their job), and personally motivating to employees. A fourth objective, often kept hidden from line management, has been ease of administration for staff. Unfortunately, the first two are almost always at cross purposes with each other, forcing an organization to sacrifice one to achieve the other, and achievement of the third means a high degree of individualization, which complicates the fourth, administration.

Risher eloquently addressed the problem of internal equity versus external competitiveness:

When internal equity is a primary goal, some positions are paid more than the prevailing labor market rate. Job evaluation systems have always overpaid some employees relative to their labor markets and underpaid others. Not too many years ago that was accepted, but when the focus shifted to cost reduction, it became important to rethink how pay levels are set relative to market-determined rates. (1998, pp. 6–7)

Simply put, the problem is that no other organization is likely to place the same relative value on a position that yours does. Thus, their concept of "internal equity" is different from yours. This is of no consequence until you start looking at pay market data. Then, because of their different internal values and the resulting pay practices, the pay market data for positions X and Y (the external value of these jobs) are inconsistent with your internal values for these jobs.

Figure 4.1 illustrates the history of compensation systems over the last half century. As the pace of change in business has increased and as more sophisticated tools and data have become available, the focus of compensation has shifted from almost total dependence on internal equity to internal equity balanced with market value to a market value plus internal value-added model. As a result, the compensation vehicles employed have shifted from standardized base salary levels dependent on evaluated job content to standardized base plus performance-based incentives to individualized salary levels plus performance-based incentives.

FIGURE 4.1   The history of compensation systems.

Element	Distant Past (50's - 60's)	Recent Past (70's - 80's)	Present/Future (90's - ??)
Business Situation	Little change from year to year	Some change from year to year	Continuous change
Tools Employed	Unique job evaluation systems + limited pay market data	Standard job evaluation systems + detailed but broad pay market data	Various approaches (Skills/Competencies, tightly focused pay market data, computer models, etc.)
Objective	Internal equity based on jobs	Same + external competitiveness based on market value	Internal equity based on person's achievement + market value
Compensation Vehicles	Job-based pay ranges	Same + person-based performance incentives	Person-based pay rates + person-based performance incentives

Figure 4.2 presents another way of looking at the changes that have occurred in reward management. Interestingly, just as in biology, where ontogeny recapitulates phylogeny (i.e., where the embryonic development of an individual organism retraces the evolution of its species), organizations tend to retrace the same evolutionary process as they move from initial entrepreneurial state to maturity. Thus Figure 4.2 is not only a description of the historical changes seen in Figure 4.1 but it is also a map of the stages through which contemporary organizations will pass.

Initially, the CEO controls reward level, based mostly on need and personal feel. As the company grows, there is some formalization of the process, and the CEO and/or line managers begin to rely on staff assistance. When the organization becomes too large for any one person to be familiar with all the jobs, a formal control process is introduced by staff, who largely manage the compensation program. As the company grows and its market matures and becomes more competitive, individual performance and motivation become more critical for many positions, and the CEO and line managers once again become deeply involved, setting incentive plan objectives and payouts. Finally, as the business situation becomes highly fluid and highly competitive, organizational effectiveness becomes central, and there is a return to an individual focus, with line management assuming control of the process from staff.

In the interim since the last edition of this handbook (1991), many "new" approaches to compensation administration have emerged—broadbanding, skill-competency–based pay, and expanded use a variety of variable pay approaches. Many organizations rightfully have shifted from administering salaries to administering total compensation, and those that have not so shifted are at a disadvantage.

Yet some of these "new" approaches are new more in name and description than in actual practice—old wine in new casks. In many instances, these approaches either represent a disguised return to older, less sophisticated compensation techniques, or, in the worst cases, they open the door to managerial confusion and inefficiency. All too often, "the emperor has no clothes," but few are brave enough to point that out.

Technobabble often reigns—a flood of the jargon of the latest management fads trapped in a human resources bucket. A recent article (Rand and Franz, 1998) on broadbanding, a subject to be dissected later in this chapter, led off as follows:

> Many organizations are transforming themselves into learning communities through an emphasis on strategic quality, process innovations and customer-in marketing alliances. This requires a number of changes in the way people think and interact with each other....
>
> The management team realized...that the organization needed to abandon the complicated multi-range, multi-structure systems for a more transparent, holistic and motivating compensation model. (pp. 24–25)

FIGURE 4.2   The evolution of reward management in an organization.

EMPHASIS ON: Job → / Person ↓	Low	Medium	High
High	**[1] Start-up or entrepreneurial phase** **Emphasis:** Expediency **Plan Type:** Person-based Discretionary Approach **Method:** Subjective ("gut feel") **Set By:** CEO 90% Staff 10%		**[5] Continuously changing, highly competitive business environments** **Emphasis:** Organizational effectiveness **Plan Type:** Person-based Integrated Reward Systems **Method:** Market Pricing/Skill-based Pay **Set By:** CEO/Line Managers 70% Staff 30%
Medium		**[2] Early growth phase** **Emphasis:** Internal job equity **Plan Type:** Job-based Qualitative Systems **Method:** Ranking/Grade Classification **Set By:** CEO /Line Managers 60% Staff 40%	**[4] Increasingly competitive markets** **Emphasis:** Individual motivation **Plan Type:** Job-based Quantitative Systems + Incentive Plans **Method:** Same as [3] **Set By:** CEO/Line Managers 50% Staff 50%
Low			**[3] Later growth phase** **Emphasis:** Control **Plan Type:** Job-based Quantitative Systems **Method:** Point Factor/Factor Comparison **Set By:** CEO/Line Managers 20% Staff 80%

PAYING PEOPLE VERSUS PAYING JOBS

As noted in Figure 4.2, compensation programs have swung from being individually focused to being job based to a recent return to individuation. Broadbanding and skill-competency–based pay represent two different approaches to paying for the person rather than for the job:

> From a different perspective, the new work paradigm, in which jobs are more flexible and duties change as required, undermines the traditional focus on jobs....
>
> The newer concepts for managing base pay—pay banding, competency-based pay and skill-based pay—shift the focus to the value of the individual. Value is now determined by what the individual can do, not on what he or she actually does from day to day. A new definition of equity, one that will need to be understood by employees, supports paying the most competent people higher salaries.
>
> As organizations move to team-pay environments, it will lead to differences in pay for people in similar jobs. The trend to multiple incentive systems will underscore the need to redefine equity. (Risher, 1998, p. 7)

Broadbanding

There are numerous definitions of *broadbanding,* but all are basically similar. Many positions traditionally covered by numerous separate pay ranges are swept into a relatively few, very wide job classifications (i.e., "bands"). Usually, differences between functional specialties are eliminated both to simplify administration and to enhance a sense of common purpose and a single-team atmosphere.

Broadbanding, as with many of these "new" approaches, is often touted as though it were a panacea:

> Most developments in compensation during the past 30 to 40 years have been modifications in methodology and technique that left the basic philosophy unchanged. Broadbanding goes deeper. By collapsing a multitude of traditional salary grades into a few wide "bands" to manage career development and administer pay, broadbanding changes the basic tenets of compensation. It takes some of the rungs out of hierarchical career ladders and tells employees that development is more important than jockeying for promotion. It threatens the use of job titles as status-markers and focuses attention on "paying for the person" rather than paying for the job. (Abosch, 1998, p. 28)

Yet many of the claimed benefits of broadbanding are based on questionable data. For example, rebutting the concern that broadbanding results in higher costs, Abosch reports, "For the 73 companies participating in the 1998 study, 82 percent of those organizations that tracked cost during the transition indicated a cost-neutral impact" (p. 30). Yet later in that article we learn that 34 percent of the companies did not track costs, while "many companies (69 percent) have not installed the mechanisms for tracking the effectiveness of broadbanding" (p. 31). If one-third do not even know their costs and two-thirds are not measuring effectiveness, any data that emerge are so seriously compromised as to be worthless.

Further, meaningful assessment of something requires that one understand what one is supposed to assess. Only 67 percent of executives and 56 percent of managers understand broadbanding as practiced in their organization (Abosch, 1998). Yet in the same Hewitt study, 70 percent of executives and 68 percent of managers rate broadbanding as "effective," while 81 and 75 percent, respectively, rate it as "favorable." Similarly, only 27 percent of employees feel they understand broadbanding, but 56 percent rate it as "effective," and 64 percent rate it as "favorable." They may not understand it, but it works and it is good for them!

The broad bands that are the essence of broadbanding turn out to be much less broad in practice:

> Broadbanding companies use various methods for managing, monitoring, and controlling individuals' pay over time. The market cluster approach, used by 28 percent of the respondents, groups similar positions into clusters based on similar market values, then uses a cluster reference range to guide pay decisions. Thirty-five percent use individual market points. This approach establishes market value for as many positions as possible and each is provided an individual market reference range. Another approach, used by 21 percent, assigns positions to a specific subrange (zone) within the band, each with its own minimum and maximum. (Abosch, 1998, pp. 32)

If we add 28 and 35 and 21 percent, we find that 84 percent of the firms are dividing each of the broad bands into narrow sections and assigning individual positions to one of these sections, probably because real-life managers cannot manage compensation effectively with true broad bands. In actual practice, broadbanding, in conjunction with market pricing, may even be moving to narrower pay points than traditional approaches:

> Actually, the overall developments may be moving in a good direction. It's fair to say that most traditional programs were "market based" in the sense that organizations took market values and statistically massaged the values to create structures with minimums, midpoints and maximums. What broadbanding is bringing to the forefront is *a direct focus on discrete market values* and offering these values to the organization *as points of reference in managing pay.*
>
> Market data are viewed as a value system that takes priority over what formal job evaluation plans, including point factor plans, used to provide. If anything, this will make it easier, not harder, to *determine a competitive salary for specific jobs* in a tight market. (Abosch, 1998, p. 32, emphasis added)

Research indicates that broadbanding often fails to improve the organization's career management processes, although improved career management is often cited by proponents as one of the main benefits of broadbanding. HR managers from 89 percent of Abosch's (1998) total sample of 73 companies rated broadbanding as effective for "skill and/or competency development," while 88 percent rated it effective for "emphasis on career development."

Yet of the 73 companies in Abosch's study, only 17 have a fully functional career planning program, while another 23 have a program under development. Since 33 participants were repeats from an earlier study who had lived with broad-banding for an average of 4.6 years, then it can be safely said that at least half of these long-term broadbanders had no functional career planning program. One can only wonder why they feel broadbanding is so effective as a development tool.

Change is inevitable, and now organizations are moving to what they describe as *second-stage broadbanding approaches.* MetLife Auto & Home went from 732 positions and 20 grades to 51 "clusters of work" that became "career bands":

> The clusters were: Leadership, Professional, Technical, Management, Administrative. Within each of those five bands, MetLife Auto & Home defined seven characteristics that would serve as a corporate vision of characteristics to be displayed by employees. The characteristics described in the Corporate Profiles were: Knowledge, Customer relations, Impact/execution, Decision making, Innovation, Communication, Ethics/quality....After narrowing down functional responsibilities, the company whittled its 732 job descriptions to 65 Function Profiles."...Within this compensation model, there are no minimums, no maximums and no profile superior to another. With CareerBanding, compensation does not have any levels, scales or ranges, and no promotions....Moreover, CareerBanding has moved compensation from an entitlement mentality to an environment where compensation recognition is based on career development, employees' contribution and market competitive pricing. (Sierra, 1998, pp. 23–24)

This brave new world of compensation raises many questions. If there are "no levels, scales or ranges," what role does "market competitive pricing" play? Why is it even a factor? Is it subordinate to "career development" or "employees' contribution," or are they subordinate to it? Is "career development" more or less important than "employees' contribution"?

Skill-Competency–Based Pay

One of the most common approaches to paying people rather than jobs is the use of skill-competency–based pay:

> For the last half-century,...organizations have hired for jobs, paid for jobs, developed job skills, appraised job performance, and planned careers as a sequence of jobs. In the 1990s, there is an alternative paradigm for HR integration, which focuses on competency structures versus traditional job structures....(Rahbar-Daniels, 1998, p. 36)

In the corresponding chapter in the last edition of this handbook, Wolf (1991) wrote the following:

All job-evaluation systems, formal or informal, essentially are based on three things: what you know, what you do, and, to a degree, what you have to put up with. These three things are the primary compensable elements, that is, the things for which employers pay people. (p. 44)

Whether one relies on old-fashioned job evaluation and traditional job-pay structures or moves to competencies and broad bands, employers still pay for what you know and what you do. No matter how you get there, those are the key compensable elements! Attempts to dress this up in modern garb abound, but the underlying premise remains as an eternal verity.

In her article, Rahbar-Daniels (1998) concludes, "This review indicates that competency-aligned HR systems have emerged as a viable alternative to traditional job-based systems for certain business environments" (p. 40). Yet despite all the invented terms and an apparent use of broadbanding, her approach fits the traditional paradigm of what you know and what you do, and within a limited actual pay range rather than a true broad band. The competency rating clearly is a function of what you know (although she considers them ratings of *applied* competencies, which would add in an element of what you do to what you know), while the results rating is clearly an evaluation of what you do.

Rahbar-Daniels provides an example of the salary process for a career band. The salary scale goes from $31,000 to $71,000, a range of some 129 percent ($71,000 is 129 percent of $31,000). This compares to a traditional salary range of 50 percent. Employees within this career band are rated for their competency on a 0.0 to 7.0 scale, apparently to one decimal place. The competency rating determines a "guide point" within the pay range. Employees also receive a results rating on a 1.0 to 4.0 scale. A results range of ±5 percent is created around the guide point, and the employees' results rating then determines their targeted salary within that results range.

While the nominal salary range is 129 percent wide, the *de facto* range is only 10 percent wide (the results range for any given competency rating). Further, the middle four competency ratings categories (2 to 5) of the eight available (0 to 7), the area where most employees are likely to be rated, span a pay range only from $41,000 to $58,000, some 41 percent. Add in a −5 percent at the low end and a +5 percent at the high end for the results ranges at either extreme, and the effective pay range for most employees is $38,950 to $60,900, some 56 percent—very close to the traditional 50 percent range.

The approach also suffers from false precision. I challenge anyone to demonstrate 80 distinct levels of employee competency (0.0 to 7.0 by 0.1 increments equals 80 possible levels) in any real-life job.

PAY FOR PERFORMANCE

Not everyone sees the trend toward paying for skills and/or competencies as a good thing:

> It would be easy to conclude from reports in the business press that merit pay is dead and organizations need to reconstitute pay plans to pay people in some new way. Suggestions include paying employees for the knowledge, skills, abilities and behaviors (personal competencies) they bring to the workplace. Although interesting, this call for wholesale reform overlooks fundamental tenets of economic and behavioral theories. (Greene, 1998, p. 26)

Pay for performance is the holy grail of modern compensation administration—widely sought but hard to actually achieve. Pay for performance is the flag, motherhood, and apple pie, but it is easier said than done. One primary problem is defining performance properly, so that the organization pays for results and not for effort. Once over that hurdle, there remains the large impediment of finding enough money to make the reward for top performance meaningful. Many different approaches are used—various variable pay (bonus) schemes, annual awards in lieu of permanent increases in base pay, and the traditional merit pay (performance-based) salary increases.

The concept of pay for performance has different meanings to different people. Many either (1) fail to recognize that pay for performance fails when the difference in reward between adequate performance and outstanding performance is inconsequential or (2) cannot solve the problem of funding adequate differentiation while dealing with essential range maintenance costs.

For example, Logue (1998) reported on the introduction of performance-based pay for unionized employees in a public university. The old system had four annual, essentially "automatic," 5 percent steps from minimum to maximum. The new system added 10 percent to the top of the salary range. All employees would move through the regular range automatically, but growth within the top 10 percent was based only on performance. Since 20 percent of all salary increase funds were allocated to performance increases, top performers could receive additional amounts over and above the automatic movement through the standard portion of the salary range.

Such *performance-based salary increases* (PSIs) went to 12 percent of the represented employees, who receive PSIs ranging from 3.9 to 5.9 percent in the first fiscal year (1995 to 1996). PSIs ranged from 0.5 to 4 percent in fiscal year 1996 to 1997 due to the greater number of employees receiving increases. One wonders what happened the third year! In any event, achieving an extra 1 or 2 or 3 percent is unlikely to stimulate anyone to significantly higher levels of performance, particularly when they are guaranteed automatic annual increases.

Others take steps to address the differentiation problem:

> Through the implementation of a new tool called the Monoline Merit Increase Matrix, one organization shows how it rewards employees based on performance and gets more mileage out of its merit increase budget....
>
> The 1998 Monoline Matrix eliminates the use of comparisons for merit increases. It is designed to create a larger distinction in the merit percent

provided between top performers and employees who meet expectations and are paid fairly for their work....

Under the new methodology, managers must examine the possibility that employees who meet performance goals do not have to receive a merit increase if they are competitively paid. (Scholl, 1998, p. 28)

What a radical idea—zero increases for those already well paid for their performance! When one examines this "new" approach, it turns out that Allstate did just what was being advocated 30 years ago when I first got involved with compensation administration. That is, they communicated to employees that "Allstate pays competitively based on extensive market analyses and that an employee's pay is not a random number." They trained HR managers in the program and in how to help line managers with it, they built training about the compensation program into new manager orientation, they improved their performance management process, and they established an ongoing communications program about the emphasis on pay for performance.

All in all, the description suggests that they did a very creditable job. However, switching from a traditional merit matrix that considers both position in the salary range and performance to one that considers only performance probably was irrelevant to the program's success, or lack thereof, with the possible exception that the shift served as a device which Allstate could use to communicate that it really meant what was being proposed.

Some approach the problem from a different perspective:

The most common flaw in execution is that organizations have tried to manage pay increases based on performance, rather than managing pay based on performance. The typical merit pay plan leads employees who receive an "excellent" or "significantly exceeds expectations" performance rating to believe they are entitled to a large increase (expressed as a percentage of their current pay)—no matter what their pay is....

The easy way out of the dilemma created by merit pay plans that do not work well may seem to be to shift to some form of person-based pay—or to use variable pay more often. This also raises big issues, however. If organizations pay people based on what they bring to the workplace (e.g., knowledge, skills, abilities and the capability to exhibit specific behaviors), they run the risk of rewarding potential even when no return on that investment is realized in the form of performance. Using variable pay to limit the growth of fixed-cost base pay levels sounds like a solid idea. Variable pay awards are variable costs and can be tied to the organization's ability and willingness to pay.

There are practical considerations, however, when replacing base pay growth with variable pay awards—not the least of which is the reluctance of employees to put their standard of living "at risk." Lending officers do not approve mortgages based on the prospect of a variable pay award, and credit card companies will not wait until the end of the year to be paid (except at great cost to the card holder). (Greene, 1998, p. 27)

Greene is not the first to recognize these issues, and various approaches have been tried to resolve them. Interestingly, Rand and Franz (1998) go "Beyond Broadbanding" to a "cluster-based" model in their approach to solving this dilemma:

> Each job carries a market-based value to the organization. Similar jobs are organized in clusters that define the incumbent's base salary (similar for anyone occupying that or similar positions). Beyond the baseline level of performance expected for every employee in a job (and for which the basic wage is intended), personal performance above and beyond the average is rewarded individually with the variable-pay portion of the compensation system....
>
> In general, pay is administered by providing all employees an annual across-the-board market adjustment equal to the amount the market moves for groups of jobs or all jobs as a whole (e.g., 1+ to 2 percent). The amount can be determined by available market information or through an annual salary survey. A cluster's base salary range is narrow: plus or minus 4 percent on either side of the target. During the transition, employees with salaries falling above the cluster-plus-4-percent receive no addition to base salary, but receive their market adjustment in a lump sum payment. All other increases are determined through a variable pay plan such as gainsharing, profit sharing, or team- and skill-based pay.
>
> The two-pronged system of market-based clusters augmented by explicit performance-based, variable pay is easier to administer and more motivating. It provides an equitable base salary while directly tying part of each person's compensation to performance (e.g., the attainment of corporate goals). (pp. 26–27)

So these authors see the step beyond broadbanding as *narrowbanding*—a very tight base salary range coupled with a range of incentive opportunities. They adopted this approach as a means to fund significant incentives for superior performance without increasing payroll costs disproportionately—a highly desirable objective—while attempting to maintain a competitive base pay level. It also serves to solve the common problem of a lack of meaningful differentiation between the size of pay increases granted for adequate and outstanding performance due to the intermixing of merit pay and salary range maintenance, using the combination of small permanent increases in base and annual, one-time performance awards. One wonders, however, where they got the data for "the amount the market moves for groups of jobs or all jobs as a whole (e.g., 1+ to 2 percent)." (For another, somewhat similar, yet distinctly different, approach to the problem of separating merit pay and range maintenance, see Wolf, 1994.)

PAY FOR WHOSE PERFORMANCE

Even if one can solve the differentiation problem, there still remains the problem of determining the locus of performance—the work group or the individual. The many different types of performance pay plans all devolve into two broad categories, depending on whether performance is measured at the group or at the individual level:

Group plans can fail to specifically direct or reward individual employee behaviors. As a result, group plans have produced somewhat limited results with respect to improvements in employee performance or organizational profitability. Further, group plans do not differentially reward individuals who perform well vs. those who do not. This may exacerbate the perception of pay inequities among better performers.

Performance pay plans based on individual performance are more effective in improving individual employee performances vs. group plans. Typically, these plans provide specific and objective goals for employees to work toward. However, rewarding individual performance may reduce cooperation among employees and focus employees on a restricted range of results. (Abernathy, 1998, p. 23)

BEST PRACTICES VERSUS PRACTICES OF THE BEST

If the new compensation approaches give superior results in terms of employee satisfaction, employee motivation, and/or administrative effectiveness, one would expect that companies that are the best must be using them. In one study, the world's most admired companies were nominated and ranked by their peers and the investment community. These companies' remuneration practices were then researched in detail by the Hay Group:

Hay did not find convincing evidence that newer remuneration approaches were favored. Broadbanding or competency-based pay, for example, were no more prevalent in the most admired companies than in their industry comparators....

There were similarly ambiguous findings on performance-related pay as the most admired companies were divided....

Regarding stock plans, the admired companies stand apart from their peers. A high proportion of these companies have share options or other share plans in which the majority of employees can participate....

Given the lack of a clear differentiation on many aspects of remuneration design, the research turned to pay levels....The companies were found to offer above-median total remuneration compared to others in their sector. But base salaries are less uniformly competitive. Although some certainly pay in the top 25 percent or even 10 percent, others hover around the median salaries for their industry. In these cases, however, higher earnings from bonuses and long-term incentives more than make up the difference in direct compensation.

But even this finding can be misleading. The most admired companies do not necessarily have policies designed to be more generous. For example, share option grants are often no more than the market median. However, because these companies are often the highest performing in their sector, bonuses and share plan gains are higher....

At these companies, remuneration practices are market aware, not market driven, and reinforce beneficial internal work cultures and business strategies rather than follow the latest fads. (Wright, 1998, pp. 21–23)

DESIGNING AN EFFECTIVE COMPENSATION PROGRAM

First, an effective compensation program should recognize that monetary rewards do change employee behavior despite what some academicians have claimed. The power of money is twofold. It not only is valued for itself, for what it can buy, but it can also serve as a powerful communication device, as a scorecard if you will.

Second, stick to the basics when designing a salary program. Pay people at a reasonable market level for base salary based on survey data (What is reasonable will depend on your ability to pay and the availability of the talent you need.) Focus primarily on external pay market data, and maintain internal equity *only within each separate pay market.* That is, internal equity is important *within* information technology, engineering, accounting, etc., but is not important *between* these groups as they are in separate external pay markets. One size never fits all!

Third, use variable pay everywhere. For those positions that cannot be individually measured, use group measures (work group, location, division, and/or corporate measures, as appropriate). For those positions that can be individually measured, use a combination of individual and group measures (individual measures to motivate individual effort, group measures to encourage cooperative behavior).

Fourth, keep the performance measures as simple as possible and limit their numbers, preferably to two or three. Remember, what you measure is what you get, so pick your measures carefully.

Fifth, communicate, communicate, communicate. Communicate the details of the program. Communicate the rationale for the measures—that is, how they fit into the organization's strategy. Communicate on an ongoing basis actual performance versus target performance.

BIBLIOGRAPHY

Abernathy, William B., 1998. "Linking Performance Scorecards to Profit-Indexed Performance Pay." *ACA News,* vol. 41, no. 4, April, pp. 23–25.

Abosch, Kenan S. 1998. "Confronting Six Myths of Broadbanding." *ACA Journal,* vol. 7, no. 3, autumn, pp. 28–35.

Greene, Robert J. 1998. "Improving Merit Pay Plan Effectiveness." *ACA News,* vol. 41, no. 4, April, pp. 26–29.

Logue, Karen A. 1998. "Implementing Pay for Performance in the Public Sector," *ACA News,* vol. 41, no. 2, February, 1998.

Rahbar-Daniels, Dana. 1998. "Aligning Total Human Resources Processes Through Competency-Based Broadbanding." *ACA News,* vol. 41, No. 10, November-December, pp. 36–40.

Rand, James F., and Randal S. Franz. 1998. "Beyond Broadbanding: Crafting a Cluster-Based Model." *ACA News,* vol. 41, no. 3, March, pp. 24–28.

Risher, Howard. 1998. "Rethinking Equity." *ACA News,* vol. 41, no. 4, April, pp. 6–7.

Scholl, Steve. 1998. "Allstate Pay for Performance Methodology Rewards Excellence." *ACA News,* vol. 41, no. 8, September, pp. 28–31.

Sierra, Lorenzo. 1998. "The Next Generation of Broadbanding." *ACA News,* vol. 41, no. 2, February, pp. 21–24.

Wolf, Martin G. 1991. "Theories, Approaches, and Practices of Salary Administration: An Overview," in Milton Rock and Lance A. Berger, eds., *The Compensation Handbook,* 3rd ed. New York: McGraw-Hill, pp. 43–48.

————1994. "A Nimble Compensation System for Managing Change," in Lance A. Berger and Martin J. Sikora, eds., *The Change Management Handbook.* New York: Richard D. Irwin, pp. 431–442.

Wright, Vicky. 1998. "Remuneration Strategies in the World's Most Admired Companies." *ACA News,* vol. 41, no. 8, September, pp. 20–23.

5

JOB ANALYSIS AND JOB DOCUMENTATION

Deborah A. Grigson, Consultant

Aon Consulting

Gerald W. Stoffel, Vice President

Aon Consulting

EMPLOYER AND EMPLOYEE EXPECTATIONS are defined through the process of job analysis. Job analysis is indeed a process. Expectations are constantly changing and evolving as a result of incumbent skills or lack thereof, technology, downsizing, organizational growth, and so on. In an effort to systematize the process, employers have developed methods of job documentation that provide "snapshots" of the agreed-upon job content.

HOW JOB ANALYSIS CAN BE USED

Job analysis and job documentation are used in a variety of human resource management functions, as demonstrated in tthe chart in Figure 5.1.

FIGURE 5.1   Functional areas in which job analysis is used.

Job Analysis					
Performance Management	Career Growth	Discipline	Legal Compliance	Recruiting and Staffing	Job Value or Worth

Performance Management

Arguably, 90 percent of all job analysis is done in an effort to manage performance. It just makes good sense to judge an employee's job performance on the basis of the agreed-upon job description. The job description should accurately describe the essential functions of the job, and these are the functions upon which the employee should be judged. Employers will take these essential functions and develop standards. These standards are then the basis of the measurement scale.

Career Growth

In addition to performance reviews, employers rely on job analysis to determine the hierarchy of jobs. From this hierarchy, the employer develops the organization maps or charts, which lead to the second function of job analysis and job documentation: career growth. Knowing the responsibilities of the other jobs in the organization's hierarchy allows both the employee and the employer to focus job training and education to prepare the employee for the next step in his or her career.

Discipline

When a job's responsibilities are well documented, employers can rely on the documentation to let employees know when they are not meeting the demands of the job. There are a variety of reasons that an employee may fall short of his or her job expectations. As jobs grow, employees may find that their current skill set is not adequately keeping pace. It may also be true that an employee is not able to fulfill the essential functions of the job. A well-written, current job description will offer good information about why the job exists. Documentation will be key to the employee's understanding of the employer's position. Should an outside agency become involved in a discipline or termination decision, this documentation is critical to the fact-finding process.

Legal Compliance

Job documentation has increased in importance over the past several years due to the enactment and enforcement of several laws. For example, employers are required to comply with the Americans with Disabilities Act (ADA). In essence, the act gives all people the right to work at any job for which the individual can perform the essential functions. The Equal Employment Opportunity Commission (EEOC) has been charged with the responsibility of enforcing ADA requirements, and this agency relies on employers' job descriptions to review compliance. The EEOC has advised employers that the focus of the job documentation should be on the purpose of the function and the result to be accomplished, rather than the manner in which the function is presently or traditionally performed. The EEOC emphasizes that the documentation should accurately reflect what the employee does. If there is a discrepancy between what the employer and employee report as the job content, the EEOC will make its own observations. Understandably, since this act was passed, a flurry of job documentation has ensued.

In addition, employers use job documentation to support claims of exempt or nonexempt status. The Fair Labor Standards Act (FLSA) says that, in general, all nonexempt employees must be paid time and one half for all hours worked over 40 per week. Of course, this is an oversimplification; however, many court battles have been fought over the issue of which positions are exempt. Exempt status is often defined by a person's job content. The employer's best defense is to have a solid job analysis in advance of the litigation.

Recruiting and Staffing

Employers use job analysis to provide recruiters and candidates with facts about an opening and the requirements for filling the job. The job analysis is used to prepare the employment advertisement, to hold the interview, and then to give a new hire a sense of what he or she will be doing for the organization.

Job Value or Worth

Employers often rely on job analysis as a basis for developing external job comparisons to determine the value or worth of a job. The employer's job content is reviewed against similar job content in published surveys. An analyst can learn two things by making these comparisons. First, he or she can learn how positions are ranked in the marketplace. Second, she or he can learn what the market is paying for similar skill sets or responsibilities. This process is usually referred to as market pricing, which is a form of job evaluation.

In summation, job analysis sets the stage for the human resource management process. Every organization should have a formal system for recognizing its expectations. This system should allow for constant change, making every attempt to maintain job documentation.

The management functions listed above are compromised by not having current and accurate job documentation. Generally speaking, organizations do not keep up as well as they should with the process of documenting ever-changing jobs. Often job documentation is unavailable, outdated, inaccurate, or poorly written.

IMPLEMENTING JOB ANALYSIS AND/OR DESIGN

Job Documentation

The *first step* toward providing a sound basis from which to document an organization's jobs is to analyze the organization's culture. This can be done by assessing where the company is heading, reviewing the organization's mission statement, compensation, and benefits philosophy, and interviewing management and employees of the organization. Consultants usually refer to this as strategic alignment. One of the objectives of strategic alignment is to ensure that the job analysis and subsequent documentation supports the organization's work culture and describes what is important to the organization.

The *second step* is to determine what categories or parameters will be analyzed. How jobs are defined lays the framework for recruiting, discipline, performance measurement, and so on. Jobs can be defined in terms of skills, competencies, abilities, responsibilities, duties, degree of decision making, supervisory responsibilities, qualifications, and output expectations and/or results. These categories should represent what the organization values. Once the organization has decided on the appropriate categories, they should be used for all job documentation. This provides consistency between jobs.

Once the categories have been determined, then a job analysis process should be prepared, one that ensures credibility, reliability, system compatibility, and cost effectiveness.

Credibility. The job analysis process is credible if the documented job content matches what the incumbent and the supervisor perceive as the job content. This can be achieved by having both the incumbent and the supervisor agree on the job content. Admittedly, the employer has the ultimate say in determining job content.

Credibility can be maintained or eroded on the basis of how the information is utilized. As an example, when a manager falsely categorizes an employee's skills and abilities as a "higher-valued" job to ensure a performance increase, the manager compromises the job analysis process. Both employees and the employers begin to see the process as corrupt.

The process may be more credible if an independent third party analyzes the jobs. Companies tend to feel that people outside of the organization's employment will be more objective. This approach will make it easier to separate the incumbent from the job content.

Reliability. Job analysis and documentation is as reliable as the data provided in the job description. The data should be current and should accurately describe the job content and the nature of the job as it is today. Some of the job analysis reliability comes from how effectively the data can be used to evaluate the position's relative value. This is a measure of both internal and external reliability.

System Compatibility. As previously mentioned, job analysis provides documentation of job content. The systems that are installed around this function must interact with the various human resource functions that rely on job analysis, recruiting, discipline, performance management, career growth, job value or worth, and legal compliance.

Cost Effectiveness. Any system that does not meet an organization's goal of cost effectiveness will surely fall by the wayside. Thus the system's administration should be carefully examined from that perspective. Prior to accepting a particular methodology, the methodology should be reviewed in terms of its acceptance inside of a particular work culture. The administration should be simplistic enough that the people who get involved in the job analysis process are willing to give the time necessary to maintain the system.

The *third step* in the job analysis process is to collect job content. Employers have used a variety of methods to collect job content. Job content can be obtained through observation, questionnaires, interviews, and/or work team analysis. These methods can be used alone or in combination.

Observation.   This method is effective for lower-level jobs that require repetitive tasks. The job analyst will spend a period of time watching employees assigned to one job identifying the skills, abilities, and results that are necessary to complete the job. The observations can then be documented for use at a later date.

Questionnaire.   Questionnaires are sent to all incumbents in a particular job. The information is then compiled and documented for the supervisor's approval. The process can be reversed.

The *final step* in the job analysis process is to document job content. Typically, this documentation is in the form of a job description. There is no magic to the format. The best job descriptions are clear and concise. One page of documentation is sufficient, provided that it captures the data collected.

Exhibits 5A and 5B provide a job description and job description questionnaire, along with instructions for completing them, to demonstrate a simplistic method of data collection and documentation. This particular form and questionnaire are provided in a computerized format. The format is designed so that the manager can answer the questionnaire, and the computer program will automatically write the job description from the manager's answers.

Another option for providing job documentation is called a position charter. Often this type of documentation is used for newly created positions. An example of a job charter is provided in Exhibit 5C.

CONCLUSION

Despite the relative importance of monitoring job content, employers repeatedly fail to maintain accurate job documentation. Most often the reason cited for this oversight is the lack of time. Job content is analyzed and documented on an as-needed basis. Many employers have turned to computer technology to help them maintain current, accurate job data.

There are a number of computer models available today that claim to meet all of the employer's requirements. Employers should review the credibility, reliability, cost effectiveness, and system compatibility of potential systems prior to investing the company's time and money.

Employers would be well served by developing a system for routinely collecting job content. It may be helpful and appropriate to attach a questionnaire to the annual performance review. The incumbent's job description could be reviewed as part of the performance management process. Employers will find that current, accurate job documentation will facilitate virtually all Human Resource processes.

EXHIBIT 5A   ABC Company: Draft Job Description/Questionnaire Instruction Sheet: Trainer's Guide

OVERVIEW

There is a lot of change going on at ABC Company. As we continue to grow and work on achieving our goals, it is important that we understand our jobs and have up-to-date job descriptions. With that in mind, we want to get your input into your job responsibilities and requirements.

The process of completing the questionnaire will give you the opportunity to think about your job and its key responsibilities and expectations. The final job descriptions will accomplish the following:

- Facilitate a greater understanding of your role and the roles of others within the company

- Define ABC Company jobs clearly enough to allow for accurate comparisons to similar jobs in the marketplace and, ultimately, to ensure that each job is placed in the proper ABC Company salary range

- Serve as a foundation for planning and evaluating performance for your position

This instruction guide, supplemented by the sample questionnaire you have been given, is designed to guide you through completing the job questionnaire.

1. Note that employee involvement in writing their own job descriptions is important to the process of redefining all the ABC Company jobs in light of recent growth and changes.

2. Emphasize that ABC Company needs employee involvement and support.

3. Make sure that all employees understand the reason for this questionnaire process, that this process is the foundation for a consistent and equitable compensation program.

4. Emphasize that someone who doesn't know the job should be able to review the job description and understand the complexity and scope of the position.

5. Discuss the procedures and goals for this meeting—that you will go through the questionnaire together, section by section, and in the end, all employees will have (individually or jointly) completed their own full job description.

EXHIBIT 5A   ABC Company: Draft Job Description/Questionnaire Instruction Sheet: Trainer's Guide *(Continued)*

I. BACKGROUND INFORMATION

This section asks for the most basic information about your position, including position title, job code, pay grade, department, unit, location, supervisor's title, number of direct and indirect reports (how many of those jobs that report to you, as well as those jobs that are in your organizational structure but don't report directly to you), and the current date.

There is a space on each questionnaire for your signature, as well as those of your supervisor and manager. The purpose of having these signatures is to ensure that you, your supervisor, and your manager have a shared understanding of your job focus.

1. Note that if they are unsure as to an answer in the background section, simply leave it blank. If they are not sure who their supervisor is, they should choose the title of the person who discusses their salary changes and gives them performance reviews.

2. Explain that "direct reports" encompasses those employees for whom they are immediately responsible There should be no other level of management between themselves and the reports. Also explain that "indirect reports" refer to those employees that they supervise through their direct reports.

3. Discuss the procedure for approval signatures. Indicate that this process is in place not to check up on them but rather to ensure that all parties have a common understanding as to the content of the job. Stress that since these signatures indicate agreement, all necessary communication should have taken place prior to "signing off."

EXHIBIT 5A   ABC Company: Draft Job Description/Questionnaire Instruction Sheet:
Trainer's Guide (*Continued*)

II. POSITION SUMMARY

This should be a brief general statement, typically 1 to 2 sentences, that summarizes the overall purpose of your position. Consider the response to this question as your job's mission statement. Someone reading your statement should come away with a good sense of your job's purpose in terms of both major activities and critical end results.

Try to answer the following questions:

- What am I being paid to achieve?

- How does my job support ABC Company's goals?

1. This section is often the most difficult section for an employee to write because of its broad focus and lack of day-to-day specificity.

2. Explain that the exact wording is not as important as getting the basic idea across clearly.

3. If the employees need further guidance, go over the examples in greater detail or make an example of your own job. It may be helpful for the employees to complete the remainder of the questionnaire first and then return here.

EXHIBIT 5A   ABC Company: Draft Job Description/Questionnaire Instruction Sheet: Trainer's Guide (*Continued*)

III.   JOB RESPONSIBILITIES

These brief numbered statements should describe those activities that are critical to your job's success. Basically, these are the actions that allow you to achieve your job's mission (as stated in section II). Essential functions should include all activities you perform that directly allow you to achieve your mission. Secondary functions should include additional activities you perform that are not as important to your mission.

Each responsibility statement should contain information on what you do in this activity and the approximate percentage of time you spend performing it during the course of a typical week or month. Percentage of time should total 100 percent. Do keep in mind that you want to give a general idea of the proportion of your work time spent on each activity. There is no need to be exact about this (that is, don't worry about small percentage differences).

1. Explain that this section basically composes the specifics of the job.
2. Emphasize that the questionnaire is not looking for a laundry list of responsibilities detailing every minute task performed by the employee. Rather, the employee should list a small number (approximately five to eight) of major accountabilities.
3. Reinforce that essential functions are those which must be performed in order for the company to continue operating smoothly. Secondary functions may be described as those that aren't absolutely necessary for continued success in the position.
4. Once again, stress that wording is not extremely important.
5. If necessary, use your position as an example.

EXHIBIT 5A   ABC Company: Draft Job Description/Questionnaire Instruction Sheet: Trainer's Guide (*Continued*)

IV. RESULTS EXPECTATIONS

These answers will describe the ongoing outputs or results or outcomes that your job produces. Generally, your answers will describe the end results of your job—that is, what you need to accomplish by performing the responsibilities described above. In identifying these results, don't put down specific measurable objectives that you want to fulfill this year (for example, increase check processing speed by 5 percent). The focus should be on those enduring results you are expected to achieve on a continuing basis. Of course, these results statements may be helpful to you as you identify specific performance goals for a particular time period.

1. Explain that this section should answer the question "Why do I do my job?" and "What does my job achieve?"

2. Generally, these statements will flow from the previously determined job responsibilities. Stress that this section is not to be seen as specific objective setting, although ultimately annual objective setting could be seen as an outgrowth of these responses.

3. Note that not all job responsibilities need to have defined results or expectations.

EXHIBIT 5A   ABC Company: Draft Job Description/Questionnaire Instruction Sheet: Trainer's Guide (*Continued*)

V. SKILLS AND ABILITIES

In this section, you should identify the key skills and abilities necessary to attain the results expectations you described above. To assist you in completing this section, broad categories of knowledge, customer influence, communication, and leadership have been provided. If your position requires a skill or ability that does not fit any of these categories, use the blank space after "other."

Make sure to describe the main skills and abilities your position requires, which may not necessarily be those that you personally have. These skill categories are defined as follows:

Knowledge: Technical, specialized, business, industry, and/or operational knowledge or understanding required in your job

Customer influence: Requirements for educating, training, selling to, serving, and/or otherwise influencing customers

Communication: Requirements for verbal communication—either oral or written

Leadership: Required ability to manage people, department(s), and/or operations or to provide guidance or counsel to others

1.   Emphasize that if their position does not require particular skills in one or more of the categories, it is acceptable to leave the category blank.

2.   Note that the questionnaire is looking for skills and abilities necessary to complete the job, not necessarily those skills and abilities which the employee possesses.

EXHIBIT 5A   ABC Company: Draft Job Description/Questionnaire Instruction Sheet: Trainer's Guide (*Continued*)

VI. EDUCATION AND RELATED EXPERIENCE

This section of the job description allows you to describe the education and/or experience requirements to qualify for your job—that is, the type of work and/or life experience, formal education and/or training, vocational training, apprenticeships, professional certifications, or any other particular background necessary to be hired into this position.

1. Once again, emphasize that the questionnaire is looking for education and experience necessary to qualify for the job, not necessarily education and experience that the employee possesses.
2. Note that if their position does not require any particular prior education or experience, it is acceptable to leave the category blank.

VII. WORKING CONDITIONS AND/OR PHYSICAL REQUIREMENTS

In order to fully understand your position, it is important to define the overall working context in which you perform your tasks. To meet this goal, it is important to describe any unusual physical or mental demands that are placed on your position.

Your response should include requirements for physical mobility (e.g., sitting, standing, running, or climbing), physical effort (e.g., lifting, carrying, or pushing), unusual sensory requirements (e.g., distinguish colors, touch, concentration, or mental effort), work environment (noise levels, air conditions, temperatures, etc.), and special travel requirements.

There is no need to list items if your work does not place unusual physical and/or mental demands on you.

1. Explain that this section is looking only for those conditions that are not found in a typical office setting.
2. Note that many individuals may leave this section blank.
3. If additional questions arise, use the accompanying checklist as a source of information.

EXHIBIT 5A   ABC Company: Draft Job Description/Questionnaire Instruction Sheet: Trainer's Guide (*Continued*)

VIII.   ORGANIZATIONAL CHART

This section will provide a general overview of your "location" in the organization. Your response should include position titles for your supervisor, yourself, colleagues who also report directly to your supervisor, and your direct reports. Place the appropriate titles into the boxes on the chart.

The box above "Your Title" should be used for your immediate supervisor's title. If there is some doubt as to who your immediate supervisor is, choose the title of the person who discusses salary changes with you and reviews your performance. The boxes to your left and right are reserved for other positions that report to your supervisor. Last, the boxes below you are for employees who report directly to you. There is also space in the lower left of these boxes for the number of employees in each of the subordinate positions. If there are more than five different positions that report directly to you, use the lines below the chart to include information on those additional positions.

1.   Note that this section must be consistent with the direct and indirect reports responses from the background information section.

2.   Explain that the purpose of this section is to provide a visual representation of the organization in which the employee works.

EXHIBIT 5B   ABC Company: Job Description

Division:		Job Title: Field Applications Engineer/Sr. Applications Engineer
Job Code: 5831 - 5834		Level: 1, 2, 3, 4
Date:	Date of Last Revision: 11/3/97	Exempt Status: Exempt/Nonsupervisory

PRIMARY RESPONSIBILITIES

Provides technical support to the company's sales staff and customers. Provides, presents, and interprets design, application, and service information. Develops product specifications and applications usable by a specific customer and explores the business feasibility of general marketing. Designs and builds test application circuits and demonstration boards.

REPORTING RELATIONSHIP

ESSENTIAL FUNCTIONS

Answers technical questions from customers. Designs and builds test application circuits and demonstration boards or software. Develops customer application seminars and sales force training material. Writes application bulletins. Evaluates new products and competitors' products.

PROGRESSION

JOB LEVEL

SENIOR LEVEL: Works on problems of diverse scope where analysis of data requires evaluation of identifiable factors. Exercises judgment within generally defined practices and policies in selecting methods and techniques for obtaining solutions. Displays thorough knowledge of linear and data-conversion specifications, applications, and component testing.

EDUCATIONAL / EXPERIENCE REQUIREMENTS

BS in electrical or mechanical engineering required plus at least five years' engineering experience. Proven experience with op amps, instrumentation amplifiers, and A/D converters.   Excellent verbal and written skills. Proven experience with commercial testing equipment.

ENVIRONMENT

All functions take place inside with optimal lighting. Employees are able to wear casual attire. The employee can expect medium levels of noise. The temperature is generally average. The position is occasionally stressful.

PHYSICAL REQUIREMENTS

The position requires the ability to use both hands in a nonrepetitive motion for up to 4 hours per day. The incumbent can expect frequent breaks during the day. The position requires the ability to occasionally lift 0-10 pounds. The employee sits constantly and stands and walks intermittently.   Excellent visual acuity is required for the position.

Supervisor's Signature:	Date:
Incumbent's Signature:	Date:

EXHIBIT 5B ABC Company: Job Description (*Continued*)

Physical Requirements Survey

Division:		Job Title: Field Applications Engineer/Sr Applications Engineer
Job Code: 5831 - 5834		Level: 1, 2, 3, 4
Date:	Date of Last Revision: 11/3/97	Exempt Status: Exempt/Nonsupervisory

Physical Requirements:

Review the chart below. Indicate which of the following are essential to perform the functions of this job, with or without accommodation. Check one box in each section.

Incumbent Uses:	NA	Right	Left	Both	Repetitive motion Y	Repetitive motion N	The job requires the use of the first category up to 2 hours per day	The job requires the use of the first category up to 4 hours per day	The job requires the use of the first category up to 8 hours per day	Frequent breaks: Normal breaks plus those caused by performing jobs outside of the area.	Limited breaks: Two short breaks and one lunch break.
Section 1					Section 2		Section 3			Section 4	
Hands: (requires manual manipulation)			X			X		X		X	
Feet: (functions requiring foot pedals or the like)	X										

Lifting capacity: Indicate, by checking the appropriate box, the amount of lifting necessary for this job, with or without accommodation.

	NA	Occasionally (As Needed)	Often (Up to 4 Hours Per Day)	Frequently (Up to 8 Hours Per Day)
0-10 pounds		X		
10-20 pounds	X			
20-50 pounds	X			
50-100 pounds	X			
100 plus pounds	X			

Mobility: Indicate which category the job functions fall under by placing a check next to those that apply.

☒ Sits constantly (6 hours or more with two breaks and one lunch break)

☐ Sits intermittently (6 hours or more with frequent changes, due to breaks and getting up to perform jobs outside of the area)

☐ Stands constantly (6 hours or more with two breaks and one lunch break)

☒ Stands intermittently (6 hours or more with frequent changes, due to breaks and getting up to perform jobs outside of the area)

☐ Bending constantly (4 hours or more with two breaks and one lunch break)

EXHIBIT 5B   ABC Company: Job Description (*Continued*)

☐ Bending intermittently (4 hours or more with frequent changes, due to breaks and getting up to perform jobs outside of the area)
☐ Walks constantly (6 hours or more with two breaks and one lunch break)
☒ Walks intermittently (6 hours or more with frequent changes, due to breaks and getting up to perform jobs outside of the area)

Visual acuity: Indicate the minimum acceptable level, with or without accommodation, necessary for the job.

☒ Excellent visual acuity
☐ Good visual acuity
☐ Not relevant to the job

Auditory acuity: Indicate the minimum acceptable level, with or without accommodation, necessary for the job.

☐ Excellent auditory acuity
☐ Good auditory acuity
☒ Not relevant to the job

EXHIBIT 5B   ABC Company: Job Description (*Continued*)

Essential Functions
Division:

Job title: Field Applications Engineer/Sr Applications Engineer

Reports to:

Required education (check the best answer):
- ☐ High school diploma or GED preferred
- ☐ High school diploma
- ☐ Completion of basic electronics courses
- ☐ Completion of basic vacuum technology courses
- ☐ Associates degree preferred; will accept equivalent education or experience in electronics
- ☐ Ph.D.
- ☐ 4-year college degree in related field
- ☐ MBA or equivalent related experience
- ☐ MSEE or BSEE
- ☐ BSEE
- ☐ AAS
- ☐ Other —
  please describe:_____

Required experience (check all that apply):
- ☐ Good math and communication skills
- ☐ Good oral and written communication skills
- ☐ Excellent math and communication skills
- ☐ Excellent oral and written communication skills
- ☐ Excellent interpersonal skills
- ☐ Excellent communication and presentation skills
- ☐ Minimum of 4 years' related experience
- ☐ Good computer skills
- ☐ 6 years on task experience or equivalent experience
- ☐ 9 years on task experience or equivalent experience
- ☐ 12 years on task experience or equivalent experience
- ☐ 15 years on task experience or equivalent experience
- ☐ 2-6 years in technical marketing with operations management experience
- ☐ 5+ years of experience
- ☐ 1-3 years of technical experience in sales, marketing, or engineering
- ☐ 4-6 years of technical experience in sales, marketing, or engineering
- ☐ 6-12 years of technical experience in sales, marketing, or engineering
- ☐ 7 years of computer technical support
- ☐ 3 years management experience
- ☐ 3 years manufacturing experience
- ☐ Other —
  please describe:_____

List in order of importance the major responsibilities of the job, and estimate the percentage of time spent on each responsibility (the main function of the job may or may not be the one where the most time is spent). Be sure to answer the following questions: Purpose of the job? Results to be accomplished? Do they supervise? Do others do the same job?

1.	%
2.	%

EXHIBIT 5B   ABC Company: Job Description (*Continued*)

3.	%
4.	%
5.	%
6.	
7. Able to react to change productively and handle other essential tasks as assigned.	100%

EXHIBIT 5C   XYZ National Bank: Position Charter

Job title: Senior vice president and chief financial officer, treasurer

Position title: Finance — accounting, treasury, deposit and loan servicing

Position summary: To manage the finance department in addition to providing support and
                        leadership to the bank as a whole.

Period: 4th quarter, 1992

Mission: By example, promote an entrepreneurial spirit as the foundation for a
                        culture by which the bank will achieve its mission.

                        A. *Quality statement:* To represent the bank as the senior financial
                           executive in dealing with the investment community, customers,
                           regulators, peers, and our staff, in a highly professional, businesslike
                           manner.

                        B. *Service statement:* Provide timely, accurate financial data. Create
                           new profit opportunities. Lead others in the pursuit of bank
                           objectives.

Success factors: a. Preferred stock offering circular
                        b. Bank acquisition analysis
                        c. Next year strategic plan and operating budget
                        d. Correspondent bank account analysis
                        e. Standard financial reporting requirements

Comment: *This charter is intended to provide guidance for the position incumbent. It also is
                        intended to be a dynamic document that will change as the company changes.*

                        *The incumbent and the incumbent's supervisor should feel free to suggest new success
                        factors, as appropriate.*

                        *Amendments to existing charters may be made on a quarterly basis. New charters will
                        be developed as appropriate. Existing charters may be discontinued, as appropriate.*

                        *The charter will be used as a guide in analyzing the market competitiveness of base
                        salaries and in assessing the performance of a position incumbent.*

EXHIBIT 5C   XYZ National Bank: Position Charter (*Continued*)

ABC Company
Position Charter/Questionnaire

I. BASIC INFORMATION

Name:	
Job title:	Division/department:
Supervisor's name:	Location:
Your signature:	
	Date:
Supervisor's signature and title:	
	Date:

II. POSITION SUMMARY

Summarize the porpoise of the position in one sentence. What is the function of the job, and why does it exist at ABC company?

III. MISSION

Indicate in no more than four statements of one sentence each, the primary mission of this position. Include the major activities for which this position is responsible.

1.

2.

3.

4.

EXHIBIT 5C   XYZ National Bank: Position Charter (*Continued*)

IV. SUCCESS FACTORS

Indicate in no more than four one-sentence statements the specific results or output that a person in this position is expected to achieve. Include description of quality and service goals.

1.

2.

3.

4.

IV. POSITION REQUIREMENTS

*Indicate particular job requirements that are **necessary for sustained success** in this position.*

Education/experience *(high school, 2, 4, or more years of college, etc./minimum years of experience)*

Specialized knowledge *(computer languages, equipment operations, certifications, licenses, etc.)*

Other

EXHIBIT 5C   XYZ National Bank: Position Charter (*Continued*)

VI. COMPLEXITY/DECISION MAKING

Indicate in no more than a three sentence paragraph the complexity of the position with respect to judgment needed, analytical requirements, diversity of functions performed or responsible for, variety of situations and conditions encountered, and consequences of error.

Indicate in no more than a three sentence paragraph the scope and range of decisions that an employee performing the job can make independently. For example, does the position require the employee to follow standard procedures, internal policy statements, work within broad business objectives, or develop new policies and objectives?

VII. TYPE/NATURE OF CONTACTS

Indicate in no more than a three sentence paragraph the type and nature of internal and external contacts required of an employee in the position. For example, are the contacts of a routine nature to other bank employees? Are there occasional contacts with outside vendors and suppliers? Does the job require frequent contacts with customers influencing their decisions to use bank service? Are there frequent contacts with senior executives of customer companies?

EXHIBIT 5C   XYZ National Bank: Position Charter (*Continued*)

VIII. SUPERVISORY/BUDGET RESPONSIBILTY

If you have supervisory responsibilities, record the total number of direct and indirect reports you supervise.

Direct reports: _____

Indirect reports: _____

Total direct and indirect reports: _____

Indicate the annual approved dollar operating budget you are directly responsible for and/or the annual approved dollar operating budget that you directly influence. For example, if you are responsible only for your own position, indicate you salary as your direct budget; if you directly influence an approved operating budget, such as a financial officer influencing the overall corporate budget, indicate the overall corporate budget you influence.

Budget directly responsible for: _____

Budget directly influence: _____

IX. WORKING CONDITIONS/PHYSICAL REQUIREMENTS

Please describe any special physical requirements, working conditions, concentration, and/or travel that are necessary to perform the job.

6

METHODS OF
JOB EVALUATION

Bernard Ingster

Consultant, Human Resources Management

I N THE UNITED STATES, attempts to establish fair methods for setting pay levels for employees can be traced back to the early years of the federal government. In 1838, in response to grievances about pay equity from clerks working in federal departments, the Senate passed a resolution that urged adoption of a method to assign clerks to pay classes based on differences in the responsibilities and required qualifications of their jobs.[1] This was a cry for "internal equity" in the payment of wages.

However, 70 years passed before this rudimentary concept of position classification was elaborated upon and extended much beyond this population. Between 1909 and 1910 E. O. Griffenhagen fully developed a classification process that was implemented by the municipal service of the city of Chicago. In 1912, Commonwealth Edison Company—a privately owned Chicago utility—also installed his process to cover 5,000 employees.[2]

In a short period between 1909 and 1926, the four methods of job evaluation shown in Table 6.1 were developed. They continue to be the dominant techniques used. This chapter describes the principal design characteristics of the four methods and lists some advantages and disadvantages associated with their application.

TABLE 6.1   Dominant Methods Used in Job Evaluation

Method of Comparison Used	Method of Analysis Used	
	By Considering the Entire Job	By Considering Job Elements
Comparing job against some scale	Classification method, E. O. Griffenhagen, 1909	Point method, Merril R. Lott, 1924
Comparing job against job	Ranking method, Arthur H. Young, George Kelday, Early 1920s	Factor comparison method, Eugene J. Benge, 1926

SOURCE: Table adapted from Eugene J. Benge, Samuel L. H. Burk, and Edward N. Hay, Manual of Job Evaluation: Procedures of Job Analysis and Appraisal (New York: Harper and Brothers, 1941), p. 20, and C. Canby Balderston, "Wage Setting Based on Job Analysis and Evaluation," Industrial Relations Monograph No. 4 (New York: Industrial Relations Counselors, 1940), p. 11.

Until the United States was drawn into World War II late in 1941, the number of employers who adopted job evaluation and related personnel administration practices was very small. However, with wartime regulation of wages under the national War Labor Board—established January 1942—job evaluation and formal salary administration emerged as a major device to adjust pay inequities without igniting a destructive wartime inflation of wages and salaries. By the end of the war in 1945, vast numbers of employers, labor unions, and employees had become acquainted with the subject of this chapter. That was the impetus for the expansive use of job evaluation in compensation program design since that time.[3]

The chapter also covers a relatively recent job evaluation method that has interested human resources professionals but which has had limited application, the *position analysis questionnaire* (PAQ), as well as contemporary efforts to automate job evaluation through the use of computers. It closes with a brief analysis of the ongoing debate that first erupted in the United States 20 years ago regarding the attempt to use job evaluation to resolve charges of discriminatory pay practices.

JOB EVALUATION AS A TOOL TO ACHIEVE GOOD MANAGEMENT

At the start of the twentieth century, two analysts of workplace management—Frederick Winslow Taylor and E. O. Griffenhagen—were urging differing but related management reforms intended to benefit both employers and employees, and, thereby, society at large.

Taylor promoted what he called "scientific management," the objective of which was to extend to all the potential benefits of living in an industrial society. He offered one of the earliest challenges to a then widely held view that employees and employers were bound in an inherently antagonistic relationship. Taylor asserted that in order for *either* group to prosper, the other must prosper as well.[4] Taylor's contribution to the development of job evaluation was his emphasizing management's responsibility (1) to use scientific methods of observation and planning to define and organize the tasks in a job and (2) to recruit and select people who, with continuing training, could perform the required tasks.[5]

While Griffenhagen also believed in the controlling importance of good definition of jobs in the employment relationship, his emphasis was on what he termed "personnel administration," which included the following:

> the processes of formulating policies, and exercising managerial functions, respecting the selection, compensation, well being, and conduct of the persons making up the human organization of an enterprise....[6]

As did Taylor, Griffenhagen believed strongly that compensation plans were important tools for the general management of an organization.

THE CLASSIFICATION METHOD

In this, as in all other job evaluation methods based on the content of the work performed, there is a requirement that the process start with formal, systematic documentation of the nature and characteristics of the jobs to be covered by the program. This step is generally known as *job analysis*. The varied techniques available to perform it will not be described in this chapter. However, that is not intended to diminish the fundamental importance of job analysis to the job evaluation processes discussed.

The classification method produces a hierarchy of jobs through the use of a common-sense, nonquantitative approach that might be adopted in any type of classification effort. The process first requires the selection of criteria appropriate to the purpose of the classification to be attempted. In this job evaluation method, the three usual criteria for grouping jobs together are the *duties,* the *responsibilities,* and the *qualifications required* of the people hired to perform the work. Existing compensation levels of the positions being studied are never referenced in the process.

The intent of the process is to develop *classes* among the jobs being considered, with a *class* defined as a single job or a group of jobs exhibiting common and distinctive qualities of the classifying criteria. In effect, a *class* is the smallest group that can be identified as deserving uniform treatment with regard to pay and other aspects of personnel administration. At the risk of some oversimplification, the process works as follows:

1. A broad, general category of positions is identified from among other broad categories of positions. For example, an *engineering group* is separated from *physical sciences positions* and *biological sciences positions,* all of which are in a category of *professional positions* in contrast with *nonprofessional, support positions.*

2. The engineering jobs are divided into subdivisions, such as *civil* and *mechanical engineering.*

3. The mechanical engineering jobs, for example, are then grouped in a hierarchy by applying the three classifying criteria cited earlier to the job content documentation for each job. *The criteria are always applied to the entire content of the job.* The question being answered in this stage of the process is: Which jobs have (a) the most complex duties *and* (b) the highest level of responsibilities *and* (c) the most demanding qualifications requirements?

4. The process is then applied to the civil engineering positions in like manner, and then extended to all remaining categories of positions.

5. Each hierarchy is then examined separately to determine the number of *classes* into which the positions in each hierarchy should be placed. This effort usually results in a compromise between groupings that are exceptionally homogeneous and narrow and groupings that are loosely inclusive. Neither too few nor too many classes are desirable.

6. Classes are then compared *across* each occupational specialty to determine the number of *levels* or *grades* of work that exist within the entire block of the positions studied. Table 6.2 illustrates the type of diagram often constructed at the completion of this step.

Prior to assigning specific pay levels to the grades, *class specifications* (or *occupational specifications*) are prepared for each class. These include such information as the class title, which is assigned to every position in that specific class; a general description of the duties common to all positions in that class; and the necessary qualifications for performing the duties—data that can be used for recruiting, selecting, and training candidates and incumbents for positions in the class.

The classification method has been widely used by government at national, state, and local levels. In very large organizations such as the federal government, the total number and diversity of positions usually require the use of additional process steps that have not been discussed here.

TABLE 6.2 Representation of the Framework of the Classification Method

Grades	Professional Positions		Clerical/technical Support Positions	
	Mechanical Engineering	Civil Engineering	Accounting Clerical	Electronics Technician
1	c			
2	c			
3	c	c		
4	c	c		
5	c	c		
6	c	c		c
7			c	c
8			c	c
9			c	
10			c	

| c | = A class of positions.
Grade 1 contains the position classes of "highest value" among the positions covered.

Compensation analysts who have administered programs based on this method indicate that (1) it is a very complex system, (2) it is very flexible in accommodating an exceptional range of differing types of jobs, and (3) it is prone toward either loose or tight interpretations of language, creating problems in maintaining appropriate grade levels.

A CONTEMPORARY MODIFICATION OF THE POSITION CLASSIFICATION METHOD

During the past several years, IBM has been working to transform its corporate culture to emphasize three new values:

- Risk taking to assure winning against formidable competitors

- Being the first company to the market with new products and systems to assure high profitability and market share

- Transforming employees' work unit commitments to a willingness to be "teamed" as required for the success of IBM as a whole.[7]

The long-prevailing compensation system did not reflect these values. It had 24 salary grades and was based on a point plan with 10 compensable factors. It was designed for rewards in an organization characterized by hierarchies and work unit insularities.[8]

A newly developed compensation plan being used increasingly is based on a simple, nonquantitative job evaluation plan that utilizes elementary aspects of a classification approach. There are 10 *bands,* each of which is divided into three job-based aspects: *skills required, leadership and/or contribution,* and *scope and impact.* Key job characteristics are provided in cells within each band, and each band has an assigned minimum and maximum base pay amount.[9]

An online library of position descriptions is available to managers. Employees are assigned to bands by the managers who match work performed with one of the descriptions.

THE RANKING METHOD

This method is a second type of *whole-job,* nonquantitative grading process. It has been described as a "card-sorting system, because under it jobs are arranged from high to low as are the cards of a playing card deck."[10] Differing jobs are ranked one against the other according to the perceived relative value of each job to the organization. The rankings create groups of jobs that can then be treated in a common manner for purposes of pay determination.

The method was used by Arthur H. Young and George Kelday at the International Harvester Company in the early 1920s, and they are usually considered to be its originators. In their use, judgments of "job value" were made without benefit of any common set of clarifying criteria.[11] However, others who have used the process sometimes introduce criteria to assist the evaluators.[12]

The virtue of the ranking method is simplicity. However, unless it is used with the discipline of some definition of differing levels of job worth that the job rankers adopt in common, it is not a good choice for establishing internal equity in a compensation program. On the other hand, in small organizations willing to assure its use in a disciplined, consistent manner with excellent record keeping, it is a viable method for establishing a formal compensation program.

THE POINT METHOD

This method is the most widely used of the four dominant methods under discussion. It was devised in 1925 by Merrill R. Lott when he was superintendent of employment at the Sperry Gyroscope Company, and he described it fully in his book one year later.[13] The point method provides job evaluators with a means of quantifying their judgments about the relative worth of various aspects of jobs by assigning points to those judgments. It produces a final statement about job worth expressed as a single total of those points. As with most attempts to quantify attributes of things that are not readily measurable, the point method has a tendency to be perceived as being "more scientific" than either the classification or ranking methods.

In general, there are approximately eight steps in the process of designing a point plan for evaluating jobs:

1. A number of factors are identified as being common to all jobs to be evaluated. These are called the *compensable factors*.
2. The factors are defined and weighted to reflect their perceived importance in the organization.
3. Each factor is analyzed to determine how many different *levels* of job content will probably need to be covered by the factor. These levels are usually called *degrees of the factor*, and they are also defined.
4. The degrees for each factor are quantified using the relative weightings of the factors. Table 6.3 is a representation of a type of evaluation scale that is used in this method.
5. The evaluators study a written description of each job. They assign point values for each factor by making judgments about the job content using the predetermined points and job requirements for the degrees of each factor. (No reference is made to the existing wage or salary of the incumbents in the job.)
6. Each job acquires a *total job content* point value.
7. The titles of the positions are hierarchically arranged according to their total point values.
8. Groupings of total points are tested to develop appropriate job grades. The grades can then be converted to pay levels.

Historically, the point method was used predominantly for nonexempt clerical and production positions. In 1975 the U.S. Civil Service Commission adopted the

TABLE 6.3   Representation of a Job Evaluation Scale in the Point Method

Factor 7: Responsibility for Operations		
Degree	Job Requirements	Points
1	Responsible only for use of own time	15
2		30
3	Must coordinate with crew in a production unit	45
4		60
5	Assures flow of individual processing and meets production schedule for machined parts	75
6		90
7	Develops schedule and assumes joint and supervisory responsibility for work unit	105
8		120

use of a point method, named the *Factor Evaluation System,* for some aspects of classifying certain positions covered by grades 1 through 15 of the general schedule compensation system.[14] The selection was made after substantial investigation and experimentation with a variety of job evaluation techniques. The choice is not surprising. Those who have administered point method plans in organizations that inform employees of all of the details of the plan invariably find that most employees understand and find reasonable the principles and rules governing the program.

THE FACTOR COMPARISON METHOD

This method was respected but never widely used after it was developed by Eugene J. Benge in 1926. The concept has been represented as having evolved out of studying the advantages and disadvantages of the three other dominant methods discussed in this chapter.[15] The method is based upon two key ideas: (1) It assumes that the rates paid for a small number of key jobs in an organization will be found to be in a proper relation to one another; and (2) it builds job content measurement scales from the rates of the key jobs that are applied to all other jobs being evaluated. These concepts can be represented as shown in Table 6.4.

The most significant derivative of the factor comparison method is the *Guide Chart-Profile Method of Job Evaluation* developed by Edward N. Hay and Dale Purves in the early 1950s.[16] Hay had used factor comparison evaluation, and he

TABLE 6.4   Building Job Content Measurement Scales for the Factor Comparison Method

Job Title	Current Pay Rate	Factors for Comparing Key Jobs		
		Technical Knowledge	Complexity of Work	Responsibility
A	$22.00/h	7.80	5.50	8.70
B	$16.50/h	6.60	4.95	4.95
C	$13.00/h	5.85	4.55	2.60

The job titles are those of key jobs, which are a cross section of all jobs and which have current rates considered to be in proper relation to each other.

The factors are considered to be of significance to all jobs. The factors selected *only* for this illustration are technical knowledge required to perform the work, complexity of the work, and level of responsibility assigned to the job.

Job analysts are asked to allocate a portion of the current pay rate to each factor according to the analysts' views of the relative importance of that factor in each job. Their differing views are rationalized, and the allocated pay rates are converted to "points" in job content measuring scales for use in evaluating all other jobs.

The resulting hierarchy of jobs is grouped into grades.

was a friend and colleague of Benge. Hay's innovations were (1) the elimination of wage rates as the basis for creating measurement scales and (2) the introduction of "profiles" that in effect substitute percentages of job content for the process of allocating a portion of wage rates to each factor. Over nearly 50 years, this method has achieved worldwide use in all economic sectors through the consulting organization founded by Hay, currently named the Hay Group.

AN ALTERNATIVE PERSPECTIVE ON JOB EVALUATION: THE POSITION ANALYSIS QUESTIONNAIRE

There is a traditional admonition given to job evaluators who are using any of the four dominant methods described: Neither the *incumbents* in a job being evaluated nor *any characteristic* of those incumbents may be considered during the process.[17] However, this restraint is challenged by the developers of the *position analysis questionnaire* (PAQ), Ernest J. McCormick, P. R. Jeanneret, and Robert C. Mecham.

The PAQ shifts the traditional focus in job evaluation from subjective judgments of the compensable factors that should be measured in jobs to statistical determinations of how the marketplace is actually valuing worker characteristics. This is accomplished through the use of a structured job analysis questionnaire, developed on the basis of extensive studies that attempted to identify every possible worker behavior. The questionnaire, copyrighted in 1969 by Purdue Research Foundation, is divided into six divisions that cover 187 "job elements." For example, one division consists of 35 job elements measuring the types of information sources that must be perceived by a worker.[18]

There is a substantial amount of published research covering the PAQ. All aspects of administration of the questionnaire—from acquiring the instrument through its processing and analysis—are very carefully controlled. I have administered the PAQ in a regulated manner and then interviewed the participants about the experience. There was a nearly unanimous feeling that probably every important aspect of their work had been covered by the questionnaire.

COMPUTER-ASSISTED JOB EVALUATION

The importance of computers to the administration of the PAQ is suggestive of possible automated applications of job content–based job evaluation systems as well. Many consulting organizations offer such systems, some with a preestablished evaluation method and others with customizing opportunities for clients. The installations are frequently built utilizing a point plan similar to that described in this chapter. All involve use of a structured questionnaire for data collection. The formats and types of the outputs vary considerably.

The vendors of the plans invariably cite the following benefits: (1) reduced time in collecting job content data; (2) consistency in the quality of data gathered; (3) the elimination or computer generation of job descriptions, if desired; (4) the elimination or reduced use of job evaluation committees, which saves executive time; and (5) the ease and relatively low cost of maintenance and updating of the database.

Much of the attraction of computer-assisted evaluation is its potential to maintain current programs with reduced staffing and cost. However, even customized automation may not be able to preserve all desired aspects of an existing program.

CAN JOB EVALUATION SETTLE CHARGES OF DISCRIMINATORY PAY PRACTICES?

If the "true worth of a job" can be determined, a useful process could be developed to address charges that a given pay practice has roots in racial or gender bias. This is essentially the matter that the U.S. Equal Employment Opportunity Commission asked the National Academy of Sciences to study in 1977. The committee appointed to review the matter reached several conclusions related to subjects of this chapter: (1) No universal standard of job worth exists; (2) existing wage rates of labor markets do not provide a measure of relative worth of jobs free of discriminatory practices; and (3) when used under certain guidelines, job evaluation plans can provide measures of job worth useful in identifying and reducing wage discrimination for those covered by a given plan.[19] General guidelines that would be helpful to plan designers are listed in Table 6.5.

TABLE 6.5   Draft Guidelines for Using Job Evaluation Procedures in a Nondiscriminatory Manner

1. Use a single job evaluation system for all employees.

2. The attributes of jobs deserving compensation should be explicit and public.

3. Factors chosen for factor-based plans should be free of radical or gender bias.

4. Factor scores should be fully consistent with the compensable factors of item 2.

5. Factor weights should not result in adverse impact upon a worker population.

6. The integrity of the job evaluation plan should be protected through:

   a. Clear and complete documentation, distributed for all to read

   b. Good training for all who must use the plan

   c. Regular, documented audits of all aspects of its administration

   d. A formal appeals process open to all employees

   e. Committees that are representative of all employee groups

7. The evaluation of specific jobs should be capable of demonstrated validity.

SOURCE: Donald J. Treiman and Heidi I. Hartmann (eds.), "Women, Work, and Wages: Equal Pay for Jobs of Equal Value," *Final Report of the Committee on Occupational Classification and Analysis to the Equal Employment Opportunity Commission* (Washington, D.C.: National Academy of Sciences, 1981), p. 96.

While the committee of the National Academy of Sciences did not advocate the universal adoption of job evaluation by all employers, it found continuing experimentation and development of these ideas to be worthwhile.[20] This is welcome acknowledgment of the socially beneficial contributions of the pioneering developers of job evaluation cited in this chapter.

NOTES

1. U.S. Civil Service Commission, Basic Training Course in Position Classification: Part 1—Fundamentals and the Federal Plan, Personnel Methods Series No. 11—Part 1, rev. ed. (Washington, D.C.: Government Printing Office, 1965), p. 25.
2. E. O. Griffenhagen, Classification and Compensation Plans as Tools in Personnel Administration, Office Executives' Series: No. 17 (New York: American Management Association, 1926), p. 17.
3. David W. Belcher, Compensation Administration (Englewood Cliffs, N.J.: Prentice-Hall, 1974), p. 92.
4. Frederick Winslow Taylor, The Principles of Scientific Management (New York: Harper and Brothers, 1911), p. 10.
5. Ibid., pp. 38–39.
6. Griffenhagen, p. 4.
7. Andrew S. Richter, "Compensation Management and Cultural Change at IBM: Paying the People in Black at Big Blue," Compensation and Benefits Review (May/June 1998), pp. 52–53.
8. Ibid., p. 54.
9. Ibid., p. 55.
10. Benge, Burk, and Hay, p. 23.
11. Balderston, p. 11.
12. Benge, Burk, and Hay, pp. 23–25.
13. Merrill R. Lott, Wage Scales and Job Evaluation (New York: Ronald, 1926).
14. Donald J. Treiman, "Job Evaluation: An Analytic Review," Interim Report of the Committee on Occupational Classification and Analysis to the Equal Employment Opportunity Commission (Washington, D.C.: National Academy of Sciences, 1979), pp. 17–20.
15. Benge, Burk, and Hay, p. 41.
16. Edward N. Hay and Dale Purves, "A New Method of Job Evaluation: The Guide Chart-Profile Method," PERSONNEL Magazine, July 1954.

17. Griffenhagen, p. 20. This is discussed in his report to the Canadian govern-
     ment upon the completion of his installation of his method for 60,000 posi-
     tions in the Dominion of Canada.

18. Robert C. Mecham, "Quantitative Job Evaluation Using the Position
     Analysis Questionnaire (PAQ); A Description and Comparison with
     Traditional Job Evaluation Methods," *Personnel Administrator,* June 1983.

19. Donald J. Treiman and Heidi I. Hartmann (eds.), "Women, Work, and
     Wages: Equal Pay for Jobs of Equal Value," *Final Report of the Committee
     on Occupational Classification and Analysis to the Equal Employment
     Opportunity Commission* (Washington, D.C.: National Academy of
     Sciences, 1981), pp. 94–95.

20. A working group in which I participated was convened by the Committee
     on Occupational Classification and Analysis on May 14–15, 1979, to
     review a draft of guidelines referenced here. While the draft guidelines were
     never published, they were fully consistent with the discussion of job eval-
     uation plans in Treiman and Hartmann, pp. 95–96.

COMPENSATION SURVEYS

D. Terence Lichty
Senior Corporate Compensation Consultant

The Raytheon Company

INFORMATION SHARING—SURVEYS—PROVIDES DATA that can be a cornerstone of your compensation communications efforts. Through participation in and competent analysis of good surveys, your organization can be assured of obtaining solid information that will develop credibility not only with those whose pay is being administered but also with the management who has to foot the bill.

PAY ENVIRONMENT

Compensation surveys are typically designed to examine the external pay levels of positions in a given industry, geographic sector, or functional discipline (such as engineering, human resources, sales, or finance). In fact, market compensation surveys may carry more weight than do organizationally sensitive job evaluation systems, as, for example, when hot information technology skills are in demand and salary levels for those skills far outpace their "normal" place in the pecking order. Salary range midpoints or ranges may also be studied to provide a broader look into an organization's pay policy for a given job.

THE LEGAL QUESTION OF INFORMATION SHARING

Many are reasonably concerned with the legality of passing around salary information. You have probably heard of class-action lawsuits brought for potential area "wage setting" in violation of antitrust laws. In fact, salary surveys are not inherently illegal: The U.S. government is one of the largest collectors and publishers of area wage surveys.

Limited information sharing, such as telling a counterpart in a neighboring company what your company's average wages are for a single position, may seem innocent. However, sharing substantial amounts of information directly with competitors and making decisions based on that data can present problems. Whether true or not, using another company's specific compensation data to establish salary levels can be *perceived* as wage setting. For this reason, one of the safest and often most efficient ways to obtain survey data is through a disinterested third party—such as a trade organization, consultant, or survey company—thereby preserving the industrial participants' data confidentiality.

SURVEY PURPOSES

In formulating and administering your pay structure, you have several goals:

- Avoid inappropriate pay expenses—paying too much (or too little) to too many (or too few).

- Be aware of what the larger (or smaller) organizations are doing, as well as those of your own size, industry type, in your own part of the country.

- Keep on top of line managers' interests in their particular areas or lines of business.

To assist you in meeting those goals, surveys should accomplish the following:

1. Help shape and increase the accuracy of management's pay decisions:

    a.   Develop market data from which to make and support individual practice and broad-based salary policy recommendations

    b.   Develop information on other, broader human resources and operating data for decision making

2. Give you timely, needed answers for management about competitive rates:

    a.   Respond to inquiries from management about pay appropriateness

    b.   Respond to outside inquiries from professional sources and counterparts

3. Provide continuity and consistency of information

4. Provide a vehicle with which to define and communicate what market and what pay is being compared (for example, base salary only, commissions and other variable pay, total cash compensation, or other combinations, including long-term incentives, perquisites, and benefits).

DEFINING THE PAY MARKET

The basic idea behind compensation surveys is to answer this question: What is the market paying? A fundamental starting point, critical to sound management decision making, is answering this question for your organization: What is the competitive labor market for this particular position or group of positions?

Certain complexities can obscure the market pricing picture. For example, most medium and large companies don't have one market but several—exempt and nonexempt; local, regional, national, and international; functional and/or line-of-business markets; and so on. Also, some organizations may *think* their market is limited to the company down the street and the bank on the corner. But, whatever your circumstances, define comprehensive markets *before* developing salary structures, and keep abreast of market data sources and market changes to keep your program current.

Once the market has been defined, the next questions are: What data should I compare? Should I compare only base salary levels or also examine total cash compensation? What about looking at competitors' midpoint structures or comparing your midpoints to their base salaries? The answers are, compare everything, show how your organization stands up in each instance, and draw your primary comparisons to complement your organization's business plans and objectives.

SURVEY TECHNIQUES

Telephone surveys, though generally not the most accurate or sophisticated, are probably the most prevalent form of surveying today. In the compensation departments of most larger companies, rarely a week goes by without another company's calling and asking what a particular job is being paid. Often this type of study is of the "short-fuse" variety and is used to support an out-of-the-ordinary, imminent hiring decision. While the personal touch can be helpful in gathering information quickly, telephone surveys often yield marginal results, forfeiting quality for immediacy; questions are likely to be inconsistently phrased, and answers are likely to be inaccurate. When conducting your own telephone survey, don't forget that, while answers to your questions are important to you, they're rarely of any interest to the person at the other end of the line. In addition, calls often interrupt whatever the person was working on when you called. The data you seek may not be readily available, and you may be getting a best-guess response rather than one that is studied and researched.

Mailed questionnaires are often used by trade organizations, personnel consultants, and survey companies to maximize the size of their databases in a given information area. Compared to telephone surveys, this method achieves far more consistent results, though rarely is this technique capable of providing a quick turnaround answer. The mailed questionnaire can be particularly effective when used in conjunction with telephone surveys and/or personal interviews. To solicit participation and show the extent of data required, the questionnaire is mailed to the potential respondent. The survey questionnaire serves as a recording instrument, increases the chances of collecting consistent data, and gives the prospective respondent the opportunity to complete it at his or her convenience. At a specified time, data are returned to you, or you contact the participant, who has had time to complete the survey. The data can be collected and qualified by mail, by fax, over the phone, or in person.

A hybrid of the mailed questionnaire is the *electronic questionnaire,* often in spreadsheet or database format. In the latter case, the participant might respond to questions through a form built into the database. Sometimes these database applications conduct internal tests and data validation on the input before it returns to the surveyor. The spreadsheet version allows widespread understanding because so many people these days have to have access to Microsoft *Excel,* Lotus *1-2-3,* etc. Both versions have the benefit of allowing the person inputting the data to sort and examine data before submitting them, to import information from other regularly used applications at the office, and to minimize keying errors and needless expenditure of time.

SURVEY SCOPE

Survey scope varies significantly. Many are limited to average salary information on a single job or two, or on early spring best guesses by first-level analysts as to what next year's merit increase budget will be. Some are of the 50,000-foot-level variety, requestion opinions of senior executives as to where the world is going to be in 5 years and what's most important in their world of work. Others, such as job-family and line-of-business surveys, may include more data on a given position or related group of positions, such as a study of an entire accounting department's positions and compensation levels.

Job-family surveys—such as Mercer's finance or human resources surveys—can provide an excellent view of compensation within a particular discipline, but participant lists are often inconsistent from family to family, making an integrated analysis of a specific group of companies difficult. Base salaries are collected in some studies; others, such as noncash and industry surveys, run a more complete gamut, including employee expense, staffing levels, total cash, long-term incentives, and benefits. Since organizational size has a significant influence on pay, most surveys will also ask for annual revenues, asset size, population, bed count, and so on, depending upon industry.

Benchmark surveys include key industry jobs common to most organizations. A good benchmark survey will include higher and lower levels, and multi- and single-incumbent positions representing all major functions of an organization. Most of these surveys define and provide specific criteria for matching each of a number of specific positions. Some, such as ORC's SIRS survey, define a host of functions and a generic list of job types and organizational levels that, when combined, allow virtually 100 percent coverage of your company. Because the survey's participant base is constant across a whole range of jobs, benchmark surveys give their users a framework for comparison, not just among individual jobs but among job families. Scope measures, such as number of employees managed, sales volume, budget size, and the like, are a means to determine the relationship between pay and magnitude of responsibility. The competent practitioner will collect data from all of these sources, assess the value of the data, and use them appropriately.

Information quantity and quality, as well as cost, can vary significantly. Some of the most common surveys and the results you can expect from them are listed in Table 7.1.

DATA DISPLAYS AND TERMINOLOGY

Surveys appear in myriad forms and formats. Some reports extensively slice and dice the data provided; some adopt a minimal interpretation stance. A good survey will return some information on everything collected, consistent with the quality and quantity of data received (always preserving the confidentiality of any one company's data). Remember, though, the underlying value of a survey is not in the numbers it presents but in the answers you are able to derive from its use.

Most survey data are presented in one of three fashions: *tabular* (numeric) *displays, graphic* (visual) *displays,* or *regression analysis* (containing formulas and chart lines that project compensation levels).

Tabular Displays

Tabular displays (see Figure 7.1 and Table 7.2) include arrays, statistical reference points, and frequency distributions.

Arrays.   Arrays are high-to-low listings of all data collected in a given category (Figure 7.1). Arrays allow the analyst to inspect each data point reported (often by company code) to see how the data distributes through the range.

Statistical Reference Points.   Also called the *arithmetic mean* (or simply the *mean*), the *average* is typically one of the following:

- The *weighted average* is the sum of all salaries (or other compensation values) divided by the number of incumbents reported. [In Figure 7.1, the weighted average is $(2 \times \$60.0) + (5 \times \$58.7)$, etc. (a total of $7,853.6; use the SUMPRODUCT function in Microsoft *Excel* or Lotus *1-2-3*) divided by 148 incumbents, or $53.1.] *This is the best indicator of the real market for a given survey position: Big companies with lots of incumbents weigh heavily here.*

TABLE 7.1   Survey Types

Survey Type		Cost	Value	Output
Irregular, phone	To/from counterparts, competitors	A little time; obligation to return favors; $0	Usually limited, except to surveyor.	None, unless you ask "What's everybody else doing?"
Group, association, club	Key jobs common to member organizations	Other than membership dues, usually small or none	Varies greatly depending upon survey design, quality of input, actual participants.	Printed report with your data typically in the averages.
One-time custom surveys	Special purpose; often difficult to replicate	Can be substantial to company commissioning survey	Typically high (unless participation is low) because design is specified.	Very precise report showing your company versus the overall competition. Participants get report, possibly with coded arrays.
Annual third-party (consultants)	Broad coverage for databases, research, speeches, projects	Usually fairly modest; profit often not an issue	Valued according to source, focus. You generally get enough value for the cost.	Often general information with high-level analysis and low-level data displays.
Annual third-party (survey companies)	Functional areas, levels of management, industry	Competitive with above, but in it for profit	Valued according to source, focus, but you can often get more value than you pay for.	Specific, focused information, often with your company displayed separately from your selected peer group.

- The *simple average* is the sum of the averages for each company divided by the number of companies providing information. [In Figure 7.1, the simple average is $60.0 + $58.7, etc. (a total of $482.2; use the = average, or @AVG, function in *Excel* or *1-2-3*) divided by 9 companies, or $53.6.] *This number can be used to compare company policy, for example, on midpoint levels; small companies with few incumbents and large companies with many weigh evenly here.*

The *standard deviation* is a measure of how widely values are dispersed from the mean. The data within plus-or-minus 1 standard deviation cover approximately the middle two-thirds of the observations: Use = STDEV (*Excel*) or @STDS (*1-2-3*). *Use this to see where the bulk of the market is being paid, perhaps to help establish range width.*

FIGURE 7.1 Array with statistical reference points.

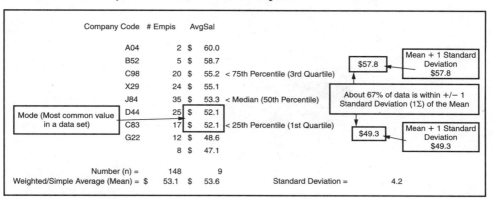

The *median* (also the 50th percentile, second quartile, midpoint) is the middle of all the data points reported. Use = or @MEDIAN. *Focus on the median when data are erratically distributed, especially when you have a small sample.*

The percentiles (also quartiles, deciles, etc.) refer to locations in an array below which a certain portion of the data lies. Formulas start with the = or @PERCENTILE. The 75th percentile is frequently viewed by high-paying companies; some analysts prefer to view data between the first and third quartiles (25th and 75th percentiles) to see the middle 50 percent of the data, instead of the middle two-thirds viewed when using standard deviation.

Frequency Distributions. These are often used in lieu of arrays if presenting individual data points strains the confidentiality concerns of the participants. Table 7.2 shows how many times a salary is reported within certain ranges of salaries; actual salaries or averages are not shown.

Graphic Displays

Graphic displays include many types of charts (line, pie, bar, and so forth) that can be used effectively in presenting data, especially to top management, when the big picture is more desirable than all the detail. See Figures 7.2 through 7.4.

TABLE 7.2 Frequency Distributions

Range	Frequency
45.0–47.9	1
48.0–50.9	1
51.0–53.9	3
54.0–56.9	2
57.0–59.9	1
60.0–62.9	1

FIGURE 7.2   Pie charts.

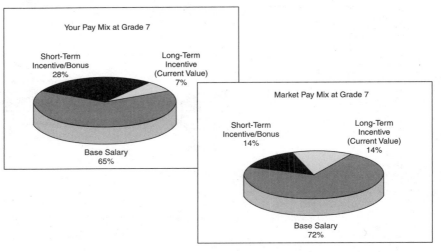

Your Pay Mix at Grade 7

Short-Term Incentive/Bonus 28%

Long-Term Incentive (Current Value) 7%

Base Salary 65%

Market Pay Mix at Grade 7

Short-Term Incentive/Bonus 14%

Long-Term Incentive (Current Value) 14%

Base Salary 72%

FIGURE 7.3   Bar charts.

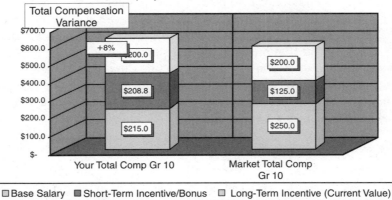

Your Company vs. Market Total Compensation

Total Compensation Variance

+8%

$700.0
$600.0
$500.0 $200.0 $200.0
$400.0
$300.0 $208.8 $125.0
$200.0
$100.0 $215.0 $250.0
$-

Your Total Comp Gr 10   Market Total Comp Gr 10

☐ Base Salary   ■ Short-Term Incentive/Bonus   ☐ Long-Term Incentive (Current Value)

Regression Analysis

Regression analysis (see Figure 7.5) is a very powerful form of presentation that relates two or more data elements and shows by formulas and charts the central data tendencies. Based on one or more measures (such as base salary or company sales), regressions forecast—where another measure (such as incentive percentage or total cash compensation) will likely be found. Regression analysis also correlates the reliability of the information to its dispersal around the line of central tendency. The closer a correlation coefficient, or R^2, value is to 1, the greater reliance you can place on the forecast. Regression charts often use logarithms because the

FIGURE 7.4 Line charts.

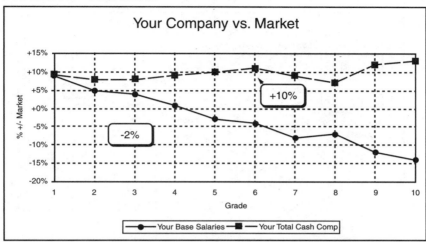

range of data covered can be so great and because the formulas often are more accurate when the data are so transformed.

A few words of caution: Regression alaysis infers that if one condition exists, then the other exists. Also, when looking at a chart, the eye and mind can lead the untrained observer to conclusions that may or may not be valid. The assumption that you should provide a 35.7 percent incentive opportunity to a $150,000 employee based on Figure 7.5 data is no more valid than if you were to conclude that $150,000 is the right amount to pay that employee just because that is the peer group average for the individual's position.

Regardless of format, "above average" does not equal "overpaid"; "below average" does not equal "underpaid." "Average" is not necessarily the proper pay posture for your organization versus your market; perhaps it would make more sense to adopt one posture for base pay and another for total cash compensation, as in the situation described in Figure 7.1. Remember the pay environment in which you operate; performance, internal organizational values, job family, and other issues come to bear on what's right for you. If your compensation policy is to pay at the 75th percentile, you may consider someone at the market average to be underpaid.

HOW TO USE A SURVEY

If they do not exercise caution, those responsible for providing compensation rec-ommendations can fall into one of two categories: (1) those who use every bit of survey data available without regard to its validity and (2) those who fail to fully exploit the data sources at their disposal. The following paragraphs give you some

FIGURE 7.5   Regression analysis.

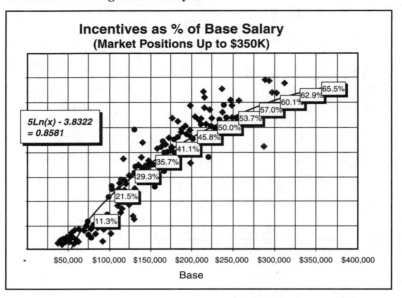

pointers on what constitutes worthwhile information and how to use the data. (In-depth quantitative analysis and methods of developing salary structures from survey data are not treated in this chapter.) The effective practitioner assesses a survey's reliability and the efficacy of the data before incorporating the information into a thought process or number-crunching software package; all survey numbers may not be as meaningful as you would like them to be. Because people are people and because organizations differ so widely in the way jobs and their incumbents relate to each other, data quality can vary markedly and should be checked before deciding to base one of your management decisions on it.

Understand that at the foundation of all surveys is the need to compare similarities, not differences. The surveyor tries to identify areas of similarity and jobs that are consistent from year to year and to include the same companies annually. The hope is that the individuals submitting the data follow directions. Unless the survey participants see how their jobs and the surveyed jobs are alike, little information will be forthcoming. When the survey results are published, that is the time to ask two questions, in this order: (1) How can I be sure that the data are correct? and (2) How similar is our job to the market comparison position?

You can feel comfortable that the data are "correct" by following a few guidelines. Choose annual survey sources that contain the majority of the positions and competitors in which your top management is chiefly interested. Don't undermine your efforts by getting only free survey information from recruiters (with their own interests to cultivate) or from magazine articles. Survey costs represent only a small fraction of the payroll costs that benefit from the data they provide. In short, surveys can be a real investment.

To begin, participate in a high-quality, omnibus benchmark survey as a fundamental data source. This allows you to see how all the major job areas and functions relate to each other, drawing on a relatively consistent set of organizations and data preparers. Augment your chief data source with other data and other surveys; don't limit yourself to one source of information. Also, don't overlook the opportunity to compare compensation data from different sources. After all, surveying is a comparative process. Increasing the number and variety of weapons in your information arsenal increases your coverage and understanding of positions, organizations, and other industries.

So, what if you've taken these steps and the numbers don't agree or if you have only one source? How do you know that the data are reliable? You can assess the number of data points. If only a small, unrepresentative sample appears on a given position, you should consider devaluing its importance in your structure development or not using the information at all. The more tightly packed the data distribution, the more confident you can feel about the comparison's validity. Realize, however, that aberrations are common in compensation. One organization will buy talent to use in a start-up or turnaround situation, and the individual's pay will be out of line with the size or profitability of the reporting unit. Another organization will pay an individual very high or very low total compensation because of individual and/or corporate performance. Rare is the survey that can capture the relationship between targeted and actual pay except when viewing top management compensation in light of corporate performance.

In addition, rates for positions in the same job family should relate to each other. Case I in Table 7.3 shows a reasonable salary progression from entry to junior level (about 33 percent), from junior to medium level (about 37 percent), and from medium to senior level (about 40 percent). Although the junior level is sparsely populated, its salary level seems plausible, given the surrounding job family data. In case II, however, the data are skewed so that the junior position is almost 70 percent higher than the entry-level job, and just $2,800 below the next level. Therefore, data in case I are more reliable than the data in case II.

If your data source covers a broad spectrum of positions—upper- and lower-management levels, staff and line functions, multi- and single-incumbent positions—most of the pay relationships should be generally consistent with the compensation program of your organization. Most companies try to have overall pay practices within ±10 percent of "their market." Be cautious of data skewed by one or two large companies weighting much of the data upward or downward. However, before discounting data affected by such circumstances, consider the following: If one company employs 60 percent of all the engineers or tellers in the state, shouldn't a pay decision on that job be heavily influenced by the pay average that includes the one large company?

TABLE 7.3   Salary Progression by Position

	Number	Case I Average Salary	Case II Average Salary
Senior-level position	12	$57.0	$57.0
Medium-level position	15	$40.7	$40.7
Junior-level position	*2*	*$29.7*	*$37.9*
Entry-level position	27	$22.4	$22.4

The participant sample should also represent your industry or labor market. Then, regardless of how odd pieces of data appear in relation to your own, if all of your company's direct and indirect competitors are submitting data, you may have to admit that *you* are out of line with the overall market. On a similar theme, realize that the more consistent the sample of participants is from year to year and the better the survey covers your competitors, the greater the value of the survey to you. Finally, the survey should describe positions that correspond closely to those in your organization so that you feel confident using the results.

GETTING THE MOST OUT OF YOUR SURVEY EFFORTS AND DOLLARS

Assuming that you are the individual responsible for using salary surveys to develop compensation programs:

Start by creating a survey library.   Set aside a file drawer, a diskette, or shared network drive, someplace where you and authorized others can find and use all of your organization's survey data. Alert others in your organization to forward all surveys and requests for survey participation to you so you can respond to them most efficiently.

Choose your surveys.   Limited resources and unlimited day-to-day work requirements often preclude participation in every survey in which a company is asked to participate. You must balance your current needs, your future needs, and the ability to get what you want from others. In other words, participate not only in those studies from which you get information but also in those that your competitors need to satisfy their information demands. Unless you help them get their data, you may well not get theirs when needed.

Use the data you have.   Take the time to examine each survey in your library. Only by using the data you have will you maximize your investment of time and money. Categorize surveys and their data by peer group, position, by family type and by date. Don't retire a survey until you have its replacement; even a 3-year-old study of a specialized, infrequently surveyed job stream can be useful if updated by prevailing salary increase rates.

Consolidate your data onto a spreadsheet or in a database.   Surveys are often consulted to respond to specific questions from a variety of constituencies. Try consolidating qualified position data from multiple survey sources onto a single electronic spreadsheet or database for more convenient consultation. By arranging your position table alongside the survey data, you have a handy matching guide for input to next year's survey and a way to develop solid answers during your annual compensation planning and structure review.

Derive a single answer from each set of data presented in a survey.   If you consolidate data from multiple sources or have several views of the data presented in one source, you have a decision to make: Of the data available, of the different numbers purporting to be "the market," what is the single number that best represents the market for your organization? Some practitioners simply aggregate all the data available from all sources, throw out odd data, then assign "company weights" to each data point to replicate what it would cost to staff your company at market rates. (In Table 7.4 this means multiplying the consolidated weighted average base by your company's population in each job, then dividing by the total population.) Some analysts feel some survey sources are more reliable than others, so they might weight that source, say, 75 percent, and data from all others sources 25 percent as they aggregate and consolidate.

Answer all survey questions to the best of your ability.   The survey designer is responsible for requesting data that are relevant to the survey output. Assume that all data requested have value in the quality of the results and that without certain data from you, the survey will be delayed or reduced in value to you and to others. In other words, share requested information to the best of your ability. After all, that's what you expect of others. Remember, as no two companies are alike, no two sets of information needs are identical.

As you develop your data, two criteria should guide the way. First, *be realistic*. Find your market answer first, then describe how your situation differs. You and others will find many reasons that your organization's situation is different from the market and your incumbent's salary level is too low, too high, or just right. Let the market give you an answer first, then decide whether or not you like the answer. Don't become obsessed with finding matches and survey data on all positions. Remember organizational differences. A good analyst can determine three reference points relative to an undefined or dataless position: one surveyed position obviously higher in your organizational hierarchy, one obviously lower, and one perceived to be of similar job value.

Second, *be creative*. While some organizations and managers will require that you produce information in a certain format, don't allow your thinking to stop there. Compensation information is like a bolt of cloth—you should see patterns of numbers within a function, from function to function, and across the entire organization. You should notice the different hues and textures from area to area, division to division. Then, from this combination of highs and lows and positive and negative variances, you should be able to fashion your organization's pay garment.

TABLE 7.4 Consolidated Survey Averages

Your Position	Your Company Code	#	Wtd Avg Base	Survey A: Omnibus Survey 24 Companies of Our Size, Type Code	#	Wtd Avg Base	% ±	Survey B: Financial Survey 62 Companies of Our Size Code	#	Wtd Avg Base	% ±	Consolidated #	Wtd Avg Base	% ±
VP Controller	FIN001	1	$175.0	AC100	23	$200.0	-12.5%	005	58	$195.0	-10.3%	81	$196.4	-10.9%
Dir Accounting	FIN002	2	$115.0	AC110	98	$125.0	-8.0%					98	$125.0	-8.0%
Mgr Accounting	FIN003	4	$80.0	AC115	256	$90.0	-11.1%	100	985	$89.0	-10.1%	1,241	$89.2	-10.3%
Accountant IV	FIN004	2	$57.0	AC120	1,456	$65.0	-12.3%	150	3,456	$69.0	-17.4%	4,912	$67.8	-15.9%
Accountant III	FIN005	7	$40.7	AC121	3,754	$54.0	-24.6%	151	4,567	$55.0	-26.0%	8,321	$54.5	-25.4%
AccountantII	FIN006	5	$29.7	AC122	2,543	$43.0	-30.9%	152	2,568	$42.0	-29.3%	5,111	$42.5	-30.1%
Accountant I	FIN007	3	$22.4	AC123	1,265	$32.0	-30.0%	153	1,345	$29.0	-22.8%	2,610	$30.5	-26.4%
Accounting Family		*24*	*$55.8*		*9,395*	*$51.8*	*7.7%*		*12,979*	*$56.7*	*-1.5%*	*22,374*	*$54.6*	*2.1%*
VP Chief Information Officer	IT001	1	$185.0	IT100	20	$225.0	-17.8%					20	$225.0	-17.8%
Dir Software Development				IT110	40	$140.0						40	$140.0	
Mgr Software Development	IT003	4	$107.5	IT115	434	$125.0	-14.0%					434	$125.0	-14.0%
Software Engineer IV	IT004	3	$89.0	IT120	1,245	$94.0	-5.3%					1,245	$94.0	-5.3%
Software Engineer III	IT005	8	$70.0	IT121	2,856	$75.0	-6.7%					2,856	$75.0	-6.7%
Software Engineer II	IT006	5	$53.0	IT122	1,756	$57.0	-7.0%					1,756	$57.0	-7.0%
Software Engineer I	IT007	5	$41.0	IT123	1,287	$43.0	-4.7%					1,287	$43.0	-4.7%
IT/Software Family		*26*	*$73.5*		*7,638*	*$72.1*	*1.9%*					*7,638*	*$72.1*	*1.9%*
Totals/Survey Averages		50	$65.0		17,033	$60.9	6.7%		12,979	$56.7	14.8%	30,012	$59.1	10.0%
Totals/Company Weights		*50*	*$65.0*		*50*	*$62.4*	*4.2%*		*50*	*$58.8*	*10.7%*	*50*	*$63.7*	*2.0%*

HOW TO CONDUCT YOUR OWN SURVEY

The preliminary thought process is critical in a good survey of any sort. You must know what the questions are and how you plan to present the answers before you involve anyone else. After establishing your objectives, you should target the appropriate markets, solicit and secure their participation, gather the data, and present them in a meaningful manner. Keep in mind four survey fundamentals: *People* gain by *getting* information; *people* gain nothing by giving information; *people* are the companies with whom you must deal; and *people* have their own agendas that differ from yours.

With the fundamentals in mind, start by choosing a survey type that is appropriate to your need for speed and content. Different circumstances may dictate different approaches. You may have extra time just for this survey, but far more likely you will need to conserve your energies and resources (data processing support, costs, etc.).

Outsourcing the task may be more cost effective while preserving the necessary hands-off posture. Always have a report format in mind when you conduct a survey—that is, know specifically what information you are seeking. This way you won't miss asking for a particular piece of important information. Too often, especially with phone surveys, followup calls have to be made to fill in additional data elements. Always construct a questionnaire, even if you're collecting information on just one position from just a few companies. A questionnaire helps you ask the same questions of all participants, and it serves as a response record. Keep your survey simple and focused on the final product. Don't collect extraneous, irrelevant information that takes extra time to input and analyze.

Keep your survey brief or use a check-box format. Asking for narrative answers reduces the ability and interest of the potential participant to provide data. Few executives and even fewer organizations are particularly altruistic. They want to get something for their time and energy. As a minimum, always plan to give your survey participants a copy of the final results of the study. Try to fashion your survey so that it answers your questions and provides value to others as well. For example, add a job or two, ask for another component, or change your description a bit. Finally, ensure that you have enough "hooks" in your survey to merge it into a larger body of survey data. In other words, collect enough comprehensive data to allow you to compare results to other data you have received in this particular area, as well as to broader market or evaluation data you have.

WHERE TO FIND SURVEY DATA

Survey sources are growing in number, and the field is becoming very competitive, so the following list is by no means exhaustive. Being omitted from the list does not impugn a survey's quality, any more than being on the list endorses it. Consider this merely a starting point in your quest for information:

- Contact counterparts in your peer group. The surveys they participate in are probably the ones you should also join. Your own functional and line managers are often aware of surveys covering their particular business or discipline.

- All of the major compensation and/or human resources consulting firms conduct compensation surveys (all domestic, and some international, as well). Hay Group (haygroup.com), William M. Mercer (mercer.com), Organization Resources Counselors (ORC; orc.com), TowersPerrin (towersperrin.com); Hewitt Associates (hewitt.com) and its survey firm Management Compensation Services; Watson Wyatt (watsonwyatt.com) and ECS/Watson Wyatt Data Services, etc. Major accounting firms—especially PricewaterhouseCoopers (pricewaterhousecoopers.com) and KPMG Peat Marwick (kpmg.com)—also produce pay studies, as do many regional, local, and niche consultants, such as DCA Stanton and The Survey Group.[1]

- Economic Research Institute (eri.com) and Reggio & Associates produce domestic geographic cost-of-living differentials, and ORC and Runzheimer International (runzheimer.com) produce international studies covering cost-of-living and currency differential reports.

- The U.S. government is a significant surveyor. Contact the Department of Labor, Bureau of Labor Statistics (BLS), Wage and Hour Division. Most major cities have BLS offices. Your state and local Chamber of Commerce may also produce surveys. BLS has a particularly good Internet Web site (http://www.bls.gov, http://stats.bls.gov). Once there, surf around a plethora of data, free and of the standard government quality. Their occupational compensation survey is at http://stats.bls.gov/ocshome/htm, and covered employment and wages is at http://stats.bls.gov/cewhome/htm.

- Many regional and local personnel and compensation associations conduct surveys. Trade and professional organizations are often good sources.

- Finally, but perhaps most importantly, several survey bibliographies are periodically published that give extensive lists of available pay surveys:

    - *Salary Survey Guidebook,* American Compensation Association and American Management Association. (ACA), 14040 North Northsight Boulevard, Scottsdale, AZ 85260   (602/951-9191). Web: http://www.acaonline.org (about 460 surveys identified), $75. Also gives additional information on how to use surveys.

---

[1]Internet addresses change frequently, and mergers can change firm names. Addresses given are currently at the time of writing. All are preceded with http://www. Some of these firms make survey data available online.

- *Available Pay Survey Reports: An Annotated Bibliography,* Abbott, Langer & Associates, 548 First Street, Crete, IL 60417 (708/672-4200). Web: http://www.abbott-langer.com (about 1,200 surveys identified), $450.

- *Stern's SourceFinder: The Master Directory to HR and Business Management Information and Resources,* Michael Daniels, Publishers, Post Office Box 3233, Culver City, CA 90231-3233 (310/838-4437). Web: http://www.hrconsultant.com (about 1,200 surveys identified), $239.

- *Survey Sources for US and International Pay and Benefits,* Personnel Systems Associates, 2282 Aspen Street, Tustin, CA 92782 (714/573-9430). Web: http://www.personnelsystems.com (about 1,037 surveys identified), $265.

RETRIEVING, MANIPULATING, AND ANALYZING COMPENSATION DATA

Diane Yellin, Director Reward Information

Hay Group

John Yurkutat, Director HIS Product Management

Hay Group

ENVIRONMENT

As we stand poised for the twenty-first century, compensation professionals find themselves in an unsettled, yet exciting environment. Major internal changes in staffing levels, role perception and stature, and technological support, coupled with powerful external forces, have created an environment characterized by:

- Lean corporate compensation functions that look to technology or outsourcing to assist in the completion of more work, more quickly, with fewer resources

- Organization management that in some cases requires—and in other cases resists—that HR, and compensation directors in particular, act as a strategic business partner and sit at the decision-making table

- A proliferation of technical tools and solutions—homegrown, off the shelf, and customer built—to store, retrieve, analyze, and manipulate compensation information

- A truly global economy, whether the organization is itself global or simply competing with global firms

This environment has come into existence at a time when the speed of job creation and role change, the disparity in market supply and demand for varying skills, and the number and types of factors that influence the worth of individuals and job roles are all increasing at ever faster rates. Within a 3 to 4 percent U.S. economy, certain jobs—not all in the IT hot skills areas—are commanding 10, 15, or 20 percent annual increases, while their colleagues down the hall are likely to receive the "common" 3 to 4 percent, or in some cases, even less.

Within this construct, a very interesting phenomenon has occurred. For perhaps the first time, the automated systems to support compensation information storage, retrieval, manipulation, and analysis are no longer the barriers to understanding and accurate decision making—the people resources and corporate infrastructures are the barriers. Just a few years ago, the systems, software, and applications were not readily available; today they are abundant, even in an environment that requires much more fragmented data and analyses, and in much shorter time frames.

What are the realities of compensation information needs today, and what kinds of automated solutions are available?

INFORMATION NEEDS

Although the concept of *pay determinants* has not changed much over the years (measurable variables and/or factors that can substantially impact the appropriate level of pay), the number and complexity of them have certainly increased. In addition, pay determinants now routinely include personal characteristics in addition to organizational and job characteristics. Some of these pay determinants primarily affect internal decisions, while others primarily come into play in relation to the external marketplace. As a result, both internal *human resources information system* (HRIS) constructs and external survey sources need to be tuned to the storage, retrieval, manipulation, and analysis of the appropriate factors.

What are these determinants of pay?

Organization-Level Determinants

Historically, general organization-wide pay levels could be related (either strongly or loosely) to variables like industry sector, size, and performance. In today's marketplace, the larger, more complex and more diverse the organization, the more likely different parts of the organization will be characterized by different sector, size, and performance descriptors. Therefore, it is less likely that a single, simple answer will emerge.

Industry. The industry in which an organization operates typically forms a natural competitive market. Most commonly, industries or industry groupings are easily defined by clusters of *standard industrial classification* (SIC) *codes.*

Size. Measures such as sales, revenues, assets, number of employees, and others typically reflect general organization size and may give some indication of the complexity of people-related issues. Large organizations often perceive that they experience more complex pay equity issues.

Performance. One would expect that high-performing organizations would have the ability, and the tendency, to pay more liberally. History would suggest that this is not necessarily true, even for the executive population.

Ability to pay. Different organizations, because of size, industry, performance, culture, philosophy, or other factors, are more or less able to pay at particular levels in the marketplace.

Location. Because the supply and demand for broad categories of workers are different in different parts of the country (or in different countries around the world), where a job is physically located can often have a significant impact on pay levels. This *cost-of-labor concept* should not be confused with *cost of living.* The cost of living deals with the value of goods and services; the cost of labor deals with the value of people with particular skill sets.

Job-Level Determinants

Job characteristics are still very relevant as pay determinants, and in certain instances, they are more powerful in setting appropriate levels of pay than organizational considerations. Some jobs, and job type groups, form separate markets for pay irrespective of industry, size group, or performance. Simply look at the market for IT professionals: Whether the EDP jobs of the 1970s and early 1980s, the MIS jobs of the late 1980s, or the IT positions of today, these critical skill–short supply positions have created their own pay market unrelated to almost anything else.

What job variables influence or predict pay?

Organization location. Is the job in a line or staff function? Is it located at corporate headquarters or at a division or plant site? Jobs at corporate headquarters tend to be staff or internal consulting positions; jobs in other units are often heavily line oriented. Many times, these differences require an organization to develop different pay programs that adequately recognize job differences at the parent level rather than other levels.

Organization level. Pay practices vary widely based on the management requirements of a job. Paradoxically, a job title is often a very poor indicator of the true management responsibility of a job. This is particularly true in functions like sales, where individual contributor sales representatives may be regional vice presidents, which affords them access to customers more easily.

Job size. Whether measured empirically or subjectively, how "big" (influential, complex, important, critical) is the job? While job measurement fell out of favor in many organizations in the recent past, automated systems and models make the process quick and easy today and a viable (perhaps desirable) approach to dealing with ever-changing job roles and newly created positions.

Employee-Level Determinants

It is at this level that the most significant changes in variables have taken place in the recent past. If we looked at employee-level determinants of pay in the 1960s, items like tenure (length of service) and performance rating would be mentioned (as well as characteristics like age, sex, and race—which discrimination legislation has made nonissues). Today, roles, skills, competencies, and other subjob metrics are constantly being defined and analyzed.

Roles. What primary roles does the individual job holder fulfill? Some of these may be inherent in the basic job design, but others (like mentor, task force member, or community organization liaison) may be specific to the individual. Do, or should, these role differences create or support differences in pay?

Skills. Many organizations today test for skills, whether obtained or demonstrated. These range from demonstrated ability to perform a new or more complex assembly process, to acquisition and use of a highly prized software language. Skills definition, testing, certification, and inventory are all required to support this pay determinant.

Competencies. What "soft" behavioral characteristics differentiate the exceptional performer from the average performer? Many organizations today base job placements, promotions, grade or broadband assignments, and other salary actions on the objective or subjective measurement of competencies.

INTERNAL AND EXTERNAL INFORMATION REQUIREMENTS

As roles, skills, competencies, and other job and personal components become the focal determinants of pay, organizations need to develop systems and databases to identify, inventory, store, and manage these additional elements. They also need to expect that external survey providers will develop techniques for market measurement of the worth of these elements. In the movement to develop these systems and techniques, it is important to remember that the application of these pay determinants is not uniform across jobs, levels, functions, or organizations. For example, IT will likely require a skills inventory, and jobs within that function will likely change rapidly within most organizations, while jobs in accounting and finance may not be differentiated by skills and will likely evolve much more slowly.

Information needs that are framed at the level of roles, skills, and competencies require a much more detailed understanding of these components and internal systems that support this greater level of detail. Recent technological breakthroughs suggest that information systems capable of supporting these more complex requirements either have been or are in the process of being developed. For example, new versions of HR information systems are coming to the marketplace with the capability of capturing and reporting critical skills and competencies on an individual incumbent basis. These systems will succeed only if they are supported by rigorous definition of the concepts and variables and if they are thoroughly inventoried at the individual employee level.

In addition, comparisons of these variables to the external market will require careful thought and planning. Do internal HR information systems have the capability to easily store, retrieve, manipulate and analyze skills, roles, and/or competencies data from external sources?

Survey providers have supported electronic submission of data for a number of years—in spreadsheet, dBase file, ASCII flat file, and other common formats—and have provided diskette and/or CD-ROM output for easy upload into the organization's HRIS. At least one has made submission and dynamic interactive analysis available via the Internet. This new information platform will have dramatic impact on the availability, customization, relevance, and common referencing of compensation information into the next millennium.

Case Study

In a global economy, multinational organizations have a wide range of information needs, differentiated by volume, type, and level of detail. They require data to support actions and decisions specific to global companies such as the centralization of policies, management of local payrolls, understanding of the costs of employment, and the understanding of pay drivers and econometric links with pay. Similar to domestic organizations, they are concerned with setting compensation policies, designing pay schemes, managing payroll, updating salary structures or policies, and recruitment, promotion, and retention. Consider the case of Whole World Company, a clothing manufacturer with worldwide revenues of $19 million.

Whole World Company's headquarters is located in the Midwest. With 15,000 employees outside the United States and 10,000 in the United States, they are faced with rethinking their global reward systems. In order to take advantage of lower labor rates, they are also considering opening manufacturing plants in Malaysia. While local conditions dominate their compensation strategy, their local customization of pay systems must support the organization's global mindset.

Whole World has assigned global reward accountability to Jill Smith at the Midwest headquarters. Regional compensation managers in North America, the Far East, and Europe are responsible for the consistent implementation of programs in their regions that support the company's global business strategy. Local managers can choose from a variety of total compensation forms to operate successfully in their markets.

Jill Smith needs to report to the CEO on the labor feasibility of operating plants in Malaysia. Working with an international consulting firm, she determines that while Malaysia is in the midst of its first recession in 13 years, it still boasts political stability and a highly productive and skilled labor force. Some of the data she receives show that compensation market practices for Malaysia reflect the following:

- For the current year, most annual salary increases were between 6 and 8 percent.

- Due to the economic downturn, over 20 percent of the companies in the study reported pay freezes with a corresponding hold on bonus payments.

- While most companies have implemented incentive programs, few companies use dynamic pay approaches, with team-based pay being particularly unpopular.

- Pay practices vary considerably between different business sectors, different functions, and different regions. Table 8.1 shows the regional differences in base salary, which may help Whole World Company determine the best plant locations.

- Typical market rates (converted to U.S. dollars) for plant managers are:

Base salary: $49,438
Total cash: $56,454
Total earnings (total cash plus fixed allowances): $56,994

Whole World Company decides to go ahead with their plans for a Malaysian manufacturing operation.

Back in the United States, Whole World Company, as have many domestic companies, has experienced the recent loss of a number of their critical IT professionals at their corporate headquarters. This is in direct contrast with their otherwise very low turnover rates. Whole World Company is challenged to review their overall pay policies and specifically to evaluate their somewhat conservative pay strategy for this key function. They focus particularly on programmer positions, as

TABLE 8.1

Region	Overall, %
KL/PJ/SA	104
Central	109
Eastern	102.6
Southern	96.5
Northern	94.1
Sabah	101
Sarawak	111

they have experienced the most difficulty in retaining and recruiting these positions. The market data they use report on three levels of programmers (associate programmer, programmer, and senior programmer) that correlate closely to the existing levels at Whole World. For these positions, they compare their average pay rates to national pay rates in their industry. Table 8.2 shows the results of this comparison.

The data show that Whole World is paying consistently below the market for these jobs. While Whole World needs to consider changing their pay practice for these jobs, they also need to consider other factors before implementing a new pay system. Some considerations are:

- Skill premiums that may be paid for specific technologies such as Java, SAP/Basis, and CICS

- Training and development issues

- Competency programs

- Special bonus programs such as sign-on bonuses, project milestones, or completion incentives

- How pay for IT professionals fits into the overall company strategy

While securing data on these factors may be more difficult, they are available, and they provide a more complete picture of the factors that influence this important labor market.

CONCLUSION

Global reach, complex organizations, expanding numbers and types of pay determinants, increasing demands on HR professionals, and ever-fragmenting pay markets strain the capabilities of traditional methods of compensation information storage, retrieval, manipulation, and analysis. Fortunately, new breeds of systems—

designed to address both internal and external information needs and to capture roles, skills, competencies, and other emerging pay determinants—have been developed to support the sophisticated, multinational analyses and modeling required.

TABLE 8.2   Annual Dollars, $000

	Midpoint	Actual Base Salary	Actual Annual Bonus Received	Target Annual Bonus	Total Cash
Associate Programmer					
Median market rate	35.5	35.0	1.7	2.0	36.0
Whole World	35.0	33.7	.5	1.5	34.2
Percent of market	99	96			95
Programmer					
Median market rate	41.1	40.8	1.9	2.5	41.2
Whole World	40.0	37.0	1.2	2.0	38.2
Percent of market	97	91			93
Senior Programmer					
Median market rate	45.1	43.9	2.2	3.0	44.8
Whole World	44.0	40.0	1.8	2.5	41.8
Percent of market	98	91			93

C H A P T E R

9

DEVELOPING COMPETITIVE COMPENSATION PROGRAMS

Bruce I. Spiegel, Senior Vice President

Aon Consulting

Trista Slobodzian, Consultant

Aon Consulting

COMPANIES CONTINUE TO BE CHALLENGED in maintaining competitive compensation programs in the face of globalization, deregulation, strategic mergers, and restructuring. Moreover, certain functions command more attention than others; for example, high demand exists for sales and information technology resources that can help a company maintain a competitive edge and keep up with rapid changes in technology. Outsourcing now offers more people new challenges and different work environments, and volatility in the global markets further exacerbates the situation by encouraging movement of resources. People with skills in demand have a multitude of options. With so many opportunities for change, people are becoming more independent and less committed to one organization, acting as contractors in a short-handed market.

How does a company capture a true picture of those opportunities, and the compensation packages that will potentially lure valuable resources away? The right mix of compensation can be a powerful tool to compete with the market and encourage people's commitment. To determine the right mix of compensation, a company must ask itself a series of questions:

- Who are my competitors for resources?

- What are the characteristics of my business that make it similar to and/or different from other companies?

- Where does our business want to position itself with respect to market pay practices? How competitive do we need to be to keep our people? What can we afford?

- What are the critical functions that will allow my business to have a competitive advantage?

- Where are my operations situated, and how does that affect my ability to attract skilled people?

Knowing the answers to these questions is the first step to understanding the dynamics that influence pay practices in the market. Once the company has set a compensation strategy that positions its pay practices competitively, it can proceed to gather and interpret market information to establish appropriate pay levels.

Gathering and interpreting competitive market information has become less time-consuming with the development of flexible, interactive computerized compensation databases. Such systems allow users to derive market data for complex, or "hybrid," positions that are not easily found in the marketplace. This chapter briefly discusses computerized databases including online surveys, multiple survey market-pricing systems, and multiple ranking technologies for hybrid positions.

WHO ARE THE COMPETITORS FOR RESOURCES?

To understand compensation opportunities in the marketplace, companies must first identify competitors for resources. Companies should consider both their direct line-of-business competitors as well as labor market competitors. A labor market competitor can be any company seeking resources with the same skill set from a common talent pool.

WHAT ARE THE DISTINGUISHING CHARACTERISTICS OF MY BUSINESS?

Companies compare themselves to others in the market based on industry and size of the organization measured by variables like financials or numbers of employees. Once the industry has been identified, the company can select survey sources that hold relevant market compensation information.

Industry

Industry groups are broad categorizations of companies with related operations and products or services. Knowing how companies in similar industries compensate employees will assist in determining appropriate pay levels. For example, differences are likely to exist in regulated industries (like banks and utilities) compared to companies operating in a traditional market-driven environment like automotive or consumer goods. Industries that are mature and typically experiencing stabilized growth, like ground transportation, will likely have compensation strategies different from high-growth industries like information technology. Table 9.1 illustrates how starting salaries for entry-level positions in high-technology companies vary by industry.

The product or service offered by the company can significantly impact compensation levels. A company producing goods using hazardous materials should compare itself to producers of similar goods because such companies may offer premiums for occupational risk. Service companies may compensate employees very differently depending on the type of service offered (e.g., management consulting versus courier services).

TABLE 9.1 Starting Rates for Entry-Level Positions (No Experience) Assemblers (Hourly), Overall

	Industry								
Starting Rates	Semi-conductor	Computer/ peripheral	Software	Network products/ services	Telecom-munications	Capital equipment	Pharm/ medical and scientific	Other	Total Results
Average	$8.12	$7.74	$7.95	$8.64	$8.94	$9.23	$7.91	$8.38	$8.22
Lowest	$5.25	$5.50	$6.70	$7.70	$6.48	$6.23	$6.00	$6.00	$5.25
Highest	$12.70	$10.50	$8.65	$10.00	$13.50	$12.50	$12.24	$13.00	$13.50

SOURCE: Copyright © 1998, Aon Consulting/Radford Division.

Size of the Company

The size of a company usually has an impact on compensation levels, as size can reflect organizational complexity. Size can be measured by the number of employees, customer base (particularly for insurers and the like), sales volume, or asset size, to name a few examples.

Judgment is required when using sales volume in dollars as a measure of size because the concept of the value added per dollar of revenue becomes an issue. For example, revenue at an energy company is highly dependent on the market price of oil or natural gas. Suppose the quantity produced per employee was a constant and the price fluctuated greatly. The same amount of work would be required to produce that quantity regardless of the price, even though total revenue would vary. Is it fair to base employees' pay levels on the revenues of a company when they are highly influenced by the market price of the product? When selecting market data, differences in the value added per dollar of revenue are most likely to be kept at a minimum if companies select their relevant industry or product market.

HOW SHOULD MY BUSINESS FIT WITH PREVAILING MARKET PAY PRACTICES?

Where does a business want to position itself with respect to market pay practices? How competitive does it need to be to keep its people? What can it afford? The answers to these questions form the basis of a well-planned compensation strategy. The art is in knowing how to balance the cost of (or budget available for) resources with gaining a competitive advantage by paying more for valuable talent.

Compensation strategies define the relative weight of all components in a company's total compensation program. For example, target salaries and incentive opportunity are balanced to ensure the proper mix of fixed and variable pay. If one is relatively high compared to established standards, the other may be adjusted downward accordingly. For example, whether or not a position is eligible for an incentive will affect the target base salary level, ensuring that the total compensation opportunity is aligned with the company's target pay philosophy.

A variety of factors are considered when establishing a compensation strategy, including the company's stage in the business life cycle: embryonic, growth, maturity, or aging. With mergers and acquisitions commonplace in today's market, a single corporate entity may have divisions or subsidiaries (frequently in different industries) at different stages in the business life cycle. Depending on the business's stage of maturity, different strategies may be used when choosing target levels of pay within the relevant labor market.

Table 9.2 outlines strategies for establishing base salary, short-term and long-term incentives, and benefits and perquisites for companies in the four business maturity stages. For example, a startup company (embryonic stage) may have a greater degree of risk built into the compensation program by offering lower base

TABLE 9.2   Typical Compensation by Business Maturity Stage

Component	Embryonic	Growth	Mature	Aging
Base	Low	Competitive	Competitive/High	High
Short-term incentives	Competitive	Competitive	High	Low
Long-term incentives	High	Competitive	Competitive	Low
Benefits	Low	Competitive	High	High
Perquisites	Low	Competitive	Competitive	High
Overall pattern	Adaptive	Adaptive	Regulated	Regulated

salaries but greater potential for earning variable pay through incentives. A different strategy, higher base salaries and lower incentives, may exist at an aging company in the stages of decline, where there is little potential to realize rewards for business growth.

The company may decide to exceed, target, or even lag competitive market pay levels depending on a variety of other factors, like those shown in Figure 9.1. As described earlier, pay targets may be set for different business units or groups of jobs, based on need.

WHAT FUNCTIONS ARE CRITICAL TO MY BUSINESS'S COMPETITIVE ADVANTAGE?

Pay is determined by the value a company places on a particular functional area of the organization. The critical nature of a particular functional area may influence a company to deviate from its philosophy to target a certain level of compensation within the market.

For example, a utility entering a more competitive arena needs to attract sales and marketing talent from outside its traditional sources. A company that is successful in this effort potentially has a competitive advantage: resources with skill sets different from those of other utilities. If another utility responds to this competitive threat by hiring away key individuals from the first company, the pendulum may shift. To protect itself from losing other trained and developed resources, the first utility may elect to "carve out" sales and marketing positions (or key individuals in these functions) and pay them differently. The company may have two or more compensation strategies: targeting 75th percentile market pay levels for key contributors in sales and marketing, and market median pay levels for all others.

Table 9.3 illustrates that individuals receive different compensation opportunities (as indicated by average salary movement) depending on the functional area of the business.

FIGURE 9.1   Pay philosophy: Targeting pay.

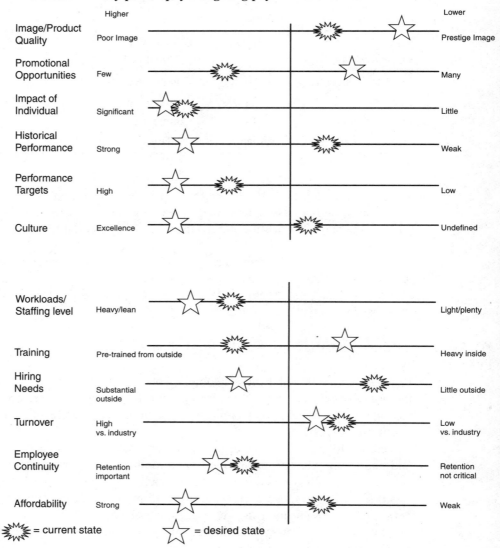

HOW DOES LOCATION AFFECT MY ABILITY TO ATTRACT SKILLED PERSONNEL?

The geographic location where the employee works, whether urban or rural, in the country or outside it, and the cost of living in the region can have a significant impact on pay levels. A pay market in urban New York, for example, may be substantially higher than the pay market for similar positions in a rural location. Premiums may exist for individuals willing to work in remote locations or out of the country.

TABLE 9.3   **Northern California functional area benchmark trends.**

Job Category	Functional Area				
	Operations, %	Engineering, %	Marketing, %	Finance and Admin, %	Total, %
Exempt Supervisory					
Average salary movement	+3.1	+3.3	+4.3	+3.7	+3.6
Exempt Nonsupervisory					
Average salary movement	+3.6	+3.6	+2.9	+3.0	+3.3
Total Nonexempt					
Average salary movement	+3.1	+4.1	+4.0	−3.6	+1.5

SOURCE: Copyright © 1998, Aon Consulting/Radford Division.

Table 9.4 shows how starting salaries for entry-level positions can be determined both by industry as well as geographic location.

GATHERING AND INTERPRETING COMPETITIVE MARKET DATA

By answering the questions regarding competitors, characteristics of the business, compensation strategy, critical business functions, and geographic locations, a framework is established for gathering and interpreting competitive market data. Several options are available to those seeking relevant market compensation information: published surveys, custom surveys, compensation databases, and individual knowledge.

Survey Participants

In all cases, the participants in the survey can have a significant impact on the market results generated. Surveys exist for different industries, company sizes, functional areas, and geographies. Based on the analysis of the relevant labor market, a company selects the most appropriate market reference. Within that survey, the user should review the participant list to understand the distribution of companies by various factors. For example, a survey may report information for "all industries" but in fact have a participant list that is 70 percent manufacturers or insurance companies. Similarly, a banking industry survey may contain the most relevant positions and functional areas for comparison, but the average size of the participants may be inappropriate.

TABLE 9.4 Starting rates for entry-level positions (no experience). Assemblers (hourly), overall.

				Industry					
Starting Rates	Semiconductor	Computer/peripheral	Software	Network Products/Services	Telecommunications Services	Capital equipment	Pharm/Medical, Scientific	Other	Total Results
Northern California	$8.14	$8.15	$7.78	$9.00	$9.51	$9.82	$8.41	$8.93	$8.69
Southern California	$7.55	$6.99	$8.50	$7.87	$8.37	—	$7.11	$6.95	$7.51
Boston/New England	$8.57	$8.00	—	$7.70	—	$9.50	$8.22	$9.89	$8.88
Pacific Northwest	$8.73	$7.21	$8.65	—	—	$7.26	$7.25	$7.65	$7.71
Southwest	$7.75	$7.44	$7.92	—	$8.08	—	$7.36	$6.83	$7.64
Other United States	$8.23	$7.76	$7.53	$10.00	$8.72	$10.00	$7.76	$7.86	$8.02

SOURCE: Copyright © 1998, Aon Consulting/Radford Division.

Premiums: Individual Adjustments to Survey Data

The pay levels for different incumbents holding the same position may be adjusted for specific skills, education, knowledge, or demonstrated competencies of an individual. Expert knowledge of a particular software application, for example, may result in a premium paid to one job holder over another in the same position.

Published survey pay levels can also be adjusted for an individual's tenure. For certain professionals, like engineers, lawyers, and scientists, rates of pay are particularly influenced by an individual's experience—that is, his or her length of time in that position.

Companies may identify particular functional groups of people as "key contributors." Key contributors are those people who directly create a competitive advantage and who if lost to competitors would be a detriment to the company's success. Companies can decide who should be paid premiums due to their relatively greater value to the organization.

COMPENSATION DATABASES

To keep compensation programs current with changes in the market, it is essential that information on pay practices for positions in those markets be readily accessible. Computers are used today to develop an inventory of positions, job content, industries, company (scope) information, and pay practices that allow a user to combine a number of variables and extract relevant compensation information. Compensation databases maintained on a computer have the advantages of flexibility, ease of access, reduced paper trail, and enhanced reporting capabilities.

Compensation databases may contain information from one survey source or multiple survey sources. Flexibility means that the user can accomplish the following:

- Select the job title or have a match generated through a keyword search

- Adjust the degree of similarity between the survey job description and the company position

- Choose the industry and company size

From the customized request, the system will generate market composite compensation information regarding base salary and total cash levels.

The Internet has become a powerful tool in managing survey information. Market-pricing models housed on local Web sites allow multiple users to retrieve compensation information efficiently and cost effectively.

DERIVING MARKET DATA FOR LARGE POPULATIONS AND HYBRID JOBS

Typically, when assessing the overall competitiveness of a company's pay levels, benchmark positions are selected to serve as a representative sample of all positions in the organization. Market data are collected for each benchmark from which assumptions are made and conclusions are drawn regarding overall external competitiveness. By using a small sample of jobs, the company can manage the costs and time required to complete the assessment. However, what should a company do when a need exists to determine market competitive rates of pay for large populations or positions that are not easily matched to survey positions?

One solution involves using existing job evaluation points (from a point factor system like the Hay system) to create a scale of values and adding survey jobs using the same evaluation points into the hierarchy. The relationship between the points for the internal job and the survey job can be applied to the survey job's market price to derive a market value for the internal job.

If a company does not use a point factor job evaluation system or if a survey has not been similarly calibrated, an alternative multiple ranking approach can be used to establish a scale of values and derive market data. In a multiple ranking exercise, a committee first determines the relative worth of each position to the organization according to its value system. By also determining the value of published survey jobs to the organization, the results can be quantified into a hierarchy of both internal and external job worth. Knowing the relationship between internal and external jobs, combined with market data from the external jobs, imputed market values for all internal jobs can be derived. The result is a complete set of imputed market values for all jobs in the organization, including those that are hybrids or jobs not easily matched to positions in the marketplace.

For example, in the chart shown in Figure 9.2, market jobs have been assigned points, and the relationship between those points and market median salary data

FIGURE 9.2   Market median salaries to multiple ranking points.

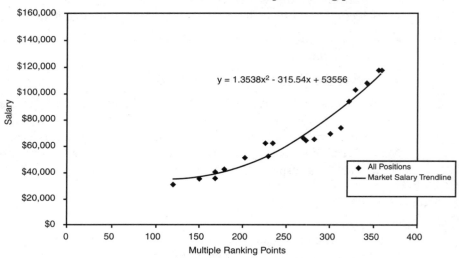

$y = 1.3538x^2 - 315.54x + 53556$

has been drawn in a trend line. The equation from the trend line can then be used to derive inputed market values for all internal jobs, using points as the x value.

The element common to both of the methods described above is that a value (or points) is created for both internal and external jobs. Having both quantified and establishing a relationship to market data allows a company to derive market data for a large population of jobs.

This chapter has outlined a foundation for companies attempting to understand variables affecting pay practices and some of the sources of information available for market pay information. Though many sources exist, interpreting the data and understanding the companies in the survey profile are critical to properly defining market compensation practices.

10

THE DEVELOPMENT OF SALARY STRUCTURES

Hilary Belanger, Consultant

Aon Consulting

Andrew S. Rosen, Vice President

Aon Consulting

COMPENSATION STRATEGY

A *salary structure* (the grades and salary ranges that are the framework for the hierarchical placement of jobs and the subsequent delivery of pay to individuals) must be developed and implemented within the context of a compensation strategy that is aligned with an organization's people strategy, which supports the mission, culture, and business strategy. Figure 10.1 depicts the business-compensation strategy flow.

The salary structure is one of the basic building blocks of a base compensation program (see Figure 10.2). How so?

- The structure is built on the relative ranking and clustering of jobs or roles (typically called *job evaluation,* or, in more person-based systems, *role evaluation* or *role placement*) according to an organization's internal valuing system and/or external market values.

- Positioning of jobs within the structure—which usually reflects the relative level or perceived impact of a job in an organization—often determines degree of participation in other programs, such as bonuses, supplemental benefits, and perquisites.

FIGURE 10.1   Business-compensation strategy flow.

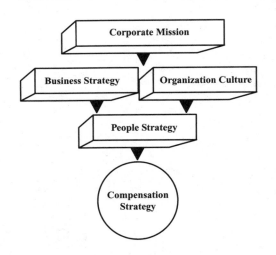

- The type of structure sends a clear message about a company's approach to job design, work process, and organization structure. For example:

  - A *layered structure*—one that encompasses many grades that overlap considerably—is typical of organizations that have many job titles, operate under a hierarchical, pyramidal structure, and view advancement as moving up rungs on a career or job family ladder.
  - A *flat structure*—perhaps a broadband framework with relatively few grades defined by broad dollar parameters—is typical of more fluid organizations that might have customer-driven organization structures and value both lateral and vertical career-job movement.

The types of salary structures often seen in organization models include those shown in Table 10.1. The structure that an organization chooses must fit its culture, business needs, and operating style. The following section discusses the advantages and disadvantages of commonly—and not so commonly—used approaches to developing a salary framework.

TYPES OF STRUCTURES

The type of salary structure you choose must be consistent with the company's compensation strategy and fit within the context of the total compensation program. Your choice will be determined within the context of a number of important program design and policy issues:

FIGURE 10.2   Base pay program architecture.

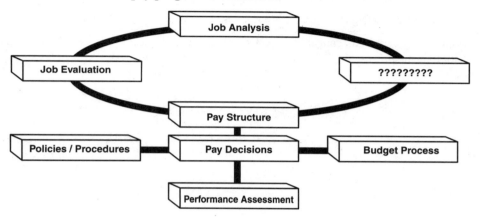

- How much variation or flexibility can we tolerate and/or support in a salary structure? Who will be held accountable for program management?

- Should we plan to pay each employee at the same level relative to the market (e.g., at the market average)? Are there some areas where we need higher-caliber employees than others?

- How many salary structures do we need? Can the dynamics of the labor markets and our staffing and career management plans be accommodated within one structure? Two? Multiple, job family–specific structures? Should the structures be based on similar concepts?

- What form should the salary structure take to support our career management plans? Do we anticipate hierarchical career paths (i.e., based on sequential promotions) or lateral-horizontal career movement? Can we anticipate how "jobs" will be defined and managed?

- How do we want to recognize and reward performance? What behaviors do we want to reinforce? Should the pay-for-performance philosophy be the same across the system? Is the way we define employee "value" going to be relatively stable over the next few years? What "message" do we want to send to employees?

- Do we know how much time is currently spent on program administration? Do we want to reduce the administrative costs? What administrative steps can we eliminate?

In light of these many questions, we consider the advantages and disadvantages of layered, or traditional, and flat, or broadband, structures.

TABLE 10.1   Organization and Salary Structure

Mature, Hierarchical Organization	Fluid, Flat Organization	Network, Virtual Organization
■ Midpoint-driven salary ranges with typical spreads of 35–50%	■ Broadbands with typical emphasis on market values and demonstrated individual competencies or skills	■ Fluid, market-driven, individually based framework
■ Numerous grades from top to bottom; heavy overlap	■ 200+% range spreads or ranges without dollar definitions; moderate overlap	■ Person-based framework, depending on capabilities, contribution, end results

Traditional Structure

Traditional salary structures are the old faithful of compensation frameworks, consisting of a series of ranges, typically well into the double digits (Figure 10.3).

Characteristics of a traditional structure include many narrow bands and a framework that is usually defined by mathematical relationships leading to generally symmetrical range spreads and consistent interrange distances. Grades are typically based on formal job evaluation methodologies. Traditional structures have found their place in organizations with more stable work flows and associated job responsibilities that remain relatively constant and that are hierarchical in their organization structure and leadership style.

Traditional structures often support pay delivery methods such as merit pay programs or step systems that reinforce a job-based, as opposed to person-based, view of the working world.

Reasons for Adopting a Traditional Structure.   The reasons for adopting a traditional structure vary from organization to organization based on alignment with the organization's strategies. However, several common reasons for adopting (or maintaining) a traditional structure are noted below:

■ There is an emphasis on promotion–career advancement through a hierarchical system; individuals can "see" their promotions in the form of moving from grade to grade.

■ Typically, these structures are predictable and easy to administer in the sense that the reasons and timing for pay movement are clearly defined by the structure and associated pay delivery policies.

■ Typically, a traditional structure has a strong technical, mathematically derived foundation, which may be viewed as more objective than a less constrained broadband structure.

FIGURE 10.3   Salary structure—traditional.

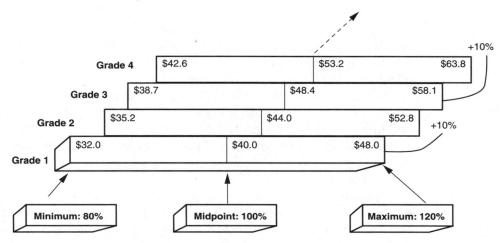

- Traditional structures are the tried-and-true approach to building compensation programs, which may be in-grained in the organizations culture and/or meet the expectations of senior management.

Disadvantages

- Traditional programs are highly structured and may not always respond effectively to changing organizational or individual needs.

- They may create perceived or real barriers between or within functional work groups because of differences in perceived value or status as defined by grade levels.

- They may be slow to recognize increased responsibility or competencies unless they warrant a promotion to a higher grade.

- Managers often do not actively participate in the pay decision-making process; rather, they follow established procedure regarding pay delivery (i.e., promotional, top-of-range, and new-hire guidelines).

- Traditional approaches recognize the job more than the individual in the job. The structure accommodates the relative worth of the job as compared to other jobs, and if the job responsibilities change, the placement of the job within the structure may change (i.e., moved up to a higher grade). An incumbent's acquisition of new skills does not typically result in a reclassification of the job within the structure.

Broadband Structure

Broadbanding could represent the simplification of a system to fewer grades and wider ranges, or, more dramatically, it could mean a deeper cultural change characterized by a leaner organizational structure, greater management responsibility for human resource management, more organizational flexibility, and greater attention to individual career planning and advancement.

Whatever its desired impact, structurally the systems are the same—a salary system with a few, very wide salary ranges. A traditional salary structure may have multiple overlapping ranges (20 or more) from bottom to top and salary range widths that may vary from 40 to 60 percent. In contrast, a broadbanding system is more likely to have 4 to 10 overlapping salary ranges with salary range widths of 150 percent or more.

Typically, broadband structures support person-based pay delivery approaches such as competency-based pay, skill-based pay, and career laddering, allowing organizations to better recognize and reward individuals and move them through the structure based on their capabilities and contributions to the organization (Figure 10.4).

Reasons for Adopting Broadbands.   While reasons for adopting a broadbanding approach vary considerably, it is paramount that the structure support the organization's strategies and not be implemented just because it is the latest trend. Most of the organizations that have modified their systems have done so to complement broader organizational changes, such as:

FIGURE 10.4   Band structure with career stages—an example.

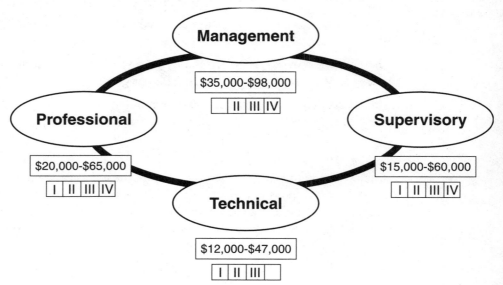

- Reducing the emphasis on promotions and grades
- Providing the organization with the flexibility to respond to changing business needs
- Breaking down the barriers to teamwork and cooperation (i.e., barriers resulting from narrowly defined job duties and responsibilities)
- Providing employees with the opportunity for personal growth and extensive performance recognition
- Placing more human resource decisions in the hands of managers
- Facilitating (and encouraging) lateral job moves
- Reducing the administrative burden of job evaluation

Disadvantages

- May not be worth the commitment of time and money if the change is only superficial (combining grades)
- Requires significant organizational and supervisory commitment to development, training, and communication
- May be considered too "loose," lacking definition and thus may be potentially difficult to manage and administer
- May not afford the same sense of promotion for individuals when they are advancing through a band as opposed to moving from grade to grade

Once a type of structure has been decided on, the technical work of creating the structure begins.

SETTING PARAMETERS

The components of the salary structure include the following:

- Grade, points, skill block, or some measure of relative ranking and clustering
- Salary target for each job or group of jobs (often called *midpoint, target, control point,* etc.)
- Spread for each range (the distance between the minimum and maximum of a range, typically expressed in percentage terms) and the method of moving an individual's pay through that range
- Interrange distance (the distance between each range, typically expressed in percentage terms)
- Range overlap (the degree to which dollar values in adjacent ranges overlap)
- The number of structures across an organization

Grade

The *grade*—or relative ranking and/or clustering of jobs—represents the relative internal valuing of a grouping of jobs, roles, or skill sets. The number of grades or bands is influenced by the number of jobs, the number of job-career levels, and the extent to which an organization wants to distinguish among job and impact levels. Let's talk about, for example, a technology-driven manufacturing company with 1,000 employees spread among 200 job titles. A traditional model might suggest 12 grades for nonexempt employees and 10 grades for exempt employees. A banded structure, on the other hand, might have 5 bands for the entire organization.

What circumstances might lead us to adopt the first model? It may be that management wants to be able to differentiate between relatively finite job levels and wants to be able to reward people accordingly (both monetarily and through enhancing status) as they move quickly up through the organization. They have a merit system that (amazingly enough!) is working, and this dovetails nicely with a minimum-midpoint-maximum structure that is the hallmark of traditional salary frameworks.

The flip side—the broadband model—would be more appropriate if most work were being done in teams and, as a consequence, the organization was looking for ways to break down boundaries between job classes. Furthermore, the company needs people who can flex easily between job duties and wants to be able to reward them as needed. In order to decide on the number of bands, we would observe the *natural groupings* of jobs, which typically reflect relative degrees of organizational or strategic impact, knowledge requirements, accountability, etc. Our 5-band model is shown in Figure 10.5.

Finally, some organizations highly value the skills an individual brings to, and demonstrates on the job, as well as the flexibility achieved through extensive cross training. In such cases, the "grades" may actually be defined skill sets or groups of skill sets, as depicted in Figure 10.6.

Salary Target

The *salary target* represents the *destination salary* (or *going rate*) for jobs in a particular grade level. The actual number depends on the organization's compensation philosophy (do we want to pay at the 50th percentile in the local market? 50th percentile in the region? Below median in recognition of our above-average variable pay plan? 65th percentile nationally, reflecting our need to recruit and retain the best and brightest key contributors?) and its selection of pay survey sources.

How that salary target is used as the foundation for developing ranges depends on whether the organization prefers the layered look or the banded approach. In the former, many organizations use regression analyses to create a line of best fit through data points that represent the intersection of market pay levels and relative job size (whether reflected by job evaluation points, grade levels, or some other measure of internal value). A similar line of best fit representing internal pay

FIGURE 10.5   Five-band model.

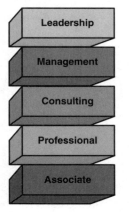

FIGURE 10.6   Skill sets.

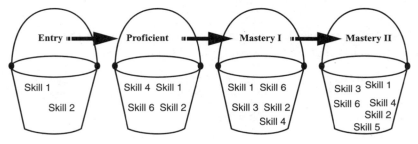

practices can then be developed, and a comparative analysis of the two conducted. See Figure 10.7 for an example of this type of analysis.

Depending on the compensation philosophy of the organization, this analysis will be used to define a *policy line,* which, in turn, can be the basis for defining the actual salary range structure.

An alternative to the line-of-best-fit approach—which is used more often in broadband implementations but could be applied in any scenario—is the *cluster analysis method.* In this process, market rates for the jobs clustered as described above are reviewed, and target pay levels are developed based on approximate average or median values (or other competitive levels depending, once again, on the organization's particular philosophy).

It is important to mention that in the development of broadband systems, target salary rates for entire bands may not be feasible or advisable, given the dollar spread for each band and the variety of market pay levels within the band. In such instances, the dollar parameters for the band are more typically defined by first reviewing the high and low market values for jobs in the band. The next step is

FIGURE 10.7   Line of best fit.

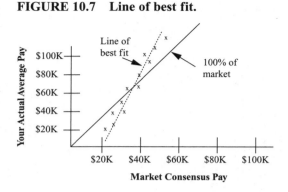

setting the band minimum at a value approximating hiring rates for the lowest market value jobs, and then defining the band maximum at a value approximating the maximum amount the company would be willing to pay a superior performer in the highest-market-value job.

Once the band parameters are set, many organizations create further *pay markers* within the band to facilitate administering pay on a more finite basis. Typical approaches include target zones or subbands:

- Tied to market levels for groupings of jobs within the band (e.g., professional band divided into four zones based on approximate market values)

- Tied to individual jobs within the band (e.g. each job within the professional band with its own target range based on actual or imputed market values)

- Based on defined competency and/or skill levels or career stages (e.g., professional band divided into three zones, with each segment identified by demonstrated behaviors and/or outputs in critical competency areas)

Spread for Each Range

The *spread for each salary range* refers to the distance from range minimum to range maximum or, alternatively, the distance from a midpoint or target (if used) "down" to the minimum or "up" to the maximum. Clearly, the spread of a broadband will be much larger than the spread of a more traditional range structure.

Typical pay range spreads in traditional structures are as follows:

- 20 to 25 percent for lower-level service, production, and maintenance

- 30 to 40 percent for clerical, technical and paraprofessional

- 40 to 50 percent for higher-level professional, administrative, and middle management

- 50 percent and above for higher-level managerial and executive

Before taking these numbers on faith, it is important to consider some of the issues inherent in sizing ranges, including the following:

- If your ranges will be built on a target rate, how much below target is the hiring rate for that job (will we, in fact, expect to hire qualified but inexperienced people at the minimum, or above it)? Conversely, how much are we willing to pay above a market competitive rate for extraordinary performance and/or contribution (in other words, is there a cap to what we're willing to pay for a particular job no matter how well it's being performed)?

- How long does it take for a newly hired, inexperienced employee paid at the minimum to achieve competence, arriving at market target pay? The longer the time period, the greater the distance between the minimum and target.

- There is no law requiring that salary ranges be symmetrical. While range symmetry may appeal to our sense of orderliness, it is more important that salary range frameworks accurately reflect hiring practices, development processes, compensation philosophy, and the degree of linkage between pay and performance and that employees and their managers understand how ranges work and how the structure affects their current and future pay opportunities.

Generally speaking, broadband spreads can range from around 75 to 200 to 300 percent. In fact, some organizations that use broadbands but price jobs or people individually do not place dollar limits on the bands themselves (see Figure 10.8 for an example). Their rationale is that a huge band is less an overgrown range than a grouping of jobs or people whose scope, job complexity, and organizational impact are similar. In these cases the actual dollar ranges are more likely to be built around a job or group of jobs. Setting dollar limits on the bands themselves is sometimes seen as raising unrealistic expectations that any job in the band has a clear path to move from, say, $50,000 to $150,000.

Interrange Distance and Range Overlap

Typical midpoint-to-midpoint differences in traditional structures are as follows:

- 5 to 10 percent for clerical, service, and technical jobs
- 8 to 12 percent for professional jobs
- 10 to 15 percent for managerial jobs
- 20 to 40 percent for executive jobs

The smaller the distance between ranges, the larger the number of ranges in the structure. As this distance gets very small, a structure may become overly layered and will offer only minimal pay differentials between an employee in one grade

FIGURE 10.8   Banding illustration.

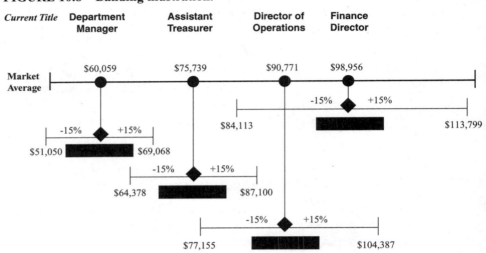

and, say, a supervisor or senior-level contributor in the next. As the interrange distance gets very large, an organization will, by definition, have fewer and fewer ranges, leading inevitably to a *de facto* broadband system (we heartily recommend a more planful approach, of course!).

In nearly all structures—whether traditional or banded--at least some degree of overlap will be found (see Figure 10.9 for an example of a strongly overlapping approach). *Overlap* ensures that moving from one grade to another (or from one zone to another within a single band) can be a smooth transition that is not accompanied by a promotional increase of windfall proportions. The greater the overlap, of course, the less sense of advancement (and accompanying pay adjustments) when moving from one level to another. Typically (though not necessarily), structures with smaller interrange distances also have greater overlap between ranges; the converse is also generally true.

The Number of Structures

The number (and type) of structures in an organization depends on many factors, including the following:

- Different lines of business that may actually be in separate industries or require skills in different functions

- Various employee groups that may represent different labor markets and total compensation profiles (e.g., nonexempt, exempt, executive)

- Divergent cultures or work environments ranging from, say, a customer service organization staffed by self-directed work teams (sounds like a

FIGURE 10.9 Overlapping structure approach.

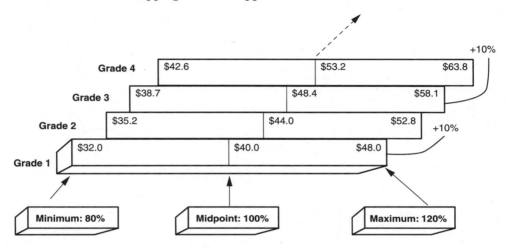

skill-based system within broadbands might work) to a functionally organized manufacturing plant (in which a more layered, step-based system may be appropriate)

- Extent to which an organization wants to, for example, create a seamless, "one-for-all" organization (single structure) versus decentralized, entrepreneurial operations (multiple structures)

Important considerations in determining the ideal number of structures include the degree to which internal equity is valued (how often do people transfer across business units or geographical sites?) and the ability of the organization to effectively support and administer a complex array of structures.

11

PAY FOR SKILLS, KNOWLEDGE, AND COMPETENCIES

Gerald E. Ledford, Jr.
Practice Leader, Employee Effectiveness and Rewards

Sibson & Company

Robert L. Heneman
Associate Professor of Management and Human Resources

Ohio State University

COMPENSATION SYSTEMS that pay for *skills, knowledge, and competencies* (SKCs) use a logic different from conventional job-based pay systems. More familiar, job-based pay systems compensate for the *job* that an employee is performing at a particular time. In contrast, systems that pay for skills, knowledge, and competencies reward the employee's repertoire of capabilities. Moreover, compensation typically follows a formal certification that the employee has acquired SKCs. In contrast, the trigger for a change in job-based pay is a change in the employee's job, not a demonstration of accomplishment. In the extreme, the employee's job-based compensation level may change during the course of the workday as the person temporarily changes jobs.

It is important to recognize that, by definition, pay for SKC plans are not a reward for performance. Rather, these plans seek to provide employees with the SKCs that *enable* greater performance. Thus, these plans are not complete pay systems by themselves. They need to be supplemented by performance incentives. Group or unit incentives such as gainsharing or goal sharing often make a potent combination with pay for SKCs. The pay for SKCs encourages increased potential and almost always rewards individuals. Group or unit incentives help overcome the centrifugal force of the individualistic SKC plan and encourage a balance between immediate performance requirements and developmental needs.

In recent years, there has been a tremendous growth in the use of systems that pay employees for their skills, knowledge, and competencies. For example, surveys by the Center for Effective Organizations (CEO) at the University of Southern California indicate that 62 percent of Fortune 1000 firms used such pay plans for at least some employees in 1996, up from 40 percent in 1987. The users of these plans consistently report a high level of satisfaction with them. For example, the CEO study found that firms were four times more likely to rate these plans as successful than unsuccessful. (Perhaps because so many plans are new, however, almost half reported that they were undecided about the success of the plans.) Similarly, a study of 97 skill-based pay plans sponsored by the American Compensation Association found that two-thirds to three-quarters of skill-based pay users found these plans to be successful on a wide range of outcome measures.

This chapter will consider two major issues concerning these plans. First, we will examine different types of plans and consider whether the differences in plan labels reflect real or surface differences. Second, we will consider the major issues in the design of these plans, including the infrastructure needed to support them.

VARIETIES OF PLANS TO PAY FOR SKILLS, KNOWLEDGE, AND COMPETENCIES

Plans discussed in this chapter have many names. Are they basically similar, or are skill-based pay plans fundamentally different from pay-for-knowledge plans, competency pay plans, or plans that pay for strategic competencies? In our view, these plans are more alike than different. They share the key characteristic of paying for the employee's repertoire of SKCs rather than for the job the employee is currently performing. However, plans with different names have origins at different places in the organization and tend to be applied to different groups of employees. Figure 11.1 depicts three major approaches that we consider here.

FIGURE 11.1   Targets and constituencies for different forms of pay for skills, knowledge, and competencies.

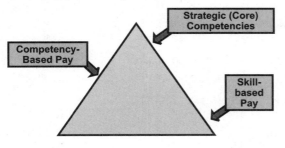

Skill-Based Pay

Skill-based pay originated as a way to reward nonexempt employees for cross skilling. These plans are also called *pay for knowledge, knowledge-based pay, pay for skills,* or *pay for applied skills.* Although versions of this approach are ancient, we can trace the modern approach to high-involvement manufacturing plants that Procter & Gamble built in the 1960s. Line managers developed skill-based pay plans to incent employees to learn the multiple jobs necessary to support self-managed teams and business involvement. Compared to the other forms of pay for SKCs, skill-based pay systems stick very closely to the specific tasks that employees perform. Characteristics of the original Procter & Gamble plans describe the classic skill-based pay plan still commonly found today. The *classic skill-based pay plan* has the following characteristics:

Compensation Approach.   The classic system is pure base pay, not a set of bonuses or add-ons to job-based pay.

Design Methodology.   The classic system is based on a relatively exhaustive analysis and cataloguing of all the skills necessary to do the work of the organization. The skills identified through this analysis are then packaged into skill blocks that represent compensable units of skill and employees are rewarded for mastering these blocks. Assessment procedures are developed to test whether employees have mastered new skill blocks and training systems are established to make it possible for employees to learn new skill blocks.

Most Common Settings.   Classic plans are most commonly found in manufacturing or manufacturing-like service settings, such as back-office operations in insurance and financial services. The term *skill-based pay* continues to be applied primarily to plans that cover employees at the lower levels of the organizational hierarchy.

Implicit Assumptions.   Classic skill-based pay plans require a significant start-up investment, and typically 6 to 18 months are required to complete the entire design process in a large plant or similar unit. These plans depend on having enough organizational stability to realize a payback on the investment in the design process.

We have far more experience with such skill-based pay plans than with other types of plans that pay for SKCs. The available research suggests that the clear majority of these plans are successful in encouraging multi-skilling and in increasing organizational performance, notwithstanding some well-publicized failures (such as one at Motorola). A relatively strong finding in the literature is that these plans work best and are found most often in settings that encourage a high degree of employee involvement and indeed involve employees in the design and administration of the pay plan. In addition to the typical advantages of employee involvement in the process of organization change, a high-involvement system is more likely than a traditional bureaucratic management system to take good advantage of the new skills that employees acquire. A system that adds skills but does not take advantage of new employee abilities simply adds cost without gaining offsetting advantages.

Competency Pay Plans

Competency pay plans evolved from the work of psychologist David McClelland and others on the importance of competencies in determining individual job performance. *Competencies* are demonstrable characteristics of the person, including knowledge, skills, and behaviors, that enable performance. Most of the work in this tradition has focused on the exempt workforce, specifically managers and professionals. In keeping with the nature of the work of these populations, the competencies rewarded in these systems tend to be more abstract and less closely tied to the specific tasks of those on the plan. Cognitive skills (such as analytic thinking), values, self-image (such as self-confidence), motivational patterns, and even personality traits have been used as competencies that are rewarded in pay plans.

Writings about competency pay often include lengthy discussions about what constitutes a competency and about distinctions among different types of competencies. Each author tends to apply his or her own classification scheme. A common distinction is between those competencies that are necessary to perform the job but are not the source of competitive advantage and those that are more difficult to achieve and more strategic in nature, offering the hope of competitive advantage. The former are called, for example, *requisite* or *threshold competencies,* while the latter are called, for example, *strategic* or *differentiating competencies.* Common characteristics of competency pay systems include the following.

Compensation Approach.   The typical competency pay system is pure base pay, not a set of bonuses or add-ons to job-based pay.

Design Methodology.   The most common approach to designing competency pay systems is to study a group of performers who are judged superior on specified performance criteria and to collect extensive data to determine how top performers are different from average or poor performers. An extensive battery of tests, interviews, observations, and ratings may be used to discover such differences. The differences are packaged into competencies that are then tied to human resource systems, including compensation.

Most Common Organizational Settings.   The term *competency pay* is most often applied to systems that cover managers, supervisors, professionals (including human resource professionals), and technical personnel. Often, these systems are applied to large numbers of personnel in different positions and locations within a company. When this occurs, the system may not be closely tied to the specific work of covered employees.

Implicit Assumptions.   Competency pay plans require considerable design and installation effort, and thus these plans make the same assumptions as skill-based pay plans about the organizational stability needed to realize a return on the up-front investment in the plan. These plans also make a strong assumption that performance at the organizational level will increase if more employees emulate the behavior and values of superior individual performers. This assumption is rarely tested, even though a fair amount of research suggests that organizational performance is not merely the sum of individual performance. The problem is that collective behaviors (such as setting a good performance strategy and coordinating effort) may be needed to generate good organizational performance but not to generate the superior individual performance captured by the competency-modeling process.

There is relatively little research about the effectiveness of competency pay systems in increasing organizational as opposed to individual performance. A 1996 American Compensation Association survey study found too few competency pay cases to draw conclusions about the organizational effects of these plans. A great many validation studies, similar in methodology to industrial psychology tests of the validity of hiring tests, offer encouragement, but these usually validate against individual rather than organizational performance.

A particular concern with competency pay plans is the risk of legal jeopardy for poorly conceived and validated competency pay systems that may illegally discriminate against minorities and other protected groups. This is a special concern with competencies that are based on personality traits and other abstract competencies far removed from the actual work. These may not pass the *face-valid test* and may invite court challenges.

Plans Based on Strategic Competencies

The third approach is the most embryonic. It has been the subject of considerable discussion because of the intense interest in *core competencies* in the business strategy literature and among senior executives during the 1990s. The *core competencies approach* argues that a small set of technological and organizational skill complexes are a more stable and effective source of competitive advantage than superiority in particular markets or products. Market leadership is fleeting as products evolve rapidly, but competencies remain. For example, Sony's core competencies in miniaturization and precision manufacturing, Toyota's prowess at lean manufacturing, and Wal-Mart's core competencies in distribution, marketing, and information technology, are underlying sources of competitive advantage that remain despite rapidly shifting markets and products.

In many companies, human resource managers and consultants have used executive interest in core competencies as an opportunity to introduce competency-based pay plans. However, it is important to recognize that the "core competencies" of the strategy literature bear no relation to those found in many pay systems. It takes extensive analysis and effort to discover the handful of core competencies that business strategists have in mind. In the competency pay literature, "core" often means basic or requisite—the opposite of the meaning in the strategy literature. Worse, simply selecting competencies from a consultant's menu of prepackaged choices, a procedure that is far too common, invites ridicule from strategists and executives interested in discovering the unique competencies that gain competitive advantage for the firm.

One of the most positive aspects of the focus on strategic competencies is that it encourages forward thinking. In contrast, the focus in the competency pay approach on identifying why some are superior performers is essentially backward looking, in that it identifies the competencies that have made some people successful in the past. For companies that are about to undergo fundamental change in response to business conditions, reinforcing old successful habits can be a recipe for disaster. Consider IBM or AT&T in 1980, at the dawn of the PC and telecommunications revolutions. If they had paid for competencies, would they have been better served by a forward-looking or backward-looking system? Many companies believe that their situation today is analogous to that faced by IBM and AT&T 20 years ago.

There are relatively few examples of pay systems based on strategic competencies. Business leaders and authors have devoted relatively little attention to how this approach might be applied to human resource systems, as opposed to business strategy. However, some characteristics of this approach seem clear.

Compensation Approach.   The typical system is a base pay compensation system.

Design Methodology.   The design methodology is top down, evolving from the top executive group's identification of the core competencies of the corporation rather than from the current work of employees. This permits identification and rewarding of forward-looking competencies that have not received significant prior attention in the corporation.

Most Common Settings.   Although experience is limited so far, it seems likely that the pay of managers and professionals is most likely to be touched by these plans.

Implicit Assumptions.   An important assumption is that highly abstract strategic competencies that may not be within the experience of most employees can serve as the basis for an effective pay plan. This places a heavy burden on management to explain their reasoning and persuade employees of the merits of the strategic competency approach.

There is no published research about this type of plan. The first author has conducted an unpublished study of a plan that fits the strategic competency definition. The plan covered nearly 1,000 managers from a variety of functions and levels within a large food company. All were rewarded by movement within a broad band for their mastery of just four competencies that applied to all those covered on the plan. The competencies were closely linked to the business strategy of the firm. For example, one competency supported the customer focus that was important to the company's then-new total quality management (TQM) initiative. The study found that across the company, the regions that were most effective in implementing and supporting the competency pay plan were the most effective on hard measures of performance (productivity, cost, and quality).

SKC Bonuses

So far, we have considered three kinds of base pay systems for rewarding the acquisition of SKCs. In general, base pay systems are advantageous. Adoption of a base pay system tends to force a relatively thorough analysis of needed SKCs rather than the casual adoption of a new pay plan. Base pay plans also are relatively difficult to remove arbitrarily. Finally, employees tend to view base pay increases as desirable and meaningful rewards. However, one-time bonuses are an underused alternative to base pay increases, and they make a great deal of sense in two situations.

First, bonuses may help preserve a competitive wage position in the market. If an existing organization is converting to a pay-for-skills plan, and if base wages are already over market, the organization may not be able to offer additional base wage increases without becoming uncompetitive. It is difficult to see how existing plans in the auto industry, for example, can offer meaningful base wage incentives for skill acquisition, but one-time bonuses may offer an attractive alternative. This is because bonuses do not have the recurring annuity cost of base wage increases.

Second, bonuses are attractive when the organization is experiencing rapid changes in the types and mix of skills, knowledge, and competencies that it needs to be successful. In high technology, for example, the competitive landscape changes so frequently that long-term planning is difficult. The rate of technical obsolescence may be so great that the organization does not have the luxury of devoting a year or two to creating a competency pay plan. The plan might be largely obsolete before the design is complete. Bonuses are an attractive option because they can be developed and implemented very quickly. Such plans can be modified frequently. For example, a new set of bonuses can be adopted each year, changing as business conditions change.

Bonuses have other advantages—and problems. They can be targeted to a select few competencies without upsetting the base pay system. Administrative support is much less than it is for a base pay system. Sloppy or even poor designs in any given year have fewer negative consequences because of the absence of an annuity feature. On the other hand, bonuses may have more limited incentive value to employees. Also, these plans are probably more difficult to sustain over time because management tends to feel more comfortable about terminating bonus plans than terminating base pay plans. A quickly executed plan may lack credibility with employees if the company fails to support it with an adequate communications and training infrastructure.

There is no research about SKC bonus plans, but such companies as Monsanto and Rockwell have used them. Anecdotal evidence is highly encouraging. One engineering-intensive company placed thousands of employees on a competency pay bonus system. All exempt employees negotiated learning contracts with their supervisors in an appraisal cycle set off by 6 months from the performance review cycle. The plan offered employees a $750 bonus for meeting the negotiated learning contract. The company experienced a fivefold increase in the amount of development activity in the company at a relatively modest cost in bonuses. The tuition reimbursement budget actually experienced a windfall, as technical personnel stopped taking classes that were not directly relevant to their work (and their learning contracts).

THE DESIGN CONTEXT

In designing plans that pay for skills, knowledge, and competencies, managers often seem to have an irresistible urge to jump into the details of skill block design. The first lesson from research and experience is that the fit of the system with its organizational context is far more important than any choice about the design of particular skill blocks. In particular, the system must be carefully married to the business context. Specifically, this means that designers should attend to the following issues.

Business-Based Objectives

Skill-based pay plans, for example, can be especially helpful in increasing employee flexibility, encouraging training, and reinforcing self-management skills. Designers need to think through what specific patterns of behavior are required of employees, whether the proposed pay plan is able to reinforce those skills, and how the intended benefits will be realized. A very important business issue to consider is how much flexibility the organization has to increase average wages levels, which will affect the availability of meaningful incentives in exchange for mastering new skills, knowledge, and competencies.

Organizational Structure and Technology

Plans that pay for skills, knowledge, and competencies can reinforce or undermine organizational structure. For example, if the organization is emphasizing the use of employee teams, cross-skilling within teams may be more appropriate than cross-skilling throughout the entire organization. The organization's technology often acts as an important constraint, and in some cases it may need to be modified to support training needs. For example, in customer service organizations, new technology can provide fully trained customer service agents with all the information they need to fully service a customer so that they do not have to make inquiries of many departments.

Organizational Culture

As we have indicated, organizations that adopt plans that pay for SKCs should have or be moving to an open, participative culture. This is one of the strongest predictors of success in part because cultures with such characteristics are far more likely to take advantage of the new capabilities employees develop through the plan.

THE DESIGN OF COMPENSABLE SKILLS, KNOWLEDGE, AND COMPETENCIES

Whatever form the pay system takes, it will be constituted of certain units of skills, knowledge, and competencies that the organization is willing to compensate. There are three major issues that must be addressed in the design of compensable units. These are depicted in Figure 11.2.

Compensation Management

First, the architecture of the overall compensation system requires attention. The nature of the SKC blocks will be determined primarily by the type of plan being implemented. A number of questions arise after the basic blocks are defined. How will SKC blocks or units be ordered, indicating career paths and minimum and maximum advancement opportunities? Decisions about these matters will give employees messages about the sequence of actions necessary to advance and to remain an employee in good standing. In general, it is best to err on the side of conservatism in these decisions early in the history of the plan. Employees rarely complain if they end up with more career opportunities, easier minimum

FIGURE 11.2   Elements of a system paying for skills, knowledge, and competencies.

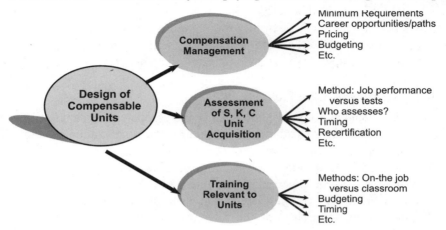

requirements, and greater maximum earning potential later, but the opposite condition feels like a loss.

An important issue concerns the pricing of plans that pay for skills, knowledge, and competencies. Often, it is impossible to price each competency or skill block to the market, in the way that each job in a job-based system can be priced. Rather, the typical procedure is to price the overall system rather than each element of it. The entry rate is set at the level just high enough to entice talented people to join the organization. The top rate is set based on market conditions as well. For example, in skill-based pay plans for semiskilled factory workers, the top end of the range may be placed appropriately near the bottom of the skilled worker classification. Finally, in some cases an average-rate pay rate is also set to market, based on labor market or industry benchmarks. Within these anchor points, skill blocks or competencies are assigned values based on their relative degree of difficulty. To take a simple example, assume that the entry rate is $10 per hour and the top rate is $20 per hour, both determined by the market. If there are 10 skill blocks of equal difficulty (as indicated by learning time or some other metric), each block an employee masters might be given a value of $1 per hour.

Employees need to have some idea of how long it will take to master competencies or skill blocks. The amount of time required to master a block or competency can vary tremendously, from a few months to several years. In general, it is desirable to break very complex blocks or competencies into several pieces so that at least annual advancement is possible within the system. If the blocks or competencies require only a few weeks to master, on the other hand, it is better to group them into a longer and more meaningful grouping or reconsider whether the plan really fits the skill requirements of the organization. The organization does not want too many blocks or competencies because this makes the plan difficult to administer and communicate and because it sets up the expectation that employees will receive compensation every time they learn something.

Assessment of SKC Acquisition

Any system requires some way of determining whether an employee has mastered skill blocks or competencies. The methods and procedures for assessment can be quite contentious if they are not thought through well. The assessment step has no counterpart in job-based pay systems. Unless it is done well in SKC pay plans, however, the plan will deteriorate into a *de facto* time-in-grade system, and the organization will receive no value for the increased wages provided under the system.

Part of the design of each skill block or competency is the specification of the standards for determining how to verify that an employee has mastered it. In skill-based pay plans for nonexempt employees, the process can be fairly elaborate, involving measurement of on-the-job performance, testing, and other methods. In general, management should rely on work samples whenever possible. Work samples are *face valid,* meaning they have natural credibility with employees. However, work samples may need to be supplemented with oral testing, written testing, or live demonstrations, if it is important to know, for instance, how the employee would respond to rare or hazardous conditions that are not likely to be encountered during the work sample of a few weeks or months.

In skill-based pay systems, certification may become one of the most time-consuming supervisory duties. Thus, it is important to think through the scheduling of certifications and the procedures for handling those who fail the tests. For example, how soon will they be allowed to retest? Is there any queuing of certification opportunities in the work unit?

Periodic recertification, perhaps annually, seems to be an increasing trend in skill-based systems. This ensures that employees maintain the skills for which they receive compensation. Without recertifications, the pay plan can result in increased wages that are attached to skills long lost through disuse.

Competency pay plans tend to incorporate competency assessments into the performance appraisal system. By their nature, most competencies are demonstrated on the job over a long period of time. Increasingly, assessments have a *360 degree component,* with reviews by peers, subordinates, supervisors, and customers who have relevant knowledge of the employee's demonstrated competency.

Training

Unless employees have the opportunity to develop the skills and competencies that make up the pay system, they will be frustrated by the incentives they have no opportunity to earn. Experience and research clearly indicate that demand for training greatly increases once employee pay is attached to the mastery of skills and competencies.

It is desirable to create a solid training plan in advance of the installation of the pay system. The starting point of the plan is the assessment of the training required to master each skill block or competency in the system, together with an estimate of the likely speed and path of progression of employees through the system. A menu of training courses relevant to the system, a specific schedule of offerings, and the assignment of instructors (which may be peers, vendors, managers, or trainers) are part of the plan. An adequate training budget is essential.

Job rotation is a critical part of the acquisition of many skills and competencies, especially in skill-based pay systems. No classroom training can take the place of the experiences on the job that are needed for mastery of most skills included in the typical system. Rotation issues can become very contentious, and it is best to anticipate the problems and plan for rotation ahead of time. Many issues need to be determined. Who will decide when to rotate, and according to what timetable? How will the organization balance production needs with employee desires for training? How will it handle slow learners and those who refuse to rotate, which can lock up the whole rotation system? Competency systems for exempt employees may require new assignments rather than something analogous to job rotation. However, the same types of issues are relevant.

CONCLUSION

Since publication of the third edition of this handbook, systems that pay for skills, knowledge, and competencies have gone from a rarity to an increasingly standard tool of compensation practice. We expect the use of these plans to continue to increase because they meet the needs of so many contemporary organizations. The need for ever-increasing employee skill and knowledge, the increasing use of work systems emphasizing employee self-management, the decline of the conventional job and the job-based pay systems that went with it, and the general pressure for improved corporate performance that drives innovation of many kinds, all will encourage greater use of these systems.

We will conclude with four summary lessons drawn from our experience and research:

1. The design of the system is important, but the quality of the infrastructure needed to support it (certification, training, communication, etc.) is a stronger predictor of success than the elegance of the design.

2. All things being equal, simpler is better. One of the major problems with SKC pay plans is that they tend to become unnecessarily complex, and sometimes they are abandoned because management comes to feel that the administrative hassle outweighs any benefit.

3. Communication is even more important than for job-based pay systems. SKC systems are inevitably unfamiliar to most employees, they are complex compared to job-based pay systems, and they are dependent on

employee understanding of certification and training requirements that add complexity.

4. Any SKC pay plan will change over time, or it will be abandoned, because of its inflexibility and lack of fit with changing conditions. A complete design includes provisions for periodically revisiting the design and its infrastructure and making revisions as necessary. This provision should be very explicit, to increase the chances that employees will greet changes with interest and appreciation rather than resistance.

ADDITIONAL READINGS

A recent, relatively comprehensive review of research on the management of (including pay for) skills, knowledge, and competencies is E. E. Lawler III and G. E. Ledford, Jr., "New approaches to Organizing: Competencies, Capabilities, and the Decline of the Bureaucratic Model," in C. L. Cooper and S. E. Jackson (eds.), *Creating Tomorrow's Organization: A Handbook for Future Research in Organization Behavior* (New York: Wiley, 1987).

The American Compensation Association–sponsored study of 97 skill-based pay plans is reported in a monograph G. D. Jenkins, Jr., G. E. Ledford, Jr., N. Gupta, and D. H. Doty, *Skill-Based Pay: Practices, Payoffs, Pitfalls, and Prospects* (Scottsdale, Ariz.: American Compensation Association, 1992). At this time, the best academic case study of skill-based pay is by B. Murray and B. Gerhart, "An Empirical Analysis of a Skill-Based Pay Program and Plant Performance Outcomes," *Academy of Management Journal,* 1998, **41:**68–78. Three case studies of skill-based pay were reported in a special issue of *Compensation and Benefits Review,* 1991, **23**(2).

The competency pay (and more generally, competency management) approach is outlined in L. M. Spencer and S. M. Spencer, *Competence at Work* (New York: Wiley, 1993). The ACA–sponsored survey study of competency management is *Raising the Bar: Using Competencies to Enhance Employee Performance* (Scottsdale, Ariz.: American Compensation Association, 1996). Skepticism about the similarity of competency systems in many different types of organizations is expressed in P. Zingheim, G. E. Ledford, Jr., and J. Schuster, "Competencies and Competency models: One Size Fits All?" *ACA Journal,* 1996, **5**(1), 56–65.

Most writing about the strategic or core competencies approach is oriented toward business strategy rather than pay and other human resource practices. The original and seminal description of this approach was C. K. Prahalad and G. Hamel, "The Core Competence of the Corporation," *Harvard Business Review,* May–June 1990, pp. 79–91. A rare application of this approach to human resource management, albeit in highly academic language, is A. A. Lado and M. L. Wilson, "Human Resource Systems and Sustained Competitive Advantage: A

Competency-Based Perspective," *Academy of Management Review,* 1994, **19:**699–727.

Data cited about the incidence of the use of pay for skills, knowledge, and competencies were from a study at the Center for Effective Organizations, by E. E. Lawler III with S. A. Mohrman and G. E. Ledford, Jr., *Strategies for High Performance Organizations: Employee Involvement, TQM, and Reengineering Programs in Fortune 1000 Corporations (San Francisco: Jossey-Bass, 1998).*

12

RELATING COMPETENCIES TO PAY

Duncan Brown, Principal

Towers Perrin

I N OUR INCREASINGLY KNOWLEDGE AND SERVICE BASED ECONOMIES, paying people for growing their level of competence, and paying the most
competent people the most money, seems an obvious and sensible practice. And there is certainly a growing trend to relate competencies and
pay. Yet it is also a highly controversial practice, which critics claim
defeats the developmental purpose of competencies and is impossible to manage effectively.

In this chapter, I will attempt to examine competency-related pay objectively, to consider what it is, why it is growing and how well, and how companies
are making and managing this relationship. My conclusion will be that
competency-related pay, as is true for any pay practice, cannot be dismissed or
endorsed universally. Its success is contingent on the objectives and circumstances related to its use.

WHAT IS IT?

Defining *competencies,* nay even spelling them, is a controversial topic in academic circles, and part of the controversy over competency-related pay undoubtedly stems from the variety of interpretations of what it is. No wonder organizations such as gas company BOC and systems firm ICL avoid the term altogether and talk about *capabilities, values, skills,* and *behaviors* instead.

In essence, *competency-related pay* is a simple concept. As Art Zintek, vice president of human resources at Mitsubishi Motor Corporation, puts it, it is about rewarding the "observable, measurable skills, abilities and behaviors which are critical to successful individual and corporate performance." Reflecting on his company's scheme, Phil Pavard of Volkswagen UK says that it is simply about "rewarding people for working better."

WHO IS DOING IT AND WHY?

As a theory, it sounds as though it is a wonderful idea. In our increasingly global, competitive, and resource constrained environment, the success of our organizations is more than ever dependent on the skills, abilities, and performance of our people, and particularly the growing number of professionals and knowledge-based workers. The development and enhancement of "core competencies" among their staff lies at the heart of the business strategy of some of the most globally successful companies in recent years, such as General Electric, Motorola, and Honda. As the head of a major U.S.-based utility told me recently, "To be a world-class company, we have to have the best, the most competent people."

Thus if we can identify the knowledge, skills, and behaviors of our most successful employees, which underpins our organization's competitive success in the marketplace, and encourage the development and application of these same attributes through our pay and reward systems, then we ought to prosper. Surveys of reward trends in the United States and Europe highlight the enormous interest in, and slowly developing incidence of, competency-related pay. Increasing the level of staff competence as the basis for competitive success in these organizations appears to be a prime driver. Towers Perrin's survey of 700 U.S. organizations found 16 percent using skill- and competency-related pay schemes, and a huge 78 percent considering their use in the future. Similarly, in Europe, Towers Perrin's study encompassed 300 organizations and found 20 percent operating pay schemes related to skills and competencies. Over half regarded paying people for competence as one of their top three reward priorities for the future.

Of these companies in the United States, and of a similar-size sample in the United Kingdom and Europe, 45 percent were aiming to "raise the bar" of competence for all employees, supported by their pay and reward changes. For example, Nokia explains its competency pay approach, which was piloted in the United States, on the basis of needing a world-class, broadly skilled workforce to enable it to compete successfully in the twenty-first century. Their people need to be more competent, learn new things, and become more flexible and adaptable—thus, their new pay scheme rewards them for doing so.

Companies using competency-related pay include many well-known and reputable names in fast-moving, rapidly changing, knowledge-based sectors, such as Hewlett Packard, Motorola, Glaxo Wellcome, and Smith-Kline Beecham. Indeed, many research-based organizations with large numbers of professionals have been rewarding personal skills and competency development for many years. Examples include the *dual ladders* of pay for research staff at chemicals producer ICI and the clinical grading schemes used in many health care organizations for nursing staff. Job and results-based pay makes little sense in basic R&D work, where people are constantly changing their roles and tasks and where a high proportion of their work ultimately fails to reach the marketplace.

Yet competency pay users span the full range of sectors, from 19th U.K. brewers Guinness and Bass in the drinks industry, through Pacificorp and Nuclear Electric among utilities, to Bank of Scotland and ABN Amro in financial services. This diversity highlights the second main driver of competency pay applications, which is the perceived failings and inflexibility of traditional pay systems. Rigid hierarchical pay structures and detailed job descriptions and evaluation, in our ever-faster-changing world, have often served to restrict the development and growth in competence and contribution of our employees. Narrowly focused, individual merit pay schemes have similarly often acted as a straightjacket on people, restricting their contribution to no more than six smart individual objectives and producing minor differentials in the resulting payments. As Gerald Ledford of UCLA explains, "The reward systems used by most organizations are too rigid and cumbersome,…[and] cannot keep pace with current business needs and the pace of change." Or, as a seasoned operations manager in a chemicals company told me recently, "We worship at the altar of teamwork, the basis for our success in the future, and then destroy it with our performance pay scheme."

Of those in Towers Perrin's U.S. study, 36 percent cited improvements in the means of relating pay to performance as a primary goal for linking competencies and pay, while Irish food company Kerrygold and travel bureau firm Thomas Cook Direct have abandoned merit pay altogether, the latter replacing it with a competency pay scheme.

WHAT'S THE BEEF?

A logical concept maybe, but also a highly controversial one, given that at least in theory, competency pay challenges many conventional pay shibboleths: Pay for the job, not the person; pay for results, rather than how results are achieved. The opponents of competency pay make three primary criticisms. First, a pay linkage defeats the developmental and improvement aims of competencies, with people unwilling to openly discuss their weaknesses and competency shortfalls if they know their pay increase will be affected. U.K. retailer Boots the Chemists, which employs competencies for selection and training and development purposes, eschews a link with pay on this basis.

Second, competencies cannot be defined and measured precisely enough to provide a valid basis for pay decisions. Ed Lawler points out that the generic competency menus used in many companies "are not only hard to measure, they are not necessarily related to successful task performance." The inclusion of personality traits, meanwhile, "is at its best trivial and at worst damaging," leading to irrelevant or discriminatory pay decisions. Courtaulds Textiles feels that the measurement of competencies is not precise enough for pay determination purposes and instead establishes and adjusts pay on the basis of market and performance considerations.

Finally, attempts at relating pay to competencies are therefore doomed to failure in practice, with overly complex competency menus and inexact but exacting measurement and assessment processes. One well-known bank initially used its entire competency menu to influence base pay increases. Managers had to select the 12 most relevant competencies and appropriate levels for each of their employees from a dictionary of over 50. Hardly surprising then that the Automobile Association, the United Kingdom's largest roadside rescue organization, abandoned its competency-based pay adjustment approach after 3 years of trying, in favor of a simpler, wholly performance based scheme.

One result of bad management is poor cost control, which has been found to be a problem by a number of companies who moved to relate pay to competencies. Research by the Center for Workforce Effectiveness in Los Angeles among 50 U.S. companies found that in 40 percent of cases, competency-related pay had failed, primarily due to the cost impact. Wage costs rose, on average, by over 15 percent, and training costs by over 25 percent. Cummins Engines in England recently took out its skills pay system on the shop floor and replaced it with a team performance bonus for this reason.

SO HOW CAN YOU DO IT? A FRAMEWORK OF APPROACHES

Recently explaining his company's competency pay scheme, Alastair Ross, head of compensation at the Royal Bank of Scotland, invited his listeners to "define it for yourself." The prevailing opinion is the same among companies who are linking competencies to pay: Forget the academic debate. It is important to do it, so let's do it in a practical way that suits our company. Actual approaches and practice are therefore highly diverse and difficult to summarize in a single chapter. Nonetheless, they can be categorized in respect of the three main ways that the linkages are being made (as illustrated in Figure 12.1):

FIGURE 12.1 A typology of competency-related pay.

		Focus of Competency Definition		
		Job	**Role**	**Person**
Method of Linkage	**Evaluation**	■ Point factor plans and grade structures e.g. Portsmouth Housing Trust	■ Role classification systems into broader pay bands, e.g. Motorola	■ Person-based pay setting in very broad bands, e.g. SmithKline Beecham
	Pay Adjustment	■ Skill/competence pay steps in ranges e.g. Pacificorp ■ Formula-based increases, e.g. VWUK	■ Pay increases based on assessment of results and competencies e.g. Woolwich	■ Pay increases based wholly/largely on personal competence e.g. ICL
	Bonus and Recognition	—	■ Bonuses related to assessment of results and competencies, e.g. U.S. Computer Company	■ Recognition awards for personal behaviors in line with corporate values e.g. South West Airlines

■ As a job-focused process that uses competencies as the criteria wholly or partly to evaluate jobs

■ As a more people-focused process that links pay levels and increases to the levels of competence attained by individuals

■ Usually in a less direct manner, as partly relating the award of bonuses or nonfinancial recognition to the display of essential core competencies

Salary increase determination is the predominant method of linkage in the United States, while in Europe job or role evaluation is equally common. Linkages through bonus and recognition schemes are least predominant on both sides of the Atlantic (used in 10 to 15 percent of cases), primarily it seems because of the measurement and valuation difficulties involved.

Considering the different approaches however, my research suggests that you also need to consider how the organization defines competencies, as well as the pay vehicle it uses. Moving to the horizontal axis of our framework in Figure 12.1, some organizations focus on a narrower and more traditional definition of the job and concentrate on relating pay through to "hard" and demonstrable competencies. Others relate pay to a much wider and more flexible concept of the behavioral competencies displayed by the individual, which represents the most radical, and also most critical, wing of the paying-for-competence movement. And in my experience, in developing their own tailored solicitor, the majority of organizations—42 percent in the U.S. survey, and including U.K. companies such as brewers Guinness and the Woolwich Bank—use more than one method of linkage and consider aspects both of the job content and the individual contribution.

So let us have a look at some examples of these different approaches, to help you to decide whether making these linkages is fantastic or foolhardy, sensational or silly.

LINKING COMPETENCIES TO PAY THROUGH JOB EVALUATION AT GUINNESS BREWING

Productivity, speed to market, and workforce flexibility are essential for success in industries. The need for radical improvement in these areas was the driving force behind Guinness Brewing's new integrated human resource management and reward approach, which had competencies in its heart. The company's new pay system, introduced in May 1996, uses a competency approach and covers the 600 employees in its Park Royal brewery. It was introduced after a significant rationalization and downsizing.

A much flatter structure was introduced, with far fewer, more flexible roles replacing the previous high labor specialization. The system employs broad role profiles and three pay bands, which replaced the previous restrictive job definitions, lengthy job descriptions, and 24-grade structure. Roles are now specified in terms of "need to do" (primary accountabilities); "need to know" (experience and knowledge requirements); and "need to be" (levels of competence). Competencies are defined as "the skills, knowledge and behaviors which need to be applied for effective performance." There are seven competency categories, and they include "commitment to results" and "interpersonal effectiveness." The competencies are used as an integrating framework for a variety of HR systems, as shown in Figure 12.2.

Roles are profiled against each relevant competency, and individuals' actual competencies are compared with the requirements through the performance management process. Roles are slotted into the broad pay band that best describes the competencies required. Thus the summary description of band 2 roles is as follows:

> Roles which fall into band two involve planning or managing work for others, as well as completing one's own tasks/projects. The focus of decision-making is longer-term, with an awareness of the broader impact on the function and the business. This is reflected in the requirement for project management, resource management, cross-functional experience and market knowledge. Typically, the role holder requires a degree and/or specialist knowledge. The role requires a range of experience in the technical/specialist skills found in the function, although the focus is primarily on delivering results in areas where the individual has sound working experience. There may be a requirement for knowledge/skill associated with other parts of the business.

FIGURE 12.2   An integrated approach to using competencies at Guinness Brewing (GB).

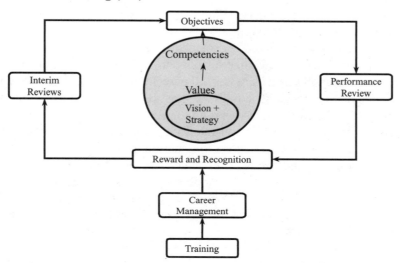

Pay ranges for each band vary by function and are set using external market data. Explaining the approach, HR director Mike Westcott feels, "We had done a lot of good work using competencies on the development side, but this was starting to conflict with the messages our traditional reward systems delivered." Now he feels the business can really value and reward the criteria that will underpin its long-term success. He also sees it as the basis for focusing more of the company's pay budget on its most talented staff, facilitating their recruitment and retention.

Since introducing the new structure, Guinness Brewing has moved on, and competencies are now also used to influence pay movement in the bands. This depends on three factors: company affordability, market movement, and the individual's contribution to the business, as shown by the results he or she achieves and his or her demonstrated level of competence assessed in the performance management process.

Summarizing his experiences, Mike Westcott feels that "although our competency work was always about contribution to the business, the link to reward has given an additional edge to it, as well as clarifying what the company really is paying for." However, making the linkages without the necessary experience in competencies for development purposes, in his view, would have been "a recipe for disaster."

LINKING COMPETENCIES TO PAY THROUGH BASE PAY INCREASES

In 1990 the Woolwich Bank began to relate the pay increases for 6,000 of its staff to their performance against agreed personal objectives and required levels of competence. Staff pay was managed within a structure of 12 grades, and pay progression was based on an assessment of individual contribution, which took place each year in the final quarter. This resulted in each member of staff receiving a points rating, up to a maximum 400 points.

As well as being based on performance goals such as customer service and sales, points were also awarded for standards of individual competence in each job. Thus for a branch service adviser, 50 percent of the total marks were related to the personal competencies. The points scores were then categorized into five levels of rating, and a fixed formula was used to relate the level of base pay increase to the performance rating. Thus a top-rated individual might receive a pay increase of twice the average, fully effective, points rating.

According to remuneration manager, Trevor Chapman, "The system has been successful in getting staff to focus on how results are achieved, as well as what is achieved. This has contributed significantly, ensuring a consistent approach to performance management in a business where standards of customer services and quality of advice are vitally important."

However, a series of changes has taken place to the system beginning in 1998. This was part of a wide-ranging review of HR and reward policies, in the wake of the Woolwich's recent conversion from being a mutual into a quoted company, providing a broader range of financial services. The general tenor of the changes has been to make reward policies more business driven and line managers and staff themselves much more involved in their operation.

Staff have been moved into a flatter structure of six broad pay bands, each defined in terms of key accountabilities and competencies (see example in Figure 12.3). The descriptions vary according to whether staff are in the operational and management, or in the professional and specialist, job families.

The competency framework has been redefined into three core areas, focusing on those competencies that really make a difference to business performance. Each is described at four levels. A looser, more flexible system of performance management and review will in the future be used to determine individual pay increases, involving regular, two-way performance discussions. The existing points system had become somewhat inflexible and discredited in the eyes of managers and staff. "HR policies consistently need to be redefined and improved to stay in tune with the ever-increasing rate of business and market change," according to the head of human resources, David Smith. "But competencies will remain at the heart of our performance management and reward approaches in the future."

PURE COMPETENCY AND PERSON-BASED PAY IN A PHARMACEUTICAL COMPANY

A few organizations have taken the ideas of the importance of personal competence and the death of the job to its logical extreme and moved to paying people very largely on the basis of their individual competence, irrespective of the imme-

FIGURE 12.3   The competency evaluation framework from the Woolwich Bank.

Competence Indicators	BAND 1 Level		BAND 2 Level		BAND 3 Level	
	Team Leader	Team Specialist	Team Leader	Team Specialist	Team Leader	Team Specialist
Planning to Achieve	C	D	C	C	B	B
Improvement Through Change	D	D	C	C	C	B
Self Development	D	D	C	C	B	B
Effective Communication	C	D	C	C	B	B
Influencing Others	C	D	B	C	B	B
Helping Others to Achieve	C	A	B	B	B	A
Managing Performance	C	C	B	A	B	A
Making Decisions	D	D	B	C	B	B
Specialist Knowledge	C	D	C	C	B	C

diate results they achieve or the specific tasks they are carrying out at any particular moment.

The obvious problem with applying any form of person-based pay is how to define, structure, and assess the skills, behaviors, and contribution that is required from each individual. The fear of most organizations is that it will result in pay anarchy, with no control on costs, inequitable pay judgments, and the money directed to those who shout loudest.

One approach is to use a model of life-cycle stages. This was developed through research by a number of U.S. academics, including Dalton, Driver, and Boyatsis. The model posits that we all have the potential capability during our career to pass through four stages of development:

- A learning stage, of learning how to do work and developing up to the required standard

- An applying stage, when we apply and further develop our skills in our own specific area of expertise, sometimes to a very high standard

- A guiding stage, when we apply our expertise more broadly to benefit our organization and develop and coach others

- A shaping stage, when we come to provide strategic leadership and promote the development of the whole organization

The research suggested that around 75 percent of people in an organization are in the first two stages, and around 25 percent in the latter two. The competencies required obviously vary in each stage, with a focus on technical and operational skills in the first two stages, relationship and business competencies in the third stage, and conceptual and strategic competencies in the fourth.

This life-cycle approach was applied in one division of an American pharmaceutical company in the United Kingdom and United States. The division had a record of poor performance, and a sequence of downsizing had left it with 400 employees and the threat of complete closure. Radical measures were called for.

The staff moved therefore to a totally flexible, team-based work approach, with no job titles. They developed seven core competencies to underpin their strategic survival and success, including innovation, use of resources, technical ability, teamwork, and customer satisfaction. Critical incident interviews helped to define the levels of these competencies displayed at each of the life-cycle model stages. Base pay is now managed on a single continuum split into the four stages, running in the United Kingdom from £17,000 up to £85,000 (approximately $27,300 up to $136,400). New entrants are slotted in by matching their initial competency and skills assessment to an appropriate market rate, and with comparable staff internally. Thereafter pay progression is wholly dependent on the development, in breadth and depth, of their personal level against the seven core competencies, and irrespective of their short-term work function. Increases are obviously constrained, however, by the size of the pay budget, and ceilings in ranges do apply, related to market rates for a sample of benchmark roles. Administrative staff are excluded from the structure.

Competencies are assessed through a quarterly performance management process, incorporating 360 degree feedback and the input of customers. Even in this setting, however, performance results are rewarded, in the form of a bonus, related to a mixture of division, team, and individual performance. The organization has survived and prospered using this approach, with markedly increased levels of customer satisfaction, declining cycle times, and more projects carried out by fewer staff.

WHAT MAKES FOR SUCCESS IN RELATING PAY TO COMPETENCIES?

We have looked at three organizations that have related competencies to pay, with some degree of success. So what are the learning points that I can draw out from them and the other companies I have worked with, in helping you to assess whether to, and how best to, progress down the competency-related pay path. I would make four key points:

1. Recognize that competency-related pay is not for everyone, nor for all the different parts of an organization. It does appear to be particularly appropriate in settings where it is recognized that employee competencies are the key to competitive success, as in scientific research, computer software, and management consulting companies. Applications are particularly evident for the knowledge workers and professional staff who predominate in these sectors, and for whom conventional performance-related pay schemes often do not work effectively. These organizations are also often characterized by flat and flexible organization designs, broad-banded pay structures, and with lateral and continuous employee development.

If your company is engaged in a highly structured activity with high labor specialization and a strategy of low-cost leadership, then competency-related pay probably is not for you. The strength of competitive pressures may also determine the approach you take and the speed with which you pursue it. The pure, personal, and competency-related pay example we have seen, where personal competence is virtually the entire focus of pay setting, are generally evident in crisis situations, or in small, highly entrepreneurial, startups. In larger, complex companies, a more balanced pay approach is generally employed.

2. If you do not have a well-established competency framework already in use for development and recruitment purposes, again, competency-related pay is probably not for you. Pay generally supports and reinforces the move toward a more competence-focused organization, rather than leading the change, as at the Woolwich. In the vast majority of U.S. and U.K. instances (75 percent of companies in Towers

Perrin's European study and 67 percent in the United States), pay has similarly followed on from the use of competencies for recruitment, development, and performance management purposes. This helps to ensure that the pay linkage does not conflict with or restrict the developmental objectives of competencies and also that the competencies themselves are well established and understood.

In the vast majority of cases today, companies are researching and developing their own competency frameworks to ensure their validity for development and pay purposes, rather than using borrowed or national generic schemes. Even when making the pay linkages, the median length of time taken to introduce these schemes is between 1 and 2 years. Competency pay is definitely not a "quick fix" for your pay problems.

As Mike Westcott at Guinness told me, not having this detailed level of preparation and years of experience would have been a "recipe for disaster." Even then, the majority of companies, such as Glaxo Wellcome, are not using personal traits and their full competency menu when making the link to pay. So be clear about what your definition of *competencies* is, how they relate to business success, and what people really do in your organization, and ensure that people are experienced in the language and application of them before making any pay link. And don't rush it!

3. Generally, don't pay only 100 percent on the basis of competence. In most organizations, there is still a need to consider job size and content, objectives and results achieved, market pay levels, and so on as well as competencies, when making pay decisions.

Competency-related pay is in the main not replacing traditional pay approaches but fusing with them. Thus 84 percent of Towers Perrin's surveyed companies with competency-related pay continue to use job evaluation. Of these, 70 percent relate base pay reviews to considerations of individual performance as well as competence. Such a combination can help to address the measurement concerns of academics and trade unionists at the use of competencies, but also the failure of traditional performance-related pay systems. At the Land Registry Agency, a public-sector body in the United Kingdom, each competency has associated performance indicators (see Figure 12.4). This ensures that they are not paying for "nice-to-have" skills and helps managers to assess the level of competence applied and its business impact. Competence is, in most cases such as Woolwich, just one factor affecting a rounded and two-way assessment of a person's contribution, resulting in an agreed pay increase. The exacting measurement requirements placed on a pay system wholly based on competencies are thereby relaxed. This is why I prefer the term *competency-related* rather than *competency-based pay,* as competencies are mostly just one influence on the pay process, not the whole basis for it.

Correspondingly, the use of competencies can help to address the traditional failings of performance-related pay systems—the excessive focus on individual results achieved and on past performance, ignoring how those results are achieved

FIGURE 12.4   Example of the definition of a competence area at the Land Registry Agency.

Elements of competence	Performance indicators	Outcome
1. Understanding scope of own role	■ knows when to take decisions without reference ■ takes an interest in what is happening in the section and keeps up-to-date ■ takes advantage of opportunities for self-development as they occur	Has the trust and confidence of their line manager
2. Managing time effectively	■ plans own workload to achieve priorities ■ delegates tasks where appropriate	Priority tasks are achieved within agreed timescales
3. Showing determination to achieve	■ demonstrates commitment by a disciplined approach to the job ■ sets a personal example of good conduct ■ adopts a flexible approach to overcoming difficulties	Gets things done

or what will create success in the future. As a car salesperson in a large dealership told me, despite his company's extravagant customer service objectives, his highly geared commission scheme incented him to "screw the customers," selling them overpriced financing packages and accessories.

Perhaps we should in fact be talking about systems that pay for contribution, rewarding both measurable results and how they were achieved, past success and future potential, performance and competence.

4. Finally, the traditional compensation mantras of "keep it simple," and regularly review, monitor, and modify appear to apply with particular force in this area of pay. The bank I referred to earlier with 50 competencies has now simplified its approach. Managers are provided with pre-prepared role profiles using 6 competencies, selected from a list of 9 core competencies.

Job families are actually often a way of structuring and simplifying the process, giving flexibility and local ownership in the competencies used, their description, and the nature of the pay link, while keeping this variety within a clear and common framework. Computer firm ICL recently reduced the number of competency-based job families it employs from 25 to 15 in an attempt to simplify their system. South West Electricity, the U.K. subsidiary of the Southern Energy Company of the United States, recently introduced a 6-monthly customer service bonus, paying all staff a cash lump sum if an index of the business's regulatory service standards improves—broadbrush certainly, but with no experience of competencies, possibly a faster and more effective reinforcer of customer service in their circumstances, than trying to assess and pay every individual according to his or her own customer service competence. Later, a more detailed approach might be required, as the impact of the bonus wears off. The experiences of Woolwich and Guinness demonstrate the constant need to review and modify your approach as business needs and circumstances change.

Obviously there are other tips and points I could make—pay for the application, not the acquisition, of competencies, take steps to control competency pay drift, etc.—but these lessons capture, for me, the major issues to bear in mind.

A CONCLUSION ON RELATING COMPETENCIES AND PAY

What I have described in this chapter may have concerned you—how complex an approach competency pay can be, how demanding of management time and skills, how potentially inflationary, and how disruptive to your other pay administration procedures and control. Yet whatever these concerns, and despite the ongoing academic debate as to the philosophical basis and measurement difficulties surrounding the subject of competencies, western organizations are slowly but surely moving toward relating pay more closely to their development and application. They are being driven by the requirement for a more highly skilled, competent, and professional workforce, in order to succeed in increasingly global and hypercompetitive markets, as well as by the need, in a world of ever faster changes, to pay for what is required for success in the future rather than the results achieved in the past.

Organizations are developing a wide range of tailored and hybrid approaches to linking competencies and pay, combining considerations of the job and the person, job evaluation and individual pay adjustment, results and competence, the what and the how.

I hope I have convinced you to look seriously at this subject as part of your reward strategy. It certainly is not for everyone, perhaps not even a majority, at least not yet. I would encourage you to raise the question of its value and application for your own organization. Even if you are currently the leaders in your industry, in a world of seismic business shifts, in which the skills and contribution of your staff are increasingly becoming the single most important, sustainable source of competitive advantage and in which key skill shortages are increasingly evident in many technical and professional areas, can you ultimately do without establishing some form of relationship between competence and pay? Or are you in danger of losing your most competent, star players or, as has happened in parts of the financial services sector, the bulk of a very successful team because someone else recognizes and rewards their competence more effectively than you do?

BIBLIOGRAPHY

Dubois, David. 1993. *Competency-based Performance Improvement: A Strategy for Organizational Change.* HRD Press.

Lawler III, E. E. 1996. "Competencies: A Poor Foundation for the New Pay." *Compensation and Benefits Reviews,* November/December.

Towers Perrin. 1998. *Compensation Challenges and Changes.* Research studies in the United States (1997) and Europe (1998).

13

BUDGETING, AUDITING, AND CONTROL SYSTEMS FOR SALARY ADMINISTRATION

Bernard Ingster

Consultant, Human Resources Management

PERSONNEL COSTS are regularly stated in the forecasts and budgets of financial and operating plans of an organization. However, there are substantial differences in the methods of documenting such costs and of using the documents in the management of an enterprise. This chapter illustrates how a budgeting process for the wage and salary aspect of personnel expenses can effectively support business strategies and objectives.

The discussion demonstrates that wage and salary planning can be an instrument for developing skills in human resources management as well as being an instrument of financial management. The principal process described in the chapter covers a budget cycle for a current fiscal year and the immediate future fiscal year, utilizing phases of budget building that integrate judgments of several levels of management.

Because of the strong contemporary interest of many organizations in using variable base salary increases to reward varying levels of employee performance, an illustration is provided of a useful form of merit salary control as a feature of salary planning. Finally, some important roles are identified for a compensation administrator in audit functions for all of these processes.

It should be noted that this chapter does not include discussion of the emerging techniques of *broadbanding*. The term currently suffers from ambiguity concerning its use as either a substitute for "traditional" job evaluation or salary administration or as a substitute for both. Those who are experimenting with the idea continue to face issues that are *conceptually,* if not in outward form, similar to those addressed herein.

TIMING OF WAGE AND SALARY INCREASES

There has been a decades-long debate over whether annual or merit wage or salary increases should be granted on a *single date* for all employees or on the *anniversary dates* of employees as they occur throughout a fiscal year. Many large employers have alternated between these practices over time, and some utilize the timing choices with differing groups of workers—for example, single dates for nonexempt employees and anniversary dates for exempt employees

The use of single dates is a popular salary administration practice with deep roots, particularly among organizations whose workers are paid predominantly by hourly wages. This practice is asserted to have significant administrative benefits:

1. It concentrates the time demands of salary administration into a single, limited period of a fiscal year and thereby relieves managers of the need to be concerned with most matters of wage or salary increases throughout the year.

2. It greatly simplifies the annual process of forecasting and budgeting personnel expenditures, particularly with regard to their impact on cash flow.

Advocates of once-a-year salary changes who incorporate formal performance appraisal into the program also claim the benefit of being able to rate employees against each other as well as in terms of their accomplishments against individual objectives.

It is true that when variable base salary increases are used in a program that is administered on anniversary dates, certain complexities are introduced in budgeting, auditing, and controlling compensation changes. However, it is also true that those same complexities provide opportunities for broader human resources management improvements. For example, staggered performance and salary reviews can reinforce the equivalent importance of human resources management with fiscal management as the latter is expressed through monthly budget variance reviews. Rarely does an employer believe that the *financial performance* of the organization can be forecasted, budgeted, and announced only on one date during a given fiscal year.

In governmental and health care organizations, which are very labor intensive, between 65 and 80 percent of the total operating budget is based on personnel costs. Thus, the management consequences of choosing either a single date or anniversary date for compensation changes will be readily apparent. On the other hand, the personnel costs of a high-technology process industry such as chemicals production constitute a relatively small percentage of operating budgets, and the management consequences of selecting either of the timing intervals will be subtle. The systems described in this chapter are applicable to both single date and anniversary date wage and salary planning frameworks.

GENERAL CONCEPTS OF A SALARY PLANNING AND BUD-GETING PROCESS

Salary planning should be a component of the general program of financial planning in an organization, and it should be conducted within the regular company cycles for planning an operating budget. The salary budgeting should cover at least a 2-year period—a current fiscal year and the fiscal year next following. Some organizations attempt to project planning to a third year or beyond, but when that is done, it is generally recognized that the projections are very soft. Beyond a 2-year salary planning cycle, the budgets for additional future years are understood to represent, at best, an early-warning system for forecasting that certain significant changes might occur. Thus, this chapter concentrates on a 2-year cycle.

Salary planning and budgeting are best done by each employee responsible for the work of others. In most organizations, the planning is done within general financial guidelines that are derived from financial forecasts prepared by the highest level of corporate management. An effective process is an iterative one in which each level of supervision completes a budget proposal that is then integrated upward in the organization, usually to the department level of a function and then, ideally, to the overall business unit level. At the latter point of integration, all of the earlier judgments are tested against each other and against the functional and business unit objectives.

Consolidated business unit and departmental budgets are then shared with all who have contributed to the process, with particular highlighting of the changes made by higher levels of management to the original entries of the contributors.

Opportunity should exist for final reconciliation of differing managerial judgments.

Salary budgeting is best performed using at least two major planning periods during each fiscal year. Assuming that the planning is for a fiscal year starting January 1, a *preliminary budget* for the new year should be prepared during May and June of the current operating year, and then a *final budget* should be prepared during October and November of the current year.

The documents required for preparing the preliminary, next-year budget should include the actual, current-year salary budget. If budget changes for the *second half of the current* fiscal year are required, they should also be identified during May and June while the preliminary budget document is being completed. The October and November budget should represent the best and final judgments of managers of the actual operating conditions they anticipate they will face during the next fiscal year. The 2-year cycle is represented in Table 13.1. (The detailed elements of the budget planning documents will be provided later.)

THE HUMAN RESOURCES MANAGEMENT CHALLENGE

A special challenge for the human resources professional exists during the period of the announcement and explanation of preliminary budgeting. This is the time during which managers should be influenced to examine the human resources management issues that are the foundations for the salary decisions they will be forecasting. They should be encouraged to ask themselves general questions, such as the following:

- Do I have the best organizational design for the achievements expected during the current and future years of the budgeting program?

- If the organization design is right, are the individual jobs structured in optimal fashion? Are there opportunities for job-content revisions that would improve overall unit performance and/or efficiencies?

TABLE 13.1 Budget Planning Cycle

	Current Year		Next Fiscal Year
January	May–June	October–November	January
	Affirm current-year budget for the second half of year	Prepare *final* budget for the next fiscal year	
	Prepare *preliminary* budget for the next fiscal year		

- Who are the star performers in this unit? Am I providing effectively for their continuing development and success within the organization? Are compensation rewards appropriate?

- Whose performance is below expectations? Is discharge a likely outcome? What provisions have been made or must be made to help such employees succeed? Are compensation rewards consistent with the performance level? (In particular, are they too generous, thus sending conflicting messages?)

- Are there employees currently meeting performance expectations who can be given assistance to exceed expectations in some or all of their responsibilities? If so, what form of assistance is required in each case?

- What are the likely employment needs during the years covered by the budgets? What are the likely replacement hiring and/or new hiring needs?

- Will there be significantly large numbers of new hires? Will there be a significant number of reductions in the staffing of the unit?

- What are the likely needs for granting leaves of absences during the periods covered by the budgets (personal, education, military, or maternity)? Is anyone planning retirement?

- What promotions and/or reclassifications are likely to be made during the periods covered by the budgets?

The process of salary budgeting should formally encourage all managers to examine at least annually the full range of issues associated with the management of the people for whom they have leadership responsibility. It is a highly useful vehicle for portraying a composite of the human resources management needs of a working unit. If the process does not clearly illuminate the paths of necessary management action but emphasizes only quantitative dimensions of a salary budget, the value of the planning effort for the management of the enterprise is substantially diminished.

VARIABLE BASE SALARY INCREASES

In some organizations that utilize variable increases in base salaries to reflect differing levels of personal accomplishments, a *merit matrix* is frequently established as a guide for decisions of managers. The matrix is a useful component of salary planning and usually attempts to relate several variables:

- The size of a base salary increase, generally expressed as a percentage of the base.

- The location of the current base salary in the salary range, commonly expressed as the ratio—called the *compa-ratio*—of the base salary to the range midpoint.

- The frequency with which the base salary increases should be given, although many companies are eliminating this variable and offering salary reviews for everyone at 12-month intervals. A merit matrix based upon uniform 12-month reviews might look as shown in Table 13.2. (This illustration assumes that the organization in which it is being used has effectively trained those who have responsibility for the work of others in the techniques that help assure valid and reliable decisions concerning performance differences.)

The merit matrix establishes the boundaries within which management may grant merit salary increases. In good practice, these matrices should be reviewed annually to ensure the continuing competitiveness of the levels of reward.

Some organizations exercise control over the total cost of merit increases by mandating or suggesting that managers limit the numbers of staff eligible for a particular performance rating. For example, the company might distribute guidelines with the salary planning and budgeting documents that suggest limiting 15 percent of the departmental workforce to the rating of "distinguished," 20 percent of the workforce to the rating of "exceeds expectations," and 55 to 60 percent of the workforce to "meets expectations." (Usually, it is not anticipated that more than 3 percent to 5 percent of a given departmental staff will exhibit deficient performance.)

Some organizations exercise control over the total cost of the merit increases by establishing a separate merit budget that cannot be exceeded for the fiscal year in which it is established. For example, managers are told that the total of all merit increases proposed for a given fiscal year may not exceed 5 percent of all base salaries of employees in a department at the start of that fiscal year. In most cases, managers in these organizations are also provided with additional guidelines for salary increases such as those found in the merit matrix.

TABLE 13.2   Merit Matrix

Performance Rating	Base Salary, %	
	Below Midpoint	At or Above Midpoint
Distinguished	9–11	7–8
Exceeds expectations	7–8	5–6
Meets expectations	4–6	3–4
Deficient performance	0	0

COMPONENTS OF A PRELIMINARY SALARY BUDGET

In almost all organizations using effective techniques for salary planning, the necessary data exist in computerized human resources information systems (HRISs) that are also integrated with the computerized financial reporting databases. It would be difficult, but not impossible, to establish and maintain the salary budget, audit, and control practices described in this chapter in the absence of such a computerized capability.

Typically, the worksheets provided for the preliminary salary budget consist of at least two sections. One section provides detailed information about the salaries of employees for the current fiscal year in which the planning is taking place. For each current employee, this section should at least include:

- Employee name and identification data
- Position title
- Salary class, including minimum, midpoint, and maximum salaries of class
- Current base salary
- Current compa-ratio
- Type, date, and amount of last salary increase
- Planned salary change for the current year (forecasted in *previous* year), including type, date, and amount

In addition, this section should include a total of all staff in the unit (a head count) and the totals of all current and all proposed base salaries. The net increase cost of the planned salary changes for the current year plus the percentage increase this represents over the total base salaries of the previous year should also be shown. Managers should also affirm or propose modifications to the current-year plan in this section of the preliminary budget. This constitutes one additional opportunity to reconsider plans for the balance of the operating year.

A second section of the worksheets for the preliminary budget should allow managers to enter a variety of codes (preferably those of the existing HRIS) reflecting planned salary changes for the next immediate fiscal year. The forms should also provide space for the entry of certain variable data, such as the percentage amount of any wage or salary increase. Thus, in addition to entries for base salary increases, there should be available codes for the following personnel actions:

- Promotions and/or reclassifications
- Planned leaves
- Planned transfers
- Planned retirements

The second section should also provide space for the entry of planned increases in staffing for the future year, including the designations of, at least, initial or temporary salary classes. The system should calculate projected costs of a new hire using the midpoint of the salary class. Dates of all planned changes should be identified, usually using the first or last day of each month in the year.

All of the proposed changes in the budgets for the current year and all of the changes planned for the future year should be automatically calculated by the computer for each contributing manager. When printed, the formats of the budget reports for both the current and future year should be the same. The accuracy of the printed reports should be affirmed by the contributors.

THE FINAL SALARY BUDGET

Toward the close of the current fiscal year, preferably in October or November, the budgets for the current and future year should be redistributed to all contributors. These reports should be accurate with regard to all salary and other personnel actions taken *to date in the current fiscal year.* The budget data for the future year might now reflect proposed corporate changes in salary ranges adopted as a result of salary surveys. Such range changes might have impacts upon the originally proposed levels of salary increases because of compa-ratio changes. These should be highlighted by the computer for attention by the managers making the original submissions. Managers should affirm or modify their proposals.

Once more, there should be an upward organization process of integration of budgets to the department level of the function and to the management of the business unit, with opportunities for reconciliation of differing managerial judgments.

SUMMARIES OF REPORTS

Most large organizations attempt additional integrations of budget planning data to increasingly higher functional levels. This process is usually accompanied by summaries of selected information. For salary planning and forecasting, it is useful to have at the department level at least summary data such as the following:

- Total base salaries (current year)
- Total base salaries (future year)
- Actual net change of base salaries for the current and future years
- Percentage of the net change in base salaries from the current year to the future year
- Head count and base salary expense in major functional groups
- Projected changes in head count and base salary expense in major functional groups

- Totals of base salary and personnel actions by type (that is, merit increases, promotions, reclassifications)
- Compa-ratio comparisons for current and future years

ONGOING AUDIT AND REVIEW OF SALARY BUDGETS

In highly labor-intensive organizations, the monthly measurement of actual performance against operating budgets primarily will be a report of performance against the salary budgets previously prepared. In these situations, month-to-month analysis of variances between planned and actual base-salary expenses is useful and necessary because in these organizations, cash flow planning is fundamentally built on salary costs. However, in non-labor-intensive organizations, a quarterly review of performance against salary planning is generally adequate, and the cash flow impacts of changes in the base salary may not be seen as particularly significant.

In good practice, a compensation administrator has responsibility for the independent audit and review of the salary budgets. While *all* department managers are primarily accountable for ensuring that plans and actual performance are fully congruent, the human resources function should also ensure that the budgeting objectives are being met. Should that not be the case, it is anticipated that direct consultations would occur between a human resources professional and the manager affected.

ADDITIONAL CONSIDERATIONS

Sometimes personnel costs for certain groups of people are not included in the salary planning and budgeting that is done by the manager for whom the people are performing work. For example, costs for part-time employees might be aggregated at an organizational level other than that at which part-timers are assigned, particularly if no insured benefits are granted to them. Similarly, the costs for per diem employees hired from a contractor for a limited time might be aggregated at an organizational level remote from that at which the work is performed. Or, more commonly, there is a discovery at the end of a year that a large number of temporary employees have been engaged to fill needs for which regular, full-time employment requisitions were denied. It is in the interest of an organization that the salary planning process identify expenses for part-time employees, temporary employees, and/or contract workers in the salary budgets of each unit that is directly accountable for the contributions such workers are expected to make.

However, with regard to the costs of bonus payments of various kinds, most organizations do not attempt to forecast those expenses in the planning processes described in this chapter. There will usually be accruals for the bonuses that are allocated to departmental budgets by the finance function. In like manner, costs for employee benefits tend to be budgeted at the macrolevel of an organization and subsequently allocated to each organizational unit on the basis of the numbers and kind of employees in that unit.

If the HRIS capability is particularly strong and well integrated into the financial computing systems, salary planning can be greatly facilitated through the automatic modification of budgets when various unplanned salary or personnel actions occur. For example, transfers into or out of the budget unit, hirings, and terminations are routinely recorded on the company's computer files. The computer system should also routinely amend the budgets of affected departments and alert the managers of the new conditions both on the worksheets used in the preparation of preliminary and final salary budgets and on the monthly or quarterly statements of budget performance.

Finally, it should be understood that salary planning and budgeting are tools for effective *general management,* not artifacts of human resources administrators. For greatest benefit, these processes must be institutionalized within the general, entrepreneurial planning programs of an organization, and they must be perceived as equally necessary with other forms of budgeted expenses.

RELATED READING

A comprehensive treatment of the salary administration practices associated with merit pay programs is provided in: Heneman, Robert L. 1992. *Merit Pay: Linking Pay Increases to Performance Rating.* Reading, Mass.: Addison-Wesley.

Two classic textbooks in compensation management contain very useful, still-relevant treatments of issues discussed in this chapter. They are: Belcher, David W. 1974. *Compensation Administration.* Englewood Cliffs, N.J.: Prentice-Hall. (See especially Chapter 22, "Control and Integration of the Compensation System.") Patten, Thomas H., Jr. 1977. *Pay: Employee Compensation and Incentive Plans.* New York: The Free Press. (Chapter 8, "Building and Maintaining Compensation Structures," is a wide-ranging study of fundamental issues to be addressed in compensation management.)

Exceptional insights into the roles of budgets and control systems in general management are provided in two chapters of: Drucker, Peter F. 1974. *Management: Tasks, Responsibilities, Practices.* New York: Harper and Row. (See especially Chapter 9, "Strategies, Objectives, Practices, and Work Assignments," and Chapter 39, "Controls, Control, and Management.")

14

COMPUTERS AND COMPENSATION ADMINISTRATION

Martin G. Wolf, Ph.D., President

Management Advisory Services, Inc.

COMPUTERS HAVE PLAYED A ROLE in compensation administration since the sixties, when payroll was put on the mainframe as part of the finance department's computerization of all accounting activities in large corporations. Then computerized payroll became available almost everywhere with the development of service bureaus such as ADP. While a limited number of standard reports were available, special analyses required difficult-to-get support from the IS department.

As mainframes grew in power and came down in price in the seventies, additional employee data were added to personnel records and HRIS became a reality, at least for the fortunate. The list of standard reports grew, but special analyses and what-if's remained difficult to come by.

With the advent of PCs in the eighties, compensation administrators began to use the computer to do more complex compensation analyses. Getting current compensation data was the problem, usually requiring time-consuming reentry of the data from a printout generated off the mainframe. External data such as surveys generally came in hard copy and had to be hand matched to internal data. By the late eighties, surveys could be obtained on disk, simplifying the analytical process.

With the arrival of the Internet and of intranets in the nineties, and the exponential increase in PC processing power, it became possible to perform highly sophisticated compensation analyses almost undreamed of only a few years before. In addition, many routine compensation administration tasks could be handled by the computer, particularly those responding to employee requests for information about either general details of particular benefit programs or the employee's specific situation.

Salary surveys are now being conducted via the Internet, allowing for faster turnaround of the output. A number of software packages are available for the collection and/or processing of survey data. Several firms offer turnkey packages for custom surveys—questionnaire design, data collection via the Internet or diskettes, and processing and reporting services.

Survey data are also available on the Internet, both to participants of some surveys and from consulting firms. A limited amount of information can be obtained free of charge, but most survey sites either require a paid subscription or a payment per view. A few professional organizations have moved to the Internet both to survey members about their compensation and to report on it. Many more will probably do so in the near future.

Increasingly, organizations are putting their benefit and pay administration information online, either via an intranet or through the Internet. Employees in the more automated organizations can check their benefit coverage, determine their available vacation or sick time, monitor the progress of their 401K or pension plan, check on claim status, and so on. Supervisors can call up present pay data on their employees, salary range information, competitive pay practices, and so on. Such systems come with two different types of access problems—achieving access and controlling it.

ACHIEVING ACCESS

In many organizations today, most employees have PC access. However, in some organizations, large numbers of employees have little or no access (for example, assembly-line workers). However, even where employees have access, they may not have enough privacy to want to delve into their pay and benefit information. For example, in my bank, there is a PC for the tellers to use to access account information. Customers waiting in line can see the screen, even if most of the data are too small to read, and other tellers can easily see what is displayed.

One common solution is employee computer kiosks, where employees can go to access the database. These are commonly placed near employee lounges, the HR department, the time clocks, and so on—anywhere that employees may gather. Some organizations allow for access via touchtone phone as well as by PC.

CONTROLLING ACCESS

It is necessary to control access to protect both the confidentiality of compensation information and its integrity. Traditionally, access has depended on identification via password. This type of protection is easily breached, either because the password is accessible to other employees (written on the keyboard or in the desk drawer, etc.) or is compromised by a hacker. Advances in identity recognition include the use of a combination of physical tokens plus a password or, most recently, of unique biometric data (retinal scan and fingerprint sensors are already commercially available, and voice print identification is under development). At the moment, the hardware for biometric identification is relatively costly, particularly where there are very large numbers of PCs that must be equipped. Costs are dropping rapidly, however, and biometrics appear to be the wave of the future.

CURRENT EXAMPLES

OSRAM SYLVANIA chose a software company which offered a flexible human resources management system based on client/server technology. This HRIS, offered by a number of vendors, allow various networked computers to process only those tasks for which they are best suited, as follows:

- Software distribution servers (relatively powerful PCs) coordinate the linked desktop PCs by "serving up" new versions of the system and restricting access as appropriate.

- The database server carries data stored in tables, all of which are related by common information such as Social Security number or job code.

- Client workstations (mainly desktop PCs) interact on their own with the servers, taking advantage of downloaded application logic to update data, perform analyses and request data in a multitude of forms....

There are two main sections of The Compensation Connection: one for all HR employees and another for all employees. These two sections assure the availability of a complete range of compensation information, from confidential communications for field HR to general program communications for all employees.

Besides providing just-in-time compensation information to end users, The Compensation Connection became the communications outlet for unique applications such as online Market Reference Values (MRVs)....

A survey management application became the foundation of OSRAM SYLVANIA's market pricing effort. This application streamlined data loads from 15 surveys, sorted them to company positions based on identified job matches, and allowed specific "cuts" of the data to be used in internal analyses.

Capabilities of the application ranged from aging data by any factor to calculating market rates to specific reporting requirements. The nuts and bolts of the implementation phase involved identifying survey sources, matching jobs, electronically loading the data, scrubbing the data and quality-checking the MRVs for benchmark (matched) positions....

Field HR can now use two dropdown menus—one for job title, another for location—to pinpoint their search. Local and national MRVs can be accessed, including average, entry and highly competitive salary levels. Besides external salaries, internal paid salaries (average, low and high) are available on the same screen for jobs with three or more incumbents. (Maloney and Stokley, 1998, pp. 31–32)

A recent consulting assignment involved the integration of position classification, performance, competency and potential assessment, and compensation. First, appropriate competencies for the unique organization were selected. All employees were evaluated by their managers both in terms of their present competency levels, as demonstrated by their job performance and in terms of their potential on these same dimensions. Custom software was developed using a commercial PC-based database program to collect and analyze these data. In a parallel process, jobs were classified into grades based on job evaluation methodology. Spreadsheet analysis of survey data was employed to price the grades. Then employees' present salary and position in the new ranges (compa-ratio) were compared to their performance and potential ratings. Based on the actual distribution of compa-ratios and performance levels, a salary increase matrix was developed that totaled to the organization's budget.

The amount of data involved would have defied analysis without a computer. Yet it was possible to develop a package for ongoing program administration and maintenance that was easily handled by the PCs and inexpensive software available to this low-tech, limited-budget, nonprofit organization.

COMPENSATION ADMINISTRATION IN THE TWENTY-FIRST CENTURY

By looking at today's best practices and hardware-software trends, it is possible to develop a likely scenario for computer usage in the near-term future:

Mary receives an e-mail reminding her that her self-appraisal of her performance is due by next week. Attached is the electronic form for her to complete. Planning to complete it at home, she e-mails the form to her home computer. At the same time, her boss, George, receives a notice that his appraisal of Mary and her compensation recommendation are due the week after next. Attached are the electronic forms for both.

When Mary finishes her self-appraisal at home the next day, she logs on to the Internet and sends the data to her computer at work. The following day, she identifies herself by retinal scan to the company intranet and posts her self-appraisal. The system e-mails it to George and stores a copy in her personnel file. Mary also checks the database to identify the current salary range for her position, noting that she is in the lower third of the range and has plenty of room for an increase. She also checks her last self-appraisal and George's appraisal at that time to see how similar they were. While she is online, she updates her benefit data, increasing her life insurance coverage and adding her new husband as beneficiary. She also adds him to her health care policy as a dependent and switches to the coverage option that includes maternity.

Meanwhile, George has completed a draft of his appraisal of Mary. After identifying himself to the intranet, he checks Mary's compensation history and her previous appraisals. He also calls up the local and national salary survey data for her position, noting that the demand for her specialty has resulted in an 8 percent increase in market value last year, while the salary range for her position went up only by the ABC company's standard 3.5 percent. While he is at it, he also checks what the average pay is at ABC for others with the same education and experience as Mary, noting that she is paid a little more than others with similar experience but noticeably less than others with the same experience and her advanced degree from Prestige University (or from similar schools).

After they meet and discuss her performance, George finalizes the appraisal and enters it into the system. Based on Mary's performance and her salary level versus both the external market and the internal structure at ABC, he recommends her for a 10 percent increase, noting his reasoning on the electronic form he completes.

Since this is a larger amount than the system is programmed to allow George to grant, the recommendation and the performance appraisal are automatically e-mailed to Alice, George's boss. She reviews the data and authorizes the full amount. The system updates the payroll records to reflect the new salary level and e-mails George to that effect. George then meets with Mary and tells her about the increase.

All of the pieces for this scenario exist today, although few, if any, organizations have all of these pieces in place, and fewer still have them connected.

BIBLIOGRAPHY

Maloney, Nancy E., and James R. Stokley. 1998. "User-Friendly Market Pricing on a Broadband Platform." *ACA News,* vol. 41, no.4, April, 1998, pp. 30–32.

C H A P T E R

15

USING INFORMATION TECHNOLOGY FOR SALARY BUDGETING AND PLANNING

Anne C. Ilsemann, Partner

Arthur Andersen & Co., S.C.

Mark Simms, Manager

Arthur Andersen & Co., S.C.

CHANGING ROLE OF THE HUMAN RESOURCE FUNCTION

In the last decade, the *human resource* (HR) function has steadily increased in visibility and importance. In leading organizations, it has become a high-profile, strategic business function.

This, in turn, has created a major change in the content of the work that the HR function performs. The low-value administrative support role is being transformed in many organizations into a *leadership* role. The HR goal now is to add value to human capital by adopting innovative, cost-effective programs that produce measurable impacts on the company's bottom line.

In this new paradigm, "HR managers must not merely monitor and communicate change; they must also *drive* it, providing their companies with the understanding, sensitivity, and knowledge they need to conduct business successfully on a global scale" (Cuthill and Bentzon, 1999).

To support this higher-level role, leading HR functions rely increasingly on advanced technology. The goal here is to provide high-quality information that is immediately accessible, incisively useful, and strategically valuable rather than merely abundant. This new capacity, in turn, enlarges the potential scope of activity: "With the help of the HR function, companies can go deep beneath the surface of each information-bearing item that resides with an enterprise-uncovering, transforming and leveraging data in all dimensions: organizational, relational, and human" (Fitz-enz, 1999).

The salary budgeting process is one area of HR that can have substantial impact on the ability of the whole organization to meet its goals. Both the human motivational elements and the financial performance of the organization intersect at this critical junction. But no one said it would be easy to create a way to measure and administer the salary budgeting and planning processes while adding value to the organization. One of the "best practices" common to all high-performing human resource departments is *partnering* with internal customers in setting organization-wide goals and in agreeing on reasonable ways to calculate results.

Because organizational structures and work flows have been evolving rapidly in recent years under a variety of reengineering and downsizing scenarios, the compensation programs and processes of most organizations need to undergo fundamental changes as well. Not surprisingly, new compensation programs are emerging in response to these changes and to the fluctuating demands of various industries and labor markets, both local and global. Examples of some newer compensation schemes include *team-based pay, competency-based pay, pay for skills,* and *market-driven pay.*

In the realm of change, however, "The most profound opportunity…will stem from providing technological support for performance development activities (e.g., hiring, selection, assessment, performance management, continuous learning and salary administration, and strategic human resource planning)" (Schoonover, 1999).

Much is happening in HR, and it is happening quickly—the ideal environment for a major assist from technology. Information technology offers tools that enable the salary budgeting process to happen logically and coherently through a number of key maneuvers: integrating functions, distributing accountability to the lowest level, streamlining storage and retrieval, manipulating data, analyzing salary budget information, and benchmarking results along the way. But most companies are not there yet.

CURRENT STATE: TYPICAL SALARY BUDGETING PROCESS

In the typical pyramid organization today, central control for all salary budgeting resides in the financial function, which develops overall budgets based on the company's fiscal year. Since merit increases are administered on employees' anniversary dates, not on the fiscal year, it is difficult to determine or prorate the actual cost of labor when salary increases jump across fiscal years. Nevertheless, the finance department hands down the overall budget and the departmental budgets for total salary cost. This initiates the next series of steps:

- HR develops a series of spreadsheets by department. These contain current employees' names, their salaries, and their previous performance ratings and increase percentages.

- HR distributes the spreadsheets to the other departments.

- Each department manager makes a projection of the total salary budget. This projection is based on anticipated employee performance ratings and their subsequent percentage salary increases.

- Each department sends its spreadsheets back to HR.

- HR reviews the spreadsheets for conformance to corporate-wide salary increase guidelines, noting any discrepancies.

- HR sends the spreadsheets, with discrepancies or issues, back to the departments for corrections.

- All of the spreadsheets are then forwarded by HR to the finance department.

- The finance department reviews the spreadsheets for conformance to overall corporate-wide budget guidelines.

- The finance department sends the spreadsheets back to HR, noting any discrepancies or issues.

- HR forwards the spreadsheets to the departments.

- The departments correct the issues.

- And so on…

If this sounds slow, unwieldy, wasteful, duplicative, and counterproductive, be assured that it is. It is old-style bureaucracy at its worst, but there is a cure. The cure resides in information technology and in changing the way departments or business units relate to the whole entity, and how they interact with each other. However, it's not a quick fix because the typical salary administration process is equally convoluted.

CURRENT STATE: TYPICAL SALARY ADMINISTRATION PROCESS

In the typical organization today, the human resource function is the central control for all salary administration. HR develops the organization's salary increase guidelines—usually in the form of a matrix depicting the allowable salary increase percentage, based on where the employee's salary falls in the salary band and on the employee's annual merit rating. The ensuing workflow looks approximately like this:

- HR develops salary increase guidelines in the form of a matrix. The matrix depicts the allowable salary increase percentage, based on a combination of where the employee's salary falls in the salary band and the employee's annual merit rating.
- HR distributes the increase guidelines to the departments.
- The department managers complete performance reviews and determine the overall annual merit rating for each employee.
- The department managers determine the salary increase percentage based on increase guideline matrix.
- The department manager forwards the performance review and the salary increase percentage to HR.
- HR reviews the performance review and increases percentage for compliance with guidelines.
- HR makes corrections (or not) and sends the form back to the department.
- The department manager conducts the performance review discussion with the employee and communicates the salary increase percentage.

What's wrong with this picture?

DISADVANTAGES OF THE PARALLEL SALARY BUDGETING AND SALARY ADMINISTRATION PROCESSES

The multi-iterative salary budgeting and salary administration processes described above are largely manual, paper driven, disjointed, cumbersome, slow, and bureaucratic. The dual process results in:

- Redundant work
- Inaccuracies

- Long cycle times

- Management's making short-term practical and/or tactical decisions rather than visionary, value-added strategic decisions that contribute to both short- and long-term outcomes for the organization

- Salary budgets and/or salary administration plans that are not aligned with company strategy and may actually interfere with or erode the company's ability to get where it has planned to go

- Frustrated managers and employees

Yes, there is room for considerable improvement.

A BEST-PRACTICES APPROACH TO SALARY ADMINISTRATION

Best practices are derived by observing and analyzing the way things work in the very best companies—organizations that are leaders in their industries, shining stars in profitability, productivity, employee and customer satisfaction, and public approval. Applying best practices to the salary budgeting process can yield spectacular results, such as streamlining the mechanics to shorten cycle times, lowering the cost of budget delivery, and reducing the disruption to the core value-adding activities of each department or business unit. And this can be accomplished without sacrificing the quality level of the budget or employee satisfaction.

Most best-practices models incorporate the key concepts and criteria outlined here.

Control (Limit) the Number of Budgets Developed. To do this, management begins afresh by evaluating how many budgets are needed and how often budgets are to be developed and revised. By focusing sharply on the true value of making frequent budget revisions, executives and managers are often able to reduce the frequency of revisions and, correspondingly, to reduce the amount of data maintained.

Standardize Budgeting Methods throughout the Organization. When consistent methods are used systematically throughout an organization, several benefits accrue: fewer errors, less rework, easier automation and delivery, less explanation needed, and fewer "exceptions noted" to slow down decisions and determinations.

Minimize the Degree of Budgetary Detail. By using rollups or consolidation of accounts to present a big-picture overview, higher-level management can use the budget information more easily to support decision making. This speeds the process and is far more economical than the old repetitive and interruptive back-and-forth motions.

Integrate the Salary Budgeting Technology with Other Financial Systems, Human Resources, and Payroll Systems.   This immediately reduces redundant data maintenance and inconsistencies among parallel systems while facilitating the sharing of common information across relevant departments.

Train Budget Developers to Use Budgeting Technology.   This will help assure the full and proper use of budgeting technology. New training will be needed after each enhancement to the technology.

Deliver Information Quickly, Accurately, and in a Useful Format.   This lays the groundwork so that tactical and strategic decisions can be made easier and faster to shorten budget cycle time.

Link Salary Planning and Budget Development to Corporate Strategy.   This is key if the organization is to evaluate progress toward overall corporate strategy. By making the linkage apparent and communicating it to all levels, the organization transmits to managers and employees a clearer understanding of strategic goals and incentives. This, in turn, generates greater organization-wide support for goals and interdepartmental coordination of tactics.

Set up Superior Communication Channels.   Leading organizations today want to use e-mail, the Internet, and intranets to communicate goals, share documentation, and create dialog with customers and employees.

Choose the Right Technology.   The right technology facilitates salary budget preparation, workflow, and analysis for the organization. A salary budgeting system should meet most or all of the following objectives:

- Incorporates best practices.

- Supports workflow-based automatic routing. This means that upon electronic approval, information is forwarded automatically to the next person in the process.

- Assigns clear version numbers for budget and forecast revisions to reduce confusion and errors.

- Allows for either vertical or horizontal control over the budgeting process, depending on the company's preferred organizational pattern.

- Permits versatility in creating salary plans in case the company uses multiple salary administration methods to handle different types of employees in each operating unit.

- Links salary plans with budget plans by organization, department, and position.

- Links employee performance with salary increase guidelines.

- Stores salary survey data and links it with a company's positions.
- Allows distributed access while ensuring confidentiality. For example, HR and finance professionals need to have access to common financial or salary information; however, employees' personal information should be restricted to authorized employees only. Similarly, departmental budget information should be restricted to the appropriate departments.
- Allows for decentralization or centralization since distribution of information may vary from business unit to business unit.
- Allows for other currencies and currency translations.
- Allows for the conversion of unit-based figures to monetary values.
- Stores salary survey data
- Uses easy-to-learn templates, allocation formulas, checklists, and rules.
- Provides for online editing to reduce the compounding of errors and to enforce compliance with salary and budget guidelines.
- Supports position pooling and job sharing.
- Contains mass-change capability for across-the-board increases or adjustments.
- Incorporates variable compensation plans and award programs.
- Provides online help and documentation on system procedures, as well as process overviews.
- Provides the ability to:
  - Compare budgets to actual.
  - Perform what-if analyses based on one or many factors, such as the average increase by department and the total monetary increase spread across departments.
  - Store history and access online.
  - Use several query and reporting tools to allow for a full range of analysis and reporting by all levels of the organization.

Human resources and financial systems that incorporate the salary administration and budgeting features outlined above are not inexpensive. However, used effectively, these systems offer a degree of control and cost savings not previously available.

Technology alone is insufficient to do the job completely. "The most beneficial changes will occur in organizations that most effectively, efficiently and quickly translate data and information into knowledge and wisdom. This can only be done by investing seriously in human, as well as, financial and technological capital" (Landry, 1999).

THE FUTURE STATE OF SALARY ADMINISTRATION AND BUDGETING PROCESSES

Information technology, if effectively used in the new paradigm, allows the human resources function to partner with the financial function and with operating departments during the salary administration process. Through this multifaceted relationship, salary programs as developed by HR will reflect the goals of the departments in support of the goals of the organization as a whole.

The ideal is for HR, the finance department, and operating departments to follow a fiscal year salary planning and budgeting cycle. In addition to simplifying the salary budgeting process, aligning salary planning and budgeting cycles creates a more focused, cohesive atmosphere in which the HR and finance functions are working toward common goals.

In this best-practices model, the information technology reflects and links salary programs, salary budgets, and employee goals, while also linking employee review factors and incentives to each department's goals and to the larger organizational long-term goals. The result is a consistent, unified, well-ordered mechanism using the same methods, strategies, systems, and understandings to move together toward a common organizational purpose.

Not long ago, the typical human resource function spent about 75 percent of its time and attention on policy transactions and 15 percent on controlling, leaving a mere 10 percent for strategic planning. Many companies still mirror that proportion. But the effective HR function of the future will spend 20 percent on administrative transactions and 80 percent on minding the strategic directional course of the human side of the organization. The power of technology is clearly poised to enable this switch, with best practices ready to be adopted by any organization that wants to make the transition.

BIBLIOGRAPHY

Cuthill, Sarah E., and Katie C. Bentzon. 1999. "Developing the Global Human Resource Manager: Meeting the Challenges of the Next Millennium," H.R. Director—The Arthur Andersen Guide to Human Capital. New York: Profile Pursuit, Inc.

Fitz-enz, Dr. Jac. 1999. "Knowledge Can Be Power: How to Turn Intellectual Capital into Intellectual Capacity," H.R. Director—The Arthur Andersen Guide to Human Capital. New York: Profile Pursuit, Inc.

Landry, James A. 1999. "Valuing Human Capital: A Guide for the Information Age," H.R. Director—The Arthur Andersen Guide to Human Capital. New York: Profile Pursuit, Inc.

Schoonover, Stephen C. 1999. "Applying Technology to Maximize the Value of Human Assets: A Blueprint for Change," H.R. Director—The Arthur Andersen Guide to Human Capital. New York: Profile Pursuit, Inc.

PART 3

Variable Compensation

16

VARIABLE PAY: AN OVERVIEW

H. N. (Rug) Altmansberger, Goal Sharing Consultant

Overland Resource Group

VARIABLE PAY IS AN EXPANDING FIELD within compensation driven by the emerging trends of pay for performance and competitive advantage. Funding these new programs and developing the processes supporting long-term effectiveness is critical. This chapter will cover the types of variable pay, as well as the legal requirements and need for communications effectiveness that accompany it.

PAY FOR PERFORMANCE

In the past, company employment was routinely assumed to be for a career. Many, many employees worked for one organization for their entire work life. Loyalty on the part of the employer and employees was taken for granted. Times have changed. Reengineering, downsizing, and talent wars have reworked the playing field for employment decisions. No longer does a new college graduate dream of working for the same company for life. In addition, worldwide competitive business pressure has focused corporations on performance. In the past and still for many organizations today, paying for performance is normally done with promotions over the career. Base pay increases over time is a normal method to reward performance.

Information technology professionals can now move from company to company with ease and can expect to receive a year 2000 bonus if they stay until the new millennium. Organizations realize the competitive demands for change and the need to motivate change. Many employees are now asking "What is in it for me if I take the risk?" Variable pay is an excellent way to answer the question. Pay for performance with variable pay below the executive level is in its infancy for most organizations excluding the sales organization. Less than 30 percent of organizations have variable pay for all employees. The majority of this 30 percent is profit sharing and does not have a line of sight to business unit performance. Fewer than 10 percent of organizations have variable pay programs for all employees that reward individual, team, and business unit performance. Variable pay has many opportunities for growth with the new organizational emphasis on performance, retention, and competitive advantage.

FUNDING VARIABLE PAY

Financially, variable pay is very attractive compared to base pay increase programs. Base pay increases compound and are a concern for permanent increased cost. In addition base pay increases have an entitlement mentality where the recipient is looking for the next one shortly after receiving the last increase. Many corporations reinforce this expectation by having an annual increase plan (normally called a *merit increase plan*) to adjust for inflation and market movement.

Variable pay is attractive because it does not compound from year to year, and the unspent funds can be reused each year or budget cycle. Having employees re-earn their performance bonus each year creates a compelling reason for them to improve instead of relaxing into an entitlement mentality, which is often the result of base pay increase programs. When business results are good, the payout can be attractive, and, when times are bad, the payout is small, reducing costs and helping to improve the bottom line.

Strategic planning can support the movement to variable pay (Figure 16.1). Moving to a strong variable pay program can take years with the need to build success along the way. The following variable pay funding example is a long-term plan to move base pay from 55 percent today to 48 percent over 10 years while taking total compensation from 55 to 72 percent when business is outstanding. In an average year, total compensation would be at 60 percent of market, which is above the 55 percent today. When a terrible year occurs, there is a 7 percent reduction in wages to offset costs during the downturn. Once management directionally agrees to support improved performance, the plan becomes the master plan for implementing variable pay.

The plan assumes a tradeoff ratio of 2:1 of variable pay to base pay. This is a very conservative approach where the expected payout is $1. In a really good year the reward is $2, and in a very bad year, zero.

FIGURE 16.1   Variable pay funding example.

	This Year	+3 Years	+5 Years	+10 Years
Base Pay	55	52	50	48
Avg Bonus	0	4	6	12
Bonus +	0	8	12	24
TC+	55	60	62	72

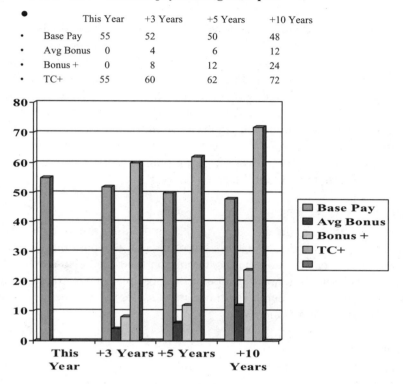

VARIABLE PAY SUCCESS

So if variable pay has such great potential, why has there been such a reluctance to implement variable pay? One answer is that the failure rate for variable pay plans is 38 percent as documented in an ACA study by Marc Wallace. The success rate in executive compensation and sales compensation is substantially greater, but the concern for excessive rewards is real. Executive compensation requires hand-holding and considerable administration. Many small-group plans require periodic redesign, which takes more compensation consulting resources than are available. These drawbacks are part of the reluctance of management to implement variable pay.

Building variable pay plans to be continuous for the long term is the key to variable pay success. Most plans need to be renewed annually to ensure ongoing success. Fairness, trust, and impact on the business are all measures of success. Plans that do not continuously evolve need extra attention every year and will fail more frequently. I helped implement two variable pay plans for all employees at Corning Incorporated, and those plans are now over 10 years old and going strong.

One is a *spot bonus plan,* and the other is *goal sharing.* Variable pay plans can indeed work very well.

Balancing individual incentives with shared business goals is important. The rewards for business success are the most critical and should be more significant in total dollars than individual rewards. The bottom line is that the business needs to succeed. Line of sight and control are also important variables. Many times this is where individual incentives come into play. People like to be judged on what is in their control. Be careful. The balance between business success and individual control is delicate. Too much emphasis on individual incentives may reduce teamwork. Too little line of sight, like profit sharing in large companies, is not motivating because of lack of impact. For a plan to work, it is crucial to design it so that it will last and support business success.

TYPES OF VARIABLE PAY PLANS

Variable pay plans can take many forms—individual, small team, business unit, or everyone. The following list does not exhaust the possibilities of variable pay plans, but it does include the most common types and also new innovative methods. This chapter will quickly summarize those plans covered in other chapters and will provide greater depth for those methodologies not mentioned elsewhere in *The Compensation Handbook.*

Executive Compensation

An executive's variable compensation is based on business results by themselves and in comparison to other executives in their industry. Stock options, restricted stock, and short-term and long-term variable pay are all part of executive variable compensation. Executive compensation has been growing at a rate comparable to the stock market growth for the past decade. All other compensation has been growing at a rate equal to or slightly exceeding inflation. Executive compensation administration is complex and not available to all employees. Many organizations have middle-management bonus plans that cover some or all of management. The intent of these plans is retention and performance. Other chapters of *The Compensation Handbook* include a complete discussion of executive compensation.

Sales Compensation

This form of variable pay is bound tightly to the purpose of the business. It is a high-stake, high-visibility pay system that requires continuous focus and comprehensive design support. Normally the primary design support comes from sales management. The amount of pay at risk is expressed in shorthand as 80/20, 60/40, or any other combination. The first number is the amount of base, and the second number is the pay at risk. The tradeoff between highly motivated sales personnel and pay at risk usually errs in favor of the salesperson. The balance between individual incentives and business results is a common design issue. Overpayments, underpayments, wrong behaviors, unexpected outcomes, and overall frustration from field sales personnel are symptoms of sales incentive plan design issues.

Profit Sharing

This is one of the most common types of variable rewards and is based on the profitability of the entire business. Some companies use profit sharing to vary the match on their 401K plan based on business results. Other companies prefer to pay the profit-sharing incentive in cash normally annually but perhaps as frequently as quarterly. A cash reward can be spent immediately and is usually more motivational than a deferred reward. A key problem with profit sharing is the tendency to lack a line of sight. *Line of sight* means the ability to influence and understand what needs to be accomplished to make the business result happen. In multiple-business-unit organizations, profit-sharing plans lack line of sight. Maintaining the line of sight can be accomplished by focusing on business unit results. A variable pay plan that balances profit sharing with business unit results is the next discussion topic.

Goal Sharing, Gain Sharing, and Other Business Team Plans

Goal sharing is a new variable pay plan for implementing a balanced scorecard for all business units and for all employees in an organization. Goal sharing was developed at Corning Incorporated and has a decade of success with over 50 business unit plans operating on an ongoing basis. Over this time the plan has paid out at target or above, and the likelihood of some payout has been very high.

Long-term business success is closely tied to the implementation of the business strategy. Goal sharing is a rewards program for implementing the business strategy and involving every employee with the key strategic goals. All employees, not just management, need to have a reason to change. Goal sharing can be that reason. The goal-sharing process vigorously communicates the key business goals, and it rewards everyone for making positive change a reality.

In contrast, gain sharing is a financial gain plan that was developed in the 1930s for manufacturing. *The Compensation Handbook* has a complete discussion on gain sharing. A common misconception is that gain sharing and goal sharing are the same. Table 16.1 summarizes the key differences.

Gain sharing plans tend to focus on a financial formula for gain in a selected area of employee control. Goal sharing focuses on the entire business and involves everyone in understanding how to help drive the business strategy. The business strategy is a balanced scorecard of financial and strategic measures of customer satisfaction, quality, process improvement, or growth measures. Gain sharing apportions the gain between the employees and the company based on a preset

TABLE 16.1   Differences Between Gain Sharing and Goal Sharing

	Gain Sharing	Goal Sharing
Focus	Financial gain	Achieving business strategy
Methodology	Financial formula	Fair, stretch goals, continuous improvement
Funding	Incremental gain	Total compensation
Business teams	Manufacturing primarily	Everyone—all business units
Process type	Rucker, Scanlon, Improshare & Custom	Common process
Process owner	Formula expert(s)	Goal-sharing committee
Typical payout	Frequently	Annually
Renewal	New formula or moving average	Annual business review

ratio such as 50:50. Funding for goal sharing is based on total compensation with the reward amount based on continuous improvement targets for each goal. There needs to be improvement over the preceding year for a payout to occur.

The key for business team success is the communications program for employee understanding. Gain sharing plans tend to have frequent payouts to remind employees about the plan. However, receiving a check does not communicate what needs to be done to improve performance. Goal-sharing plans require monthly communications and have been documented to have better than 80 percent employee understanding after 2 years of monthly communications. The local goal-sharing committee is responsible for the effectiveness of the communications. Goal sharing normally pays out annually to make the amount significant, minimize administration, and reward sustained results.

Renewal for gain sharing is usually done when the formula changes or is based on a moving average such as 3 years. Every goal-sharing plan is renewed annually for continuous improvement and to align the goals with the business strategy. Having a strong renewal process is critical to the ongoing success of variable pay.

Small-Team Incentives and Team-Based Pay

Team-based pay is a timely topic that is thoroughly covered by Steve Gross. Rewarding collaboration and teamwork with a mutual-advantage process is a superior methodology to individual incentives. Permanent process teams and strategic process teams are logical candidates for small-team incentives. A team-based incentive is one reward method, and a spot bonus process is an additional consideration.

Spot Bonus Programs

These programs are relatively easy to implement and can truly reward exceptional performance. Like other variable pay programs, spot bonus plans need to be designed correctly the first time. There is no room for process failure. Process failure occurs when the program is perceived to play favorites, becomes another entitlement, or is not managed as a reward process.

The reason for instant, lightning, or spot awards is to provide immediate feedback with a significant financial reward. This requires a simple approval process with the check available on the next payroll cycle. To comply with the Fair Labor Standards Act (FLSA), there should be no promises or automatic awards. This is a bonus that is awarded after the fact, and there should never be a promise or incentive announced beforehand. The key criterion is performance above and beyond the normal job scope. Rewards could also be given for taking ownership and extraordinary success, effort, or initiative. The reward criteria should be developed to fit the culture and terminology of the business group or unit. This should not compromise the requirement for rewarding above-and-beyond performance.

Eligible employees are normally permanent employees working individually or in teams or entire teams of employees. Normally all team members receive an equal dollar award, but this may vary when the situation warrants. Any individual or team may receive more than one award in a year but not for the same reason. Financing these awards is from a separate fund based on a very small percent of payroll. A starting point for funding would be to reserve 1 percent of payroll for spot awards. Setting the number of awards expected in a year will determine the average award percent. For example, if 1 percent of payroll is budgeted and the number of spot awards are expected to be 25 percent of the number of employees, then the average award will be 4 percent. Lowering the number of spot awards expected will raise the average award percentage. If the number of awards is too high, the criteria are not being followed, and an entitlement attitude is likely to follow. The amount of the award can vary based on the culture and the funding criteria. However, the minimum award amount should be carefully considered. The net amount received by the employee should be significant. I would suggest $300 or greater is a good starting point for establishing the minimum award. It is better to have the minimum set too high than too low. If the minimum is set too low, the program can be viewed as cheap and demeaning. There are companies with spot bonus minimums of $1,000 net.

The compensation function should track the number of awards and the amount spent on exceptional performance. This is necessary to promote the reward process and encourage managers to reward performance. This role of encouraging managers to spend more is unusual for compensation professionals and will take some adjustment time.

The issue of public-versus-private awards is a cultural one. Every organization needs to decide on an appropriate award process for them. For many organizations, recognition of the accomplishment is made very openly, but the monetary transaction is private. For other organizations, the entire process is openly celebrated.

Spot bonus awards have the potential to reward and encourage exceptional results. A simple but solid process must encourage and reward outstanding performance. Existing programs have demonstrated that the majority of the awards are given to recognized high performers and that the process rewards excellence.

THE FAIR LABOR STANDARDS ACT

Any new variable pay plan being considered for implementation should be reviewed with legal counsel for compliance with the Fair Labor Standards Act (FLSA). FLSA compliance is necessary for nonexempt employees. The following guidelines should be reviewed with your legal counsel for correctness.

If you are considering a profit-sharing or spot bonus plan (with no promises), the overtime provisions of FLSA are not applicable. If you are implementing any incentive (pre-determined reward) plan other than profit sharing, then the overtime provisions apply. The easiest method for compliance is to pay the incentive as a percent of wages plus overtime for the period applicable. Again, please get a legal opinion before proceeding with the implementation of a new variable pay plan.

VARIABLE PAY COMMUNICATIONS

The need for excellent variable pay communications is very high. The variable pay program, especially the performance requirements necessary to earn a reward, should be widely publicized to all eligible employees. For incentive awards, the plan should keep score on the current performance measures. Employees will not think they earned the reward if they do not know what they did to receive the reward. A reward viewed as a gift by the employee may be appreciated but will not be considered earned. Excellent communication is necessary for employees to understand how they can make a difference, how the program is progressing, and how the reward amount was calculated.

When variable rewards become significant, the need for total compensation communication is apparent. It becomes important to summarize the total compensation an employee receives for financial planning and net-worth calculation.

SUMMARY

Variable pay has many opportunities for growth with the new organizational emphasis on performance, retention, and competitive advantage. Goal sharing is a new business team reward program that can be implemented to balance the scorecard and pay for performance. The major differences between gain sharing and goal sharing are summarized in Figure 16.1. Spot bonus plans can reward exceptional performance with timely feedback. Given the historical failure rate of variable pay, plans need to be implemented correctly the first time. There is no room for process failure. Process failure occurs when the plan is not communicated, or renewal does not occur, or the plan is not managed as a reward process. Solid process design and excellent communication will make variable pay plans the growth segment of compensation for the foreseeable future.

BIBLIOGRAPHY

Altmansberger, H. H., and M. Wallace. 1998. "Designing a GoalSharing Program." *American Compensation Association (ACA) Building Blocks,* Scottsdale, AZ.

Beer, M., R. Eisenstat, and B. Spector. 1990. "Why Change Programs Don't Produce Change." *Harvard Business Review,* Nov–Dec.

Fishman, C. 1998. "The War for Talent." *Fast Company,* August.

Kaplan, R., and D. Norton. 1996. "The Balanced Scorecard." *Harvard Business School Press,* Boston, MA.

O'Malley, M. 1998. "Are You Being Paid What You're Worth?" *Broadway,* New York.

Pfeffer, J. May–June 1998. "Six Dangerous Myths About Pay." *Harvard Business Review.*

Wilson, T. Summer 1998. "Reward Strategy: Time to Rethink the Methods and the Messages." *ACA Journal.*

VARIABLE PAY: NEW PERSPECTIVES

John G. Belcher, Jr., President

J.G. Belcher Associates

VARIABLE PAY PLANS, which we will define as *compensation systems that pay cash bonuses to a defined group of employees based on pre-determined measures of group or organizational performance,* are quite prevalent in American industry today. Survey data suggest that about two-thirds of large and medium companies now have some form of variable pay for their employees.

The widespread use of variable pay programs, however, is a relatively recent phenomenon; 20 years ago, these systems were hard to find.

What is behind this tremendous increase in the use of variable pay? This growth is driven by fundamental changes in the business environment, particularly those related to the growth of international competition. Specifically, two forces have made variable pay a desirable and effective approach to compensation for many companies:

1. Because of global competition, companies in many industries today have little pricing power and are therefore unable to pass through to customers any increases in labor costs. Increases in base pay in this situation represent an unrecovered cost and therefore come directly out of the profits of the business. Variable pay, on the other hand, produces bonuses that are *funded* by performance improvements and therefore do not detract from profitability. As a result, American industry is according greater emphasis to variable pay as a vehicle to deliver pay increases in highly competitive environments.

2. American management has come to realize that it cannot survive the rigors of international competition without the commitment and involvement of employees at all levels. This realization has led to fundamental changes in management practices. The traditional, autocratic style of management is slowly but surely being replaced by team-based, participative management systems. As these cultural change processes unfold, it becomes readily apparent that traditional compensation systems are not adequate to support this transformation; what is needed is a pay system that communicates business priorities and reinforces the behaviors (teamwork, continuous improvement, etc.) that are critical to success in a highly competitive environment. There is a clear need, in other words, to *align* compensation practices with the business strategy and the new management philosophy.

There are many program features that must be addressed when designing a variable pay plan (the payout frequency and the establishment of baselines or goals, for example). More than anything else, however, the variable pay formula, or measurement system, defines the character of the program. While many names are given to these plans, such as *pay for performance, success sharing, team incentives,* all variable pay plans can be categorized, based on the type of formula employed, into four basic approaches:

- Profit sharing
- Gain sharing
- Goal sharing
- Combination plans

We will review each of these categories in turn.

PROFIT SHARING

Profit sharing is the oldest form of variable pay (dating back to the late 1800s in this country) and undoubtedly the best known. The term *profit sharing* describes any plan in which the payout is determined by some measure of profits or returns, such as the company's *return on investment* (ROI).

Profit-sharing plans can take a variety of forms. In its simplest form, a company might pay out to its employees a fixed percentage, say, 15 percent, of its after-tax, fully accounted profits. Or it might choose to share only those profits in excess of a threshold amount, for example, 25 percent of profits in excess of a 12 percent ROI.

An alternative approach is to establish the budgeted or planned levels of profitability as the threshold, such as would be the case in a plan that pays out 50 percent of profits in excess of its budget.

Profit-sharing plans are not limited to those that are based on after-tax profits of an entire corporation. They can also be found at a division, plant, or any other organizational unit that is a profit center. In these cases, the typical measure is *operating profits*, rather than fully accounted profits, because nonoperating costs, such as interest on corporate debt and income taxes, are not generally attributed to individual business units. An example of this type of plan is shown in Table 17.1.

The primary advantage of the profit-sharing approach to variable pay is that it aligns the interests of employees and owners; employees do well only when the owners of the business are doing well. With profit sharing, employees cannot earn substantial bonuses when the profitability of the business is poor.

As an organizational change vehicle, however, profit sharing may leave something to be desired. In a large company, employees will not be able to relate changes in the company's profits to their behaviors on the job, and they will not feel that they have any real impact on corporate profits. Thus they are unlikely to materially change their behaviors on the job, and the system will therefore have little effect on the organization's work culture.

This is not to say that profit sharing is of no value. It offers a simple and convenient way to deliver additional compensation, when business results justify doing so, without increasing base pay. It also gives employees a more direct stake in the success of the company and thus increases their interest in and awareness of business issues.

The effectiveness of profit sharing as an organizational change vehicle can be improved through various types of combination plans, such as one that employs a

TABLE 17.1

Division Operating Profits versus Plan, %	Payout as % of Gross Earnings
125 or greater	12
120–124	10
115–119	8
110–114	6
105–109	4
100–104	3
90–99	2

measure of profitability as a funding mechanism, while requiring that more controllable operating goals be achieved by employees in order to earn the funded payout. These approaches will be discussed in a later section of this chapter.

GAIN SHARING

Gain-sharing plans, as the name implies, *share* with employees the financial *gains* associated with improvements in measures of organizational or team performance. Gain sharing differs from profit sharing in that the measures employed are operating or performance measures rather than measures of profitability.

In the United States gainsharing dates back to 1935, when the *Scanlon Plan* was introduced at the Empire Steel and Tinplate Company in Mansfield, Ohio. This plan shared with employees the cost savings associated with reductions in the ratio of labor costs to sales value of production.

Gain-sharing plans were difficult to find, however, until the late 1970s and early 1980s, when international competition forced companies in many industries to rethink their traditional management practices and to seek the involvement of their employees in cost reduction and productivity improvement activities. Reflecting the performance emphasis of the time, the great majority of gain-sharing programs during this period focused exclusively on measures of cost or labor productivity.

Gain-sharing plans built around cost formulas remain popular today because cost is almost always a competitive issue, and cost reduction provides a clear and easily calculated financial benefit to any organization. These plans usually employ one of three cost measures in their gain-sharing formula:

- Costs as a percent of sales

- Costs per unit of output

- Costs versus budget

As the performance emphasis in the 1990s shifted first toward quality, and then toward customer satisfaction, cycle time, and other variables, gain sharing adapted to the changes. As a result, an extraordinary variety of measures can be found in today's gain-sharing programs. An example for a manufacturing facility is given in Table 17.2.

A baseline is established separately for each of the measures, usually (but not always) based on past performance. Gains versus the baselines are then quantified, and the financial value of these gains to the organization is calculated. The sum of these financial values (net of the value of any losses) represents the gain-sharing pool, which is shared between the company and the employees based on some predetermined sharing ratio.

The use of multiple measures, as in the example above, serves to focus employee efforts on a variety of performance issues and, unlike cost formulas,

TABLE 17.2

Variable	Measure
Productivity	Units produced per hour
Quality	No. of defects (parts per million)
Material waste	Material losses as % of production
Safety	No. of OSHA recordable accidents
Customer satisfaction	% on-time delivery

ensures that employees do not ignore quality, customer satisfaction, and other key business priorities. It also fits well with the *balanced-scorecard approach,* developed by Robert Kaplan and David Norton, that many organizations use for goal-setting and performance management processes.

GOAL SHARING

The third major category of variable pay plans is *goal sharing.* In contrast to *gain sharing,* in which the financial value of gains versus a baseline contribute to a pool to be shared between the company and employees, a goal-sharing plan involves a predetermined payout for the achievement of goals. Thus there is no complicated quantification of the value of gains and no pool of money to be shared.

In its simplest form, goal sharing involves a single goal for each of the measures, such as the example in Table 17.3, taken from a continuous process operation.

One advantage of goal sharing over gain sharing is its simplicity. There are no gains to measure and value, there is no pool of money to share, and there is no formula for distributing the employee share to the individuals involved. The payout is predetermined, and everything the employee needs to know about the system appears in one simple table.

A disadvantage of the simple form of goal sharing is the all-or-nothing aspect of the payout. There is no reward for performance improvements that fall just short of the goal, and there is no additional reward for performance levels that exceed the goal.

TABLE 17.3

Measure	Goal	Bonus, %
Average daily production	1,200 units	2
% first quality	97%	2
Facility expenses	$24.6 MM per month	2
No. of lost-time accidents	0	1

These shortcomings can be addressed through a plan with multiple goals and payouts for each measure, such as the example in Table 17.4 taken from a service organization. More elaborate forms of goal sharing can also be found, such as one in which points are awarded for achieving various performance levels on a variety of measures, with a weighting system applied to determine an overall score. This score then translates into a payout amount.

COMBINATION PLANS

An organization's choices are not limited to a pure form of profit sharing, gain sharing, or goal sharing. Many variable pay plans today employ a combination of these formula alternatives.

The most prevalent combination approach uses a form of profit sharing to fund a bonus at a corporate or division level, with the payout contingent upon the achievement of controllable goals at the operational level. In Table 17.5, the funding mechanism for the variable pay plan is a measure of corporate profitability.

Only 40 percent of the funded amount, however, is distributed to all employees without further condition. The remainder is contingent on the achievement of goals at each of the company's operating units, as shown in Table 17.6.

This plan, a combination of profit sharing and goal sharing, is designed to achieve the best of both worlds. Since a measure of profitability funds the bonus, any payouts from this plan will track closely with the profitability of the company. At the same time, the existence of qualifying goals at the operating level serves to focus employees on performance areas over which they have some degree of control and therefore should bring about more behavior change than would profit sharing alone. Employees, in other words, have to *earn* the bonus that has been funded by corporate profitability.

TABLE 17.4

Measure	Minimum	Target	Stretch
Cost per transaction:			
■ Goal	$6.42	$6.28	$6.16
■ Payout	$100	$175	$250
No. of complaints:			
■ Goal	60	50	40
■ Payout	$50	$100	$150
Growth in revenue:			
■ Goal	12%	16%	19%
■ Payout	$75	$125	$175

TABLE 17.5

Pretax Profits versus Plan, %	Funded Bonus, %
120+	7
116–119	6
112–115	5
108–111	4
104–107	3
100–103	2

TABLE 17.6

Goal	% of Funded Amount Paid
Unconditional	40
Productivity	20
Quality	20
Response time	10
Customer survey results	10

This combination approach, with the bonus funded by a measure of financial results, offers another advantage: A company is now free to incorporate measures of employee development or cultural change as qualifying goals without worrying about how these bonuses will be funded. This sends a powerful message to employees about the importance of change. Examples of such goals include the following:

- Employees receive an average of 40 hours of training.

- Each department develops a performance measurement system.

- Teams take on three additional responsibilities (e.g., minor maintenance, managing costs, dealing with customers).

The primary disadvantage of the combination formula is that there is no reward, regardless of the level of goal achievement, if the funding measure does not reach the level necessary to fund a bonus. If this is a regular occurrence, the plan may lose credibility with employees.

SUMMARY

While there are many design issues that must be addressed in developing a variable pay plan, the formula is the heart of the system and defines its character more than any other plan feature. The four general approaches, based on their formulas, are profit sharing, gain sharing, goal sharing, and combination plans.

Variable pay plan designs have evolved greatly over the last two decades, and companies' choices are no longer limited to a small number of standardized plans, or even to a pure form of one of the three main approaches. There is every opportunity for plan designers to be creative and design a plan that uniquely meets the needs of their businesses.

BIBLIOGRAPHY

Belcher, John G., Jr. 1996. *How to Design & Implement a Results-Oriented Variable Pay System.* New York: AMACOM.

————1994. "Gainsharing and Variable Pay: The State of the Art." *Compensation & Benefits Review,* May–June.

Greene, Robert J. 1997. "Effective Variable Compensation Plans." *ACA Journal,* spring.

Lawler, Edward E. 1990. *Strategic Pay.* San Francisco: Jossey-Bass.

Masternak, Robert. 1997. "How to Make Gainsharing Successful: The Collective Experience of 17 Facilities." *Compensation & Benefits Review,* September–October.

O'Neill, Darlene. 1994. "Blending the Best of Profit Sharing and Gainsharing." *HR Magazine,* March.

Turnasella, Ted. 1994. "Aligning Pay with Business Strategies and Cultural Values." *Compensation & Benefits Review,* September–October.

Schuster, Jay R., and Patricia K. Zingheim. 1992. *The New Pay.* New York: Lexington Books.

————1993. "The New Variable Pay: Key Design Issues." *Compensation & Benefits Review.* March–April.

IMPROSHARE: SHARING PRODUCTIVITY GAINS WITH EMPLOYEES

Mitchell Fein, President

Mitchell Fein, Inc.

THE TERM IMPROSHARE is derived from *improved productivity through sharing.* This incentive plan encourages employees to increase productivity so that they may share in the gains from doing so. The we-they adversarial relationship between management and employees is changed to a cooperative environment in which the organization and its employees gain as they mutually strive to produce more product or services per employee hour. Both groups are affected by productivity impediments and losses. The three components of improshare are the following:

This chapter is an adaptation of Chapter 12 from the third edition of this handbook.

1. A philosophy of managing that encourages employees to cooperate in raising productivity so as to share the resulting productivity gains
2. A formal work measurement system for ascertaining productivity changes
3. An involvement program that establishes productivity teams of employees and management to help promote improvements in operations and product that will benefit both the employees and the organization.

Improshare productivity measurements use traditional work measurement standards and practices of a selected base period.

EMPLOYEE INVOLVEMENT

Numerous experiences in companies of all sizes have demonstrated that when employees are involved in the production process, the outcome is substantial benefits and improved productivity. Improshare rewards employees for their efforts. Reduced production costs result in increased compensation and more secure and rewarding jobs.

PLANTWIDE PRODUCTIVITY MEASUREMENT

A plan to share productivity gains must measure the contributions and inputs of the employees and processes being measured and exclude factors outside their control. Money values should not be used in productivity measurement because many factors that affect money costs do not affect productivity.

Traditional work measurement establishes the time it should take to perform a task under prescribed conditions. Such normal or fair day's work standards are established through performance ratings with a stopwatch time study or through predetermined standards against a defined measurement base. This normalizing of observed data is the keystone of traditional work measurement.

The differences that arise between employees and management in setting traditional time standards are avoided under improshare by measuring productivity against the average level of an agreed-upon base period. Using a method called *measurement by parameters,* standards are set at the average time of the past, using historical data, with no need to performance rate the observed data. Yesterday's performance is established as the *accepted productivity level* (APL). Future measurements will be made against this APL base.

Improshare is a macromeasurement system that measures productivity by comparing the labor-hour value of completed production to the total labor-hour input. Since only acceptable product ready for shipment is counted, this approach is indisputable. This overall measurement of productivity avoids the arguments that occur with conventional accounting practice that separates workers into those who work directly on product and those who do support and service work.

Productivity Measurement for Improshare

When measuring groups or a plant under improshare, a reliable measurement base is the average productivity over a past period. Considering the total output of the group against the total hours worked by the group permits the establishment of valid measures that include all employees.

This principle of measuring and sharing productivity is illustrated by the following: Assume a single-product plant of 100 employees produced 50,000 units over a 50-week period; the employees worked a total of 200,000 hours. The average time per unit is 200,000/50,000, or 4.0 hours. This becomes the measurement base. Suppose an improshare plan is introduced and the employees and management share productivity gains 50/50 below the past average of 4.0 hours per unit. In a given week, if 102 employees worked a total of 4,080 hours and produced 1,300 units, the value of the output would be $1,300 \times 4.0$, or 5,200 hours. The gain would be $5,200 - 4,080$, or 1,120 hours, within one-half, or 560 hours, shared by all the employees. Translated into pay, this would be 560/4,080, or 13.7 percent, additional pay to each employee based on each employee's weekly pay. Management would also gain 560 hours. Where originally the unit-labor value of the product was 4.0 hours, the new unit time including productivity-sharing payments is (4,080 + 560)/1,300, or 3.57 hours. Thus, the unit time after productivity-sharing payments to the employees has been reduced.

In plants with multiple products, a measurement base must be established to reflect the past average productivity for all products and of the entire plant. An example of such a plant is a company with 350 factory hourly employees, which does not include those who are salaried, that produced 475 different products made of sheet metal components. The plant operates under measured day work; no incentives are used, but conventional, engineered time standards measure the productivity of individual employees. Since these standards include only the work of production or direct employees and omits the work of those who do all sorts of so-called nonproduction work (about one-third of all employees), it is necessary to compute the composite productivity of the entire plant.

The engineered time standards for all the operations needed to produce each product, established using traditional work measurement methods, is totaled to obtain the overall, engineered standard time by product. This includes all direct labor and excludes all nonproduction labor. Working from records of finished product transferred from production to the warehouse, the total is obtained for each product made during the prior year. These totals are then multiplied by the respective overall standard time for each product to obtain the total standard hours produced for all products. Then, the total hours worked by all employees in the plant for the year, including all the indirect workers, is obtained from the payroll ledgers.

In this year, the workers have produced 367,500 standard employee hours based on product time standards and have worked a total of 700,000 hours. The hours worked are much higher than the produced hours because the time standards do not include the time for receiving, shipping, maintenance, materials handling, machine setups, waiting for work, rework, salvage, and so forth. The actual time is in excess of standard time because the performance of the measured employees is below the 100 percent standard level. To convert the engineered standards to reflect the previous year's productivity and to factor in all actual time, a *base productivity factor* (BPF) is computed as follows:

$$BPF = \frac{\text{total hours worked}}{\text{total standard hours produced}}$$

The BPF represents the relationship, in the base period, between the hours worked by all employees and the value of the work in hours produced by these employees, as determined by the measurement standards. In effect, the BPF is a means to use up all hours worked and to factor into the original standards all occurrences that are not included in the standards. This approach is equitable to both employees and management when management is willing to use the past average productivity as the base from which to measure improvements. In this example, the BPF = 700,000/367,500, or 1,905 hours.

Multiplying all engineered product time standards by 1,905 creates base standards to be used for the improshare plan, which groups the entire plant. All 350 hourly workers are included in the product standards and the productivity measurements. The BPF states the total clock hours required during the base period to produce a 1.0 standard hour of work. A BPF would be calculated to develop product standards for the improshare plan.

Relationship of the BPF to Time Standards

Standard time multiplied by the BPF will reflect fully the average operating conditions and productivity that prevailed in the base period. These modified standard times, called *improshare product standards,* then are used to measure productivity in any other period. The BPF adds all plant labor hours not included in the standard times, excluding holidays, vacations, and nonworked time.

Productivity measurement must be made against a defined base if the measurements are to have any meaning. This requires that measurement standards be frozen, or at least clearly identified as to the base, at the beginning of the improshare program. The accounting department will continue to update its standard costs following accepted accounting practice, but the standards used as the basis for the improshare product standards must not be changed.

In the example, the BPF was calculated as 1,905 based on 700,000 total hours worked and 367,500 hours transferred to finished goods, representing standard time. Suppose the time standards in this plan were cut in half; the calculations would be as follows:

$$\text{BPF} = \frac{700,000}{367,500/2 = 3.810}$$

The BPF would be doubled, but the improshare product standards would be the same, reflecting the average operating conditions and productivity that prevailed in the base period. Once the BPF is established, it is carried on into the future with no change. The assumption is that the relationship between standard time and total improshare product standards is fairly constant.

Standards for new operations and products in the future must be set to the same work performance base used to set standards in the base period. Exceptions are new capital equipment and technology, which are specifically defined. The BPF established for different plants cannot be compared because each plant has its own base-period characteristics and measurement practices.

Once established, the BPF concept can be used to measure productivity changes from one period to another by calculating the *operating productivity factor* (OPF) for a period, just as the BPF was calculated. Suppose the OPF of a period is 1.89 and the base period BPF is 2.0. The change in productivity is calculated as $(2.0 - 1.89)/2.0$, 0.055, or 5.5 percent improvement. Conversely, if the base period BPF is 1.89 and the new period OPF is 2.0, the change is $(1.89/2.00)/1.89$, or -0.0582, or 5.82 percent reduced productivity.

ESSENTIALS OF THE IMPROSHARE PLAN

An improshare plan can be developed for all sorts of operations. The plan can be applied to one person or a thousand, to groups or to an entire plant. It can be used to supplement incentive plans or to replace them. Several plans can operate in a company. The versatility of improshare comes from the way productivity is measured—hours of input against output, expressed as hours. A full improshare plan contains details of how to establish measurement standards and calculate productivity changes and how to make calculations under changing conditions.

The plan limits management to following a set of rules but puts few restrictions on employees. It is an unusual agreement because the employees are not held to any conditions. The improshare plan does not require the signature of union representatives. The plan's ground rules specify how productivity will be measured and shared, who will be included, how various types of production changes will be handled, and other details. All of these are binding only on management. The proposition to share does not obligate management to make any payments unless productivity actually increases as measured by management's yardsticks and records. Management does not enter a blind arrangement or give up any traditional prerogatives and rights. Employees' interests are protected since all productivity records by operations and products are open to inspection by employees. Current benefits and wages are protected since no one can earn less than before.

The improshare plan measures only final results, usually as finished product ready for shipment. The system encourages employees to become concerned with matters they previously ignored. Ideally, the employees will use underutilized skills and abilities to make more good products per hour. When employees become oriented to the bottom line, a new world of potential improvements opens up.

CONTROL OVER THE IMPROSHARE PLAN

The improshare plan provides that measurement standards are frozen at the average of the base period and are not changed except for capital equipment and material changes or a buy-back of standards. Control over the improshare plan is maintained in the following way:

1. A ceiling on productivity improvement, generally set at 160 percent, which is 30 percent in earnings

2. A cash buy-back of measurement standards when productivity exceeds the ceiling

3. An 80/20 share of improvements created by capital equipment

The improshare plan establishes a ceiling on earnings. When productivity exceeds the ceiling in any measurement period, the excess hours produced are banked and moved ahead to the next period. Banking the excess is an inducement for the employees to produce as much as they can in order to create a cushion for subsequent periods when productivity may be lower than the ceiling. Should productivity rise above the ceiling and continue at a high level, the improshare plan is able to respond because it provides a simple formula for a one-time cash buy-back equivalent to 50 percent of one year's savings created by the changed standards. The process is voluntary, and employees and management must agree to the buy-back. The ceiling and buy-back provision does not limit productivity; instead, it provides an extra inducement to employees to raise output further, and it rewards the company for contributing the efforts of its experts and specialists to help the employees gain half the improvements.

The ceiling and buy-back work as follows: Suppose productivity averages 180 percent and the ceiling is 160 percent. The excess hours produced are banked for future periods. If productivity remains over the ceiling, the standards can be bought back with employees' agreement to the 160 percent level, or any other level, reduced by a factor, so that, in this case, 180 percent becomes 160 percent. The employees receive a cash payment of 50 percent of the 20 percent, projected for a year, at their regular pay. A $10-an-hour employee would receive a cash payment of $10 \times 2,000$ hours $\times$ 50 percent $\times$ 20 percent = $2,000. Simultaneous with the buy-back, all time standards are reduced by a multiplier of 1.6/1.8, or 0.8889.

Capital equipment and material gains are also shared. Expenditures for equipment of $15,000 or more (varies by plant) are identified as capital change. Of the savings attributed to the equipment, 80 percent are removed from the measurement standards, and 20 percent are left in. Since productivity gains are shared 50/50, management retains another 10 percent, so that management receives 90 percent of the gains created by the equipment. Employees share 50 percent of all gains from equipment that costs less than $15,000 and 10 percent of all gains from equipment costing more than $15,000. Material changes are treated the same way. Over several years, the shared gains from capital equipment can be substantial.

ESTABLISHING AN IMPROSHARE PLAN

Since valid output and input measurements are essential to establishing an improshare plan, one of the first steps in designing a plan is to develop the measurement system following the improshare principles.

Output is measured by counting finished product ready for shipment. Parts and subassemblies used in the production process are not counted. When parts and subassemblies are shipped as spare parts, these then are designated as *products*. Under the plan, *product* is anything that is packed for shipment. For output measurement under improshare, the total hours required to manufacture product must include the hours of all employees involved in the plan, as reflected in the improshare product standards, at the average productivity level prevailing in the base period. When direct labor standards are not available, the direct labor content of each product can be estimated and then the BPF can be calculated. Various estimating procedures can be devised. Some plants list the operation sequence by part and obtain, or estimate, the direct labor by operation. Other plants develop matrix charts with two or more variables from which to determine the labor content.

USING IMPROSHARE WITH OR WITHOUT TRADITIONAL INCENTIVES

An improshare plan can be designed to operate in conjunction with traditional incentives, or the incentives can be replaced by improshare.

When a plant operates without incentives, the average productivity during the base year is reflected in the BPF. Dividing the hours worked by all employees included in the plan by the total produced hours at standard provides a BPF that reflects the base-period productivity. When an incentive plan operates before the introduction of an improshare plan, in calculating the BPF, it is necessary to include in the BPF numerator the incentive premium hours earned by all employees on incentive and to include the total hours worked by all employees. The sum of hours worked plus hours earned as an incentive premium is termed *charged hours*. The time standards used to generate the standard hours produced for the base period would show standard productivity at the level where incentive earnings start. Since the employees earned incentive pay in the base period, the actual productivity level was higher than standard; the amount by which it exceeded the standard is calculated for the base period for all employees on incentive (expressed in hours). Incentive premium is paid in dollars and converted to equivalent hours earned by dividing the total dollar premium incentive pay by the average hourly rate of all employees on incentive.

In calculating the BPF for a plant in which incentives will be retained or replaced by improshare, the numerator of the fraction must be the charged hours, equal to the total hours worked by all employees in the plan, plus the premium incentive hours earned during the base period by all incentive employees. In calculating productivity after the plan is established, the charged hours concept must also be followed.

A traditional incentive plan can be discontinued and replaced by improshare. To protect the employees who have been on incentive against reduced earnings, they are guaranteed their former average premium hourly earnings as personal red-circle add-ons. All employees, those formerly on incentive and those not, will then receive the same percent share from productivity improvement on their base earnings. The company is protected against loss by the charged-hours concept; all red circles paid each period are added to hours worked as charged hours. Output hours must exceed the charged hours for productivity sharing result in a net gain.

When incentives are retained and improshare involves only nonincentive employees, the productivity calculations are the same for the entire plant, except that only the nonincentive employees share in the gains. Productivity of the entire plant is calculated by total product made. The input hours are the charged hours of the entire plant, which includes all hours worked plus incentive premium hours. In calculating the productivity share to all employees eligible to share, divide the 50 percent hours gained by the hours worked by only the nonincentive employees.

SHARING MATERIAL SAVINGS

Establishing productivity sharing with measurement only of completed product always saves materials yields since employees become quality conscious in order to produce fewer defects. Inevitably there are savings in materials.

Labor savings and materials savings can be shared in separate plans. Labor savings are usually measured weekly on a moving average with gains included in a regular paycheck. Material savings are generally distributed several times a year. When materials usage can be calculated in short periods, improved yield can be reflected as equivalent hours and integrated into the labor-productivity calculations. Using the records of several years' usage, a company can calculate the dollars spent on materials per standard hour produced, which can be established as standards for the various items. Since materials prices change, a constant dollar base must be established using a suitable product price index published monthly by the U.S. Department of Labor. Each month the actual usage is compared with the standard usage, and the difference is posted on a spreadsheet. The cumulative gain or loss for the month is carried forward to following months so that all can see the gains accumulating in the material plan. At the end of the period, 50 percent of the total dollar gains are divided by the total pay of all eligible employees, and the fund is distributed to each employee in relation to his or her annual pay.

IMPROSHARE FOR HOURLY AND SALARIED EMPLOYEES

Managers who see the potential for productivity improvements through improshare agree that all hourly employees should be included in the improshare plan. Many also agree that supervisors of hourly employees are important to the success of the program and they should be included. However, there are differences as to whether to include other salaried employees.

Proponents of including salaried employees believe the following:

- All employees can contribute to productivity improvement. The argument that direct employees make a greater contribution than indirect employees is unsound.

- Offering earnings gains to hourly and not to salaried employees will cause resentment on the part of the latter. Labor relations are improved when everyone is included.

- The wage structure is preserved when all employees share in the gains. Permitting increases only to hourly employees will compress earnings between the two groups.

- Salaried employees are drawn closer to the production operations and will be more effective in their work.

Reasons for not including salaried employees are the following:

- Salaried employees are traditionally expected to represent management's interests in the relations of managing the plant. Many are in managerial positions and are expected to perform effectively without extra compensation.

- Salaried employees do not affect factor productivity to an appreciable extent.

- Extra compensation paid to the salaried employees will increase costs if increased productivity could be attained without the extra pay.

Mechanics of Including Salaried Employees

Salaried employees can be included in an improshare plan by using one of two methods: (1) Include salaried hours in calculating the BPF and in measuring productivity or (2) do not include salaried hours and pay the average of the plan. When salaried employees are included with hourly employees, their productivity is also measured, and the BPF is calculated the same way as it is for hourly employees only. Paying salaried employees the average of the plan is the more appropriate method to use if the salaried employees can affect plan productivity but their hours are expected to remain fairly constant.

Including the Total Company

When hourly and salaried employees are included in the improshare plan by including them in the BPF, care must be used to account for fixed and variable employees. When only the factory hourly employees are included, the BPF is fairly constant at different volumes of business. When fixed salaried hours are included in BPF future calculations, variations in volume can distort the productivity measurements.

To measure the entire company of hourly factory and salaried employees, an effective approach is to include hourly factory employees plus variable nonfactory employees in the BPF.

SUMMARY

The success of the improshare plan depends on the involvement of the employees in efforts to raise productivity. Employees and management must be dedicated to creating more effective operations. An important element in the success of improshare is that the employees see the fruits of their efforts in their paychecks. Since productivity losses affect them, employees are actively involved in reducing costs and facilitating output. Managers should consider utilizing the skills, efforts, and knowledge of the workforce. Higher productivity levels will be attained by encouraging the entire workforce to assist in raising productivity and reducing costs.

C H A P T E R

GAIN SHARING: SHARING IMPROVED PERFORMANCE

Timothy L. Ross, Codirector

Ross Gainsharing Institute

Ruth Ann Ross, Codirector

Ross Gainsharing Institute

THE CONCEPT OF SHARING GAINS with employees is certainly not new. The term *gain sharing* was used as early as 1889 in an article written by Henry R. Towne. In a very broad context, most companies use some form of gain sharing, even if limited to higher management. Some consultants and writers promote packaged plans; others say that only narrow employee-controlled measures work; and still others say that only a broad measurement plan, close to and including profit sharing, works. Unfortunately, gain sharing today can be very confusing because a few "experts" now include even individual incentives under its banner, which was never done in earlier years. This article reviews the concepts and procedures associated with what could be referred to as *traditional* (not necessarily old) *gain sharing* but includes "modern" terms such as *goal sharing, gain management, variable compensation,* and *multiple pool calculations. Nontraditional gain sharing* includes just about anything an organization or consultant can think of including spot bonuses, individual incentives, recognition systems, and so on without any real underlying values and is not part of this article. Nor are small-group or team bonuses included even if the concepts discussed could be applied to such systems.

WHAT IS GAIN SHARING?

In its most elementary form, gain sharing is typically referred to as a *group bonus plan* that shares improved performance with most or all employees of a unit. In earlier days, these boundaries were much more clearly defined since many applications were "packaged" approaches known by names such as *Scanlon, Rucker,* and *improshare.* Scanlon, which emphasizes heavy employee involvement, Rucker, which promoted value added as a calculation, and improshare, which uses a standards-based calculation and does not require a formalized employee involvement system, are still being installed. However, the trend today is moving toward more customized plans that meet the needs and sophistication of a particular organization, although some people still promote narrow- or broad-packaged plans as the panacea to solve most, if not all, problems. Frankly, we don't know which system works best in all situations; research and case study articles generally report on successful plans, which tells us little about unsuccessful ones. There are, however, some common characteristics of gain sharing about which most people agree. They are as follows:

Performance Improvement Related

A goal of most gain-sharing plans is to improve performance by changing employee behavior. Performance can be measured narrowly, by using total actual time versus standard time or physical measures of output versus physical measures of input (for example, 40 tons of coal in 40 hours), or broadly, by using calculations based on *improving* profits or return on investments although most people relate it to more employee controlled measures of performance. Some people like the idea of basing it on goals such as quality, productivity, and safety, which also allows management to control how much they pay; that is, if you do this, you get so much money.

Based upon Something

Historically, most gain-sharing plans were based on some measure of past performance, from periods as short as a few months to as long as several years. There seems to be a trend today toward basing the bonus on a combination of past and expected performances. The advantage of using past performance is its ease of building trust; employees can more easily accept what the desired performance is and that it is attainable since they achieved it in the past. Some "experts" promote using the most recent past year. Basing the plan on goals entirely can, of course, become manipulative, but some combination of past performance and targets may make sense in these competitive times.

Shared with All or Most Employees

Most plans today include all or most employees *or* are team or small group oriented. This is another source of confusion because in the past, almost all plans included all hourly or almost all employees. As we said earlier, this article covers primarily organization-wide gain-sharing plans. Double-dipping into two bonuses is discouraged, so some executives or sales-commissioned people may be excluded on all or part of their wages. In fact, the idea of including most people and basing it upon past performance fairly well excludes all managerial bonus plans from gain sharing.

Employee Involvement Related

Most, but not all, plans include considerable employee involvement since the emphasis is on developing better cooperation, communications, teamwork, and identity. In fact, gain sharing would have a hard time surviving in the long run without extensive employee involvement and communications. Most consultants of gain sharing are behaviorally oriented and often view gain sharing as a fairly refined form of organizational development that makes significant employee self-control as its ultimate goal; much time is spent in developing the concept of working smarter, not just working harder.

Not Individual Oriented

Since gain sharing is normally large group oriented, individual-oriented and team-based systems are still typically excluded. Before installation, most, but not all, firms eliminate individual-oriented systems, such as piece-rates and pay-for-suggestion systems, neither of which seems to work well after a period of time for a variety of reasons. *Variable compensation* normally refers to all forms of bonuses—individual, group, and organization-wide of which gain sharing is just one component.

Site Specific

Although exceptions can be found, most plans are site specific—being conducted within a single plant, for example—and, therefore, generally companywide plans—such as the Ford and General Motors profit-sharing plans—are excluded from the definition. These companywide systems probably do little, if anything at all, to change behavior by themselves.

Long-Term Oriented

Most gain-sharing plans are not installed for short-term results because the employee involvement aspect makes doing so difficult. Nor are many installed on a pilot, small-department basis for the same reason. It is hard to isolate a group because of the emphasis gain sharing places on interdependency within the organization.

Not Part of Wages

Traditionally, gain sharing has been maintained separately, set apart from market-based pay systems. That is, it has not been considered part of normal compensation. Consequently, it has almost always been excluded from union contracts, for example. Variable compensation typically tries to make a closer link; that is, an employee's pay includes base pay plus the bonus, so in theory, some pay is at risk.

Paid Frequently

Most gain-sharing plans pay earned bonuses more than once a year. Monthly, quarterly, bimonthly, and even weekly payouts are being made in gain-sharing plans today.

WHY COMPANIES INSTALL GAIN-SHARING PLANS

The outcomes of a successful gain-sharing plan can be numerous. These include increased competitive position; more emphasis on quality and cost reduction; more economic education and communications; increased commitment to change and employee involvement; and more responsive managers. The reasons for installing a gain-sharing plan are as numerous as the plans' potential results, but most interested companies can be grouped into one of three broad categories, as follows.

Troubled Companies

Their need to change is apparent. A variety of problems are often present: low or no profits, poor labor relations, limited trust, declining business, and so forth. In these situations, gain sharing leads the organization through a change process. Major change is expected. Gain sharing has been proven to change behaviors and performance in a very short time period. In fact, one of the fathers of modern gain sharing, Joe Scanlon, was hesitant to install it in other than troubled companies.

Successful Companies

These companies install gain-sharing plans because they believe in sharing, capitalism, more employee self-control, and employee involvement. They install gain-sharing plans because they *believe* in it, not because they *have* to. A large number of successful firms, such as Motorola, General Electric, and 3M, have installed gain-sharing plans for these reasons. In these situations, gain sharing follows organizational change.

Contingent-Compensation Situations

More firms are starting to tie pay, or part of it, to business performance. Many organizations do at least talk about variable pay or pay for performance of which gain sharing is part. Traditionally, the gain-sharing bonus was paid *over and above* normal and equitable wages, but this is no longer true in all situations. Because of increased competition, particularly from foreign countries, many organizations can no longer afford the automatic pay increases they awarded to employees in the past. Companies now look to gain-sharing plans to help instill in employees the notion that more pay results when the company makes more profits or has improved other performance. Unions, in general, are not big proponents of gain sharing because firms may and have used gain sharing as a substitute for normal wage increments.

TYPES OF ORGANIZATIONS INSTALLING GAIN-SHARING PLANS

Most gain-sharing installations are made by manufacturing firms with 100 to 1,000 employees, although some have over 1,500 employees; about 40 percent of these are unionized. Most of them are plants or divisions of larger companies rather than small, privately owned companies, as was true in the past. Gain-sharing plans are slowly gaining acceptance by service-sector organizations, such as hospitals, banks, and insurance companies. Certainly bonus plans are more numerous today in service-sector firms than in the past. This trend is likely to accelerate in the future.

The government is also installing some gain-sharing plans at various local, state, and national levels. Various initiatives at these levels are expected to continue at an increasing rate.

GAIN SHARING'S RELATIONSHIP TO PROFIT SHARING

Most gain-sharing plans stop short of sharing profits with employees, but about one-third of the plans are profit oriented, and some proponents heavily promote such an approach if coupled with extensive employee involvement. Some firms base the amount of sharing on profit levels. We believe that some people will include profit sharing as one form of gain sharing, and others will exclude it. For those organizations that base their bonus on profit improvement (that is, a hurdle rate) and include the other components discussed earlier, such as including most employees as eligible bonus recipients, promoting employee involvement, making payments more than once a year, and being site specific, there is no difficulty in classifying their plans as gain sharing. To summarize, some people classify profit-oriented systems based on improvement, not just a percent of profits, as a form of gain sharing, and others do not. To say that employees cannot understand profit-oriented calculations is erroneous; broad calculations just require more education effort if changed behavior is desired.

WHY GAIN SHARING WORKS

Many successful companies already do or should espouse the tenets of gain sharing. Gain sharing integrates communications, teamwork, goal orientation, improvement in quality and performance, employee involvement, and financial rewards into one system. There are no secret tenets, and successful firms work on them continually. The benefits of gain sharing include more long term identity with the company, improved communications, employee involvement, and shared rewards from improved performance. We do not believe that management would install gain sharing without expecting to get something in return for both the company and hopefully all employees. Possible benefits for management include emphasis on improved performance through cooperation, rewards tied to improved performance, use of a goal-oriented system, a structured approach to the change process that is needed, and getting people to relate to economics and identify with the company. Possible benefits for employees include improved long-term employment security; a way to make changes and get things done; learning more about the company; a way to get recognized for performance; improved communications, teamwork, and cooperation; a way to get involved with the company in many capacities; and the possibility of earning more money.

KEY ISSUES UNDERLYING GAIN SHARING

If you were to read the more than 100 articles and books written on gain sharing, you would find that most deal with the two issues outlined in Figure 19.1.

A relationship exists between these two major issues. For example, if a coal miner produces 40 tons of coal in 40 hours in the first week and 44 tons in 40 hours in the second week, physical performance has increased by 10 percent (1 ton per hour to 1.1 tons per hour). This increase could be caused by capital improvements, the person's working harder, easier coal to mine, and so on. If between the first week and the second week the price of coal decreases by 25 percent, the financial performance has decreased. No doubt, most employees relate more to physical performance, but financial performance is most important to the long-term success of the company. The two key calculation issues are to what degree you need employee involvement, education, and communications if you want to change behavior, and what the company wants to pay for.

FIGURE 19.1   The two key issues of gain sharing.

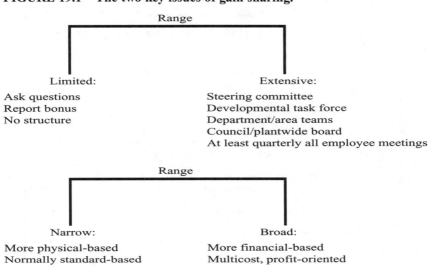

Range

Limited: Extensive:

Ask questions   Steering committee
Report bonus   Developmental task force
No structure   Department/area teams
                                              Council/plantwide board
                                              At least quarterly all employee meetings

Range

Narrow: Broad:

More physical-based   More financial-based
Normally standard-based   Multicost, profit-oriented

Involvement

Does a company need a major commitment to employee involvement? Although some people may disagree, most successful long-term gain-sharing plans have a considerable amount of employee involvement in some form.

A fairly typical overlapping-team concept of employee involvement in its installation and operation is outlined in Figure 19.2. The approach shown in Figure 19.2 seems to work quite well. It has been used for many years and could probably be called an intermediate level of employee involvement. It may not materially change the daily operations of a department. Although many other options can be found in practice, many consultants recommend this type of approach.

Types of Calculations and Payment Issues

In actual practice, one can find a wide range of calculation from physical measures of output (for example, board feet of lumber, standard time earned, documents processed) as related to hours of labor input to much more profit oriented calculations. Some successful gain-sharing plans measure improvements in return on investment. The ultimate success of any calculation will depend on several common factors. It must be perceived as fair by the employees, company, and customers; it must meet management's objectives; and it must be understandable and relatively easy to administer. Several examples will be discussed after outlining some of the key measurement and distribution decisions that must be made. Most calculations relate inputs, such as labor, to some ratio of outputs, but some are goal

FIGURE 19.2   An example of an organization's team structure.

INVOLVEMENT BEFORE INSTALLATION

STEERING COMMITTEE
Sometimes permanent
Usually top management
Study of various plans
Develop draft of plan document
Monitor and evaluate plan periodically
Gain higher tentative approval
(Could include union)

DEVELOPMENTAL TASK FORCE
Typically not permanent
Cross-section of all employees
Review, advise, refine, and present plan document to all employees

INVOLVEMENT AFTER INSTALLATION

DEPARTMENTAL OR AREA TEAMS
One person for each 8–15 people in department or area
Meets at least monthly
Selected or elected to some term of office
Management member-appointed
Defined decision-making authority

COUNCIL
One nonmanagement person from each team
Some management members
Meets monthly to review team activities, bonus results,
and economic activity

oriented—if you do this, you get so much bonus. When deciding on calculations, keep in mind the following considerations:

- Development of a measure of output from the broad (for example, sales) to the narrow (for example, physical units) and a measure of input from the broad (for example, most or all costs) to the narrow (for example, labor hours).

- Determination of a historical base period or one based on expectations or some combination of the two (which is increasingly common).

- Percentage going to employees (ranges from 10 to 75 percent of improvement with 50/50 being fairly common for narrow calculations). Goal-oriented systems normally eliminate this issue since people are paid so much for each change in behavior.

- Frequency of payment (often monthly with some set aside for year end to reinforce long-term attitudes; in actual practice, it ranges from weekly to yearly depending on the orientation and the degree of changed behavior expected). Bimonthly and quarterly are also frequently used.

- Distribution (percentage to each employee or some other method, which is a sensitive issue because of overtime provisions of the Fair Labor Standards Act; unless profit oriented, one must give consideration to the overtime provisions of the act, which is why most firms use a percentage of wages for time worked, including overtime).

- Basis of pay (time paid or worked; this also is a sensitive issue in actual practice).

- Participation (normally includes most employees, but caps are frequently formed for higher-paid salaried employees).

- Adjustment procedures (some require adjustment for capital, mix, and so forth, which have to be specified before installation).

- Separate check or not (most pay as a separate check).

- Moving base or not (some experts are strongly against moving the base, and some do not believe that one should pay for a one-shot improvement in performance—obviously, a very sensitive issue). Some continuous improvement is normally built in today.

The developmental task force previously outlined *may* be allowed an important say in many of these decisions.

Although many calculations are found in practice, we have outlined four of the most common forms: one based on a broad measure of performance, one based on physical performance, one based on a multiple-pool concept, and one based on goals.

The calculation in Table 19.1 is fairly broad, and the more costs included, the closer one gets to profit sharing. Line 1, output, is generally a broad measure of output, such as sales or sales plus or minus changes in inventory to make it more production oriented. From line 2, allowed costs in this orientation, usually felt to be those over which employees have more control, are determined from which actual costs are deducted. The bonus pool is on line 4. If the employee share of the improvement is 50 percent (line 5), one-third is set aside for the year end (line 6) to protect against normal ups and downs and reinforce long-term attitudes (distributed at year end if positive, and normally absorbed by company at year end if negative) to yield the net bonus (line 7). When divided by participating payroll (line 8), one arrives at the net bonus percentage (line 9).

If there is no reserve, as shown in Table 19.2, each employee would typically receive a 4.3 percent increase in the hours paid for the period; overtime hours

TABLE 19.1   Multicost Calculation Example (Broad Measure of Performance)

	Period A
1. Output (could be revenue, total standard cost, or some other measure)	$1,000,000
2. Costs allowed (assume 80 percent of line 1 from history or targets)	$800,000
3. Actual costs	− 770,000
4. Bonus pool (line 2 minus line 3)	$30,000
5. Employee share (assume 50 percent of line 4)	$15,000
6. Reserve for year end (assume 1/3 of line 5)	− 5,000
7. Net bonus (line 5 minus line 6)	$10,000
8. Participating payroll (all participating payroll)	$200,000
9. Bonus percentage (line 7 divided by line 8 or $10,000 divided by $200,000)	5%

normally count at $1\frac{1}{2}$ of normal hours. This is similar to the improshare type of calculation based on more physical measures of performance. It has been used by gain-sharing companies for over 30 years, including some Scanlon-oriented systems.

The expanded labor-calculation method, or multiple-pool concept, typically has a series of pools, as shown in Table 19.3. *Decisions* are needed as to how the split should be apportioned to employees, reserve, and so forth. One could distribute a different percentage of each pool, which is common. Three pools are fairly common: labor productivity, quality and/or customer service, and expenses and/or safety. This is an expansion of the allowed-labor calculation and may well become the most common gain-sharing calculation in the long term because of its flexibility. For those firms so inclined, profit goals can be easily tied into the year-end reserve to develop an even closer tie to total performance.

A goal-oriented system can be very simple, as shown in Table 19.4.

Obviously, any scaling is possible (these are all pluses, but they could also be minuses), and one could add and delete items over time as goals change. This could be applied to any group or the entire organization, even a new company startup.

CONDITIONS SUPPORTIVE OF SUCCESS

If one assumes that a major, long-term change process is desired with significant changes in employee behavior, some specific areas among others are important for success:

1.   Management commitment (this must be fairly specific)

2.   Need to change or strong desire to improve or continue to improve (one or the other is strongly needed)

TABLE 19.2 Allowed-Labor Calculation Example (Physical Performance)

	Period A
1. Allowed labor (for example, standard hours allowed or physical units times hours per unit, generally from history)	5,000
2. Actual hours	− 4,600
3. Performance improvement	400
4. Hours to employees (assume 50 percent or ½ of line 3)	200
5. Percentage improvement (line 4 divided by line 2)	4.3%

TABLE 19.3 Expanded Labor-Calculation Example (Multiple-Pool Concept)

Pool 1—Labor Productivity	Period A
1. Allowed hours (based on historical standard hours earned)	5,000
2. Actual hours	− 4,600
3. Performance improvement	400
4. Percentage improvement (line 3 divided by line 2)	8.7%
5. Participating payroll (assume)	$ 100,000
6. Net addition (line 4 times line 5) before split and reserve	$ 8,700

Pool 2—Other Costs or Quality	
7. Examples of costs allowed as a percentage of revenue, or standard hours, or standard cost (based on history or targets): scrap, overtime, material quantity variance, supplies, travel	8%
8. Revenue (as an example)	$1,000,000
9. Allowed costs (line 7 times line 8)	$ 80,000
10. Actual costs	− $ 75,000
11. Net addition (line 9 minus line 10)	$ 5,000

Pool 1	$ 8,700
Pool 2	$ 5,000
Total bonus pool	$13,700

TABLE 19.4   Goal-Oriented Approach

Goal	Bonus Percent
1. Labor productivity	
60 < efficiency	0
60–65	1
65–70	2
70–75	3
75–80 >	5
2. Quality measure: On-time shipments	
< 80	0
80–85	1
85–90	2
90 >	3
3. Safety: Lost-time incidents	
4 or >	0
3	$\frac{1}{2}$
2	1
1	2
0	4

3.   Management acceptance and encouragement of employee input and education

4.   High interaction and cooperation

5.   Lack of major threats to job and employment security or lack of major problems with business volume

6.   Adequate information on productivity and costs

7.   Goal setting

8.   Commitment on part of all people to the change or improvement process

9.   Agreement on a calculation that is relatively simple, perceived as fair, and meets management objectives.

WHAT THE EVIDENCE ON GAIN SHARING SHOWS

Dozens of case studies and government studies document the merits of gain sharing. Perhaps the most comprehensive study, done by the American Compensation Association,[1] included over 633 gain-sharing companies. Some of the results from the study are the following:

---

[1]Jerry L. McAdams and Elizabeth J. Hawk, *Organizational Performance and Rewards* (American Compensation Association, 1994).

1. Organizations gained 2.3 times for every dollar they paid to employees.

2. Bonuses seemed to average around 3 to 4 percent, depending on the plan.

3. Gain sharing works in all kinds of environments, and operational and combination (both operational and financial measures) plans perform better than financial. Gain-sharing companies disclosed much more information to employees than non-gain-sharing firms.

4. Many benefits occur to such plans from education, identity, involvement, communications, and so on, and the more these are emphasized, the less the importance is placed on the size of the bonus.

5. Plans must have broad management support at all levels.

6. Firms with such plans generally performed better than competitors.

Another recent study illustrates the importance of politics in such systems, especially in unionized firms,[2] and a recent book reviews most of the relevant research and approaches in detail.[3]

HOW TO START THE GAIN-SHARING PROCESS

Perhaps the most common approach is to start with a presentation for top management or someone attending a seminar. Frequently a steering committee, made up of higher management, is then formed to accomplish the following:

1. Evaluate the different plans.

2. Visit locations and read materials.

3. Decide on the need for involvement of outside consultants.

4. Develop a draft of a plan including:
   a. Purpose and goals
   b. Involvement system
   c. Calculation
   d. Policy issues

5. Consider the timing of union involvement, if applicable (sometimes on a steering committee).

6. Formulate a corporate approval process.

This process varies greatly by firm. Packaged plans obviously do not include all of these steps, but all interested firms should keep an open mind in deciding what might be best for them.

---

[2]Denis Collins, *Gainsharing and Power* (Cornell University Press, 1998).

[3]Brian Graham-Moore and Timothy L. Ross, *Gainsharing and Employee Involvement* (Washington, D.C.: Bureau of National Affairs, 1995).

THE OUTLOOK FOR GAIN SHARING

If current trends are any indication, gain-sharing applications will continue to grow, but for many different reasons. Some firms will install a gain-sharing plan because they are in trouble, which is how the concept really got started. Others will use it to help eliminate a deteriorated individual incentive system. Still others will install it as a form of contingent compensation to totally or partially offset wage increases. And some will implement it because they truly believe in employees and in sharing financial and other improvement with them. Gain sharing will also show significant application in service-sector firms and periodically will be applied in government units. Most plans will be customized to meet the needs of the organization.

20

NONMONETARY REWARDS: CASH EQUIVALENTS AND TANGIBLE AWARDS

Jerry L. McAdams
National Practice Leader, Reward and Recognition Systems

Watson Wyatt Worldwide

TOTAL REWARD OPPORTUNITY

The 1990s saw a significant change in the employee-employer relationship with the accompanying change in how compensation plans were viewed. As we have seen, organizations introduced multiple pay schemes besides just base compensation. In fact, the term *compensation* was expanded to "total reward opportunity" in acknowledgment of the broader spectrum of rewards being deployed. Recognition and noncash awards were included in this expanded view.

Additional contributions to this chapter were made by Michael Lockwood, Vice President, Maritz, Inc., Fenton, Missouri, and Roger Stotz, Vice President, Maritz, Inc., Fenton, Missouri.

The use of this term, *total reward opportunity,* also forced compensation and human resource professionals to consider two additional, important elements in plan design: alignment and integration. The alignment of the overall reward system, plus each of its parts, with the business strategy and objectives was determined to be critical in communicating and reinforcing desired behaviors. In addition, having multiple plans—that is, organizational unit incentive plans, profit sharing, project incentive plans, recognition and so on—required plan designers to view the plans from both the individual plan and the total reward system perspective.

This expanded view, the total reward opportunity, has fostered the understanding that noncash awards, which can be used in both incentive and recognition plans, are mainstream, not just an afterthought.

If you are considering alternative reward strategies, consider alternative award types. Ask employees what type of award motivates them, and the answer will probably be "cash." Compensation professionals, consultants, and practitioners rarely consider any other type of award. We think of and design for cash awards because it is how we pay and get paid. It is not, however, the only effective type of award; ask anyone who has earned a special holiday or a new stereo system for outstanding performance.

We also understand the power of a pat on the back as social reinforcement from people we respect. In fact, recent surveys show that being recognized for a job well done is the most often mentioned motivator to do a better job.[1] Also listed as important are "challenging work" and "knowing that my opinions matter"—cash is usually lower on the list. (These surveys, as well as this chapter, assume that the respondents are presently being fairly compensated.)

To begin with, you should appreciate the difference between performance improvement plans and recognition plans. *Performance improvement plans* identify what needs to be accomplished, engage people in the work, and reward on performance. *Recognition plans* honor outstanding performance after the fact and are designed for awareness, role modeling, and retention of the recipients. To improve performance, a reward plan must be behaviorally sound, measure performance improvement and its value, provide measurements that can be affected by the people, and use awards that are perceived as valuable by the recipients. A reward plan must also be well communicated, and the participants must thoroughly understand how the performance improvement system and its components work. Participants must know what the organization's objectives are and why they are the objectives; what those objectives mean to them as employees; how they, as employees, can impact those objectives; how they are going to be measured and how the measures are developed; and finally, if the employees do all that is expected of them and the objectives are accomplished, what's in it for them. Management needs to ensure

---

[1]American Productivity and Quality Center, "What Motivates Center Members," *Consensus,* Houston, Tex., vol. 1, no. 4, July 1988, p. 1.

that everyone understands the direction of the organization and how they can help achieve their vision, mission, and objectives; what their contribution can and should be, and what the value is to both the organization and individually. Effective internal communications and education are crucial to driving change and ensuring that the reward plan is effective.

As we enter into the next millennium, the business world is faced with an increasingly tight labor market—a labor market that is demanding more knowledgeable workers, and these workers have skills and motivational needs that differ from previous generations. It is therefore imperative that we examine, design, develop, and implement performance improvement systems that reflect the needs of the new economy, new organizations, and the new knowledge worker.

Nonmonetary awards assist in the overall framework of fulfilling these needs. Nonmonetary awards are unique in that they do double duty: They are of sufficient value and attractiveness to motivate people to improve performance, and they provide the recognition that is increasingly important to today's workforce.

REASONS FOR USING NONMONETARY AWARDS

1. *Supplements a fair compensation plan.* If people generally believe they are being fairly compensated and you don't want to change your compensation plan, consider using nonmonetary awards for reinforcing performance against specific objectives. If people do not believe they are being fairly compensated, fix the basic compensation plan before you try to add new objectives with nonmonetary awards.

If you have an existing cash incentive plan, it is generally not a good idea to replace the cash with nonmonetary awards. You can create an additional plan with different criteria using nonmonetary awards or stop the cash plan for a time (at least a year) and introduce one with nonmonetary awards and different objectives and performance measurements.

2. *Eases the transition to an organizational unit incentive plan.* There is ample evidence that a properly designed performance improvement plan will work effectively using nonmonetary awards. You can test all aspects of the new strategy, get the bugs out, and refine it without upsetting employees. If the measures you are going to be using in the gain-sharing plan are new or you are not sure of the proper historical base period from which to measure improvement, you may wish to consider noncash as a transition strategy. Likewise, if you are unsure of the measurement goals or if you are going to change the measures frequently, you may wish to consider noncash. It is much easier to extract from a noncash program than a cash program. Even a small amount of cash quickly becomes imbedded into the compensation of the employee and makes disengagement from an improperly designed process difficult. After a 2- to 3-year test period, conversion to a cash plan can be more easily done, if you choose to make it permanent. Obviously, if you decide not to make it permanent, you can withdraw without a significant negative employee reaction.

3. *Helps introduce an objective-driven or cost reduction/gross profit enhancement plan.* If you have an established cash gain-sharing plan, both team-based programs to generate ideas from employees to reduce costs or enhance gross profit and objective-driven plans (group based programs that reward for group performance in reaching an objective or objectives) can be run very effectively using nonmonetary awards. In fact, using cash as an award in these situations is probably not as effective as using nonmonetary awards. The special attention and focus that nonmonetary awards bring with them will allow the employees to differentiate more easily between the productivity objective of your existing cash gain-sharing plan and the other objectives. Using cash for everything reduces the ultimate effectiveness of all the plans.

If you are introducing gain sharing with nonmonetary awards, you can also introduce an objective-driven or CR/GPE program using nonmonetary awards. This approach has been followed successfully in manufacturing, health care, service, and white-collar organizations. When introducing new plans, mixing award types (cash for gain sharing, nonmonetary for objective driven, and/or cost reduction programs) is not a good idea. Most organizations cannot adjust quickly enough to absorb and act upon new plans and different types of awards all at the same time.

4. *Recognizes outstanding performance.* Nonmonetary awards carry the element of recognition. They can be shown with pride to peers, family, and neighbors; the awards are visible. They are much more "promotable" than cash. An employee will brag about the new stereo system he earned and show it to his friends and family. The same employee would not readily discuss the dollar value of the bonus received. The noncash award thus becomes a "trophy," and the value received by both the employee and the organization is much greater than nonpromotable cash.

5. *Works well with most employee populations.* In the private sector, nonmonetary awards do well with nonsales, individual or group, exempt or nonexempt, with any existing incentive plans, except piece rate; sales, individual or sales team, with existing salary, salary-plus-commission or straight-commission plans; sales support, individual or group, with any compensation plan; and service or technical support, with any compensation plan.

And in the public sector, symbolic awards are frequently used, but there is little use of merchandise, travel, or earned time off (the nonmonetary awards of significant value). Public hospitals, however, have used merchandise and travel awards with success to improve productivity, patient care quality, attendance, and cost reduction. The limited use of nonmonetary awards in the public sector does not mean that they cannot or should not be used. It probably reflects the sector's limited use of any form of incentive for improving performance.

TYPES OF NONMONETARY AWARDS

There are a few companies that specialize in full-service performance improvement, whether the performance to be improved is that of employees or the company's customers, such as dealers, distributors, or jobbers. These agencies offer research, training, communications, promotion, and reward systems design and implementation. They supply merchandise, travel, and symbolic awards. The largest of these agencies are the Maritz Motivation Company (a division of Maritz, Inc.), Carlson Marketing Group (a division of Carlson Companies), and BI Performance Services.

A distinction should be made between these full-service performance improvement agencies and those that are limited to supplying awards, known as *fulfillment sources.* An example of a *merchandise fulfillment source* would be a local retail store of the incentive division of a merchandise manufacturer. An example of a *travel fulfillment source* would be a local travel agency, and a local broker of promotional and advertising items would be an example of a *symbolic award fulfillment source.* The decision of whether to use a full-service agency or a fulfillment source depends on how much you want to accomplish with your alternative reward strategy. The more you want to accomplish, the more services you will need. The decision will also depend on how much of your internal staff you want to dedicate to the design, implementation, and administration of the strategy.

The five basic types of nonmonetary awards are *social reinforcers, merchandise awards, travel awards, symbolic awards,* and *earned time off* (see Table 20.1).

Social Reinforcers

These awards should be an integral part of all management practices. Examples of social reinforcers include a pat on the back, respect, training, and various activities (picnics, tailgate sales, charity days, and so forth). These awards can be used as morale boosters and acknowledgment of the value the organization puts on its employees.

Merchandise Awards

These are given for improved performance, and they can be preselected items or a broad offering of merchandise. The merchandise award is of significant financial value, usually totaling over 2 percent of the employee's annual salary. Merchandise certificates that can be used at a local branch of a national retail chain often are used as awards, although merchandise awards, in general, are most effective when delivered via an awards catalog.

. There are two types of merchandise awards catalogs: an awards catalog and a general-purpose catalog. Books of awards come in various sizes. Some catalogs offer 1,800 or more items of the highest quality, selected as appealing awards for

TABLE 20.1   Types of Nonmonetary Awards

Social: Involvement, listening, pats on the back, respect, feedback, training, and activities (picnics, tailgate sales, charity days, etc.). Should be an integral part of all management practices. Most of these are a function of management's style and can be used for morale and acknowledgment of the value the organization puts on its people.

Learning and development: Not normally considered an "award," learning and development are beginning to become very important motivational factors as people need or want to increase their skills to match the ever-changing demands of the work world. This type of award has shown to be effective particularly in the high-technology arena where staying current or being on the leading edge is considered very desirable.

Merchandise: Preselected items or a broad offering earned through the accumulation of points applied to a catalog; of "significant" financial value, generally totaling over 2 percent of annual salary as an award for improved performance. Merchandise certificates can be issued and used at a local branch of a national retail chain.

Travel: Trips awarded to an individual, family, or group from the organization; generally valued from $250 to $4,000 per person. Certificates of $10 to $100 in travel are also used. These certificates are accumulated over a period of time and applied to a trip's costs.

Symbolic: Awards with more "meaning" than financial value; often referred to as "recognition awards." Examples are plaques, rings, pins, desk sets, publicity, free lunches, jackets, hats, reserved parking places, or memberships in advisory councils.

Earned time off: Time off with pay. This is in addition to time off with pay as a result of sickness, vacation, or disability. These are considered an entitlement or part of the agreement for employment; they are not considered an award.

Flexible work schedules: Ability to adjust working hours to fit personal needs. As the labor market continues to tighten and skilled workers are harder to find, this type of award is growing in appeal.

The most popular nonmonetary awards for improving or recognizing outstanding performance are merchandise, travel, and earned time off with pay. Symbolic awards are most popular for awareness (focus on a specific objective or message) and role modeling.

a broad range of tastes. While it offers a broad selection of functional items, its intent is to focus on items with special value to the individual or family. The next smallest catalog generally has about 800 items. The smallest catalogs are really booklets that are made up of 10 to 15 items, each in value groupings of $25, $50, to $500.

Accompanying the catalog is a price list in points or award credits. When a plan is introduced, levels of performance are directly related to the award value in points. Checks are issued by the agency for the appropriate number of points. The employees can redeem them immediately or accumulate them for a larger award. About 90 percent to 95 percent of employees accumulate the checks to get the award they have selected. An awards catalog itself also enhances the merchandise as an award by providing an attractive and exciting promotional vehicle. Of the two ways to offer and promote merchandise as awards, the awards catalog is the most popular and has the highest motivational appeal.

Awards catalogs are supplied by full-service performance improvement agencies. They issue and mail the point checks, based on performance information supplied by the company or directly from the participants. They handle lost checks and refunds (when participants send in more points than necessary for their order). All record-keeping, tax and management reports, order entry, shipping, customer service, auditing, and billing are also handled by the agency.

Some agencies also offer a bank account system. This system deposits the points into an account in the participant's name, issues balance statements, and allows for ordering by telephone or mail.

Some of these organizations have also developed Internet capabilities. This allows the participants in many instances to view their award earnings and to shop online.

In the last few years, another type of award media has been introduced, the debit card. The *debit card* allows an organization to deposit *points* to an employee's individual performance account. The employee then has the option of selecting merchandise from a variety of vendors. There are two main types of debit cards: open and closed ended. The *open-ended debit card* allows the participant to shop at any retailer that accepts the debit card supplier (American Express, MasterCard, Visa, etc.) while the *close-ended debit card* limits the employee to certain retailers. Both have their advantages. Open-ended cards allow the employee to select an award of his or her choosing but may also be used for such things as gasoline purchases, which hold little trophy value. This option is very much like giving the employee cash. The closed-ended card limits the award earner to the vendors selected. This has the advantage of ensuring that the award has more trophy value. There are several companies that offer debit card technologies: Maritz, Carlson, and Hinda Incentives as well as several other smaller suppliers.

To award earners, service is a critical element. People have higher expectations in product quality, delivery, and customer service than when they purchase something for cash. They have earned the award, and they want it as soon as possible and without problems. If there are any problems, they demand quick, fair, and empathetic service. A good agency will stock items that make up from 60 percent to 75 percent of their orders. Some items, such as clothing, furniture, and large appliances, have to be shipped from the factory. The size and buying power of the agency has a strong influence on the service that an award earner will receive on these "drop" shipments. If the desired item is not in the awards catalog, a special service is also offered by some agencies.

People earning merchandise awards feel that they have been cheated if they have to pay taxes on the awards. For this reason, firms "gross up" the award value when reporting it on each W-2 form and pay the federal tax, usually based on 20 percent withholding. Assuming this does not move an employee to a higher tax bracket, there is little or no tax cost to the employee. Many firms extend this practice to cover state and local taxes as well.

Agencies usually bill the firms for the award points redeemed plus transportation and sales tax. This gives firms a cash-flow benefit unique to merchandise incentives. The vast majority of merchandise award earners save their checks until they have enough to get their selected (and often larger) award. This time lag between the actual performance improvement and the billing for awards can be as much as 8 months to a year. The performance has improved, and the company has the benefit of that improved performance without the cost of an award until redemption and billing. Depending on the interest rate, the positive cash flow can be significant. Obviously, there is no cash-flow advantage when the award is made in cash. Bank accounts are generally billed on point issuance, providing no cash-flow advantage.

The second type of merchandise awards catalog, a general-purpose catalog from a traditional department store, is designed to meet every-day functional needs. These catalogs provide a range of items within each category, from basic TV to an expensive, big-screen TV. The majority of the catalog items, however, are low-end merchandise and would not be considered as awards. While the individual may find a number of desirable items in the catalog, the catalog is not designed to be an award vehicle.

Firms using this type of catalog issue merchandise certificates redeemable at the store. As opposed to the award points approach, merchandise certificates are essentially directed cash and lose much of the award appeal. Little goal setting is done.

Most retail stores with catalogs do not offer administrative services for certificate issuance, record keeping of participants' performance, stop payments, tax reporting, and all the other administrative demands of a program. If a company arranges its fulfillment directly with a retail store, the company handles all the administrative duties. Also, the tax considerations are not the same as those associated with the book-of-awards program. Merchandise certificates are billed on issuance, eliminating the cash-flow advantage over cash. The service the employees get from the store is purely a function of the store itself. As with the agency approach, the service, good or bad, will be perceived as the responsibility of the sponsoring firm.

Companies can also buy merchandise awards directly from a manufacturer. Many major manufacturers of popular consumer goods (GE, Motorola, Sony, Thomasville, and so forth) have an incentive division that focuses on selling a limited selection of their products directly to companies for their incentive plans. The buyer—in this case, the company—has to decide what will be most appealing to the targeted population. A common approach is to create a booklet of a few items (TV, VCR, camera, golf clubs, and so forth), at least one of which will be of interest to anyone in the audience.

The risk of preselected items is that they might not be appealing to the people who are targeted. If you have three TVs, it is hard to get excited about earning another. Trying to guess what is valuable to people is a frustrating and often hopeless task. Offering a broad range of awards is the safest approach.

Agencies are generally not involved in the incentive plan when companies purchase their merchandise awards, although brokers often represent a number of manufacturers for the incentive market. Generally, they do not offer any additional services.

If a company decides to purchase merchandise from a manufacturer, then the company handles all the administrative work. This may not be very burdensome if the number of items is limited and all merchandise is drop shipped. If the company buys a number of items and stocks them for redistribution, it must take all of those costs into account when designing the alternative reward strategy. Because of the complexities involved, few firms take this approach, at least not the second time around.

The tax considerations are the same as described for the award catalog approach, and unless the purchasing arrangement is drop shipped only, there is little cash-flow advantage with this approach because award payment is made when shipment is made to the company's stock.

Demands for good customer service exist with a preselected merchandise approach and when the company's staff is responsible for providing the service.

Travel Awards

Trips can be awarded to an individual, family, or to a group from the organization, and they are generally valued from $250 to $4,000 per person. Certificates of $50 to $100 for travel are also used. These certificates are accumulated over a period of time for a trip. Travel awards have a special motivational appeal to people, particularly when delivered as a group incentive.

Group Incentive Travel. In group incentive travel, all earners of a travel award go to the same location and are entertained as a group. A sales force is the most common user of this form of incentive. While some trips are for the earner only, the majority is for the award earner and spouse or guest. Everything is arranged in advance: airline tickets (often including charters), ground transportation, hotel accommodations, cocktail parties, group dinners, sightseeing, sports activities, and so forth. The program can be as deluxe or as economical as the company wishes.

The appeal of a travel award is hard to overstate. An all-expense-paid trip to Hawaii (still the most popular destination), Europe, the Caribbean, the Far East, or a cruise offers what many consider the "giant carrot" for motivating people to improve performance. It is not unusual for people to extend travel awards into vacations that they could not otherwise afford.

One of the most overlooked benefits of group incentive travel is the good feeling that naturally develops on a trip. It is a relaxed opportunity to lay the groundwork for networking and bolstering company loyalty. It is not unusual for the highlight of the trip to be the announcement of the next year's destination and how it can be earned. If the spouses are also there, the company has more motivators on its side for future incentive plans.

Because of the logistics involved and the importance of quality service for the earners, most companies use a full-service performance improvement agency rather than a local travel agency (fulfillment source). Although most travel agencies claim to offer incentive travel, is not as attractive as that of the awards catalog approach. The Internal Revenue Service generally has established that group incentive travel programs are taxable to individuals. Consultation with the firm's tax attorney is strongly recommended. If the trips are taxable, most firms gross up the trip value (as with merchandise awards) and factor this increased cost into the financial rationale of the plan itself.

Group travel, with all its motivational appeal, is a sensitive business. Weather, strikes, and airline operations, for example, are often out of anyone's control. The sponsoring company, however, is held accountable in the minds of the award earners. The power and experience of the full-service agency is the firm's insurance policy. Most companies have learned the hard way to use the major agencies for consistent performance because they are in the business of working with the same hotels, airlines, and local service supplies on a yearly basis.

Individual Incentive Travel.   Individual (or family) travel awards are becoming more popular because they feature many benefits of an awards catalog plan. Travel awards operate in two ways:

1. Travel certificates can be issued in various denominations of "travel value" ($10, $25, $50, and so forth) according to a preannounced schedule that relates levels of performance to a number of certificates. A book of travel destinations is given to the employees at the beginning of the program. Certificates are accumulated by the award earners and redeemed for the travel awards. The certificates may be used to pay for any part or all of the cost of the award.

2. Points earned for performance improvement could be used for individual travel. The certificates are given a point value. The rest of the process is the same as above. This approach allows a company to offer both merchandise and travel awards without the expense of group incentive travel or having a lot of people out at one time. (Nonsalespeople often prefer to travel with family than with a group of coworkers.)

Both approaches have a high motivational appeal because they offer the glamour of travel customized to individual needs and desires. Individual incentive travel also has a great appeal to the family.

It is possible to use local travel agencies for individual incentive travel. Local travel agencies rely on a collection of brochures or a stock airline promotional piece for your company to use with your participants. If your participants are located in offices in other than the local area, the agency must be staffed to handle these travel arrangements as well.

One of the appeals of this approach is its ability to offer a wide range of destinations (100 or more) in a promotional kit to the participants. All administration services, including redemptions and all arrangements, are generally made by the individual award earner directly with the airlines, hotels, and other travel suppliers. The certificates are used in payment directly to the supplier for the travel award cost.

Full-service agencies offer a catalog of award travel destinations designed to promote the resorts and locations. Their primary award travel business is to serve participants from any part of the nation or world, and they are staffed to deliver this service. Customer service is a function of the travel supplier (hotel, airline, and so forth) with the support of the agency. In either case, the sponsoring company will be held responsible in the participant's mind for the quality of service.

Taxes can be handled by grossing up. Billing for the cost of the travel certificates is done on issuance, so there is no cash-flow advantage over cash. If the certificates are issued in exchange for points, however, the cash-flow advantage is the same as with the awards catalog plan.

A WORD OR TWO ABOUT TAXES FOR NONCASH AWARDS

The tax code regarding taxable income and tax withholding for payroll taxes is both extensive and subject to periodic changes. However, anyone designing and/or implementing a noncash award plan must take the tax code into consideration or risk being in violation of the law. It is not the intent of this chapter to provide legal advice. However, there are several general conceptual approaches that, once the appropriate tax interpretation is determined, provide alternatives for addressing tax withholding.

The approach generally acceptable only for independent contractors or other nonemployees is not to withhold taxes. In these cases the individual or organization recipient of the award has the responsibility to report and pay the taxes. The sponsoring organization, although not required to withhold taxes, has reporting responsibilities to the IRS depending on the amount of the award.

The approach for employees by necessity involves withholding appropriate payroll taxes. For this reason two conceptual approaches tend to be followed: grossing up the award or netting down the award. Let us start with the more familiar one: netting-down. The *netting-down approach* is most familiar to employees because it is the process used with their paychecks. Their gross pay is "netted down" by the withholding of various federal, state, and local taxes. What they receive in their paycheck is the net amount.

Likewise with noncash awards of financial value, the total or gross value of the award being offered can be reduced by the obligatory taxes, and the employee receives the net amount. An example of this would be an award plan that issued "points" for improved performance. The employee would be issued a check for the points earned minus the taxes withheld. The employee could then redeem the award point check (the net amount) for merchandise or travel. The withheld points would be converted to dollars and credited to the employee's appropriate payroll withholding accounts.

The *grossing up approach* is more often used with merchandise and travel awards since frequently the award item or trip is promoted, not its dollar value or award credit amount. As such, the employee expects the item or trip to be earned to not be encumbered with taxes. In fact, providing an award that requires the recipient to pay taxes from their "own pocket" is a sure way to demotivate the employee.

The process of grossing up the award is somewhat straightforward and, if you have a computer, easy. It requires the calculation of the various taxes that are generally based on the gross amount of the award, which to the taxing agencies is the net award plus all taxes withheld. A formula that accomplishes this calculation is the following:

$$X = Y + wX + sX + lX + fX$$

where X = gross award value, \$
Y = net award value, \$
w = federal tax rate, 28 percent
s = state tax, percent
l = local tax rate, percent
f = FICA tax rate, individual percent

The following example uses a \$100 item, 28 percent federal, 3 percent state, 1 percent local, and 7.65 percent FICA:

$$X = \$100 + 0.28X + 0.03X + 0.01X + 0.0765X$$
$$X = \$100 + 0.3965X$$
$$0.6035X = \$100$$
$$X = \$165.70$$

The gross award value for a \$100 item is \$165.70. Conversely, an employee would receive a net award value of \$100 from a taxable award of \$165.70.

The bottom line is that employee noncash awards of deemed taxable financial value require that taxes be withheld per IRS guidelines. It is not different from cash awards except that noncash awards can be positioned and promoted very positively, especially when they are grossed up. The employee receives the desired award and additionally has the required withholding taxes paid.

Symbolic Awards

Symbolic awards include plaques, coffee mugs, photographs, mementos, T shirts, hats, rings, pins, and so forth—the list is endless. These awards have symbolic but little financial value to the employee. That does not mean that these awards have to be inexpensive. Company rings or pins can cost hundreds of dollars, but the average symbolic award budget per person is $8 per year.

Symbolic awards are used for two purposes: awareness and recognition. Awareness is acknowledging the importance of an objective or goal. A company could have program themes printed on selected items to distribute to all members of the organization, regardless of their performance. These items are excellent communication tools and tangible, ever-present reminders of the company's focus.

The more common use of symbolic items, however, is as recognition. Offering a T shirt or coffee mug to each employee who reaches a preestablished goal is an inexpensive way of getting focus. Few would argue that this award is significant enough in financial terms to get people to improve performance, but there are a number of cases in which group dynamics and pride take over. The symbolic award is a way for employees to publicly display their accomplishments. Most companies have some form of individual recognition for display in the workplace—plaques, pictures displayed in the cafeteria, and so forth.

Membership in advisory councils, upgrades in company cars, reserved parking places, free lunches, special business cards, and so forth are also used extensively as symbolic awards for recognizing individual outstanding performance. A word of caution about such programs as "employee of the month": The concept is great, but the execution is generally poor. Nominations from management of their employee population often degrade into a lottery or rotation. Credibility and the reinforcing power of these programs tend to erode. Unless you truly can identify and defend the nominations to the rest of the employees, the worth of such programs is questionable.

There are hundreds of advertising specialty and promotion brokers that supply symbolic awards. Full-service agencies offer symbolic awards as an accommodation to their clients. They also offer artistic symbolic awards rarely available elsewhere. These awards are often limited-edition sculptures, designed and produced just for the company and/or event. As with the awards catalog approach, these full-service agencies offer the design, communication, promotion, and distribution services not available with fulfillment sources.

Administration of symbolic awards is much the same as described in the awards catalog plan. Because the value of each item tends to be low, many firms stock the awards and handle most of the administration themselves, particularly if the awards are issued throughout the year. If the plan is to send out the awards all at one time, it is considerably easier to have the full-service agency or fulfillment source handle the distribution from a mailing list supplied by the company.

Generally, symbolic awards are valued at less than $25 each and are tax free to the employee. Under certain conditions, such as with the cost of service awards, the tax-free allowance goes up to $600. The tax law tends to be interpreted differently over time, so be sure to consult your firm's tax attorney.

Earned Time Off

Americans value their leisure time more than ever. With the increasing demands of work, time off can become an award in itself. Having an unplanned day off is becoming a very attractive award. Vacations, of course, are entitlements and are planned in advance.

Most companies make the time off with pay because they feel it is hard to consider it an award otherwise. Time off without pay, however, can be a positive way of capturing productivity improvements. There are lots of employees who would be quite happy to get a day off without pay if it would not jeopardize their job status.

Selectively used, earned time off can be a very powerful incentive. Earned time off has been used as an organizational incentive in two ways. One is for all employees to take a day (or days) off when a specific goal or objective has been reached. Some companies allow employees to accumulate days for additional vacations or extensions. There could be, however, a philosophical conflict with earned time off. What message does such a plan send? Do we really want to reinforce the idea of not coming to work? Some believe such a plan should be applied only in organizational units in which attendance is not a problem or customer contact is not part of the job.

A second way to use earned time off is through company celebrations that take people, as a group, off the company premises. Most of these activities are considered entitlements, such as company picnics, but they can also be effective awards. When goals are met, everyone gets to celebrate. If your company already has traditional events that are not considered awards, it would be unwise to try to convert them into awards. Some creative thinking, however, can bring a company real benefits through group activities. One firm uses special team-building training as an award. The event takes place in the Rocky Mountains, lasts a week, and is highly prized both as a benefit to the company and as an award to the employees. To be the latter, however, participation must be purely voluntary. Even implied pressure to participate eliminates any award aspect of such an activity.

Administration for this type of plan must be handled by the company and tends to be more complex with nonexempt and shift workers than with the exempt and professional ranks. Unlike the other types of awards described, the cost of this award is something to consider.

Because of the limitations of accounting systems, the real cost of this award gets lost in the system. Many firms consider professional, exempt, and management earned time off is given. Nonexempt and shift worker's earned time off is generally considered to carry a real cost. Earned time off is probably most effective when used on a limited basis, driven by the nature of the operation, timing, workload, and how critical the individual is to the organization. Also, earned time off generally has no tax consideration to the employee.

PLAN DESIGN

Regardless of the type of award, the plan must be effectively designed to meet the strategic objectives of the organization. This sounds rather obvious, but it is common to become wrapped up in mechanics of the plan and have little consideration of whether or not the plan is the right type to meet the company's objectives. Too many plans have been installed because "it seemed like a good idea" or "everyone else seemed to be doing it." The strategic objectives of each organization must be fully explored to develop and create plans that motivate employees to meet and exceed those objectives.

The report by the White House Conference on Productivity, Reward Systems and Productivity describes the elements of a productive organization, which are also critical elements for a well-designed performance-improvement plan.[2] They are:

- *A high degree of information sharing, including business, financial, competitive, performance, and planning information.* Not to be overlooked is a consistent plan for feedback to management.

- *A general sense of employment security.* This does not mean lifetime employment guarantees but regularly communicated statements of the relationship between business realities and employment. These statements have legal considerations, particularly with recent court decisions on employee rights. The point, however, is that you cannot expect employees to work cooperatively to improve performance if they live with the constant fear of losing their jobs. As our labor pool continues to shrink, this element will become increasingly important.

- *A mechanism for involving employees in meeting business objectives.* If the employees really can make a difference, a productive organization must provide an easy way for them to make a contribution to improve performance. Quality circles, labor-management teams, multifunctional task forces, advisory councils, and cost reduction–gross profit enhancement teams are but a few examples of such mechanisms. Employee involvement often requires a proactive, program-based process. The answer is not just to install quality circles,

---

[2]White House Conference on Productivity, Reward Systems and Productivity, American Productivity and Quality Center, 1985.

for example, but to make it easier for all employees to make a contribution by offering all-employee programs focused on specific objectives. It is a dynamic process, requiring effort and commitment at all levels of the organization.

- *A reward system that rewards for performance.* It is unfortunate that most pay plans do not effectively pay for individual performance improvement. Across-the-board increases, most individual merit increase plans, and even some sales commission plans have become entitlements.

- *A behaviorally based plan design.* An effective plan incorporates the basic behavioral science rule: "Behavior is a function of its consequences."

RECOGNITION PLAN VERSUS PERFORMANCE-BASED REWARD STRATEGIES

Most compensation professionals relegate nonmonetary awards solely to recognition programs. The most common recognition plan design involves picking out the top 5 to 10 percent of your sales force and recognizing them with a trip or merchandise awards. Non-sales recognition programs include "employee of the month," "customer service person of the year," and "president's award." Although large lump-sum bonuses are common for this kind of plan, they are almost always accompanied by such symbolic awards.

These types of recognition plans are important to creating role models, retaining outstanding performers, and motivating these performers. They do little, however, for the majority of the employees. In fact, when the plan includes an organization-sponsored competition for the top slots, it can be counterproductive. Organizationally imposed competition will not encourage teamwork and can pull focus from the real competition in the marketplace. Within an organization, you want everyone to be winners. To accomplish this, design plans in which everyone understands what it takes to become a winner or earner by improving his or her own or his or her group's performance.

The difference between a recognition program and a performance improvement system is best depicted by the graph in Figure 20.1. The more an organization moves to implementing a true performance improvement process, the more impact that plan will have on organizational performance. Companies need both—one to create role models and acknowledge truly outstanding performance, the other to move the majority of employees closer to attaining the company's objectives and goals.

Figures 20.1 through 20.3 provide a comparison of three basic plan designs: Recognition plan for top performers, earning threshold for performance improvement and recognition of top performers, and performance-based reward plan. The recognition plan for top performers defines winners as a top percentage of the eligible population, rather than those who reach a specific goal. An example would be that the top

10 percent of the workforce would win, rather than everyone who reaches 120 percent of the goal. In the top 10 percent (or "employee of the month") case, people compete with each other rather than focus on the more important competition in the marketplace or against previous performance. This is an effective plan for retaining and motivating winners, but it has little effect on the rest of the employees, as indicated in Figure 20.1 by the relatively small area defined as people likely to be motivated.

With a plan for earning threshold for performance improvement and recognition for top performers, the message is clear: Do this, get that. The focus is on improvement over past performance or toward a new goal. In this case, everyone meeting 120 percent of the objective would earn rather than just the top 10 percent. Winners become earners, determined by achievement of a goal. The earning threshold could be set to generate the top 10 percent of the people as earners. For example, if last year the lowest performance of the top 10 percent was 120 percent of the objective, then 120 percent could be the earning threshold. As indicated in Figure 20.2, this plan design motivates a larger portion of the population.

In a performance-based reward plan, thresholds are set for each individual (usually salespersons) or groups (work groups, organizational units, or the whole organization) or combination of individual and groups. As shown in Figure 21-3, this plan design offers the greatest opportunity for improvement by moving the whole performance curve to the right.

Most organizations have installed versions of either of the first two plans—the recognition for top performers or earning threshold for performance improvement and recognition of top performers—primarily because they are relatively easy to implement. Unfortunately, management often believes these plans are improving the performance of everyone in the organization. This is clearly not the case. The greatest performance improvement opportunity (and highest return on investment) is achieved with a performance-based reward plan.

FIGURE 20.1   Recognition plan for top performers.

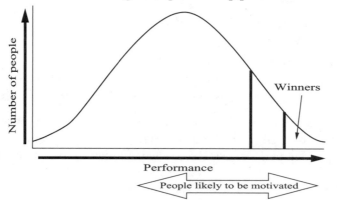

FIGURE 20.2   Earning threshold for performance improvement and recognition for top performers.

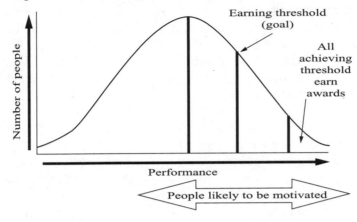

FIGURE 20.3   Performance-based reward plan.

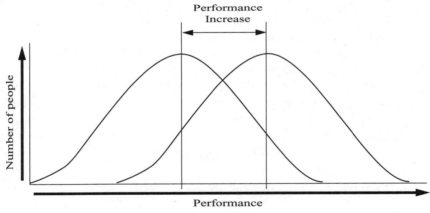

All achieving individual or group goal earn awards

WHY NONMONETARY AWARDS WORK

In *People, Performance, and Pay,* Carla O'Dell and I reported on why organizations using nonmonetary awards chose them over cash.[3] The reasons are as follows:

- *Trophy value.* Every time a person looks at the award, a TV, VCR, furniture, and so forth, or remembers the trip to Hawaii earned for being a top performer or for improving performance, he or she is motivated to continue to improve.

---

[3]Carla O'Dell, in collaboration with Jerry McAdams, *People, Performance, and Pay* (American Productivity and Quality Center: Houston, Tex., 1987).

- *More promotable than cash.* It is easier and more effective to promote the value of a nonmonetary award than its cash equivalent. There is an excitement and recognition factor built into nonmonetary awards that are not present with cash.

- *More flexible than cash.* Because nonmonetary awards are clearly not cash, they cannot be confused with the compensation plan. There is little or no entitlement. The use of nonmonetary awards allows the organization to adjust the measurements and objectives, within reason, without argument from the people who believe that their cash income standard of living may be reduced.

- *Less expensive than cash.* Performance generally increases the same amount whether cash or nonmonetary awards are used, assuming that the award is consistent with the degree of performance improvement required.

  Also in *People, Performance, and Pay,* we asked sales managers who have the most experience in using nonmonetary awards to tell us how cost effective they were versus cash. There was about a 13 percent performance improvement using either nonmonetary awards or cash awards. The cost of nonmonetary awards was 4.1 cents for every dollar of increase. This reflects a significantly better return on investment for nonmonetary awards.

  These data pertain to sales, but my experience in nonsales is about the same. The three-times return on investment advantage of nonmonetary awards over cash in sales populations may slip to 2.0 or 1.5 in nonsales populations, but the point is the same: When organizations want increased performance, the return on investment is often better using nonmonetary awards than cash.

- *Promotes family involvement and goal setting.* Nonmonetary awards have the unique attribute of getting the family involved. A catalog at a family's home provides the opportunity for everyone to participate in the award selection. The catalog is used for the family members to pick out what they want and as encouragement for the employee to make his or her personal goals. The family focus and involvement provided by nonmonetary awards are important advantages to consider when choosing this award type.

CONCLUSION

This chapter is an argument for a broader mix of awards to complement the broader mix of reward strategies that will be installed in the new millennium. It is a suggestion that there are many types of awards as well suited as cash to meet the performance improvement challenge. In many situations, nonmonetary awards are more suitable than cash and can provide a better return on a company's investment.

21

TEAM-BASED PAY

Steven E. Gross, Principal

William M. Mercer, Inc.

S HOULD PEOPLE WHO WORK IN TEAMS BE PAID FOR TEAMWORK? The obvious answer is, Yes. People tend to behave the way they are measured and paid. If they are paid as individuals, they will view themselves as individuals who happen to work on a team. If they're paid for teamwork, they're far more likely to work together as members of a team. If you tell people that you expect them to work in teams but you continue to pay them as individuals, the message they may hear is that teams don't count. When it is deployed properly, team-based pay can be a powerful means of driving or reinforcing a team-based culture.

Yet the subject of team-based pay is more complex than that common-sense "yes" implies. For one thing, not all teams are equal; there are many different types of teams, drawing on different talents and levels of commitment of members. For another, not all team members are equal; on any team, some members will bring much more than others to the table. To pay everybody equally for unequal contributions is patently unfair.[1]

With that in mind, we plan to discuss some of the more problematic issues about team-based pay—and seek to provide answers that, while not immediately obvious, make good common sense. These questions include the following:

Under what conditions should companies align pay with teamwork?

If team members' base pay is unequal, then how should team success be rewarded and recognized?

What is the proper balance between a team member's individual and team-
based pay?

What's the best timing for implementing team pay?

A common mistake among companies that are newcomers to team-oriented
work design is to assume that only variable pay should reflect the new team orientation. A recent Mercer study indicates that is where team-based pay has made
its greatest inroads: of the 1,800 companies surveyed, 24 percent were using team-
based variable pay, and another 24 percent were considering implementing it.
While that's an impressive showing, the fact is that all of the available reward
mechanisms—base pay opportunity, increases to base pay, recognition awards and
incentives—should be aligned with the team structure and culture in order to make
teams work.

THERE ARE TEAMS, AND THEN THERE ARE *TEAMS*

Let's start by defining what a *team* is. The definition offered some years ago by
Jon R. Katzenbach and Douglas K. Smith is still widely accepted within management circles: "A small number of people with complementary skills who are committed to a common purpose, set of performance goals, and approach for which
they hold themselves mutually accountable."[2]

Using those parameters, we can define the three types of teams that most
often occur within corporations: the parallel team, the process team, and the project team (see Figure 21.1). Each has a unique set of characteristics, applications, and pay architecture. In the real world, admittedly, such distinctions are
rarely so neat. Companies may use all three types of teams for different purposes,
and they may have their employees serve simultaneously on more than one type
of team. Furthermore, there may be considerable overlap—hybridization—
between team types.

Parallel Teams

Parallel teams are arguably the most common type of team, occurring in any kind
of organization. They are formed to address a particular problem or issue. They
may be temporary if that problem is resolved within weeks or months, or permanent if it is ongoing. In either case, what is unique about the parallel team is that
it is part-time: Members commit only a partial and limited amount of their time to
teamwork. They have a range of other jobs within the organization that, as a rule,
make greater demands on their time than their parallel team jobs.

In the sports world, gymnastics or skiing teams are examples of parallel teams.
Most of the time, the team members may be stars in their own right, perfecting
their mastery of their sport and seeking individual gold medals, but for brief periods of time, these individuals coalesce as a team to seek the highest possible
aggregate score.

FIGURE 21.1 Team types.

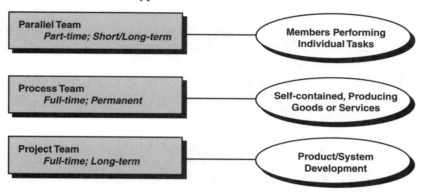

In the corporate world, parallel teams may be formed for a number of purposes. Factories may form teams to monitor safety issues; white-collar teams may work on quality concerns or redesign a work process. At the top of the management ladder, there may be a permanent steering committee to review compensation structure.

Process Teams

The process, or work, team is the workhorse of corporate teamwork. It is a full-time, permanent team whose members together carry out the work or process. The majority of these teams consist of people with comparable training and education, performing similar work. Their goals are more uniform than those of the other team types; they are working, for example, to maximize productivity or customer satisfaction, and they are measured according to the performance of the group overall.

Team sports such as soccer or basketball are examples of processes in which the team is paramount. In the corporate world, process teams may be found in assembly "cells" in manufacturing or as work units that process orders or claims in a service organization such as an insurance company.

Project Teams

This team type is the antithesis of the parallel team; it demands a full-time commitment of its members for the duration of the project. Unlike the process team, the project team typically includes members from numerous functions and ranks throughout the organization. A typical project is the development of a new product or service or the reengineering of one that already exists. The emphasis is on speed, as time to market is critical.

Outside the business world, project teams can be found in the entertainment world, where musicians or actors perform together for a limited, but intense, period of time. In corporations, project teams form in Detroit to design a new car, in

Silicon Valley to create a new computer, or on Madison Avenue to craft an advertising campaign.

How should members of each of these team types be compensated? Later in this chapter, we describe the different pay architecture for each of these teams. But first let's explore the different forms of compensation that make up that architecture: base pay opportunity, increases to base pay, and variable pay, consisting of recognition awards and incentive compensation.

BASE PAY

Although growing numbers of companies are implementing some form of variable pay such as profit sharing or gain sharing[3] for all levels of employees, base pay remains the system that delivers most of the pay for most people. Because their teamwork is only part-time, people who work on parallel teams receive base pay much as individuals who work alone. However, for process and project team members, base pay may be calculated differently. Overhauling the base pay system is enormously time-consuming and disruptive, so normally we recommend it only for those companies with permanent full-time process teams. Those companies may want to implement *broadbanding*—a pay system that simplifies salary structures by consolidating numerous pay grades into a series of broad bands.

Although broadbanding can be useful in a more hierarchical organization, it's especially well suited to teams. On process teams, where members generally have similar backgrounds and expertise and the work is shared, broadbanding makes obvious sense: It puts many employees in the same pay band or range, thus creating a sense of equality. And because it has the potential to minimize differentiation, it's also suited to project teams that bring together employees with diverse pay histories and prior work assignments; people from functional areas as unlike as marketing and engineering, for example, can be placed within the same pay band.

Unfortunately, there is no formula that dictates the ideal number of bands on a team. As a rule, however, less is more. In establishing bands, companies should use a "noticeable difference approach"—that is, if two jobs aren't different enough to be detected by most people, they should probably be in the same band. Within each band, however, there may be a few pay "zones," which allow members to be rewarded based on seniority, acquisition of skills and knowledge, contribution to the team, or other criteria. There should also be an overlap in pay between bands, to reflect the comparative value of a newcomer who enters in a higher band and the veteran who plays a key role on the team but who, because of limited capability or other factors, will remain permanently in a lower band.

Once a company has bands, it needs to define the parameters for wages or salaries within each band. In any organization, base pay is generally determined by two criteria: market pricing (what the market will bear) and job evaluation or work comparison (how the company rates or values the job). Market pricing is relatively straightforward as long as there are comparable companies whose workforce is organized similarly. When only one company in an industry or a market uses process teams, for example, it may be necessary to estimate market pay by evaluating several jobs that together represent the mix of work the team members perform and weigh them accordingly.

The traditional work comparison approaches are attuned to the traditional functional model of the organization. While there are many different approaches, they tend to use three broad categories of factors in valuing jobs: know-how, problem solving, and accountability. *Know-how* represents the sum total of every kind of capability or skill—technical depth, managerial breadth, human resources skill—needed to do the job. *Problem solving,* in a sense, takes know-how one further step: It's the self-starting use of know-how required by the job to identify, define, and resolve problems. These two categories measure not only book-learned skills but also competencies—those underlying "best practices," such as leadership or flexibility, that can be shown to predict effective or superior performance in a job or other situation. The third category, *accountability,* describes the extent to which the job holder is answerable for his or her actions and their consequences.

These categories need to be overhauled when they're applied to teams. In the case of the process teams, in which each member has a role, know-how is replaced with *process capability*—the total of all skills, knowledge, and competencies that are likely to support the team. For project teams, the primary work comparison is *impact*—a measure of the scope of the mission and its potential importance to the company. In both cases, one of the most pervasive differences involves the valuation of competencies. Research (and common sense) indicate that the competencies that best promote teamwork are very different from those likeliest to guarantee a good individual performance. The list of competencies valued for teams—whether parallel, process, or project—includes teamwork and cooperation, interpersonal understanding, oral communication, organizational awareness, and commitment. For parallel teams analytical thinking is crucial; for process teams, there is a subset that emphasizes continuous improvement; and for leaders of all teams, an additional subset includes leadership, developing others, self-confidence, and empowerment. These competencies enter into the calculation of base pay for teams.

How should increases in base pay be handled for teams? Again, this depends on the type of team. For parallel teams, the key consideration is how much of the person's time and energy is allocated to the team. The company can base merit raises on the employee's performance on both the team and in his or her regular job. However, many companies are understandably reluctant to raise base pay permanently as a reward for what is only a temporary team role. In that case, they should consider rewarding members for their contributions by means of recognition awards.

Process teams have arguably the greatest variety of possible approaches to increasing base pay. Some companies prefer an across-the-board wage increase, particularly for teams consisting of hourly and/or nonexempt workers. However, companies that want to reward individuals—and encourage a climate that fosters continuous improvement—should consider using a mix of components in determining raises. Team members could merit raises if they acquire new skills or demonstrate competencies that are considered useful to the team effort. In some companies, peer evaluations or *360-degree/multirater assessments*—evaluations by peers, superiors, and possibly customers and/or subordinates—may be used to affirm members' contributions to the overall performance of the team.

Because project team members usually have the greatest range of base pay and also make widely varying contributions to the work of the team, individual merit raises—as with parallel teams—probably make the greatest sense. Top performers may receive raises twice the size of those given to average performers; alternatively, everyone may share a small merit increase, with the rest of the gain from the project used to fund a team-based incentive program contingent upon achieving predefined results. For project teams, where time is of the essence, raises should reward the immediate demonstration of the skills and competencies deemed critical to success—not the acquisition of skills or competencies that may never have a chance to be applied.

RECOGNITION AWARDS

It's the rare worker who doesn't feel the need for recognition. When workers are asked about job satisfaction, a common complaint is the lack of recognition for their contributions to the company. In a team environment, where people may feel their identity has been subsumed by the team, the need for recognition can be even greater. So since solitary workers and team members alike crave—and, studies also show, respond favorably to—recognition, the only question is how best to deliver it to teams.

First, a brief definition of what's at stake. Recognition can come in two shapes: noncash and spot cash. ("Spot" cash awards are different from incentive pay, for which management has established—and informed workers of—goals and timetables at the outset.) Noncash awards, which are the most common, tend to be given out for a job well done and are usually of nominal value; a typical noncash award would be a baseball cap, T shirt or mug with the company's logo (less than $200 per award). Cash awards are usually small bonuses, but they can be substantial, running well into the thousands of dollars. Many corporations give such awards only for efforts that have had a measurable financial impact. The implicit distinction is that noncash awards are for a job well done; cash is for results. But, the team type also determines the appropriateness of one form of recognition over another.

For parallel teams, both cash and noncash awards can be used as forms of recognition, although in practice noncash is much more widely used. In either case, the award is likely to be relatively modest. One reason is that a parallel team is typically chartered for a specific task that is far less ambitious than a project team's mission. Second, because the members have full-time jobs, the company's expectations of success may not be as high.

Studies show that both process and project teams are almost equally likely to receive noncash awards and spot cash. Because their achievements are generally a matter of incremental improvement, however, process teams are much more likely to receive incentive compensation as a reward for excellent performance. Still, noncash and spot cash awards may be distributed to process teams in recognition of certain milestones, such as the training of every member in a new skill. It's with project teams that cash awards tend to be their most substantial. However, not every project team achieves a scientific breakthrough or develops a breakout product, and typical cash awards may be generous but not dazzling. The award should be linked to a real financial measure.

Should all team members be recognized equally? Team members tend to say yes, although that all-for-one, one-for-all spirit may evaporate when the award is actually given out. Management, for its part, tends to favor individual recognition. Who's right? That depends, again, on the team type and the situation. On parallel and project teams, where members are likely to come from different functions and layers in the hierarchy and to contribute accordingly to team results, there may be occasions where different levels of reward are justified. If some members do feel they've been treated inequitably, the good news is that these teams dissolve when the job is completed, so that members aren't left to nurse grudges.

The situation with process teams is very different. Their members typically come from more uniform backgrounds and make more uniform contributions; singling out one or two members with a special award may create a sense of injustice. On the other hand, equal recognition may leave some members feeling slighted. That's why noncash awards may often be the most appropriate for process teams—and, if they take the form of a pizza party or some other shared celebration, may even help to bring members together. However, recognizing all members and then highlighting a most valuable player profiles a sense of community and recognition for stars that can provide the appropriate balance between individual and team contribution.

INCENTIVE COMPENSATION

There are many powerful arguments for incentive pay. It reinforces cultural change and communicates values to employees, aligns pay with business results, suppresses employees' "entitlement mentality," and encourages them to feel like stakeholders in the organization, and focuses their activities. The same arguments can be made on behalf of team incentives. If incentives influence employee behavior, then team incentives influence team behavior.

Team incentives are the logical extension of paying for teams. Incentives work best when they reward performance that is within the control of the employee. For team members, that means team performance. Properly designed, incentive plans that reward superior team performance should help engender feelings of teamwork, reinforcing team members' sense of accountability and mutual dependency.

That's particularly true for process teams, which work together over the long term to achieve the kind of incremental improvements that incentive plans typically reward. However, as we discuss here, not all team types are equally well suited to incentive pay.

How large should the incentive be? To be meaningful, the payout should be at least 8 to 10 percent of income, or about a month's pay. That represents true discretionary spending. But should everybody get the same amount? Companies are taking a variety of approaches; some pay the same lump sum to all team members, others pay the same percentage of income, and still others pay incentives based on their assessment of individual members' contributions. All the approaches have their pros and cons, but, as with spot cash awards, the distribution of incentives can be a hugely contentious issue—and, as with spot cash, it's best determined by team type (see Figures 21.2 and 21.3).

For process teams, where the goal is to minimize differentiation among members even if they perform somewhat different tasks, a plan that pays equal dollars to all members is probably the best choice. That's generally not true for parallel and project teams. In the case of project teams, members usually receive a wide range of base pay, reflecting their different skills, competencies, and contribution to team results. To pay them the same lump-sum incentive would diffuse the impact of those differences and thwart the intention of the overall compensation structure. Incentive pay that is an equal percent of base pay is more consistent with this structure. Alternatively, members could be paid for their individual contributions.

In general, incentive plans for parallel teams are ill-advised. The danger is that they will create conflict between the members' regular jobs and their team jobs, with employees working harder for the higher bidder. Furthermore, paying incentives to parallel team members could create a sense of inequity among company

FIGURE 21.2   Incentive compensation payout.

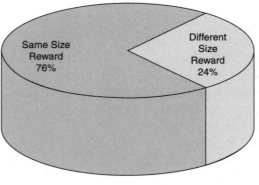

Distribution of
Team-Based Rewards

FIGURE 21.3   Incentive compensation distribution.

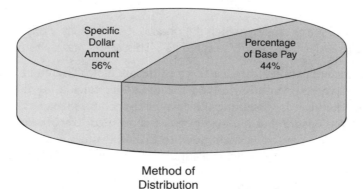

Method of
Distribution

employees who were not chosen for the team. If incentives are used, however, the most equitable plan—given the likelihood that members' contributions will be unequal—is a payout based on individual contribution. Still, most companies recognize that noncash recognition and spot cash are the best rewards for parallel teams, and incentives are relatively rare.

There are a couple of other key factors to consider in establishing an incentive pay program for teams. How are results to be measured? How is incentive pay to be funded? Because financial measures tend to be generated by larger units, such as divisions, measurement for process team results must usually be operational and productivity based—transactions per hour, say, or cycle time. Parallel and project teams, on the other hand, may produce readily quantifiable financial results—either money saved or revenues generated. As for funding incentive plans, the ideal arrangement is self-funding—the important exception being a safety committee, which is typically a parallel team activity. To calculate the funds generated or saved by process teams, companies typically extrapolate from productivity gains.

THE ARCHITECTURE OF TEAM PAY

Now that we have examined the various components of pay, we need to assemble it into an architecture that supports productive employee behavior—in this case, teamwork. Each team type has its own unique architecture (see Figure 21.4). However, four factors must be addressed within any compensation architecture: value, process, activity, and results:

■ *Value* refers to the way an organization values work, creating the opportunity for pay. It is by means of valuation, generally through work comparison, that the company determines base pay ranges.

■ *Process* describes how the job is done and determines which skills and competencies should be rewarded with base pay increases.

- *Activity* refers to one-time events for which employees should be recognized and rewarded.

- *Results* are the means by which the organization evaluates ongoing performance in order to establish variable pay. This refers mainly to process teams.

In the case of parallel teams, activity is the key factor. Members of these teams bring their own compensation package to the table; calculating their base pay is not a team exercise. In designing their pay architecture, management's particular challenge is to ensure that the members are motivated to work at their part-time assignment while remaining committed to their full-time, permanent jobs. If the company promises to pay the team a stipulated amount of cash for results, the danger is that members will neglect their day job. As a result, predetermined incentives are generally not recommended for parallel teams. For this team type, as indicated earlier, recognition rewards work well—preferably noncash are best for efforts while cash awards should be reserved for tangible results. An after-the-fact strategy seems to work best.

The pay structure for process teams is both simpler and more complex. For a start, base pay and base pay increases must be viewed as key building blocks in the compensation architecture. Paying for skills and competencies lays the groundwork. To function effectively, the members of process teams generally must be able to do each others' jobs and work together well. To encourage cross training, the company may have a pay-for-skills program that will result in individual base pay increases; similarly, it will need a pay-for-competencies program to encourage the acquisition of team-based and team-building behaviors. Team members must have similar opportunities to grow and to be rewarded.

FIGURE 21.4   Team pay architecture.

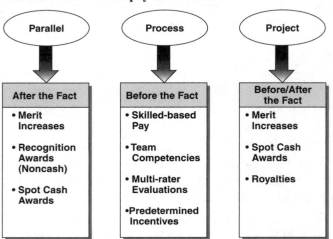

For members of process teams, a plan that explicitly defines the rewards for performance before the fact is considered the most motivating. Thus, predetermined incentives are an essential part of their compensation architecture. But how much incentive? Or, given that the opportunity for incentive pay should result in above-average compensation if the goals are reached, what's the best balance between fixed (base) pay and variable (or incentive) pay? Management—sometimes in conjunction with the team—must decide how much it wants to guarantee and how much it wants to put at risk. As the company and employees gain more experience with incentives and if the experience is positive, their willingness to put more pay at risk—in return for greater rewards—may grow.

Members of project teams are usually employees who have been taken from a permanent assignment to work temporarily on a key company venture. On such teams, base pay and merit increases tend to play their customary (preteam) role. The real variability comes from spot cash awards and, occasionally, incentive plans, based on the success of the team. For project teams, spot cash is widely—and sometimes generously—used to reward performance after the fact. While before-the-fact incentives are not a building block in the compensation architecture of these teams to the extent they are for process teams, they are still sometimes used to reinforce the essential charter of the project team: Do it within budget, on time.

There are drawbacks to offering incentives to project teams. For one thing, their work is usually harder to quantify than that of process teams. Furthermore, events—a change in competitive strategy, innovation, the introduction of new technology—may make predetermined goals obsolete. A more fundamental danger arises if the project is relatively open ended; sometimes a target incentive becomes the end point. A possible alternative, at least for the upper corporate echelons, is royalties or phantom stock—paper shares that mirror the equity growth of a new venture as if it were publicly traded. Depending on how it's structured, these forms of compensation can be either an after-the-fact reward or a before-the-fact incentive.

TIMING

Once an organization has accepted the need for team pay and determined how it should be structured, the temptation is to institute it immediately. While such enthusiasm is gratifying, it's mistaken—particularly if the company has adopted teams relatively recently or is only just beginning to implement them. All teams go through a developmental process during which they solidify as teams; to introduce team-based pay prematurely would impede this progress. In the initial stage, *forming,* there is widespread confusion among team members over the precise nature of their roles, and often there is comparatively little team orientation. In the next stage, *storming,* the conflict and turmoil may grow as people seek to pursue their personal agendas. Only in the next stage, *norming,* when people have begun to accept their roles and openly share information, is it appropriate to impose a team pay architecture. See Figure 21.5, Stages of Team Development, for a more complete description of the stages of team readiness.

Figure 21.6, Team Effectiveness, Alignment, shows in more detail the ways in which several other fundamental aspects of the workplace should be aligned before team-based pay is implemented. These aspects include the following:

- *People.* Do team members have the appropriate mix of skills and competencies? If they lack the behavioral skills to work together as a team, no team pay architecture will enable them to perform successfully.

- *Organization of work.* Are people sharing work appropriately? If it's a process team, is the workload organized in such a way that employees can pinch-hit for each other? If it's a parallel team whose members have other jobs, is the workload manageable?

- *Managerial control.* Who's in charge? Is the team empowered to hire, fire, or conduct peer evaluations? In most cases the answer is no, but the team does need enough autonomy for members to feel as though they function as a self-contained unit.

- *Information and knowledge flows.* Is there effective communication within the team, and between the team and management? Without wide-scale information sharing, members will feel excluded, and the team will be unable to function as a team.

- *Decision making.* How does the team make decisions? Is all decision making top down? Is it one man, one vote? Or is it some compromise between those extremes? To function as a team, members need to feel that they have a voice in its decisions.

FIGURE 21.5   Stages of team development.

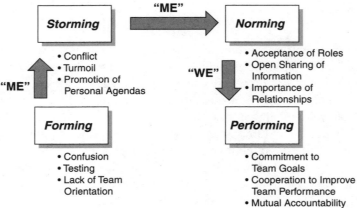

FIGURE 21.6   Team effectiveness: Alignment.

The last spoke on this wheel is rewards. In the best of all worlds, the aspects described above are aligned before the company rolls out team-based pay. As the chart indicates, leadership lies at the core. Strong leadership can help bring these aspects into alignment by sending a consistent message throughout the organization. Its gist: Teamwork pays—and we pay for teams.

ENDNOTES

1. Steven E. Gross, *Compensation For Teams,* AMACOM, 1995.
2. Jon Katzenbach and Douglas K. Smith, "The Discipline of Teams," *Harvard Business Review,* March–April 1993, p. 111.
3. *Gain sharing* is generally defined as a system by which a percentage of the value of increased productivity is distributed to employees, under a prearranged formula.

C H A P T E R

OPTIMIZING TEAM-BASED INCENTIVES

Theresa Welbourne, Ph.D.

Business School, University of Michigan

Luis R. Gomez-Mejia, Ph.D.

College of Business, Arizona State University

A GROWING NUMBER OF CORPORATIONS are moving away from the long-held belief that individual achievement and success, often through brutal competition with fellow workers, is to be encouraged and reinforced. Instead, there is an emerging emphasis on a more cooperative environment in which employees learn to share their talents and information with each other by working as a team on common tasks. Increased foreign competition, more educated employees, excessive turnover and absenteeism, the aftermath of the social revolution in the 1960s and 1970s, and fewer management positions during the 1980s and 1990s are some of the key factors often cited for this trend.

Redesigning work using a team concept provides the organization with flexibility to blend employees with unique skills and backgrounds to tackle common projects or problems. It also provides workers with more freedom, greater independence, and the ability to improve skills and use talents that might not have otherwise been tapped in a narrowly defined position. For example, General Foods Corp. created a network of interfunctional work teams as part of a new strategic direction emphasizing greater cooperation and integration in the workforce.[1] The multidisciplinary teams were formed to encourage maximal performance from every member. Although trained in a particular area of specialization, such as finance or marketing, these individuals in the new system are expected to cross boundaries within the team and contribute in those areas in which they had not previously worked. The result of the experience at General Foods is what M. Bassin describes as "peak performance of each and every employee."

Another example of team performance, reported by M. S. Fisher, indicates that even within 3 months of employing a team concept, one can observe improved productivity, reduction in costs, fewer employee grievances, and less turnover.[2] Fisher reports that after 4 years with the team design, one plant derived a 69 percent improvement in productivity, and after 5 years the figure had jumped to 92 percent. The nature of the work in this plant required extensive, cooperative work relationships among employees, and changing from an individual- to a team-based work environment allowed this plant to achieve remarkable improvements in productivity. Examples of companies employing teams within their manufacturing operations include General Motors Corp., TRW, Inc., Digital Equipment Corp., Shell Oil Co., and Honeywell, Inc.

Many firms are also providing team incentives to reinforce the team concept. These include well-known companies in a variety of industries—Unisys, Hallmark Cards, Blue Cross-Blue Shield, Rockwell, Motorola, Signicast Corporation, and Smithkline Beecham, among others.[3] Based on a survey of 2,500 corporations during 1996 and 1997, William Mercer, Inc., found that approximately 20 percent of these firms are currently using team-based incentives and that another 21 percent

---

[1]M. Bassin, "Teamwork at General Foods: New and Improved," *Personnel Journal,* 67(5), May 1998, pp. 62–70.

[2]M. S. Fisher, "Work Teams: A Case Study." *Personnel Journal,* vol. 60, no. 1, January 1981, pp. 42–45. Also Bassin, pp. 62–70.

[3]E. W. Straub and A. S. Rosen, "Supporting the New Business Contract," *HR Focus,* vol. 73, no. 12, December 1996, pp. 11–12. See also the following: S. E. Gross, "When Jobs Become Team Roles, What Do You Pay For?" *Compensation and Benefits Review,* vol. 29, no. 1, January/February 1997, pp. 48–51. E. J. Hawk, "Aligning Stakeholder Interests: The Power of Group Incentives." *Compensation & Benefits Management,* vol. 13, no. 3, summer 1997, pp. 8–17. N. Isaacs, "Team Structures Can Complicate Reward Programs." *Infoworld,* vol. 20, no. 21, May 25, 1998, p. 132. B. Nagler, "Recasting Employees into Teams," *Workforce,* vol. 77, no. 1, January 1998, pp. 101–106.

are considering it.[4] A wide variety of formulas and approaches are used to link incentives to team performance.[5]

Based on our personal experience and interviews with managers, the most common reasons given for redesigning work into teams are the following:

- Teams are portrayed as a more effective mechanism to improve quality than traditional quality control approaches.

- A greater accumulation of knowledge can be brought to bear on a particular problem. Facilitating innovation by breaking down barriers among people and improving the flow of expertise throughout the firm are also advantages.

- Companies have greater flexibility as the organization becomes less dependent on particular individuals. This provides a mechanism to absorb turnover and downsizing because other people can "fill in" as necessary.

- There is greater cross fertilization of ideas as people from different backgrounds share their views and experiences. This combination of diverse talent can stimulate innovation.

- The company is less dependent on supervisory formal hierarchies, which produces more autonomy, discretion, empowerment, and emergent leadership within the firm.

- Employees are more committed to the organization if they participate in decision making.

- Employees gain a corporate-wide or an organization-wide perspective so that they can see how different parts of the company fit together.

Like any other personnel program, team-based management approaches do not function in a vacuum; they need the support of other human resources systems to be effective. By putting money behind the policy, compensation can play a leading role in communicating the organization's commitment to the team concept. As Bassin noted when describing the experience of General Foods, "In terms of support for team activity, nothing is symbolically more important than compensation."[6] Therefore, in addition to the institutional mechanisms by which team-based pay programs are coordinated with other compensation methods, the way group rewards are linked to performance will be pivotal in establishing and maintaining effective team arrangements.

---

[4]P. Pascarella, "Compensating Teams," *Across the Board,* vol. 34, no. 2, February 1997, pp. 16–22.

[5]D. Antrim, "How to Get Employees to Commit to Agency Goals," *Rough Notes,* vol. 141, no. 5, May 1998, pp. 81–82. J. McAdams, "Back to Basics," *Incentive,* vol. 172, no. 8, August 1998, p. 22.

[6]M. Bassin, "Teamwork at General Foods: New and Improved," *Personnel Journal,* vol. 67, no. 5, May 1988, pp. 62–70. And M. S. Fisher, "Work Teams: A Case Study," *Personnel Journal,* vol. 60, no. 1, January 1981, pp. 42–45.

REWARDS TIED TO TEAM PERFORMANCE

Team incentives can be based on the concept of either pay-for-performance or pay for skills and/or knowledge. *Pay-for-performance* is the more common design, and outcomes of team effort are used as payment criteria. Objectively measured consequences might include cost savings, number of products manufactured, meeting agreed-upon deadlines, parts rejected, or the team's successful completion of a new product design and successful patent. The goals, methods of measurement, and bonus amount can be determined in advance and communicated to group members, thereby serving as an incentive for the entire team.

Bonus payments can be made in cash, corporate stocks, or through noncash items such as trips, time off, or luxury items. Payment may be distributed equally to all team members or differentially in an effort to reward those who made greater contributions to the team's objectives. If rewards are to be distributed based on the individual's contribution to the team's goals, then the organization must employ a method of individual-based performance measurement. Rather than granting a lead or supervisor the responsibility for evaluating individual contributions, team members may rate each worker's performance, and the group's consensus can be employed for distributing rewards.

When team rewards are distributed differentially to individuals, the element of competition among team members creeps into the team concept. Team bonus payments can easily evolve into simply just one more scheme for merit pay, and the processes of dividing bonus money among individual members can then be contaminated with the multitude of errors cited in traditional pay-for-performance systems. There is also the added problem of differentiating between true performance and the results of a popularity contest when using peer evaluations.

Team-based pay for skills and/or knowledge is a second approach. It is important to differentiate this from other pay-for-skills plans based on individual performance. Manufacturing plants are experimenting with skill-based pay plans in which members of the organization increase their pay when they acquire additional skills and can master new tasks within the plant, usually as a result of extensive cross-training efforts within their team. Although the members might be working in teams, each individual increases his or her pay by improving personal skills. This form of knowledge-based pay is individual oriented rather than team based and reinforces individual accomplishments in the same manner that merit pay traditionally rewards workers for self-improvement.

Skill-based pay, at the team level, on the other hand, rewards group members for increasing their ability to work as a team. Cooperation with other teams might be an important criterion for payment; ability to work effectively together on problem-solving assignments might be another. The important distinction is that all team members are rewarded when the skills of the entire team, not just the skills of specific individual members, are improved. Corporations experiencing problems with competition among various teams might find this type of incentive useful to increase cooperation among teams.[7]

This same approach can be used to reward the team when each member has attained new skills. Rather than rewarding one person for learning a new job, the entire team might be compensated when all team members are satisfactorily cross trained or the team's evaluation can be dependent upon its ability to bring each team member up to speed. This provides incentives for the more competent employees to assist the struggling employees. It also motivates team members to evaluate each other's performance in a more open, honest environment. Because team members are aware that one person's nonperformance can hinder the rewards to all members, a poorly performing employee is likely to be quickly discovered and dealt with by members of the team.[8]

REASONS FOR CHOOSING TEAM INCENTIVES

Rewards based on team performance will affect the business's ability to attract, retain, and motivate employees and will mold the corporation's culture. Team compensation plans should be chosen when they are consistent with both the nature of the work and the goal setting of the organization and the team.

Nature of Work

Recent efforts to redesign jobs have focused on enhancing cooperative work relationships among employees to attain desired outcomes, such as improved quality, increased quantity, enhanced communication, and lower costs. Manufacturing programs, such as just-in-time inventories, require constant communication among sales representatives, field engineers, and inventory personnel. Since the nature of much work today requires cooperation among team members, incentive plans that reward the team's performance provide workers with feedback that will reinforce the organization's goals and strategies.

A *cooperative work environment* was defined by M. Deutsch as one in which the objectives of individual employees are mingled together in such a way that there is a positive correlation among the group members' goal attainment. In other words, no one individual can achieve success without the willingness of coworkers to contribute to the desired performance outcome. This type of work requires

---

[7]B. E. Garson and D. J. Stanwyck, "Locus of Control and Incentive in Self-Managing Teams," *Human Resource Development Quarterly,* vol. 8, no. 3, fall 1997, pp. 247–258. See also M. Ezzamel and H. Willmott, "Accounting for Teamwork: A Critical Study of Group-Based Systems of Organizational Control," *Administrative Science Quarterly,* vol. 43, no. 2, pp. 358–396. M. A. Campion, E. M. Papper, and G. J. Medsker, "Relations between Work Team Characteristics and Effectiveness: A Replication and Extension," *Personnel Psychology,* vol. 49, no. 1, summer 1996, pp. 68–78.

[8]B. Murray and B. Gerhart, "An Empirical Analysis of a Skilled-Based Pay Program and Plant Performance Outcomes," *Academy of Management Journal,* vol. 41, no. 1, February 1998, pp. 68–78.

compensation programs that emphasize group outcomes rather than individual outcomes.[9]

The concept of individual pay programs stems from economic theories that indicate individual contracts between employees and the organization are formed in a working relationship. Thus, the sum of all individual employment contracts forms the corporation. This concept has a number of problems associated with it due to the intercorrelated nature of most work. A group of employees independently working on separate goals and objectives is inefficient in an organization that does not have a number of individual goals but rather one objective that requires cooperation among individual workers.

An often-cited example of the failure of this concept can be found in traditional sales commission plans. The sales representative is commonly paid strictly for units sold, representing an individual contract between the salesperson and the employer. Unfortunately, the contract only delineates the amount of money the sales representative receives based on the quantity of goods sold rather than on the quality of information delivered to the customer. This may create a tremendous customer relations problem that is only realized after the sale. The customer service representatives and field technicians are often extremely frustrated due to the salesperson's disinterest and inability to effectively relay information to either the customer or to headquarters offices. The employment contract between the salesperson and the company specifies only units sold. Therefore, the contractor is not concerned with cooperating with the customer service group, home office, or field representatives. By narrowly defining the jobs, the firm's goal of effective sales and service is not realized. The result is confusion within the organization and a poor image conveyed to the customer. This type of work is intrinsically team oriented, and team rewards could assist in realizing the organization's true goals for both volume and quality.

Goal Setting

There has been an abundance of research concluding that goal setting leads to improved performance.[10] Most of the studies have focused on individual goal setting and resulting individual performance, although a few studies have considered the issue of group goals and subsequent group performance. In general, it appears

[9]S. Johnson, "Plan Your Organization's Reward Strategy through Pay-for-Performance Dynamics," *Compensation and Benefits Review*, vol. 30, no. 3, May/June 1998, pp. 67–72. See also R. Seaman, "Case Study: Rejuvenating an Organization with Team Pay," *Compensation and Benefits Review*, vol. 29, no. 5, September 1997, pp. 25–30. S. T. Johnson, "High Performance Work Teams: One Firm's Approach to Team Incentive Pay," *Compensation and Benefits Review*, vol. 28, no. 5, September/October 1996, pp. 47–50. M. Erez and A. Somech, "Is Group Productivity Loss the Rule or the Exception? Effects of Culture and Group-Based Motivation," *Academy of Management Journal*, vol. 39, no. 6, December 1996, pp. 1513–1537.

[10]G. P. Latham and E. A. Locke, "Goal-Setting—A Motivational Technique That Works," in R. M. Steers and L. W. Porter (eds.), *Motivation and Work* (New York: McGraw-Hill, 1987).

that group goal setting does lead to improved group performance when the goals are accepted by the group members.[11] The goals should be difficult, therefore providing a challenge for the team members, but not unattainable.[12] It has also been suggested that group goal-setting processes persuade individuals within the team who have not accepted the team's goals to personalize the group's goals.[13]

Research has also found that linking group rewards to the achievement of group goals has a positive effect on team performance.[14] When combined with consequences, such as rewards, it appears that goal setting has a long-term effect on the team's performance.[15] Compensation programs provide an essential feedback link for the goal-setting process. Pay related to the goals set by the team signifies that the organization is committed to the program, and the feedback provided regarding the team provides employees with positive reinforcement in addition to an incentive to continue pursuing the team's goals.

TWO EXAMPLES: SELF-MANAGED WORK TEAMS AND RESEARCH AND DEVELOPMENT TEAMS

As the traditional corporate hierarchy continues to evolve into a more egalitarian structure with emphasis on participative management, new organizational forms are being introduced. Self-managed work teams are currently utilized by manufacturing and nonmanufacturing firms that have found the traditional form of supervisor, lead, and worker ineffective in promoting autonomous decision making and high levels of cooperation.

Self-managed work teams are formed by a group of employees, usually all at equal status within the hierarchy, who work together in identifying goals and objectives, solving problems, and completing stated performance objectives. The team's responsibility can also encompass personnel matters such as hiring,

---

[11]C. R. Gowen, "Managing Work Group Performance by Individual Goals and Group Goals for an Interdependent Group Task," *Journal of Organization Behavior Management,* vol. 7, Fall 1985/Winter 1986, pp. 5, 23.

[12]J. Forward and A. Zander, "Choice of Unattainable Goals and Effects on Performance," *Organization Behavior and Human Performance,* vol. 6, 1971, pp. 184–199.

[13]J. T. Austin and P. Bobko, "Goal Setting Theory: Unexplored Areas and Future Research Needs," *Journal of Occupational and Organizational Psychology,* vol. 58, no. 4, December 1985, pp. 289–308.

[14]R. D. Pritchard and M. Curtis, "The Influence of Goal Setting and Financial Incentives on Task Performance," *Organizational Behavior and Human Decision Process,* vol. 10, no. 2, October 1973, pp. 175–183.

[15]Austin and Bobko, pp. 289–308.

disciplining, evaluating, rewarding, and firing team members. Such teams are currently being used in many manufacturing firms in which individuals need to closely cooperate to perform tasks. The Sherwin-Williams Co., for example, has emphasized work teams in an effort to allow employees to more effectively handle the numerous product changes required in their plant while also maintaining high-quality standards.[16] A flat organizational structure with emphasis on operators' contributions to their teams' tasks was developed and complemented by an open-plant design allowing workers access to all stages of the production process.

Moving to the concept of team management versus individual workers reporting to a supervisor enhances an environment of close cooperation and allows workers to contribute more effectively to job completion. Employees are more committed to the goals of the group than they are when individuals are competing under traditional systems. The effectiveness of these teams has been greatly enhanced with the employment of compensation mechanisms that reward the team for accomplishment of team objectives, whether these are performance based, such as meeting a stated output goal, or process based, such as improving management skills. The pay system that rewards team members for accomplishment of team goals delivers an important message to workers that management supports team performance and team goals are important to the corporation.

Luis Gomez-Mejia and D. Balkin studied 175 scientists and engineers and found that aggregate rewards were more effective for research and development teams than individual rewards. The nature of research and development work requires teamwork and cooperation by scientists and engineers who often have competing personal goals due to their scientific training and interest in pursuing strictly research-oriented activities versus customer-oriented projects. Aggregate incentive plans help bring their personal objectives into alignment with the organization's needs.

These authors found that an additional reason for the effectiveness of team incentives, was the absence of adequate individual measures of performance for these professionals. Research and development teams make progress in leaps rather than gradually, and it is hard to measure the contributions of one individual to the team's success in ventures such as designing a new product or creating a unique technology. Team-based bonus programs were also found to provide the organization with more flexibility in timing the reward to match team accomplishments.

Two primary advantages of using team incentives for research and development work rather than individual-based programs or organization-wide plans such as profit sharing were uncovered by Gomez-Mejia and Balkin. First, compensation

---

[16]E. J. Poza and M. L. Markus, "Success Story: The Team Approach to Work Restructuring," *Organizational Dynamics,* vol. 8, no. 3, winter 1980, pp. 2–25.

is more closely tied to performance of the workers within teams that control both the quantity and quality of their research results. Second, pressure can be exerted on individuals to perform their best in alignment with the team's goals.[17] Gomez-Mejia, Balkin, and Milkovich describe the case of a Boston-area high-technology firm that allows engineers to earn up to 25 percent of their salary as a result of successful team performance. The program is administered competitively, and each research and development team is required to submit a written report showing how the team's efforts resulted in significant cost savings or other benefits to the firm. A committee of technical and nontechnical supervisors and managers reviews the proposals and may or may not grant bonus money.[18]

The team approach may also be used to motivate the research and development department to work more closely with individuals within the marketing department. These two divisions have traditionally been in conflict due to their responsibilities and training; research and development is interested in pursuing technology while marketing focuses on selling products based on consumer needs and perceptions. Although these two goals are not always in alignment, pay mechanisms can be used to create teams of technical and marketing personnel. The result can be products that are both technologically advanced and marketable.

INTEGRATION

Team incentives can be combined with individual, business unit, and organization rewards programs. The key to success is integrating all of these compensation methods so that they are consistent with the organization's strategy. If they are not developed to be consistent with the business strategy, then each individual method of payment can conflict with each other's or the corporation's objectives, therefore transmitting extremely mixed signals to employees. When team incentives are utilized, individuals continue to possess personal goals in addition to their incorporated team goals. The rewards system can be effective in ensuring that individual and team goals are consistent rather than in conflict with each other.

Rewards programs are important for supporting or developing either hierarchical or egalitarian business structures. If the firm is primarily hierarchical and if individual employees know that success comes only after rising through supervisory and management levels, there will continue to be a struggle among team members who are trying to ensure that their individual performance is noticed by upper management. Incentives, in addition to promotional opportunities, must be carefully tailored to anticipate the needs of individuals who desire successful movement within the organization. Tall, hierarchical structures are consistent with

[17]L. R. Gomez-Mejia and D. B. Balkin, "The Effectiveness of Individual and Aggregate Compensation Strategies in an R&D Setting," *Industrial Relations,* vol. 28, no. 3, fall 1989, pp. 431–445.

[18]L. R. Gomez-Mejia, D. B. Balkin, and G. T. Milkovich, "Rethinking Your Rewards for Technical Employees," *Organizational Dynamics,* vol. 18, no. 4, spring 1990, pp. 62–75.

individual rewards. Therefore, firms that desire flat organizations must change their rewards methods to be consistent with the desired structural goals.

Organizations must also consider the desired relationships among teams. Teams can work in either a competitive environment, in which teams are competing with each other for performance outcomes and subsequent rewards, or they can work cooperatively on common objectives. The atmosphere will reflect the corporation's goals and culture. Team membership can be designed so that only individuals within one department work together on a team, or department members can cross over their traditional boundaries to join teams that are multidisciplinary. Again, the form of the team is dependent upon the goals of the business.

INDIVIDUALISM AS A CULTURAL VALUE

Although many organizations are moving to the team concept, relatively little attention has been given to the nature of the American worker in a team environment, which is foreign to the basic culture from which the employee has emerged. G. Hofstede, in a comprehensive study employing a database with over 116,000 questionnaire responses, found that the United States ranked number 1 on a construct that he called "individualism." High-individualism countries are characterized as places where the culture emphasizes the individual rather than the group. Each individual is expected to care for himself; the organization is not committed to care for individuals on a long-term basis. Pay policies within these countries tend to emphasize individual rather than group performance.

An employee's ability to demonstrate his or her successful individual achievements to others is important and evidenced by the accumulation of rewards for performance, such as salary, company cars, job title, number of subordinates, and other rewards found in traditional compensation systems. As team concepts are employed, it must be asked how the mentality of individualism, which is typical of the American worker, can survive in this atmosphere. The compensation program can be one tool for satisfying both individual and group needs. Awards for outstanding individual performance cannot be ignored in a society so insistent on individual accomplishment; rather, they must be carefully incorporated within an organizational environment whose survival depends on team rather than individual effort. Turnover should be carefully monitored when a business moves from individual to team programs. This will provide feedback on the types of personnel who are challenged by the team concept and those who are not satisfied within the environment. This information will be essential for future recruitment efforts, succession planning, and program evaluation.

Creative compensation management, in which pay is tailored to the needs of the organization, the nature of work, and the characteristics of the workforce, is playing an important strategic role in organizations. The team concept is rapidly gaining popularity due to the positive outcomes that many organizations have experienced after implementing such programs. Team-based, rather than individual, criteria for pay should be used when the goals of the business are to strengthen the team's performance—not only the individual employee's performance within the team. In a culture so dominated by individual goals and objectives, organizations must strive to be creative in their deployment of effective team incentive programs that communicate to the worker that group, rather than individual, performance is critical to success.

HOW TO MAKE TEAM-BASED PAY MORE SUCCESSFUL

Compensation is an important aspect of the success of team-based work designs, as discussed in this chapter. Exhibit 22.1 provides a checklist of best practices and key issues to consider when linking pay to team performance. We have created this list based on our own consulting experience and the literature. One important caveat is that effective compensation design is only one aspect that contributes to improved team performance. The firm also needs to consider other important issues in tandem. Additional practices in conjunction with team-based incentives that can enhance team performance are noted in Exhibit 22.2.

KEY ISSUES AND BEST PRACTICES WHEN DESIGNING TEAM-BASED INCENTIVES

- Never forget that you get what you measure and reward!
- The best way to reduce free-riding is through group pressure:
  - Group pressure increases through cohesion.
  - Cohesion increases by providing group rewards.
  - Rewards should go to the entire team and not be associated with one person, for example, "Walter's shop."
- Evaluation and rewards must take into account the difficulty of the assignment and the probability of failure. People will not take risks if they are penalized for taking on difficult assignments, especially if there are easier ways to be recognized.
- Space out rewards so that they are linked to different stages of projects to reinforce short-term accomplishments without losing sight of long-term objectives—for example, from key intermediate landmarks through patenting of innovations through commercialization of a project.

- If an employee works for multiple teams, utilize all available inputs for measuring team performance and allocating rewards.

- Identify "internal and external customers" of each group, and measure their expectations and assessments of teams.

- Reduce hierarchies (e.g., Technician I, II, III, etc.) as a way for promoting and rewarding people. Hierarchies create status and power differentials that are dysfunctional in a team environment.

- Use broadbanding as a flexible way to provide rewards without creating tall career-grade structures.

- Reward teams through lump-sum payments for landmark accomplishments. These are more noticeable and less contaminated with other factors, such as cost of living.

- Identify and reward key contributors through group nomination, utilizing cross-functional groups for the evaluation of nominees.

- Be creative in providing nonfinancial rewards that promote a team spirit such as trips, picture of the team in the company newspaper, and company events such as banquets or picnics.

- Use peer appraisals with the supervisor's consolidating and integrating this feedback so that it is provided to the employee in a manner that is useful.

INTERNAL TEAM ORGANIZATION

- Ensure that each team has an effective facilitator.
- Each individual should have a loosely specified role within the team; thus team composition needs to be carefully thought out, considering both personality and technical issues.
- Recognize major challenges to innovation: Being able to work with people and technical expertise are often at odds with each other. "Mavericks" need to be protected because they are crucial for innovation.

INCREASING SALES FORCE EFFECTIVENESS THROUGH COMPENSATION

Jerome A. Colletti

Colletti-Fiss, LLC
Management Consultants

Mary S. Fiss

Colletti-Fiss, LLC
Management Consultants

SEVEN YEARS HAVE PASSED since this chapter first appeared in the handbook. A great many changes have taken place in business in the intervening years. Total quality management, reengineering, and cost reduction are three examples of change initiatives that companies have pursued in recent years.[1] After a time of fervent cost cutting, business growth is now a top priority at many companies. Businesses have costs under control, and managers have, therefore, concluded that growing the top line is the key to future profitability and increased shareholder value. This desire to grow—by creating new markets, winning new customers, and continually improving processes to retain current customers—increases the pressure on the sales organization to achieve outstanding results. One of the consequences of this situation is that many companies are compelled to examine the effectiveness of their sales forces with a particular focus on existing compensation arrangements.

The old saying "The more things change, the more they remain the same" is certainly true about the role of sales compensation in helping companies increase sales effectiveness. The business environment today (and most likely for the near-term future) is very different than it was in 1991. However, sales compensation is very much on the minds of top managers in many companies today.

There are three reasons why this is so. First, our research shows that, depending on the industry, sales compensation makes up between 30 and 70 percent of the selling expense budget. The magnitude of this expense is large enough for concern on the part of top managers about a proper return on compensation investment regardless of the economic cycle of business. Second, the sales compensation plan is a powerful "signaling system" to the sales force about what is important to focus on. Ideally, a well-designed plan should direct, motivate, and reward a sales force for achieving business objectives that top managers desire. However, when the plan is out of sync with business objectives, the consequences can be as disastrous as a plan "in sync" can be positive. The popular business press regularly reports on companies who have experienced financial disaster only to discover that one of the root causes of their problem was how the sales force was paid.

And, finally, sales compensation plans do grow obsolete over time. Plan obsolescence is largely a function of the changes that take place in how customers buy or in the way they expect the purchasing process to work. This requires companies to rethink their processes for selling to and interacting with customers. This reexamination often results in the conclusion that the sales compensation plans require change to complement new sales roles, new customer relationship management processes, or both.

---

[1]For a discussion about how these three change management initiatives have impacted sales organizations, see Jerome A. Colletti and Lawrence B. Chonko, "Change Management Initiatives: Moving Sales Organizations from Obsolescence to High Performance," *The Journal of Personal Selling & Sales Management,* vol. 17, no. 2, spring 1997, pp. 1–30.

The overall objective of this chapter is to discuss how to design a sales compensation plan that contributes to and ultimately enhances sales effectiveness. *Sales effectiveness* is defined as an organization's ability to attract, retain, and expand business with its customers profitably. To achieve increased sales effectiveness, it is important to ensure that the sales compensation plan is designed and managed to be consistent with current business objectives.

In this chapter, we first describe the five positive outcomes that top managers look for in a successful sales compensation plan. Second, we describe a model, with related techniques, to use during plan design to help ensure that the compensation plan supports business objectives. Third, we introduce several incentive formula approaches. Fourth, we discuss the major challenges that top managers must address to manage the sales compensation plan effectively in the future.

FIVE POSITIVE OUTCOMES OF A SUCCESSFUL SALES COMPENSATION PLAN

Sales compensation is one of the most powerful tools available to management to achieve business results. The plan's principal objective is to direct a company's salespeople to sell to and interact with customers effectively. Whether a company wants increased volume, a better mix of customers or product sales, or more new accounts, the right compensation plan can help accomplish those objectives. In most sales organizations, the sales force is extremely interested in the sales compensation plan. In fact, sales representatives typically judge the plan by a single criterion: "Am I making more money now than I did a year ago?"

Management, on the other hand, typically judges the sales compensation plan's success on multiple criteria. In companies where sales compensation plays a key role in shaping the effective performance of the sales force, top management looks to the plan to contribute positively to five business outcomes: growth, profits, customer satisfaction, sales talent, and sales productivity.

Growth

The desire to grow—by creating new markets, winning new customers, and continually improving processes to retain current customers—is a top priority at most companies. The Alexander Group's "1997 Survey of Executive Confidence in Sales Growth" reported that 64 percent of the respondents expected to achieve sales growth of 15 percent or more. Our in-depth investigation into how companies achieve their sales objectives shows that the growth strategy they pursue is "deeper penetration of current customers." This suggests that these companies have gone back to the basic blocking-and-tackling approach to growth—selling more to current accounts, either new product sales to current buyers or more sales to new buyers within the same account. This sales strategy suggests a compensation plan that rewards the sales organization for (a) retaining and growing sales volume in current accounts and (b) booking sales with new customers. The challenge is to motivate and reward the sales force for profitable top-line growth. The biggest obstacle to doing so is often overcoming the inertia associated with "annuity"-oriented compensation—particularly plans that place a disproportionately high percentage of the variable compensation, 80 to 90 percent, on reaching volume objectives tied to last year's sales.

Profits

Increasingly, companies want salespeople to focus on profitable business. The availability of meaningful information about purchase transactions at the account level and the intense pressure in many industries on operating-profit margins are motivating executives in many companies to examine the mix of business sold to customers. Selling the right mix of products may produce better profits; therefore, a key question to investigate is this: Is the sales force motivated to and rewarded for selling the right mix of products?

Marshall Industries is a billion-dollar electronics distributor, headquartered outside Los Angeles. It was founded in 1954 on the simple idea of buy low and sell high, but its world became infinitely more complicated. Marshall continued to grow, says Rob Rodin, president and CEO, "but only through staggering manipulation and brute force."[2] The bigger the company grew, the worse the problems became. As Rodin told *Fast Company* magazine, the problem wasn't inside the system; the system was the problem. "It made sense for one division to hide inventory from another; they were paid to compete. It made sense for salespeople to ship orders ahead of schedule or hide customer returns; they were paid to make their monthly numbers. The system persuaded good people to make bad decisions."

Rodin's solution: Eliminate all pay for performance. In 1992, "we eliminated commissions, incentives, promotions, contests." The entire system now "encourages salespeople to invest months, even years, prying companies away from other distributors and turning them into Marshall customers." As one Marshall sales rep told *Fast Company,* "I can look out for the interest of the customer. I can take the long view. I can invest time with a new customer without worrying about paying my next gas bill." This is an extreme example of the action a company will take to ensure that its salespeople are selling the right products and services to customers—ones that meet their needs. It is, nonetheless, just one example, and, therefore, by reporting it, we do not mean to imply that companies are rushing to eliminate their sales incentive plans.

Customer Satisfaction.   In the early 1990s, we found a large number of companies embracing the idea of rewarding employees for customer satisfaction

---

[2]Curtis Hartman, "Sales Force," *Fast Company,* June/July 1997, pp. 134–146.

improvements. The tremendous interest in and recognition associated with the quality movement provoked the trend. The Baldrige Award acted as a lightening rod that focused top management attention on achieving excellence in quality and customer satisfaction. Virtually every company we met with in those days was focused on quality and customer satisfaction, and the sales organization felt the impact. Many companies took aggressive action to implement sales management practices and changed their sale compensation programs to reflect the importance they attached to customer satisfaction. Companies actually paid their salespeople as much as 25 percent of their variable compensation based on improvement in customer satisfaction scores.

While companies look to the sales organization as an integral player in sustaining and improving levels of customer satisfaction, a relatively recent update on the prevalence of paying sales incentive compensation based on customer satisfaction suggests that this trend may have peaked.[3] We have found (and other experts in sales compensation also report) that while the concept of paying the sales force based on customer satisfaction seemed attractive initially, the major stumbling block in doing so has been measurement. Defining what "customer satisfaction" means and then measuring it so that it can be linked to the sales compensation process has discouraged companies from hard-wiring it to the sales force's variable pay. Jim King, the director of sales at Boehringer-Inglheim, marketers of ethical pharmaceuticals, told us he is not convinced customer satisfaction surveys are valid. He gave an example: "We can take a survey out to a managed care customer and ask, 'What do you think of Boehringer-Ingelheim?' The response really depends on whether the customer has had any contact with Boehringer-Ingelheim in his present position, and it depends on the latest contact. If we are having a lot of trouble signing a contract with them, they tend to—at least in my opinion—think that Boehringer-Ingelheim are a bunch of clowns. If we give them a hard time on rebates, they think we're clowns. If we give them a lot of rebate money, and we're pretty easy to deal with, then we're great guys."

The net result is that today a smaller portion of pay—whether merit increases, special rewards, or incentive compensation—is tied to customer satisfaction because in many companies, the sales force, and, in fact, all customer contact personnel, have learned how to meet and exceed customer requirements.

Sales Talent

In most companies, top management looks to the compensation plan to help attract and retain the caliber of people it needs to successfully sell to and interact with customers. Attracting and retaining top-notch talent is one of the most serious

---

[3] "Sales Compensation: Are You Getting What You're Paying For?" *Sales Manager's Bulletin,* Bureau of Business Practices, December 30, 1995, pp. 6–7.

challenges faced by companies today according to a recent McKinsey & Company research study.[4]

The study indicates that the number of 35- to 44-year-olds in the United States will decline by 15 percent between 2000 and 2015. Our own experience shows that this is the very age group that represents approximately 60 percent of the typical sales force. Top managers will be challenged to develop processes and programs to win the talent war and, as the McKinsey study also points out, to use "differentiated compensation" more effectively because it is among the top five factors that motivate talented people to select and remain with a particular employer.

A strong sales force is a major competitive advantage, especially in highly contentious markets—markets characterized by high product parity, markets in which all the major players offer virtually equal high levels of product quality and customer service. In such situations, a company's advantage is the relationship between the customer and the salesperson. As one executive told us, his company's objective in this type of competitive environment was to "shrink-wrap" the salesperson around the product offering so that a company employee became the source of differentiation. The sales compensation plan plays a pivotal role in attracting and retaining talented salespeople. Thus, a question to ask about a current plan is: Does it help the company hire and keep the right salespeople?

Sales Productivity

Today, most companies view their customers as "assets" of the business. Thus, investments in salespeople, who regularly interact with customers, are periodically reviewed for improvement. Three years ago, a sales job well done in a given industry produced $1 to $1.5 million in revenues. To justify that salesperson with today's potentially smaller margins, one or both of two things may have to happen: (1) Volume will have to be higher, usually twice as much or more, and/or (2) the mix of business will have to change, both in what customers buy and in which customers to address. If the salesperson's average productivity was $1.2 million a year, it may now have to be $2.4 to $3 million with an improved product and customer mix so that a company will get the better margin with volume.

Moreover, the productivity issue is dynamic. Today, an entry-level person may have to produce $700,000 in sales while a senior salesperson may have to produce $2.5 million, but those numbers are not fixed. Each year they must rise by some significant factor if the company plans to continue investing in direct resources. Top managers often ask us what they should expect a salesperson to produce—a figure that varies by industry—and once we get the figure, they want to know if it stays set. The unhappy answer is no; it has to go up.

---

[4]Elizabeth G. Chambers, Mark Fouler, Helen Handfield-Jones, Steven M. Harkin, and Edward G. Michaels III., "The War for Talent," *The McKinsey Quarterly,* November 3, 1998, pp. 44–57.

LINKING SALES COMPENSATION TO BUSINESS MANAGEMENT

The sales compensation plan needs to support the company's business strategy. Three of the more important elements of business strategy include: business objectives (e.g., financial goals—growth, profit, shareholder return); marketing strategy (e.g., offerings, value proposition, markets targeted, channels used); and sales strategy (e.g., the plan of action that defines how to sell to and interact with customers). The sales compensation plan design effort should follow a series of decision-making steps that, when successfully completed, ensures that the plan is consistent with business strategy. Figure 23.1 illustrates the interrelationship between business management considerations and the five essential components of sales compensation plan design.

Designing a sales compensation plan is a derivative process. In other words, the design of the proper plan is derived from the circumstances and objectives unique to that company. Over the years we have found that the most significant

FIGURE 23.1   Model for optimal sales compensation plan design.

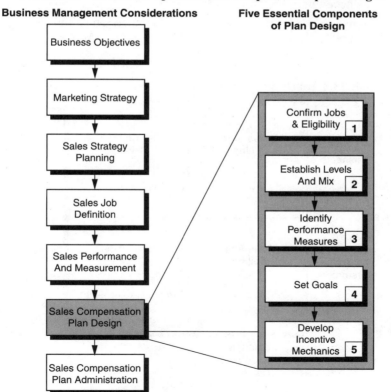

challenge faced by companies during the design process is to understand exactly how to link strategy, jobs, performance measures and goals, and pay together into an optimal plan. Doing so requires a clear definition of the type of selling to be performed by the sales force.

We have found the *Sales Strategy Matrix* to be a helpful tool in clarifying sales jobs and in aligning those jobs with the company's business objectives. As Figure 23.2 illustrates, there are two variables: buyers and products. Buyers fall into two groups: prospects and customers. Products also fall into two groups: existing and new and/or additional in-line products. This two-by-two matrix defines the types of selling opportunities facing a company in each quadrant of the matrix. The four selling opportunities are the following:

Retention selling. The objective of retention selling is to sell established customers current products on a reorder basis. The sales job is to successfully retain the revenue stream of business with those customers.

Penetration selling. This type of selling involves maximizing the customer relationship by selling a broader range of products (new or existing) to current customers or selling more to customers within an established account.

Conversion selling. The objective of conversion selling is to get competitors' customers to switch to the company's products.

FIGURE 23.2   Sales Strategy Matrix.

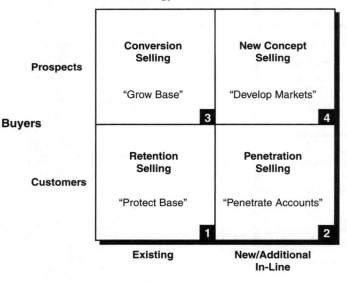

New market selling. This type of selling is probably the most difficult; its objective is to attract new customers to the company by selling new products.

While every situation is individual, one of the principal values of the Sales Strategy Matrix is to provide a framework to define and deploy a company's sales jobs. Figure 23.3 illustrates one likely set of sales jobs that a company could deploy in attracting, retaining, and expanding business with customers. The four jobs illustrated in this figure are the following:

FIGURE 23.3   Sales Strategy Matrix.

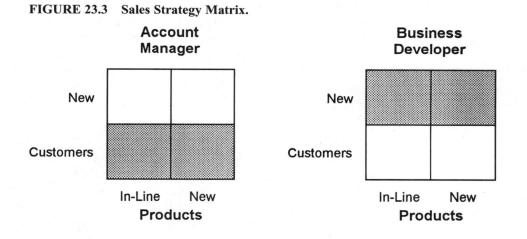

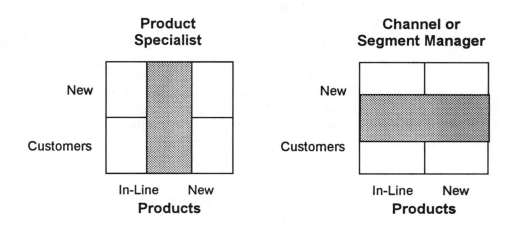

Account manager. Our research shows that it is typical for an established company to realize 60 to 80 percent of its business from selling in-line products to current customers. When this is a company's goal—to retain current business and to expand by selling additional products or new products to buyers within the current account base—an account manager's job is established. In recent years, companies have learned that account managers can be deployed in a variety of ways—by assigned geographical area, by an assigned industry, by assigned accounts covered telephonically—and, by doing so, the percent of revenue realized through customer retention can be substantial and profitable.

Business developer. Many companies have discovered that the sales cycle differs by the type of customer. For example, winning business with a new customer often takes three to four times longer than doing more business with a current customer. Thus, some companies adopt a *business developer* job. The focus of that job is to attract new customers to a company by selling current in-line products, new products, or both.

Product sales specialist. A company with a single, large sales force that represents the products of many business divisions often finds that it is impractical for its sales representatives to be experts in the application of all products. Thus, one form of sales specialization that is used is the *product sales specialist job.* This job specializes in understanding a buyer's (current customer or new buyer) unique requirements and then tailoring the solution with the right mix of a company's products and services. Product sales specialists typically work across a broad slice of a market (as illustrated in Figure 23.3); however, it would not be unusual for individuals in this job to be dedicated to either a defined set of customers or to new accounts.

Channel or segment sales manager. As a business grows and matures, management comes to realize that the only way it can address the diversity of sales opportunities available in the markets in which it competes is to consider new routes of access to customers. Often times it is more efficient and effective for a company to reach customers through a nondirect sales force channel. Figure 23.3 illustrates that, across the product line, for a defined segment of the market, an *alternative sales channel* (also referred to as a *segment*) could be covered by a specialized resource.

The number and type of sales jobs (and sales channels) derived from applying the Sales Strategy Matrix to a particular company is largely influenced by the growth and profit expectations of top managers. Our research shows, however, that when a company is examining the effectiveness of its sales compensation, the top three reasons for doing so are to accomplish the following:

1. Improve sales productivity.
2. Improve sales coverage to current customers.
3. Grow sales overall profitably.

Thus, to achieve these objectives, we observe that companies that are most satisfied with their sales compensation plan start with a review and clarification of the types of sales jobs used to do business with customers.

ESTABLISHING THE GROUND RULES FOR PLAN DESIGN

Prior to the actual plan design process, it is critical to establish the basis for decisions about sales compensation plan elements. The two key areas that require management's attention are the company's philosophy of pay and the principles or rules that establish expectations for the program.

Philosophy of Pay

To develop an effective sales compensation plan, its design should be consistent with an organization's compensation philosophy. Frequently, this philosophy is informal, undocumented, or both. Therefore, we suggest that plan designers discuss with management and then document the company's compensation philosophy, using the following list of key criteria:

1. *Objectives.* Confirmation of the strategic purpose of compensation and its elements
2. *Labor market comparison.* Identification of relevant companies and job matches.
3. *Competitive positioning.* Percentile standing for pay levels.
4. *Salary-to-variable pay ratio.* Based on the company's philosophy of risk versus reward, competitive practice, and the influence of eligible job(s) in getting and keeping business with customers.
5. *Base salary determination.* Factors and practices that will be used in setting and adjusting base salary
6. *Short-term incentives.* Eligibility and type of incentives considered appropriate
7. *Long-term incentives.* Eligibility and type of incentive considered appropriate
8. *Communication.* Roles and responsibilities

Confirming this information is the first step to ensure that the sales compensation plan will be designed to be consistent with other compensation programs in the company.

Compensation Principles

Typically, the design of a sales compensation plan is influenced by the compensation philosophy and practices used throughout a company. In fact, in many companies top managers ask human resources or the compensation function to ensure that the sales compensation plan is in alignment with the enterprise's programs because employees are moved in and out of the sales organization as part of a companywide career development initiative. With that background in mind, sales compensation plans should be grounded in core principles that are compatible with those that guide a company's overall compensation and reward system. While there are many publications—including this handbook—that provide details about the tenets of effective and appropriate compensation, the following briefly summarizes essentials that a sales compensation plan designer should keep in mind:

1. The compensation philosophy must actively reinforce the company's strategy and vision to achieve its objectives.
2. Compensation programs must be consistent with legal and regulatory requirements.
3. Compensation should be consistent with the financial requirements and administrative capabilities of the company.
4. Compensation must be consistent with both internal equity and external requirements to attract, retain, and motivate talented employees.
5. Compensation program details must be based on clearly defined jobs and their role within the buying and selling process.

In addition to these core principles, it is generally useful to establish other ground rules specific to a company's needs. Consideration should be given to the following topics:

1. *Business objectives.* What objectives are critical for this year? What objectives must the plan reinforce?
2. *Strategy.* What are the company's marketing and sales strategies?
3. *Job definition.* What jobs will be required to achieve the company's strategies?
4. *Performance measurement.* How should performance be defined and tracked over time? How should performance objectives be set? What level of achievement should be expected? What is the range of performance that can be used in sales compensation plan design?
5. *Compensation plan.* Who should be involved in the design process? What mechanics are most appropriate to direct and motivate the sales jobs?
6. *Administration.* When should we credit performance for incentive purposes? What is our communication strategy? Who should be involved?

Once the ground rules have been established, an efficient, five-step design process can be initiated.

FIVE ESSENTIAL COMPONENTS OF PLAN DESIGN

There are five essential components of sales compensation. Figure 23.1 illustrates the relationship of these components to business management considerations addressed prior to plan design. The ideal design process, including the sequence of decisions required, is a derivative process. That is, the design of an effective and appropriate plan is based on the solid foundation provided by business management decisions for the plan year.

Design Team

In order to address the objectives and strategy of complex business environments, companies generally charter a design team, or a designated group of cross-functional resources that bring to the process the necessary knowledge and focus. Functions most frequently represented on this type of team are marketing, sales management, human resources, finance, sales administration, and information systems. Using a teamed approach to plan design results in more widespread acceptance of the new sales compensation program, earlier ability of key executives to affect the decision-making process, and a plan that is aligned with multiple objectives.

Whether designed by a team or by one or two key individuals, the following five essential components must be addressed through the design process.

Step 1. Confirm Jobs and Eligibility

Key concept: Determine incentive eligibility based on degree of impact in the buying decision and participation in the process to access and/or persuade and fulfill customer needs. Typically, positions that initiate, persuade, and fulfill in the customer coverage process, and those positions' line managers, are eligible to participate in the sales compensation program. Corporate philosophy is also a key determinant in eligibility to participate in a sales compensation program. For example, team members may be eligible for sales compensation only as long as they are on a customer team.

Step 2. Establish Pay Levels and Mix

Key concept: Ensure that pay levels are externally competitive, and internally equitable, based on the roles and responsibilities of the job. The total target cash compensation is the cash compensation (including base salary and variable incentive compensation) available for achieving expected results. Use of market data and application of the company's philosophy of pay result in a reference point for decisions about the level of compensation the company is willing to pay for each job. The total target cash compensation level for each job must be large enough to motivate and to pay for performance to drive business results.

Determination of the pay level for each job serves as a foundation for decisions related to the *mix* (ratio of base salary to incentive opportunity as percentages of the total target compensation; expressed as two portions of 100 percent) and *leverage* (the amount of "upside" opportunity beyond total target compensation that outstanding performers are expected to earn). The mix is determined by defined criteria, including the type of sale, sales cycle duration, number of transactions in a year, and degree of influence the job has on the decision to buy. The sales compensation plan should provide upside opportunity (leverage) consistent with the job, the company's philosophy of pay, and labor market realities. Outstanding pay should generally be available for excellent performers (i.e., the plan should provide increased dollars on the upside after target performance is achieved).

Step 3: Identify Performance Measures

Key concept: You get what you pay for. Three or fewer measures should be used, based on the key objectives of the organization, and the key accountabilities of the job. This is perhaps the most critical design component to address effectively. Several decisions are required to ensure that the performance measures selected are aligned with the business and the job, as follows:

Confirm business objectives impacted by the job(s). Examples include growth, profitability, productivity improvement, cost reduction, or customer loyalty and retention, or some combination of those five.

Select the indicators that are associated with achievement of those objectives. Ensure that systems or processes are in place for measurement. If a key indicator cannot be consistently tracked and achievement calculated, potential alternatives must be identified and examined.

Ensure that the measures are consistent with the job. Measures used in the sales compensation plan should be influenced through reasonable effort and behavior. Measures must be based on job roles and the salesperson's ability to impact results.

Determine the level of measurement. The unit of aggregation of results (territory, accounts, team, etc.) for the purposes of sales compensation calculation should be based on the level at which results are impacted by the job and the level to which company systems can accurately track, credit, and report results.

Confirm the relative importance of each measure. The weight of each measure in the plan is based on the strategic importance of each to the achievement of business objectives. In addition, the relative weight among measures helps the sales force understand how to deploy its time, based on the plan message and its alignment with management requirements.

The sales function is primarily responsible for the maximization of top-line results. Therefore, a measure of total volume is generally the first consideration for any sales job. The design process determines the appropriate measure of overall volume that can be associated with a salesperson's performance. This may mean total sales dollar volume, sales volume from new business, new business and recurring sales dollar volume from regular customer ordering (a measure of retention), revenue derived from volume, or number of units sold. In most plans, one measure should be a volume measure that rewards growth.

Additional criteria should complement the volume measure, communicating what type of volume is best, where the volume should come from, or how it should be achieved. Additional categories to consider include profitability (financial measures), sales productivity (may include both financial and nonfinancial measures), and strategic planning (generally nonfinancial measures).

Step 4. Set Goals

Key concept: Assign expectations for key performance measures based on job influence, and a uniform process. Once performance measures have been selected, many companies assign goals to the sales force for one or all of the selected measures. Particularly for volume or profitability-focused measures, these goals are frequently referred to as a *quota.* In the past, companies used primarily financial measures of performance in the sales compensation plan, and perhaps 50 percent of all companies established quotas. Many companies simply assigned a uniform percent or dollar increase across the sales force, based on the growth objectives for the plan year.

In today's competitive environment, many more companies are establishing performance expectations for both financial and nonfinancial measures. The process to arrive at goals varies widely across industries, companies, and types of measures. Regardless of practices, many firms find quota setting to be difficult and express frustration at both the process and the outcomes. However, giving proper attention to setting goals is essential to the success of the sales compensation plan. Properly assigning goals provides the opportunity to manage for results, allows for maximum flexibility, and visibly aligns the success of field resources with corporate resources.

Once goals are established, attention should be given to the *performance standards,* or the performance range associated with incentive payout. The sales compensation plan has varying degrees of payout depending on performance levels. Below a certain level of performance, no payout should occur. A threshold level of performance is used to communicate minimum standards of performance. Above a certain level of performance, many companies provide higher amounts. While a ceiling, or *cap,* is used in cases where it is difficult or impossible to set realistic ranges, an *uncapped plan* is generally desirable. However, earnings above an excellence level should become increasingly difficult to achieve. Some statistical rules of thumb for the performance range are based on an optimal performance distribution (e.g., 90 percent achieve threshold, 60 to 70 percent achieve or exceed goal, 10 to 15 percent reach or exceed excellence).

Step 5. Develop Incentive Mechanics

Key concept: Select plan mechanics based on desired relationship between pay and performance. Sales compensation in its broadest sense includes all elements of remuneration for sales and sales management positions. While base-salary-only plans are appropriate for nonpersuasive selling environments, many companies are moving to putting some percent of pay *at risk,* even for "nonselling" jobs in customer coverage organizations. Therefore, in this final component of plan design, all previous components are aligned through the plan mechanics associated with the incentive (or variable) element of total cash compensation. *Mechanics* refers to the type of plan, plan formula, and the ways in which incentive elements interact to calculate payment.

Plan Type

There are two primary plan types: commission plans and bonus plans. Either may be used in conjunction with base salary, or both may be used. In addition, either a bonus or commission may use a quota or goal; however, bonus plans always use some type of goal, while commissions may or may not use a goal or quota as one element in the calculation.

A *commission plan* provides a percent share or dollar amount tied to gross dollar sales, product unit sales, or gross profit dollars. Commission programs support absolute measurement systems—the more of a product or service sold, the greater the incentive paid. Commission may be *capped* or *uncapped.* This type of plan is most commonly used in new-market selling situations where individual persuasion skills and short sales cycles are key differentiators. Organizations use commission programs to reward individual effort and drive results, with payout directly tied to sales results. In some industries, commissions have typically been used to push new products and gain market share with specialized sales forces.

Bonuses are a percent of base pay, or a fixed dollar amount, for accomplishing objectives. They are most appropriately used in more complex sales environments, and are always goal-based, whether the goal is financial (volume, profitability, productivity) or nonfinancial. These programs support a relative measurement system—payout depends on performance against individual goals. They may be capped or uncapped. A salary-plus-bonus plan manages the amount of incentive payout to a preferred market rate while accommodating goal-based measurement.

Plan Formula

Plan formulas may be linked or unlinked:

- An *unlinked formula* means that additive payouts will be made in a series over time.

- A *linked formula* means that payout for one measure depends on achievement of another. Linking measures together within the formula ensures a clear message that two performance measures must receive the salesperson's attention. There are three ways to accomplish a linkage:

  - *Gate (or hurdle)*. *Hurdles* are the minimum performance levels a salesperson must achieve in one plan component to be eligible for variable pay in a different component.
  - *Multiplier*. *Multipliers*, or *modifiers, increase or decrease* the salesperson's earnings in that plan component based on performance in another measure.
  - *Matrix*. The *Matrix design* is used when there are two competing performance measures against which the salesperson must perform. The salesperson has to manage performance between two measures.

IMPLEMENTATION OF THE SALES COMPENSATION PROGRAM

Even the best-designed plans will fail if they are not implemented properly. A successful implementation will test the new plan, gain support throughout the organization, educate the company, and limit transition inefficiencies. Successful implementation uses various principles of adult learning to effectively and efficiently communicate and install a new sales compensation plan. As the implementation plan is developed, four elements critical to learning need to be addressed:

- *Motivation*. Adults are goal oriented and want to see the reason for learning what is being taught, for example, how to succeed under the plan.

- *Reinforcement*. Media and techniques should ensure that the message the company intends the plan to convey is consistently and positively reinforced.

- *Retention*. Adults must see a purpose for what is being communicated. The materials and media should include practice sessions to ensure that the participants have direct experience in how the plan works and how they can affect the payout.

- *Transference*. The information that the media and materials convey must be transferred into positive action on the part of the participant. The participants should be excited and want to use the information to enhance their current situation.

The thought of change in any aspect of sales compensation is daunting to most salespeople. Successful change management initiatives require an understanding of potential issues in order to anticipate the types of difficulties that may arise when something is new or done for the first time with the sales compensation plan.

It is a good idea, therefore, to use a structured change management process to guide planning and decision-making tasks related to the implementation of a new sales compensation plan. The objectives of a change process, as it pertains to introducing a new sales compensation plan, are to help in the following areas:

- Define specific changes and accountabilities.

- Explain why change is important now.

- Provide a framework for guiding the change process.

- Determine whether desired benefits and improvements are being achieved.

- Provide feedback to work associates who need to remain "in the know" about change results.

We have found that a three-step process to address these objectives is required for effective implementation. Briefly, the process involves the following:

1. Field managers who manage with the plan, and headquarters resources that administer the plan, should be fully knowledgeable about the company's philosophy of compensation, the principles used to guide plan development, the benefits of the program, and how plan participants can succeed under the plan. In addition, all aspects of administration should be thoroughly documented and understood. A special training program for these individuals will contribute significantly to plan success. Electronic "incentive calculators," plan announcement brochures, Q&As, and formal documentation provide managers with the tools to implement and manage with the sales compensation plan.

2. Once field management and headquarters resources are trained, the program should be introduced to the sales organization. A group presentation that is led by executive management and individual follow-up sessions to answer specific questions are both required. Full communication including detailed descriptions of the reports that will be available to the plan participants are keys to successful implementation.

Note that the calculation of the incentive payment is not, and should not, be the responsibility of the sales resource. Calculation is based on information from various systems, and reports should be timely and accurate. Even the best-designed plan is likely to be considered a failure if salespeople feel they need to constantly verify the accuracy of these reports.

3. A formal assessment process should be completed at least annually. However, an interim evaluation may be undertaken after one or two payout periods to determine the extent to which the plan is supporting the behaviors and delivering the results for which it was designed. The design team, or designated personnel, should examine the results of the evaluation and assess any need for change.

MANAGEMENT OF SALES COMPENSATION IN THE FUTURE

For most companies, the essence of business success is the ability to attract and retain customers. Because the sales force is a vital link between a company and its customers, it holds the key to business growth and profitability. A properly directed, motivated, and rewarded sales force will make a significant contribution to the achievement of these business measures. We believe that the sales compensation plan is one of the more powerful tools available to management to achieve optimal sales force motivation and performance.

In the future, we believe that top management will continue to ask for increased sales performance and profitability. Sales compensation plan designers will be challenged by three strategic forces, as described below.

1. *Global expansion and business consolidation.* In the quest for growth, many companies will continue to expand their business presence around the globe by organic growth, through mergers and acquisitions, or both. As a result, the sales organization is often characterized by a mix of globally and locally deployed resources focused on meeting the shifting needs of increasingly complex customers. Additionally, as companies are merged or acquired, sales organizations, often with widely different sales cultures and value systems, must be brought together successfully to realize the benefits of consolidation.

The key to successful design of sales compensation plans in this ever-changing business environment is to consider three guiding principles: "focus, flexibility, and simplicity."[5] *Focus* means knowing what to concentrate on. One of the most effective ways to establish focus for a sales organization is through the measurement system. Often times what gets measured, gets rewarded. Whether a company is expanding globally or integrating sales organizations, a common set of metrics—usually no more than three—increases the likelihood of success.

Flexibility is required in the design of sales compensation plans because selling situations vary widely not only in local markets within the United States but also outside it. The challenge faced by the plan designer is how much flexibility to provide in the elements of the compensation plan. We find that the creation of *design templates* is an effective approach to help guide the customization of plans.

Simplicity in plan design is required so that sales personnel not only understand how they are paid but also can easily move throughout the company's national or global sales organization. Typically, simplicity is most important in constructing payout formula. If participants in a sales compensation plan cannot readily calculate their actual earnings under the plan, our research shows that a significant amount of motivational value is lost.

---

[5]David G. Schick, "Developing Incentive Compensation Strategies in a Global Sales Environment," *ACA Journal,* autumn 1996, pp. 54–67.

The challenge plan designers face is, thus, how to keep in their line of sight the importance of balancing these requirements—focus, flexibility, and simplicity— with the constantly changing business environment in which plans must operate.

2. *New sales roles and talent requirements.* A growing number of U.S. and foreign companies are introducing new sales roles into their organizations to retain current customers and gain access to new customers. A *sales role* can be defined as the part an employee plays in the process of interacting with a customer. Top managers introduce new sales roles into a company based on an evolution in the number and types of customers served, the size of the product line, and the basis for doing business—transactional versus relationship. Virtually no company is immune to the changes that are taking place in the ways customers want to do business. This means that companies are constantly adjusting the sales coverage process and the roles—and thus impact on its jobs—to meet customer needs.[6]

The challenges related to how to compensate employees for performing new sales roles falls into three categories:

- Clarifying or redefining jobs—sales and other customer contact positions— as a result of assigning or reassigning responsibilities to employees for playing a part in retaining, expanding, or acquiring a revenue stream through interaction with customers.

- Altering compensation plan(s) to reflect job accountabilities associated with new sales roles.

- Implementing new sales compensation plans to support new sales roles that are often objected to, resisted, or both because the sales force is reluctant to accept change

Sales roles in companies are constantly changing to meet and exceed the requirements of the competitive environment. Add to this the fact that companies will be challenged to attract and retain talented people as revealed earlier by McKiney's study. Thus, it is not likely that the current situation will reverse its course any time soon. To successfully meet these challenges, a company must come forward with new and innovative compensation solutions.

3. *Automated sales compensation management systems.* The days of spreadsheet sales compensation administration could come to an end within the next 2 to 3 years. As a result of advances in computer hardware and software, plan designers will have available to them new options to truly manage all facets of the sales compensation plan's design, cost, and administration. One of the more difficult, yet exciting challenges companies face is how to take advantage of the new sys-

---

[6]For a more in-depth discussion of this topic, see Jerome A. Colletti and Mary S. Fiss, *Compensating New Sales Roles: How to Design Rewards That Work in Today's Selling Environment,* AMACOM, a division of American Management Association International, December 1998.

tems that are either available or will be available to give the plan designer more flexibility in adapting sales compensation to changes in business strategy and objectives. Plan administration software ranges from standard, prepackaged solutions to highly sophisticated, customized solutions. Currently, there are five companies that are competing for business in the automated sales compensation management environment: Again Technologies, Callidus, Incentive Systems, Synygy, and Trilogy. Knowing the right solution to choose will require a careful examination of the needs and requirements of a particular company.

Trilogy, for example, suggests in its marketing literature that arriving at the right solution requires careful consideration of four decision criteria: (a) functionality, (b) administration and ease of use, (c) reporting, and (d) system architecture. Ultimately, the business goal for many companies is to select the right automated sales compensation management solution to reduce the cost and increase the efficiency of plan administration. Our research shows that it is not unusual for a company to spend between $1,000 to $2,000 per sales representative in plan administration. Obviously, if an automated plan administration system can help a company reduce this cost and, at the same time, improve plan reporting and communication, it is essential that plan designers learn about and take advantage of the opportunity.

CONCLUDING REMARKS

The purpose of this chapter is to help the reader design a sales compensation plan that contributes to and ultimately enhances sales effectiveness. We will have succeeded in that objective if this chapter clarifies when there is a need to act and how to go about taking that action. We hope our readers will better sense and respond to the need for change in order to optimize their business opportunities as a result of reading this chapter.

C H A P T E R

THE ROLE
OF COMPETENCIES
IN SALES FORCE
SUCCESS

Jay Jacobsen, Performance Practice Manager

Holden Corporation

Jim Holden, Founder and Chief Executive Officer

Holden Corporation

Todayʼs selling organizations compete in an environment characterized by frequent shifts in customer buying patterns, changes to the traditional organizational construct, greater recruitment and selection risk, and rapid technological advances. To successfully meet these challenges, sales forces must strive for new and innovative ways of gaining a competitive advantage. This demands rigorously assessing and updating their skills, knowledge, and behaviors, thus ensuring they are armed with the precise *competencies* to remain competitive. Successful organizations must also become learning organizations, fostering their ability to sell differently and respond rapidly to competitive threats and new markets. It requires sales forces to have well-designed internal processes and mechanisms for continuously determining the right competencies and an organizational infrastructure that applies this knowledge to gain a competitive advantage. Competency-based management systems provide a structural tool for achieving this. Implemented correctly, competency programs can be leveraged as a learning tool to drive sales forces' success through increased intellectual capital, performance management, recruitment and selection, innovative compensation, and strengthening of the sales manager's role.

For most sales forces, the marketplace is becoming more complex and fluid. Markets open, close, and change rapidly due to influences such as demographic shifts, technological advances, increased globalization, and evolving customer buying patterns. Domestic customer buying patterns have been altered as a result of changing age structures, geographic shifts, white-collar employment growth, and population diversity. The explosive growth of new technologies such as the Internet, telecommunications advancements, and software development has created new markets and expanded the ability of organizations of every size to reach new customers.

The Internet is being leveraged by sales organizations as a powerful tool for communicating internal information and researching potential markets and opportunities. Changes to the global geopolitical map have opened new markets in Asia and the former Soviet block. These forces present both opportunities and competitive threats. Insightful organizations have responded by revising their marketing plans and business strategies. However, that alone will not ensure success. Sales organizations must have the know-how and competencies to effectively compete at the customer level and execute a global, complex marketing plan. The sales force must remain intellectually "nimble" and in possession of the correct competencies to exploit these new and rapidly developing opportunities. Through flexibility, they can gain a competitive edge by maximizing their sales planning, understanding their customers' needs, and delivering value-added solutions.

Changes to the traditional, hierarchical reporting structure and organizational construct of the sales force are driving the need to implement new and innovative learning and performance management systems. Reporting relationships are becoming more complex, frequented by team selling, matrix management, "virtual-office" environments, and sales force specialization. As a result, consistent mentoring and learning opportunities for individual sales representatives have been adversely impacted. The traditional practice of the sales representative's "learning" under the tutelage and development of a single manager and chain of command is no longer the norm. This phenomenon provides additional incentive for sales organizations to "fill the coaching void" by implementing competency-based management programs as a means of maintaining themselves as learning organizations and introducing a dynamic and consistent coaching element.

Additionally, changes to the organizational construct have made it more difficult to effectively and consistently communicate corporate strategy and clearly articulate what is important to be learned. Well-designed competency programs not only provide a framework for individual learning, they also align themselves with and communicate the corporate strategy and values.

To be fully effective, competency programs should be integrated into the recruitment and selection process, ensuring that sales organizations are hiring and retaining only those individuals who possess the desired competencies and know-how. Sales organizations are faced with rising recruitment costs and a job market characterized by significant employee movement from one entity to another. Keeping in mind the need to continuously ensure that the sales force possesses the precise competencies to effectively compete, a competency-based recruitment and selection process can be critical to an organization's competitive readiness. Sales force mis-hirings are costly, both in direct costs and revenue opportunities lost. Effective competency programs, however, fully aligned with the recruitment and selection process, increase the hiring success rate, shorten the learning curve, and increase employee retention.

Thus, the enlightened sales force can generate great benefits from well-executed competency-based programs. Implementing a competency-based management system begins with the determination of key success competencies. This is followed by the construction of a behaviorally based competency model used as the foundation for developing performance management, organizational development, recruitment and selection, and competency-based reward programs

COMPETENCY-BASED MANAGEMENT SYSTEMS IN A SALES ENVIRONMENT

Within a sales environment, a well-executed, competency-based management system results in three important benefits:

- It reinforces and communicates the high-level business plan and tactical sales plan.

- It conveys that ferociously competitive sales organizations are also learning organizations, and it emphasizes that learning is important and specifies what should be learned.

- It serves as a basis for communicating a "revised compact" with the sales force, stressing that the organization values competencies as a method of gaining a competitive edge. As a result, competency development is critical to personal and organizational development. Therefore, when employees increase their proficiency in the key competencies, they become more versatile and valuable, and they will receive greater rewards and opportunities, both vertically and horizontally in the organization.

Successful implementation of competency programs in selling organizations will depend as much on program delivery, effective integration, and communication as it depends on the precise accuracy of the competencies selected. Competencies will continue to evolve, but sales organizations will have few opportunities to "get it right" when launching a new competency-based program. Many sales organizations select strikingly similar competencies (Schuster and Zingheim, 1996). Therefore, an organization's opportunity to gain a competitive edge results from its ability to leverage a competency program to advance individual development, recruitment of new hires, and improved compensation systems.

When implementing a competency program in a sales environment, it is essential that the following objectives are successfully met:

- *Internal marketing, not just communication.* It is surprising how many sales organizations fail to understand that simply communicating the introduction of a competency program is not sufficient. Instead, organizations must "market" the program and demonstrate personal benefits to the participants. Communication creates victims; marketing enrolls participants!

- *Alignment up and down the sales chain-of-command.* Competency programs require active endorsement. Sales management must not only openly endorse the program, they must demonstrate it through their actions by completing required tasks, meeting deadlines, and insisting on subordinate compliance at all levels. Failure to do so will result in rampant cynicism.

- *Flexible and self-correcting mechanisms.* Organizations readily acknowledge that competency requirements change. However, many fail to implement a process for capturing competency changes and updating competency models, training programs, and recruitment and selection tools. Therefore, a process for reassessing competency requirements must be in place when initiating programs.

- *Validating the competency model.* Demonstrating that there is a correlation between superior performance and competency development is critical to the program's credibility.

DETERMINING THE KEY COMPETENCIES

An initial and vital step in implementing a competency program is the determination of desired key competencies. *Competencies are skills, knowledge, and behaviors, measurable and observable in terms of performance, that are linked to successful or superior job performance.* Competency selection can focus on an individual position, title, job level, or sales team.

Sales organizations with an in-depth knowledge of the marketplace, their competition, their customers, and strategy will have a decided advantage in accurately determining their key competency requirements. Competencies must also include behaviors and skills that are accurate predictors of superior performance. In addition, because of the rapidly changing marketplace, the competency selection must be visionary and include anticipated competencies needed for future success. The ability to accurately select competencies, therefore, has dependencies to the organization's strengths in areas such as competitive intelligence, business planning, and customer needs awareness.

There are a number of alternative methods that can be used to determine an organization's key competencies. They include:

- Strategy discussions with senior management

- Behaviorally based interviews at all levels of the sales organization

- Customer interviews, focus groups, and Delphi techniques

- Think-Tank sessions focusing on future needs

- Competitive intelligence reports

- Examination of business and marketing plans

Competency selection must also focus on those behaviors that are predictors of success. One method of ascertaining this information is success profiling. *Success-profiling programs* expand beyond knowledge and skills by determining job-related behaviors of the most successful members of the sales force. This may include how well an individual utilizes technology, galvanizes internal resources, keeps abreast of internal sales support systems, or seeks outside training and development. Because these behaviors do not easily surface during traditional interviews, success-profiling methods require that successful sales force members be studied over a period of time to ascertain job-related behaviors.

Once the competencies have been determined from the selected data gathering method, the organization can assemble a detailed competency model to be used as the basis for assessing the current state (current level of competency proficiency of the sales force), training and development, recruitment and selection, and reward systems.

COMPETENCY MODELS

After determining the desired competencies, organizations should develop a competency model, or map, that delineates the key competencies deemed critical to success for a given position, level, or title. Competency model development is grounded in the belief that excellent performers have knowledge, skills, and behaviors that are identifiable and distinguishable from those of employees performing at less successful levels. Competency maps should identify the key competencies and include clear descriptions of behaviors at varying degrees or levels of competency proficiency. These varying degrees of proficiency are commonly referred to as *behavioral anchors* and describe, in behavioral terms, the type of desired behavior demonstrated at each graduation of competency proficiency. For a given competency, the descriptive anchors vary at different levels by the degree of application, complexity, frequency of use, and amount of effort expended (Spencer and Spencer, 1993). Detailed, descriptive behavioral anchors are critical for the following reasons:

- The sales force must be able to clearly understand the type of behavior(s) required of them if competency maps are to be effective.

- Sales managers must be able to recognize, assess, and coach to the behavioral anchors.

- Trained assessors must evaluate individuals and teams against the anchors.

- Recruitment and selection criteria will be developed around the anchor descriptions.

As a result of these key dependencies, the competency model serves as the foundation and fulcrum from which personal development, recruitment, and competency-based pay programs are developed. Consequently, the model must be viewed as a "living document," continuously revisited to examine the competency content and behavioral anchors.

Aligning sales force competencies to the business strategy is frequently mentioned as a goal of competency model development. However, the discussion focuses on the selection of the competency itself, neglecting an equally important decision—what level of individual competency proficiency is optimal for a sales position or title? Organizations that automatically assume their sales force must be at the highest level of competency development (for a given competency) will fail to align their competency program to an important aspect of their sales strategy—their "approach to market." Organizations with well-defined approach-to-market strategies have a keen awareness of the desired level of competency proficiency required to maximize their effectiveness. For example, a key competency for sales organizations is *competitive adeptness or awareness.* For telemarketers selling magazine subscriptions, however, the selling experience is limited to a brief customer encounter, with little opportunity to apply *competitive awareness,* perhaps with the exception of pricing. Investing substantial training time and financial resources to develop a telemarketer to attain a high level of competitive awareness would be unnecessary. Conversely, in a complex sales environment with long sales cycles, the sales force must operate at a higher level of competency proficiency. In this case, an account executive must analyze competitor strategies, utilize competitive counter tactics, seek ongoing competitive insight, and develop a competitive, value-based sales plan. Understanding the company's approach to market, therefore, allows organizations to develop competency models that accurately reflect their individual needs, thereby gaining a competitive advantage in resource allocation, recruitment, and organizational development.

PERFORMANCE MANAGEMENT AND COMPETENCY DEVELOPMENT

After a competency model has been fully developed, the organization must evaluate the members of the sales force against the selected competencies and appropriate desired level of proficiency as an initial step toward building a competency-based performance management system. In order to successfully apply a competency model to performance management, several key integrated processes must be in place. These include:

- Clearly established levels of acceptable performance within the model

- Assessment tools to accurately evaluate individuals

- Formal and informal programs for increasing competency proficiency, including a focus on management coaching

The organization must establish criteria for acceptable levels of deviation, the speed at which individuals are permitted to get to the acceptable level, and the consequences for failing to do so. This is often the Achilles heel of many competency-based programs. In a sales organization, however, without clearly stated consequences (and rewards), the program will quickly lose credibility.

There are a variety of approaches for evaluating individuals against the desired state for each competency. Essentially, each approach involves evaluations by trained observers and other key parties. The goal is to rate individuals numerically according to the behavioral anchors for each appropriate competency. Many organizations use a team-based or multisource approach. In some cases, the individual being evaluated can supply information to the evaluation team. Moreover, in some organizations, customers provide insight. Whichever technique is used, the employee should be quickly informed of the results in behavioral terms that are easy to understand. Once the results are determined, the manager, along with the employee, must agree on a developmental plan and timeframe for increasing the employee's scores.

One of the most powerful applications of competency models is that it provides the front-line sales manager with a behaviorally based coaching tool. Although much has been written about the need for front-line sales managers to focus on coaching, sales organizations often fail to develop their front-line sales managers into effective coaches. The common belief is they lack coaching skills and only focus on "hard" sales results; therefore, they should be provided training in basic coaching. After their training, however, even with increased coaching acumen, the typical performance conversation with a subordinate still reverts to hard sales results and performance against quota—perhaps with a kinder, gentler tone, or equally as limiting, a Knute Rockne type of speech. Unfortunately, too often overlooked is that a front-line sales manager lacks the tools and information to be an effective coach. The competency model can provide the missing link, the play book, that changes the nature of the coaching experience and the performance management dynamic. In a competency-based performance management system, the manager can focus on both hard results and success behaviors as described in the competency model. Put another way, the coach has the information to focus on the mechanics of the golf swing, not just how far the ball travels. Placed in the hands of the sales manager, the competency model changes the coaching dynamic by emphasizing competencies and skills required for success, not just reviewing hard numbers and past results.

The challenges and requirements of competency-based performance systems, changes to the traditional organizational sales model, and sales automation technology have created new competency requirements for front-line sales managers themselves. They must possess the skills, knowledge, and abilities to successfully develop their subordinates in the key competencies deemed necessary for success. This includes the ability to behaviorally identify, articulate, and describe the desired behaviors in terms that the subordinate can understand and apply toward account planning, executive-level calling, and value proposition development. The challenge will become increasingly complex as organizations continue to migrate toward remote and matrix management reporting constructs. The amount of direct face-to-face interaction between the manager and the subordinate will continue to be reduced. The successful sales manager must have the competencies required to be effective within this newly evolving environment.

In addition to direct coaching from sales managers, the organization should provide other learning vehicles to enhance competency development. This can take the form of working with more seasoned sales representatives, formal internal training, external training, education, and outside readings. However, the employees must recognize as part of the new compact that the organization will provide vehicles for competency development, but the employees themselves are ultimately accountable for their personal success.

APPLYING THE COMPETENCY MODEL TO RECRUITMENT AND SELECTION

As organizations face the challenge of competing in markets that demand new or different competencies, they have an opportunity to gain a competitive advantage by applying the competency model to the recruitment and selection process. Executed correctly, the sales force can quickly move up the competency learning curve by recruiting individuals who either possess the desired competency or show a strong capacity to learn rapidly. Those organizations that best identify their key success competencies and implement hiring systems with well-trained recruiters will have a decided advantage over their competition in improving their hiring "hit rate." Properly implemented, a competency-based recruitment and selection process will identify only those candidates who have demonstrated, through past behavior, that they possess the competencies required for success.

While there are a number of alternative processes and systems that integrate competencies into sales recruitment, a viable plan should include the following elements:

- It must be comprehensive, beginning with the initial phase of résumé screening or exploratory conversations and continue through the more interactive levels of the hiring process.

- It must incorporate behaviorally based interviews that permit candidates to demonstrate their level of proficiency for each competency. Interview questions should be developed requiring candidates to cite examples from their past experience. Answers should be complete and specific—not vague or theoretical. The focus is on demonstrated behaviors, not hypothetical speculation.

- It should be a collaborative interview involving more than one interviewer. This increases the objectivity of the process.

- It should include an opportunity to observe the candidate in a live sales simulation.

To be fully effective, the process must be rigidly adhered to. The process should not be intended to determine who are the best candidates out of a pool in a forced ranking approach. Rather, it must be seen as a "gate" requiring a successful rating against predetermined hiring criteria.

SALES COMPENSATION AND COMPETENCIES

Because of the relationship between competencies and superior performance, organizations are attracted to the concept of linking compensation to competency attainment and development. However, the relationship between individual performance and competencies is only one compelling justification for implementing competency-based pay. An examination of traditional sales compensation plans reveals that many compensation plan components, beyond standard commissions, are independent remedies for current behavioral problems within the sales force or short-term business strategies. Generally, a sales plan is introduced and remains in place throughout the plan year despite the potential for changing priorities. In subsequent years, the organizations must examine their strategic priorities and redesign various plan elements to align with the current business strategy. As a result, the sales force must be subjected to plan changes requiring reeducation, often resulting in distraction and cynicism.

Competency-based pay programs, on the other hand, provide an opportunity to reduce major overhauls and redesign fallout. By assiduously maintaining the competency model, competency-based pay plans can be "self-correcting" in that, at a snapshot in time, they include only those key competency requirements deemed critical to an organization's success. Changes to corporate strategy will directly translate into changes to the competency model, not necessarily requiring changes to the compensation plan elements. This will reduce the need to make major plan design overhauls each year.

To be effective within a sales organization, competency-based pay programs must include or accomplish the following:

- Represent enough monetary significance to get attention and make a difference.

- Not replace overall sales results as the primary success measure.

- Send a cultural message that the organization recognizes the vital link between competencies and achieving individual and organizational strategic objectives and values.

- Reward both competency attainment as well as the speed at which it is achieved.

- Include compensation mechanism to reward sales management for both their own personal competency development as well as the development of their subordinates.

Currently, there is no universally accepted, best-practice methodology for linking competency development to pay. Linking competency attainment to individual base pay or base pay structure appears to be the most popular method for nonsales positions. However, within the sales environment, the application of competency-based pay is more complex as a result of the following:

- Base salary for a sales force member represents a smaller proportion of total target earnings than those in staff positions. Therefore, restricting competency pay to the base salary treatment process has a reduced effect and deemphasizes the program.

- The culture of sales organizations has traditionally focused primarily on hard sales results as the predominant success metric.

- Front-line sales managers, when introducing competency-based pay, are often reluctant to emphasize the program in the year of introduction.

To counter this, the alternative that seems most attractive for sales representative compensation is the establishment of a separate reward mechanism or plan component for rewarding competency development. Further, the separate incentive should be included within total targeted earnings as a means of spotlighting the importance of the competency program and to shift the cultural bias. Because of the direct linkage to pay, the use of multiple source assessment of individuals is essential for improving objectivity. In addition, it is critical that all other aspects of the program are executed well to maintain the credibility of the program. This includes effective pay plan communication, initial individual competency assessments, and defining behavioral anchors so that the sales force is clear as to what they are being asked to develop and master. Performance objectives must be established and communicated up front, with all participants fully aware of what is required to attain a given reward level.

For sales managers, competency-based rewards should be aligned to the success of their sales team in achieving their predetermined competency development objectives. A "participation bonus" that rewards managers based on the number of individuals within their team who achieve their own individual developmental targets motivates the manager to coach across the entire force of direct reports. Again, multisource assessment should be used to avoid conflicts of interest.

CONCLUSION

Implementing a competency-based management program provides an opportunity to seek new ways of gaining a competitive edge through knowledge, personal growth and development, hiring accuracy, and unique reward systems. While internal departmental structures are becoming more complex, competency programs offer consistency of message and an exhalation of the sales manager's role. To be successful, competency programs within sales organizations require solid commitment of sales leadership and the support and active involvement of other internal departments such as marketing and human resources. This presents a unique opportunity for human resource practitioners to position themselves as a strategic resource and *business partner* to the sales organization.

REFERENCES

Dewey, Barbara. 1997. "Six Companies Share Their Insights: The Challenge in Applying Competencies." *Compensation & Benefits Review,* March/April.

Drucker, Peter. 1993. *Post-Capitalistic Society.* New York: Harper Business.

Edwards, Ph.D., Mark R., Ann J. Ewen, and Sandra O'Neal, CCP. 1994. "Using Multisource Assessments to Pay People, Not Jobs." *ACA Journal,* summer.

Holden, Jim. 1990, 1992. *Power Base Selling: Secrets of an Ivy League Street Fighter.* New York: Wiley.

Ledford, G. E., Jr. 1995. "Paying for Skills, Knowledge and Competencies and Knowledge Workers." *Compensation & Benefits Review,* July/August.

Schuster, J. R., and Patricia K. Zingheim. *The New Pay: Linking Employee and Organizational Performance.* San Francisco: Jossey-Bass, 1996.

Spencer, Jr., Ph.D., Lyle M., and Signe M. Spencer. 1993. *Competence at Work: Model for Superior Performance.* New York: Wiley.

Zingheim, Ph.D., Patricia K., Gerald E. Ledford, Jr., Ph.D., and Jay R. Schuster, Ph.D. 1996. "Competencies and Competency Models: Does One Size Fit All?" *ACA Journal,* spring.

P A R T

Executive Compensation

C H A P T E R

EXECUTIVE COMPENSATION STRATEGY

Marvin A. Mazer, Vice President

Aon Consulting

Eric C. Larre, Vice President

Aon Consulting

THIS CHAPTER DEFINES A FRAMEWORK AND PROCESS that facilitate the development of an executive compensation strategy, which can be used to rationalize and communicate organizational philosophy and decision making related to pay levels, pay mix, and performance measures and standards.

Why? Because one critical challenge for strategic compensation practitioners is convincing their employers that executive compensation strategy goes well beyond simply knowing how much their competitors pay. Unfortunately, in some organizations, the human resources function continues to be viewed merely as a cost center that is incapable of contributing to the company's strategic direction.

Thus, no opportunity is provided to probe deeper into how and why compensation structures should be developed in certain ways.

The one-dimensional approach of obtaining detailed competitive compensation data does not and cannot address the need to understand all the factors that drive and constrain the employer's compensation structure. The difficulty posed by this one-dimensional perspective is that it fails to identify and prioritize the many other aspects of the industry, the company, and the workforce that affect the choice of compensation tools available and how they should be used to attract, retain, and motivate employees. This is true even when a seemingly rigorous process of peer group selection is used to select companies that are like the subject organization, either due to revenue size, market capitalization, number of employees, or numerous other objective measures of supposed comparability.

A valuable executive compensation strategy provides the linkage between an organization's mission of optimizing shareholder value and the programs and policies used to compensate the employees who execute the business strategies designed to achieve that corporate mission. This business strategy is premised on management's conclusions regarding the company's business model, including economic and industry conditions, its culture and history, stage in the business cycle, financial situation, customer base and, most relevant to this discussion, its people.

An organization's people strategy articulates the skills, competencies, and behaviors required of its workforce to execute the business strategy. By identifying and prioritizing these necessary employee attributes, the company is in the position to begin developing the compensation programs that will be used to attract, retain, and motivate its workforce.

For example, technology industry companies typically seek highly skilled entrepreneurial employees. These employees are required because technology companies survive and succeed on the basis of their ability not only to develop superior products but also their ability to do so before any of their competitors. Thus, the very best employees, those with an appetite for risk taking and leadership, are the most highly sought after. These employees generally are willing to forego some level of current cash compensation in return for the opportunity to earn much higher levels of equity compensation delivered if the company is financially successful. These pay needs are fortunately consistent with the employers' needs to preserve cash for critical investment in research and development.

In contrast, consider the expectations of employers in the retail industry, where employees generally need to have a focus on customer satisfaction and companies succeed on the basis of their ability to serve and retain customers. Employees with required behaviors and skills in this environment are more likely to require less variability and more predictability in their compensation mix. This also is consistent with the employers' economic model, which relies significantly on high volume and narrow profit margins—an environment that cannot support unpredictability in pay levels.

All of this is not to say that a good understanding of the competitive references is not critically important because that information is very relevant to the organization's ability to understand how its executive compensation cost structure relates to those of its competitors. We also know that pay levels need to approach a given minimum rate of market comparability to assure that employees don't leave strictly for pay reasons. Rather, the point is that organizations need to be able to rationalize why their pay practices are and should be different from those of their competitors.

The remainder of this article describes the ideal contents and foundation of a robust executive compensation strategy, and it defines a process for developing an executive compensation strategy that can be rationalized by reference to the organization's internal and external needs, not simply by reference to external data.

WHAT IS AN EXECUTIVE COMPENSATION STRATEGY?

How does a company develop an executive compensation strategy? We need to start with a common understanding of what compensation strategy is. A *compensation strategy* articulates the company's philosophy regarding the linkage between the corporate mission and its specific compensation policies and programs.

The actual compensation strategy consists of statements that address specific facets of compensation policy that are developed within the context of the organization's assessed risk-reward profile. These facets of compensation policy are the following:

- Competitive positioning of compensation

- Optimal mix of compensation components

- Performance measures and standards

To articulate a strategy with respect to *competitive positioning,* the company must answer the following questions:

- How does the employer define its competitive marketplace? By reference to product or service competitors, by reference to labor market competitors, or both?

- How does the competitive marketplace vary by organizational level and function?

- Where does the employer need to position its compensation levels in comparison to the relevant competitive markets? Does this positioning vary by component of pay?

- Are there elements of employment rewards that are not viewed as compensation but that nonetheless provide economic value that should be evaluated in measuring total compensation?

An organization's compensation strategy with respect to *component mix* addresses the following issues:

- What are the components of compensation that should be used by the organization?

- What is the appropriate mix of fixed and variable components of pay?

- What is the right balance of current and deferred elements of compensation?

- What is the right balance of short-term and long-term incentives reflected in the variable component of compensation?

- With respect to all of the foregoing, how do the answers vary by organizational level, business unit, or corporate function?

Finally, the ability of compensation programs to reward employees for meeting the organization's goals is assured through *performance measures and standards:*

- Will performance be measured objectively or subjectively?

- How will programs balance emphasis on organizational, business unit, team, and individual performance?

- Should performance measures be financial, operational, or milestone goals?

- Should performance measures be applied on an absolute (budgeted) basis or on a relative (comparative) basis?

- Over what period(s) should performance be measured?

- As in the case of pay mix, how do the answers vary by organizational level, business unit, or corporate function?

It bears mentioning that organizations are likely to need multiple compensation strategies, which will vary by function or by business unit. For instance, one of the biggest challenges for employers in the late 1990s has been the ability to attract and retain critical talent for their *information technology–information systems* (IT/IS) *functions.* Very strong MIS capabilities are required to respond to the approach of the year 2000 and the myriad problems associated with that development, the day-to-day issues presented by the commercialization of the Internet, and the integration of constantly improving hardware, software, and telecommunications capabilities. Employers frequently are forced to employ special compensation policies and programs that apply only to MIS employees. These programs, which are not used in other parts of these organizations, include hire-on bonuses, special stock option grants, above-market base salaries, and special retention bonuses.

Consider also the predicament of the non-U.S. conglomerate that acquires a U.S. information services company. The pay paradigms applicable overseas rarely translate well to meet the expectations of American employees, who now have become accustomed to the pay-for-performance mantra and the variable pay and equity ownership opportunities associated with it. Very different compensation strategies are required for these organizations because of the very different needs and expectations of the multinational parent company and its U.S. employees.

WHAT ARE THE INPUTS TO EXECUTIVE COMPENSATION STRATEGY?

As noted earlier, an organization's business and people strategies standing alone will support certain compensation strategies. However, these preliminary indications must be processed through specified internal and external constraints that can either drive or constrain an organization's ability to adopt certain plans or policies. The operation of this thought process is illustrated through the framework presented in Figure 25.1.

Internal constraints consist of items such as organization structure, culture, financial capabilities, communications capabilities, company life-cycle stage, current plans, and employee demographics. For example:

FIGURE 25.1

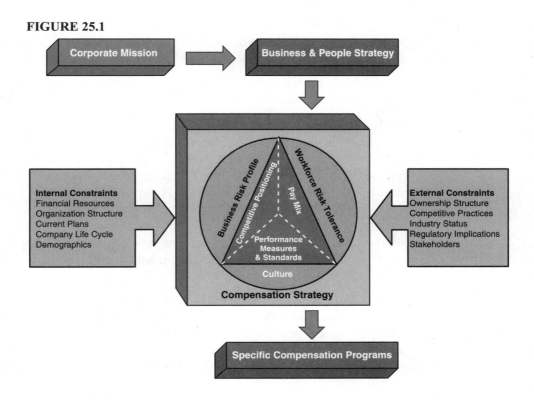

- An *organization's structure* almost always will influence how performance is measured for purposes of variable pay plans. This is because line of sight is required in order for employees to understand how their efforts and contributions impact organizational performance. Some companies believe that employees affect the corporate bottom line every day, while others believe that employees can affect the performance only of their specific business unit or division.

- *Financial capabilities* will influence how the organization chooses to use its resources in delivering the right mix of pay. Companies with limited access to financial resources will emphasize variable components of pay, while cash-rich organizations may be willing to use high base salaries as a key attraction and recruiting tool.

- *Company life-cycle stage,* which is, the organization's risk and success horizon, significantly impacts an executive compensation strategy design. Emerging and high-growth companies reinvest earnings extensively to fuel growth and new product offerings, thus defaulting to noncash and/or performance-sensitive forms of compensation. Mature and declining businesses frequently face employee retention issues due to the limited viability perceived for the business. This requires companies to pay at above-market fixed compensation levels to make it more difficult for employees to find comparable paying positions in other firms. Table 25.1 provides a somewhat general but universally accepted assessment of how a company's life-cycle position impacts the competitive aspects of establishing rewards.

    External constraints include items like ownership structure, industry attributes, regulatory constraints, and, of course, competitive practices. For example:

- *Ownership structure* affects pay mix and sometimes performance measures and standards because shareholder needs and requirements can vary dramatically from company to company. Non-U.S. shareholders more frequently than not are uncomfortable with the use of equity vehicles to reward employees, although this trend is slowly changing. These companies tend to focus exclusively on cash compensation. Privately held organizations will develop compensation programs differently, depending on their long-term investment strategy (i.e., going public versus long-term family control). They also differ significantly from their publicly held competitors with respect to the use of stock as a compensation medium.

- *Regulatory constraints* can include tax regulations, SEC reporting requirements, financial accounting rules, and ERISA requirements. Most significant are financial accounting rules, which tend to limit the types of long-term incentive alternatives available to smaller companies, which cannot afford the compensation expense ramifications of several performance-oriented plan design options.

TABLE 25.1

	Life-Cycle Stage			
	Embryonic	Growth	Mature	Declining
Base salary	Low	Competitive	Competitive/high	High
Annual incentives	Competitive	Competitive	High	Low
Long-term incentives	High	Competitive	Competitive	Low
Benefits	Low	Competitive	High	High
Perquisites	Low	Competitive	Competitive	High

- Finally, *competitive practices* must be considered to the extent that they drive both competitive positioning of pay and pay mix. Organizations must respond to the fact that employees are very knowledgeable regarding the compensation practices of their competitors, which frequently are used as levers to gain compensation concessions.

HOW IS AN EXECUTIVE COMPENSATION STRATEGY DEVELOPED?

The process of developing an executive compensation strategy involves in the first instance the exercise of identifying and prioritizing these inputs for one's own company because no two companies are alike. Only after completing this internal and external examination can the organization start to identify and rationalize the policies and programs that will best respond to the company's needs and strategies.

The ideal process for developing an executive compensation strategy consists of the following steps (see Figure 25.2):

- Understand what the organization and executives should expect to gain from having a compensation strategy and identifying the benchmarks that the organization will use to measure successful implementation.

- Understand the organization's business and people strategies, and identify and prioritize all of the drivers and factors that impact the delivery of compensation in support of those strategies. This requires substantial internal investigation of management and nonmanagement opinions and perceptions regarding the needs and values of the company and its people.

- Develop a preliminary executive compensation strategy. Identify the gaps between the organization's current programs and the preliminary compensation strategy, develop recommended alternatives for closing those gaps, and model transition plans for moving from the current to the desired state.

FIGURE 25.2

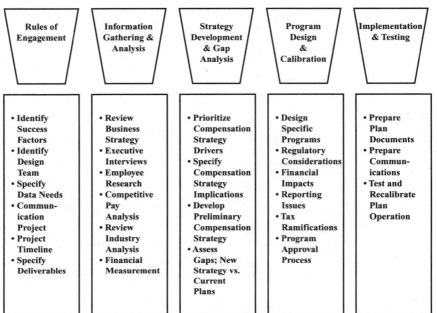

- Devise a final executive compensation strategy, including specific program design features and pros and cons for each recommended policy or program, and calculate the cost of each element of the new strategy in comparison to the existing cost structure.

- Test the executive compensation strategy and programs against the business and people strategies, and the identified success indicators, and recalibrate as required.

CASE STUDY

Newco, an organization engaged in a very regulated industry, has more than 2,000 employees. The company was successfully emerging from a very difficult and stressful set of circumstances that had, 5 years before, almost resulted in the declaration of bankruptcy. The company is organized primarily under an *employee stock ownership plan* (ESOP), and during the turnaround period, management voluntarily accepted uncompetitively low levels of cash compensation to assist in the turnaround of the company.

During that period, management believed that it would be difficult to justify stock option grants for management, largely because of the philosophy behind the ESOP ownership model. However, having successfully avoided complete financial disaster, the company's management was successfully positioning the company for an initial public offering (IPO) as a means to raise capital to fund debt reduction and growth through acquisition. On another tack, the successful turnaround of the company had focused industry attention on the management capabilities of the company's senior management, and competing offers were being fielded by the CEO on a regular basis. It was at this time that management determined to change the compensation structure of the organization to meet its changed circumstances and to be in a position to reward its executive group for their past and future efforts to bring the company to a financially successful state.

Applying the compensation strategy framework, an executive compensation structure was built that prioritized the following drivers and constraints:

Business Strategy.   Newco needed to preserve cash resources for debt reduction and future acquisitions. Thus they wanted to create an emphasis on financial performance measures for variable pay plans and to use equity (which had only rarely been used in the past) as a compensation tool.

People Strategy.   The existing management team had increased the value of the company significantly (without sharing in that value creation) and was believed to be capable of continuing that trend. However, it was also true that a few key recruits were required to provide skills in financial management and business development. These individuals would ideally be recruited from environments that were highly entrepreneurial in nature. These factors suggested that the use of highly leveraged variable cash compensation, stock options, or other equity vehicles would be required as key reward elements.

Risk-Reward Profile.   Although Newco had made substantial financial gains, the highly competitive nature of the industry, ongoing debt burdens, and outstanding litigation suggested a relatively high-risk profile to the organization. The perception of management, outside legal counsel, and investment banking advisors was that higher levels of reward opportunity were appropriate to compensate for this increased-risk profile.

Ownership Structure.   ESOP ownership had over time fostered an environment of relative equality within the organization. Therefore, the ESOP trustee perceived that disproportionately enriching management through stock option grants would be difficult to justify. The trustee favored very moderate stock option grant levels with a focus on cash compensation. This argued in favor of a traditional mix of pay components, which was not historically highly leveraged on the equity side by reference to other companies like Newco (ignoring the company's risk-reward profile).

Financial Capabilities.   The optimal uses of cash were reducing existing debt, cleaning up the balance sheet, and allocation to future acquisitions. All parties shared this view. Thus, compensation expenditures were to be linked to financial performance goals and the use of noncash vehicles to deliver rewards that would contribute to preserving those liquid resources.

Regulatory Limitations.   As a representative of the ESOP, the ESOP trustee was statutorily bound under the Employee Retirement Income Security Act (ERISA) to protect the interests of the ESOP participants. The retention of existing management and the ability to recruit top talent could be justified from a long-term performance perspective. However, the ESOP trustee also was faced with rationalizing the significant dilutive impact on ESOP participation that would result from creating a stock option pool from which substantial initial grants would be made. In addition, the consideration of a near-term IPO made it almost impossible to use any long-term incentive vehicle that would generate a compensation expense on the company's P&L due to its adverse impact on earnings.

Competitive Practices.   Research supported the position that management teams in entrepreneurial and turnaround situations typically received significant equity stakes in the employer (1) to provide them with a share of the value created and (2) to counterbalance the acceptance of cash compensation that was below competitive levels. However, by the same token, stock options were not used in significant amounts by industry-specific competitors, largely due to a concentration of founder-owned companies in the industry. Research showed that most of the management team had received cash compensation (and no equity compensation) that was well below competitive norms for similarly situated companies. A difference of opinion arose as to the competitive practice reference points that should be used for the analysis: industry-specific companies, turnaround companies, or ESOP-owned companies. Findings from all three perspectives supported the extensive use of equity compensation. Industry-specific companies appeared to support extensive retirements, *supplemental executive retirement plans* (SERPs), deferred compensation, and perquisites programs for their executives.

SAMPLE EXECUTIVE COMPENSATION STRATEGY STATEMENT

Under the foregoing circumstances, the following compensation strategy was recommended and ultimately approved by the board of directors (including a representative of the ESOP):

- *Compensation mix.* Executive compensation will consist of the following components of pay:
  - Base salary, to compensate executives for performing to expected levels of experience and competence.
  - Annual incentive awards, to reward executives for attaining aggressive strategic, financial, and operational goals viewed as critical to the continued growth and profitability of the company.

- Long-term incentives, in the form of stock options, to allow executives to share reasonably in the future growth of the company, to align their economic interests with those of the ESOP, and to serve perceived retention needs. Restricted stock may be used in rare circumstances to address specific retention or recruiting needs.

- Retirement programs and perquisites will not be offered to executives, given the general lack of performance orientation to such plans and the absence of such programs for other facets of the workforce.

- *Competitive positioning.* Newco's compensation programs will have the following attributes:

  - To avoid the likelihood that Newco's executives will be recruited to competitors for reasons of compensation, executive annual cash compensation will be determined by reference to a peer group of companies of similar revenue size that are in the same industry as Newco or are in other regulated industries that are similar in nature to Newco's industry.

  - To manage the company's finances efficiently while providing reasonably attractive levels of compensation, annual cash compensation, consisting of base salary and annual cash incentive awards, will be calibrated to provide market 50th percentile total cash compensation for the attainment of quantifiable financial, strategic, and operational goals for the year and to provide up to market 75th percentile total cash compensation for performance in excess of company expectations against such goals.

  - To assure fairness with respect the company's employee shareholders, initial long-term incentive grants will be determined by reference to their dilutive impact, as compared to the dilution rates experienced generally by companies with significant ESOP ownership and companies that are viewed as troubled or in turnaround situations.

  - For ease of administration and consistency, ongoing long-term incentive grants will be determined by reference to the same group of companies used for purposes of assessing cash compensation for executives.

  - Vesting schedules for significant initial grants of long-term incentives will be longer than market prevalent vesting terms to ensure retention of key individuals.

- *Performance measures and standards.* The alignment of Newco's executive compensation with the company's mission will be supported as follows:

  - To support organizational financial success in the best interests of the shareholders, annual incentive award opportunities will be dependent primarily on organizational performance, with modest flexibility for awards to vary on the basis of distinguished individual contribution to organizational goal achievement.

- In support of the organization's goal of completing an IPO within the next 2 to 3 years, performance measures will be quantifiable and objective and will relate directly to the organization's strategic growth and profitability initiatives.

- To promote the company's strategic financial needs, performance will be measured primarily on the basis of financial results including EBITDA (earnings before interest, tax, depreciation, and amortization), cash flow, and year-over-year revenue growth.

- To position the company favorably from the perspective of the investment community, performance will be measured by reference to both internally budgeted financial goals and the relative performance of industry-specific peer group companies.

- To focus executives on generating stable yet sustained financial growth, performance will be measured within relatively narrow bands, such that no awards will be earned for financial performance that is less than 90 percent of expected levels, and awards will be capped after company performance exceeds 110 percent of expected levels.

- The opportunity for executives to continue sharing in the financial growth of the company through ongoing stock or stock option grants will be determined on the basis of the CEO's subjective assessment of each executive's efforts and contribution to the company's success. This assessment will be subject to the review of the board's compensation committee.

CONCLUSION

No two organizations are alike. They have different people, resources, missions, and different people and business strategies to achieve those missions. As such, there is no reason for them to compensate their people the same way. Compensation practices and policies should be determined on the basis of the organization's individual internal and external business, demographic, and organizational attributes. If your organization is unique, treat it as such, and avoid the trap of "keeping up with the Joneses."

DESIGNING AND IMPLEMENTING TOTAL EXECUTIVE COMPENSATION PROGRAMS

Alan M. Johnson, Managing Director

Johnson Associates

IN DESIGNING AND IMPLEMENTING THE TOTAL COMPENSATION PROGRAM, one of the most important considerations is maintaining the proper perspective. Essentially, that means approaching the exercise not from the direction of the individual components of pay but rather from the perspective of the total program. This applies to issues such as how much we should pay executives, as well as to what the compensation program is supposed to achieve in support of the company's overall objectives.

The executive compensation landscape has changed dramatically in recent years driven by the focus on shareholder value creation and the continued rise in

U.S. and European stock markets. It is safe to say that having an effective total compensation program has never been more important to satisfy increasingly knowledgeable and vocal shareholders, directors, executives, and various political and public groups.

One way to begin is to think in terms of a compensation philosophy, the guiding principles that underpin all design elements. At the same time, it is important to understand the likely issues and tradeoffs, the role of the advisor, and the mistakes others have made.

THE COMPENSATION PHILOSOPHY

There are many details that must be attended to in designing the executive compensation program of any company, large or small. These range, for example, from the relatively simple questions of how closely the base salary and annual bonus reflect the market to the more arcane but significant issues surrounding stock option valuations and the latest accounting changes. Although all the details are important to the development of a sound, well-designed program, probably the most important factor is that there be absolute clarity on the purpose and objectives of the total program.

One key step a company can take to achieve clarity of purpose is to articulate a meaningful compensation philosophy. The philosophy is an embodiment of organizational beliefs and values in the area of compensation practices, but it should be also a practical guide that links those values to the strategy and direction of the business, as well as a way to coherently bring together the various elements of compensation, such as base salary, annual and long-term incentives, agreements, perquisites, and executive benefits.

Unfortunately, in many if not most organizations, the compensation philosophy is a general statement of values without the specificity and necessary tradeoffs present to form an actionable document. Most compensation philosophies are so broad and noncontroversial they fail to identify and address the key issues that should guide the design and administration of the total compensation program. For example, a company may state that it believes in pay for performance, but what does that really mean? How much should pay vary between the top performer and the average performer? Are we willing to use forced ranking to ensure that there is some dispersion in performance ratings? The following example, which focuses on only a small aspect of a compensation philosophy, may better illustrate the kind of specificity companies should strive for.

Original Version.   The mission and goals of our company will be achieved by attracting, developing, and involving the most highly qualified people. The objective is to provide highly competitive and excellent compensation. There will be a focus on shareholder value creation and stock ownership by executives.

Revised Version. The purpose of our compensation program is to help the company achieve its mission and goals (for example a 20 percent *return on equity* (ROE) with growing market share and new products) by attracting, motivating, and retaining the most highly-qualified people. Pay opportunities will be fully competitive (for example, targeted at the median of the appropriate comparator groups) for average performance, and above-average pay (for example, 75th percentile pay for 75th percentile performance) for superior performance. Variable components of pay, including both annual and long-term incentives, will be a significant element of compensation, building on median base salaries, and they will be truly variable on the basis of performance. Executives will retain 50 percent of the net shares from option exercises until meaningful ownership guidelines are achieved.

In short, the fatal flaw in most compensation philosophies is that they fail to be sufficiently specific. By not addressing the issues, by not fully understanding their implications, and by not taking a stand one way or the other, companies end up with compensation philosophies of little value and compensation programs that don't do what they're supposed to accomplish. An effective and meaningful compensation philosophy is likely to cover 3 to 4 pages and address 15 to 20 specific issues in some detail.

A LINK TO BUSINESS DIRECTION

By insisting on specificity, the compensation philosophy becomes a link to the direction management intends the business to take. For example, by identifying return on equity relative to comparator companies as the key financial measure for the annual incentive plan, management makes a statement about the progression of the company's culture. That is, what's important is not performance versus budget or whether this year is better than last year; what's important is how the company is doing versus the competition and market expectations.

As another example, the compensation philosophy would address the mix between fixed and variable pay. In a fairly stable or regulated environment with predictable short-term results, having a highly leveraged annual incentive plan makes little sense. For a company in transition, however, trying to adapt and change under great stress, a highly leveraged plan could be an effective vehicle, creating a sense of urgency and purpose. The philosophy clearly identifies the link between the business direction and the program design.

THE SIZING OF THE OVERALL PROGRAM

One of the trickiest questions addressed in designing the compensation program is, How much money is really required? Many approaches are very good at establishing annual pay accurately in terms of some target competitive position. They are less effective, however, when integrating the prospective value of long-term incentives into a fully competitive, total pay program.

For example, determining salaries and median annual pay (base salary plus bonus) for average performance is fairly straightforward. On the other hand, data on long-term incentives are much more difficult to obtain and interpret, particularly when multiple vehicles are in use among competitors. How should stock options be valued relative to restricted stock or performance units, and should that relate to target annual pay levels? It requires careful thought to reconcile participant expectations from historical or Black-Scholes perspectives on the likely value of management equity awards. Another questions is, How does the company position itself with respect to competition in terms of the total pay opportunity? If the answer is to pay executives at the 75th percentile in total compensation, does that mean providing 75th percentile long-term incentives on top of 75th percentile base and bonus? In reality, as Table 26.1 shows, it does not because such an approach would probably position a company close to the 90th percentile, or better, in total compensation.

Using the illustrative data from Table 26.1, it would be correct to add the $200,000 median long-term pay opportunity directly to the $250,000 median annual pay to arrive at the correct $450,000 median total compensation opportunity. Adding a $300,000 long-term opportunity—representing the 75th percentile of the data—directly to the $250,000 75th percentile annual cash, however, yields $625,000 in total compensation opportunity. This is a subtle and often misunderstood point. The "correct" long-term opportunity to achieve a 75th percentile total compensation target (say, $525,000) on top of $250,000 annual compensation would be $275,000. This mix of pay profile is, of course, completely different from that achieved at the median competitive level, and it sends a different message about the relative importance of long-term versus short-term pay.

One of the most vexing issues involved in compensation program implementation is how to value and consider long-term incentive awards, especially stock options. It is crucial to be aware how small changes in modeling assumptions can change significantly the size of potential awards, either positive or negative, with a meaningful impact on both shareholder cost and program attractiveness. Award sizing must reflect both individual and aggregate competitive data regarding recent awards, shares granted as a percentage of outstanding stock, and the aggregate exercise dollar value of grants. The recent volatility in the stock market, while generally in a positive direction, has made it more difficult to rely on historical public or proxy data since share prices (and perspective valuations) may have

TABLE 26.1   Total Pay Positioning: An Illustration, Survey Data (Assumed)

	Annual Cash	Long-Term Value	Total Pay
Median	$250,000	$200,000	$450,000
75th percentile	$325,000	$300,000	$625,000

changed significantly. Experience has shown that considering awards from several perspectives is likely to improve the quality of decisions and acceptance by both participants and directors.

Benefits and perquisites are another area in which problems can arise with valuation and integration into the complete program. What alternatives are available to a company that believes in a competitive total program and also wants to have as few supplemental perks as possible (to promote egalitarian values and avoid administrative headaches), yet is in an industry in which extensive entitlements are the norm? One way to deal with the situation is to simply convert a typical package into a fixed dollar amount that the executive can take as cash compensation·or spend on cars and clubs, if that is what is valuable. This is an especially effective (and administratively simple) way of handling the issue, given that there are practically no tax advantages for supplemental entitlements.

Benefits are more complicated: Although most companies agree that it is important to have a competitive benefits package, whether executives should have something extra is an important issue. For example, should executives have a pension formula more attractive than that provided to the broad employee population? Are there tradeoffs that might be attractive between additional benefits versus current compensation? Another important factor to consider is the safety and security of unfunded benefits-related liabilities. What type of protection should be provided against loss of benefits in the event of a change in control? These are all complex problems that need to be addressed with the total compensation program in mind.

ISSUES AND TRADEOFFS

One of the important lessons visible in the marketplace is that across a wide variety of issues there is not just one way to run the show. Design alternatives can make profound statements about how an organization is going to be managed. One of the most important roles of the human resources professional is to ensure that management is aware of possible alternatives and fully understands their implications.

The issues to be addressed and the tradeoffs to be resolved extend to all elements of the program. For example, the choice of job evaluation systems can send a powerful message about priorities. Is the system primarily concerned with internal equity, that is, getting the internal hierarchy of jobs right? If so, then one of the "analytical" job evaluation systems (for example, point factor or factor comparison) would probably best fit the company's needs. On the other hand, if the organization needs to be more externally oriented with a greater focus on what the competition is doing, then a market-pricing system would be more appropriate. There are, of course, shades of gray between these two extremes, and only top management can decide which is more important.

In the area of annual incentives, examples of issues and tradeoffs abound. For example, should performance measures include nonfinancial criteria, and, if so, how would data be gathered and evaluated in a timely fashion? Should performance be measured primarily at the corporate level (to encourage team performance), or should division managers operate largely as independent business units or profit centers (the "entrepreneurial" approach)? Although both approaches can be effective, someone will surely have an opinion as to which appears more appropriate in the current situation. However, the type of environment to encourage is a key senior management and board decision.

Other common issues, and their implications, that need to be addressed include the following:

■ Should annual incentives make up for low salaries or be a reward for outstanding performance?

■ Should plans be highly leveraged?

■ Should payouts be based on the "first dollar" of achievement, or should there be some threshold?

■ What, if any, should be the nonfinancial business objectives of the annual incentive plan?

■ Should the focus be on absolute results, relative performance, or budget achievement?

■ What is the role of individual, as opposed to corporate or unit, performance?

The issue of business versus individual performance is particularly interesting in light of the way many companies have handled it over the years. At the urging of advisors, companies have often decided that about 20 percent, typically, of an executive's target bonus should vary according to individual performance. The incentive balance would then be derived from the company or business unit results. Thus, the intent, in most cases, was that a $50,000 target bonus (to illustrate) could vary from at least $40,000 to $60,000 based on the individual's efforts assuming full achievement of business objectives (Table 26.2).

In the context of a total program, including base salary, long-term incentives, benefits, and perquisites (none of which are typically tied to individual performance except the base salary via the annual increase and often modest adjustments to option awards), such a narrow band of pay variability shrinks to insignificance. This sends an important, and often unintended, message about what the company does or does not value.

In the area of long-term incentives, all the preceding issues apply as well as a few others—what the balance between long-term and short-term pay should be, for example. The central issue here is how to structure the reward system to encourage the executive to properly weigh the tradeoffs between what may be "right" in the short term with what is consistent with the long-term best interests of the organization. Many companies, intentionally or unintentionally, put an excessive amount of emphasis on achieving what are essentially short-term

TABLE 26.2   Potential Pay Variability Based on Individual Performance*

Compensation Element	Target/Est. Value	Variable for Individual Performance	Minimum	Maximum
Benefits	$45,000	No	$45,000	$45,000
Perquisites	5,000	No	5,000	5,000
Long-term	50,000	No	50,000	50,000
Annual incentive	**50,000**	**Yes**	**40,000**	**60,000**
Base salary	150,000	No	150,000	150,000
Total	$300,000		$229,000	$310,000

*Assumes full achievement of business objectives.

objectives, often to the detriment of the long-term health of the business. It is important to recognize that the excessive focus on short-term stock price movements coupled with rapid stock option vesting and executive mobility has converted stock options into, at best, a medium-term incentive vehicle.

One of the most important issues in designing the long-term component of the program deals with the tradeoff between risk and reward. To what extent is an executive's long-term compensation truly at risk for poor performance? For example, stock options are probably the best vehicle for capturing risk because a deteriorating stock price will have an immediate impact on the value or potential value of an executive's holdings. Companies, however, often question the ability of the stock market to fully appreciate their company's true worth, and they have therefore granted performance units along with options, have repriced existing grants, or have made "outsized awards." If the market fails to reward executives, these practices provide a form of insurance. Although such practices reduce an executive's exposure to market risk, a protection that shareholders do not typically enjoy, they can represent valid decisions in certain limited circumstances.

Restricted stock provides another analogy. Like options, restricted stock responds immediately to fluctuations in the stock price. It is clearly less risky than options, however, because its value will almost certainly be greater than zero, whereas options can easily be underwater. At the same time, by providing the immediate tangible rewards of ownership (voting rights and dividends), restricted stock is probably a more effective retention device than options. Thus, the tradeoff between options and restricted stock involves more than the risk-reward issue. It also includes value judgments regarding the importance of executive stock ownership and the need for additional retention features.

Other issues and tradeoffs that need to be addressed with respect to the long-term plan include:

- Real shares versus phantom shares, especially for subsidiaries
- Incentive stock options versus nonqualified options
- Accounting costs and tax issues versus resources available for compensation programs
- Broader participation versus more limited participation
- Importance of executive and employee stock ownership

Another area with important issues and tradeoffs that can have a significant morale effect—as well as an impact on hard and soft dollar costs—is executive perquisites. Although very few, if any, executive perquisites are particularly tax efficient, some companies still maintain elaborate perk programs. This may or may not be intentional, but there are valid reasons for having executive perquisites. For example, they can be an effective and useful symbol of power and authority in some companies.

In summary, there are many important issues to be addressed in designing the total compensation program that deal with how the business is going to be managed and led. These issues involve tradeoffs between competing yet totally valid ways of running a business, and they cannot be settled by human resource professionals in isolation. Rather, these are issues and alternatives whose implications should be fully explored with the CEO and then resolved with senior management and the board of directors.

COMMON MISTAKES

Even when companies do a good job of defining the purpose and objectives of their compensation program, there are still a number of mistakes that can destroy the effectiveness of a well-designed total compensation program.

One of the most common mistakes is poor communication. Companies regularly fail to communicate to employees what the intent of the program is, how it is supposed to work, and why the program is designed the way it is. An example of this can often be found with stock option plans. There are few sound reasons to employ stock options unless one of the objectives the company wants to achieve is increased ownership by executives. If that is not desired, then there are other ways to achieve some of the objectives a company may have for its long-term compensation programs. The problem is that even when companies recognize ownership as an important objective, they fail to communicate it adequately. As a result, executives perceive stock options as another form of compensation, exercising the option when the time is right and selling the stock. One of the important features of an articulated compensation philosophy is that it can serve as a vehicle for clearly communicating to executives that stock ownership is a desired and expected objective of the program.

One communication hurdle commonly occurs with companies that determine stock option awards as a multiple of annual pay. For example, a company may determine that a $250,000-per-year executive has a long-term stock option opportunity equal to 100 percent of annual pay, or $250,000 in stock option grant value. At a $50-per-share stock price, the executive will receive 5,000 options. If the stock price goes up to $75 per share, however, next year's grant will only be 3,333 options. Unless communicated properly, executives will wonder, and with good reason, what they did wrong to warrant a decrease in options. This may seem to be an easy-to-avoid problem, but many companies have stumbled over this communication problem.

Another common communication failure happens when companies have a lot of good things to say about their compensation programs, but just don't say it. For example, the benefits package may be terrific by objective standards, but no one knows about it. Or a company may have a policy where the pay line is set at the median of a competitive group and at the same time target pay to a 1.05 compa-ratio. What that means is that, on average, employees are paid above the market, but if that message never gets out, the company loses a lot in terms of employee goodwill. In short, poor communication probably means a company is not getting the most for its money.

THE ROLE OF THE ADVISOR

In many companies, compensation programs have developed piecemeal over the years. Annual incentives were added on as an afterthought on top of a salary administration program developed for a hierarchical organization that rose up in a different time and place. Long-term incentives were added later because everyone seemed to be doing it. In many companies, no one had the vision to provide a comprehensive view of the total program. One of the important contributions the human resources adviser can make is to provide that comprehensive perspective. There are essentially three key roles the human resources advisor can play, as follows.

The first, and perhaps most important, is to articulate the issues and strive to keep the issues and tradeoffs in focus. Many companies have problems with their compensation programs not because top executives are particularly ill-willed or shortsighted but because they simply have never had anyone explain to them the real implications of their actions. This often happens because companies have a tradition of not making the best use of their human resources professionals, or outside consultants.

The second important role the advisor can, and should, play is that of the advocate. Given the unique knowledge and experience base of the top human resources professional, it is inevitable that his or her opinion will be solicited in weighing and resolving the tradeoffs involved.

A third role, and this probably applies more to the in-house professional than to the consultant, is that of *product champion,* with the product being the compensation program. As an important disseminator of information on design issues and the intent and purpose of programs, the human resources professional can play a crucial role in building the kind of consensus needed to ensure the success of a new compensation program. In short, much of the burden of communication and of the success of the program falls on the shoulders of the human resources professional.

SUMMARY

There are four keys to designing a successful total compensation program. First, formulate and articulate clearly the compensation philosophy. By defining the purpose and objectives of the compensation programs, and by identifying specifically how those translate into the strategy and direction of the business, the problems some companies have with their executive compensation programs will be avoided.

Second, maintain a total program perspective. This is crucial not only in determining how much but also in helping top management understand the issues and tradeoffs involved in the various design alternatives.

Third, stress the importance of good communication not only so that the purpose and objectives of the compensation program are clear but also so that the good news gets out.

Fourth, remember that human resources professionals have a crucial role to play in developing the total program. Part of that utility derives from their organization-wide perspective. A second part derives from their knowledge of how upper management wants to run the business. The third part derives from their position as the disseminator of the information, which has the practical effect of their also being the recipients of feedback from employees.

ANNUAL INCENTIVE PLANS FOR MANAGEMENT

Peter Chingos, National Director
Executive Compensation Consulting Practice

William M. Mercer, Inc.

AN ANNUAL INCENTIVE PLAN REWARDS INDIVIDUALS OR TEAMS for achieving specific financial performance objectives. Directly linked to financial performance over a relatively brief period of time, an annual incentive plan supports better than other pay elements a pay-for-performance strategy, and it is a powerful tool for motivating desired employee performance, which ultimately leads to improved business results.

Almost universal in large, publicly held organizations, annual incentive plans are now frequently found in private companies and not-for-profit organizations as well. Ninety-six percent of executives and 83 percent of other management employees in William M. Mercer's 1998 *Policies and Practices Survey* are eligible for annual incentives. In many organizations, annual incentives extend down through the employee ranks. Sixty-six percent of companies in the Mercer survey offer some kind of incentive to their technical-professional employees, and 47 percent offer incentives to their nonexempt employees. Many of these incentive plans are specially designed team or functional incentives or profit-sharing plans. In the paragraphs that follow, we will limit our discussion to corporate management incentive plans.

CONDITIONS FOR EFFECTIVE ANNUAL INCENTIVE PLANS

Annual management incentive plans work best when the following conditions exist:

- The organization is willing and able to identify and measure financial performance goals.

- The result cycle is relatively short and related to the performance period recognized by the incentive plan.

- Critical factors affecting short-term results are within the control of plan participants and traceable to them.

- Top management is willing to judge performance by comparing and rating each participant's output and to make awards accordingly.

In designing an annual incentive plan, top management and human resources professionals must address the following issues: eligibility for participation, target awards for participants, the funding mechanism, the performance measures, and the allocation of funds to participants. Other issues should also be addressed, such as the form of payment, voluntary deferred arrangements, and the tax deductibility of payments to senior executives.

ELIGIBILITY

Salary or salary grade midpoint is usually the primary determiner of annual incentive eligibility, and the trend has been to extend eligibility down through the management ranks. In most large companies across major industries, employees at a salary (or salary midpoint) of $55,000 or higher are typically eligible for an annual incentive, compared to approximately $70,000 in 1991. Criteria other than salary, however, frequently influence decisions on eligibility. For example, companies that seek a significant level of pay at risk tend to include more employees in the annual incentive plan than companies that stress fixed pay. Annual incentive plans designed to measure performance in decentralized organizations often include more employees than organizations that are centralized. Competitive practice can also influence eligibility, especially where recruiting and retaining top performers are management priorities.

There is a tendency over time to include more employees in the annual incentive plan. This, of course, adds to the cost of the plan and should be monitored.

Since many organizations have multiple incentive plans (e.g., team incentives, sales or commission plans, productivity-related incentives), care must be taken to avoid rewarding employees under more than one plan for achieving the same performance goals. It may be that certain employees would be better motivated and rewarded if they participated in an incentive plan other than the management plan. Line of sight is the important consideration here. Employees should participate in the plan where they have the most direct influence over results.

TARGET INCENTIVE AWARD OPPORTUNITIES

Incentive-eligible employees are usually assigned a target incentive opportunity expressed as a percent of salary or salary range midpoint. For example, at a salary of $80,000, the targeted incentive opportunity could be $20,000, or 25 percent of salary. The maximum award could be set at two times the target, or $40,000. Targeted total cash compensation would be $100,000 ($80,000 plus $20,000) with a maximum potential of $120,000 ($80,000 plus $40,000). Whether or not the target incentive is paid depends on the employee's reaching his or her goals and the organization's achieving its performance goals. Figure 27.1 gives sample target and minimum to maximum ranges for selected executive positions.

Incentive award targets depend chiefly on three factors, as follows.

Compensation Strategy

An organization's compensation strategy typically specifies the desired balance between annual and long-term incentive opportunity. Because senior executives

FIGURE 27.1 Sample target awards expressed as a percent of salary.

	Target Award	Potential Range	
		Minimum	Maximum
CEO	70%	0	140%
President/COO	60%	0	120%
Subsidiary President	50%	0	100%
CFO	45%	0	90%
CIO	40%	0	80%
VP Marketing and Sales	35%	0	70%
VP HR	30%	0	60%

are responsible for the long-term success and strategic direction of the organization, they are often given a long-term incentive opportunity that exceeds the annual incentive opportunity. For middle management, a balance of annual and long-term incentives is often desirable. An incentive strategy heavily weighted toward annual incentives is often suitable for those in the lower management ranks who principally affect short-term results.

Business Strategy

An organization's business strategy can also influence annual incentive targets. In high-risk, entrepreneurial organizations, management will often place a significant percent of cash compensation at risk through lower-than-average salaries and substantial bonus opportunity. In low-risk environments, organizations will typically pay above-average salaries with more modest annual incentive opportunity.

Industry Practice

In setting incentive targets, organizations often look at industry practice for an external barometer of what is typical at various job levels. Considerations of industry practice can be a major factor in setting incentive targets where retention and recruitment are important management concerns.

DETERMINING PERFORMANCE LEVELS FOR PLAN FUNDING

As described in the following paragraphs, an organization can use several approaches to funding an annual incentive plan.

Budget-Based Plans

Seventy-nine percent of companies in Mercer's 1998 *Policy and Practices Survey* fund their annual incentive plans through the budget process. Under this widely used approach, the achievement of specified profit budget or business plan goals results in payment of targeted incentives. Targets may be keyed to a single index of performance, such as net income, return on sales, or return on equity, or to several indexes, and they may also include nonfinancial goals. Figure 27.2 illustrates a typical budget-based plan using return on equity as the single performance goal. If the organization achieves 100 percent of target, the incentive pool would generate sufficient dollars to pay plan participants 100 percent of their target incentives. Outstanding performance at 125 percent of target return on equity would generate a maximum incentive of 200 percent of target.

Budget-based incentives are most effective when management is able to set financial goals and forecast performance targets accurately. They can also accommodate different business unit or profit center goals. Concerns about the budget-based approach center on the integrity and sophistication of the planning process and the possibility of budget gamesmanship if stretch goals are not realistic.

FIGURE 27.2   Funding a budget-based plan using return on equity.

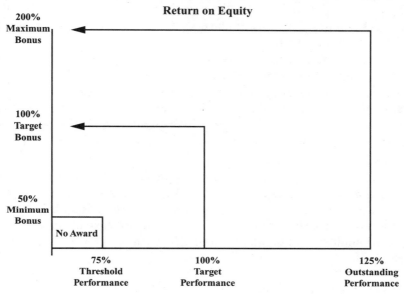

Percent of Budget Achieved

Prior Year's Performance

The performance level required to generate an incentive compensation pool is based on a fixed increase in one or a combination of financial indexes, such as earnings per share, return on equity, or net income. For example, a plan may specify that an incentive pool will be established when annual revenues and net income increase by greater than 8 and 15 percent, respectively, over the preceding year. The amount in the pool typically increases on a sliding scale depending on the degree to which the performance attained exceeds the prior year.

The strength of this approach is that it motivates management to achieve sustained improvement and is easily understood and communicated to employees and the investment community. It may, however, conflict with other strategic objectives, and outstanding performance in one year may penalize management in subsequent years by creating unrealistically high performance thresholds. Prior-year-performance comparisons, which often remain in place over several years, need to be reviewed periodically to accommodate changes in business conditions.

Peer Group Comparisons

Under this approach, the size of the incentive pool is determined by comparing the organization's performance against average industry results or a selected group of competitors. For example, a plan may state that the organization will pay target awards if performance is at or above the 65th percentile of competitor companies. No award will be paid unless the organization ranks at least in the 40th percentile of competitors, and a maximum award will be paid if the organization is at or above the 90th percentile.

A peer performance approach provides an objective measure of performance and factors out industrywide economic events beyond the organization's control. A peer group, however, may be difficult to define, and valid information may be difficult to obtain on a timely basis, thus delaying awards and eroding the link to performance. Also, shareholders may object if an incentive is paid when industry results are poor or show a decline, even if the organization has performed relatively better than its peers.

Because each of these funding approaches has the goal of driving desired behavior and performance, they share basic similarities. It is important to consider the merits of each and combine the characteristics that best meet organization objectives. Care should be taken, however, not to make the incentive plan too complex. Simplicity is important, especially when the plan applies to large groups of employees.

FORMULA APPROACH TO FUNDING

Some organizations fund the incentive plan by means of a formula that requires a minimum level of financial success before an incentive pool is established, for example, 10 percent of pretax earnings that exceeds a 6 percent return on capital. That is, an incentive will be paid out only after shareholders have received a return of 6 percent of capital. Thus, if excess pretax earnings equal $50 million, the incentive pool would equal $5 million ($50 million times 10 percent). Funds may be paid out on a discretionary basis or allocated through a formal goal-setting process.

A fixed-formula approach is often found in organizations that are composed of a portfolio of businesses where corporatewide financial results cannot be forecasted confidently. Once a credible financial planning process is in place, most organizations move to an approach that relies on the business planning process to establish performance parameters. The most positive characteristic of a fixed-formula approach is that it usually provides for a fixed return to shareholders before management receives an incentive. There are, however, several concerns with a formula plan. One is that it is essentially a profit-sharing plan with little direct correlation to the business planning process or industry results. Another is that the formula tends to stay in place for many years irrespective of changing business dynamics and strategies. Formulas also typically relate to corporate performance and may not reflect differing performance opportunities and the strategies of business units.

ALLOCATION OF FUNDS

Once the amount of the incentive pool has been determined, management must decide how to allocate the pool among the participants. This is done through the goal-setting process. Goals, which apply to teams as well as to individuals, should be measurable, related to specific objectives, and simple to understand and communicate. Most important, goals should be challenging, achievable, and within the control of the individual or team being evaluated. Goal setting should not be determined by individuals and their immediate supervisors but rather should result from a formal process that begins with business unit goals and flows down through the unit, thus ensuring that individual and department goals support overall unit goals.

Individual awards are typically based on a combination of business unit and individual (or team) goals. The relative weight assigned to business unit and individual performance usually depends on the level of responsibility and influence over results. For example, a CEO's annual incentive may be based entirely on corporate performance whereas that for the head of a business unit may be split between corporate (50 percent) and business unit (50 percent) performance. Similarly, a divisional manager's incentive may be split equally between divisional and individual performance. Today, balanced scorecards, 360 degree feedback, and review teams are frequently used as part of the annual incentive process to assess individual employee contribution.

FORM OF PAYMENT AND DEFERRED ARRANGEMENTS

Almost all organizations pay out annual incentives in cash (or sometimes a combination of cash and stock) soon after the annual performance cycle has ended and performance results are known. In rare circumstances, payments may be held back where retention is an issue or where performance levels are highly volatile and may not be sustained. Voluntary deferrals, however, are widespread, and most annual incentive plans allow participants to defer income recognition until a future date, typically a specified number of years following the award or until retirement. If the plan is structured properly, both the incentive amount and any interest paid over the deferral period accrue on a tax-deferred basis. The executive must, however, elect to defer all or part of the incentive prior to the service period and must specify the period over which the incentive is to be deferred. Such deferred amounts are not unsegregated from the organization's other assets and are liable to the demands of creditors.

IRS SECTION 162(m)

Publicly held corporations should design their annual incentive plans to take advantage of the exemptions under IRC Section 162(m), the "million dollar cap" on compensation deductions. Section 162(m) states that compensation in excess of $1 million paid to any "covered employee" (i.e., the CEO and the four other named officers in the company proxy for SEC reporting purposes) will not be deductible as a compensation expense unless the following general conditions apply: (1) The amounts paid are based solely on attaining one or more performance goals established by a compensation committee consisting solely of two or more outside directors, (2) prior to payment, the shareholders have approved the material terms under which the compensation is to be paid, and (3) prior to payment, the board or board compensation committee has certified that the performance goals have been satisfied. Today, almost all large publicly held corporations have structured their annual incentive plans to qualify for the exemptions under Section 162(m).

CONCLUSION

Properly structured annual incentive plans can enhance an organization's performance and serve as a powerful management tool to influence behavior in a positive way. Designing, implementing, and administering an annual incentive plan, however, are activities that can be undertaken only with the full cooperation of top management and the human resources department. Human resources professionals can provide top management with expertise on how compensation can be used to support business objectives. To do this, they must be knowledgeable about their organization's products and services and familiar with the principles of financial management and the tax and accounting rules affecting incentive compensation plans. When human resources professionals work with management to create incentive compensation programs tied to the strategy of the business, they contribute in a real way to the future direction and success of the organization.

C H A P T E R

LONG-TERM INCENTIVES

Jeffrey S. Hyman, Principal

Hewitt Associates LLC

THERE IS NO DOUBT THAT THE DECADE OF THE 1990S WILL BE REMEM-BERED by compensation professionals as the era when long-term incentives grew to prominence in the aggregate executive remuneration package. Spurred by a record-setting bull stock market and ever-increasing demands for enhanced investment value, management has increasingly turned to long-term compensation programs to reinforce value-added mandates and recognize executive contributions to increasing share-owner wealth. Even the federal government has played a role in enhancing the emphasis on long-term incentives. When Congress imposed penalties on excessive base salaries, long-term incentives remained an unencumbered channel through which to deliver the promise of escalating compensation levels. And long-term incentive compensation became a bridge between executives and the rest of the employees when the performance benefits of broad-based ownership sharing manifested itself in all-employee stock option programs that benefited workers at all ranks within the organization. As a consequence of these factors, long-term incentives have become one of the most popular—and certainly one of the most publicized—

forms of executive compensation today. No treatment of executive compensation is possible without a comprehensive review of long-term incentives.

To understand the extent to which long-term incentives are embedded in the compensation landscape, consider a recent Hewitt Associates survey through which it was found that 92 percent of major companies offer their executives at least one long-term incentive opportunity. This figure has remained unchanged for the last 10 years.[1] Furthermore, organizations with more than $1.0 billion in annual sales generally maintain at least two different types of long-term incentive plans, and it is not at all uncommon for executives in these firms to participate in multiple award opportunities, whether in a tandem relationship or independently of one another.

Not only is the prevalence of the long-term component growing, but its relative value within the total executive compensation package has changed, too. What was once considered a relatively incidental fringe benefit has become a substantial and integral part of the corporate executive's overall pay opportunity. Studies indicate that while the long-term incentive component was just 16 percent of a senior executive's total pay in 1982, it contributed 31 percent in 1989 and 45 percent in 1997—almost triple the impact in 15 years.[2] This represents a growth rate of over 7 percent per year, far outpacing the rate of increase in cash compensation for most executive program participants.

CHARACTERISTICS OF LONG-TERM INCENTIVE PLANS

Before choosing a long-term incentive program, careful thought should be given to the overall corporate strategy driving the plan implementation. As is true for all management systems, soundly designed compensation programs should not be structured in a vacuum, so it is essential to understand the purposes for which the long-term incentive plan is being implemented and the specific objectives the program is expected to help satisfy. Well-articulated compensation objectives are instrumental in the process of selecting the long-term incentive program design that best supports the organization's business and human resources needs.

Most often, long-term incentives are designed to accomplish the following:

- *Share the company's success with executives.* By allowing executives to share in the company's success, long-term plans serve to focus executive attention on certain key aspects of the company's performance.

- *Promote long-term thinking.* Long-term plans effectively balance the short-term focus of annual incentive plans.

---

[1]Hewitt Associates private survey.

[2]Hewitt Associates private survey.

- *Align executive interest with that of shareholders.* By making a portion of an executive's compensation contingent on company performance, long-term plans help correlate management's personal interest with those of shareholders, thereby promoting decision making that enhances the value of the firm's capital investment.

- *Attract and retain talented executives.* Long-term incentive awards often represent a sizable percentage of an executive's total compensation. When these awards are structured so that they vest over a period of years, they can act as an effective retention device. Additionally, the prevalence of long-term incentives in American industry makes it increasingly difficult for companies without such plans to attract and retain talented people.

- *Supplement broad-based, tax-qualified employee retirement income programs.* As tax laws continue to limit the benefits that can accrue on behalf of the highly paid, many companies implement long-term incentive plans to supplement the capital accumulation opportunities available to executives under broad-based, tax-qualified retirement programs.

Since the effectiveness of a long-term plan depends largely on how well the program suits the intended objectives, it is important to be familiar with the full range of program designs. Keep in mind, however, that unlike the broad-based benefit programs typically offered to all employees, executive long-term incentive plans generally are not tax qualified (with the exception of incentive stock options) and, therefore, are not usually restricted to a format that complies with stringent legislative regulation. The range of possible program structures is limited only by the creativity and resourcefulness of those challenged with developing the overall plan.

Notwithstanding the flexibility permissible in executive incentive plan design, the format of a long-term program typically falls into one of three categories, depending on the company's primary considerations. Plans that are *market based* relate incentive earnings opportunities to increases in the price of a company's common stock. *Performance-based arrangements,* on the other hand, correlate payout with more internally focused performance targets. *Hybrid formats* incorporate elements of both internal and external performance in determining the value of the earnings available to the plan participants.

Whether a market-based, performance-based, or hybrid plan is right for an organization depends entirely on the operation objectives, overall corporate strategy, and underlying management philosophy of the company itself. Remember, the long-term incentive plan is best characterized as a communication device through which the company identifies for its executives the mission it expects to fulfill, the strategy by which it will do so, and the goals that, when accomplished, will indicate the satisfaction of the corporation's purpose. Consequently, the structure of the long-term incentive is impossible to separate from the objectives it is expected to support.

Many factors affect the choosing of an appropriate long-term incentive plan, especially the related tax and financial accounting implications. Given the magnitude of long-term incentive awards and the breadth of participation in the plans, it is important to consider the impact of charges to the financial statements, the potential for earnings dilution, and the timing and characterization of income and deductions.

Still, the primary consideration when constructing a long-term incentive plan is whether the plan framework supports the organization's objectives. Understanding how these programs can work to deliver the right messages is probably accomplished best by understanding the mechanics of specific program formats. The remainder of this chapter, therefore, characterizes the most frequently used long-term incentive plans, which is followed by a discussion comparing the different approaches.

MARKET-BASED PLANS

Stock Options, in General

Stock options are by far the most popular form of long-term incentives found in American industry. Roughly 80 percent of all major companies have an option program in place. Stock options provide employees with the right to purchase company stock at a stipulated price over a specific period of time. If the stock value appreciates within that time frame, the employee then has the right to acquire the stock at a price below its market value.

There are two types of stock option plans—the nonqualified version and the incentive stock alternative. While the mechanics of both types of plans are similar, they each have distinct characteristics.

Nonqualified Stock Options. The more prevalent of the executive stock option plans is the nonqualified variety. *Nonqualified stock option plans* are the more flexible of the two kinds of stock option programs. They are unfettered by statute or regulation concerning minimum-price requirements, maximum grant periods, or maximum exercise and holding periods. The absence of regulation enables companies to tailor their plans to fit their individual objectives (for example, some companies may wish to offer options at below fair market value, others may wish to extend the term of an option over an employee's career, and so forth).

On the accounting side, if the option is granted at 100 percent of the market price at the date of grant, the employer incurs no compensation expense for accounting purposes. If the employer grants a nonqualified option at a discount (i.e., an exercise price below market value at the date of grant), the excess of the market price over the exercise price is deemed a compensation expense for accounting purposes, and it must be charged against earnings.

Generally, the employee who receives nonqualified stock options incurs no tax liability at the time of the grant. However, at the date of exercise, the excess of the stock's market value over the option price is taxable as ordinary income. Any subsequent appreciation that is realized at the time the acquired share is sold is taxed as a capital gain. Figure 28.1 presents a graph of an employee's tax consequences with nonqualified stock options.

With a nonqualified stock option plan, the employer receives a business expense (compensation) deduction in the amount and at the time the employee realizes ordinary income.

Incentive Stock Options. The second type of executive stock option plan is the *incentive stock option,* which is designed to be a tax-favored way to deliver stock to employees. The operational aspects of incentive stock options are largely the same as those of nonqualified stock options, but the employee and the plan itself must comply with several restrictive tax law provisions that have no application to the nonqualified variety of option. If the rules are adhered to, employees benefit two ways: They avoid taxation both at the grant and the time of option exercise, and any gain ultimately recognizable on the sale of acquired shares is treated as capital in nature rather than as ordinary income.

The rules that ensure favored tax treatment for incentive stock options are delineated in Section 422A of the Internal Revenue Code. In short, the options must be designated "incentive stock options," they cannot be exercised at a price less than 100 percent of the underlying stock's fair value on the option grant date, and no more than $100,000 worth of options can vest in any one year. In addition, a statutory holding period must be satisfied. If the stock is held for at least 1 year following the date of exercise and 2 years from the date of the grant, then when the stock is disposed of, the aggregate difference between the option price and the sale price is taxed as a long-term capital gain.

FIGURE 28.1   Nonqualified stock option. (*Source: Hewitt Associates.*)

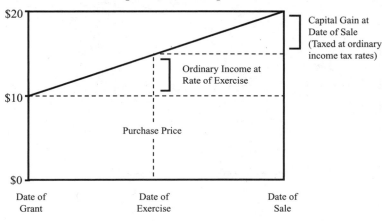

Essentially, there are two principal advantages to incentive stock options: favorable long-term capital gain tax treatment and the deferral of taxation until the date the acquired shares are sold. However, the *bargain element* (the difference between the option price and the market price) at exercise is a tax preference item subject to the alternative minimum tax. The tax effect of incentive stock options on the employee is shown in Figure 28.2.

For most employees, the tax deferral and capital gain treatment attendant to incentive stock option awards makes them quite appealing. But employers typically object to their issuance because of their less-than-optimal consequences for the company. More specifically, the employer generally earns no business expense (compensation) deduction on option exercise unless the employee fails the requisite holding-period requirements. In that event, the employee will be forced to recognize any accrued appreciation as ordinary income, and the employer then will become entitled to an offsetting tax deduction.

Stock Appreciation Rights

Stocks with appreciation rights (SARs) allow an employee to realize the appreciation in value of a specified number of common shares without making a cash investment in the stock or causing dilution of the employer's shareholder equity. SARs work in the following way.

Suppose an employee is granted 1,000 SARs when a single share of the company's stock is selling for $20. Further assume that the price of a single share appreciates in value by $10 during the exercise period, and the employee exercises all 1,000 SARs when the market value of the stock reaches $30 per share. In this scenario, the employee becomes entitled to a cash award from the company equal to $10,000. It is at this time, when the SARs are cashed out, that tax ramifications materialize.

FIGURE 28.2   Incentive stock option. (*Source: Hewitt Associates.*)

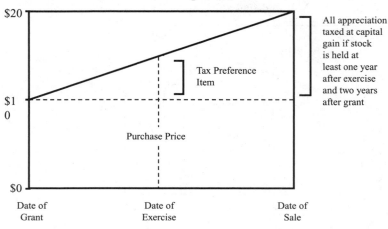

On the date the SARs are exercised, the employee recognizes ordinary income in the amount received in satisfaction of the award. Sometimes the SARs are satisfied in the form of shares of the company's common stock instead of in cash. When this happens, the recipient becomes, in effect, an investor in the company, so, later on, when the acquired shares are sold, the amount received at the time of sale is subject to tax in accordance with the rules governing the sale of a capital asset. These results are displayed graphically in Figure 28.3.

Because the employee is taxed at ordinary income rates at the time the SARs are exercised, the employer may claim a business expense (compensation) deduction equal to the amount of the employee's ordinary income in the year that the employee first incurs a tax liability. The employee's subsequently earned capital gain or loss on the disposition of acquired shares has no effect on the company.

SARs may be granted alone or in conjunction with nonqualified stock options and/or incentive stock options. When SARs are granted in tandem with stock options, the number of shares covered by the appreciation rights normally equals the number of shares granted to the employee under stock options. The exercise of an option typically cancels an SAR account and vice versa. In this manner, the SARs act as a tax offset or financing vehicle for the exercise of options. When SARs are granted independently of stock options, any appreciation in company stock that occurs between the date of the grant and the date of exercise may be payable to the executive in cash, stock, or a combination thereof.

An accounting consequence associated with SARs, however, greatly distinguishes them from stock options. Remember that options usually generate no earnings change. But the estimated expense of appreciation rights has to be accrued quarterly from the date of the grant to date of exercise, and the expense is

FIGURE 28.3 Stocks with appreciation rights. (*Source: Hewitt Associates.*)

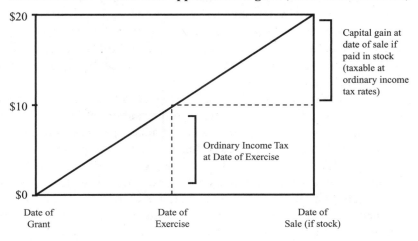

generally considered to be equal to the amount of appreciation realized during each quarter. If the plan is a combination plan permitting a choice between options or rights, the compensation cost is measured according to the most likely choice. Because of the volatility of this accounting treatment, however, many companies have severely restricted the number of executives eligible for SARs and, in some cases, have eliminated the plan altogether.

Restricted Stocks

Restricted stock programs permit the transfer of the employer's stock to an executive, usually free of charge to the employee. In this sense, restricted stock plans are outright equity grants. Full rights to stock acquisitions are conditional, however, and are predicated on the occurrence of certain events, like the continued employment of the individual for a specified period of time. Some plans provide restricted stock to vest when certain corporate or individual performance goals are met. However, imposition of these types of conditions is relatively uncommon.

In most restricted stock plans, the executive enjoys full shareholder rights during the restricted period, except for the right to sell or transfer stock. If the conditions placed upon the transfer of stock are fulfilled, then at the end of the restricted period the executive owns the stock outright. However, if the conditions are not met, the executive must forfeit the stock completely.

A variation on restricted stock is a TARSAP feature. TARSAP stands for *time-accelerated restricted stock award plan*. The time-accelerated feature allows restrictions to be removed faster than originally scheduled if the executive or the company meets certain performance goals. In this sense, the TARSAP constitutes a hybrid format.

For example, if XYZ Company awards restricted stock to executive A, then the stock becomes A's outright if A is in the employ of the company at the end of a 10-year period. In an alternative scenario, the company might set up certain income goals for the corporation and its business units. If executive A's business unit achieves 110 percent of its budgeted pretax income each year, the vesting period would be shortened by 3 years (for example, if the 110 percent goal is reached in the first year, the restricted stock will vest to executive A at the end of 7 years, rather than 10 years).

Another variation among restricted stock plans is a *restricted stock performance plan.* It offers restricted stock in the traditional manner but also sets forth a performance schedule that can generate a cash payment related to the restricted stock award. The cash payment often is intended to pay taxes on the restricted stock when the shares vest. As with a time-accelerated plan, a restricted stock performance plan awards restricted stock to executive A, with full rights conditioned on A's being employed with the company 4 years later. If executive A's business unit achieves, on average, 105 percent of its budgeted pretax income over the 4-year period, the plan also will make a cash payment large enough to pay all taxes due on the restricted stock, which becomes vested in the fourth year, and on the cash itself. Performance to a lesser or greater degree than target likewise will provide a lesser or greater cash payment.

A third variation on traditional restricted stock is a plan that bases restrictions primarily on performance rather than continued employment with the company. For example, an executive may be granted restricted stock that becomes vested in 4 years only if the company achieves an average earnings per share of $2 over the 4-year period and the executive is employed at the end of those 4 years. If the performance goal is not satisfied, a smaller number of shares may be vested, or none at all.

The compensation expense associated with restricted stock is recognized as of the date of the initial grant and is not affected by any subsequent appreciation or depreciation in the stock. The amount of the expense is the difference between the stock's fair-market-value grant date and the price paid for it (if any) by the employee. This amount is amortized for accounting purposes over the restriction period.

The accounting treatment differs if full rights to the restricted stock depend solely on whether the employee is to meet performance goals or has a TARSAP. When goal achievement is the only prerequisite to payment, compensation expense for the restricted stock is not based on the value at the time of the grant but instead on an estimate of its full fair market value when the restrictions lapse. In the case of a TARSAP, the compensation expense equals the market value of the shares on the date of the grant, but the timing of the financial statement charges depends on the timing of the accomplishment of the performance goals that accelerate the lifting of the restrictions.

Ordinarily, an executive who gets restricted stock incurs no tax liability at the date of the grant. When the restrictions lapse, however, ordinary income needs to be recognized on the current fair market value of the stock less the employee's cost to acquire the shares, if any. After restrictions lapse, the executive is viewed as an equity investor in the company, so, for tax purposes, any subsequent appreciation or loss is treated as capital in nature.

In the instance where the employee expects there will be a substantial increase forthcoming in the market price of the shares, the employee may elect to pay the tax on the initial bargain value of the restricted grant within 30 days of the grant date. When this election is made, the income recognized is taxed as ordinary income, but any subsequent appreciation is capital gain. Given the disparate treatment accorded ordinary income and capital gain, some employees find this "Section 83(b) election" to be an attractive alternative to the standard tax posture. Figure 28.4 depicts the usual [non-Section 83(b) election] tax consequences for an executive who receives restricted stock.

As is the case in all other nonqualified compensation plans, the employer granting restricted stock becomes entitled to a deductible compensation expense for tax purposes at the same time, and in the same amount, as the employee

FIGURE 28.4   Restricted stock. (*Source: Hewitt Associates.*)

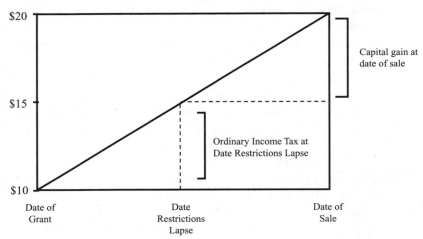

realizes taxable ordinary income. Typically, this means that the employer gets a deduction when the restrictions on share transferability lapse. In addition, any dividends paid on the restricted shares are also tax deductible during the period restrictions on the shares are in force.

Note that, to obtain this deduction, the company must withhold income taxes on the shares granted. However, the nature of a pure restricted stock program is such that there may be no cash payment from which to withhold. Consequently, the company must either ask the recipient to make a cash payment to the company for the withholding taxes or the company must withhold taxes from other sources, such as salary or bonus compensation.

Also consider that the employer obtains a tax deduction equal to the value of the stock at vesting, while the accounting charge is limited to the value of the share on the grant date. This means companies whose stock has appreciated will accrue a tax benefit that is disproportionately high relative to the accounting expense. Any such excess benefit cannot be added to income, however, but instead must be charged to capital.

Phantom Stocks

This form of long-term deferred compensation uses the employer's stock as the measuring device for calculating the value of the ultimate award payment. Designated executives are given units called *phantom stock,* which incorporate a value equal to the price of shares of common equity. Unlike real shares, however, the phantom stock does not represent any true ownership interest in the company. The employer simply credits these phantom shares on its books, and as the company's stock price rises and falls, so does the value of the phantom stock. Typically, phantom shares are "put" back into the company after a stipulated time has elapsed, and the amount of any accrued appreciation during the holding period is paid out in cash. A variation on this theme pays out the full value of the stock plus any accrued appreciation, as opposed to appreciation alone, after the stipulated time frame.

As a rule, the value of one phantom share at any time equals the market price of one share of the company's stock. Nonetheless, when a public market for the company's shares does not exist, the employer may relate phantom stock values to the firm's book value per share. Note also that phantom stock accounts may be credited with any dividends declared on a number of shares of stock equivalent to the number of phantom shares in an executive's phantom stock account.

Sometimes phantom stock plans are used to defer compensation earned from an annual incentive plan. The employee's incentive dollars are used to purchase a number of phantom shares at the then-current value of the employer's stock. At the end of the deferral period, phantom shares are revalued, and final payments are made in cash, in stock, or in a combination of cash and stock. Dividend equivalents may be either credited to the executive's account or paid directly upon declaration.

The estimated expense of phantom stock grants needs to be accrued quarterly by amortizing the appreciation in award value over the maturity period. The payment or crediting of dividend equivalents is expensed at the time of payment or credit.

The tax treatment of phantom stock plans closely resembles that of plans that include stocks with appreciation rights. Participants incur no tax liability on the initial grant of phantom shares. However, final payments in satisfaction of the award accrual are deemed "ordinary income" in the year paid out, and it is at that time that the employer sees an offsetting deduction. Sometimes dividends are paid to holders of phantom shares. When this happens, the payments are treated as additional compensation and are subject to ordinary income tax when received by the employee. If final phantom stock redemptions are made in stock, subsequent appreciation represents capital gain (see Figure 23.5).

PERFORMANCE-BASED PLANS

Performance Shares or Units

Performance shares or units plans typically offer awards payable in stock or cash and are contingent on the organization's meeting preset, long-term performance objectives. Generally, an employee receives an unsecured promise from the company to pay the employee cash or stock at no cost to the recipient. The employer then designates some objective measure of company performance and relates the magnitude of the award opportunity to varying levels of goal achievement. This yardstick is typically based on the performance of the entire corporation, but it could also relate to group or division performance. Commonly, performance is measured over a multiyear cycle in terms of return on equity, return on assets (or capital employed), or compound growth in earnings. Increasingly, however, it is defined relative to a standard set by the performance of other companies.

The employee earns the right to receive some or all of the promised cash units or shares at the end of the performance cycle. The number of performance shares or cash units to be received depends on the employer's long-term performance. The value of the cash units is a fixed dollar amount determined at the time of initial grant. The value of the shares, however, is based on the market value of the employer's stock at the conclusion of the performance period. Regardless of how the value is determined, the full amount of all payments made to plan participants needs to be fully amortized and charged to earnings throughout the performance period on an as-accrued basis.

Taxation of performance shares or units is a function of cash-basis accounting. Employers do not get a deduction until they pay out awards, which also is when participants realize ordinary income on the full value of all the amounts received. If final payments are made in stock, then the recipient is an investor with respect to those shares, and any subsequent appreciation in stock price is treated as a capital gain. Figure 28.5 presents a graph of the recipient's tax consequences.

Formula-Value Shares

The *formula-value share plan* is a variation of the previously discussed phantom stock program, but this plan is generally applied in private companies or at the divisional level of public organizations. Like the phantom stock concept, the formula-value share plan awards participants with stock-like units priced to reflect a share in the company or division.

FIGURE 28.5   Performance share per unit. (*Source: Hewitt Associates.*)

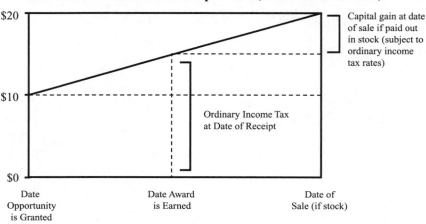

Generally, the value of a formulated share is a function of the organization's earnings, revenues, cash flow, or other combination of measures that the market might be expected to consider in assigning value to the company or division. Shares generally are valued at the time of the grant and again after a stipulated performance period, at which point any appreciation in value is paid to the executive in cash. The variable accounting rules associated with stock appreciation rights also apply to formula-value shares. Reserves need to be created over the performance period to reflect postgrant appreciation in award value as it accrues.

Recipients of formula-value shares incur no tax liability when they first receive their shares. When the shares are redeemed at the completion of the performance or measurement period, however, the plan participants realize ordinary income on the amounts received. Figure 28.6 illustrates how an employee is taxed on the receipt of formula-value shares. A tax deduction accrues to the company in the same amount and in the same year as the participant realizes ordinary income.

MARKET-BASED VERSUS PERFORMANCE-BASED PLANS

After considering the workings of commonly used long-term incentive plan formats, it becomes clear that the selection of a preferred design format depends on balancing the company's objectives in implementing the program with the realities of the operating environment in which the executive group serves. For example, an organization whose management philosophy exhorts executives to continuously maximize the value of its shareholders' investment might quickly conclude that any of the market-based programs are well suited for implementation since the value of the participant's earnings directly relates to increases in the price of the company's stock. This is a logical conclusion to draw, yet it ignores many

FIGURE 28.6   Formula-value shares. (*Source: Hewitt Associates.*)

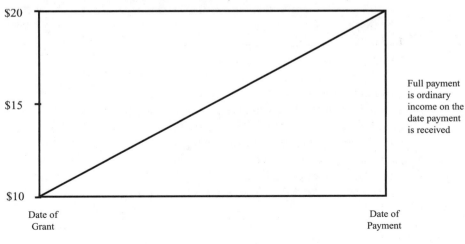

compelling arguments that suggest stock prices move in response to many stimuli wholly unrelated to individual executive decision making. If we believe that factors pertaining to macroeconomic events, market psychology, industry cycles, and other external factors strongly impact share value, then introducing a long-term compensation system that relates individual earnings opportunities to stock price appreciation alone may amount to an overzealous and futile attempt to encourage executive activity that enhances shareholder value.

Certainly, the effort to match executive rewards with shareholder value enhancement is an admirable goal, one from which the human resources professional ought not to be distracted. But while market-based plans such as stock options and stocks with appreciation rights can be very effective vehicles for sharing organization success as defined by appreciation in shareholder return, they tend to reward plan participants through a retrospective, after-the-fact view of performance. In this sense, they are passive arrangements that, because of the uncertain connection between management decision making and stock price movement, represent ineffective instruments for communicating the specific goals that are within management's grasp and that the company wants its executive team to achieve.

In many instances then, performance-based awards, such as performance units or formula-value shares, or even the hybrid formats (for example, performance shares or TARSAPs), might offer better approaches to plan structure when the company is clear about its performance targets and confident that goal achievement eventually will drive stock price appreciation. Under this assumption, it is incumbent upon the organization to identify those measures of internal performance that correlate well with share price movement.

As noted earlier, when selecting performance targets, most companies identify earnings, return on assets or investment, or some other reflection of financial performance founded on traditional accounting principles. At the frontier of performance measurement thinking, however, are the advocates of economic-based planning. They argue that of all the common yardsticks of success, it is the metrics that reflect economic value—measures like net operating profit after tax after capital charges, and discounted inflation-adjusted cash flow and asset growth—that correlate most directly with stock price appreciation.

As a result, organizations that utilize sophisticated financial planning techniques and information systems are increasingly recognizing that there is a profound inconsistency in promoting a management philosophy that advocates shareholder value creation while rewarding executives for maximizing traditional accounting measures. Those organizations are moving away from the more common focus on book earnings and returns on equity and capital. Instead, they are beginning to relate long-term incentive opportunities to value creation models whose foundations rest in economic value-added theory and discounted cash-flow analysis.

CONCLUSION

The significance of long-term incentives in the overall executive compensation package has grown substantially over the past decade, and few compensation professionals expect the growth trend to abate any time soon. As long as shareholder value creation directives continue to characterize the direction and nature of management initiatives, then one can anticipate that the long-term incentive component of the executive compensation package will maintain its special prominence in the compensation landscape.

For the human resources professional, it will become increasingly important to possess a clear understanding of how long-term incentives work to help organizations accomplish their operating objectives. Part of the challenge will be to ensure familiarity with the mechanics of plan design. But equally critical will be an ability to discern how the workings of each program will fit within the organization's culture, how effective they will be in promoting the firm's business and human resources objectives, and how well they will support the company's overall management philosophy.

EXECUTIVE COMPENSATION SYSTEMS: DRIVERS OR RESULTS FROM STRATEGIC CHOICES?

Johannes M. Pennings
Department of Management

The Wharton School, University of Pennsylvania

EXECUTIVE COMPENSATION CONTINUES TO BE A MATTER OF CONTROVERSY among academics and practitioners. Debates continue on how to optimize the incentive structures of top decision makers in organizations. Criticism in the popular business press abounds about senior executives being overpaid, and when benchmarked with peers and their firm's performance, many executives appear to be rewarded at a level that is excessive. Lately such criticism has gained new dimensionality. For example,

The New York Times[1] reported that while the pay of top executives continues to swell, the wages of the workforce have grown only piecemeal. The ratio of CEO pay to that of workers grew to 326 to 1 in 1997, compared to 44 to 1 only 20 years earlier. Cross-nationally, American CEOs also far out-earn their counterparts in other societies.

Numerous academic researchers have countered such criticism by their findings on the link between pay and performance, even if as little as 1 or 2 percent of the variance in executive pay might be accounted for by differences in accounting or market-derived indices of firm performance. Yet, this skepticism resurfaces if the focus is on strategic performance. Unlike such short-term, relatively unequivocal performance measures, strategic measures are surrounded by a good deal of ambiguity. Executive pay has also become a complex, intricate phenomenon with little transparency, further blurring the pay-performance link. Thus, there are issues to address, such as what constitutes executive compensation and strategic performance and how to construe their connection. This chapter reviews these issues. Executive compensation systems are now widely diffused among U.S. corporations. Usually, they cover a comparatively small number of executives, although in some cases this number might exceed 50 people. The underlying assumption is that these top managers have a disproportionate influence on corporate performance and have the leverage to direct their firm's strategic destiny. Executive compensation plans, therefore, can be labeled as "strategic reward systems." Most of these plans have been devised by compensation consulting firms. Although each firm's system might have its own unique attributes, there is also an increased convergence among corporations in the manner in which these systems are designed. The mechanical features and the formal attributes for making compensation decisions should be distinguished from the behavior and attitudes among those involved. We should ask why firms maintain compensation plans, separate from those aimed at other classes of employees. Compensation plans are often very complex, particularly in the United States, and they raise the question as to whether such plans are truly effective, whether they matter. It boils down to the issue of whether firms in the United States do indeed pay their executives for corporate performance. Such issues acquire an interesting dimension when we make international comparisons and spot determinants of pay that seem to be unrelated to actual performance. In this chapter we explore some of these issues.

CONCEPTUAL ISSUES IN EXECUTIVE COMPENSATION

Linking executive pay to performance is surprisingly difficult because it is not easy to define the proper terms. *Executive pay* includes myriad elements, some of which defy attempts to assign them to a specific time period. Some are entitlements such as a company car or club membership fees, and there is some question

---

[1]*The New York Times,* "Pressing the Issue of Pay Inequality," February 7, 1999.

as to whether we should include them in executive compensation. Other components can vary temporally. For example, the pay associated with stock options can be measured at the time they are granted. They can also be assessed at the time they are exercised, at the time the exercised options are sold by the beneficiary, at the time of distribution of the stock or cash dividends associated with those stock options when they were exercised but not yet sold, and so on. Valuing the option in the present through some form of discounting further exacerbates the difficulty of determining executive pay. After a stock market correction, many firms adjust the strike price of options, thus further complicating an assessment of this variable component of compensation. Similar problems exist in the interpretation of "deferred" compensation, pension contributions, and golden parachutes, where one or more executives are to receive a generous cash payment in the event of being forced to resign through some jolt such as a hostile takeover or some palace revolution. Even more difficult to interpret are perks, whose cash value may be small but whose symbolic meaning is highly salient. This latter aspect cannot be sufficiently emphasized. Compensation is only one of a variety of incentives. Power, status, and achievement rival compensation in their prominence for executives. In European and Pacific Basin cultures, such nonpecuniary outcomes may even exceed pay to top executives.

As we will see, the pay profile of CEOs in different countries varies widely, thus calling into question the benefits of perks, pay components, and other incentives as vehicles for inciting executives. It should therefore also be obvious that one should not only look at the level of compensation but also at the profile. The profile represents the relative size of base salary, bonuses, long-term incentive compensation, stock options, and the perks' cash value. The profile is often depicted with a pie chart, showing the relative magnitude of the various compensation components. The compensation mix has a time-and-risk aspect. Table 29.1 spells out these aspects. From these compensation components we can derive some architecture and calculate some important ratios. The architecture is often depicted with a pie chart in which short-term versus long-term or the fixed versus the variable compensation component is highlighted. Two ratios are useful in uncovering differences in incentive regimes among firms, industries, or even countries:

$$\text{Compensation risk} = \frac{\text{annual bonus} + \text{long-term compensation}}{\text{salary} + \text{benefits} + \text{perks}}$$

$$\text{Compensation time horizon} = \frac{\text{long-term compensation}}{\text{annual bonus}}$$

The underlying premises can be spelled out in a neoclassical (orthodox economic) way: Managers often act in their own self-interest rather than in some

TABLE 29.1   Computation of Executive Compensation Mix

	Short-Term Time Horizon	Long-Term Time Horizon
High compensation risk	Annual bonus	Long-term bonus
		Stock options
		Restricted stock
Low compensation risk	Salary	Deferred compensation
	Benefits	
	Perks	

altruistic or even corporate interest. Corporations (which are usually not owned by the managers) have divergent objectives regarding R&D, production, and financial decisions. When managers are the owners of the firm, such divergence is often absent. Likewise, if managers are the founders and still retain a substantial stake in the firm, we would also assume their interest to be highly overlapping with those of the firm. However, the separation of ownership and control has the potential to create all kinds of problems, which economists refer to as *agency problems,* which we will review later.

Sources of conflict between executives and the owners of the firm are manifold. For example, unlike a "regular" investor, executives are constrained in diversifying their wealth. Such constraint might render them risk averse and in fact might induce them to commit to projects that produce low (but highly probable) returns. Many executives do not reach their level of power and compensation until they come close to retirement age and are prone to make commitments that will have a short time payoff. For example, they may refrain from R&D expenditures whose rents do not materialize until after they retire. R&D expenditures suppress internal rates of return. In general, managers might value certain expenditures differently than do owners.

All this also assumes that performance in general, and strategic performance in particular, can be readily articulated, but its antecedents cannot easily be identified. Firms resort to financial, short-term operational and accounting indicators, such as return on investment or return on equity, in choosing the criteria for decisions regarding executive compensation. When trying to endow performance with some strategic meaning, they tend to stretch such indicators over a multiyear period, the assumption being that elongating the time frame renders such performance measures strategic. More recently firms tend to substitute accounting performance measures for (capital) market measures in order to draw executives' attention from short-term to long-term time horizons. Unlike accounting measures, market-derived performance indices are less likely to be manipulated. They also tend to be more future oriented than historical. Whether such pay bases deserve the label "strategic" is not quite evident, however. Examples of such long-term pay systems are those whereby cost of capital is related to return on equity over a 5-year period—the so-called par line—and the executives are given some long-term bonus (phantom stocks or performance shares) based on the latter's exceeding the former. Such procedures tend to blur the meaning of performance and can be challenged on their strategic relevance because the essence of "strategic" may reach further than merely the time frame under consideration. The matter becomes far more nebulous and complicated when the issue of tying pay to performance pertains to the marginal contribution to (strategic) performance, which can be attributed to the CEO or any other executive. Economists consider the marginal productivity of labor to be equivalent to compensation: The higher an executive's marginal productivity, the greater his or her pay. It is particularly this issue that confronts the practice and research on executive compensation systems.

The link between pay and corporate strategy can be examined in two distinct ways. Compensation plans might emanate from a firm's strategy, or they may be significant antecedents through which strategic objectives are realized.

Linking pay to strategy, therefore, can be decomposed into two questions: (1) What is the meaning of executive compensation derived from or as part of the firm's strategy? and (2) What role does it play in the implementation of strategic objectives? For example, the adoption of golden parachutes can be construed as part of the firm's strategy to fend off hostile takeovers and to further tie executives to their firm. Yet those golden parachutes may result in conservative choices and discourage executives from taking risks or being innovative.

In this chapter we view strategy broadly. Strategy formulation entails the long-term decisions about markets, products, customer segments, technology, and human resources. Strategy represents an effort to match corporate resources with environmental opportunities. The strategic choice to operate in a given market with a given technology and other resources is relatively enduring and long lasting. For example, committing vast resources to a new technology, establishing a solid tradition of lifetime employment and promotion from within such that the firm becomes an "internal labor market," or diversifying to overseas markets all represent significant decisions with profound strategic implications that are mirrored in decisions about executive pay. Compensation practices are part and parcel of such a long-lasting strategic posture.

Strategy implementation represents a set of decisions to preserve ongoing strategic commitments but also to succeed in turning a firm's strategic trajectory around. The reorganization of a firm's design, changes in culture and human resources, and the use of compensation as a lever of strategic change are elements of strategic turnaround. Of course, they can also function as a vehicle for preserving the strategic status quo. The point is that executive compensation systems can have profound strategic unanticipated consequences regardless of whether or not those practices emerged from a given strategic posture. The implication is that executive pay may be the result of a given strategy, or it may be the cause of a strategy.

To better grasp this paradox, it is useful to consider the contribution of Chandler. In his classic 1962 monograph, *Strategy and Structure,*[2] Chandler advocated the argument that strategic changes—such as the move from single-product to multiproduct offerings—necessitates changes in organizational structure, planning processes, and staffing; in short, structure follows strategy. In the absence of such restructuring, the firm's strategic turnaround falters. Others have criticized this thesis. Hall and Saias[3] suggested that it is the change in structure, personnel, planning, and other organizational practices that enable a firm to change its strategy; strategy follows structure. Both views might have a kernel of truth in that the firm's strategic posture sets the stage for various decisions regarding people, structure, and planning. Yet, the results of those decisions often acquire their own momentum and have their own consequences.

A similar argument can be developed on the role of executive compensation and strategy. Compensation practices might trigger certain strategic behaviors on the part of those who are governed under a certain compensation system, but those very systems may mirror strategic decisions that are an integral part of the grand strategic design. Separating cause and effect may be tenuous.[4] This chapter further reviews these issues. On one hand, we are exploring questions on the design of executive reward systems, particularly how such designs may reflect a strategic frame of mind. On the other hand, we also are reviewing the strategic implications or consequences of executive compensation. In the first case, one might say that executive pay emerges as part and parcel of the intended or formulated strategy, whereas the consequences of pay can be construed as elements of the strategy as realized or implemented.

STRATEGIC DETERMINATION OF EXECUTIVE COMPENSATION

The strategic posture of the firm and the markets in which it has chosen to compete are crucial to shaping the level and profile of executive compensation. The pay profile is also a function of the degree of strategic diversification and the competitive conditions in the industry. The compensation practices vary a great deal depending on whether firms compete in a discretionary versus constrained industry and on whether they are proactive versus reactive in the strategic orientation they assume. As we will see, they vary also considerably cross-nationally.

---

[2]A. Chandler, *Strategy and Structure* (Cambridge, MA, MIT Press, 1962).

[3]D. J. Hall and M. A. Saias, "Strategy Follows Structure," *Strategic Management Journal,* vol. 1, pp. 149–163.

[4]Johannes M. Pennings, "Executive Reward Systems: A Cross-National Comparison," *Journal of Management Studies,* March 1993, pp. 261–280.

Firms reveal different compensation profiles. Those in discretionary industries have a proactive posture stressing variable and contingent pay, such as bonuses and long-term incentive compensation. In contrast, more passive firms in constrained industries tend to stress fixed and noncontingent pay, such as base salary.[5] Ironically, even so called variable forms of pay, such as bonuses or profit sharing, may be set in such a way that they become a fixed feature of executive pay. Likewise, when the stock market goes through a correction, many firms will reset the stock's strike price in order to preserve the option value for managers who may want to exercise their options. The implication is that these variable forms of pay were not at risk, and construing them as "variable" would be somewhat deceptive.

A *discretionary industry* is one in which the firm enjoys a great deal of latitude in crafting its own strategy. Whether or not firms operate in a discretionary industry hinges on their ability to measure and anticipate market developments. Thus, marketing research and geopolitical forecasts enable some firms to tune in to strategically important trends and to take anticipatory action. Furthermore, they may enjoy some leverage in shaping consumer demands or diffusing product innovations. Commodity markets or public utility firms tend to have little discretion, whereas firms in the financial services, cosmetics, and entertainment industries have selected relatively free markets. Particularly in such free markets, one would expect strategically aggressive firms to adopt compensation practices with high variations in levels of pay and to differentiate the profile of pay. For example, it has been found that pay levels or pay profiles vary considerably among firms in discretionary industries with a proactive posture.

Diversified firms have the potential to tailor an executive's compensation package to the very market to which he or she has been assigned. This lies at the heart of so-called strategic reward maps, as drawn by strategic compensation consultants such as the Boston Consulting Group and Booz Allen. The strategic product matrix of the firm is mapped on to its compensation plan—taking the general template as described in Table 29.1. Its fixed and variable pay components dovetail with the strategic imperatives of the various product markets. These consulting firms propose to design the firm's compensation profile in such a way as to reflect the riskiness and time horizon of the different marketplaces together with the corresponding strategic intent of the firm. For example, Booz Allen furnishes a two-by-two matrix that is to match the strategic mandate of various divisions.[6] A cash-cow division (large market share, low growth) requires a package with a low-risk posture and short time horizon; the bulk of its executive pay could consist of a salary. The evidence to date suggests, however, that firms are reluctant to strongly differentiate compensation practices by divisions; rather, they adopt a uniform system.

---

[5]Johannes M. Pennings and David T. Bussard, "Strategy, Control and Executive Compensation," *Topics in Total Compensation: Fitting the Incentive Plan to the Company,* vol. 1, 1987, pp. 101–112.

[6]Louis J. Brandisi, *Creating Shareholder Value: A New Mission for Executive Compensation* (New York: Booz Allen, 1984).

COMPENSATION NORMS IN INDUSTRIES, COUNTRIES, AND EXECUTIVE LABOR MARKETS

A relevant part of a firm's strategy for compensation considerations centers on the recruitment and retention of members. Firms prefer to conform to industry norms of compensation, but, as with strategy in general, human strategies can also be compared on their reactivity. It is likely that conformity to compensation norms is stronger when firms resort to a great deal of external recruitment of executive talent. A strategy of bolstering an internal labor market might render a firm somewhat immune from such norms, which are a key ingredient in strategic choices about human resources and executive labor markets. Compensation consultants such as Booz Allen or Towers, Perrin, Forster, & Crosby, and the Hay Group have a great impact in promoting and institutionalizing certain compensation plans. They solidify existing practices or disseminate novel ones, thereby setting certain trends. In the management literature such tendencies are referred to as *institutional pressures:* Firms are pressured into adopting distinct practices (compensation) plans, procedures for incenting executives as a way to signal compliance with sound management and widely held standards of corporate conduct.[7] Such standards differ between industries and societies. There are both industry norms and compensation norms for various societies. Compensation innovations proliferate, but, as in the world of fashion, the compensation consulting industry has its own designers of pay systems whose diffusion reflects the eagerness of companies and their boards to stay competitive. For example, the adoption of long-term incentive compensation plans by American corporations reveals a certain degree of faddishness. Organization theorists would argue that such limitations are less induced by the desire to create an optimum incentive for strategic behavior than to conform in order to acquire legitimacy and to convey the illusion of sound management. Sophisticated compensation plans, disseminated in 10K or proxy statements, confer public credibility and preserve the competitiveness in attracting and retaining high-level executives. An even more controversial standpoint would hold that compensation plans represent fossilized practices that have become uncoupled from the actual compensation, serving only to placate the external audience. The announcement of a new compensation plan has often intriguing effects on the short-term fluctuations in stock prices: The announcements produce what financial economists call "abnormal returns" as they cannot be accounted for by systematic or nonsystematic risk.

For high-level executives, such plans disclose how well the firm is in tune with the marketplace for executive talent. The numerous executive compensation

---

[7]Paul J. Dimaggio and Walter W. Powell, "The Iron Cage Revisited: Institutional Isomorphism and Collective Rationality in Organizational Fields," *American Sociological Review,* vol. 48, 1983, pp. 147–160.

surveys have contributed to the specification of the price of managerial labor—both the level and the proportion that is fixed versus variable. They permit a firm to set a pay range with relative, precise bounds for executives in certain industries. A great amount of research remains to be done here, however. For executives as a labor pool, there are issues such as who is in it and who is not, especially if we define the pool to coincide with a firm's industry or its strategic group. Executive search firms, together with compensation consultants, may assist firms in their human resources strategies, but they themselves may blur the boundaries between industries. Also, many firms are reluctant to go to the "external labor market"; they prefer to bolster internal succession. In this case, the firm is more likely to resemble an internal labor market. We know very little presently about whether internal versus external labor markets affect the level or profile of executive compensation. As suggested before, when the firm represents a well-established internal labor market (and its executives have high-quitting barriers because their human capital is vested in and idiosyncratic to their firm), compensation may be modest or below the industry norm. Yet, compensation is likely to exceed the level that would be required to retain its executives.

We should also be aware that the recipients of executive pay often have a major impact on the design of the compensation profile, how it is administered, and by whom it is enforced. The CEO is likely to have appointed many if not all the members of the board of directors, and by implication its subset that has responsibility for compensation issues—the so-called compensation committee. The CEO enjoys a good deal of overt and covert power in manipulating the compensation for his or her own benefit. Overt power derives from such sources as social capital and seniority. The CEO might have recruited board members to whom he or she owed certain favors or whose very recruitment amounts to a creation of a favor that greatly diminishes their independence. The CEO thus might be surrounded by friends and acquaintances who are unlikely to challenge him or her (those acquaintances often reciprocate by inviting him or her on their firm's board). The CEO is the author of his or her very own social network, enjoys a good deal of structural autonomy, and might in fact broker much of the information or knowledge among the various individuals who surround him or her, as researched by Barkema and Pennings.[8]

Covert power is associated with more visible sources of power, including ownership and position in the firm. For example, the CEO who founded the firm is likely to enjoy considerable leverage in the firm, especially because most of the individuals in his or her network arrived after the CEO. He or she is likely to have some ownership stake in the firm. Having a substantial proportion of ownership

---

[8]H. Barkema and J. M. Pennings, "Top Executive Pay: The Role of Overt and Covert Power," *Organization Studies 19*, vol. 6, Nov./Dec. 1998, pp. 975–1004.

will make his or her power even more overt. Under these conditions, we would expect the CEO to manipulate his or her pay to favor his or her personal interests, and factors other than performance will determine level and mix of compensation.[9] The significance of these conditions cannot be overstated. That is why the correlation between compensation and performance is often modest, and even infinitesimally small. The correlation is also small in relation to institutional factors, such as industry customs and national culture, that strongly shape norms about level and mix of executive pay.

The role of institutional (and therefore nonmarket) forces on executive compensation levels or the configuration of executive compensation is dramatically illustrated when we consider these practices in different countries. Both level and compensation mix show dramatic variations across national cultures. Table 29.2 provides an indication of the differences in both level and internal differentiation across a select set of countries. The U.S. chief executive officers' compensation exceeds the level of that of peer individuals in other countries. Furthermore, these differences are primarily attributable to large payouts in variable compensation, most notably bonuses and stock options. As we have argued, such differences in compensation practices can be attributed to differences in national culture.[10] The work on national differences in culture has been pioneered by Hofstede.[11] This economic anthropologist identified variations in values such as individualism versus collectivism and the degree to which countries embrace or shun uncertainty and ambiguity. The U.S. system of core values scores highest on the individualism index and manifests also high tolerance for uncertainty. We similarly observe that countries with little tolerance for uncertainty (e.g., Germany) also express little proclivity for compensation profiles with a substantial compensation risk—for example, stock options.

Table 29.2 displays the unique position of the United States, where firms tend to reward their executives much more generously. The results come from a survey conducted by Towers Perrin.[12] Furthermore, we observe that the compensation mix in the United States is strongly slanted towards a longer time horizon and toward a much higher compensation risk level. The survey points out that U.S. chief executive officers have close to 0.4 of their total compensation at risk. If we exclude entitlements, such as perks, this proportion exceeds 1.5. Compared to most other countries, the Anglo-Saxon countries, like Canada and

---

9 Ibid.

[10]Johannes M. Pennings, "Strategic Reward Systems: A Cross-National Comparison," *Journal of Management Studies,* 1992.

[11]Geert H. Hofstede, *Culture's Consequences* (Beverly Hills: Sage, 1980).

[12]Towers Perrin, *Worldwide Total Reward,* New York, 1999.

TABLE 29.2   Strategic Consequences of Executive Pay

Country	Basic Compensation	Variable Bonus	Company Contributions: Compulsory	Company Contributions: Voluntary	Perquisites	Long-Term Incentives	Total Remuneration
Argentina	$386,827	$123,788	$14,917	$48,279	$19,604	$61,894	$655,309
Australia	246,794	74,038	3,827	48,000	49,359	9,872	431,890
Belgium	230,921	62,347	107,072	38,125	23,842	18,474	480,781
Brazil	302,077	82,714	134,676	41,465	58,706	81,581	701,219
Canada	257,280	90,048	8,579	54,029	16,158	72,024	498,118
China	—	—	—	—	—	—	—
France	250,443	47,859	111,134	3,597	32,780	74,575	520,389
Germany	248,022	67,842	12,265	45,800	24,500	—	398,430
Hong Kong	345,678	100,683	—	45,023	105,330	83,902	680,616
Italy	255,710	76,880	86,582	16,998	23,035	27,855	487,060
Japan	263,779	41,771	9,329	51,827	54,148	—	420,855
Malaysia	136,389	41,983	21,405	656	59,178	37,768	297,379
Mexico	324,494	84,495	5,204	9,421	25,241	8,047	456,902
Netherlands	262,515	56,415	6,576	54,272	24,979	45,131	449,889
New Zealand	109,816	18,584	—	14,377	16,116	—	158,894
Singapore	300,912	106,952	29,695	2,894	39,006	66,059	545,517
South Africa	192,492	38,122	—	42,421	53,185	35,307	361,526
South Korea	78,470	21,526	34,665	1,000	15,050	—	150,711
Spain	203,956	56,169	9,398	33,965	34,673	—	338,160
Sweden	190,404	37,334	75,222	40,993	11,444	—	355,398
Switzerland	284,621	80,661	43,870	39,572	10,486	16,132	475,342
Taiwan	—	—	—	—	—	—	—
United Kingdom	296,546	66,723	35,220	110,101	24,263	112,687	645,540
United States	402,200	156,400	18,374	70,326	35,000	390,100	1,072,400
Venezuela	202,941	158,395	36,784	32,529	28,614	—	459,264

the United Kingdom and surprisingly France, come somewhat close to the U.S. model. These results show that compensation practices in various countries mirror their institutional environments. We should view executive pay in a rather different light depending on the national context in which the firm operates. The discretion to vary the pay mix, or the actual compensation level, is conditional upon the national setting. Correlations between pay and performance should also vary by national context. Finally, it is obvious that such national differences present major challenges to multinational firms or to firms that emerge from a cross-border merger or acquisition.

It seems more interesting to consider the strategic implications of the level and profile of executive compensation. After all, executive compensation can be paraphrased as a strategic reward system. Top executives in general and the CEO in particular are governed by a reward system that is usually segregated from the general compensation systems affecting other employees. The reasons for establishing a separate compensation system are numerous. Presumably, executives have an undue impact on the strategic results of the firm. Furthermore, as we have seen, such reward systems are often linked to long-term performance criteria, such as the spread between return on equity versus the cost of capital over a 5-year period. Although such criteria are financial and reflect the vicissitudes of the market, many view them as strategic in that the choice behavior of senior executives might be conditioned by such criteria.

There has been a greater deal of research done on pay as a motivator of job performance, but virtually all this effort has been confined to lower-level employees. Thus, we do not know whether executive motivation is different from that of other occupational groups, nor do we know much about the motivational efficacy of executive compensation systems. Theoretical developments among management researchers have also failed to produce comprehensive statements on these issues.

To fully explicate this state of affairs, it may be helpful to highlight two theoretical traditions that are deemed crucial in understanding work motivation and job performance. They are expectancy theory and agency theory.

EXPECTANCY THEORY

Expectancy theory originates in organizational psychology and holds that a person's motivation is a function of two expectancies. The first one is the expectation that a certain level of effort will lead to a given performance level (for example, "If I try, it is very likely that I will succeed in meeting my sales quota"). The higher this subjective probability, the greater the level of effort.

Performance should be viewed in very general terms. It includes both job performance, such as productivity and return on investment, as well as membership performance. Membership includes decisions about joining or staying, but also other commitment-revealing behaviors such as long working hours.

The second expectancy consists of the subjective belief that performance results in outcomes or rewards having an attractive value to the person. They include pay but also the earlier-mentioned rewards of power, status, and challenge. Crucial is the assumption that individuals differ in their values such that each and every individual may not be equally motivated by the same rewards. Executives might value rewards that are different from those of other groups of employees; even among themselves, there may be differences in values. Yet, most executive compensation systems treat executives in a standardized way, thereby ignoring their differential sensitivity to levels or profiles of pay. They differ also cross-culturally. It may be these differences in values that render the executive compensation systems of Towers, Perrin, Forster & Crosby, and the Hay Group less effective in societies other than the United States.

Apart from the fact that U.S. compensation practices may have limited applicability elsewhere, there are two other issues to consider. First, it is essential that strategic performance criteria be unequivocally related to executive pay. If the time lag between effort and performance is long, the individual is less likely to perceive a clear relationship. Furthermore, under such conditions, factors other than those related to an executive's effort or business acumen may be perceived to affect strategic performance. They may include acts of God, government intervention, technological breakthroughs, executive labor markets, or business cycles. Furthermore, executive compensation plans, including golden parachutes, cover a group of executives in spite of performance accruing from an individual effort. It may be an opportunity for a free ride. These considerations are also at the heart of the question of "whether the CEO makes a difference"—a question that involves a great deal of contemporary research on executive succession and, by implication, executive compensation.

The second issue involves the expectancy that strategic performance is related to pay. As was already mentioned, strategic performance is a complicated phenomenon. Apart from financial performance indicators that have been stretched out over a long time period, most firms have tried little to expand the criteria by which strategic performance can be gauged. Financial performance bases of compensation are tied to either accounting measures, such as the efficient use of corporate or divisional assets, or to market measures, such as those that link shareholder wealth with equity cost of capital to the well being of the executives. Other nonfinancial criteria could include the development of successors, the creation of embryo businesses, or a sustained level of technological innovation and the nurturing and commercial introduction of new products or services. Such performance yardsticks are not necessarily embedded in short-term or long-term measures of financial performance.

"Corporations get the behaviors they reward" is an often-heard lament of expectancy theorists, and in principle, this should also hold for executives. If corporations like to entice executives to certain types of behavior and performance, they should make sure that such performance is feasible and convey a clear connection between certain performance criteria and pay. Also crucial is the assumption that pay itself should have a strong inducement, or "valence"—whether symbolic or by virtue of its buying power. Accounting criteria-based incentive plans tend to direct managerial motivation to short-term behaviors to improve performance on the indexes chosen. Furthermore, such indexes are susceptible to accounting bias and manipulation. In contrast, market-based performance indicators, such as 5-year earnings per share, could induce executives toward high-risk decisions, particularly those involving external debt financing. A study by David Larcker is particularly intriguing.[13] This accounting researcher found that the adoption of long-term performance plans lead to subsequent increases in capital expenditures. The effect disappeared, however, after the first year of adoption. From an expectancy theory standpoint, this suggests several concerns. First, it is important to have a sustained and unabating link between rewards and motivated behaviors and performance. Second, it is important to preserve the immediacy and saliency between rewards and performance. Long time periods or routinization of compensation decisions may dissipate the initial trigger that a new compensation plan has brought about. Third, long-term performance plans may be flawed in that the market does not always recognize the strategic strength of the firm. Ultimately, the firm (or its board of directors) seeks to reward those behaviors or performances that it considers most desirable, which may be at variance with executives' behaviors or performances, due to the executives' motives.

AGENCY THEORY

According to *agency theorists,* executives are controlled by a "contract" drawn up between them and the board of directors. The contract can pertain to behaviors (for example, implementation of strategic budgets) or to performance (for example, maintaining return on assets for certain markets or augmenting earnings per share). Such contracts are fraught with all kinds of difficulties. For example, the senior executives may have knowledge to which the board has no access. Agency problems can be alleviated by establishing more elaborate information systems. Also, and here executive pay considerations come in, the board makes the executives part of the payoff structure in the form of contingent rewards systems. Such contracts alleviate the need for highly sophisticated monitoring devices, but they also result in the sharing of risks between shareholders and executives. The interests of shareholders and executives may not always be congruent. Unlike the former, the latter do not enjoy much flexibility in diversifying their risks. Particularly when executives hold large amounts of stock or their pay profile shows them to be

---

[13]David Larker, "The Association Between Performance Plan Adoption and Corporate Capital Investment," *Journal of Accounting and Economics,* vol. 5, 1983, pp. 3–30.

heavily saddled with risk, they may be tempted to shun risky alternatives, even though pursuing them may be in the best interests of the shareholders.

Jensen and Meckling have indicated that senior executives, the CEO not excluded, often avoid risk because they attempt to preserve their status and tenure in the company.[14] By modifying the pay profile, these authors believe that risk-taking behaviors can be encouraged. In contrast, the level of pay may be dysfunctional for motivating certain behaviors or results. Although the evidence to date is scant, there appears to be support for such an opinion. Rapoport showed, for example, a direct relationship between the magnitude of long-term incentive compensation and the amount of research and development expenditures.[15] The profile of executive compensation appears to foster specific strategic decisions. Such findings suggest that under certain conditions it is possible to evoke comparatively desirable types of decisions. One should be alert to dysfunctional or strategically undesirable behaviors as well.

The research by Healey is noteworthy here.[16] He found that executives "tinkered" with their information and control system to inflate the size of their bonus payments. By refashioning the way financial results are reported, they were focusing their attention on the management of appearance rather than the management of performance. The research also highlighted a major example of agency problems (for example, the asymmetry of information between the CEO as "agent" and the board or stockholders as his or her "principal"), which the former may be tempted to exploit for his or her own advantage. As we observed earlier, our own research also suggests that CEOs use their power to manipulate their level and mix of compensation.

EXPECTANCY AND AGENCY THEORIES: A SYNTHESIS OF EXPLANATIONS FOR EXECUTIVE PAY

This discussion suggests that there is some overlap and complement between expectancy theory and agency theory. Although the former has psychological origins and focuses on the motivational effects of reward systems on the incumbent, the latter has an economic-accounting origin and stresses the contractual relationship with the incentive structure designed in such a way as to align the interest of the executives and the shareholders. It would appear that these two traditions provide enough support for some propositions on the strategic consequences of

---

[14]M. C. Jensen and W. H. Meckling, "Theory of the Firm: Management Behavior, Agency Costs, and Ownership Structure," *Journal of Financial Economics,* vol. 3, 1976, pp. 305–360.

[15]A. Rapoport, "Executive Incentives Versus Corporate Growth," *Harvard Business Review,* vol. 56, 1978, pp. 81–88.

[16]M. Healey, "The Effect of Bonus Schemes on Accounting," *Journal of Accounting and Economics,* vol. 3, 1985, pp. 85–107.

executive compensation. Expectancy research assumes that individuals are different and will respond differently to a given situation; it would answer questions such as, "What behavior is motivated by a given reward system?" and, "What values and other motivational attributes (for example, tolerance for risk, need for financial success, and so on) of various executives are present such that their response to a given reward system can be anticipated? "Agency theorists tend to have an economic-rationalistic view of people and assume that each person will respond to an incentive package in a predictable way. Its major advantage is that it forces the questions: What objectives are to be attained in this time horizon? Are they short term or long term? What milestones should be furnished to direct executives toward strategic targets? In concrete terms, such questions translate into specific statements, such as the amount of risk taking desired.

The firm's information and control system provides data on either operational (accounting) and/or strategic (market) performance indicators. The former includes return on equity, return on sales, return on investments, and net cash flow and might pertain to overall corporate performance or group, divisional, or *strategic business unit* (SBU) *performance.* Strategic indicators include 5-year earnings per share, book-to-market value, or other measures. Such indicators tend to apply to corporate-level performance only. In other words, they cannot easily be disaggregated into organizational subunits unless one resorts to accounting measures such as research and development/assets, new product development/assets or even softer measures, such as the amount of new management talent nurtured.

Assuming that information and control systems embody a variety of performance evaluation criteria, their link with pay can be represented bidirectionally. The arrows from reward to performance belong to the realm of expectancy theory, whereas the reverse arrows fit agency theory. It should be obvious that these bidirectional linkages should overlap, or should at least be consistent. Only under such conditions will the pay strategy relationship be optimal.

CONCLUSION

Under the auspices of expectancy theory, a number of outcomes or rewards can be tied to these performance indicators. Conventional types include salary, short-term bonuses, long-term bonuses, stock options, stocks with appreciation rights, phantom stocks, and performance units. For such rewards to have a motivational impact, it is important that the connection to performance be direct, immediate, and salient. Random fluctuations of the stock price, the tightening of executive labor markets, the influence of national values in setting compensation levels, and compensation profiles tend to diminish the correlation between pay and long-term, comprehensive performance indicators, resulting in a less-than-effective motivational impact. Expectancy theories stress the importance of individual differences. Such differences suggest the necessity of differences in compensation mix. Some executives might prefer deferred compensation. Others might prefer golden parachutes as a protection against unemployment. Still others might prefer risky stock options. Some executives might even prefer nonfinancial rewards, such as time for family, sabbaticals, and a variety of other perks. Their tax situation might be an important consideration as well. Of course, taxation mirrors the national institutional context in which it exists! Last, but not least, particularly when a firm is a multinational corporation, there is probably even a greater need to customize executive pay systems. Ideally, the executive compensation system should dovetail with the motivational makeup of the executive in order to render it most efficient.

Efficiency of executive compensation systems is, however, not the only issue. The reward system should also yield the type or quality of performance that is strategically desirable. Agency theory spells out the conditions under which this is most likely. Stock options and stocks with appreciation rights, for example, may diminish risk-taking behavior and promote a temptation to stimulate dividend yield. Other long-term incentive compensation tools, such as phantom stocks and performance units, may be too complex and unwieldy, and they may fail, therefore, to align the direction of an executive's efforts with the long-term interests of the shareholders. Such plans require thorough communication and coaching so that the plans become meaningful and significant. It appears that this is the major challenge of current executive compensation consulting and research.

The employment arrangements of America's senior corporate executives have become a favorite topic for the financial press. Coverage of the details of lucrative compensation packages has become commonplace, with special emphasis being placed on the amounts earned by the executives. For example, *Business Week's* May 1999 publication of the results of its forty-ninth annual survey of executive compensation indicated that, for the first time ever, the average annual salary and bonus for CEOs of surveyed companies topped $1 million, and their aggregate annual compensation exceeded $2 million. *The New York Times* frequently invites Graef Crystal, a compensation consultant and corporate gadfly, to articulate the discrepancy between a CEO's actual pay and the pay he or she should have received if pay systems were consistent across firms and within and across industries. Among academics, there are authors, such as Murphy, who wonder about the prominence of executive compensation and the success of the compensation consulting industry given that the marginal effect of corporate performance on pay is often trivial. The debates continue.

EMPLOYMENT AGREEMENTS

Bruce E. Clouser, Director

Global Human Resource Solutions
PricewaterhouseCoopers LLP

T**HE EMPLOYMENT ARRANGEMENTS OF AMERICA'S SENIOR CORPORATE EXECUTIVES** are a favorite topic for the financial media. Examining the details of lucrative compensation packages has become an annual pastime, with special emphasis being placed on the amounts earned by senior officers. For example, the median CEO received total compensation of more than $3 million in 1997, according to a William M. Mercer survey in *Fortune Magazine* (September 7, 1998). This represents an increase of 30 percent over 1996. The article notes that just under half of the median CEO's 1997 compensation came from realized option gains; Mercer estimates that the median CEO is sitting on another $9 million in unrealized gains. Substantial signing bonuses to attract executives are becoming more common. Annual bonuses and other variable pay are also becoming even more significant components of executive pay. Sixty percent of top executive remuneration packages now include bonuses.

In response to escalating executive compensation practices, Congress enacted Section 162(m) of the Internal Revenue Code in 1993. This was an attempt by

Congress to curtail what was perceived to be excessive compensation practices. In general, this provision limits the ability of public companies to deduct compensation in excess of $1 million paid to the chief executive officer and the four highest-paid officers unless the compensation meets certain performance criteria. Thus far, this provision has done little to curtail ballooning compensation practices.

The Executive Compensation Reports (ECRs), published by Harcourt Brace & Company in 1997, reviewed 100 agreements filed at the Securities and Exchange Commission (SEC) during 1995 and 1996. A substantial majority (80 prcent) of the 100 companies in the study established the executive's employment terms in a formal contract. Nineteen detailed the terms in an employment offer letter. The breakdown suggests that employment contracts have certainly become the norm with respect to public companies.

Taking into account the substantial investments that many companies make in their key executives, this chapter highlights some major reasons that an employer might want to offer an employment agreement to an executive to protect and enhance this investment. It also offers practical guidance on principal terms and issues to consider when drafting agreements.

HISTORICAL PERSPECTIVE ON THE USE OF EMPLOYMENT AGREEMENTS

In the past employers resisted using employment agreements. Their resistance was based on the premise that in the absence of such written agreements, the employment relationship was "at will," giving the employer maximum flexibility in hiring and firing. Under the *at-will doctrine,* the employer could terminate an employee for any reason, with or without cause, giving the employer substantial control over the relationship.

In contrast, an employment agreement often obligates the employer to retain the executive for a specified term, unless the employee breaks the terms of the contract. And if the employer chooses to terminate the employee before the end of term, the agreement typically provides for some form of monetary damages to be paid to the employee. Accordingly, employers viewed employment contracts negatively as eroding their right to control, over-formalizing the employment relationship, and increasing the risk of being saddled with an unproductive employee during the remaining term of the contract. Employment at will is no longer a reality, as legislation such as Title VII of the Civil Rights Act, the Americans with Disabilities Act, the Fair Labor Standards Act, the Immigration Control and Reform Act, and various states' "wrongful discharge" laws continue to undermine the modern employer's unilateral authority.

THE USE OF EMPLOYMENT CONTRACTS TODAY

Employers today face great challenges in hiring key executives. For example, executive talent is increasingly difficult to attract and retain because the competition for experienced, successful CEOs and other senior executives is intense and global. In addition, we live in an increasingly litigious society, so employers can encounter costly litigation when an employer-employee relationship sours. Even the protection of confidential information and trade secrets can become a major issue, as seen in high-profile cases such as the *Volkswagen vs. General Motor's* corporate espionage litigation involving General Motors' trade secrets [984 F. Supp. 684 (E.D. Michigan 1996)].

Employment agreements, if properly drafted, can help address or mitigate many of these concerns. By setting forth executives' rights clearly and candidly, employment contracts can be effective tools in attracting executives and in preventing future misunderstandings. Although an employer can't force an executive to remain employed, items such as "golden-handcuff" provisions or punitive forfeiture clauses can be used to deter or discourage an executive from departing prior to the specified employment term.[1] Restrictive covenants such as confidentiality clauses, covenants not to compete, and injunctive relief provisions can be powerful tools in protecting trade secrets and in discouraging unfair competitive practices by former employees. Carefully crafted language regarding the employee's duties and responsibilities and the inclusion of arbitration clauses can help mitigate costly litigation, even if the relationship terminates on unfriendly terms.

Last, those employers with offices in more than one state often include a *choice-of-law provision* specifying the particular state law that will apply in the event of litigation. Because state laws can vary significantly, these employers generally specify a state that has more employer-oriented laws.

PRINCIPAL TERMS OF THE AGREEMENT

Four areas will generally be addressed in any employment agreement negotiation between an employer and a prospective executive: (1) the position and duties of the executive and the term of his or her employment, (2) the salary and benefits to be received by the executive during this employment, (3) the consequences of a termination or resignation during the term of the contract, and (4) restrictive covenants (such as agreements not to compete and not to solicit the employer's customers or employees).

1. Position, Duties, and Term

The employment agreement typically states the executive's title and reporting obligations. In the case of the CEO, it is not uncommon for the contract to provide that

---

[1]*Golden handcuffs* are employee benefits linked to an employee's continued employment with an organization. Leaving the organization would result in forfeiting the benefits or the value. When such amounts become large as compared to offers from other organizations, the employee no longer can afford to leave the organization.

the executive reports directly to the employer's chairperson or board of directors. For other senior executives, the contract may specify that they report to the CEO.

The degree of specificity provided in the description of an executive's duties and responsibilities is a function of the negotiation process. Because a breach of a term of the employment agreement by the employer commonly provides the executive with the right to resign and recover damages under the contract, it is generally in the interest of the executive that the agreement define duties precisely. This is in contrast to the employer, who will generally want to draft the position, duties, and responsibilities broadly, with as much flexibility as possible, to retain the ability to respond to unforeseeable situations without having to renegotiate the contract. For example, an employer may want freedom to move the executive among various positions or among various companies within the employer group.

Employment agreements will often prohibit the executive from performing work for any unrelated companies. By carefully defining the scope of the employee's duties and specifically identifying the employer's interests, the employment agreement can serve as a tool to alleviate the employer's potential liability for intentional torts or crimes of the executive that are outside the scope of the defined duties. In addition, by specifying the performance standards expected of an executive, the contract can also serve as a deterrent to an executive's bringing a lawsuit claiming age, race, or sex discrimination when an employer terminates the executive for subpar performance.

The term of employment for a senior executive typically ranges from 3 to 5 years. Care must be exercised when determining the appropriate contract term. If the term is too short, the employment relationship may not be long enough to achieve the employer's business objectives. Conversely, if the term is too long, the employer is put in the position of either continuing to employ the executive for the full term or terminating the executive early—most likely paying monetary damages as a result.

2. Compensation and Benefits

The executive's base salary is typically expressed as a minimum annual rate, with a provision for periodic review. Sometimes the annual salary will rise automatically at stated intervals, either by a specified percentage or in relation to a designated measure such as the inflation rate or the consumer price index.

Incentive payments for senior executives generally take two forms: short-term incentive compensation or annual bonus and long-term incentive compensation. Short-term incentives are generally designed to reward annual executive performance based on meeting objective and/or subjective performance criteria. Long-term incentives are designed to reward executive performance over a longer period of time, typically 3 to 5 years. More and more frequently, employers today are tying executive compensation pay to performance. Another notable trend is that long-term incentives are becoming an increasingly more significant component of executive compensation. Often, they are used to align the interests of executives more directly with those of shareholders. Stock options continue to be a popular form of long-term incentive because of the favorable accounting treatment and ease on cash flow for employers. The employment agreement will sometimes describe in detail the executive's rights under the company's short- and long-term incentive programs or simply state the executive's right to participate in these programs.

Employment agreements usually contain a benefits section, stating the executive's participation in applicable pension, medical, dental, and other insurance programs offered by the employer to executives of similar status. If pension or other benefits accrued with a previous employer were forfeited as a result of joining the new employer, the employment agreement sometimes provides for a hiring bonus to "make the executive whole." Also, the executive may negotiate for supplemental retirement benefits or special benefits such as disability or life insurance.

Employment agreements typically address fringe benefits such as automobile allowances, financial consulting, and club memberships. However, the executive should take into account the taxable nature of many perquisites. Also, reimbursement of business and travel expenses are usually covered in employment agreements. When top executives are involved, the agreement may define reimbursable relocation expenses, housing loans, guarantees, tax gross-ups, or other perquisites.

3. Termination

a. Termination for Cause or Good Reason. The termination provisions of an employment agreement define the rights of the parties if the term of employment is cut short by the action of either the employer or the executive. The goals are to provide clarity if a potential termination situation arises and to attempt to avert costly litigation over damages. While an employment contract cannot foresee or forestall every possible circumstance, it can set the stage for a more amicable settlement by establishing relative bargaining positions.

The termination provisions state in detail those situations in which an employer is permitted to terminate an executive's employment prior to the expiration of the term—without incurring an obligation to make severance payments. This is known as *termination for cause.* It is not unusual for termination provisions to delineate also the circumstances in which the executive is entitled to resign without forfeiting incentive compensation and, in certain circumstances, to collect severance pay. Such an instance is known as a *resignation for good reason.* Both *cause* and *good reason* should be clearly drawn and adequately defined to clarify the legal positions of both parties. Employment agreements often include provisions concerning a warning period to the employee before termination can be effected for cause.

At a minimum, cause will typically include the executive's conviction of a felony and any willful act or omission by the executive that is materially injurious to the financial condition of the employer (or its affiliates or subsidiaries, where appropriate). Occasionally, injury to the reputation of the employer is included. Some agreements are written to give the executive an opportunity to *cure* the situation and to have a *hearing* before the employer's board of directors. An employee will want to avoid a provision that allows termination for cause based on what might be perceived as subpar performance because of the subjective nature of such a provision.

Resignation for good reason is often more narrow in scope. It will generally encompass a material breach of the employment agreement by the employer. Often included are provisions covering a reduction or failure to pay the stated compensation and benefits and a change in the executive's duties or reporting responsibilities. It may also include a relocation of the executive's principal place of employment. From the employer's viewpoint, *good reason* should be carefully constructed so as not to give the executive an unfettered right to resign and collect severance benefits.

b. Consequences of Termination. Severance provisions are fast becoming the most critical component of employment agreements, demonstrated by one of the most controversial pay packages in recent memory. To dispose of Michael Ovitz, Disney CEO Michael Eisner paid Ovitz $70 million in severance pay (about half in cash, the rest in options) for just 16 months of service when their working relationship soured, as noted in *Fortune Magazine* (February 3, 1997).

Whether an employer fires an executive with cause or the executive resigns without good reason, the result is usually the same: The executive forfeits all future claims to salary, bonus, and benefits after the termination or resignation. Further, the executive will also usually forfeit any unvested long-term incentive compensation, and certain restrictions may be placed on vested portions of such compensation—for example, the executive may be limited in the amount of time in which to exercise any vested stock options.

However, if the executive is terminated by the employer without cause or if the executive resigns with good reason, then the executive will generally be entitled to specified severance benefits, based on what the executive would have earned over the remaining term of the contract. Severance benefits might also cover the cost to the executive of loss of coverage under the employer's pension and health benefit plans. If these amounts are paid in a lump sum, they are often discounted to present value.

Sometimes employment agreements contain a provision requiring the employee to exercise his or her best efforts to mitigate damages—such as the executive pursuing employment with another employer before the end of the period specified in the employment agreement. If an employee does not attempt to mitigate (i.e., find another comparable job), the employment agreement can provide for a reduction of severance benefits.

c. Dealing with Death or Disability. Obligations of the employer in case of the executive's death should be specified in the employment agreement. Also, an employment contract will typically reserve the right of termination by the employer in the event of disability. Sometimes the determination of disability is left to an independent physician agreed upon by both parties or some other means of arbitration. Nevertheless, the ability to enforce this provision may be subject to limitations provided by applicable law, such as the Americans with Disabilities Act.

Payment on death or for disability are usually limited to amounts payable under the employer's insurance policies covering those events, although employers will occasionally agree to additional payments or benefits, such as limited salary continuation during disability. It is advisable to make a special provision in the contract for the payment of the annual bonus that the executive would have earned for the year in which the death or disability occurs. Frequently, this is accomplished by pro-rating the amount for that year.

4. Restrictive Covenants

The protection of confidential information and trade secrets has become a top-level concern of companies in today's competitive economy in which employee mobility is commonplace. It is estimated that businesses lost $1.5 billion in 1995 due to theft of trade secrets. Employment agreements are increasingly becoming the vehicle for enforcing covenants that protect the employer's confidential and trade secret information.

Recently, General Motors successfully reached a settlement in its lawsuits against Volkswagen for claims that former senior executives of General Motors had stolen trade secrets and given them to their new employer, Volkswagen. This lawsuit has made clear the risk that companies face in failing to prepare properly for the possibility that senior executives may depart, taking with them not only other personnel but also intellectual property.

Examples of restrictive covenants that are being used with more frequency to protect a company follow.[2]

> *Confidentiality clauses* prevent the employee from disclosing confidential and trade secret information, both during and after the cessation of employment.
>
> *Covenants not to compete* are valid as long as they are supported by consideration, are reasonable in time (e.g., seldom more than 1 or 2 years) and geographic scope, and as long as they seek to protect against the dissemination of trade secrets.

---

[2]Philip M. Berkowitz and Mary Elizabeth Cisneros, "The Volkswagen-General Motors Trade Secrets Lawsuit, Its Settlement: Avoiding the Lope Effect," 1997, http://www.ebglaw.com/newstand/volkswagen-gm.html.

Nonsolicitation clauses prohibit employees from soliciting the employer's customers and coworkers while the employee is employed by the employer. They also prohibit the departing employee from soliciting customers and/or key employees for an extended period of time after leaving the employer's employment.

Liquidated damages clauses provide agreed-upon liquidated damages if employees breach their fiduciary duty or contractual obligations.

Return of documents: The company should demand the return of all company documents upon the employee's resignation.

Computer software: Employers should consider reserving their right under the U.S. Electronic Communications Privacy Act to examine all hard-drive files and soft files of employees.

It is important to refer to governing state law when crafting these provisions. Despite the protection seemingly gained under restrictive covenants such as these, they may be difficult to police and enforce. However, the act of committing these covenants to writing succeeds many times in creating an atmosphere and an awareness that protects the employer's interest.

5. Other Considerations

a. Disclosure to Public.   The proxy rules of the Securities Exchange Act of 1934 require public companies to disclose the content of employment agreements with their five most highly compensated senior executive officers. The rules also require disclosure of employment arrangements with directors and executive officers that provide for one or more payments upon a change in control of the employer if the payments in aggregate exceed $100,000. Therefore, public companies must consider as part of the negotiation process the impact of employment agreements on their disclosure statements to shareholders and the public. Because change-in-control arrangements that might disclose multi-million-dollar employment contracts are closely scrutinized, public companies must be cognizant of that disclosure and how it might be negatively interpreted by the media, the public, or the SEC.

b. Arbitration.   Employment agreements may contain an arbitration clause requiring the parties to resolve disputes before an arbitrator rather than a court. Some employers feel arbitration can produce better outcomes than the court; others feel just the opposite. The arguments favoring the inclusion of a provision for arbitration are powerful. They include speed, cost, confidentiality, finality, and friendliness, which is why more companies are using broad mandatory arbitration clauses. However, some people question whether arbitration is truly advantageous to the employer. They suggest, among other things, that the speed and cost of the process increase the likelihood that employees will file claims, and, accordingly, they question whether it is truly more cost effective in the long term.

c. Change-in-Control Clauses. Many employment contracts provide for payments in the event of a *change in control* (COC) of the company. One of the primary purposes of a COC provision is to provide some protection to the executive in the event of a COC, thus encouraging retention in situations where a COC is likely.[3]

In some cases, the payments and other benefits are initiated by any termination following the COC, such as when another entity acquires more than 20 percent of the company's outstanding shares. The arrangement is said to have a "single trigger." A *single trigger* is a mechanism that permits severance payments immediately upon a COC.

In the alternative, COC payments and benefits are granted if one of two additional conditions are met after a COC occurs. Typically, the conditions are either (1) the executive is fired by new management (except for unethical or inimical behavior) or (2) the executive has justifiable grounds for quitting (for example, if he or she is demoted, if pay is slashed, or if a significant relocation is required). These arrangements are said to have a "double trigger."

COC arrangements can exert a major influence on merger and acquisitions scenarios. Typical termination benefits include:

1. A payment equal to two or three times annual salary, plus annual target bonus or the highest bonus ever received by the executive
2. Accelerated vesting and cash-out of outstanding long-term incentives including, in some cases, stock options
3. Continuation of basic employee health and life insurance benefits
4. Possible continuation of certain perquisites

One pitfall to many single-trigger change-in-control agreements is that payments are automatic, with no distinction made between friendly or unfriendly changes in ownership. If a potential acquirer wants to retain the target company's management after the acquisition occurs, single-trigger agreements can lead to an unintended result: a significant windfall payment when no termination of employment has occurred. Thus, double-trigger provisions have been quite popular.

Other technical issues also arise. For example, employers who want to include change-of-control clauses in employment contracts must take care to ensure that the provisions are drafted in a way to avoid inadvertently preventing the company from accounting for future acquisitions as a "pooling of interests," which can provide significantly more favorable accounting treatment of the transaction. Payments made to some executives following a change in control may be subject to the *golden-parachute provisions* of Internal Revenue Code, which can cause

---

[3]L. Bickford, "Mergers and Acquisitions: How Executive Compensation May Affect A Deal," *Compensation & Benefits Review,* September/October 1997, pg. 53.

adverse tax consequences to the employer and executive. Employers and executives should consult with their tax advisors when negotiating COC provisions.

CONCLUSION

Many employers view an employment agreement as offering more benefits to the employee than to the employer. It establishes minimum compensation and benefit levels, but it does not necessarily ensure any level of performance on the part of the employee. Further, an employment agreement limits the employer's freedom to terminate the employee without incurring an obligation to pay severance benefits. Consequently, most employers continue to offer employment agreements only to their most senior executives and key employees.

Yet, the employment agreement can clearly benefit the employer as well. An employee contract lays a solid foundation of understanding of the employer's expectations from the beginning. It also increases the goodwill of the new relationship and eases the road to success for both parties. In addition, negotiating the scope of termination for cause and resignation for good reason can often lead to an expansion of the employer's rights. By carefully spelling out severance benefits in the event that the employer-employee relationship sours, the employer can limit the damage it sustains. Best of all, an employment agreement can greatly enhance the employer's ability to protect trade secrets, to retain valued people, and to protect the employer against unfair competition should an executive depart. Many companies will attest that it is "the ounce of prevention" that has spared employers considerable trouble and backlash.

C H A P T E R

31

THE CHANGING LANDSCAPE OF BOARD REMUNERATION

Pearl Meyer

Pearl Meyer & Partners, Inc.

A CONFLUENCE OF FACTORS HAS RESULTED IN FUNDAMENTAL CHANGES in the way nonemployee directors are being paid as the millennium draws near. This changing landscape of board remuneration looks entirely different from its earlier terrain for many reasons:

- Growth and dominance of equity compensation
- Rise in board remuneration based primarily on the stock element
- Growing use of share ownership guidelines for directors
- Introduction of discretionary board stock grants under SEC Rule 16b-3
- Proposal by the Financial Accounting Standards Board to charge earnings for director options

- Flight from pensions

- Decline in the use of meeting attendance fees for both board and committee service

- Decline in multiyear terms for directors

These changes in board remuneration have been prompted by changes in the very nature of the director's role.

ROLE OF THE DIRECTOR

In the earliest days of corporate America, directors were founders and direct investors (or their representatives) in the companies on whose boards they served. As independent boards gained favor, a certain gentility, "clubbiness," and prestige, along with nominal payment in gold coin, accompanied "rubber stamp" board service. But today, serving on a board means standing in the line of fire—accountable to and under the tough scrutiny of not only the shareholders but also the media, general public, corporate governance activists, legislatures, regulators, and powerful institutions. The responsibilities, risks, and performance expectations associated with independent directorship have risen exponentially.

Prior to the mid-1980s, corporate governance activism—especially with regard to directors—was little more than a gleam in the eyes of a handful of forward-thinking pioneers. Today, influential activists from varied arenas proliferate. To understand how the corporate governance movement has gained momentum, it is helpful to trace the development of American capitalism and the concomitant growth curve of executive compensation.

CAPITALISM AND CORPORATE GOVERNANCE

American capitalism originated with small-business owners—bakers, blacksmiths, merchants—who worked hard and reaped the direct financial results of their labors. Equity was in their hands and their hands alone. But, as successful small operations grew into larger enterprises financed by external capital and staffed by multiple layers, significant management ownership disappeared. Chief executives were employees, and the clear correlation between performance and reward dissipated. Stock incentives were then created in the endeavor to restore this linkage by shifting into equity a portion of compensation formerly paid 100 percent in cash.

By the 1950s and 1960s, stock options designed to tie executive compensation to the fortunes of the company and its investors comprised a mere 10 percent of CEO total pay. With the rise of the pay-for-performance movement more than a decade ago, a major cash-to-equity shift was initiated at the senior executive level, causing corporations to move a growing portion of management as well as employee remuneration into company stock to motivate and reward the creation of shareholder value. By the late 1990s, stock options accounted for over 50 percent of the present value of CEO total remuneration among the top 200 U.S. corporations, and the stock options were accompanied by a whole panoply of other equity incentives and stock investment vehicles. Today, the terms *CEO* and *owner* have again become virtually synonymous.

Once equity became firmly entrenched inside the corporation, governance activists turned their attention to outside directors. Thus began the initial stages of a similar movement to directly align director remuneration with long-term stock performance and, thereby, with shareholder interests. Director compensation has come full circle, with restoration of this all-important ownership stake at the board level.

CORPORATE GOVERNANCE AND THE DRIVE FOR EQUITY

Directors and their compensation—once seemingly beyond reproach—came under attack in the early 1990s from institutional shareholders and activists. It was not how much directors were being paid that was in question. It was how they were being paid. Aggressive corporate governance initiatives propelled equity to a position of indisputable prominence in compensating the outside director for board service.

Stock ownership for directors is a breakthrough advancement in board governance. Indeed, due to the introduction of equity, 1998 was a record-breaking year for board pay—which has always been one of the best buys in American business.

A broad range of constituencies converged upon board pay as a prime target for change. It is no small coincidence that public pension funds, led by the California Public Employees' Retirement System (CalPERS), which invest in broad-based equity index funds, have become powerful governance activists—pension fund assets in the United States have grown almost 10-fold since the mid-1970s to multi-billion-dollar levels. Large union pension funds such as the AFL-CIO and Teamsters also have their eyes on top-level pay practices. Mutual funds are rapidly playing catch-up, as small investors have taken advantage of the recent stock market boon. Mutual fund managers' stock picks are influenced not only by levels of CEO and director pay but also by the amount of pay that is stock based. With huge investments at stake, it has become increasingly difficult for these funds to unload large holdings if they are unhappy with a company's performance. The potential for negative impact on share price impedes such action. Instead, fund investors have been compelled to work within the system, striving through various means to improve a company's governance and thereby, hopefully to favorably impact its performance.

Companies have responded by creating new executive positions in charge of corporate governance, and boards have established corporate governance committees. Varied organizations, such as TIAA-Cref, The Business Roundtable, General

Motors, CalPERS, and the National Association of Corporate Directors (NACD) have all issued corporate governance guidelines for executives and Directors.

Regarding director's compensation, the pro-active establishment by the NACD of a blue-ribbon commission to study board pay in December 1994 provided the catalyst needed to set change in motion. The commission's findings, and most importantly, its recommendations, have resulted in sweeping alterations in how directors are paid today.

GROWTH AND DOMINANCE OF EQUITY COMPENSATION

Equity compensation, which accounted for an estimated mere 2 percent of board total remuneration in 1985 among the top 200 U.S. corporations, followed on an annual basis by Pearl Meyer & Partners, had risen to 26 percent in the last year prior to the issuance of the NACD report. By 1998, equity doubled to average over 50 percent of total direct pay and can be expected to rise even further. A principal goal of the NACD Blue Ribbon Commission to see that a minimum 50 percent up to 100 percent of board compensation would be paid in stock was achieved by our largest corporations in a few short years, due in large part to the following:

- The introduction and increase in value of the stock component of the annual retainer

- The increase in the value of the option component due to the rise in stock prices and large grants made by companies first introducing options to their director pay packages

The movement to stock compensation and ownership has received almost universal endorsement, and the value of the directors' pay package has grown dramatically. There is a consensus within the business and investor communities that all stakeholders benefit when board members are on an equal at-risk footing with the stockholders. Directors who own meaningful amounts of stock are clearly more focused on long-term shareholder value and are more pro-active, meeting potential problems head on before there is a chance for those problems to snowball out of control.

Figure 31.1 illustrates relentless 4-year growth in the prevalence of equity from 65 percent of the top 200 U.S. corporations prior to issuance of the NACD report, accelerating to 81 percent in 1995, with 95 percent reported in 1998 proxies.

When companies offering elective deferral programs, which permit tax-sheltered investment of current cash, 98 percent of the top 200 corporations included some form of equity in their board remuneration programs by 1998.

THE PREVALENCE OF STOCK VEHICLES

The two principal board equity vehicles utilized are full-value stock grants and stock options. Among the major companies using some form of stock in compensating

FIGURE 31.1   Prevalence of equity compensation*

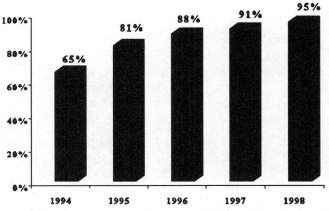

*Increase to 73% in 1994, 89% in 1995, 94% in 1996, 95% in 1997, and 98% in 1998 when elective payments of cash retainers and/or fees in deferred stock is included.**

their outside directors, full-value share grants continue to far outweigh stock options, although the use of both types of vehicles is increasing. Most recently, full-value grants were used by 75 percent of the top 200 companies versus stock options at 54 percent, as compared to 69 and 49 percent, respectively, the previous year (Figure 31.2).

Looking at full-value grants individually, unrestricted stock grants have become the most prevalent, with deferred stock on the rise while the prevalence of restricted stock has declined slightly (Figure 31.3).

With 54 percent prevalence reported by the top 200 corporations in 1998, stock options are also at an all time high. The vast majority of options are granted on a free-standing basis (52 percent), while 2 percent of the options are granted as part of stock retainers. Forty-one companies utilized stock options as their sole equity vehicle, and 67 granted options in combination with full-value awards. Among the 149 companies using full-value shares, 45 granted restricted or deferred stock that does not vest until retirement. In addition, 18 of the 83 companies that use stock retainers also restrict such shares until after retirement. In all, 60 companies defer or restrict vesting of stock awards until retirement (nonadditive because some companies offer two or three types of equity vehicles restricted until retirement).

From a governance perspective, full-value grants are deemed the more appropriate vehicle for board remuneration. Unlike options, grants place directors in a position of immediate ownership with both upside opportunity and downside risk, as well as full voting and dividend rights on a par with stockholders. In addition, stock awards are a boon to the increasing challenge of director recruitment by providing one-time-only,

FIGURE 31.2   Prevalence of full-value grants versus stock options.*

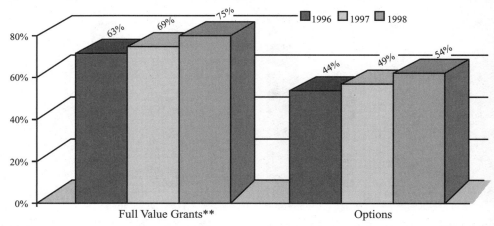

*Non-additive since 67 companies utilize both full value grants and stock options.

**Includes current stock, restricted stock and deferred stock.

FIGURE 31.3   Growth in use of full-value grants.

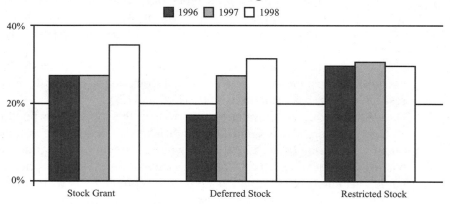

welcome-aboard grants to new board members, as well as ownership at entry, both of which encourage immediate motivation and commitment.

Some commentators have observed that stock options may focus directors too heavily on short-term stock price performance, rather than on strategic progress and long-term value creation. Notwithstanding this concern, significant option grants are the vehicle of choice—especially as recruitment tools in turnarounds, pre-IPOs, spinoffs, startups and high-growth companies—clearly identifiable situations in which maximum leverage is needed to attract and compensate desired board talent and in which cash may be in short supply.

In fact, heavy use of stock options in the strong, but volatile stock market of the late 1990s has led to wide fluctuations in director pay in many companies, some of which have experienced underwater board options for the first time. Such occurrences provide timely reminders of the inherent shortcomings of over-weighting stock options in the pay package of directors, whose attention should be focused on long-term shareholder value creation versus short-term variances.

ACCOUNTING TREATMENT OF DIRECTOR OPTIONS

A recent development may help to solidify the dominance of full-value grants over stock options. The Financial Accounting Standards Board has proposed changing the treatment of option grants to outside directors, consultants, independent contractors, and others who are not "common-law employees," resulting in an accounting charge to earnings to be accrued over the vesting period. It appears that the charge will equal the fair value of the option (as calculated by the Black-Scholes Option Pricing Model) at the date of the grant plus variable "mark-to-market" charges for changes in fair value from the date of the grant to the vesting date(s). Such variable treatment from grant to vesting dates will also be accorded to full-value grants subject to vesting, such as restricted stock.

Since board option grants are generally not significant in relative size, such charges should not have a major impact on board pay other than to shift the balance slightly further in the direction of full-value grants. Variable charges after the grant for both options and restricted stock may be avoided or limited by short-term vesting.

Early responses from a number of companies to the proposed accounting treatment indicate that changes in compensation practices will be minimal.

THE RISE IN BOARD REMUNERATION

By 1998, total direct compensation for board service among the 200 largest corporations reached an all time high, averaging $112,221 (Figure 31.4). This represents a 20 percent increase in 1 year and 57 percent in 3 years.

Outright stock awards in full-value shares and options, excluding the stock portion of the annual retainer, increased 45 percent in only 1 year to $48,262, surpassing the annual retainer as the largest portion of the director's pay package for the first time. Annual retainers in cash and/or stock averaged $39,227, and meeting and chair fees and/or retainers averaged $19,875 and $4,857, respectively.

While total direct pay has increased substantially over the last several years, the major element contributing to this rise is equity—in the form of stock retainers and outright stock awards. During the same period, cash retainers and board and/or committee meeting fees and/or retainers have remained relatively flat (Figure 31.5).

THE CONTINUING INCREASE IN RETAINER STOCK

Although retainers in total (cash and/or stock) increased 24 percent over 3 years, the cash portion has consistently hovered around $28,000 on average. In sharp

FIGURE 31.4   1998 total direct compensation for board service.*

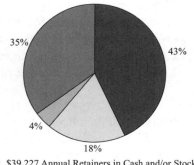

■ $39,227 Annual Retainers in Cash and/or Stock
■ $19,875 Meeting Fees/Committee Retainers
▢ $ 4,857 Committee Chair Fees/Retainers
▢ $48,262 Stock Awards/Options

*Cash and stock retainers, meeting and chair fees/retainers, plus stock-based pay. Total remuneration including pension present value averages $114,568.

FIGURE 31.5   Total direct compensation.

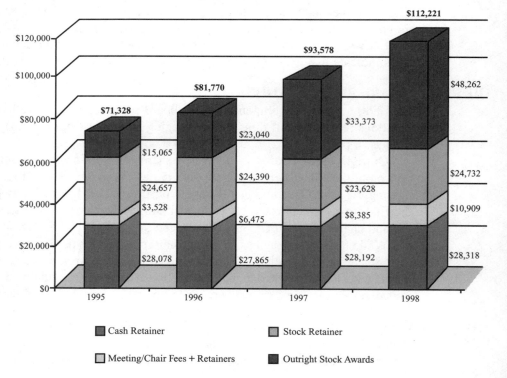

contrast, the stock portion of retainers has surged more than threefold since 1995, with its average value increasing from $3,528 to $10,909 (Figure 31.5). Growth in outright stock awards is equally dramatic—a 220 percent increase in 3 years, driven by a 45 percent jump from $33,373 to an average $48,262 in the last year alone. Putting it another way, stock retainers and outright stock awards have more than tripled in 3 years.

To highlight the increased prevalence of equity as the principal component of board pay, 70 of the 200 top companies used no equity in 1994; by 1998 that number had dwindled to a mere 4.

In most companies, stock grants and options preceded the use of retainer stock and were originally awarded as part of the total package, with the retainer generally taking the form of a cash payment. Thus, one of the most striking manifestations of the cash-to-equity shift in board remuneration has been the growing number of companies now paying all or part of the traditional cash retainer in some form of stock. In just 3 years, the prevalence of stock retainers has doubled. In 1998, 83 of the top 200 companies paid all or a portion of the annual retainer in stock versus 77 the previous year and 41 only 3 years ago. This accelerating conversion from cash to stock retainers is a significant step forward in institutionalizing equity as a vital component of board remuneration, rather than using it as add-ons as was the case in past years.

Notable examples of the use of stock retainers are those paying 100 percent of their retainers in stock, which include major corporations such as Campbell Soup, Chrysler, Colgate Palmolive, and ITT Industries.

CURRENT VERSUS FUTURE BALANCE OF BOARD PAY

It is clear that cash compensation (retainers and meeting and/or chair fees) has been overtaken by the sweeping use of stock, and director's pay will never be the same. Equity compensation has risen so significantly as to constitute 53 percent of total direct pay by 1998, up from 26 percent in 1995 (Figure 31.6). The use of cash, on the other hand, has declined steadily each year to represent only 47 percent of total direct pay (excluding pensions) in 1998, down from 74 percent in 1995.

On an overall basis, adding cash pensions to the equation modestly decreases the stock portion from 53 to 52 percent among the top 200 companies. The average balance among the three elements of board total remuneration is 2 percent pension, 46 percent cash, and 52 percent stock.

Corporate America has responded to the NACD's 1995 initiatives, which have been resoundingly endorsed by all constituencies. The NACD threshold for the "ideal" balance of board compensation has been reached in a remarkably short period. Going forward, the shift in the balance of pay elements should become even more dramatic, especially in a rising stock market (Figure 31.7).

Looking at specific industries provides a unique perspective on the balance between cash and stock as a percent of total remuneration (Figure 31.8). In 10 of

FIGURE 31.6   Cash versus equity as a percent of total direct pay.*

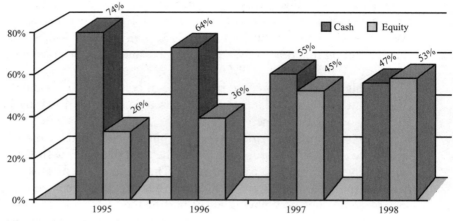

***Excludes the value of pensions.**

FIGURE 31.7   Cash to equity shift in total remuneration.

		Ideal Balance			Current Balance
Stock	↑	50%	to	100%	52%
Cash	↓	50%	to	0%	46%
Pension (Cash)		—			2%

23 industries, stock outweighs cash as a percent of total remuneration, led by technology at 77 percent stock (historically a heavy user of stock) and health care at 68 percent stock. Commercial banks and metals and metal products companies are the lowest users of stock on a percentage basis, at 32 and 26 percent of total pay, respectively.

DEFERRAL LEADING TO THE DOMINANCE OF EQUITY

By 1998, just over three-quarters of the top 200 corporations offered their outside directors the opportunity to defer board earnings on a tax-sheltered basis for receipt at a later date, with greater use of stock than ever before as the deferral vehicle. While elective cash deferral (investment in an interest-bearing cash account) is down, elective stock deferrals (investment in a company stock account whose value is based on total shareholder return—stock price plus reinvested dividends) have risen significantly. In all, 136 companies (versus 118 the previous year) provided the opportunity for elective tax-sheltered investment in company equity by 1998.

FIGURE 31.8 Cash and stock as a percent of total remuneration. Averages by industry.

Industry	Value Cash*	Stock	Percent of Total Remuneration Cash*	Stock
Aerospace	$57,372	$54,896	51 %	49 %
Chemicals	58,008	44,706	56	44
Commercial Banks	67,347	31,450	68	32
Consumer Products	52,010	60,905	46	54
Diversified Financials & Brokerage	60,899	80,641	43	57
Electronics & Electrical Equipment	65,708	49,778	57	43
Entertainment	52,740	59,481	47	53
Food/Beverages & Tobacco	66,204	49,325	57	43
Food/Drug Stores	38,834	42,384	48	52
Forest/Paper Products	56,519	35,447	61	39
General Merch./Specialty Retailers	46,317	45,300	51	49
Healthcare	52,106	109,555	32	68
Industrial & Farm Equipment	58,000	55,314	51	49
Insurance	51,306	63,466	45	55
Metals/Metal Products	65,250	23,158	74	26
Miscellaneous	56,750	40,379	58	42
Motor Vehicles and Parts	54,338	49,236	52	48
Petroleum Refining/Pipelines/Energy	56,649	50,946	53	47
Pharmaceuticals	67,175	76,203	47	53
Technology	41,966	143,648	23	77
Telecommunications	60,608	75,633	44	56
Transportation	52,772	43,179	55	45
Wholesalers/Distributors	39,671	39,511	50	50
Average (200 Companies)	*$55,397*	*59,171*	*48%**	*52%*

$114,568

SHARE OWNERSHIP GUIDELINES FOR DIRECTORS

Matching the rise in board equity-based pay, 1998 proved to be a year of tremendous growth in share ownership guidelines for directors. In the few short years that companies have voluntarily disclosed formal share ownership guidelines in their proxies, the practice has skyrocketed. Of the 200 top companies, 40 discussed ownership guidelines for directors in their 1998 proxies, a stunning 60 percent increase over the previous year, and an 81 percent increase in just 2 years. Since such disclosure is voluntary, actual prevalence of guidelines, both formal and informal, in all likelihood, far exceeds disclosure.

Several companies with share ownership guidelines require directors to own from three to five times the annual retainer in stock within a few years of joining their boards. Honeywell goes one step further, requiring the attainment of six times the retainer in 6 years. The highest multiple of ten times is found at Kellogg. Chrysler and American Express mandate that directors own 10,000 shares within 3 and 5 years, respectively. Chubb requires that one-half of the annual retainer plus fees be deferred into a stock account each year.

Rewards are also being offered to those who meet or exceed guidelines. For example, BellSouth makes a supplementary grant of options if the number of shares owned exceeds its five-times guideline. Dow Chemical grants a special option when 1,500 shares are held by a director, and ownership of 2,000 shares is required for a director to be eligible for the next grant in 5 years. Kroger directors who own a minimum of 1,000 shares receive annual options grants on 2,000 shares.

To place heightened emphasis on director ownership, for the first time in 1998, a handful of companies disclosed that directors are required to buy stock in the company as a condition of board membership:

- PNC directors must purchase stock equal to 25 percent of their annual retainer.

- Safeway directors must purchase stock as a condition of board membership, and they receive an equal number of options at 80 percent of FMV.

- USX director fees are supplemented with stock grants equal to the number of shares purchased by the director, up to 500 shares.

- And last, AIG directors must purchase 675 shares for which they are reimbursed by the company.

While a growing number of companies voluntarily disclose formal director ownership guidelines, the fact remains that many companies are paying their board in stock irrespective of guidelines. This means that directors in significant numbers of companies—both large and small—are annually accruing real ownership stakes on a direct, meaningful basis—with or without the imposition of ownership guidelines.

INCENTIVE PAY FOR DIRECTORS

The key to preserving director independence is recognition of the fundamental difference between the duties of a public corporation's board and its management—and the need to reflect those different roles in the design of their compensation. A program that subjects nonemployee directors to the same annual pay-for-performance standards as management threatens to undermine outside board members' capacity to act in a truly disinterested manner.

In the last several years, a shrinking number of the top 200 companies continue to link board remuneration to annual corporate performance, with 10 percent the magic number. Four companies require a 10 percent performance improvement over the prior year. Two of these companies award options if annual ROE increases by at least 10 percent. One grants options if annual earnings from continuing operations rise by at least 10 percent; and the fourth grants options provided the EPS increases by at least 10 percent and vests such options only if "rigorous performance goals" are met. At the fifth company, the one-time restricted stock grant vests only if 12 percent compound annual growth in the stock price is attained.

The far wiser avenue adopted by most corporations is to take definitive steps to put meaningful amounts of company equity in the hands of directors. Stock-based compensation applies the pay-for-performance concept to directors' remuneration by tying the long-term results of their corporate oversight to the long-term value of their shareholdings and those of all stockholders.

On the other hand, a positive trend in incentive pay for directors has emerged—a move that is in keeping philosophically with the goal of making directors owners to link their interests with shareholders. A small group of major corporations have begun to offer their directors a premium if they elect some form of stock payment in lieu of receiving some or all of the annual retainer in cash.

Innovative examples of this approach include the following:

- Offering a stock option at a discounted price from fair market value with and without a commensurate cash give-up

- Electing to exchange the cash retainer for options based on a Black-Scholes valuation

- Crediting directors' deferred stock accounts with a premium ranging from 10 to 70 percent above the value of the foregone cash retainer

Such incentives reward directors for electing stock over cash payment; annual corporate financial performance plays no role whatsoever.

INTRODUCTION OF DISCRETIONARY STOCK GRANTS

A significant change in Rule 16b-3 by the Securities and Exchange Commission in 1996 has brought us to the threshold of a new era in board compensation, as traditional predetermined formula stock awards may be replaced by discretionary awards for the first time. As a result, public companies have far greater flexibility in granting options and stock-related awards to directors.

An initial review of new and amended stock plans submitted in 1998 for shareholder approval by 40 major companies yields 12, or 30 percent, that provide for participation by directors in their employee omnibus plans. However, most of these plans specify stock awards identical to prior-year grants. One company that initiated a discretionary stock plan for directors is Office Depot, where the new omnibus plan replaced the directors' stock option plan, and both the size and terms of the grants are established at the discretion of the compensation committee. Also worth noting is Dillard's, a company that through 1998 has used no stock in compensating its board members. Under its 1998 ISO & NQSO plan, Dillard may now grant stock options to outside directors.

Joint employee-director omnibus plans offer several benefits. For the first time, directors are eligible to participate in compensation vehicles ranging from stocks with appreciation rights to performance shares, dividend equivalents, and stock unit bonus awards. In addition, combining the plans simplifies the shareholder approval process. Perhaps most important, the flexibility offered by discretionary omnibus plans permits the type and size of the grants to be more easily adjusted in light of changing circumstances including stock volatility and marketplace practice. Going forward, it is likely that new plans will move away from mandating awards of a specific type and size to permitting board discretion. There is no evidence thus far that boards are making distinctions among directors on an individual basis, other than to compensate for committee, chair, and special services. If, however, as advocated by some corporate governance activists, individual director performance appraisals take hold, differentiation in pay among individual directors could be introduced. The appropriateness of such an approach to board remuneration is, of course, highly questionable.

THE FLIGHT FROM PENSIONS

Director ownership has received a boost over the last several years from what once would have been deemed an unlikely source—the dramatic move to abandon director pension plans, also prompted by conclusions drawn in the NACD Blue Ribbon Commission Report on Director Compensation in 1995. As a result, board retirement benefits are disappearing before our eyes.

For years, pensions flourished as a graceful approach to the introduction of mandatory retirement ages for directors, as well as recognizing long years of valued service. Pensions were subsequently used as a vehicle to increase and provide for tax-sheltered deferral of a portion of total board remuneration. By 1994, 141 companies, or 71 percent, of top 200 corporations were providing pensions to their directors.

Regarded today as an inappropriate and expensive perquisite, 41 major corporations in the survey group eliminated board pensions in 1997, taking the lead of the 49 companies that did so in the previous year. In 1998, an additional 16 companies discontinued pensions. Pension prevalence has eroded in the last 2 years from 42 to 12 percent—representing greater than a twofold decrease—and is certain to decline further. In fact, by the millennium, director retirement plans may be obsolete.

At this rate of decline, the pension now amounts to only 2 percent of the average board total remuneration, which has risen to a record $114,568 (Figure 31.9).

With respect to terminated pension plans, in almost all cases, companies have set aside the present value of accrued benefits in deferral arrangements. While these funds may be paid out currently, such accrued benefits more frequently have been converted into vehicles for director stock ownership. For example, the directors of Fleet Financial and General Re may elect to convert their accrued benefits

FIGURE 31.9   Total remuneration and the decline in pensions.

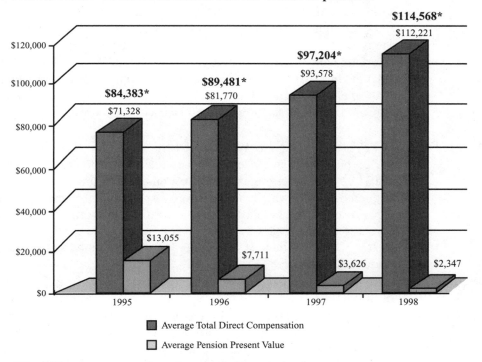

■ Average Total Direct Compensation

□ Average Pension Present Value

*Total direct compensation plus pension present value.

into deferred stock units. At TJX, present values have been credited to deferred stock accounts, while Phillips Petroleum is converting the present value of accrued retirement benefits into restricted stock.

The primary focus now is ensuring that directors maintain a meaningful equity stake in their companies during board service, rather than holding out the promise of cash pension payments once directorship has ended.

DECLINE IN COMPENSATION DERIVED FROM BOARD ATTENDANCE AND COMMITTEE SERVICE

The landscape of board compensation is changing, not just due to the tremendous growth in the use of equity and the disappearance of pensions but also because of the decline in meeting fees. In 1995, 92 percent of the companies paid board and/or committee meeting fees and retainers. By 1998, companies paying meeting fees dropped from 183 to 164. In fact, approximately 20 companies appear to have actually folded meeting fees into the board annual retainer over the last several years.

On the other hand, many companies recognize the greater responsibility thrust upon board committees in the current climate by providing chairs with special retainers or higher meeting fees. Notable by 1998 were 9 companies using equity to pay part or all of their chair and/or meeting fees. Six pay part or all of the chair retainer in equity—CBS, Kmart, Lucent Technologies, Monsanto, Occidental Petroleum, and Toys "R" Us. Three additional companies go one step further, paying part or all of their meeting fees, including the chair retainer, in stock: Chrysler, Coca-Cola Enterprises, and Federated Department Stores.

DECLINE IN MULTIYEAR TERMS FOR DIRECTORS

Major corporations have been slowly reducing director term length since 1995 (Table 31.1). This emerging trend is a response to institutional investor antagonism to staggered boards, which are perceived as potential obstacles to future lucrative changes in control. The shift from 3-year to 1-year terms is also advocated by those corporate governance activists using board elections to express their views on current issues of interest as well as the qualifications and/or performance of individual directors.

THE FUTURE OF BOARD PAY

Board pay has undergone a total transformation since 1995 as equity has risen to an unprecedented position of dominance. As the effects of corporate governance initiatives on board selection, service, and compensation continue to unfold, growth in the practice of establishing a lead director, separating the positions of chairman of the board and chief executive officer, term limits, appraisal of board and individual director performance, and of course—a further shift from cash pay into stock with increasingly sophisticated stock plan design—can be expected.

One thing is clear: Establishing parity with shareholder interests works. With ownership as the link, all stockholders have benefitted and will continue to do so.

TABLE 31.1   Length of Term (Number of Companies)

	One Year	Two Years	Three Years
1995	89	1	110
1996	91	1	108
1997	92	2	106
1998	96	4	100

Elements of Nonemployee Director Compensation*

Board service
- Annual retainer
- Meeting fees
- Stock grants or options

Committee service
- Meeting fees or annual retainer
- Committee chair fees or annual retainer

Special service fees or retainers
- Consulting
- Special committees
- Lead director or nonexecutive board chair

Benefits
- Insurance coverages
- Pension
- Free or discount products and services
- Charitable contributions

*Fees and retainers payable in cash, stock, and/or stock options.

Performance and Compensation

PERFORMANCE MEASURES: AN OVERVIEW

Gloria A. Nofsinger, Senior Manager

Arthur Andersen & Company, S.C.

THE MULTIFACETED VALUE OF ASSESSING PERFORMANCE

Most measures of individual performance take the form of performance appraisals. When properly designed, constructed, and conducted, appraisals can be the basis for decisions on whether to give an employee a pay raise or promotion—or to withhold such rewards. Such decisions can then be made objectively and for sound business reasons. Appraisals can also document that decisions to compensate and otherwise reward employees are made equitably. If ever challenged in court or by the Equal Employment Opportunity Commission (EEOC) on the grounds of discriminatory treatment, an organization can use its appraisals as crucial proof that the employer's compensation and promotion policies are based on performance rather than favoritism, prejudice, personality, or physical traits.

The value of traditional performance appraisals usually lies in their use for compensation decisions (such as incentives, variable pay, or pay-for-performance programs or rewards). Also, employers can use appraisals to coach employees to improve their performance. The appraisal process can spot strengths and weaknesses or highlight areas where retraining would prepare the employee for a new or different position or a promotion. More then simply rewarding past performance skillfully conducted appraisals can help shape employees' future accomplishments.

Although performance appraisals are considered effective management tools, they can result in legal nightmares when handled improperly. Employers must be sensitive to the surrounding legal considerations.

This chapter examines the changing workforce and demographics, as well as the changing economy, to see what impact these factors are having on the methods and practices used for measuring and evaluating performance criteria for today's human capital.

CHANGING WORKFORCE AND ECONOMY

In the old "social contract," employers looked for employees to fill positions and perform specific functions. The employee's path was identified by the employer; it was up to the employee to follow it. This old model is being replaced by a concept where employers invest in employees who will be "key value creators" for the company. Value creation is closely linked to identifying and leveraging core competencies—those unique drivers that have the power to make a company the best in its industry or best in the world. In this new paradigm, employers want to encourage employees to grow, achieve higher performance levels, and be part of the "contributory team" in terms of creating and adding value.

Employees in the new scenario expect to be recognized and rewarded in terms of the value and results they create. Value creation for the corporation will therefore become more closely aligned with employee risks and rewards, creating an entrepreneurial environment within the corporate structure.

Those in the new labor market look increasingly to competency-based models in which the employer says: "I will invest in you as a person; these are the competencies I require; here are the rewards attached to them." This model suits many baby-boomers just fine since they are aware that they are bringing considerable experience to the table and can demand particular fees or salaries for services performed.

Just as the social contract has been changing, so has the economy. The most obvious change is its evolution from a collection of isolated regional businesses to a seamless web of interconnected businesses operating globally. The new ballgame is a lot bigger and faster-paced. If employees expect to stay at the top of their game, they need to be in tune with the global implications of their jobs, and they need to be cross trained for maximum flexibility in meeting the customer's diverse needs worldwide. While employees need to take some responsibility for their personal and professional development, employers must take an active role as well.

Another distinguishing change affecting work and the economy is the nature of change itself. Futurist Paul Shay says: "In the past, change was predictable, incremental, and evolutionary. In other words, it was linear. In modern times, however, change is the opposite: It's 'nonlinear.' It's unpredictable, rapid and revolutionary."[1]

---

[1] Arthur Andersen, HR Director, New York: Profile Pursuit, 1999, p. 37.

Such an environment requires an exceptional workforce if an organization is to succeed. Through the appraisal and rewards process, we can help bring that exceptional workforce to the forefront. Recruiting and retaining competent employees was always important; however, it is intensely critical now—as is rewarding employees for performance, which in turn calls for performance measurement.

MEASURING AND EVALUATING HUMAN CAPITAL

Over the years, we have repeatedly heard that "no one takes performance management seriously." Performance management for the most part has been viewed as an "HR program versus a strategic component of the business." Another issue has always been that "no one is penalized for not giving reviews, but rewards are withheld if certain standards are not met."

Old-style performance appraisals were built like checklists. Each job at each level of the organization had a set of standards, and the standards were weighted in various ways. Points or numbers were filled in and totaled for a "score," which fell somewhere on a grid of acceptable, unacceptable, or perhaps superior performance. The employee's immediate superior conducted the appraisal in a rather linear fashion.

Newer methods are anything but linear. Often, they are *360 degree assessments*. Employees are appraised not only from above by superiors but also from below by subordinates and from peer-level coworkers. Some appraisals even go beyond that point, to a *450 degree assessment* that includes client or customer feedback. The objective is to evaluate the employee from different, meaningful perspectives. It is this kind of an interactive, data gathering process that builds a more complete, multidimensional picture of performance. Some appraisal systems even permit the employee to choose who will conduct their reviews.

In these new modes of performance appraisal, being an integrated "team player" carries weight. Individuals are assessed not only on what they do (expertise) but also on how they do it (process).

Time frames for today's appraisals have changed, too. Why should performance be assessed annually? Since work in many organizations is primarily project driven, it's logical to conduct the evaluation at project completion rather than at an arbitrary end of year. This is especially true when seeking client input on total job outcomes.

At the highest levels, executive appraisals are also changing. The top executives continue to be evaluated along the traditional guidelines, including operating results, financial soundness, market viability, and how well the company is being managed. At the same time, the best-performing organizations are placing considerable emphasis on how well management is doing in the realm of *training and developing employees* to enhance their ability to create value, contribute their special talents, and generate growth for the company.

In these high-performing organizations, employees no longer occupy neatly charted niches: they are truly *human capital,* with the ability to expand, stretch, learn, solve, imagine, and bring forth the best, to the benefit of their organizations and their own fulfillment as human beings. Executives in these forward-thinking organizations are being evaluated not only on financial success but also on how well they manage the performance of their company's human capital.

WHAT IS PERFORMANCE MANAGEMENT?

Performance management is a process-oriented approach to identifying, measuring, communicating, and rewarding core competencies and performance levels for employees so that the organization can achieve maximum productivity. It is oriented toward both the individual and the organization—as integral parts of the same "organic" entity. To manage performance, top executives must have a keen ability to communicate organizational goals and strategies, while never losing sight of individual employee contributions to "the greater whole."

As Jack Welch, CEO of General Electric Corporation, put it, "The 1990s is the decade when soft becomes hard. Being able to manage the unpredictable human side becomes a significant differentiater between winners and losers."

Bob Lutz, president of Chrysler Corporation, agrees: "I think there are indeed great rewards for organizations that pay as much attention to the engineering going on in the so-called `soft' side of their business as the `hard' side."

An enterprisewide management system requires great vision at the top. It necessitates having a comprehensive process for deploying an organization's mission, vision, values, and strategy. It means aligning operations with strategy; it ensures consistency of measurement as applied to strategic objectives and between functional groups. An ongoing process focuses on priorities and results; it integrates measurement, analysis, and action. Above all, it defines and reinforces accountability and promotes continuous improvement.

LINKING REWARD TO ACHIEVEMENT

The notion of pay for performance is virtually ingrained in management's thinking around the world today. From ventures sketched on the back of an envelope to far-flung multinational empires, the notion of rewarding effort is universal. But how do you define, measure and reward these efforts? It all begins with defining performance as achievement of stated goals.

Rewards (perks) and perquisites are used to positively reinforce desired behavior; withholding rewards (such as a bonus or extra time off) serves as negative reinforcement, discouraging undesirable or unproductive behavior. To link rewards to achievements, employers need to set up employee objectives that are:

- Measurable

- Controllable by the worker

- Capable of being observed or monitored by management
- Realistic and attainable
- Part of the larger organization's strategy and directional goals

A sample model of behavior and rewards is given in Table 32.1. In this process model, performance expectations are established, performance is measured, then feedback is given to the employee, rewards are distributed, then the next level of performance expectations are established and communicated. This model creates a self-perpetuating cycle in which each employee continues to grow. When performance is appraised this way, in an ongoing review process, most employees feel involved, up to date, motivated, fairly treated, and important.

PERFORMANCE MEASUREMENT MODELS

Some organizations are opting to move directly into behavior-based performance measurement. That is, people are paid for exhibiting the desired behaviors; and they are appraised by management and by team members, peers, subordinates, suppliers, and vendors, or a combination of them. Meanwhile, other organizations are retaining aspects of the traditional pay-for-performance model while adding more process-oriented components to appraisals. For example, their employee appraisals focus on agreed-upon outcomes as determined jointly by the manager and the employee.

Both the traditional approach and the behavioral approach are valid, and both have a best-practices model for guidance. The side-by-side comparison in Table 32.1 reveals similarities and differences. In general, the behavioral approach is broader based and more far-sighted, seeking to develop employees on many desirable fronts, not just to measure their current status.

A CAUTIONARY NOTE

Although performance measures are effective management tools and crucial in evaluating compensation, they can result in legal nightmares when conducted improperly. Employers should be sensitive to the following issues:

Implied contract claims. Employers need to be aware that they must follow to the letter any statements made in the company's employee handbook about performance reviews. For example, if the handbook states that reviews are to be conducted every 6 months, then failure to do so could give rise to a legal claim since a court of law might view it as a breach of an implied contract.

Negligence claims. The way reviews are conducted is very important. Employers need to ascertain that their managers and supervisors are conducting reviews in a sensible, conscientious way, are filling forms out on time and accurately, and are communicating the contents of the reviews clearly to the employees.

Table 32.1   The Performance-Rewards Process Model

Traditional approach to best practices	Behavioral approach to best practices
Pay for performance	Pay for exhibiting desired behaviors
Traditional appraisal completed by one's manager and communicated to the employee	Appraisals completed by management *and* team members, peers, subordinates, suppliers, and vendors, or a combination of them
Appraisal dealings with predetermined and agreed-upon measurable outcomes	Behavior based including the acquisition of new skills, development of core competencies, and personal and professional growth
■ Process oriented ■ No required competencies ■ Strengths and weaknesses ■ Wish list for training	■ User friendly ■ Position requirements ■ Scale of competency ■ Educational priorities
Best practices for senior managers	Best practices for senior managers
■ Annual revenue ■ Net profit before and after taxes ■ Return on assets or equity (ROA/ROI) ■ Earnings per share ■ Revenue or cost per employee	■ Strategic vision ■ Implementation of tactical approach ■ Team building ■ People development ■ Personal leadership characteristics
Best practices for middle managers	Best practices for middle managers
■ Budget performance ■ Solving major people and process problems ■ Controlling turnover	■ Planning and organizing skills ■ Quality focus ■ Energy ■ Verbal and written communications ■ Decision making and decisiveness ■ Personal and professional development ■ Flexibility and tenacity ■ Leadership
Best practices for nonexempt employees	Best practices for nonexempt employees
■ Attendance ■ Fit with team and is a team player ■ Conformity with safety and health program ■ Quality of "work" ■ Timeliness of efforts ■ Willingness to do more than asked	■ Teamwork ■ Entrepreneurialism ■ Problem solving ■ Desire to learn ■ Team leadership roles ■ Communications

Adverse-impact claims. Employers need to be sure that any criterion used for making employment decisions (including hiring, promotion, demotion, retention, and compensation) does not have an adverse effect on legally protected groups. The evaluation criterion must be clearly related to job performance.

Subjective evaluation claims. As stated above, evaluation criterion must be directly related to job performance. Similarly, employers need to ensure that the evaluation process is as objective and job-related as possible.

Employers typically address these legal issues by conducting training sessions, workshops, and legislative update seminars with their employees to assure internal compliance. It is particularly important for human resource staff members to partner with legal counsel and outside HR consultants who specialize in this area when clarifying and periodically reviewing all aspects of employee evaluation.

SUMMARY

The pace of change, the expanded global marketplace, and the need for employees who can create value for customers or be creative in product-service development all argue for new kinds of worker behavior. It is imperative that executive management teams rethink how they plan to attract, recruit, retain, and reward the kind of workers their organizations need to be successful.

The value of human capital as resources has never been so evident. Only a top-flight, well-motivated workforce is prepared to carry out the company's strategies, fulfill its objectives, and meet customer expectations. Clearly, rewarding the best performance provides a strong competitive edge, while also bringing out more of the best.

33

PERFORMANCE MANAGEMENT

Tracey B. Weiss, Ph.D.

Tracey Weiss Associates

MANAGING THE PERFORMANCE OF OTHERS is increasingly important in a competitive, global marketplace. Strategy implementation requires attention as never before so people management, and performance management could be the framework to drive strategy and business goals. Instead, it has languished as a system associated with forms, rules, levels of review, and meaningless bureaucracy. Frequent criticism of performance management is directed at lenient ratings, sugar-coated feedback, and ambiguous standards that don't reflect the need for greater productivity and profitability.

Despite these problems, it is more critical than ever to manage the "soft side" of performance—how people communicate performance expectations, progress, and results against those expectations. As James Shillaber, director of human resources at Berlex, an international pharmaceutical company, points out: "Performance management is always talked about as a program. There are lots of bells and whistles, but not too much on how it can be used as a tool to do your work better. Too often, these programs just become another pile on an employee's desk."

There needs to be an increase in awareness and skills in what is required of managers to lead and motivate people. To facilitate this change, managers need to break free of the bureaucratic and emotional restrictions of the performance "appraisal" and make the performance management process as powerful a management tool as the balance sheet or the organizational chart. It is not only a matter of training people in the skills of performance management. It requires raising the discipline to a whole new level. Far from a pile on someone's desk, performance management should be the link between personal achievement and organizational effectiveness.

DEFINITION

We define *performance management* as a process for establishing a shared understanding about what is to be achieved and an approach to managing people that increases the probability of achieving success (Weiss and Hartle, 1997).

- *A process*…It is not just about a set of forms—the annual appraisal ritual or the bonus scheme. It is about the everyday actions and behaviors people use to improve performance in themselves and others. It cannot be divorced from the management processes that pervade the organization.

- …*for establishing a shared understanding about what is to be achieved and how it is to be achieved*…To improve performance, individuals need to have a common understanding about what performance (and success) in their jobs looks like. It can be a list of tasks, objectives, or results. It can also be a set of behaviors. Often, it is both. These goals need to be defined clearly and by agreement with the job holder so that people know what they are working toward.

- …*that increases the probability of achieving success.* Performance management has a clear purpose. It is about achieving success in the workplace for individuals and the organization in which they work. Achieving means everyone wins. By establishing a continuous management process that delivers clarity, support, feedback, and recognition to all staff, leaders will take a major step in ensuring significant performance improvement in the organization.

Yet performance management programs often fall short of these goals because they become ensnared in trying to accomplish too many things at the same time. Three performance management dilemmas can be identified that characterize frequent problems encountered in implementing these programs. The remainder of this chapter identifies these dilemmas and then discusses approaches required to overcome them.

CLASSIC PERFORMANCE MANAGEMENT DILEMMAS

The Dilemma of Judging and Coaching

More than 30 years ago, Norman Maier, writing what has now become a *Harvard Business Review* classic, suggested that it is incompatible for a manager to serve as both a judge and a coach or counselor in the same meeting. He noted that when a supervisor appraises an employee for administrative purposes, such as pay, he is serving as a judge. When the supervisor is providing feedback for the purposes of development, he or she is serving as a counselor (Maier, 1965).

The review process in most organizations still maintains the focus of a judgment; the supervisor is in control, the review is retrospective in nature, and the appraisal is typically connected in some way to a potential pay increase. On the other hand, to be successful, development should be driven by the employee. It should look to the future, and the employee should not be preoccupied with the immediate consequences in pay. When both of these objectives are addressed in a single meeting, presumably to save time for managers, the rating and the raise become the focal point—at the expense of employee development. As a result, personal and professional development that support such popular corporate values as "continuous improvement" and "continuous learning" get short shrift.

The Dilemma of Linkage to Pay

The impossibility of accomplishing both a review for pay purposes and discussing an employee's development in the same meeting is further compounded by the negative consequences of tying performance into a merit increase that may seem negligible to the employee. Research conducted by E. E. Lawler indicates that a pay increase of 3 to 4 percent, while noticeable, is not sufficient to improve performance. The Hay Group reports that over the past few years, annual merit increases have been around 4 percent. A 4 percent increase on a $50,000 check, if taxes are around 30 percent, is a new paycheck that is only $27 higher than the old paycheck. Thus, it is understandable how a frequent survey finding on employees' perceptions of the relationship between pay and performance is that there is no meaningful distinction for outstanding performance.

The Dilemma of Measurement

Both measuring the right things and precision in measurement are important to effective performance management. However, in practicality, supervisors and employees have difficulty setting goals that are specific enough to be measurable and yet not so specific that they do not take into account the comprehensive nature of the overall performance that is expected. Particularly, when ratings are to be used to compare performance for pay or promotional considerations, it is usually preferable to formulate job functions that must be observed at a broader level so that performance among employees can be legitimately compared. However, there are also occasions where more specific tasks, behaviors, or other activities provide the criteria to be assessed when scores must be compared for administrative purposes. It is important to note that performance criteria that are more specific are more defensible for litigation purposes. (Bernardin, Hennessey, and Peyrefitte, 1995).

A second measurement dilemma is that performance appraisal programs often measure the wrong aspects of performance. When narrow role definitions are the foundation of performance goals, everyone works to meet a functional target: Close four new accounts, ship 800 units, submit accurate sales forecasts monthly. Sometimes the goals are related to bigger corporate objectives—grow market share by 20 percent; maintain a 95 percent defect-free rate—and sometimes not. Measures are frequently established that optimize particular departments at the expense of overall business goals. Sales goals are established by the sales organization and can run afoul if production doesn't keep up with sales. If a distribution center is measured on product turns, it takes only the number of products it has ordered from the factory, regardless of the quantity the factory produced, potentially resulting in unfilled orders even though the organization has produced the product.

WHY NOT ELIMINATE APPRAISALS?

Given these unsolved dilemmas of performance management, why not eliminate the appraisal altogether? A 5-year trial study completed in 1993 with 1,200 blue- and white-collar U.S. Navy employees for whom the performance appraisal was eliminated concluded that employees, who initially were in favor of the appraisal being abolished, changed their minds once it was eliminated. The researchers concluded, "The elimination of performance appraisal resulted in a weakening of the pay-for-performance link, and the introduction of productivity gain sharing based on organizational performance did not make up the loss. Moreover, the evaluation results showed no significant productivity gains were achieved....While eliminating performance appraisal seems to be a popular one, less than 50 percent of employees were actually in favor of it" (Shay, 1993).

Findings from the private sector also support the need for performance management. A recent study of 437 companies demonstrated that those with programs to manage performance outperform companies without such programs on a wide range of financial and productivity measures. Further, companies whose performance lagged behind their competitors showed significant improvement once they instituted a performance management program (McDonald and Smith, 1995).

The theoretical underpinnings of performance management date back over 40 years. Peter Drucker, writing in 1954, was one of the first to lay the foundation for management by objectives. Since then, research has continued to substantiate how setting clear goals increases the probability of successful performance outcomes. Simply put, employees are better able to direct their performance when they know what is expected from them. Bobko and Colella (1994) provide an extensive review of the literature and make a compelling case that performance standards impact self-set goals, goals regulate actions, and challenging and specific goals produce higher levels of performance than goals that are vague or easy.

The conclusion of this research is that eliminating appraisals is just another way of avoiding the difficult issues and creates more problems than it solves. People and pay decisions still need to be made in a systematic way that is perceived to be fair. In the next section, six characteristics of effective performance management programs are explained. To a large extent, these six characteristics are universal. However, how they are applied should be tailored to the unique culture and strategy of each organization. The last section of this chapter illustrates how to tailor and adopt these characteristics by presenting several case studies in different organizational settings.

SIX CHARACTERISTICS OF AN EFFECTIVE PERFORMANCE MANAGEMENT SYSTEM

Given the dilemmas of performance management, our research and consulting experience has shown that there are six fundamentals to making performance management work. While we support the idea that a performance management program needs to be tailored to individual cultures and business strategies, these six characteristics should be fundamental to all systems.

1. Create and Reinforce Performance Management As an Ongoing System of Planning, Coaching, Reviewing, and Rewarding. The four pillars that support all people management processes are still the fundamentals of planning, coaching, reviewing, and rewarding. Weaken any one of them and the integrity of the entire system is compromised. It is a continuous process, working together to establish key objectives, monitor progress toward results and give feedback on relevant course corrections, and provide rewards and recognition for results. Much detail has been written elsewhere on each of these four phases, which is summarized in Table 33.1 (Weiss and Hartle, 1997).

2. Performance Management Needs to Be Linked to Specific Business Objectives and Driven by Top Management. To overcome the measurement dilemmas, it is imperative that goals be specifically tied to the business strategy and communicated clearly so that employees are able to understand the relevance of their goals to the organization's bigger picture. Performance management becomes the way strategic change is achieved, and business drivers such as customer service or quality improvement go from being words into being operationalized as a part of everyone's job.

3. Performance Measures Are Based Both on Quantifiable Objectives and Behavioral Competencies. Until recently, most organizations were able to navigate solely by the numbers like market share, profits, and revenues. Most of these

TABLE 33.1   Four Supports for Managing People

	Planning	Coaching	Reviewing	Rewarding
Needs of the business	■ Align employees with strategies, vision, values.	■ Improve performance through feedback. ■ Track performance. ■ Reinforce progress toward goals. ■ Modify priorities and resources as required.	■ Assess performance against expectations. ■ Link results to the team and organization. ■ Document.	■ Attract and retain a motivated and able workforce.
Questions employees need answered	■ How do I fit in? ■ What do I need to do to be successful?	■ How am I/we doing? ■ What do I need to work on? ■ Are the priorities still the same? ■ How can I get help?	■ How was my/our contribution valued? ■ How does my view of my own performance compare to the evaluation of others?	■ What does this mean in terms of pay and opportunities? ■ Am I being treated fairly?
Critical process variables	■ Employee participation. ■ Challenging and attainable goals. ■ Explicit and agreed-upon standards and measures. ■ Links to employee development.	■ Systematic observation and documentation. ■ Frequent feedback that is behaviorally specific. ■ Immediate and clear consequences.	■ Document both hard data (when available) and behaviorally specific observations.	■ Separate out discussions of compensation from coaching discussions about employee development.

measures focused primarily on short-term financial performance. In recent years, a variety of nonnumeric measures such as customer satisfaction or new product development have become increasingly important. While cascading objectives help link individual to organizational performance measures, they often are inadequate to capture how a job is actually accomplished.

Competencies are the behaviors, skills, attitudes, and motives that make up the characteristics that are proven to drive superior job performance. Competencies establish a causal link between certain behaviors and the achievement of success.

How companies choose to incorporate competencies varies. Praxair, the industrial gas company, has assembled a cross-functional task force to identify core professional and managerial competencies that would support the new corporate strategy. All employees are asked to focus on the same set of competencies that will support the new corporate vision. Performance planning for competencies involves discussing how the employee can demonstrate desired behavior toward the accomplishment of objectives, along with which competencies should be prioritized for the coming year. As with other parts of the performance planning process, this takes place as a two-way dialogue between the employee and his or her manager.

Other companies give more latitude to individuals, teams, and business groups to select competencies to meet their needs. Rather than using competencies to drive a singular corporate vision, these companies see the need to tailor them to the individual and team level. In one case, we assisted a large pharmaceutical company in developing over 25 functional models for individual business groups within the company. In this case, each manager described competencies that were specifically aligned with the methods used to get work done in his or her functional area.

Behaviorally anchored rating scales, or BARS, is one commonly used method for utilizing competencies in a performance management program. A BARS approach is simply a way of labeling points along a rating scale with behavioral descriptions differentiating levels of complexity. To measure the quality of an employee's performance, the rater checks the description that most closely matches the actual observed behavior and provides examples and comments substantiating the rating. Table 33.2 is a sample from a BARS instrument.

4. Management Commitment and Accountability Must Exist at All Levels.
Lack of management accountability is often a critical flaw in performance management. The program is often viewed as belonging to human resources rather than to line management. Line managers view it as extra work, requiring them to complete forms to administer salary increases. Frequently the managers are unskilled and therefore uncomfortable giving people feedback.

Many companies have introduced supervisory training in the behavioral skills required for effective performance management. Building the requisite skills in all managers is a requirement for making a performance management system work; therefore, many companies require this training of everyone who has supervisory responsibilities.

In addition to training, building competencies in the area of leadership and developing others can build accountability for performance management right into the system itself. Managers at all levels need to feel that they are being evaluated not only on the specific projects to which they have accountability but also for the performance and the development of the people they manage.

5. There Must Be Linkage to Other Systems, and Goals Must Be Communicated Clearly.
Pay communicates. When a company changes its

TABLE 33.2   Sample from a BARS Instrument

Job Competency	Behavioral Indicators	Rating (Circle One)
Interpersonal skills	3 = Is able to modify approach when dealing with others, even in critical or hostile situations, to a satisfactory and beneficial result for all parties.	
	2 = Understands differences among people and senses reactions of others. Consistently uses this information when responding.	1 2 3
	1 = Responds to all interpersonal situations in a similar manner. Does not modify communication style.	

compensation system, it is conveying what is important and what it wants employees to take seriously. New priorities and new behavior may be required to take a business in a new direction. If competencies in customer service or teamwork are added to the performance management program, it becomes a strong statement of the company's strategies, values, and mission. (Milkovich and Milkovich, 1992).

6. Multiple Sources Must Be Accessed for Input into the Performance Review.   The role of the manager is changing, and this directly impacts performance management. Organizations are flatter and demand greater responsibility on both the parts of individuals and teams. This involves both defining work that needs to get done and measuring their accomplishments against self-defined objectives. Managers are often busy with their own project work and team commitments and are less directly in touch with the work that their direct reports might be doing. As the world of work is changing, expanding the list of who should have input into all phases of the performance management process also needs to change, if the process is to continue to add value.

The role of self-appraisal has never been more important. Research has consistently shown that when the performance review is based on the employee's self-review, the discussion is significantly more constructive and satisfying to both parties than it is when based on the manager's appraisal alone (Meyer 1991).

Who else should have input into appraisals? Much of the answer lies both in the culture of the organization as well as the nature of the work the employee is doing. Much has been written recently about the importance of companies' maintaining a focus on customers. In this respect, London and Beatty (1993) argue that internal and external customer feedback provides a competitive advantage, providing that the feedback is translated into specific outcomes that directly impact performance. While there is a good deal of debate about using multirater, or 360 degree, feedback directly in performance reviews, how these processes should link should be tailored to the unique characteristics of an organization's culture. In the next section, we discuss several case studies that feature how to tailor a performance management program to be more consistent with different business strategies.

ONE SIZE DOES NOT FIT ALL

While all six of these characteristics are universal to all effective performance management programs, how they are applied can vary a great deal. Below are three case studies, which illustrate the typical cultures and the performance management many organizations are employing. These examples are not meant to be comprehensive but merely to illustrate how performance management processes need to be tailored to specific environments to be effective.

Traditional Environment

The traditional functional culture is the one with which we are the most familiar. The multilayered organizational bureaucracy as well as assembly-line production are all examples of this type of organization. Designed to emphasize reliability of technology and stability for people, work is organized into functional specialties with well-defined jobs and accountabilities. Job levels are clearly and narrowly defined and are central to pay, with work comparison and grading being the controlling elements of the pay process. The effects of perceived competence and performance moderate this.

Fairness and stability are what employees are looking for in this type of environment. Effective performance management should focus on alignment of goals throughout the organization. Annual planning, coaching, and appraisal meetings should be scheduled on a regular basis. Policies and procedures should be clearly communicated.

Over the last few years, there has been a tendency to view the traditional method of managing performance as antiquated and lacking in relevance. Yet, it is often faulty implementation, not the design, of this system that is flawed. For many organizations, especially for business units that need to emphasize safety or limiting the downside of risk, emphasizing quality checks for consistency of work and/or respecting the chain of command, all suggest the need for a traditional performance management program. China Power and Light, a major utility for Hong Kong, asked us to redesign their performance management program and make it more relevant to employees. The focus of the redesigned program involved a cascading goal-setting process, starting at the top of the organization. A BARS approach to competencies was included in the planning, coaching, and reviewing of all employees. Four competency levels were defined for senior management, middle management, first-line supervisors, and professional individual contributors. A similar approach was developed for hourly employees. Focus was on training all supervisors in how to give behavioral feedback. This program was a dramatic shift from an uneven process with poor documentation and little focus on what it took to be successful in the organization.

Team Environment

There is a clear movement to team-based work in all sizes of organizations, from the Fortune 500 to small businesses. Competitive pressures have led to flatter, downsized organizations that require employees to play a greater role in how work gets done. The increasing complexity of many jobs makes it difficult for one person to perform them, leading to using teams in many companies as the basic work unit (Reilly and McGourty, 1998).

Employees are attracted to a team-based environment and expect more flexibility in roles, a greater sense of team spirit, and more interdependence. Distinctive characteristics of performance management processes prevalent in team environments include setting group goals, using multirater feedback on competencies for appraisal purposes, and peer as well as supervisor coaching.

A case study that illustrates the team approach to performance management is an accounting division from a major computer manufacturer that had the opportunity to start a new operation, or "greenfield" site, when the operation moved from New Jersey to Bismarck, North Dakota. The advantage of having a newly hired group to organize work into self-managed work teams was immense. Each team had about 10 members and took on much of the responsibility typically relegated to management, such as hiring new members and scheduling work. As a result, the performance management process needed to be designed to support this team process. The system was designed so that at the beginning of each performance cycle, each team would collectively set their goals. Ongoing data collection on key measures such as customer satisfaction, turnaround time, and error rate provided benchmarks for setting performance standards for the upcoming year. Competency models were specifically developed to give employees guidance on how to be successful in a team environment.

Much of the responsibility for coaching fell to team members. Because these teams had to manage their performance in some basic ways, they also had the authority and responsibility to correct situations when they were counterproductive to team goals.

Feedback was an integral part of the culture throughout the year as well as in the annual review. In addition to measurement on the quantitative goals set by the team, multirater feedback on competencies was also used as input into the performance reviews. The multirater instrument was designed based specifically on this organization's identified competencies of exceptional behavior. Rewards were directly linked to performance against the team targets and could be modified for individuals based on the competency feedback.

Sales Environment

Sales divisions are notably different from their counterparts in other corporate sectors such as manufacturing or research and development. While many organizations are integrating a team concept into their management style, for the most part sales managers are looking for individual "star" performers, who have a healthy sense of competition, can focus on both short- and long-term results, and take initiative. A high-performance sales culture is frequently characterized by a sustained sense of urgency and attention to windows of opportunity. This culture is also true of many parts of entrepreneurial businesses, such as a high-tech startups for whom getting to the market before the competition can be a matter of survival.

In a sales culture, competencies are important but frequently are detached from the pay program and focused instead on employee development. Performance against goals is closely monitored and frequently reported. All sales representatives are updated regularly on how they are performing against others. Authentic performance reviews are linked to the accomplishment of milestone goals, which are not necessarily neatly linked to a calendar cycle.

At Berlex, performance management is a continuous process within the sales force. District managers typically spend at least a day in the field with each sales representative on a monthly basis. These "ride-alongs" are opportunities for both direct observation and coaching. The sessions are documented in an ongoing computer notes file that can be downloaded by either the sales representative or his or her manager. There is a line-of-sight read access to the files by senior management who can monitor the process to ensure that the district managers are providing appropriate coaching and mentoring. The notes database serves as ongoing documentation of the performance management process and should correlate with the results achieved against quantifiable sales targets. Incentives are paid out against the sales targets achieved. Then end-of-the-year performance review serves merely as a summary of these monthly coaching sessions.

It has been a commonly accepted practice for years that sales may have a pay plan separate from other parts of a business. In fact, while many sales organizations comply with corporate requests to complete annual forms, the process is not often as tailored as that at Berlex.

It is appropriate for other parts of organizations to tailor their performance management practices in a way that is dynamic and appropriate to their needs. Some parts of an organization may be very team based while other parts of an organization may not. It is appropriate to fit the performance management techniques to the culture that will best support the business strategy. Consistency, corporatewide, can be achieved through unified principles, which can capture the performance management philosophy of the organization. Such arrangements may not be the tidy one-size-fits-all approach of performance management in prior years, but they will encourage the development of useful tools that will help drive the business strategy.

REFERENCES

Bernardin, J. H., C. M. Hagan, J. S. Kane, and P. Villanova. 1998. "Effective Performance Management: A Focus on Precision, Customers, and Situational Constraints. In James W. Smither (ed.), *Performance Appraisal: State of the Art in Practice.* San Francisco: Jossey-Bass, pp. 3–48.

Bernardin, H. J., H. W. Hennessey, and J. Peyrefitte. 1995. "Age, Racial, and Gender Bias as a Function of Criterion Specificity: A Test of Expert Testimony." *Human Resource management Review,* vol. 5, pp. 63–77.

Bobko, P., and A Colella. 1994. "Employees Reactions to Performance Standards: A Review and Research Propositions." *Personnel Psychology,* vol. 47, pp. 1–36.

Drucker, P. F. 1954. *The Practice of Management.* New York: HarperCollins.

Goleman, D. 1998. *Working with Emotional Intelligence.* New York: Bantam Books.

Lawler, E. E., III. 1990. *Strategic Pay.* San Francisco: Jossey-Bass.

———. 1995. "The New Pay: A Strategic Approach." *Compensation & Benefits Review,* vol. 28, no. 6, pp. 20–26.

London, M., and R. W. Beatty. 1993. "360-Degree Feedback as a Competitive Advantage." *Human Resource Management,* vol. 32, pp. 353–372.

Maier, N. 1965. "Split Roles in Performance Appraisal." *Harvard Business Review.* A shortened version of the article was republished in 1989 as an "HBR Retrospect," because the original 1965 article was one of HBR's 10 best-selling reprints, vol. 43, pp. 123–129.

McDonald, D., and A. Smith. 1995. "A Proven Connection: Performance Management and Business Results." *Compensation & Benefits Review,* vol. 27, Jan/Feb., pp. 59–64.

Meyer, H. H. 1991. "A Solution to the Performance Appraisal Feedback Enigma." In James W. Smither (ed.), *Performance Appraisal: State of the Art in Practice.* San Francisco: Jossey-Bass, pp. 252–259.

Mohrman, A. M., Jr., S. S. Resnick-West, and E. E. Lawler, III. 1989. *Designing Performance Appraisal Systems: Aligning Appraisals and Organizational Realities.* San Francisco: Jossey-Bass.

Reilly, Richard R., and Jack McCourty. 1998. "Performance Appraisal in Team Settings." In James W. Smither (ed.), *Performance Appraisal: State of the Art in Practice.* San Francisco: Jossey-Bass, pp. 244–277.

Schay, B. W. 1993. "In Search of the Holy Grail: Lessons in Performance Management." *Public Personnel Management,* vol. 22, no. 4, pp. 649–668.

Schneier, C. E., D. G. Shaw, and R. W. Beatty. 1991."Performance Measurement and Management: A Tool for Strategy Execution." *Human Resources Management.* Reprinted in J. W. Smither (ed.), *Performance Appraisal: State of the Art in Practice.* San Francisco: Jossey-Bass, pp. 3–19.

Spencer, L. M., Jr., and S. M. Spencer. 1993. *Competence At Work: Models for Superior Performance.* New York: Wiley.

Weiss, T., and F. Hartle. 1997. *Reengineering Performance Management: Breakthroughs in Achieving Strategy through People.* Boca Raton: St. Lucie Press.

34

MEASURING THE HARD STUFF: TEAMS AND OTHER HARD-TO-MEASURE WORK

Jack Zigon, President

Zigon Performance Group

TWENTY YEARS' EXPERIENCE MEASURING THE "HARD STUFF" have yielded best practices that can save time and improve the quality of performance measures for teams and other hard-to-measure work. This chapter will describe a process for creating performance measures for any kind of work and the learning resulting from implementing these systems. It will conclude with a case study that illustrates the how-to steps and their products.

WHY MEASURE PERFORMANCE?

Most people measure performance for one of these reasons:

- *You can't manage what you can't measure.* Managers, as well as self-managing professionals and teams, cannot define what they expect, give feedback, and provide recognition without performance measures.

- *You can't improve what you can't measure.* It's easy to say, "Let's try this new program," but without data before and after, you can't see if performance is actually improving.

- *High-performance teams and individuals require clear goals.* Creating high performance requires a definition of it so you'll know it when you see it. In addition, all high performers get there because they have a clear picture of where they're going.

- *Pay for performance requires metrics.* If you want to pay based on performance, you need to have some way of knowing when the payout has been earned.

RECENT INSIGHTS INTO PERFORMANCE MEASUREMENT

For years, I separated the techniques of team and individual employee performance measurement because team performance usually required a more complex methodology to handle the more complex performance measurement task. In the last year it has become clear that almost all these techniques can be used for groups, teams, and individuals. A more robust measurement technology is a function of a larger repertoire of techniques and models. The reader is asked to use his or her common sense to choose and apply the model that appears most likely to produce a useful measurement idea.

The approach outlined in this chapter has the following benefits:

- *It provides a road map for a difficult task.* Measurement is hard enough when you know how to do it. Having a clear path allows you to concentrate on creating measures instead of wondering what to do next.

- *It reduces cycle time.* The first generation of this process took 2 to 3 days for an individual and months for a team. The latest generation, when coupled with a large collection of measurement ideas, takes anywhere from 3 to 8 hours.

- *It handles difficult-to-measure work.* Not all work can be measured with numbers. This process handles the qualitative, hard-to-measure jobs as well as the easily quantified.

- *It provides multiple ways to align or link.* Linkage or alignment with organizational goals is more and more important in today's business environment. This process provides two ways to provide that line of sight.

- *It can be taught.* This process is not rocket science. It can be taught and learned by any workforce with a high school education.

COMMON PROBLEMS OF TEAM AND EMPLOYEE MEASUREMENT

Measurement is difficult for at least three reasons:

- *It is not always obvious what results should be measured.* Most teams and hard-to-measure individuals will use the obvious measures without asking what results they should be producing and how they will know they've done a good job.

- *Even if you know what to measure, it is often not clear how the measurement should be done.* Not everything can be easily measured with numbers; thus teams and individuals give up when they face measuring something like "creativity" or "user friendliness."

- *Teams are made up of individuals; thus measurement must be done at both the team and individual levels, effectively doubling the size of the measurement task.* Developing individual measures that support the team and don't conflict is difficult without direction.

Because there are many types of teams and individuals with different measurement challenges, the measurement process presented is not a linear one. You'll need to have a clear understanding of where you want to end up and then make choices along the way to find the most efficient path to your goal.

For both teams and individuals, we want to end up with a measurement system that includes the following:

- A list of the value-added results of the team and team members

- Performance measures and standards for each of these results

- A clear picture of the priorities and *relative importance* of the team and individual results

- A way to track how the team and individuals are performing compared to the performance standards

Based on almost two decades' experience measuring hard-to-measure work like research and development, design engineering, graphic design, marketing and customer service, and five years of helping teams create measures, I have refined a third-generation process for measuring performance:

1. *Review the organizational measures.* This step makes sure that the measures "above" and "around" the team and individuals are known and can be linked to their measures.

2. *Define measurement starting points.* This step offers five alternatives for identifying starting points for measurement. Selecting the best alternatives and using them to identify the team and individual results provide the basis for all further measurement.

3. *Weight the results.* This step allows the relative importance of each result to be discussed and agreed upon.

4. *Develop performance measures.* This step identifies the numeric and descriptive yardsticks that will be used to gauge how well the results have been achieved.

5. *Develop performance standards.* This step defines how well the team and individuals have to perform to meet and exceed expectations.

6. *Decide how to track the performance.* This step identifies how the data for each performance standard will be collected and fed back to the team and individuals.

Step 1. Review the Existing Organizational Measures

Why review organizational measures? Teams and individuals don't operate in a vacuum. The measures above and around them are usually the goals they need to support and align with. Dysfunctional organizational measures will sometimes cause a team or individual to exhibit dysfunctional behavior.

Organizational measures can cause problems with performance if they are unknown to the employees, unbalanced, or unable to be affected by them.

■ Many times the team or individuals are buried deep within an organization, unaware of what measures are important to the organization. They can't affect what they are unaware of.

■ A team or individual who is asked to improve customer satisfaction in a company solely interested in profit will find few supporters when they make suggestions requiring additional investment to improve customer service.

■ If the same team trying to improve customer satisfaction is made up of only auditing employees, it is likely to be unsuccessful because few aspects of front-line customer satisfaction can be affected by a support organization.

Unidimensional measures, which focus only on financial measures like profit or return on net assets, direct the team to change only those facets of the business that can be measured with dollars. Kaplan and Norton's balanced-scorecard concept suggests that organizations will be more successful if they add three other perspectives to the *financial perspective* when defining organizational measures of effectiveness. The *customer perspective* describes what customers think, the *internal business perspective* asks what measures of internal efficiency are important, and the *learning perspective* asks what aspects of employee development and learning are critical to the organization's success. See the Kaplan and Norton 1966 book, *The Balanced Scorecard, Translating Strategy into Action,* for a discussion of the concept.

In addition to informing the team and/or individual of the measures, the most important thing to determine is whether or not they can *affect* the measures. If they can't, you have two choices: Change the membership of the team so that it can affect the measures, or change the measures. Asking a team or individual to affect organization measures that are beyond their control will eventually weaken or destroy their motivation.

For example, a greeting card manufacturer organizes all the employees responsible for a particular holiday onto one cross-functional team. This particular team is responsible for developing, selling, and distributing all products related to Father's Day.

The company is trying to break out of its company-owned store distribution channel and is interested in increasing its profit, sales, and diversifying its sales channels. The organizational measures the team and creative individuals can affect include dollar profit, dollar sales, and sales from outside their company-owned stores.

Step 2. Define Measurement Points

Measurement is easier if you understand the *result* of the performance you are trying to evaluate. All measurement should flow from either the team and/or individual's value-added results. *Value-added results* are the contributions the team or individual makes to the organization that result from their activities and add value to the organization; they are the valuable products they leave behind after they go home at night.

Value-added results are the best starting point for three reasons:

- *It takes less time.* Agreeing on the *result* to be produced takes less time than agreeing on the best *activities* to achieve the result. While there can be many ways to achieve an end, everyone will usually agree more quickly on the "end" and less quickly on the "means."

- *Tracking the performance will be less costly.* Evaluating activities means someone has to be there to watch the activities happen. Evaluating the results of the activities can be done by just looking at the result.

- *It focuses everyone on what is really important.* Measuring activity makes activity seem more important than the results of the activity. Unless what you want is activity, focus the performer on results.

There are five techniques for identifying the starting point for performance measurement: constructing a customer diagram, identifying results that support organizational measures, constructing a results pyramid, mapping the work process, and constructing a role-result matrix.

Constructing a Team Customer Diagram.   The first technique makes use of a *customer diagram.* This technique works best when customer satisfaction is one of the main drivers of performance. Since almost all teams and individuals exist to satisfy some customers' needs, the technique nearly always creates useful starting points for performance measurement.

Because "a picture is worth a thousand words," a good way to describe who your customers are and what they need from you is to draw a customer diagram. The customer diagram will show the team or individuals the types of internal and external customers they serve and the products and services these customers need from the team or individuals. When completed, the diagram shows the linkages between the performers and their customers.

The team or individual draws a diagram with the team or individual performer in the center of the page and the individuals, departments, functions, and so on shown as boxes around the team or individual. Lines are drawn connecting the team to the customers with the products and services these customers need from the team on the lines.

Figure 34.1 is an example of a customer diagram for the Father's Day Team. The customers are listed around the team. The arrows contain statements of products and services each customer needs from the team. The same kind of diagram could be drawn for an individual.

FIGURE 34.1   Father's Day Team customer diagram.

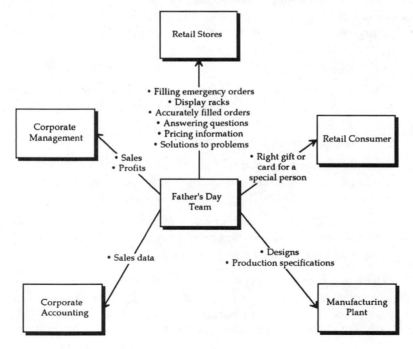

Identifying Results That Support Organizational Measures

The second option for identifying value-added results answers the question, "What value-added results does the team or individual produce that can help the organization achieve its goal?" Answering the question helps the performers identify the results they have control over that will lead to the organization's success.

This technique works best when the team or individual is asked to help the organization make an improvement in a measurable goal such as reducing cycle time or product costs or increasing sales or customer retention rate. In each case, the goal is one that can be measured with numbers, and the team or individual is supposed to help move the numbers in the right direction.

The performer answers two questions to use this technique: "Can the I/we affect the organizational measure?" And if the answer is yes, "What value-added results do I/we produce that can help the organization achieve this goal?"

The Father's Day Team is part of a larger organization that is interested in increasing its profits and sales and in diversifying its sales channels. The first two organizational goals are measured in dollars, while the diversification of sales channels is measured by the dollar sales from outside the franchise or company-owned network.

The team first decided whether it could affect these measures, and the answer was yes to all three. Because the team controls costs and makes sales, it could affect both profit and sales. Since it is charged with finding new retail outlets, it could also affect the dollar sales from new outlets. Then they answered the question, "What value-added results does the team produce that can help the organization achieve each of these goals?" In this case the answer was *signed retail outlets* and *profitable sales.*

Constructing a Results Pyramid. The third option for identifying performance measurement points is to identify the hierarchy of results that the organization must produce and select those that link the team or individual to the organization's results.

As mentioned earlier, employees do not operate in a vacuum. They exist to serve the purposes of the organization and its customers. Linking the team and individual results to the organization's results ensures that the performer's success benefits the organization.

Most teams and individuals are linked to their organization's results using *measures.* If the company is trying to increase sales and profitability, they are told those are the measures by which they will be judged. If the performer is in marketing, the dollar sales measure is probably correct, but since it can't control expenses to any large degree, the profit measure may not apply. If an individual is a graphic designer or customer service rep, neither sales nor profits may make sense. Using measures to link performers to their organization sometimes puts the team or individual in a position of trying to affect a measure over which it has little or no control.

The second problem is one of abstractness. The formula for calculating profit in most publicly held companies can be very technical and subject to wide swings due to investments, tax writeoffs, and other events over which teams usually have no control. Trying to "help" a mathematical formula produce a better number is difficult to get excited about.

By linking the team or individual results to the organization's *results,* you can avoid the problem of measuring them on something over which they have no control. While a human resources team has no direct control over profit, they do produce "qualified new hire candidates" and "trained employees." But both of these results will be measured very differently than the methods used to measure "profitable sales."

As the Father's Day Team looked for ways to further link their results to the organization's result, they drew a results pyramid linking them to the organizational result of "profitable sales" (Figure 34.2). Every other result leads to this. While the team will be responsible for a number of the results in this pyramid, a particular individual may be assigned the "competitive summary" result.

FIGURE 34.2   Results pyramid.

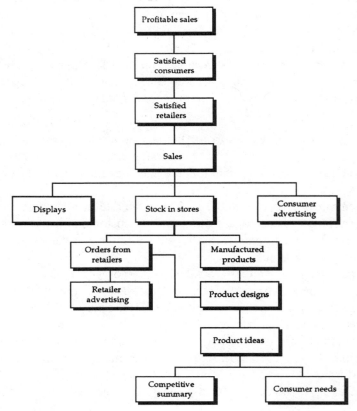

Mapping the Work Process. The fourth method of identifying measurement points is different from the first three techniques. The first three all use results as part of the process, while this technique identifies points in a work process that are worth measuring.

Work processes are a series of steps that usually cut across departments and provide some value-added service or product to a customer. The customer may be internal or external to the organization. A *work process map* is a diagram of that work process. The boxes represent the steps in the process where activity occurs. The arrows represent the "hand-offs" between the steps.

Mapping the work process and using it as a tool to identify team or individual measurement points has several advantages:

- Quality and process improvement programs can be linked to performance management.

- Teams and individuals who support an obvious work process can evaluate their effectiveness in terms of the performance of the process.

- Mapping the process may identify opportunities to simplify and reengineer, resulting in better work processes and performances.

To create a work process map, the performers identify the valuable end result of the work process and draw it in a box in the lower right-hand corner of a page. Then they identify the first step required to produce this result and place the step in a box in the upper left-hand corner of a page. The remaining steps required to go from step 1 to the end result connect the two boxes with a series of boxes and arrows. Finally, they answer the questions, "Where in this diagram should the *entire team* be measured? Where should any particular individual be measured?"

The Father's Day Team mapped out their work process and used the map to identify three additional measurement points (Figure 34.3):

- The final product to the retailer and consumer

- The quality of the design step (Is everyone involved and signed off on the designs?)

- Cycle time across the entire process (If these products are late and miss the Father's Day ship date, they are worthless to the consumer and the retailer.)

The finance person might be responsible for how well the financing and business planning steps go.

Constructing a Role-Result Matrix. The fifth technique applies when you are measuring team performance and you want to have a way to measure both the team and the individual team members. Measuring both has the following benefits:

- Individuals raised in the North American culture expect to be evaluated on both a team and an individual basis. While comfortable with being evaluated

FIGURE 34.3   Work process map.

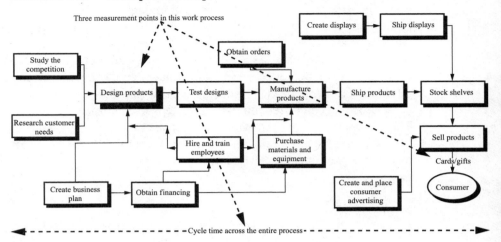

on things only a team could achieve, they want to also be recognized for their individual contributions to the team.

- Even in cultures where individualism is not as prevalent, the existing performance evaluation systems are usually individual based. Measuring both team and individual performance allows a smoother transition to a team-based appraisal.

- Evaluating individual performance provides the data for coaching individual employees who are not supporting the team well enough with their individual contributions. Without this data, the discussions may degenerate into personality conflicts and arguments, instead of becoming constructive coaching sessions.

- Evaluating individual performance provides the data for rewarding outstanding individual contributors who might otherwise be unrewarded on a "losing" team. A basketball star such as Michael Jordan might leave a professional basketball team of which he is member unless his contributions are rewarded independent of the team's results for the season.

Unless designed otherwise, team and individual measures will usually conflict. Most team members complain that their individual-based performance assessment and pay systems do not reward them for any team results they have produced. In fact, their bosses see the time they spend on the team's work as taking away from their "real job."

To prevent these conflicts and achieve the benefits mentioned above, use a role-result matrix to identify the individual results that are needed to support the team's results.

A role-result matrix is a table that identifies the results each team member must produce to support the team's results (Table 34.1). Its name comes from the function of the table: It defines the roles of the members in terms of the results they must produce to support the team.

The team results are listed across the top of the table, and the team members are listed down the left side of the table. Inside each cell is written the answer to the question, "What result does this particular team member have to accomplish to help the team produce the particular result?"

The Father's Day team identified the results the individual team members produced to support the team's results using the role-result matrix in Table 34.1. Inside the cells are the results each team member is to produce to support a particular team result. Note that only three team results and five team members are in this partial example.

To support the creation of new product designs, production determines the costs of various product ideas that the team generates. Marketing brings customer needs from focus group research, their own product ideas, and a summary of what the competition is doing. Creative produces their own product ideas. Fulfillment contributes their requirements to ensure safe and economical shipping of any

TABLE 34. Role-Result Matrix

| | Team Results | | |
Team Members	New Product Designs	Shipped Products	Profitable Sales
Production	■ Product cost estimates	■ Manufactured products	■ Cost-saving ideas
Marketing	■ Focus group results ■ Product ideas ■ Competitive summary		■ Retail sales ■ Orders from retailers
Creative	■ Product ideas	■ Product designs	
Fulfillment	■ Shipping requirements	■ Correctly filled orders	■ Cost-saving ideas
Human resources	■ Skills and experience inventory of existing employees	■ Trained employees	■ Trained employees

given product design. Human resources helps the team decide if they can produce a given design with the human resources of the company.

Notice that marketing has no contribution to the result of "shipped products" listed in the second column. When defining the individual contributions to a team, it is OK that some team members might not have a contribution to a particular team result.

Step 3. Weight the Results

Weights can be used to help a team discuss priorities and agree on what is really important. An individual can use weights as the basis for a conversation with his or her manager concerning priorities. Because the weights reflect the *importance* of the results, and not just the amount of *time* spent working on them, weights can help the team or the individual manage its time better.

When individual assignments are made in a team environment, weights help the individual team member prioritize their team and individual results.

Failing to discuss priorities and define the relative importance of results can cause the following problems:

- Team members can get confused about what is important, and when time is limited, they may make the wrong decision on where to put their efforts.

- A shared vision of the team's priorities and the reasons for those priorities may not exist, leading to unnecessary conflicts.

- Without weights for their team results showing up on their individual performance plans, most individual team members will complain about "not receiving credit" for their team efforts.

- Team leaders on cross-functional project teams will find that they do not have the attention of some team members because these members' supervisors control the rewards they receive in what is most often an individual-based compensation system.

Weights are set by spreading 100 percentage points across the team and individual results. First, the 100 points are divided among team and individual results. Then the percentage given to the team results as a whole are divided among the list of team results. Finally, the percentage given to the individual results as a whole are divided among the list of individual results. The most important results have the largest weights, the least important have the smallest weights, and those results with equal importance have the same weights.

When it came time to set weights, the Father's Day Team decided that the team results were worth 60 percent and the individual results were worth 40 percent. The 60 percent was distributed across the following team results while the 40 percent was distributed in the following manner for the marketing team member.

Team Results (60 Percent)

- Profitable sales (20 percent)
- Satisfied retail outlets (10 percent)
- Shipped products (10 percent)
- New product designs (5 percent)
- Signed retail outlets (5 percent)
- Satisfied consumers (10 percent)

Individual Results for the Marketing Team Member (40 Percent)

- Focus group results (5 percent)
- Product ideas (10 percent)
- Competitive summary (5 percent)
- Retail sales (20 percent)

Step 4. Create Measures for Each Result

Now that you have defined and prioritized the results for your team and the individual team members (or a single individual), the next step is to decide how to measure each result. From now on, the steps are exactly the same for team or individual performance.

Measures are the yardsticks used to judge how well the team or individual produces each result. While most managers see quantifiable measures as the best, *not everything can be measured with numbers*. Trying to quantify everything sometimes results in meaningless measures. Good measures are those that can be verified by someone else and are observable. While you can't always use numbers, you can always use words to describe how someone could observe an excellent job.

The first place to look for measures is the list of organizational measures listed in step 1. In some cases these organizational measures apply to the team or individual with only minor modifications.

The second way to create measures is to borrow and modify—reviewing measures already created by teams elsewhere in the organization and modifying them to fit this particular team is easier than creating new measures. The performers can also review measures created outside the organization and then borrow and modify those that look useful. A searchable, free collection of measurement examples for this purpose can be found on the Internet at the URL http://www.zigonperf.com/performance.htm.

If borrowing measurement ideas doesn't work, you'll need to create measures. This is done by breaking down the measurement problem into smaller parts by first identifying a general measure, then a more specific one.

General measures tell what is important, *in general,* about each result. They are used when you have difficulty identifying measures for a particular result. There are four general measures: quantity, quality, cost, and timeliness.

Specific measures describe in numeric or descriptive terms which parts of the result the team wants to track. They define how you will know whether the quantity, quality, cost, or timeliness standard has been met. There are two kinds of specific measures. *Numeric measures* use numbers to evaluate the result. The numeric measure identifies the units that will be tracked. *Descriptive measures* use words to evaluate the result. The descriptive measure identifies who will judge the performance and what factors they will be evaluating.

To create measures for any result, answer these questions:

- "In general, what do I care about when evaluating this result? (*quantity, quality, cost, and/or timeliness*)"

- "How could I measure (*quantity, quality, cost, and/or timeliness*)?"

- "Is there some number or percent I could track?" If the measure is numeric, list the units you will keep track of.

- If there is no number and the result can only be judged, ask "Who could judge that the result was done well? What factors would they look for?" If the measure is descriptive, identify the judge, and list the factors that the judge will look for.

Step 5. Create Performance Standards

The next step in measuring team performance is setting the level of performance you expect for each of the measures you have identified.

If a measure is the yardstick used to judge a result, then a *performance standard* is the range of points on the yardstick that represents *excellent performance.* The measure is *what* you evaluate, and the performance standard is *how much* you require.

After you have defined the measure, creating the performance standard is usually easy. For numeric measures, answer, "How many is the team or individual expected to produce?" or "What level of performance must the team or individual achieve to help the organization achieve its goals?" and set the standard as a range. The top of the range is the beginning of "exceeding expectations." The bottom of the range is the beginning of a performance problem worth discussing.

For descriptive measures, ask, "For each factor the judge is looking at, what would this person see that means the performer has done a job that meets expectations?" Or what would this person hear the performer's customers saying that means the team or individual has done a job that meets expectations?" List the judge and the factors, and then list what constitutes a meets-expectations job for each factor. Repeat the process to define what "exceeds expectations" would look or sound like. Repeat these steps for each of the results.

TABLE 34.2   Sample Measures and Performance Standards

Results /Weights	General Measures	Specific Measures	Performance Standards
Profitable sales (20%)	Quantity	Annual dollar sales	$24M to $35M annual dollar sales
		Percent profit before taxes	15 to 21% profit before taxes
		Expense budget variance	±5% expense budget variance
New product designs (5%)	Quality	Corporate VP marketing's judgment of:	Corporate VP marketing's satisfaction that the new product designs:
		■ Fit with other product lines	■ Maintain the corporate feel
		■ Innovation	■ Contain at least 3 products that are different from anything the competition is selling
		■ Corporate image	
		Focus group opinion of:	■ Enhance and maintain the corporate image through high-quality art, text, and materials
		■ Value	
		■ Preference compared to competition	Focus groups say the following about the new product designs:
		■ Uniqueness	■ The value of the product exceeds the price.
		■ Fit	■ I would be proud to purchase this for my father.
		■ Durability	■ They prefer our designs to the competition's designs in a blind preference test.
			■ They are different from anything they have ever seen.
			■ They have something they think their father would enjoy.
			■ They have at least two cards that express the exact feeling they want to communicate to their father.
			■ Gifts look as though they will last as long as the gift will be meaningful.
	Quantity	No. new ideas generated	■ 30 to 50 ideas generated that are different from those suggested during the last 3 years.

Table 34.2 is an example of the general and specific measures the Father's Day Team created as well as the performance standards for each of these measures.

Table 34.3 is an example of performance standards for the marketing person on the Father's Day Team.

Step 6. Decide How to Track the Performance

Now that you've developed a performance plan and know *what* is to be measured, the next step is to decide *how* to collect the information the teams and individuals need to stay on track.

The goal is to answer the question, "How will you know you met each performance standard or not?" You'll need to identify the data required to answer that question for each measure. In the end, the value of the data must exceed the cost to collect it. Otherwise the measurement system will be more trouble than it is worth to maintain.

If the cost is too high, consider sampling the work. Make the sample size large enough to be seen as fair to the participants, but small enough to be practical.

The tracking data should be provided often enough to avoid major performance problems. New employees will need to be given data more often. Experienced employees may do well with data only once a quarter.

When possible, the team or the individual employee should collect the data unless gathering the data disrupts the work flow and takes too much time or the completed work is seen only by another person.

Data can be summarized in a table or graph to allow easy comparison to the standard.

To summarize how the Father's Day Team is doing compared to its team goals, Table 34.4 was created.

LESSONS LEARNED AND SUMMARY

Twenty years' experience has resulted in many mistakes and almost as many successes. In either case, learning resulted. Here are the highlights:

- *First measure to help the work get done, then use the information for the PAS/PMS.* Too often, revising the *performance appraisal system* (PAS) or the *performance management system* (PMS) is the goal. This leads to a hard-fought implementation and makes compliance an issue. Better to create a system that helps managers and employees get their work done *better* and then use it as an appraisal system.

- *Revise the PAS/PMS to avoid overall ratings; they add little value.* Overall ratings cause more problems than they are worth. They do nothing to help improve employee performance and can damage morale. Eliminate them whenever you can.

TABLE 34.3   Performance Standards for Father's Day Marketing Person

Value-Added Results/Weights	General Measures	Specific Measures	Performance Standards
Retail sales (20%)	Quantity	% sales gain compared to last year	Sales are 8 to 10% higher than last year.
Product ideas (10%)	Quantity	No. of ideas	At least 20–25 new product ideas are offered each year.
	Quality	Team judgment of: ■ Innovation ■ Uniqueness ■ Build on team's strengths ■ Buildability ■ Support profit plan	The team is satisfied that the ideas: ■ Take advantage of the unique strengths of the team (writing, laser-die cut) ■ Are not offered by the competition ■ Can be manufactured with the existing facilities, equipment, and people ■ Can be manufactured and sold so that they support the team's business plan
Competitive Summary (5%)	Quality	Team judgment of: ■ Thoroughness ■ Usefulness of data	The team is satisfied that the competitive summary: ■ Covers all products of all known competitors ■ Provides data on the products' description, likely production costs, advertising and merchandising, and success rate
	Timeliness	Supporting production schedule	Competitive summaries are provided by the agreed-upon deadline.
Focus group results (5%)	Quality	Team judgment of: ■ Usefulness of data	The team is satisfied that the data allow them to make data-based decisions on alternative product designs.
	Timeliness	Turnaround time Supporting production schedule	Focus group results are provided within 3 weeks of the request and early enough to prevent delays to the production schedule.

TABLE 34.4 Father's Day Team Tracking Report

Value-Added Results	Performance Standards	Actual Performance
Profitable sales (20%)	$24M to $35M annual dollar sales 15 to 21% profit before taxes ±5% expense budget variance	$26M in sales 18.1% profit 1% over budget
New product designs (5%)	Corporate VP marketing's satisfaction that the new product designs: ■ Maintain the corporate feel ■ Contain at least 3 products that are different from anything the competition is selling ■ Enhance and maintain the corporate image through high-quality art, text, and materials Focus groups say the following about the new product designs: ■ The value of the product exceeds the price. ■ I would be proud to purchase this for my father. ■ They prefer our designs to the competition's designs in a blind preference test. ■ They are different from anything they have ever seen. ■ They have something that they think their father would enjoy. ■ They have at least two cards that express the exact feeling they want to communicate to their father. ■ Their gifts look as though they will last as long as the gift will be meaningful. 30 to 50 ideas generated that are different from those suggested during the last 3 years	Corporate VP says that: ■ All but two of the new product designs maintain the corporate feel. ■ Five of the products are different from anything the competition is selling. ■ All but two products enhance and maintain the corporate image. Four out of five of the focus groups said that the value exceeded the price. Three out of five said that they would be proud to purchase the gifts for their fathers. Five out of five said they preferred our designs to the competition's. Two out of five said the gifts are different from anything they have ever seen. Five out of five said that the line has some gift their fathers would enjoy. Five out of five said that the card line has at least two cards that expressed the feeling they wanted to express. Four out of five said that the gifts look as though they will last. 57 ideas for new products generated
Shipped products (10%)	90 to 95% complete orders 96 to 98% orders shipped within 48 hours Reduction in cycle time for entire design/production process from 16 months to 11 months	94.5% complete orders 98% orders shipped within 48 hours Cycle time reduced to 11.5 months
Signed retail outlets (5%)	150 to 250 new outlets signed $5M to $8M in sales from new outlets	212 outlets signed $9.5M in sales
Satisfied customers (10%)	Less than 0.5% returns due to defective products Less than $100K in gift returns to retailers 90 to 95% of surveyed retailers say they are satisfied that: ■ The product line contains products at the price points and product types their customers want. ■ The price of the products seems to match the quality of the products.	0.1% returns due to defective products $75K in gift returns 96.2 percent of retailers satisfied with the product types and value of the products

■ *Wait to link performance to compensation.* Tying performance to compensation before the performance data are stable causes morale problems. Wait until you can trust the data before you tie money to it. If you can't wait, explain to employees that the performance standards may go up or down as you learn more about measurement.

■ *Cascade measures when you can; otherwise, develop simultaneously and refine later.* Top-down cascading of measures is ideal. But if stopping at each level of the organization and spending weeks negotiating keeps the lowest level of employees from having goals before 6 months into the process, do things differently. Try creating measures at all levels of the organization simultaneously in the first 4 weeks of the year. At the end of the month, trade papers, and make refinements based on what you see. It cuts months out of the process.

■ *Use a balanced scorecard only at the top; use other models at lower levels.* Norton and Kaplan's model is the tool of choice for creating measures at the president and division manager level. While it can be forced to work at lower levels in the organization (much like a shoe can be used to pound in a nail), the other models presented in this chapter work much better below the division manager level.

■ *Align based on results and measures.* If line of sight is weak, build a chain or pyramid of results, and show the team or individuals how their results builds and fits into the organization's results. Using measures alone may be too abstract.

■ *Let those being measured create first drafts.* This process works best when those being measured actively participate in creating the measures for their work. Many kinds of work are "one of a kind" where only the person doing the work can create the measures. In these cases you have no choice but to have the person doing the work create the first draft for management review.

■ *Large teams: Develop measures in subteam and review in a larger group.* Create the measures using representatives of the target group, and then ask for input and feedback from the entire group. The buy-in will be worth the extra time and effort.

■ *Examples save time and increase quality.* The number 1 step you can take to help speed up this process, improve the quality of the measures, and help employees and managers feel as though it is an easy way to manage is to provide examples of performance measures—lots of them! A critical mass seems to be achieved when you have 50 to 100 kinds of work measured in an organization. Everyone who follows has a much easier time creating measures for their work.

- *Borrow examples from anywhere.* Measurement ideas cross functional and industry boundaries, and there's no way to predict how and when this will occur. Provide everyone in the company access to all examples created anywhere in the company. Purchasing will borrow from customer service; R&D will borrow from sales; everyone will borrow from other industries. I have has seen warehouse teams borrow ideas from a nursing patient care team and CIA managers borrow from oil company geophysicists!

- *Publish all current and future examples.* Publish your examples on a LAN, WAN, intranet, extranet, on CD-ROM, paper, or whatever. Just make sure employees don't have to reinvent the wheel unnecessarily. See http://www.zigonperf.com/performance.htm for an extranet-based example of performance measures tied to a search engine.

- *Link individuals to a team, and teams to the organization.* Look for ways to make sure that the team members' results directly support team results and that team results directly support organization results and measures.

- *Allow time for review and revision.* Don't rush to use your first-draft measures without taking the time to allow review and revision. Rushing will just make people uncomfortable.

- *Weights are only a communication tool.* If they become the focus of nonproductive discussions or conflict, remove them from your system. If engineers and accountants begin calculating weighted averages to 16 decimal places, drop the weights. Use a discussion of weights to help promote a shared vision of priorities.

- *Always start with value-added results.* This is the way to save time and improve the quality of your measurement. Use behavioral measures when results are inadequate or missing some important aspect of performance. Behavioral measures are proportionately more expensive than results-based measures, but sometimes they are the only alternative.

- *Verifiability is the key, not quantifiability.* Give up on quantifiability as the gold standard for measurement. For work not easily measured with numbers, verifiability gives you the flexibility to measure work that couldn't be measured until now.

- *The value of data must exceed the cost to collect it.* If the tracking system is more trouble than it's worth, then the measures were designed incorrectly. Cut down, change the nature of the measures, or sample the data.

Team and hard-to-measure employee performance measurement, while time-consuming and sometimes difficult, can pay off big dividends in improved performance. The number 1 cause of poor performance is lack of clear goals. This process outlines how to lay the foundation for team and employee success based on verifiable goals and a tracking system to help the team and individuals know where they stand.

REFERENCES

Gilbert, Tom. 1978. *Human Competence: Engineering Worthy Performance.* New York: McGraw-Hill.

Kaplan, Robert S., and David P. Norton. 1996. *The Balanced Scorecard: Translating Strategy into Action.* Boston: Harvard Business School Press.

Lawler, Edward E., and Susan G. Cohen. 1992. "Designing Pay Systems for Teams." *American Compensation Association Journal,* vol. 1, no. 1, pp. 6–18.

Lynch, Richard, and Kelvin Cross. 1991. *Measure Up! Yardsticks for Continuous Improvement.* Cambridge, Mass.: Blackwell Business.

Zigon, Jack. 1998. *How to Measure Employee Performance.* Media, Pa.: Zigon Performance Group.

—. 1998. *How to Measure Team Performance.* Media, Pa.: Zigon Performance Group.

—. 1995. *How to Measure the Results of Work Teams.* Media, Pa.: Zigon Performance Group.

—. 1995. *How to Measure White-Collar Employee Performance.* Media, Pa.: Zigon Performance Group.

—. 1994. "How to Measure White-Collar Employee Performance." *Performance and Instruction Journal,*

—. 1998. *Performance Measurement Examples.* Media, Pa.: Zigon Performance Group.

—. 1999. *Performance Measurement Examples—CD-ROM.* Media, Pa.: Zigon Performance Group.

—. 1995. *Sample Employee Performance Measures.* Media, Pa.: Zigon Performance Group.

—. 1993. *Performance Appraisal Lessons from Fifteen Years in the Trenches.* Media, Pa.: Zigon Performance Group.

—. 1994. "How a New Appraisal System Saved Yellow Freight System $20.8 Million," in *Return on Investment in Human Resource Development: Cases on the Economic Benefits of HRD,* Jack Phillips (ed.), Alexandria, Va.: American Society for Training and Development.

JOB AIDS

COMMON PROBLEMS AND THEIR SOLUTIONS
Table 34.5 lists typical performance planning problems along with their solutions.

TABLE 34.5

Common Problem	Examples	Solution
Wrong value-added results.	■ No result of "satisfied customers" for a team that provides a service to specific customers.	■ Add the missing results. ■ Remove results that don't match the purpose of the team.
Activities disguised as results.	■ Meetings attended. ■ Evaluations scheduled. ■ Reports written.	■ Identify the value-added contribution made to the organization as a result of the activity, and make that contribution the result. ■ "Meetings attended" becomes "new product decisions" or "solved problems."
Too many results.	■ List of 15–20 results.	■ Combine results by making some into *subresults* of other larger results.
Measures not verifiable, or descriptive performance standards lack a judge or verifiable checklist.	■ Evaluate work in a high-quality fashion. ■ Demonstrate positive interface with other departments. ■ Write meaningful agenda specific to needs.	■ Decide who will make the judgment. ■ Identify what factors the judge will look for. ■ List what the judge will see or hear to indicate that the performance meets expectations.

TABLE 34.5 (*Continued*)

Common Problem	Examples	Solution
Specific measures don't match the general measures.	■ General measures list "quantity," "quality," and "timeliness" as important, but specific measure is "number of meetings held with customers."	■ Create specific measures for each general measure.
Measures would take too long to track.	■ Number of typos. ■ Answering the phone by the third ring.	■ Track a sample of the work when tracking all of it is too time-consuming. ■ Instead of tracking the "percent correct," track the "number of errors." ■ Drop the measure.
Numeric performance standards lack a range.	■ 98% of customers say they are satisfied. ■ Three errors per quarter.	■ The manager or customer may have in mind a range of performance that "meets expectations." If so, make it explicit.
Performance standard defined in such a way that it can't be exceeded. ˘	■ Performance standard contains words such as *zero, never, always, less than, more than, all*. ■ Performance standard uses a range with zero or 100 percent as one of the ends of the range.	■ If perfection is absolutely necessary, keep the performance standard the way it is. ■ If perfection is not likely to be attained, set the performance standard so that perfection represents "exceeds performance," not just "meets expectations."
Performance standard written as if performance happens only once per year, when the performance occurs many times per year.	■ Report has no errors. ■ Progress reviews are held on a timely basis. ■ Applications approved within 3 days of receipt.	■ If result occurs more than once, then state either the number or the percent of results that must meet the performance standard. Examples: % reports with no errors, no more than 1–2 progress reviews are late per year, 95–99% of applications approved within 3 days.

CHANGING MEASURES FOR CHANGING TIMES

Jack Dolmat-Connell
Vice President and Managing Director

Wilson Group, Inc.

YOU CANNOT MANAGE WHAT YOU CANNOT MEASURE. If you can't measure it, you can't reward for it. If you can't reward for it, you probably won't get it since reward systems send strong signals about what is important and what isn't. This chapter discusses the evolution of measures, the strategic context of measures, the development process for a strong measurement system, and two of today's hottest measures—the *balanced scorecard* and *economic value added* (EVA).

TODAY'S COMPETITIVE ENVIRONMENT

The environment that organizations operate in today is characterized by ever-accelerating organizational change—it isn't a question of whether or not you have to change; it is a question of how fast. Today's organizations are very different from those of the recent past. They have new structures resulting from downsizing and the quest for efficiency, new models for competing, new employee demographics, and a new "employment relationship" with the workforce. Expectations for performance are very different: Wall Street is unforgiving of unmet earnings and growth expectations, and employees want to work for a high-growth winner. The competitive environment that organizations operate within today has changed enormously. Have your performance measures?

HISTORY: EVOLUTION OF PERFORMANCE MEASURES

Performance measures have evolved dramatically over the past four decades. In the 1960s stock price was the primary measure of focus. As companies began to discover that at times executives had little control over the price of the company stock due to outside market forces, their attention turned to *earnings per share* (EPS) growth in the 1970s. The 1980s saw movement to those financial measures that were thought to be the most accurate predictors of stock price movement: *return on assets* (ROA) and *return on equity* (ROE). Finally, in the 1990s, we have seen a very strong orientation toward the balanced-scorecard and certain value-based measures such as economic value added and *cash-flow return on investment* (CFROI).

Why do so many companies use accounting or financial measures? There are five primary reasons:

1. They are understandable.
2. They are still emphasized by many financial analysts.
3. They are measured systematically by the financial department.
4. It is common practice to use them.
5. They are convenient for comparison purposes.

Does this continued focus on financial measures make sense? Are traditional measures still valid today? Would they work for your company? Let's consider these questions, beginning with the strategic context in which measures are set.

THE STRATEGIC CONTEXT OF MEASUREMENT SELECTION

There are no universally applicable measures—the measures used should always be derived from and support the business strategy. How then do you select the right performance measure(s)? The questions that your organization needs to think about are the following:

Is what I am measuring strategically important?

What do the market or key stakeholders value?

What can participants impact?

What can be measured?

It is critical to remember that measurement is about (1) competitive advantage and (2) alignment. The measures you choose should track whatever is necessary to deliver the competitive advantage to your organization. Alignment focuses people on the right levers to help you achieve that competitive advantage.

Another key point to remember when thinking about selecting measures for your organization is that measures differ industry to industry, company to company, and even within companies. Your choice of measures is influenced by the following:

1. Industry
2. The strategy or positioning of your organization
3. Organizational level

A simple matrix that can help you think about selecting appropriate measures for different levels of the organization can be seen in Figure 35.1. It is necessary to look at the object of the focus of employees at different levels, why that focus is critical, what needs to be done in order to execute against the area of focus, and how that will be accomplished. This careful consideration will give you excellent insight in determining the measures that are appropriate and aligned.

When thinking about appropriate measures for different levels of the organization, always consider whether the individuals have the appropriate line of sight to be able to make a meaningful impact on the results? If they do, you have a measure appropriate for a given level of the organization. If not, you must rethink the measure because if individuals cannot impact the results, the motivational aspects of the rewards are lost, and the measure is meaningless to those individuals.

When selecting measures, it is also critical to remember that compensation programs carry powerful messages, and as a result, so do the measures upon which

FIGURE 35.1 Matrix for selecting appropriate measures.

Level	Focus	Why	What	How
Board				
Executive Management				
Division/SBU Management				
Unit Management				
Employees				

these programs are based. Compensation programs, and measures, accomplish the following:

- Reinforce strategic direction and help generate targeted results
- Communicate focus and priorities
- Clarify linkages between value creation and specific actions
- Reward and penalize behaviors
- Introduce discipline
- Signal cultural change

Therefore, the selection of your measures and the linkage that they create to the compensation programs can have a major impact on your organization. Spending the up-front time to select appropriate measures is as important as selecting the right strategy for your organization as the world's best strategy has yet to be executed.

Your organization's choice of measures also has to be set within the context of your ability to gather, analyze, and report out information about the measures. Many organizations that we work with have the desire to dramatically rethink the measures that they use to guide their programs, but they do not have the ability, from either a manual or an information technology perspective, to track and report out information about these measures. Consider this issue early on in the process, and if a measure is critical to the business but cannot be tracked or reported, begin development of a process and a system that will enable you to get what you need.

This section has focused on several key considerations in selecting appropriate measures for your organization. Thinking about these considerations early in the selection process will save you enormous time in the long run. Once you have selected appropriate measures, it is important to assess their effectiveness and applicability on a regular basis. Some questions to consider for assessing your measures are as follows:

1. What is the purpose of performance measures in your organization?
2. How well are the performance measures aligned with key business strategies and objectives—both short-term and long-term?
3. How well do people understand what drives the measures?
4. How well do people see that their actions impact the measurement areas?
5. How committed do people feel to achieving the desired performance levels?
6. How well are the measures integrated with your reward systems (formal and informal)?

DEVELOPING A STRONG MEASUREMENT SYSTEM

Developing Good Measures

When deciding upon the measures for either a short-term or long-term incentive plan, it is critical to ensure that the measures meet the following criteria:

Specific. The measures focus on the desired behaviors and provide a clear line of sight between the action and the result.

Meaningful. The value of the reward must be "worth the effort" to both the executive and the organization.

Achievable. The results are viewed as achievable, though not easy.

Reliable. The rewards are contingent on taking an action or achieving a result. The plan works as designed.

Timely. The rewards are provided as timely as necessary to reinforce the desired behaviors that achieve desired results.

Additionally, it is imperative to ensure that the measures meet these additional criteria:

- They are indeed measurable.

- They are connected to the strategic (LTI measures) or operational objectives (STI measures).

- They have no unintended or unexpected consequences.

There are several different perspectives from which to look at measures—financial versus nonfinancial measures, single versus multiple measures, and absolute versus relative measures.

Financial Versus Nonfinancial Measures

Financial Measures.   Almost every executive incentive plan, both short-term and long-term, has financial measures included. This is important in that most businesses, both public and private, must demonstrate appropriate levels of shareholder return. Common financial measures include the following:

Earnings per share (EPS)

Return on investment (ROI)

Revenue growth

Profitability

Because most measurement systems consist mainly of financial indicators, they focus organizations on past performance and encourage a short-term view of strategy. Financial measures are mostly short-term focused, resulting in tradeoffs that limit the search for investments in growth opportunities.

Nonfinancial Measures.   Nonfinancial measures have come into widespread use, most commonly in addition to, not instead of, selected financial measures. These measures often focus on areas such as quality, customer satisfaction, and teamwork. They have increased in importance as the management trends that accompany them have gained attention and focus.

Our belief is that both areas are important. Organizations need to ensure that one is not emphasized to the exclusion of the other, that they are appropriately weighted, and that all measures chosen are integrally linked to the strategic and operational objectives of the organization.

Single Versus Multiple Measures

Single-Measure Plans.   Another important dimension to consider is using single versus multiple measures in the overall plan design. Single-measure-based plans are those that have one, and only one, measure that is considered in the funding and payout of the plan. It could be based on economic value added, ROIC, revenue growth, market share, customer satisfaction, and so on. What is important is that it is based on a single measure.

Single measures are used when there is one clear, compelling area of focus necessary to achieve success. These measures can be, and are, successful, but they are most often focused on the short term. The downside is that organizations and businesses are incredibly complex, and it is very difficult to categorize success into one single measure.

Multiple-Measure Plans.   Multiple-measure plans are those that have two or more components to them. An example is a plan based on both revenue growth and profitability, or a *balanced scorecard.*

Multiple-measure plans generally more accurately capture the complexity of the business environment, and they provide managers with feedback on the several key levers generally required for achieving an organization's strategic objectives. The downside to multiple-measure plans is that they can be too complex (3 to 5 measures should be the maximum), and they can cause executives to have conflicting focuses. However, well-designed plans can minimize or eliminate these difficulties.

Absolute Versus Relative Measures

The final area for consideration is whether to have the plan based on absolute or relative measures of performance.

Absolute Performance Measures.   Absolute performance measures are internally focused; they describe how the organization performed against its plan, budget, or target. Using the return on invested capital, for example, an organization would set its measure at the level of ROIC derived from the business plan figures—easy to track and communicate. The shortcomings are that it can be difficult to set multiyear objectives, and internal goals may not be challenging.

Relative Performance Measures.   Relative performance measures consider performance vis-à-vis a defined peer group—how the organization did *relative* to its peers. They adjust for industry or economic factors beyond the executives' control and are consistent with the investment community perspective. The shortcomings are that they are more difficult to track than absolute goals, and they can reward for "being the best of a bad lot."

We believe that where practical, given the available information and the ability to accurately define the peer group, relative measures are very powerful. Business is inherently competitive, and how well an organization does relative to its peers is meaningful in so many ways—from a shareholder perspective, from a customer perspective, and from an employee perspective. For example, assume the organization above had a planned ROIC of 20 percent. This may be very good, average, or below average depending on how it compares to its peers. If the peer group is at 40 percent, there are significant issues. If the peer group, however, is at 10 percent, the organization is doing extremely well.

TODAY'S NEW MEASURES FOR CHANGING TIMES

There has been a strong move to new measurement systems over the past few years. Two primary measures or measurement types have dominated this movement: the *balanced scorecard* (a model created by Kaplan and Norton)[1] and value-based measures (led by Stern Stewart's EVA model).[2] The balanced scorecard has gathered a substantial following because it focuses on employees, customers, financials, and internal operations—those areas that drive successful businesses. Value-based models, such as EVA and cash-flow return on investment, have gained favor because cash flow drives shareholder value, market economics and competitive position drive shareholder value, and not all company growth creates value. The remainder of this chapter will look at the balanced scorecard and EVA in more detail.

THE BALANCED SCORECARD

The balanced scorecard is a tool for translating vision to action. It translates vision and strategy into a tool that effectively communicates strategic intent and motivates and tracks performance against the established goals. It also strengthens an organization's focus on future success by setting and measuring performance from four distinct perspectives:

1.   *Learning and growth.* Directs attention to the basis of all future success—the organization's people and infrastructure. Adequate investment in these areas is crucial to long-term success:

- Employee satisfaction
- Employee retention
- Employee productivity
- Competencies to deliver required results

2. *Internal.* Focuses on the development of a true learning organization. The internal perspective focuses attention on the performance of key internal processes that drive the business. Improvement in internal processes now is a lead indicator of financial success in the future:
   - Innovation
   - Operations
   - Service

3. *Customer.* Considers the business through the eyes of a customer, so that the organization retains a careful focus on customer needs and satisfaction:
   - Market share
   - Customer acquisition
   - Customer retention
   - Customer satisfaction
   - Customer profitability

4. *Financial.* Measures the ultimate results that the business provides to its shareholders:
   - Revenue growth and mix
   - Cost reduction and/or productivity improvement
   - Asset utilization and/or investment strategy

Together, these four perspectives provide a balanced view of the present and future performance of the business.

What Makes a Good Balanced Scorecard?

A good balanced scorecard should tell the story of your strategy. Three criteria will help determine this:

1. *Cause-and-effect relationships.* Every measure selected for the balanced scorecard should be part of the chain of cause-and-effect relationships that represent the strategy.

2. *Performance drivers.* Measures common to most companies within an industry are known as *lag indicators*. Examples include market share and customer retention. The drivers of performance (*lead indicators*) tend to be unique because they represent what is different about the strategy. A

good balanced scorecard should have a mix of lead and lag indicators.

3. *Linked to financials.* With the proliferation of change programs underway in most organizations today, it is easy to become preoccupied with a goal such as quality, customer satisfaction, or innovation. While these goals are frequently strategic, they must also translate into measures that are ultimately linked to financial indicators.

Designing a Balanced-Scorecard Measurement System

There are four steps to designing a balanced-scorecard measurement system:

1. *Define the measurement architecture.*
   Develop a distinct strategy.
   Incorporate the dimensions of the balanced scorecard.

2. *Build consensus around the strategic objectives.*
   Build a shared understanding of the overall strategy.
   Build consensus around the long-term strategic priorities.

3. *Select and design measures.* Select the measures to track the achievement of the strategic objectives.

4. *Develop the implementation plan.* Integrate the balanced scorecard into the management system:

   ■ Identify the current practices in various management processes.
   ■ Evaluate opportunities for integrating the balanced scorecard into the management process.
   ■ Develop an implementation plan.

Linking the Balanced Scorecard to the Reward System

For the scorecard to create cultural change, incentive compensation must be connected to the achievement of scorecard objectives. The process of linking the reward system to the balanced scorecard is essentially based upon a process similar to the scorecard development:

1. The four major categories (financial, customers, internal, and learning and growth) are weighted in terms of their impact on strategic objectives.

2. Measures for each category are determined.

3. Performance levels for each of the measures are determined.

4. The measures themselves are weighted in terms of their impact on the success within the category.

An example is shown in Figure 35.2.

FIGURE 35.2   Weighting balanced scorecard objectives with incentive compensation.

Category	Measure	Weighting
Financial (40%)	Margin vs. Competition	10.0%
	ROCE vs. Competition	10.0%
	Cost Reduction vs. Plan	10.0%
	New Market Growth	5.0%
	Existing Market Growth	5.0%
Customers (20%)	Market Share	10.0%
	Customer Satisfaction Survey	5.0%
	Physician Satisfaction Survey	5.0%
Internal (20%)	Medical Management System	10.0%
	Billing and Payment Processes	5.0%
	Innovation	5.0%
Learning/Growth (20%)	Employee Satisfaction	5.0%
	Strategic Skills Development	5.0%
	Strategic Info. Availability	5.0%
	Leadership Competency Development	5.0%

Pros and Cons of the Balanced Scorecard and Its Link to Reward Systems

There are several pros to using a balanced scorecard and linking it to your reward system. First, it translates individual vision into a galvanizing shared vision, which creates organizational alignment. Second, it balances the short-term and long-term objectives of the organization. Finally, it focuses the organization on its multiple objectives. There are, however, a few cons that need to be considered. First, the balanced scorecard can become quite complex, with many measures in the four categories. Also, it requires extensive communicating and goal setting throughout the organization to achieve successful results.

ECONOMIC VALUE ADDED

Developed by Stern Stewart & Co., economic value added (EVA) is the financial measure that comes closer than any other to capturing the true economic profit of an enterprise. It is also the performance measure that is most directly linked to the creation of shareholder wealth over time.

The EVA is a conceptually simple and operationally practical tool—one that gives managers information on which to make both day-to-day and long-term decisions in the best interests of the shareholder. The system allows management decisions to be modeled, monitored, communicated, and compensated in a single and consistent way, and always in terms of the value added to shareholder investment.

Summary of Basic Principles and Underlying Theory

The EVA is a simple concept. It is the spread between the rate of return on capital r and the cost of capital c multiplied by the economic book value of the capital committed to the business. The formula is as follows:

EVA=(r−c)×capital

=(rate of return−cost of capital)×capital

Another way to compute it is to multiply through by capital, as follows:

EVA=operating profits−a capital charge

The EVA rises if operating efficiency is enhanced, if value-adding new investments are undertaken, and if capital is withdrawn from uneconomic activities. To be more specific, the EVA increases when the following occur:

1. More operating profits are generated without more capital being tied up in the business.
2. Additional capital is invested in projects that return more than the cost of obtaining the new capital.
3. Capital is liquidated from, or further investment is curtailed in, substandard operations where inadequate returns are being earned.

A final area of substantiation of the EVA as a performance measure is that it ties directly to the intrinsic market value of any company. When it is projected and discounted to a present value, the EVA accounts for the market value that management adds to, or subtracts from, the capital that is employed:

MVA=market value−capital=present value of all future EVA

The *market value added,* or MVA, is the absolute dollar spread between a company's market value and its capital. Unlike a rate of return that reflects the outcome of one period, the MVA is the cumulative measure of corporate performance. It represents the stock market's assessment as of a particular time of the net present value of all of a company's past and projected capital projects.

The Four M's of EVA

There are four M's to keep in mind relative to the EVA: *measurement, management systems, motivation, and mindset:*

1.   *Measurement.* Purports to be the only performance measure that always gives the right answer.

2.   *Management systems.* Managers get three clear directives to increase value: increase operating efficiency, pursue expansion that returns more than the cost of capital, and shed value-destroying businesses.

3.   *Motivation.* A powerful basis for incentive compensation. Offering managers a share of improvements in the EVA with an unlimited upside (and deferring exceptional bonuses to ensure that they are truly earned) makes managers highly motivated to pursue aggressive plans. Managers can earn more only by creating value for shareholders.

4.   *Mindset.* A fully implemented EVA management and incentive compensation system can transform the corporate culture by turning managers into owners and driving everyone in the firm to strive for continuous improvement, the only thing that leads to continuous increases in value.

Linking Compensation and EVA: Turning Managers into Owners

This is more than a question of incentive compensation alone. The people must become involved as owners in the fullest extent of the word; they must be dedicated to personal excellence and the quality of the product or service; responsive to their customer's needs; willing to take sensible entrepreneurial risks; and above all, be committed to the success of the enterprise.

These ideals are little more than platitudes, however, unless the potential for economic rewards (what's in it for me) backs them up. To link the EVA to compensation, Stern Stewart suggests the following:

- One cash bonus plan, and not a short- and long-term plan. Mass the payout.

- Long-range goals, resource allocation decisions, and operating performance should all be evaluated in terms of the EVA.

- The EVA targets should be decoupled from the budgetary and strategic planning processes and should be revised according to some predetermined formula.

- The potential bonus should be unlimited in both directions.

- The exceptional parts of exceptional bonuses should be banked forward with their full payout contingent upon continued successful performance.

- Managers should be encouraged to buy into and not merely participate in the plan as a quid pro quo for aggressively amplifying their reward for success.

Pros and Cons of Using EVA and Linking to Compensation

As with the balanced scorecard, there are pros and cons of using the EVA and linking it to compensation. The pros are that the EVA drives shareholder value creation, and thus executives get rewarded for delivering this value creation and do not if they don't. Second, it is a single, simple measure, and easy to communicate. Finally, it has both short- and long-run applicability, and thus it can be used for both short-term and long-term incentive plans. The cons of using the EVA and linking it to compensation are that it is not a tool with equal applicability for all types of organizations. Second, it is somewhat difficult to translate this down to the employee level—what is their line of sight on impacting the EVA?

CONCLUSIONS

Selecting appropriate measures is one of the most important roles within compensation and human resources. Its impact on the organization cannot be understated. Select measures that are aligned with your strategy and driven consistently throughout the organization and you have a tremendous chance at achieving a competitive advantage. Select measures that aren't aligned and even with an A+ strategy, you'll have at best probably a B implementation. And, as Michael Porter once said, "I'd rather have an A implementation of a B strategy than a B implementation of an A strategy."

BIBLIOGRAPHY

1. Kaplan, Robert, and David Norton. 1996. *The Balanced Scorecard.* Boston: Harvard Business School Press.
2. Stewart, G. Bennett, III. 1991. *The Quest for Value: The EVA Management Guide.* New York: Harper Business.

PERFORMANCE-BASED REWARDS: WHAT ARE THE BEST PRACTICES?

Thomas B. Wilson, President

Wilson Group, Inc.

THE CURRENT STATE OF AFFAIRS

Most pay-for-performance programs that organizations have used historically delivered pay, not performance. Merit pay increases in recent years have averaged only 4 percent, which has left little to reward truly high performers. If the average increase has been 4 percent, in most organizations 80 percent of the people have received between 3.8 and 4.2 percent pay increases. Even in years when the merit pool was 7 to 10 percent, inflation was 5 to 8 percent, leaving the same differential as in today's pay increases. Finally, many managers have used the performance management process to justify whatever increase they had already decided to give employees. Few employees or managers have been satisfied with this overall program.

Bonuses have become for many organizations the managerial equivalent of an entitlement program. Many traditional bonus programs are discretionary. The senior managers determine the amount of bonus based on subjective goals that may have little direct relationship to the business's performance. While the funding of these programs may be based on corporatewide performance, people realize the pool size often has little impact on their payouts. In a recent study of the primary determinant of bonus amounts in a client's organization, we found that the previous year's bonus correlated with one's current bonus more significantly than did individual performance, divisional performance, or company performance.

Stock options have become a favorite source for rewarding people over the last several years. Buoyed by a robust stock market, many receivers of stock options have profited well, if only on paper. While once stock options were the exclusive right of executives, more and more organizations are using options further down. Companies like Pepsi, Du Pont, and Boeing have provided stock options to all their employees. But are stock options an employee benefit, a performance reward program, or something else? By not being clear about what stock options are intended to mean, employees, executives, and shareholders treat their distribution as a potential windfall. This implies that this form of reward may not be having the desired impact on commitment or performance.

Finally, special recognition for many employees is neither special nor effective recognition. The basic problem is that these programs are seen by many executives as existing for the "little people." They are given to operational and support employees, but they are regarded as meaningless to professionals or managers. While most organizations have some form of special recognition, the great majority of these programs are for years of service (e.g., 5 years, 10 years, 20 years). Further, when awards are given on a monthly or annual basis, the experience is often meaningful to only the recipient and the provider. Those who can share in the success often feel they had a role in enabling the individual to receive the award, but they are seldom recognized. The executive enjoys the opportunity to demonstrate support and appreciation. Some companies ask that the special awards be kept secret, in order to prevent a backlash from other employees. Does everyone leave the award ceremony more motivated to achieve than before?

If your organization experiences symptoms similar to those discussed above, do not feel alone. These are the conditions for most organizations. It is no wonder that reward programs are seen by many as responding ineffectively to individual performance, as amounting to meaningless entitlements, as sending conflicting messages to employees, and as creating discord within the company. Is the desired path then to eliminate all reward programs? Should we retreat to doing nothing because these programs have a negative or controversial impact on the organization? If so, then how do we create conditions in which people are truly valued for the contributions they make to the performance of the organization? If the organization succeeded because people worked hard and effectively, are they left with only an informal pat on the back or some general thank you? If executives and shareholders gain from this performance, shouldn't the people that made it happen share in the process?

WHAT ARE BEST PRACTICES?

There are organizations that have found a successful approach to providing awards that is based on performance. They have been able to implement a process that achieves two important results:

1. Aligns the rewards with what is critical for the organization to succeed
2. Creates conditions in which people feel a strong commitment to the results

A new model is emerging for rewarding people in a manner that strengthens the organization's ability to compete and serve its customers well. These companies have developed ways to make an impact on people's lives and on the culture of the organization, on the short-term performance as well as the long-term capability.

There is no universal right way to reward people, but neither is every reward system equally effective. Therefore, there are several principles that need to be adopted to make these systems work. Further, the systems are fundamentally inanimate. People, through their words and actions, give reward systems meaning and impact. The best-designed program is only as good as its weakest implementer. In determining what is a best practice, one needs to consider both the program's structure and how it is managed within the organization.

In recent studies of high-performing companies and those recognized as the best places to work,[1] several common themes have emerged. This chapter will describe these themes and provide case study illustrations to help the reader understand the possibilities.

"Best practices" is both a relative and temporary concept. Organizations regarded as adhering to the best practices in one industry may be regarded as ineffective in other industries; organizations that are viewed as high performers at one time often become laggards at other times. Therefore, one needs to examine best practices in terms of what works to drive desired performance and foster the culture the organization needs to succeed. If the reward systems do these things, then they are the best practices. We can learn from what others do; but in implementing what others do, do not expect success to naturally follow. Success depends on the unique situation each organization faces in terms of the present realities and the historical context for change.

LESSONS FROM THE BEST PRACTICES

Companies that have used reward systems effectively share five primary characteristics. These characteristics provide a framework for examining "why things work" and should be instructive to readers who want to assess or develop their own reward systems. Illustrations from some very exciting companies are also provided.

---

[1] T. Wilson, *Rewards That Drive High Performance: Success Stories from Leading Organizations,* (AMACOM, New York: 1999).

1. There Is a Direct Alignment between Performance and Rewards

Each organization pursues different strategies to establish a competitive advantage. The marketplace is dynamic and requires highly adaptive organizations. Those who understand the market create demand for their products and services, become the preferred vendor for the customer, and can do this profitably are usually the most successful. Michael Porter's work on defining business strategies provides a useful framework for understanding differences in organizational strategies.[2] He indicates that highly successful companies focus on one of three primary strategies while using the other strategies as supporting elements. The core strategies are the following:

- *Producing products and services at a low cost.* Providing the customers what they want at the lowest relative price

- *Providing customer service.* Providing the customers what they want and when they want it

- *Producing innovative products and services.* Providing the customers with the best, newest, and most advanced products or services

Reward systems need to focus clearly on what the organization needs to succeed. For a company that needs to be a low-cost producer, the compensation plan should reward for operational efficiency and cost reduction. Another company that needs to lead the market for innovation needs a compensation plan that enables the company to attract and retain highly talented people and that encourages risk taking and learning. There are various compensation tools the organization can use to emphasize this strategy, but they need to be in alignment with what is critical to the firm's success.

Amazon.com is clearly regarded as one of the most successful companies in the electronic commerce market. They have, in just a few years' time, created a market for selling books over the Internet. However, they do not see themselves as a book distributor but as an Internet commerce organization that has been selling books. They have now become a leader in selling music compact discs over the Internet, and they are exploring other similar products and services. They are a technology company.

For Amazon.com to be successful, it needs to provide customers with products that are less expensive than traditional retail channels and more convenient (i.e., less time required of the customer) in order to make up for the delay to individuals who would not have to wait if they were purchasing products at a retail store. They are clearly pursuing a low-cost-producer strategy. Their reward strategy therefore is to pay salaries that are below market but to make up the difference in stock options. The historical record of the stock has made many investors and

---

[2]M. Porter, *Competitive Strategy,* (Free Press: New York, 1980).

employees quite wealthy. The stock options provide people with a "stake in the success" of the organization, which further supports the core values and management practices of the company.

When Sears began its major turnaround efforts, it developed a strong strategy, involved thousands of people throughout the organization, and redesigned their reward systems. They found through research that the way in which employees are treated often determines how well they treat their customers and that how customers are treated often determines the revenues and profitability of the company. Therefore, company profit is a direct function of how they treat their employees.

With this simple concept, they aligned their reward system with these measures. For the managers' variable compensation, one-third is based on employee satisfaction, one-third on customer satisfaction, and one-third on financial results for their respective units. For employees in the stores, the variable pay system emphasizes customer satisfaction and financial performance. This alignment between their strategy and rewards has been a major contributor to this organization's return to prosperity.

In summary, compensation and other reward systems send messages about what is valued by the organization. If the programs are effective, they encourage or discourage certain behaviors. The extent to which the messages sent are the messages received determines the system's impact. The more the messages sent are those that are aligned with the key success factors of the organization, the more likely it is that the system will have the desired impact.

2. Rewards Can Reinforce Commitment

Few companies can succeed in the long term, over a complex array of challenges without the strong commitment of their people. The stronger this commitment, the easier it is to adjust and respond effectively to changing market conditions and opportunities. One of the challenging aspects of employee commitment is that it can only be given, never mandated. Employees choose to "go the extra mile," and they will do so when they feel that it is important to do so. Employee involvement, communication and reward programs can only encourage people to "sign on." The decision to be committed and to act accordingly is usually a response to what one has experienced in the past as well as what one expects for the future. Different people regard these two conditions—the past and the future—with different degrees of importance.

Do executives really know what is meaningful to their people? If you don't understand what people value, you are likely to design a reward system that is only partially successful—if you're lucky. One of the most important conditions for rewards to be effective is that they need to be meaningful to the performers. The meaning is not always defined by the amount. Some companies are able to create significant value from their reward program in the way in which the rewards are presented. It is a far different experience for an employee to receive an incentive payout personally than to receive it in a public celebration meeting or having it directly deposited into his or her checking account with little recognition for what was accomplished. One of the key practices of high-performing companies is to make the value of rewards greater than their costs.

Finally, rewards work because they give people a stake in the success they help create. If rewards are viewed as a transaction—a quid pro quo—then individuals will value the reward in relation to the effort expended. High-performing companies have found that they use rewards to provide opportunities for people to gain personally and reinforce the success they achieve.

Commitment is not achieved solely by a reward system. People need to like the work they do. People need to find meaning and importance in their activities. They should see an opportunity to add value to something that is important to them and find their efforts treated with respect. If these conditions exist, then rewards play a reinforcing role within the workplace environment. If these conditions do not exist, rewards may be viewed as a bribe. Hence, rewards support and become an important manifestation of the role, contribution, and importance of the individual. People receive value from the value they create.

At Saturn, the subsidiary of General Motors, they created and implemented a variable pay program that includes everyone in the company. As the company prospers in the marketplace, union and nonunion members alike participate in the financial success of the company. Their incentives are tied to cost-reduction results as well as the quality, training, team effectiveness, and delivery times.

The program at its inception was highly regarded by both union and management. The company was able to bring a new product to market in record-setting time, and the marketplace responded to the car's uniqueness, quality, and cost with great enthusiasm. The company and the people prospered for several years. Then, as the market demand changed and Saturn began to experience declining revenues and profits, the labor union called for another vote on the program. Even though the margin of victory declined from the original vote, employees still supported the program by a 2:3 majority. Commitment to the success of the car company and the reward program that gave them a share in the performance continued. Now the company is seeking to expand marketing efforts internationally and introduce new products to the market. Saturn has remained a different kind of car company.

Cisco System, Inc., is the world's leading supplier of products to the computer networking market. It has grown dramatically since its inception in 1984. Its growth strategy has included both providing leading-edge technology and acquiring aspiring companies in its market. A critical ingredient to its success has been the use of stock options and the encouragement of independent thinking and innovation. Companies that are acquired are quickly integrated into the Cisco culture, but the culture supports entrepreneurial spirit and rapid adjustment to market opportunities. They support the concept of a total company through the use of a common variable compensation plan. This program uses companywide and unit-specific measures, and it provides aggressive payout opportunities. This helps to retain a total company focus. The targeted use of stock options also promotes a one-firm philosophy. The results have led to highly successful integration of new companies and a strong performance orientation.

To summarize, commitment is not based on how much the employee is provided but how. People share directly in the results they achieve, and the metrics of performance are very clear. Further, goals are seen as achievable, and awarding the rewards is an important ceremony in the organization. Individuals share in the success and the downside of performance as well. Rewards are truly contingent on performance. It is a common-sense formula but not common practice.

3. Flexibility Is Built into the System

Companies that adopt someone else's reward program as is are destined to fail. Effective reward systems are custom tailored to the unique attributes of each organization. Further, no design can account for every condition or situation the organization is likely to experience. Therefore, judgment and real-world flexibility are needed to make the programs successful.

The reward systems of high-performing companies have an unusual feature in their approach. They adjust the programs, measures, and goals periodically to meet changing business requirements so that they reflect the dynamics of the marketplace. They do not make these adjustments to ensure there is a payout or award. If the results are achieved, there is a payout; if they are not achieved, there is no payout. They don't feel that people will leave the firm; instead, they believe that people will seek to solve problems and take actions necessary to return to prosperity. The rewards are highly contingent on actual performance, but there is an understanding of reality and the permission to use judgments. Their reward systems have integrity.

These companies address two important aspects of business: results and process. For results, they determine whether desired outcomes are achieved. For process, they examine the way in which results are achieved (the "how") and assess whether the actions were appropriate. They want their compensation plans to reward for results *and* encourage the desired behaviors needed for success.

Keane, Inc., is a rapidly growing systems development and integration consulting company based in Boston, Massachusetts. It helps companies build and maintain high-performance information systems that strengthen their competitive advantage. The company has grown because of the dramatic need for compliance with Year 2000 system requirements, the value companies receive from outsourcing their information technology functions, and the strong desire to use technology to gain a competitive advantage. The company has also been actively engaged in acquiring companies that add value to their capabilities and portfolio of services. Their reward systems orient individuals to both financial results and customer relationships.

The company is organized around a network of branch offices that serve the needs of local clients. This gives them the ability to respond quickly to customer requirements and attract a talent base that is able to serve clients that are near where they live. This reduces the travel costs and stress and provides the company with a solid competitive advantage. Further, the company emphasizes its learning process and the sharing of innovations across practices and industry lines, so that Keane develops its capabilities to serve clients. The result of these efforts is dramatic growth in both market share and financial results.

Their reward programs support this strategy in several ways. First, the local branch office maintains its own growth and profitability reward systems. This keeps the line of sight close to the performers. Second, they double credit revenues and associated costs for projects that involve practice areas and branch offices. This encourages customer focus, collaboration, and capability development. Third, stock options are provided to key leaders and contributors through the organization and are provided based on how they achieve results, not just the level of results achieved. This reinforces their values in very meaningful ways. Finally, the company makes extensive use of special recognition programs to employees throughout the organization. These programs and practices reinforce learning and sharing of innovations across the company. By so doing, Keane has become successful in growing a high-performing company with high-performing clients.

Starbucks has grown very rapidly and developed the market demand for coffee and its related products nationwide. It decided to build a common company rather than utilize a franchise network for its retail outlets. They have emphasized customer service and financial growth in many ways. Each store maintains a similar incentive plan in which all employees can share in the results. Key managers and employees can participate heavily in the stock options of the company. This creates an identity with the company, its mission, and its services. The stock program, called "Bean Stock," enables employees at all levels to share in the growth of the company. Since the incentive plan is highly related to each store's success and the success is directly focused on serving customers, both results and behaviors are reinforced. This is one reason why Starbucks has been propelled into being a leader in the market and has become a benchmark and focus for many other companies.

4. Take a Total Systems Approach to Rewards

Companies that treat each reward program—base salary, incentive plans, stock options, or special recognition—as a unique, independent program are losing a major competitive advantage. People look for consistency in the messages they receive in their reward programs. They look for balance and alignment with the strategy and values of the organization. Companies, however, often treat these programs as separate, and consequently they are not able to leverage the value that is created by their integration. They see one type of program as more important than another, and they try to do too much with that one program. The result is that people see the rewards as fragmented and conflicting.

Base pay is often a major reason an employee is attracted to an organization. It may serve to retain an individual as long as other factors in the company are positive, and it serves as an indicator of growth and success in the company. However, it has limited impact on driving performance. In contrast, variable pay programs can have a strong impact on driving results if the programs are designed and managed well. They may also enable a company to retain people if the pay opportunity is highly attractive. However, they are both limited by the timeliness in which awards can be given.

Recognition programs can be highly effective from a timing perspective and can provide a meaningful award for contributions or achievements. However, recognition programs have a limited reputation for being effective with managers and professionals. They are highly dependent on management effectiveness, and therefore they have a mixed impact on an organization. Receiving stock options is usually highly regarded because of what they communicate rather than what they can deliver. Cash compensation communicates that you performed well; stock options communicate that you are important to senior management. Consequently, each program has inherent strengths and weaknesses.

High-performing companies use these features to their advantage. They see that each program is focused on a specific theme and is designed and operates to serve a specific purpose. The weakness of one kind of program is offset by the strengths of another. This enables the reward programs to operate as a total system, with interdependent parts. One program may focus on results, and another may reinforce the process in which the results are achieved. One program may focus on short-term results, while another balances the value of the long term. One program may drive team or organizational performance, while another encourages and rewards individual contribution. The key is to create and manage the programs as an integrated set or a portfolio series of rewards that support the organization's strategy and values.

Levi Strauss is engaged in a multitiered strategy to retain its market leadership. The company used to be a publicly traded company, but they found that responding to the pressures of the stock market compelled them toward actions that were antithetical to the values of the founding family and key executives. They went back to their private corporate status through a leveraged buyout. If the company is able to meet or retire the debt payout ahead of schedule, individuals are eligible to receive a special award that is equal to a full year's salary. The rather large "carrot" focuses people on cost control and cash management.

To survive and prosper in the retail garment industry, the company needs to produce product at competitive prices, deliver products the customers want, and provide outstanding quality for service and merchandise. To that end, the company has a variety of special recognition and variable compensation plans that touch every employee in the organization. This enhances their ability to guide the organization and create a meaningful stake in the immediate- and long-term performance of the company. In this way, Levi Strauss can retain its values as a desired employer and retain its market leadership.

Fleet Financial Group was facing a situation that is all too common in today's hot technology market. They were experiencing rising turnover in their information technology organization that was significantly impacting their ability to compete and provide reliable services to customers. They studied the situation extensively and developed a comprehensive retention program for IT professionals. When they began to communicate the program, they realized that it was not having the desired impact. After a serious review, they realized that what they needed to do was to simplify the system so that it supported one clear message: "We value your contributions, we need you to help us be successful, and we are entrusting our future to you." They communicated this message to employees directly through a variety of meetings, and they backed up the message with a retention bonus that supported the key objectives of the function. If individuals remain with the company and continue to perform, then they will receive an aggressive bonus. The senior managers continue to reinforce this message through employee meetings, presentations, and discussion groups with key employees. Everyone has been impacted by this simple, but direct approach to retention.

The results have been dramatic. Employee turnover at Fleet has declined dramatically. The development programs are at or ahead of schedule in many areas, and the morale is much improved. They used the situation to send a message and used rewards to reinforce it.

High-performing companies use rewards to drive better results and actions. They interlace the programs so that people clearly see the key requirements for success. They see rewards as a strategic process of the organization. Whether each organization is aware of it or not, they have used a total systems approach to their rewards.

5. Integrate Rewards into How People Are Managed

Reward programs do not run themselves. As stated earlier, reward systems gain their value by how they are managed within the organization. Organizations that introduce new reward programs come to realize that the program does not begin until after the first payout is made. It does not start with the approval, announcement, or communication of the program. When it begins technically is not the same as when it begins operationally (i.e., people start performing because of the program). Employees are initially skeptical of the intention and sincerity of management to truly pay for performance. Their past experience, in most organizations does not support confidence. But after the program has generated a payout, then they realize that management is serious. They also wonder whether the program will last or be curtailed because of the lack of interest and enthusiasm by the employees.

High-performing companies have learned that the effect of these programs takes time to materialize. They realize that the results cannot be achieved unless people start doing "some" things differently. With this realization, these companies set long-term expectations for their reward systems. They don't expect immediate turnarounds; they do expect long-term improvements that will shape their ability to implement their business strategy. But, as stated earlier, these programs succeed because they serve as a catalyst for change.

Some of the most important changes that reward systems create are the process for setting goals, tracking performance, and managing people. In high-performing companies, you see the following types of activities occurring on almost a continuous basis:

- Managers communicate what is needed to be successful in clear, concrete, and meaningful terms.

- Feedback systems emerge, and people see how they are progressing during the performance period.

- People seek and receive assistance on how to improve performance.

- Problems in systems or work process are highlighted and resolved, so that people can achieve desired performance.

- As performance progresses to the goals, there is a significant amount of encouragement and reinforcement.

Reward systems either support desired management practices or highlight what needs to change. They are not a replacement for effective management. Further, a well-integrated set of reward systems makes managers even more effective—it has a multiplier effect. This transforms reward systems into a process of management that is inexorably linked to the culture of the organization.

At Southwest Airlines, reward systems are regarded as basic. Herb Kellerher, founder and chief executive officer, views rewards as important—to a point—but they become meaningless unless they are associated with a workplace filled with pride, excitement, fun, and fulfillment. This organization has become well known for its unique environment as well as its superior success in the marketplace. This is an environment where the culture and the actions that drive and reinforce it are of paramount importance. They believe if they place the right person in the right environment, they will win every time. But this simple reframing is backed by a well-developed process of performance management and rewards.

While there are few incentive compensation plans and base salaries that are at or slightly below market standards, the workplace is shaped by a wide variety of special recognition events. Recognition is both informal and formal, occurring at local units or broadcast across the organization. Almost every hour of every day someone in Southwest Airlines is being recognized for helping a customer, supporting team members, or improving the efficiency of the organization. They have hundreds of "culture committees" that involve people in all aspects of their workplace conditions. These committees create involvement in continuous improvement and are a powerful vehicle for communication throughout the organization.

Salaries, variable compensation, recognition programs, and stock options—all are viewed as tools of management. They are the devices managers use to encourage and support the actions that lead the airline to be highly competitive. They have special award programs, with titles such as "Together We Make It Great," "Walk a Mile," and "Winning Spirit." The process of recognition is both verbal and social as well as tangible. People understand why they receive what they do, and they take great pride is both giving and receiving recognition. The effectiveness of their recognition programs derives from the company's using the programs for establishing criteria for both manager selection and accountability standards. Because Southwest Airlines handles recognition so effectively, there is little need for management to place a strong emphasis on financial rewards.

At MathWorks, Inc., of Natick, Massachusetts, they have created a program to encourage continual learning and growing the company. MathWorks is a rapidly growing software systems company that specializes in various engineering and mathematical programs for the scientific community. It is a privately held company, and it seeks to remain that way. As the company grew, it faced the challenge of retaining a small company spirit and a commitment to the total organization.

After extensive research, the senior management team developed its "Stakeholders Program." Essentially, the program is a cash incentive program for all employees of the company. On a quarterly basis, 10 percent of the company's profits are placed into a pool and distributed to all eligible members (employees who have been with the company for over 18 months) based on their performance and salary. If major investments are made during a particular quarter or if a large number of new people become eligible, the payout portion will likely be reduced. However, if these actions create greater value in the company and increased profitability, then the payouts increase. This links people to the decisions made to invest in the growth and development of the organization.

The payouts are made in person. In several departments, individuals meet as a team to discuss major achievements and challenges. In other departments, managers meet with employees in one-on-one sessions; these are an important responsibility of managers. They occur at least every 3 months, and managers place significant emphasis on goal setting, performance tracking, feedback, coaching, and recognition. The program enables individuals to share in the growth and success of the company without using stock options or other equity-based devices. This keeps the pressure on to remain a privately held company, and it keeps people focused on the critical drivers of success.

IMPLEMENTING BEST PRACTICES

This chapter has outlined many of the common features found in the reward systems of high-performance companies. It should be clear that there is no perfect system, but some are more successful than others, and these programs share common characteristics. Organizations that effectively implement systems similar to the ones described in this chapter may not become high-performance companies, but they are likely to become better than their competitors. But the task is not just to design high-performance reward programs; rather, it is to enhance the organization's ability to utilize and manage their programs over time. This means they must make a strong commitment to seeing the potential advantage of linking rewards to the strategic success of the organization.

These companies have found unique ways to implement their strategy. They have sought and achieved alignment. They have created conditions in which employees feel a strong sense of commitment, as well they should. Their fortunes are linked beyond just retaining a job or having career promotions. They will share in the success that they help create.

A reward system does not need to be just a compensation plan; it does not need to be just a recognition program or stock option program. As these companies have demonstrated, rewards should be a combination of formal and informal, and immediate- and long-term, vehicles with which performance contributions are fully recognized.

The companies described in this chapter may not always be the top performers in their respective fields, but they have what it takes to be successful in any competitive environment.

37

MEASURING AND ASSESSING TOP EXECUTIVE PERFORMANCE

Craig Eric Schneier, Ph.D. , President

Craig Eric Schneier Associates

Douglas G. Shaw, Principal

Craig Eric Schneier Associates

THERE IS LITTLE DISPUTE that the most important measure of top executives' performance is the creation of additional shareholder wealth. And to grow shareholder value, not many would argue that top executives should be striving toward greater free cash flow and growing earnings over the company's cost of capital.

But is measuring top executives' ability to generate shareholder value a sufficient measure of their performance? A number of organizations do not think so.

Organizations are increasingly using intermediate measures that they believe help lead to the creation of quality earnings and shareholder value.

Some organizations are systematically identifying and developing measures that they believe lead to financial and shareholder success. Some, for example, Sears, develop sophisticated *correlational models* that identify measures that "predict" specific outcomes. Most however, identify and track the factors they believe lead to success, without the use of the more sophisticated correlational models. For example, PepsiCo determines its annual incentives for its officers based not only on the financial success of the company or one of its units but also on several less quantitative factors including the quality of strategic plans, organizational and management development, and what PepsiCo calls "idea leadership."

THE CASE FOR "NEW" EXECUTIVE PERFORMANCE MEASURES

A case for using nonfinancial executive performance measures is often made when an organization can establish empirical reasoning, or "proof," for why a particular measure can make a difference. If a meaningful relationship is established between customer satisfaction and the bottom line, an organization is likely to use measures of customer satisfaction in assessing top management's performance. Figure 37.1 lists several examples of organizations that have established linkages between a "new" performance measure and their company's bottom line.

There are several trends that point to the increasing need for measuring top executive performance in newer, less traditional ways.

1. *More organizations are focusing on measuring factors that contribute to financial performance and shareholder gains.* The balanced scorecard has been embraced by a significant number of organizations—see Figure 37.2 for a sample of executive performance measures from the four perspectives of a balanced scorecard.

FIGURE 37.1   Nonfinancial measures correlating with financial performance.

Company	Rationale Non-Financial Measures
American Express	Travel offices with highest levels of ROA have higher levels of employee satisfaction than travel offices with lower ROAs
MBNA	A 5% increase in customer retention results in a 60% growth in profits over five years
Taco Bell	Top 20% of restaurants in employee retention have twice the sales and 55% greater profits than bottom 20% of restaurants ranked by employee retention
Waste Management	• Operating divisions with higher levels of customer satisfaction are 65% more profitable than those with lower levels of customer satisfaction • Operating divisions with highest customer satisfaction levels have the highest levels of employee satisfaction
Xerox	Completely satisfied customers are six times more likely to repurchase than merely satisfied customers

FIGURE 37.2 Identifying measures from four perspectives. *(Adapted from Robert S. Kaplan and David P. Norton,* The Balanced Scorecard *(Boston: Harvard Business School Press), 1966.*

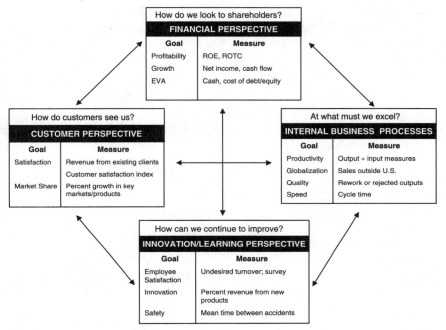

Sears, for example, has examined the interrelationship of various measures, to the extent that it has traced direct links among employee satisfaction, customer satisfaction, and revenue growth.[1] It knows that an increase in employee satisfaction in a store in one quarter will lead to a rise in that store's customer satisfaction ratings in the following quarter, which will subsequently result in above-average growth in revenue for that store.

With these "causal" relationships, Sears has based a significant portion of its officers' bonuses on levels of employee and customer satisfaction.

In its *Measures that Matter* research, Ernst & Young has demonstrated that 15 nonfinancial measures contribute to the success of an IPO, ranging from the quality of management, to strength of corporate culture, to strategy execution.[2]

2. *With the increasing correlations between customer loyalty and improved financial performance, more organizations are likely to begin to systematically measure customer loyalty and use it as a key performance measure for top executives.* Recent studies have found more companies in some industries are basing a piece of

---

[1]Anthony J. Rucci, Steven P. Kim, and Richard T. Quinn, "The Employee-Customer-Profit Chain at Sears," *Harvard Business Review,* January–February 1998, pp. 82–97.

[2]Ernst & Young, *Managing the Success of the IPO Transformation Process,* 1998, New York.

their executives' variable compensation on customer loyalty measures.[3] Several well-known companies base their executives' bonuses at least partially on measures of customer satisfaction, including AT&T, Federal Express, Kodak, and Xerox.

3. *There is an emerging emphasis being placed on the importance of the "people side" of the business to a company's success.* This emphasis on the people side of the business is bound to heighten with the demographics in the United States shifting to a reduced number of 35- to 44-year-olds in the first 15 years of the new millennium. These trends, together with thought leaders such as McKinsey & Company noting that "executive talent has been arguably the most under-managed corporate asset over the last two decades,"[4] suggest that more companies are likely to begin to search for ways of measuring top management's ability to manage its people assets.

ABB Asea Brown Boveri, for instance, uses executives' track record of developing others—measured by how many qualified managerial candidates a leader's unit offers for open positions outside their unit—as a key executive performance measure. Kodak measures employee satisfaction as one of the determinants of executives' bonuses.

4. *With proportionately greater amounts of executives' compensation shifting to variable pay plans[5] and therefore being linked to pay, companies (and their boards) are likely to place greater scrutiny on selecting executive performance measures that actually impact companies' bottom lines.* Base salary is being replaced by variable pay opportunities, usually less dramatically than IBM's CEO who exchanged 25 percent of his salary for an increase in his annual and long-term incentives. Non-U.S. companies—such as Matsushita—are increasing their pay-for-performance orientation by increasing annual incentive opportunities.

5. *Companies are measuring an increasing number of factors of executives' performance.* Figure 37.3 identifies several examples of executive performance measures used by a variety of companies. A significant percentage of "most admired" companies are using 360 degree, or multisource, feedback on their top executives.[6] Companies such as Merck have such performance systems implemented for all top executives, including the CEO. Although some organizations use data from these processes solely for development, many use them as input to their executives' performance reviews.

Although currently there is a significant emphasis placed on a variety of executive performance factors, these five trends are likely to accelerate the focus on less traditional measures of executive performance and increase their prevalence.

---

[3]J. B. Wood, "Customer Satisfaction and Loyalty: Basing a Portion of Executive Compensation on Performance in the IT Industry," *ACA Journal,* summer 1998, pp. 48–61.
[4]Ed Michaels, "The Hunt for Talent," *Leader to Leader,* fall 1998, pp. 10–13.
[5]Thomas A. Stewart, "CEO Pay: Mom Wouldn't Approve," *Fortune,* March 31, 1997, pp. 119–120.
[6]Francis J. Yammarino and Leanne E. Atwater, "Do Managers See Themselves As Others See Them?" *Organizational Dynamics,* spring 1997, pp. 35–44.

FIGURE 37.3   Examples of qualitative measures used to assess top executive performance.

Company	Qualitative Measure(s)
Compaq	"Individual contribution levels," succession plans, retention
Fidelity	Completion and implementation of development plans
Goldman Sachs	Teamwork (e.g., avoid "political" behavior, share information and credit resources with others)
Hewlett-Packard	Employee morale, marketing plans, new product success
Kera Vision	Organizational leadership, management succession, team building
Kodak	Employee satisfaction
Motorola	Respect for individuals, personal integrity
PepsiCo	Quality of strategic plans, organizational and management development, "idea leadership"
SAS Institute	Attraction and retention of talent

MEASURING EXECUTIVE PERFORMANCE IN TWO COMPANIES

Acme Manufacturing was experiencing a record year in earnings and sales. Its 5-year expansion plan was beginning to produce anticipated results, with several of its recent acquisitions turning a profit for the first time. Overall, there was a winning spirit within the organization and widespread confidence that continued good times were ahead. Not so at nearby Ajax Manufacturing. Competition from abroad had obliterated the company's sales forecasts. Persistent rumors about a pending foreign acquisition were doing little to inspire key managers and other employees. So when their respective board compensation committees divvied out annual bonuses and stock options, there were few surprises. Acme's CEO and senior management team were well compensated for their efforts, with each receiving a significant incentive payout. At Ajax. the CEO and his top executives were held accountable for the company's poor performance and uncertain future. Bonuses were cut and options were not forthcoming.

Considering what has traditionally been the norm in U.S. companies, it would be difficult to argue with the actions of these two fictional compensation committees. Companies have always assessed executive performance and provided some form of reward for good results. In the past, these rewards often took the form of increased annual compensation. Today, they are typically provided as bonuses and stock options.

This appraisal method raises important questions. Consider Acme and Ajax:

- *What are the specific quantitative measures used to evaluate executive performance?* In other words, do sales, earnings, cash flow, working capital, turnover, returns, and other financial figures provide the most accurate assessment of an executive's performance? Acme's high annual earnings may indicate that its CEO and top team have managed to move the company forward. It may also mean that external forces—including government regulations, interest rates, or the mood on Wall Street—were positioned just right to produce a winning year. Other quantitative, nonfinancial measures are useful to somewhat neutralize these external forces, including measures such as productivity, customer satisfaction, or even employee satisfaction.

■ *What qualitative measures—leadership, strategy, communication skills— should be considered as part of the performance assessment process?* Because it is not uncommon for a troubled company to take several years to right itself, the performance of Ajax's top team may show little progress on the quantitative side but very positive strategic movement on the qualitative end. In addition to assessing the extent to which financial goals are met, for the last several years GE's chairman Jack Welch has assessed top managers on the extent to which their actions are consistent with the company's values. In the mid-1990s, he cautioned that of the five officers that had been replaced, four had consistently met their financial targets but had failed to behave consistently with the company's values.[7] That sends a strong signal to top managers that the company is serious about measuring more qualitative aspects of executive performance.

QUANTITATIVE PERFORMANCE MEASURES: NECESSARY BUT NOT SUFFICIENT

Compensation committee members agree that the CEO's impact on strategy, management team building, and leadership are more critical than certain quantitative measures, particularly in the long run, but they often use measures of corporate financial performance as the criteria upon which top executive performance evaluation is based. The reasons are expediency and familiarity. Directors can easily assess executive performance based on certain "objective" (that is, quantitative) measures, but subjective (that is, qualitative) measures are another story. Quantitative measures should not be replaced as appraisal criteria, but they should be considered in concert with qualitative measures. As mentioned earlier, many people in the business community believe that the best long-term measure of top executive performance may be shareholder returns. Yet, in the short term, such quantitative measures as stock movement or earnings may tell very little about executive performance. More relevant is an examination of certain qualitative measures, including the "quality" of corporate strategy and success in implementing the strategy, similar to the PepsiCo criteria mentioned earlier. Other useful

---

[7]Dave Ulrich, "Measuring Human Resources: An Overview of Practice and a Prescription for Results," *Human Resource Management,* fall 1997, vol. 36, no. 3, pp. 303–320.

quantitative measures could include discounted cash flow, market share, return on equity, or return on net assets. Each, as well as others, tells an important part of the story.

QUALITATIVE PERFORMANCE MEASURES: TELLING THE COMPLETE STORY

In today's company, the rapidly changing business environment makes new measures—and a new performance appraisal system—necessary for top executives. Mergers and acquisitions, leveraged buyouts, global competition and markets, deregulation, and other factors dictate a new set of performance expectations. Today's CEOs and other top executives must be able to juggle administrative, financial, strategic, and leadership responsibilities with the short- and long-term interests of their shareholders, customers, and employees in mind. In fact, instead of simply asking their top executives, "What have you done for us lately?" boards and shareholders are now trying to find out, "What do you plan to do for us tomorrow?"

The emphasis on qualitative measures doesn't represent a new way of thinking for some of the most successful companies. International Business Machines and Hewlett-Packard, beginning with their founders, have recognized their importance, placing particular emphasis on contributions made by individual employees and initiative. More companies have followed suit. One major insurance company realized that its combined ratio and market share alone did not accurately reflect its success in implementing a new strategy and a new culture. The classic low-cost and product-differentiation strategies were augmented with a focus on customer service as a competitive advantage (see Figure 37.4). Other companies have been less willing to change their ways. For some, particularly those that are currently performing well, fixing a system that doesn't appear to be broken seems unnecessary. But there are a number of arguments that can be made in defense of a careful qualitative analysis.

Why Measure Qualitative Aspects of Performance?

One reason to measure qualitative aspects of performance is that there is a growing body of research that ties qualitative management factors directly to quantitative, financial outcomes. For example, there are several studies that show significant positive correlations between providing advancement opportunities (i.e., having a bias toward internal hires over external hires) and customer satisfaction, productivity, profitability, and growth. Figure 37.5 summarizes significant correlations that have been established among various people management processes (many of which can be described as "qualitative") and specific outcomes and quantitative results.

A second reason is that a company may be in trouble and not even know it. Not all problems bubble to the surface quickly. It takes a proactive company to

FIGURE 37.4   How a major insurance company developed a set of qualitative top executive performance measures to implement a new strategy and culture.

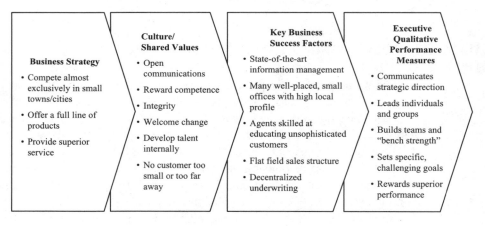

look beyond the obvious—the quarterly earnings—and determine that, for example, its leadership talent is below par as it enters the new millennium or that, even though sales are coming in, the company has failed to cement supplier relationships, invest in new technology, develop the next generation of products, or anticipate customers' expectations. Sears has recently transformed the retail side of its organization significantly. However, one could argue that Wal-Mart managed many of these qualitative aspects of its business better than any of its competitors—from supplier management, to logistics, to technology, to store manager development and succession. And that may be a large reason Wal-Mart has grown from being smaller than Sears in 1993, to being almost three times it size in 1998 in revenues and profits.

It is safe to say that three kinds of companies exist: those that are running ahead, those that are running behind, and those that are running in place. How, then, do companies apply qualitative measures in each of these instances?

Designing a Qualitative Performance Measurement and Management Process

Once a company accepts the fact that both quantitative and qualitative measures must be merged into an effective performance measurement and management process for its top executives, it can then begin to set the parameters for such a system.

An effective top executive performance appraisal system requires six actions:

1. *Select performance measures.* Top executive performance can be measured across several quantitative and qualitative dimensions. One framework for quantitative measures is the *balanced scorecard,* noted in Figure 37.1, which groups measures into four perspectives: financial, customer, internal business processes, and innovation and learning.

But how well do the CEO and his or her team perform as leaders? The second dimension addresses individual responsibilities for improving company performance and represents that aspect of performance largely within an individual executive's control. An example of a set of such performance areas appears in Figure 37.6. These become the basis for assessing strengths and weaknesses and provide a framework for the board to provide constructive performance feedback to the CEO and the top executives. The key is to let strategy and business goals, coupled with the requisite culture or shared values, drive these measures.

2. *Develop performance indicators.* Next, such measures as leadership must actually be assessed using some type of consistent and effective yardstick. Each performance area should contain "elements of accountability," which define the specific accountabilities within each broad area of an individual executive's responsibility. Consider succession planning, for example. The best CEOs and top executives spend a considerable amount of time identifying and developing the "bench strength" their companies will need to succeed in the future. Succession planning involvement, then, is an accountability. If viable succession is part of an executive's long-term vision, then a commitment must be made to developing

FIGURE 37.5 **Significant correlations between selected people management practices and quantifiable performance results.**

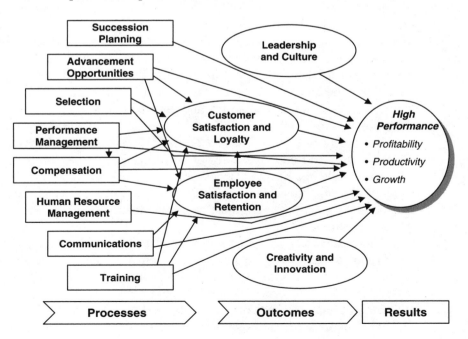

FIGURE 37.6   CEO appraisal: Roles and responsibilities.

Participants*	Design System	Determine Measures, Set Targets	Gather Performance Data	Provide Performance Data	Appraise Performance	Provide Feedback	Determine Consequences
Entire Board	X	X	X	X	X	O	X
Board Compensation Committee	●	●	●	X	●	●	●
Board Executive/Management Committee	X	X	X	X	X	O	X
CEO	●	●	●	●	●	O	X
CEO Direct Reports	O	O	X	O	X	X	O
Various Levels of Employees	O	O	O	X	O	O	O
Outside Parties	O	O	O	X	O	O	O

*Members of some participant categories overlap.

● Major
X Some
O None

those with potential in key executive positions throughout the organization. The performance areas and elements of accountability should be affirmed (or reaffirmed) by the board and CEO prior to the start of each year.

To make measurement less subjective, the board and CEO should also agree on the specific "indicators" of performance in each area, with the understanding that more than one indicator may be developed in each area of responsibility. These indicators can be either quantitative measures (for example, results of employee surveys) or observable qualitative evidence (for example, observations of the CEO's behavior in presentations to financial analysts). Indicators clearly define performance expectations up front and provide the facts needed to accurately appraise performance at year end. Of course, the board will still need to exercise considerable judgment in applying these facts. Figure 37.3 lists several qualitative measures used by companies in assessing their top executives' performance. Elements of accountability and illustrative indicators for one performance measure are provided in Table 37.1.

3. *Identify resources and mechanisms.* There is a good reason that boards desire to use qualitative measures of performance yet may shy away from them. They are rarely in a position to observe *how* an executive performs the job—only *what* results are obtained. Hence, in order to evaluate top executive success in each performance area, the board must determine the necessary resources and mechanisms to gather data.

The most effective systems rely on data from many relevant sources. The board should attempt to gather data in a systematic manner. After all, random comments, overheard conversations, and infrequent observations will provide a weak case if a CEO or top executive must be confronted with lackluster performance.

Because many aspects of executives' performance are difficult for a board or a CEO to observe or assess, getting input from others in a systematic fashion can

TABLE 37.1 Illustration of Elements of Accountability and Performance Indicators for Performance Assessment Area: "Organizes, Develops, and Utilizes Management Team"

Element of Accountability	Performance Indicators
Establishes, evaluates, and as necessary, changes the management structure to improve organization effectiveness and efficiency	Ratio of overhead to operational costs is better than industry norms. Number of management layers is below industry norms. Management structure supports business strategy.
Attracts, selects, grows, and keeps the best available management talent	Voluntary management turnover is below industry norms. Quality of management team, as reflected in the appraisal process and financial and nonfinancial results for each business unit, consistently exceeds standards. When necessary to recruit from the outside, the company is consistently able to hire leading candidates for open positions. Management development plans are in place and being executed for all management positions.
Ensures continuity in the management team through appropriate succession plans	Management succession plans are in place for all executive positions. Company is able to fill key positions with high-quality candidates from within the organization.
Successfully utilizes the management team through effective and appropriate: 1. Delegation and empowerment 2. Involvement in overall corporate decision making	Decision-making roles for key decisions have been clearly articulated in writing to executives. Decisions are made at the lowest possible organizational level without sacrificing corporate interests (for example, as evidenced by the decision-making roles described above and a retrospective analysis of key decisions made during the prior year). Senior executives actively participate in corporate decision making (for example, as evidenced retrospectively by the degree of involvement of senior executives in key corporate decisions during the prior year).
Stimulates collaboration and cooperation among members of the management team	Potential synergies among business units have been clearly identified and exploited (for example, joint strategies have been developed among two or more business units). Where feasible, resources are consistently shared among business units—management succession plans cut across business unit lines; where feasible, duplicative systems have been eliminated; cross selling is the norm, rather than the exception.
Sets clear performance expectations for the management team, provides appropriate feedback and coaching, and acts decisively to terminate executives who do not meet standards	A performance management system is in place for senior executives that establishes performance expectations in writing and formal feedback at least once per year on a timely basis (results of which are transmitted to the board). Nonperforming executives have been terminated.

provide valid and helpful measurement and feedback. Multirater, or 360 degree, performance measurement and feedback systems collect input not only from leaders' direct reports but also from colleagues and, in some cases, customers. Some studies have estimated that a large majority of Fortune 500 companies are currently using 360 degree systems, from IBM, to Procter and Gamble, to Merck, Ford, Hewlett-Packard, Levi Strauss, and Motorola.[8] Some of these organizations use 360 degree performance data for developmental purposes only; others use the data for development and performance assessment.

4. *Determine the importance of measures.* Few boards weigh both financial and nonfinancial measures of performance equally; most use nonfinancial measures to "modify" the appraisal of financial measures. This is consistent with the notion that financial measures are necessary but not sufficient to describe or assess top executive performance. For example, the CEO of a large consumer goods company met financial targets but failed for a second year to develop a viable top management decision-making team, choose a successor, or deal effectively with the media. If the board chose to consider heavily the nonfinancial aspects of performance and communicated this viewpoint to the CEO, then an appraisal of that CEO's performance would result in an "adequate," or even "marginal," evaluation. In assessing its CEO's performance, Dayton Hudson's board, for example, places equal weight on the financial performance of the company and the extent to which board members believe the CEO has carried out overall responsibilities and strategic objectives.

Whatever the relative emphasis of the measures, it is important that there be no mathematical system or computed weights. The reason: Doing so would add unnecessary complexity. The critical point is setting and communicating relative priorities, not agreeing on a numerical or percentage weight.

5. *Provide for changes in priorities.* No performance measurement and management process for top executives can work if it is too time-consuming, paper driven, or complex. Informal discussions and candor must prevail at the top levels. In addition, no performance plan for top executives, no matter how detailed, will survive a year intact. Internal and external events are too numerous, complex, and unpredictable. The measures, indicators, targets, and priorities may change. To ensure that the appraisal system reflects these changing priorities, periodic informal reviews, perhaps twice a year, are advisable.

If takeover becomes a threat, if a new tax law is enacted, if an acquisition suddenly presents itself, or if financial conditions change appreciably, so must the performance expectations for the top executives. In a mature durable goods company, the CEO was told to look for acquisitions that would complement the company's strong national brand awareness. Halfway through the year, a proposed hostile

---

[8]Francis J. Yammarino and Leanne E. Atwater, "Do Managers See Themselves as Others See Them?" *Organizational Dynamics,* spring 1997, pp. 35–44.

takeover loomed. The acquisition goal was shelved in favor of a stock buy-back plan and a search for a "white knight." A key nonfinancial performance measure for the CEO became his ability to negotiate effectively with other CEOs whose companies could become white knights and position the company as a solid, long-term performer in the financial community.

6. *Determine uses of results and provide feedback.* To make any attempts at top executive appraisal effective, the results of the appraisal must be linked to consequences. For the CEO, these consequences are largely financial but, of course, could include continued employment in the most severe cases. The objectives of the appraisal process are not only to hold individuals accountable for performance but also to foster a better working relationship between the CEO and the board, as well as the CEO and his or her direct reports. Measuring performance will focus the attention of the people at the top on those key financial and nonfinancial areas that will facilitate strategy implementation.

The assessment of nonfinancial measures should be undertaken each year by the board and/or the CEO, and feedback should be given to individuals. In those areas where improvement is needed, a goal, complete with target and indicators, can be established for the subsequent year. The attainment of this goal, along with any others, both financial and nonfinancial, should have an impact on compensation.

One CEO of a financial services company was found to have problems delegating authority, even to business unit heads. Consequently, implementation of strategy suffered. For instance, the strategy called for changing the positioning of its different units to provide services to specific markets. To do so, business unit heads had to understand and respond quickly to changes in those markets. By requiring all decisions to be pushed to the top, time and market share were lost in two business units. The board set a goal for the following year that required the CEO to develop and implement a plan revising the decision-making process and delegating certain marketing decisions to business unit heads. After one year, the board did not feel, based on data gathered in a systematic fashion, that the CEO had made significant progress in this area. As a result, the CEO's annual incentive was decreased, even though short-term financial targets were met. There is a moral here: If the board feels that a measure is important enough to include in a CEO's goals, it is important enough to have a bearing on compensation.

Implementing the System

Once the system has been designed, successful implementation can be carried out in four steps:

1. *Determine timing.* Boards often take the initiative to implement a top executive performance management process as a result of a shift in strategy, a new competitive environment, growth, or some other significant event. The best-case

scenario would be to address performance measurement when performance is good. After all, putting off this task, especially when performance is a problem, will only worsen the situation when and if decisive action must be taken.

2. *Determine roles and/or responsibilities.* For CEO performance assessment, those directors who will take primary responsibility for the appraisal process must be identified. Often, this is the compensation committee. But roles for other relevant parties exist (see Figure 37.6 for general guidelines). Above all, only those with relevant data should participate in the process. The roles must be spelled out in advance of the system's implementation. For the CEO's appraisal, the normal operation of the board and its key committees will determine how much, if any, participation each director will have.

3. *Determine relationship to other systems.* As the appraisal system is implemented, its impact on compensation—and on strategic planning, succession, and other systems—must be determined. The linkage from appraisal to compensation also must be spelled out in advance. The CEO performance areas should be consistent with appraisal criteria for executives below the CEO level. Likewise, data considered by the board as it reviews succession plans and identifies "high potentials" must be consistent with CEO assessment areas. In this way, a common, well-articulated, and specific picture of success emerges for the company. What it takes to "make it" becomes less of a mystery, and the shared values that top executives must adopt to drive strategy are shaped.

4. *Review strategy.* As previously noted and shown in Figure 37.4, the appraisal system for top executives must be tied to the company's strategy. As the chief architect and implementor of corporate strategy, the CEO must have his or her goals come directly from this strategy. Each year, prior to establishing the CEO's individual performance goals, a review of strategy is required. Those aspects of CEO performance that drive strategy in the nonfinancial arena (for example, how well the CEO delegates decisions) should be emphasized. When strategy shifts, additional goal areas surface, but each goal set for a CEO must be traced to strategy implementation.

FINAL THOUGHTS

Designing and implementing a performance management process that provides an instrument to capture top executive performance, evaluate it, and feed the evaluation back to individuals is not a simple undertaking. It requires commitment on behalf of directors, the CEO, and other top executives. In the words of retired CEO Robert Lear, "All the logic in the world says that the CEO should not be measured strictly on financial results. The trick is how to do it."

Sleight of hand aside, it takes an effective performance management system—one that is well designed, practical, and whose mechanisms are firmly rooted in the company's strategy and culture.

MERIT PAY AND PERFORMANCE APPRAISAL

Frederic W. Cook

Frederic W. Cook & Co., Inc.

MERIT PAY is the permanent increase in a person's salary rate based on his or her evaluated performance. By being individually driven and permanent, merit pay is easily distinguished from profit sharing and gain sharing, which are group driven and based on company or business unit performance. General increases (which are also group driven but are based on competitive conditions or inflation), promotional increases (which are individually driven but based on moving to a new, higher-level job category), incentive or spot bonuses (which are based on individual con-

---

Note: The scope of this chapter is the administration of salaries based on individual performance. The perspective is that of a company that employs large numbers of salaried employees (exempt and nonexempt) and desires to pay them based on individual performance. The administration of salaries for executives is within the scope of this chapter, but pay for hourly employees represented by collective bargaining is not.

tributions but paid in a single lump sum), and piecework (which is individually driven but based on actual output of the employee) are not merit increases for purposes of this chapter.

Because it is a permanent increase in pay, merit pay represents the best way to reflect a permanent increase in a person's value to the company. A person's singular contribution, no matter how valuable, is more suitably recognized by a reward that is also singular in nature, such as a spot cash bonus. It is very important in compensation to match the pay device correctly to the nature of the services performed so that the value of the employee's contribution is matched to the company's costs, both in amount and duration.

WHAT IS THE PURPOSE OF MERIT PAY?

Before addressing that question, three questions must first be asked:

- *What is the purpose of base salaries?* To attract and retain the number and caliber of employees necessary to accomplish the organization's mission.

- *What is the purpose of job evaluation and job grading?* To recognize and reflect the hierarchy of jobs in the company in terms of responsibilities, skills required, impact, and reporting relationship. Also, to create pay equity among dissimilar positions.

- *What is the purpose of a salary structure (grades, ranges, and midpoints)?* To provide a competitive range within which individual salaries can be determined.

What, then, is the purpose of merit pay? Answer: To motivate and reward performance on the job and to realign an individual's base salary to a new level of sustained contribution and value to the organization.

The purpose of merit increase is *not* to recognize differences in performance but to result in *salaries* that recognize differences in performance. Excellent performance might deserve, for example, a 10 percent increase regardless of the person's current base salary. However, proper salary administration requires the existing salary rate to be taken into account, as well as the individual's performance, when setting the new salary rate. For example, excellent performance may warrant a 20 percent increase if the person is paid low in the pay range, 10 percent if paid in the middle, and 0 percent is paid high in the range. This is not universally understood or accepted.

A merit increase is an adjustment between the current base salary and the new salary rate. The new salary rate should reflect the person's relative individual performance and value on the job. The size of the adjustment necessary to do this is the amount of the merit increase. This size of the increase, measured as a percentage of the old base salary, is derived from the relationship of the new rate to the old rate.

TABLE 38.1   Suggested Percentage of Average Salary for Target Salary Based on Performance Rating

Performance Rating	Target Salary as a Percentage of Average Salary for 3 Rating
5	120
4	110
3	100
2	90
1	80

If the purpose of merit pay is to result in salaries that are differentiated by individual performance, how much of a difference do we want? There is no agreement on this within the compensation community, but if a company employed a 5-point performance rating scale (with 5 being the highest), it might find the target salary relationships given in Table 38.1 to be appropriate.

So far, nothing has been said about length of service in merit pay. Should longevity on the job affect one's level of pay? Certainly it should if longevity adds value and aids performance. If it does, it should be reflected in the performance rating in the resulting pay. If not, then there is no place for rewarding longevity, per se, in a modern salary administration program. Most would readily acknowledge that a relatively short-service employee need not, and should not, be paid at the same or higher rate as more experienced people. But after a period of time in most salaried jobs, 3 to 5 years for example, relative service should make no real difference and performance alone should drive pay.

Is that how it is now? Unfortunately, no. Several companies have attempted to correlate the differences in salary levels within the same job grade with factors such as age, company service, sustained performance rating, or time in grade. They found no significant correlations with any factor, except a slight correlation with time in grade, meaning that the pay level was more strongly influenced by service than by performance. That is an indictment of current practices, and it is incompatible with pay-for-performance philosophies.

WHY IS MERIT PAY IMPORTANT?

Base salaries are the foundation of the total compensation program, and for most employees, they represent the largest component of total compensation. Many benefits, such as death and disability benefits, pension plans, and savings and profit sharing, tie directly to salary level. For management, annual incentive compensation and stock options often relate directly to one's salary. So it is important that salaries are established correctly. Therefore, merit pay is important because it affects the absolute level of salary and related benefit costs.

Merit pay is also important because, for most salaried employees, it is the embodiment of "pay for performance," which is one of the two most significant compensation themes of current times (the other being shareholder value alignment). Most employees want to be paid based on their performance, and merit pay is the traditional vehicle for accomplishing this. Profit sharing and gain sharing are also important, but they are group driven and hence, are not a substitute for merit pay, which is individually driven.

Although nonfinancial incentives and rewards are powerful, merit pay is the most important way companies have to recognize and reward individual performance, Money talks, and merit pay speaks with a loud voice. The power of merit pay cuts two ways, so it is important to get it right. The way a company administers merit pay says a lot to its employees about its standards of performance, what is valued, and what behavior is rewarded and not rewarded. Turnover among higher-performing employees, the ones companies want to lose least, can be strongly influenced by a company's merit pay policies. The same is not true of less-valued employees.

Finally, merit pay is important because in a time of delayering while improving productivity and staffing, there are fewer promotional opportunities in large companies. This means that even high-performing people will stay in a grade longer, and merit, rather than promotional, increases are the way they will be recognized and rewarded.

REQUIREMENTS FOR SUCCESS

Despite the fact that virtually everyone is in favor of merit pay and most companies are trying hard to make it work, it is not very successful in many companies. The problem from the company's point of view is that there is often too little spread in the size of merit increases and the resulting salary levels based on performance. From the employee's perspective, there is widespread cynicism and lack of trust, as revealed by attitude surveys, that good performance will, in fact, be recognized and rewarded.

There are two simple requirements that must be met if a merit salary plan is to be successful in motivating and rewarding differences in performance. First, there must be a credible system of measuring and evaluating performance. Second, employees must perceive that differences in performance will be recognized and rewarded.

Performance Management

Performance management is the process by which a supervisor evaluates or appraises the performance of a subordinate in meeting the requirements of the job and contributing to the organization's success. The appraisal is usually conducted annually and involves a discussion with the employee and written documentation that is made part of the employee's personnel file. Beyond that, there is very little commonality in approaches among companies. Each company develops its own system to meet its own needs and philosophy. The human resources department is usually charged with developing and maintaining the performance management program In decentralized companies, different divisions may be charged with developing their own programs, or the program might remain centralized. Often, the programs adopted are different for exempt and nonexempt jobs, with the appraisal of exempt positions being more complex. Within the exempt ranks, the program for evaluating management positions may be different from that for evaluating technical-scientific positions, given the differing nature of the jobs. In many companies, formal, documented systems at lower levels give way to informal evaluations at the executive level or no evaluations at all.

Performance appraisals serve many important purposes, which include letting employees know what is expected of them, setting and communicating job standards or objectives, relating individual objectives into overall organizational needs and objectives, evaluating employees' performance of job requirements and objectives, and telling employees how they are doing, including when things are going well and when performance needs improvement.

The results of the appraisal process are used primarily as a basis for merit pay actions, but they also are used as input in establishing training needs and making transfer, promotion, and termination decisions. Performance management programs, however, do not exist just to support merit pay or other decisions. They exist because it makes sense for managers to let employees know what is expected of them and how well they are performing against those expectations. Managers likewise benefit by getting feedback from their employees.

Types of Performance Management Programs

The best performance management program would be one in which an individual's performance and contribution are measured quantitatively and objectively. Unfortunately, this is not possible for most salaried positions. Qualitative assessments are required because of the nature of white-collar work. But if the program is to be perceived as effective, these judgments must be seen by employees to be valid, germane to the job, and free from bias, discrimination, or favoritism.

There are four basic types of performance appraisal programs for salaried employees:

- Job requirements
- Management by objectives (MBO)
- Trait
- Value based

A performance appraisal program that focuses on *job requirements* relates directly to the employee's job description and evaluates the employee on how well each of the assigned responsibilities has been performed. Under an *MBO system,* finite (often quantitative) goals or tasks are set for the employee each year. These objectives are goal oriented and have expected target completion dates. The employee should be involved in setting the objectives, but ultimately the manager must ensure that the objectives tie into the overall objectives of the business unit or company. In some quantitatively oriented companies, the individual's objectives are weighted in terms of importance, with performance scales built around the objectives so that overachievement or underachievement can also be assessed. At year end, a precise numerical evaluation of total performance can be enumerated. Whatever the degree of precision, an MBO appraisal process requires the annual resetting of objectives.

Trait appraisal systems are not currently popular, although they may be making a comeback as part of a more comprehensive performance management program. Traits include such judgmental and difficult-to-measure concepts such as leadership, communication skills, quality of work, adaptability, teamwork, interpersonal skills, and dependability. Trait appraisals fell into disrepute because they were highly subjective, did not directly relate to job performance, were not under the control or ability of the employee to affect, and were used to justify actions that could be perceived as discriminatory or biased. On the other hand, personality traits *are* important characteristics that often lead to success or failure on the job and define promotability. So, can they be totally disregarded? There is a place for trait appraisal in a modern performance management system, but in a supportive rather than a dominant role.

Value-based appraisal systems attempt to define the value each employee brings to the company and to identify activities on a four-part continuum: value building, value adding, value maintaining, and value destroying. A *value builder* is one who creates value that lasts over multiple accounting periods and, hence, has a high present value. This is the most valued employee, and she or he should be rewarded accordingly with a high salary level. A *value adder* is one who creates value whose duration is relatively short. This is also a valued employee, but perhaps he or she is better rewarded with a one-time bonus. A *value maintainer* is one who neither creates or destroys value but who is perhaps best characterized as delivering "a fair day's work for a fair day's pay." A *value destroyer* is one who costs the company more than he or she is worth. The purpose of a value-based appraisal system is to encourage all employees to identify areas where they can add value and to move up the value continuum and be rewarded accordingly.

Frequency of Appraisal

An individual's performance should be formally appraised at least once a year by his or her supervisor, typically at year end. More frequent appraisals should be given to newly hired employees, typically at the end of a 3- or 6-month probationary period. Transfers, promotions, and changes of supervisor are also times for performance appraisal. This is a matter of good housekeeping and planning, so that the new requirements and objectives are set for the rest of the performance period under a new supervisor. Finally, off-cycle appraisals are appropriate in cases of performance deterioration; they can identify areas in which the employee needs to improve and lay the groundwork for dismissal if the employee does not do so.

A formal, yearly performance appraisal does not replace the need for periodic "coaching" or interim reviews as needed. Instances of good or poor performance should not go unnoticed or unmentioned until the year-end appraisal. On the other hand, frequent coaching does not replace the annual comprehensive evaluation that considers performance during the past year and performance planning for the next. Both are necessary characteristics of a good appraisal program, which helps the employee improve performance, avoids surprises, is seen as fair by the employee, and provides valid input for personnel decisions.

Many managers dislike giving performance appraisals. They regard them as time-consuming and awkward, and they dislike being placed in a judgmental role that has such an important effect on a person's career. It is likely that, unless required to do so, many managers would not give annual appraisals at all. That is unfortunate because employees want feedback on how they are doing. Indeed, employees have a right to know how their supervisor views them. To relieve the time burden on managers, some suggest that evaluations be spread throughout the year. But there is overriding merit in doing them all at once at year end, when performance can be evaluated relative to others similarly situated and with respect to business achievements for the year.

An important development that would improve performance appraisals is training management in their use. Of particular benefit to managers would be training for evaluating employees who are acceptable but who have the potential to do better. The problem is not evaluating top performers; that's easy and even fun. The issue is also not evaluating the failing employee who is on the way out; that is neither easy nor fun, but most managers know how to do it when necessary. The issue is employees who are good, solid contributors but who have the potential to improve; the difficulty is in delivering criticism in a way that motivates rather than demotivates him or her. Most of us do not like to be criticized and do not respond well to criticism. Delivering criticism in a way that evokes a positive response is a skill most of us do not have. If managers could get help in this critical aspect of their job, the leverage for improving organizational performance would be immense.

The Performance Appraisal Process

The process of doing a performance appraisal can be as simple as filling out a form once a year about an employee's performance and sending it to wherever it is supposed to go. Or it can be as complex as the following multistep approach:

Start of the Year

1. Review with the employee the requirements of the position for the forth-coming year, reach an agreement on qualitative and quantitative objectives for the year, and identify areas of weakness that the employee should work on.

2. Ask the employee to summarize the discussion in writing on an appropriate form.

3. Review the completed form, sign it, return a copy to the employee, retain a copy, and send a copy to the next higher level of management.

During the Year

4. Conduct periodic review sessions with the employee to track progress, offer assistance, and make changes in objectives as appropriate.

End of the Year

5. Arrange a meeting with the employee at which he or she will be asked to do a self-appraisal of the year's performance.

6. At the meeting, listen carefully to the employee's review and offer comments and your own perspective on the employee's performance (this is also a good time to ask the employee to evaluate your own performance as a manager and to identify your strengths and areas in which you could do a better job).

7. After the meeting, commit in writing your evaluation of the employee's performance and contribution, taking into account the employee's self-appraisal but giving more weight to your judgment of the real accomplishments.

8. Give a copy of the completed appraisal to the employee before you sign it so that the employee has another chance to give you his or her perspective in an area in which you might disagree.

9. Ask the employee to add any amplifying comments he or she wishes and to sign the completed form.

10. Sign the form yourself, give the employee a copy, keep a copy for yourself, and send a copy to the next level of management for review and approval.

There are many variations between the extremes of the 1-step and the 10-step processes. But there are good reasons to recommend the multistep approach in our complex industrial society where jobs, pay, and performance are of critical importance to a person's self-esteem and the company's performance.

Overall Performance Rating

Most, but not all, companies with formal performance management programs require that the supervisor provide an overall performance rating for the employee at the end of the process. Overall ratings exist despite the fact that it is somewhat simplistic to sum up a whole year's performance in one word or number. Furthermore, single ratings are not a necessary ingredient in appraising someone's performance and deciding how much his or her pay should be. The reasons for ratings seem somewhat bureaucratic and include simplifying record keeping, aiding in analyses of performance distributions, providing comparison and trends, forcing managers to be specific in evaluating and categorizing performance, simplifying the sorting process when selecting people for transfer or promotion, and facilitating the application of merit matrices in merit salary systems.

Ratings take many forms and carry many definitions in different companies. The simplest is a 5-point rating scale of outstanding, superior, fully satisfactory, needs improvement, and poor. Because few employees want to be "satisfactory" or "average," companies go to great lengths to define the middle rating in positive ways, such as "meets high standards." However, employees can catch on quickly; the more astute employees want to be rated no lower than the second category from the top no matter how it is labeled or defined.

Some companies use 4-point rating scales instead of 5 to force managers to categorize employees on one side or the other of average. Five choices, however, seems the most common. Some companies create subcategories within the overall five, such as a "high 3" or a "low 4," or permit rating along a continuum, such as 3.2.

If a company feels it needs to have an overall performance rating, then it should define the middle categories broadly and positively. Otherwise, the rating distribution will become excessively skewed to the high side. Some skewing is to be expected; the best that can be hoped for is that it will be kept within reasonable bounds. In Table 38.2 there is a five-point rating scale that meets the preceding definition.

These definitions evaluate performance in terms of job requirements or standards that are established for a particular job but that are common for all people holding that job. In other words, the requirements are not tailored to the particular individual's abilities. Under the definitions listed, job requirements are established with the expectation that they will be met by most people. They are minimum but nonetheless solid standards of job performance; they are not "stretch" objectives.

Forced Distributions

Most companies find that managers skew the ratings to the high side, particularly in small groups and at upper levels. There is a natural tendency of managers to rate most people positively as long as things are going well. This need not be a source of concern unless it becomes so excessive that the rating definitions risk losing their meaning.

TABLE 38.2   Five-Point Rating Scale

Rating	Definition
5	Exceeds all requirements
4	Exceeds most requirements
3	Meets all and exceeds some requirements
2	Meets most requirements
1	Does not meet requirements

Companies have two choices in controlling skewed ratings: require forced distributions or communicate encouraged distributions but not require rigid adherence. The distribution chosen as appropriate might vary from one company to another, depending on the number and definition of rating categories and manpower dynamics. Without trying to promulgate a singe standard for all, Table 38.3 might be an expected distribution for a large population.

Forced or encouraged distributions are artificial and potentially harmful to teamwork because they mean that, for one to get ahead, someone else must fall behind. This is inconsistent with what most people understand the term *performance* to mean. Specifically, performance is not a zero-sum game. If someone performs well, someone else does not have to fail; both could perform well, in which case total performance expands. Employees know this and, hence, tend to resent forced or encouraged distributions. Forced or encouraged distributions have nothing to do with absolute performance; rather, they are measures of comparative performance among employees.

The ultimate in forced distributions is ranking, a process whereby employees in the same job level or category are ranked from high to low in terms of performance, value, and contribution. In ranking, there are no performance categories or ratings; rather, each individual's rating is his or her place in the rank order. In large units, managers must get together to discuss and merge the relative rankings of their employees. This leads to concerns about favoritism, politics, and the relative strength or weakness of a manager's ability to argue for and against the rank ordering of his or her subordinates.

COMMUNICATING PERFORMANCE

It is unarguable that an employee should know how his or her performance is viewed by the company. But does it necessarily follow that an employee has a right to be told his or her performance rating, to see the appraisal form completed by his or her mangers, to sign it, to add comments, or to appeal it to a higher authority? The answer is apparently yes because the trend in large companies is clearly in that direction.

TABLE 38.3 Suggested Rating Distribution for a Large Population

Definition	Rating	Percentage in Category
Exceeds all requirements	5	10
Exceeds most requirements	4	25
Meets all and exceeds some requirements	3	50
Meets most requirements	2	15
Does not meet requirements	1	—

The reasons for openness are logical and compelling. Performance evaluations and ratings have an important influence on the employee's career, which includes pay and promotion opportunities. Employees who are performing poorly have a right to know it so that they can either work hard to improve or leave for better opportunities. Employees who are strong performers also should know that their work is valued so that they will be motivated to stay and do even better. And good performers who can improve should know the areas in which they are weak so that they can decide whether these are areas they want to work on.

Another reason is that, if merit pay is to be based on performance ratings, it makes sense for employees to know their ratings so that they can see the connection between their pay and performance.

A final reason for open communication is often not stated. Requiring supervisors to tell employees their ratings and to let them see their completed appraisals prevents supervisors from deceiving employees about their performance. The specific problem is a supervisor who submits a negative evaluation of an employee but who is not willing to discuss it with the employee. Not only is this fundamentally wrong, but it can cause legal problems if the employee is terminated for poor performance and subsequently sues for wrongful dismissal.

So the best solution is to encourage accurate evaluations of performance and open discussion of results with employees. Having performance ratings and requiring that employees be told their ratings and sign the completed evaluations is a check on the supervisor that the appraisals are being accurately communicated. And encouraging a relatively normal distribution of ratings (if a company has ratings) forces the supervisor to be discriminating in the evaluations so as not to mislead the employee.

MERIT PAY: HOW MUCH?

Earlier in this chapter, merit pay was defined, its purpose discussed, and a target spread in salaries for employees at different performance levels was described. Having now discussed performance appraisal, let us look at the details of actually administering merit pay.

Conventional wisdom says that a merit increase should be no less than 4 percent if it is to be meaningful to the recipient and that an increase of 10 to 12 percent would be outstanding. Of course, this range is subject to a number of variables. For example, in times of high inflation and competitive movement, the range might shift from 6 to 15 percent. At the other extreme, in times of severe economic hardship when there is very little money available for merit increases, a 2 percent increase may be regarded as outstanding, perhaps only for its symbolic recognition value. Other variables include the time interval between increases and the actual pay level of the person receiving an increase.

HOW OFTEN?

Most companies award merit increases on an annual basis (12-month intervals). This does not mean they grant increases all at the same time. Many do, but perhaps an equal number spread the increases throughout the year, using the anniversary date of the person's employment or promotion as the time to grant salary increases. Although there are great advantages to evaluating employees' performance once a year at year end (for purposes of making comparisons or defining objectives), it does not necessarily follow that salary increases have to be made at the same time.

Annual salary reviews may be the norm for a company, but more frequent reviews and salary increases (if warranted) should be given to newly hired or promoted employees, for example, 3 or 6 months after hiring or promotion. The reasons are to give rapid feedback on the performance of a new person's duties and to recognize the person's progress through the learning curve.

Conversely, it is also common practice for the interval between salary increases to be stretched out to 18 or 24 months once the person becomes mature in the job and is paid well into the range. This is quite logical and easily explained because, after a person has become experienced and proficient in performing the responsibility of the job, incremental changes in job value become smaller. Some companies keep everyone on an annual-increase cycle but grant smaller increases (as a percent of salary) to those who are experienced on the job and well paid. This accomplishes the same objective of slowing down the rate of growth in salary once growth in performance slows down. On balance, however, the stretched-out interval has advantages because it permits the increases, when granted, to be healthier and more motivational in amount, and it dampens the sense of entitlement and peer competition that builds if companies grant increases at regular 12-month intervals.

SALARY INCREASES AND INFLATION

The rate of inflation and competitive movement obviously have a lot to do with the frequency and size of merit increases. In times of high inflation merit budgets of 8 to 10 percent is the norm, and the 12-month merit interval becomes common (some companies grant increases even more frequently). In times of lower inflation and smaller competitive movement like the 1990s, merit budgets of 4 percent are more common and it makes a lot of sense to lengthen the merit interval.

Despite this general connection, companies should avoid linking salary movement to changes in the cost of living because this creates entitlement and reduces the amount of money available to differentiate for performance. Specifically, *cost-of-living allowances* (COLAs), once common in union contracts, are not appropriate for salaried employees. They are nothing more than general increases that are outside the company's control, and they are not based on performance. A company has no obligation to increase its employees' salaries as inflation rises. Its obligation is to pay them competitively and in line with their performance and the company's ability to pay.

MERIT PAY VERSUS PROMOTIONAL INCREASES

A promotion moves an employee to a new salary grade with higher responsibilities. A promotion calls for a special salary increase, which is different from normal merit treatment. It is larger, often at least to the minimum of the new grade range, and occurs at the time of promotion rather than at the normal merit interval. It is only appropriate to combine a merit and promotional increase if the promotion occurs at about the same time as normal merit treatment; otherwise, it is best to keep them separate.

Some companies do not give promotional increases. They pay the employee at the level appropriate for the old job until the employee has proven himself or herself in the new job. But this is a minority practice and should be discouraged unless the promotion is, in fact, a trial appointment.

An interesting issue is title promotions in which job responsibilities do not change but the employee, for example, is elected or appointed a vice president. On the surface, a title promotion would not seem to justify an increase as would a job promotion. However, it may be even more important because title promotions reflect individual performance on the job and should go only to the best contributors in the grade.

LINKING MERIT PAY TO PERFORMANCE

Merit pay is for improved performance on the job, not for taking on new job responsibilities. The size of merit increases and the resulting salary levels should relate to performance as defined and evaluated by the performance appraisal system discussed previously.

If all employees in the same job grade started out at the same salary rate, then the size of each employee's merit increase could be a direct function of his or her evaluated job performance, with higher-rated people getting the higher increases. However, the starting point is rarely equal, and, therefore, the size of the merit increase must take into account the employee's relative salary rate as well as his or her evaluated job performance. The reason for this subtle, but important, complexity is that the purpose of merit salary administration is to result in salary levels that are differentiated by performance. Merit salary increases are the means by which salaries are differentiated, not the end in themselves.

The common tool for taking into account both the employee's performance and his or her current salary rate is the merit matrix. The example shown in Figure 38.1 is fairly typical. It is designed to move the employee who performs well up to the midpoint of the range, which should be the competitive going rate. Better-performing employees can move past the midpoint up to the maximum of the range under this matrix.

A problem with the merit matrix shown is that the ranges (and midpoints) in a typical company increase every year in response to inflation and competitive pay movement. Thus, the employee needs an increase every year that is at least equal to the range change to avoid the deterioration of his or her compa-ratio. An annual change of 3 percent and a merit budget of 4 percent would be common in the late 1990s. If everyone gets an increase each year equal to the range change, how much can be left for true merit, which many would define as moving up in the range? Answer: Not much! One of the problems with salary systems that try to target employees' salaries to various positions in a range and that also increase the ranges every year is that most of the merit money is spent keeping up, and little is left over to differentiate for performance. Thus, salaries become differentiated more by time in grade than relative performance.

THE MERIT BUDGET

Merit matrixes take many different forms, but all are built around the concept of spending a certain amount of money called the *merit budget*. This is the amount

FIGURE 38.1 Sample merit matrix (built around assumed 5 percent merit budget and performance ratings).

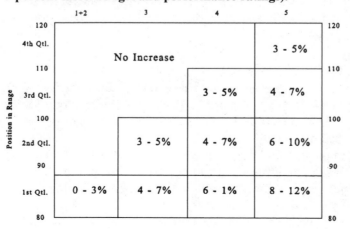

the company has decided it can spend for merit increases that year. The purpose of the merit matrix is to help managers allocate the available merit funds in a pay-for-performance fashion.

Where does the merit budget come from? It is a combination of three factors: (1) the company's current salary position versus the market (that is, average company salary divided by going market rate), (2) anticipated competitive movement for the forthcoming year, and (3) the point at which the company wants (and can afford) its average salary position to be at year end versus the market. For example, if a company's current salaries were 100 percent of market averages, it anticipates a 3 percent movement in competitive averages and it wants to still be at 100 percent of the market by year end, then it would authorize a 3 percent merit budget for the year.

How does one go about projecting competitive salaries ahead to some point in the future? First, you have to know where you are now. This involves taking the latest and best competitive survey data you have and bringing it forward to the present time using anticipated competitive pay movements (for example, 0.25 percent a month). Then you project ahead to a future point using survey estimates of what other peer companies are planning to do in the same time period. The sources of survey data on projected pay movements include industry associations, various consulting firms that survey their clients, and an annual survey conducted by the American Compensation Association (ACA) for its numerous members. The ACA survey shows projected merit budgets for various classifications of employees. It also shows how much was spent in the previous period versus what was projected.

Care must be taken in using these survey projections to derive your own merit budget because they are often biased upward. They are estimates of what compensation professionals in various companies are planning to *recommend* as merit budgets; they are not approved merit budgets. Top management may knock down the compensation manager's recommendations once profit goals are taken into consideration. Even if accurate, they are projected *merit* budgets, not projections of competitive pay *levels* to some future point. The difference is changes in population, which typically means lower-paid individuals entering the grade (through promotion and new hires) and higher-paid people leaving the grade (through retirements and promotions). Hence, merit increases for those staying in grade may be offset by a decrease in average salaries through population changes. A 4 percent merit budget may result in a less than 4 percent increase in average competitive rate. Of course, if you anticipate the same population changes as others, this factor may be disregarded.

Two final notes of caution: First, adopting the same merit budget as the survey average assumes that everyone is starting at the same point. However, your company's average paid rate may be lagging or ahead of the market. Varying the size of your merit budget versus the merit budget of others is a way to make fine-tuning corrections in market rates. Second, in a large, complex organization, it is overly simplistic to adopt a singe merit budget. Employees in different job classifications, functions, or levels in the company may be at widely varying positions versus their own relevant markets and the company average. Hence, different merit budgets and different merit matrixes may well be appropriate within the same company to achieve a competitive result. Avoiding a focus on a single number also prevents a situation in which large numbers of employees feel unappreciated and demotivated if they do not get an increase at least equal to the company average, even if they are well paid to begin with.

COMMUNICATING THE MERIT PROGRAM

There are two schools of thought on communicating a merit pay program. The first, called the *open-salary system,* believes that employees have a right to know and should be told their salary grade, their salary midpoint and range, when the salary range is changed and by how much, the merit budget, the merit matrix or increase guidelines, and the average merit increases. Proponents say open-salary systems build trust and motivate employees to improve their performance because they will see clearly that above-average performance leads to above-average pay increases.

The second, called the *confidential-salary system,* believes that employees should be told the company's pay-for-performance philosophy and how it works, the performance factors that are important in determining raises, and the employee's performance rating. But the employee should not be told his or her range, the amount of range movement, the merit budget, the merit matrix, or the average increase. Proponents of the confidential-salary system say it reduces the sense of entitlement to the average increase, maintains the average employee's self-esteem, reduces conflict and disgruntlement, and results in a wider dispersion of merit increases and resulting salary levels by performance.

Some companies, that have confidential-salary systems, will let an employee know his or her grade if asked. Hybrid systems communicate the salary structure but not the merit increase budget or merit matrix. Most large companies employ open-salary systems, whereas smaller organizations tend to employ confidential-salary systems.

SOME PERENNIAL ISSUES

Range Minimums and Maximums

Should range minimums and maximums be treated as absolute limits, below and above which salaries are not permitted to go? Or should they be treated as guides that can be violated for good reasons? I strongly prefer the latter because it is consistent with the merit concept. To illustrate: Should someone who is a poor performer being paid at the minimum receive an increase just because the minimum is increased? Obviously not. Any salary increase that is not earned by performance undermines the merit principle. And should an outstanding performer be denied an increase just because he or she happens to be paid above the maximum? Again, obviously not. Arbitrary rules should not supersede common sense.

Merit Increases and Company Performance

Should the size of merit increases relate to how well the company is performing? If the company has just concluded a poor (or great) year, should this affect the size of the merit budget going forward? Generally, no. Merit increases affect future salary levels and are not an appropriate vehicle for recognizing a prior year's performance. Bonuses, profit sharing, or other forms of variable pay are better vehicles for rewarding for past performance.

But should a company's future outlook affect the size of its salary increases? A reasonable answer is yes because these salary increases would be paid for by future performance. Whether this outlook is poor or great, however, the effect on salary increases should not be great. The reason is that base salaries should be kept reasonably competitive over time if they are to be effective in attracting and keeping good people. Some lagging and leading is acceptable, but wide swings are not appropriate. Even in a disaster scenario of layoffs and shutdowns, when a company has to tighten its belt, a company should retain the ability to recognize and reward those who are significantly underpaid in relation to their contributions.

Achieving Job Objectives

Should merit increases be granted for achieving job objectives? On the one hand, this seems quite reasonable, and many companies do it. But on the other hand, it is not logical to do so because the costs of the reward are not aligned with the economic values created. A salary increase is a permanent increase in costs. Consider benefits roll-up. The present value cost of a $1 increase in salary is probably $10 to $12. Achieving a job objective is a finite event that may have no residual value to the company. It is better recognized and rewarded by a bonus. Salary increases should be for permanent increases in job value, based on how well the individual performs the ongoing responsibilities.

Entitlement

Everyone in the compensation community is against the concept of "entitlement" when it comes to salary increases, bonuses, and other variable rewards such as stock options.[1] Entitlement is bad when it comes to variable rewards because the absence of a reward when one is expected is a disincentive and demotivator. If the

---

[1]No one is against entitlement when its comes to employee benefits because these are something that the employee is entitled to as a condition of employment.

reward is only what one expected, then it taken for granted and devalued. When entitlement exists, positive motivation is created only when one receives more than one expected (or was entitled to).

Why does entitlement exist and what can be done about it? Entitlement is caused by two factors at work in an organization's environment. The first is administrative systems that we in the compensation community create and that result in regular delivery of rewards at periodic intervals, with minor variations. Once the pattern is established, the employee logically expects it to continue, and entitlement has been created. The answer is to break the pattern of expectancy and use much more variability in the amount and timing of rewards but always base them on performance.

The second factor is the language of entitlement—the words that have evolved for expressing the delivery and receipt of rewards. Words such as *you have been granted, awarded,* or *given* an increase or a bonus imply power in the hands of the giver and subservience on the part of the receiver, which leads to entitlement. The phrase *you have earned a salary increase or bonus* would be far better because it transfers a sense of control over the reward to the employee based on the employee's performance.

Equity Increases

Most companies that have pay-for-performance philosophies have only two types of salary increases: merit or promotion. A minor exception is a salary increase to induce a relocation to a higher-cost area. Everything that is not a promotional increase is presumably based on merit and justified by improved performance. But there are many types of increases that are not really merit increases at all, such as general or cost-of-living increases; equity adjustments such as when two organizations or units are merged and the pay levels of one are brought up the higher level of the other; competitive adjustments to reflect a pay survey that shows the company has fallen behind; equity adjustments such as when recently hired college graduates receive increases to keep them ahead of escalating rates for new graduates; retention adjustments to keep someone who has received a competing offer; and adjustments for disadvantaged groups of employees to correct salary disparities that are not based on relative performance and contribution. These types of increases are not based on merit and should not be labeled as *merit increases.* Rather, they should be termed *equity increases* and communicated as such.

Confidentiality

Finally, a word on salary confidentiality. Most compensation professionals believe employees talk about their salaries, and they accept this as a fact of corporate life. Whether this is true or not, open communication of salaries should be discouraged by strong statements of corporate policy. An individual's salary, just like his or her performance appraisal, should be a strict matter of confidence between the employee, the supervisor, and others with a valid need to know. Companies that condone open communication of salaries and merit increases are condoning practices that will lead to incorrect and unfair comparisons and undermine merit pay practices to differentiate salary levels by performance.

CONCLUSION

There are only two tests of whether or not a merit salary plan is effective. First, employees have to believe their performance directly affects their pay. Second, there should be a significant difference in salaries for those in the same grade based on relative value contributed. For the first requirement to be met, employees must know the requirements of their jobs and the basis on which their performance is measured. There must be an objective and credible performance evaluation system that is used in a fair and open manner by supervision. Also, differences in performance must have a direct bearing on the size of employees' increases and resulting salary levels. For the second requirement to be met, a company needs to consider not only the employee's performance in allocating merit increases but also the employee's current salary in relation to others. Differentiated merit increases are not the goals but the means to the goal, which is differentiated salaries.

Corporate Culture and Compensation

CHAPTER 39

CULTURE AND COMPENSATION

Louise R. Fitzgerald, Principal

William M. Mercer, Inc.

Pay is not the most important thing that makes organizations attractive places to work. However, it is much more important than whatever comes third or fourth.   *Anonymous*

IN THE NOT-TOO-DISTANT PAST, INFORMATION ABOUT PAY SCALES AND SALARIES was kept close to the vest. Employers didn't share much information, and employees weren't talking. For all intents and purposes, in most environments, compensation was a secret enterprise.

Things are different these days. Companies struggle with pay communication at both the macrolevels and microlevels: namely, how does the overall system work? And how does it affect individual employees? At the same time, generation

X-ers are inclined to talk much more openly about starting salaries and pay adjustments. With more openness in the workplace, inconsistencies in the way a company's pay system is communicated and applied will be glaringly obvious. As an anonymous person once observed, "Pay is not the most important thing that makes organizations attractive places to work. However, it's much more important than whatever comes third or fourth."

Companies need to do a better job. All too often they neglect the critical tasks of communicating and consistently applying their compensation programs. They spend a great deal of time and money designing sophisticated and sometimes elaborate compensation programs to accomplish strategic business objectives. Then, they leave it to an insert in the employee handbook or, worse yet, to an ill-advised supervisor, perhaps with a video, to explain the new pay structure. But a compensation plan, no matter how brilliantly designed, will not accomplish its objectives without a communication strategy that is just as brilliantly designed as the plan itself.

A strategy for communicating a compensation plan must accomplish three critical tasks:

- Demonstrating the link between the compensation plan and the company's overall business strategy

- Applying the program in the day-to-day operations of the company
- Communicating the plan details

DEMONSTRATING THE LINK BETWEEN THE COMPENSATION PLAN AND THE OVERALL COMPANY STRATEGY

In the drive to enhance their positions in the global marketplace, companies are increasingly competing on the basis of expanded market share, greater efficiency or lower cost, and their ability to attract, retain, and motivate the top talent. To fortify their talent pools, companies are hastening to design more attractive and innovative compensation packages. Creative programs for compensating executives, sharing profits, managing performance, and developing employee competencies all stand to help companies achieve their key business goals in an environment of intense global competitive pressure.

If it is designed properly, a compensation plan will align with the company's overall strategic business objectives. For example, if a company's future success depends on reorganizing from a hierarchical chain of command to a structure that is more flat, then a compensation plan featuring a profit-sharing component or group incentives might help increase teamwork and diminish cross-departmental silos.

Whatever the link is between a company's key goals and the compensation plan, it must be clearly and persistently communicated to the entire workforce. Virtually every compensation-related speech by top management, every print piece explaining the program, every employee meeting rolling out the plan should reiterate the *purpose* of the program. Typically, employees greet any change in the way they are compensated with skepticism and even fear. While clear communication may not entirely eliminate negative employee responses to the program, it will go a long way toward gaining people's commitment to, and belief in, the value of the plan.

APPLYING THE COMPENSATION PROGRAM IN THE DAILY OPERATIONS OF THE COMPANY

Applying the compensation program—consistently and fairly—so that it actually accomplishes what it was designed to do is difficult. For example, are managers making meaningful pay distinctions between truly outstanding performers and average and poor performers? Is the pay system resulting in the desired behaviors and achievement of goals? Are individual goals appropriately linked to department, division, and company goals? Are managers effectively involving employees in the goal-setting process? Are managers providing ongoing feedback and performing effective performance reviews? Are managers successfully guiding employee career development? All of these considerations and more are aspects of communicating about a compensation program.

Supervisors play a critical role in the successful day-to-day communication of a compensation program. After all, their one-on-one interactions with employees bring the program to life. Their ability (or inability) to foster an open, two-way exchange with employees helps determine the tenor of individual performance reviews; it also builds a healthy climate of give-and-take in the department.

Truly inspired supervisors rarely distinguish between *employee* relations and *human* relations. They exercise great care in the ways they interact with people, and they spur their employees on to peak performance by maintaining the following attitudes:

- Candid and forthcoming (except with sensitive issues, which demand discretion)

- Enthusiastic coaches and mentors to the people they supervise

- Skilled listeners

- Constructive critics (They should always provide *helpful* feedback, with a measured dose of compassion.)

Of course, the reverse is also true: Supervisors who are not candid and who are not skilled listeners, coaches, and critics can undermine a well-crafted compensation plan by offending and alienating people rather than motivating them. Management should cautiously select and maintain people to serve in leadership roles because while some interpersonal skills can be taught, a caring and outgoing nature cannot.

Because of the key role supervisors play, a successful compensation communication strategy must involve a comprehensive process for training, evaluating, and motivating supervisors.

Training Supervisors

Training should equip supervisors with the tools and techniques they need to administer compensation. It should help them understand the following:

- The way the program supports the business strategy of the organization

- The details of the compensation program and how it works

- The key role they play in promoting and supporting the pay program

- The importance of fairness and consistency in compensating employees

Training That Links the Compensation Program with the Business Strategy. Supervisors must be thoroughly trained in how the compensation program links to the overall business strategy for the same reason that the link should be clearly communicated to all employees: Supervisors will be much more committed to the company if they understand the rewards for contributions to the business. Moreover, this training will enable them to take ownership for the program and garner support for it among the rest of the company's employees.

Training in Program Details and How It Works. Clearly, supervisors must understand the compensation program in order to carry it out. They conduct performance reviews, calculate pay raises, and help valuable contributors continue to develop their competencies. They serve as a key resource to employees who have questions about the program. Without a thorough understanding of the compensation program, supervisors simply cannot support it adequately. Traditional techniques for training supervisors in the plan design include handouts, group presentations, explanatory videos, and sample exercises. More exciting are some of the newer technology-based tools that model the effects of the compensation program. Additional information and training tools are available on the Internet.

In addition to receiving nuts-and-bolts training in how the program works, supervisors must also be equipped to conduct effective performance reviews. Performance reviews should reward and motivate employees and should correct problems, not simply make employees "feel better" about their work for the company. Messages that supervisors give employees during reviews should accurately reflect the employees' performance, should not contain avoidable surprises, and should support the compensation program even if it means delivering bad news about an employee's performance. Role playing, skits, case studies, and group exercises are all excellent methods of training supervisors in how to conduct effective performance reviews.

Supervisors should also be equipped with tools to help talk about pay with employees, such as the following:

- Market data showing pay ranges for similar jobs at similar companies (Some data are available on the Internet.)

- Figures showing the company's competitive position in the marketplace

- Historical trends in the company's pay policies and projections for the future

Training Supervisors to Support and Promote a Compensation Program. Additionally, supervisors need to understand their role in conveying (either symbolically or literally) to line workers the priorities of top management. Through their words and deeds, supervisors communicate to employees what the company as a whole values and seeks to reward. If supervisors show a lack of awareness or concern about the compensation program, they betray a lax attitude on the part of management toward the program. Supervisors also must demonstrate ownership of the compensation program and take responsibility for decisions they make in accordance with it. They should not blame human resources for unpopular decisions, and they should not disparage the program. Even a casual negative remark about a compensation program by a supervisor can sabotage the best efforts to unveil and promote the program—wasting vast amounts of both time and money.

Training Supervisors in Fairness and Consistency. The compensation program must be applied fairly and equitably across the organization, or employees will view it with suspicion. Fairness is often evaluated subjectively, however. Especially in an environment of change, some people will perceive threats to their pay where none exists, and some will find fault with even the most earnest attempts at fairness. Supervisors must be prepared to face diverse reactions to change, and they should also be equipped with plenty of data to demonstrate the basis for their pay decisions whenever they are called into question.

Supervisors must practice fairness by not giving secret deals or preferential treatment to some employees and by not allowing their individual biases or personality quirks to corrupt their appraisals of employees' performance. Role playing and case studies are two ideal ways of training supervisors in consistency. For example, supervisors can observe role-played performance evaluations and then discuss the outcomes: Should the "employees" be given a raise (if so, how much?), encouraged to develop new competencies (if so, which ones?), or coached in ways to enhance job performance? Similarly, supervisors can read a series of case studies, discuss the pros and cons of employee performance, and come to a general consensus on how each sample employee should be treated.

Evaluating, Motivating, and Rewarding Supervisors

In addition to thorough training of supervisors, the communication strategy for applying a compensation program must also include evaluating supervisors. Are they consistent and fair in assessing employees' performance? Do they support the program in their day-to-day communications with employees, and do they strive to make the program accomplish what it was designed to do? Supervisor performance along these criteria can be difficult to measure, but some useful methods exist. For example:

- *Assessment comparisons.* Two or more supervisors can evaluate the same employee, and their assessments can be compared. Does one supervisor consistently over- or underrate the employees he or she evaluates?

- *360-degree evaluations.* Employees who all come in contact with the same supervisor can be asked to complete (anonymous) questionnaires about the supervisor's performance relative to the compensation program. Are there any patterns in employee responses that support general conclusions about the supervisor's performance?

Human resources staff can facilitate the use of these tools and others, as well as monitor the processes to ensure that they are managed equitably.

Supervisors who effectively administer compensation in the company's day-to-day operations should be rewarded accordingly. Privately, their efforts can be rewarded in their paychecks, in thank-you notes and positive feedback from management, and in favorable performance reviews. Public recognition can include general acclaim (awards, memos, articles in the company newsletter) and increased leadership opportunities. A combination of both public and private recognition should be afforded to supervisors whose actions support the spirit of the compensation program.

COMMUNICATING THE DETAILS OF THE COMPENSATION PROGRAM TO EMPLOYEES

Last, but not least, explaining the actual details of a compensation program involves careful preparation, effective communication, and evaluation.

Preparation

Before information about the program can be communicated, the purpose of the compensation program must be clear. Purpose will become an important component of the message that ultimately is delivered. Some key questions include the following:

- Why was the compensation program designed?

- What business goal is it designed to accomplish, and how does it link to the company's overall business strategy?

- How competitive is the program? What behaviors will it motivate?

- How does the compensation program affect individual employees? Does anyone stand to gain or lose anything under the program?

After evaluating the purpose of the compensation program and the way it aligns with company strategy, the next step in preparation is to assess the current situation. That is, the existing compensation environment and people's perceptions of it should be measured. If a new compensation model is being introduced, learning the details of the existing plans will show how the new program differs from the old, and it will identify the potential "winners" and "losers" under the new program. Learning people's current perceptions about the plan will show where misinformation needs to be corrected, and it will suggest what kind of communication campaign needs to be mounted.

The best way to measure people's current perceptions is to conduct focus groups and employee surveys. Both must be carefully designed to capture employees' responses in as objective a manner as possible. Otherwise, they could turn into dangerous and unproductive forums for griping and sabotaging of supervisors. Incidentally, focus groups also present a chance to ask people what information they'd like to receive about the pay system and in what manner they'd like to receive it.

COMMUNICATION

The next step, communication, requires knowing the audience and tailoring the message and methods accordingly. The most enlightened companies will exploit an array of techniques to communicate a compensation program, including personalized information, face-to-face presentations, open-ended question-and-answer sessions with supervisors, audiovisual presentations, print pieces, and technology-based communication such as the company's intranet site, CD-ROM programs, teleconferencing, and other forms of electronic communication. In selecting from the array of options and in deciding how to pitch the message, it is useful to consider some of the following factors.

Who Wins and Who Loses If the Compensation Program Changes?　Letters mailed to employees' homes will not suffice for people who stand to lose something under the program (e.g., those who might have received a merit increase under the old program without actually having done anything to merit the increase). They will need one-on-one discussions, group meetings, and lots of question-and-answer opportunities to assuage their fears and anger. Moreover, the message itself will not be pitched the same way to each group; high-impact–high-potential employees, those who have the greatest potential to grow with the organization, may need solid evidence of the plan's merits before they buy into it.

Where Are Employees Located, and What Is the Best Way to Reach Them? If employees work on the factory floor, employee meetings might be an appropriate and efficient way to capture their attention and explain the program. If, however, they work in a virtual office, renting a desk for a few days before traveling to the next virtual office, technology-based communication may be the only way to unveil a new compensation program to them in a timely manner.

What Is the Communication Environment of the Organization? What forms of communication have traditionally been effective with the workforce? Are employees independent minded and willing to read printed pieces on their own, or do they need more guidance in the form of a group setting with lots of question-and-answer time? How active is the rumor mill? Can it be circumvented with carefully timed and orchestrated employee meetings?

What Are the Audience Demographics? What is the age of the audience? The young employees of a fast-food chain might be receptive to information delivered with a catchy theme and dynamic audiovisual materials. Older, more staid executives, on the other hand, may not find the plan credible if it is presented this way. What industry do the employees work in? People working in information technology may best respond to material presented in technology-savvy formats. People in manufacturing, on the other hand, may favor more traditional approaches, such as employee meetings and brochures mailed to employees' homes.

Evaluation

After a compensation program has been communicated to the workforce, it's important to assess how effectively the information was communicated and how well the program works. Any problems that turn up in the evaluation should be addressed and corrected, or employees will view future attempts at evaluation with skepticism. Effectiveness can be evaluated by the following means:

> Returning to step 1 (identifying the purpose of the pay program) and determining whether the pay program is having its intended effects.
>
> Conducting employee attitude surveys and focus groups again. If misconceptions or widespread confusion about the program exists, the plan has been communicated poorly.
>
> Examining other factors such as employee turnover and job satisfaction. If people don't complain about compensation but simply leave for more competitive pay elsewhere, the plan is not working.

CONCLUSION

No matter how innovative a compensation program is, if it is going to increase a company's competitiveness, it must be communicated and rolled out to the workforce effectively. In most cases, the success of communicating a compensation program hinges on:

- A clear link between the plan design and the company's business strategy
- A carefully designed communication strategy
- Optimal use of supervisors' communication talents

- Use of a variety of tools and techniques to appeal to a variety of audiences

In short, the compensation program must be literally *incorporated* into the culture of the organization so that it ultimately becomes fundamental to the company's way of doing business. Effective communication is the way to make that happen.

40

PASSING THE BATON: CONNECTING COMPENSATION, BEHAVIORS, CULTURE, AND STRATEGY TO WIN

Debra K. Besch, Principal
William M. Mercer, Inc.

Eugenie S. Dieck, Principal
William M. Mercer, Inc.

N A RELAY RACE, SPEED COUNTS. All of the runners must be well conditioned to deliver their best. But the hand-offs make the winning difference. If the pass of the baton between runners is flawed, even the fastest team can lose.

Think of the connection between compensation, employee behaviors, organizational culture, and business strategy as being much like that between members of a relay team. Like relay team members, each of these components exists independently and "runs" at a different speed. That is, in most organizations, each component will typically be at a different stage of progress toward the desired state. Rarely are they exactly in step with one another.

In designing its compensation programs, a winning organization will know how fast each component is running and will focus on effectively "passing the baton" between them, recognizing how they connect or fail to connect. Like the final relay runner, an organization's compensation program can make the winning business difference, provided the hand-offs have been effective. Only then will a compensation program effectively match rewards to organizational and individual performance, the goal of virtually every organization.

WHY THE HAND-OFFS MATTER

The need to pay attention to the hand-offs—the connections between strategy, rewards, culture, and behavior—is well known. However, it often stops short of leading to a winning compensation program. For example, much has been written about culture and compensation. The debate has often focused on whether compensation is more effectively used to signal, drive, or reinforce the desired culture, or on how best to match compensation programs to certain cultural profiles. Similarly, much has also been written about matching compensation programs to business strategy in order to reward employees for business results. More recently, motivating and rewarding desired employee behaviors—competencies—has gained the spotlight. But these are fragmented perspectives.

What is essential is to approach all these components from an integrated perspective, recognizing their individual and collective influence on compensation design. To return to our analogy, just as the four individual relay runners must come together as a team, so must these components. Designing compensation programs around just one or two of these components, or without an awareness of the inevitable interactions between all of them, will result in a program that fails to deliver expected results, or worse, is counterproductive.

Effective compensation design is built on an informed awareness of the state of and fit between each component and on a definitive choice about whether compensation plays a reinforcing or leading role.

A CLOSER LOOK

What are the connections between strategy, culture, behavior, and compensation? Some are obvious, some are less so. The framework that follows helps to keep each hand-off in perspective (see also Figure 40.1):

FIGURE 40.1   Focusing on the hand-offs in designing effective compensation programs.

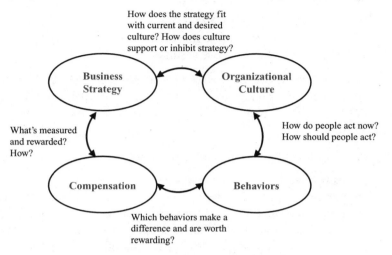

- *Business strategy to culture.* Business strategy defines the requirements for a culture's values, such as customer orientation, innovation, risk acceptance, and teamwork. The key determinant for this hand-off is the extent to which the culture supports or inhibits achieving the business strategy. At the same time, the business strategy also:

  - Influences the behaviors needed to make the culture live
  - Defines the results that should be measured and rewarded, which should directly influence compensation design

- *Organizational culture.* This is created as the norms and values that govern behavior:

  - Influence the efficacy of the strategy
  - Direct how people in the organization behave
  - Influence the kind of compensation design needed to effect change and how well certain compensation approaches will work

The direct hand-off here is understanding how the culture directs employees' actions today and how those actions may need to differ in the future to support the strategy. That leads to defining desired employee behaviors and the compensation design question of whether and how to reward the demonstration of desired values and behaviors.

- Behaviors can

  - Reflect and shape the culture
  - Support or hinder the strategy
  - Be rewarded when an organization values not only results but how employees achieve those results

The crucial hand-off here to compensation design is determining which behaviors make a difference to the culture and strategy and which are worth rewarding in order to directly reinforce selected behaviors that support the strategy and culture.

- *Compensation* connects with all three components:

  - Rewards influence behaviors.
  - Culture can be a barrier to certain rewards programs. At the same time, the "right" rewards program can accelerate cultural change, when combined with other influences like communication.
  - Rewards should reflect results against the strategic goals.

In short, the connections between these components are complex and organic. Changing—or not changing—one affects the performance of all.

CONNECTION VERSUS ALIGNMENT

We hear much today about the importance of aligning compensation programs with strategy. The real goal for an effective compensation program is not alignment but connection through an informed awareness of reciprocal impact and a common direction. While the four components (strategy, culture, behavior, and compensation) are inextricably linked, true alignment is an elusive state. Since organizations are dynamic, alignment is like the Holy Grail for most organizations—highly desirable, but virtually unattainable.

Alignment tacitly makes three assumptions: that business strategy, culture, and employee behavior are relatively static, that they are at the same stage, and that they merely need to be explicitly linked. However, strategy is aspirational and looks forward in time. Organizational culture—the values and norms that govern employee behavior—naturally tends to reflect the status quo. While the desired culture may be aspirational, the organization has to deal with the current culture on a day-to-day basis. Employee behavior is likely to be a mixed picture, with some employees moving aggressively toward the desired state, some stuck in the past, and all the rest. Compensation design may be aligned with one or two of these components, or none. Even when the attempt is to match compensation to an aligned, desired state for the other three components, the gaps between the actual and desired states may be so great that the compensation program simply fails because it is too far ahead of reality. In short, the reality is that alignment is a moving target.

That is why it is critical to be fully aware of each of these components in designing compensation solutions, and also of the gaps between them—where the baton is passed. A well-designed compensation program will neither be held back by a lagging component nor run so far ahead of it to be out of sight.

THE APEX SOLUTIONS STORY

In the real world, the process of connecting is not as simple as the schematic presented in the beginning of this chapter. In the following example, the executives of Apex Solutions, respond to changes and growth within their company by implementing planned and deliberate hand-offs and devising a clear, common purpose and mission to be shared by all employees.

Apex Solutions was formed in 1985, and the company has grown largely through acquisition. In the past, the CEO felt it was best to let each acquired group retain significant autonomy, with minimal common infrastructure and policies. Today, however, cost and customer service pressures are driving Apex toward streamlining and standardizing, as well as creating a common focus and identity.

With the four components in mind, we will eavesdrop on conversations between the CEO, Bob, and Apex's vice president of marketing, Vera, that have occurred over the course of a year.

CONNECTING STRATEGY TO CULTURE

It's Apex Solutions' annual strategy meeting. "Apex Solutions is a provider of technology solutions through programming services and systems infrastructure development," said Bob, the CEO.

As she listened, the VP of marketing, Vera, thought to herself, "That's who we say we are, but we are really a company built through acquisition. We are like 14 different companies, each with its own agenda."

Debriefing after the meeting, Vera raised the issue, "Bob, we need to face facts. If we are going to grow, we have to decide which products and services to pay attention to and tell everyone. And we better all act as one company."

"Vera, I felt that when I was talking. It's time to focus on making Apex work. That means shedding some of our products and...if I keep going here...some of our people."

"That's probably true, Bob. And we have to get to the point that the employees we have all care equally about Apex and not their own little world. Apex has to stand for something."

"I know, Vera, but needing it and actually getting it are two different things."

The Compensation Implications. The strategy-culture connection is necessary but easily passed by, often in the belief that sharing too much information about the business strategy will put the organization at a competitive disadvantage. Yet how will people understand it if they do not learn about it?

The strategy needs to be communicated in meaningful terms throughout the organization and translated into and transmitted through the culture. Not only that, the organization needs to assess objectively where the current culture will advance or hinder implementation of the strategy. This is where the next critical pass of the baton comes in. Everyone in the organization must know exactly how they need to act and behave to execute the strategy.

At Apex, the strategy may be clear, but the different cultures represented by each of the acquisitions means that people are acting in accordance with different values and exhibiting behaviors that do not necessarily support the strategy.

Again, compensation can help operationalize the desired culture and send clear messages through rewarding (or not) risk, teamwork, flattened hierarchy, and other values.

CONNECTING CULTURE TO BEHAVIORS

Back to Apex Solutions, where Bob and Vera are talking about how to move from the idea of how they want people to behave to the actual behaviors:

> *Three months later, the first quarter results are in and they are mixed. Vera and Bob are returning from a trade show. Bob observes, "You know, Vera, we still came across in a fragmented way at the show, and our results reflect that. One customer said that we have consistency problems in what we sell, what we produce, and how we act."*
>
> *"Bob, we have to agree to being one company and elect a set of values and behaviors to guide us. So what do you think? For the exercise, describe the ideal Apex executive."*
>
> *"Well," said Bob, "team player, risk taker, strategic thinker, and visionary leader are some descriptions. That's the thing: This is how I want our executives to act, but we can't legislate behavior."*
>
> *"Hold that thought," said Vera. "First, what is a `team player' to you?"*
>
> *"Vera, you know it when you see it. I can tell you who is one and who is not. And I know that having team players is important to our results, but I'm not sure which behaviors will really make a difference."*
>
> *"Bob, I'm not suggesting that we tell our people how to behave, but I believe we can identify what helps us carry out our strategy."*
>
> *"I absolutely want us to do so. Right now, it feels as though people are grasping for straws. I know I'm supposed to be a role model, but after I wore a cardigan 2 weeks ago and a half-dozen guys showed up in cardigans a week later, I felt more like a fashion model."*

The Compensation Implications.   Since culture is the amalgam of values and norms that guide behavior, actual employee behaviors, in turn, express the culture.

To change or reinforce culture, it is essential that the organization clearly delineate and communicate in very specific and concrete terms how it expects people to act—individually and as teams. Some of these behavioral expectations will apply uniformly across the organization. However, even in the strongest culture, there are subcultures that reflect differences in function, different lines of business, employee populations, and geography. Those subculture behaviors need to be accounted for, too.

When Bob and Vera talked about articulating core values and behaviors, they are talking about transforming their organization and their workforce. Finding a way to change behavior is even more challenging. Organizations are increasingly turning to *competencies*—the set of behaviors characteristic of outstanding performers—as the engine for change because they achieve the following:

- *Raise the performance bar.* Because competencies are based on the behaviors that distinguish excellent performers, the goals set for individuals are higher than before. This increases everyone's performance level.

- *Help align individual behavior with business strategies.* Organizations that are relentless in linking their competency models to the organizations' strategic values report that individuals' actual behaviors are more consistent with these values. Just as important, individuals see this linkage.

- *Provide a new employer-employee contract.* Many organizations are trying to create a new contract through which the organization provides individuals with the opportunity to develop and use new skills and knowledge in exchange for their commitment and labor. For these organizations, competency-based human resource systems provide a vehicle for assessing needs and developing the necessary competencies.

In short, competency-based human resource systems have the capacity to drive organizational—and cultural—change rather than simply enabling it to take place.

CONNECTING BEHAVIORS TO REWARDS

The following January, Bob and Vera were traveling to visit a major client:

"Vera, those competencies we developed seemed to have made a difference at first. But now people seem to think it's just talk. We need to do more with them. I believe they can help us drive change."

"I've been thinking that, too. We talk about them, but we don't use them to select or promote people. We could structure our development programs around them. What's more, we could pay people for demonstrating them. Right now, all of our bonuses are based purely on profits—not a very balanced approach to compensation."

"Vera, that's a hot issue. We've identified how we want people to act, but we're not rewarding them for doing so. People do what they're paid for doing, after all. Let's go the next step and pull what we do together."

The Compensation Implications. With employee behaviors key to culture and strategy, the issues that are central to the connection of employee behavior and compensation are the following:

- What behaviors are crucial to the strategy's success?

- Are they worth paying for?

- How and for whom?

There is little doubt that desired results are worth paying for. However, increasingly, how people achieve those results is also considered worth paying for, too—especially when people are a competitive differentiation.

The impact of behaviors on the business may differ, depending on how critical people are to the business success of an organization. For example, in a volume-driven business, behavior may matter only for those jobs that directly affect volume. In a customer service–driven business, behaviors may matter for everyone in the organization.

Rewards may also need to be tailored to the specific behaviors of the groups involved:

- To encourage teamwork behaviors, pay must be related to the results of the teams.

- To encourage innovation behaviors, rewards must be linked to the new ideas and initiatives.

In the end, you will get what you pay for. The question is *how* you pay for it and *when* you pay for it, which is a strategic investment decision. For example, suppose risk taking is a defined competency. Further suppose that an individual or team demonstrates all the "right" behaviors and makes the "right" business decisions, but the risk fails to deliver the desired results. How should demonstrating this desired behavior be rewarded? This is the kind of crucial decision that needs to be addressed.

CONNECTING REWARDS TO STRATEGY

It is often stated that compensation should reflect business strategy and that what is measured will be done. Returning to Bob and Vera, it is now 2 years later, again after the annual strategy meeting:

> *"Vera, we've come a long way in a couple of years. We're not there yet, but I think we've taken the right steps to define what matters to us most at Apex."*
>
> *"We're getting better as we go, Bob. I hear my people talking about our goals in more concrete terms than ever before."*
>
> *"Clarifying for ourselves what matters most has made our strategy more real, Vera. I think our next challenge is to keep an eye on spending our pay and incentive dollars on what counts. We need to decide what we're willing to pay for."*

The Compensation Implications.   The need for a compensation-strategy connection is clear, as seen in the Apex example. If an element of Apex's strategy is to focus on existing high-margin products and develop selected new ones for new markets, then rewarding sales revenues alone will encourage continued sales of old products to old customers. Alternatively, a compensation strategy that features higher rewards for the desired product and customer focus will further operationalize the business strategy.

IN CONCLUSION

Strategy alone, culture alone, or behaviors alone can drive compensation design—and sometimes do. Some organizations aim to understand each component and design a compensation approach that reflects an alignment among them all. A more realistic approach is to set aside ideas of alignment and look to the spaces where the strategy, culture, employee behaviors, and compensation meet—where the baton is passed—and make sure the hand-offs are sound and strong. An organization's compensation approach is best designed on the model of a relay team, with awareness of the goal, the track to run on, or common desired direction, winning behaviors and awareness of the influence of each component on the next, and with compensation.

41

REWARDING SCARCE TALENT

Patricia K. Zingheim, PhD, Partner

Schuster-Zingheim and Associates, Inc.

S CARCE TALENT IS HOT TALENT. Companies have competed for scarce talent for decades. When more jobs of a specific type exist than people, there is a talent shortage. Most recall how the cold war created a major buildup of electrical and mechanical engineering talent in the aerospace industry just to create an engineering oversupply once the concern for defense was mitigated. The severe shortage of registered nurses during the 1980s dramatically changed the talent picture in the health care industry.

Now the strong focus on getting and keeping information technology consultants and professionals has created a major scarce talent challenge that will last into the new millennium. But around the corner may be the next talent shortage and the next oversupply. There never seems to be a balance, and this imbalance strongly impacts the workplace and how people are rewarded. This chapter addresses the scarce talent challenge and suggests how a company might best turn this challenge into an opportunity by designing a more responsive pay solution.

THE BETTER WORKFORCE DEAL

For companies that look continuously to all the elements of a positive workplace, including total compensation (base pay, variable pay, and benefits), talent shortage and oversupply can be managed. But it is too late to worry about getting and keeping needed skill and competency when the wolf is at the door. Short-term, fadlike responses have not provided continuing advantage in workforce effectiveness or company performance. The reengineering movement's failure proves that companies are not able to "shrink to greatness." Taking company shortcomings out on the workforce does not result in organizational success. People are the only potential source of sustained advantage a company has, and the deal the company and workforce make is of the greatest importance. No company can become an *employer of choice* unless they can sustain a stable and talented workforce.[1]

Businesses are tested by scarce talent circumstances. In many instances, companies mount huge critical talent acquisition initiatives only to find attrition is so aggressive that they are at a lower staffing level at the end of the year than at the start. This adds to the cost of talent and challenges the stability of the company's business processes.

The cost of turnover is significant. This expense is often measured in terms of not only the financial resources consumed in the recruitment and training process but also in the disruption the company experiences as a result of needing to reestablish fractured working relationships and unsettled customer relationships and of changing the people who comprise the work group. Companies find it challenging to create collaborative work environments and a positive working atmosphere in the absence of a stable workforce. It is better business to be an attractive place to work.

People work for more than pay. Wise companies focus on the entire work experience—the culture, work environment, leadership, learning, career development opportunity, and the work itself—as well as pay. They are looking to make a *better deal* with their workforce based on trust. Where the "new deal" created a workplace of change and more accountability for people, the better deal focuses on creating a workplace where the company and workforce both gain from successful adaptation to necessary change.

Where pay fits in relative importance is subject to debate. However, pay is such a powerful communicator of values and directions that it must partner with other elements of the work experience.[2] Pay needs attention. Many companies are finding their existing pay approaches are not up to dealing with the severity of the scarce talent situation. While pay solutions are changing, talent shortages will likely quicken the pace to change pay, for a number of reasons:

- Most existing pay designs are not sufficiently agile for a scarce talent workplace.

- Skill and competency pay may offer lasting promise, but the move to these pay approaches is hardly universal, and existing solutions are often cumbersome and anything but agile.

- Variable pay can provide performance pay for more competitive times, but individual "merit" approaches that ignore a focus on shared goals remain predominant.

- Leading pay change rather than benchmarking others may save considerable agony when more jobs exist than critical talent to fill them. However, companies feel comfortable when they can copy the practices of others rather than break new ground.

The scarcity of information technology professionals is an example worth noting. At the time I am writing this, companies are competing with initial public offering opportunities that promise wealth from stock options and with other companies that may be more willing to risk stock dilution by making stock options more broadly available. Many companies must not only compete aggressively for talent but must also enlist the support of their workforce to energize their performance. The pressure to either sustain or regain high performance and to fill talent requirements at the same time is a major challenge. It is troubling enough to find scarce talent when things are going well for a company. When company performance pressures and scarce talent needs must be simultaneously addressed, human resource practice is severely challenged.[3]

AGILITY OR TRADITION

Numerous company pay programs are being left behind by their inability to adapt to a changing workplace. The customary solution to dealing with competitive talent markets has been to conduct or participate in market surveys, analyze the results of the data as compared to existing pay levels, and crank up pay as necessary. Because of the emphasis on internal relationships among jobs and people, pay adjustments tend to be more like spreading butter on bread than targeting short-supply skill and competency areas. This tends to inflate the entire pay system while not fully responding to situations such as where the price for scarce talent is growing at a rate requiring attention more frequently than annually or even every 6 months. Also, survey data are often 6 to 12 or more months old. Delays caused by the pay decision-making process can result in circumstances in which pay solutions may be responding to markets that were measured longer than a year ago. Because scarce talent markets are so dynamic, they change while companies are still contemplating what to do. Speed counts, and seldom more than when scarce skill is at stake.

Companies tend to rely on solutions that have worked well in the past. Customary scarce talent responses may include, in addition to increasing base pay, paying hiring bonuses, retention bonuses, instituting infrastructure changes such as adding broadbanding, or making counteroffers as people are going out the door. These solutions are proving to be too slow, too costly, and too easy to duplicate. They are more reactive than proactive. Further, they fit within the realm of expected solutions that members of conservative executive leadership teams are willing to accept. These responses are symptoms of "thinking in the box" and actions everybody can take with little challenge. As a result, they provide no unique advantage.

No evidence shows that these solutions make companies more or less talent or business competitive in the longer or shorter term, and this is especially true because of the propensity of companies to mimic the most common practices. It would be startling if any company were actually able to gain advantage over another in competing for talent by copying their practices. Often, while companies are surveying the best practices, the company being benchmarked is contemplating changing because its solution is no longer of contemporary value.[4]

WHAT PEOPLE WANT

As the saying goes, "Show me the money!" Everyone wants to make more money. During exit interviews, people frequently suggest that they are leaving because they were able to negotiate a better economic deal with their next employer. For scarce talent people, this deal may even involve new stock options because they either have already cashed in the options at their present company or have an uncertain chance of getting more or because current options are "under water." Is this practice of going to another company for more pay creating a generation of scarce talent "gypsies"—a transient workforce that moves from company to company in search of "gold at the end of the rainbow"?

People want to work for exciting and well-respected companies with solid leadership and able colleagues. They want a better workforce deal. This is true of everyone without regard to skill or competency, but those with very scarce skills with high market value have more opportunities to shop for the best companies. All people want an opportunity to grow and learn, to become more valuable and to keep their skill and competency fresh and applicable. They want to understand what they must do to add value. People want to be important to the success of a company and need the chance to make a difference. They want interesting, challenging and leading-edge work, like the chance to participate in special assignments and important new projects, rotational development opportunities, and a stint as a coach or trainer to help others grow.

Everyone wants to work for a company with pride in what they do. If a company wants to devise a proactive pay approach to attracting scarce talent, it will include making the work experience special, interesting, educational, important, and positive—a place people want to be. Solid pay solutions in the common sense of the word are just one component in reward solutions that match scarce talent business environments. Does this apply *only* in scarce talent times? Clearly no, these are things companies should do all the time to become or remain an employer of choice.

What are the implications of a changing workforce situation? The "deal" companies made with people at the end of the 1980s and the start of the 1990s was one of sharing shortage and changing expectations. This is because fewer jobs were chasing more people. Late in the 1990s, this situation changed remarkably. It was not possible to ask the workforce to make all the sacrifices necessary to making the company a success. Thus, a better deal is necessary where the company invests in the people whom they are asking to add value in exchange for a revised pay solution.

Companies that do not try to make themselves special are becoming commodity talent buyers. Such companies will find it increasingly necessary to "pay to buy"—to pay more than reasonable levels of pay to make up for a less-than-outstanding workplace. It takes more than just a proactive pay approach to remain viable. Despite this, pay does play a role if companies keep in mind that pay works in parallel with other elements of an attractive workplace and that pay is a communicator of key business initiatives. Two of the values and directions in which pay can communicate are in meeting a company's need for skills and competencies and workforce performance.[5]

SKILLS AND COMPETENCIES

When there are more jobs requiring scarce skills and competencies than superior people to fill them, it makes less and less sense to remain with reward approaches that focus only on jobs and not on the people who occupy them. Ed Lawler predicted an aggressive move from job-based pay to person-based pay.[6] The accelerating scarce talent market could make this prediction a reality sooner than later. What is the logic of pay solutions focusing on the skills and competencies that people use to generate results?

- People, not jobs, are the potential source of competitive business advantage.[7]

- People, not jobs, are the "warehouse" of skills and competencies a company needs.

- Jobs do not learn, people do.

- Shortages exist for skills and competencies, not for jobs.

- People, not jobs, are able to move from company to company.[8]

Investing in a pay solution that addresses these issues is a long-term proposition, not a quick fix. While companies may find it necessary to take many of the traditional stopgap actions to address the challenges of the competitive talent market, it will be essential to begin the transition to a new approach to total pay and other rewards.

Skill and competency pay has taken many forms since gaining some momentum. Many of the early pay approaches are proving to be extremely cumbersome and are likely to fail as a result of their complexity and communications challenges. Companies spend extensive amounts of effort developing "competency and skill models" when it seems likely that advantage comes more from how skills and competencies are actualized through people than from which specific competency and skill models are employed. The most common competencies are customer focus, communication, team orientation, technical expertise, results orientation, leadership, adaptability, and innovation.[9] Most companies would agree they could benefit from communicating key messages about one or more of these opportunities to improve. Do companies need to spend excessive amounts of time finding unique competencies when people are the key?

Job-based pay communicates little about necessary skills and competencies. Job-based pay focuses instead on duties and responsibilities. Job-based pay systems operate under the presumption that people assigned to the jobs have the capabilities to perform the jobs. Most of us know that this is not always the case. If the pay approach is instead designed around the skills and competencies needed to do the required work, it could keep up with competitive pressures to pay for people who have scarce skills and competencies.

However, just any skill or competency pay solution will not do. For a scarce talent market, design a pay approach having the following features:

- Select skills and competencies from the business's scarce talent requirements. The business strategy determines the key skills and competencies.

- Design a pay approach that delivers these skills and competencies as simply as possible—the "nimble" pay system.[10]

- Pay lump-sum awards when skills and competencies are acquired.

- Link base pay growth with the timing of increases in skill and competency market values.

- Implement developmentally focused performance management to keep track of changes in skill and competency acquisition and application.

- Don't overdesign the pay solution. Keep the approach as simple and straightforward as possible, consistent with addressing needed skills and competencies. Complexity is one thing that is killing job-based pay.

These guidelines reflect what is needed to make the company competitive from a business perspective, not just in the area of scarce talent but for communicating with the entire workforce.

WHERE SKILLS AND COMPETENCIES COME FROM

The business must be the source of skills and competencies. It is the business that defines what a company must pay to get needed skills and competencies. It makes no sense to have a competency model that does not place a priority on the scarce skills a company needs to do its business. In many cases these are technical skills in areas of short supply such as engineering, information systems, and science. However, this may also involve getting and keeping people who can behave and apply these technical skills and competencies in ways that are effective in a specific company.

This means seeking not only information technology capabilities but also, for example, the capability to work in a culture that requires teamwork and collaboration, to work with creativity and innovation, and to apply what is known to get results rapidly. In addition to competing for people with functional area and technical skill, companies must also compete for such skills as those involved in project leadership and management, team development, understanding the business, and process improvement. All of these have high market value in competitive times.

As straightforward as all of this may seem, selecting skills and competencies from the business does require a more strategic approach. This eliminates a skill and competency model that is developed from what already exists in the company because what already exists may not reflect the business strategy and may miss the capabilities the company needs to compete in the future. The benefits of a strategic approach are enormous because, as the workforce grows in needed skills and competencies, pay remains aligned with what the company needs to pay for most.[11]

LUMP-SUM AWARDS

Conventional pay solutions are too sluggish and cumbersome to respond as individuals acquire and apply new capabilities having high market value. Annual pay increases based on a budgeted amount of salary cost just cannot keep up with how people acquire critical skills and competencies. Individuals acquire and apply skills and competencies at different rates that defy the calendars driving conventional pay management systems. This means individuals' pay may fall behind their market value by as much as a year depending on how often conventional pay approaches provide the opportunity for pay review.

Pay solutions can use a combination of base pay increases and lump-sum awards to ensure that pay remains aligned with skill and competency growth. For example, when a skill or competency is acquired or demonstrated, a one-time pay award can be granted to recognize the achievement. Subsequently, when the skill or competency is applied to the advantage of the company, a base pay increase that acknowledges the increased value in the marketplace of the individual's capabilities is granted. The inclusion of a lump-sum award provision in the pay solution provides considerable flexibility especially if the granting of the award is not associated with the calendar but with the assessment of skill and competency growth. Thus, the lump-sum award can be closely associated with a performance management approach that calls attention to the career development process and subsequent successful improvement in capability on an individual basis. Remember, skill and competency needs change, and the pay solutions must be sufficiently flexible to make the acquisition and application of new skills a way to prosper from a pay perspective.

During a work session with human resource executives in Silicon Valley technology-based companies, several in the audience who were challenged by the scarce skill issue in information technology and other technical areas added an important reason for using lump-sum awards. Their companies had been granting base pay increases to correspond with expanded skills and competencies. However, they had to shift to a combination of base pay increases and lump-sum awards because they needed professionals to acquire fresh skills and competencies to replace those that were no longer highly valued economically by the company's customers. This meant granting lump-sum awards to acknowledge acquiring a new skill and keeping base pay at the former level since the present pay level assumed contemporary skill and competency.[12]

PAY PROGRESSION MATCHES SKILL AND COMPETENCY GROWTH

Traditional pay adjustments often cannot keep up with the rapid market changes that accompany a scarce talent market. We are all familiar with the rapid changes in the cost of information systems talent to address the continuous software and hardware evolution, including such areas as enterprise solutions and the Internet. Pay approaches must be responsive to these changes. It is not viable to permit the pay of an individual with important skills and competencies to fall substantially behind the market and then adjust pay by as much as 20 or 30 percent to catch up. This is just not acceptable for employers of choice. It means "they choose me back only after I am leaving."

The way to match pay progression to skill and competency growth is to associate them in the same pay system. This can occur by one of a number of methods that include the following:

- Design pay increase budgeting to allocate dollars according to a prediction of how rapidly the market value of skills and competencies are expected to increase during the upcoming performance period. This means having enough money available to match scarce skill- and competency-driven market changes.

- Design the pay approach to emphasize market value rather than internal equity. This means skills and competencies with different external market values will be paid for based on their market value. If Internet development is a faster-moving market than chemistry, the company will pay more for Internet development at any particular skill and competency level.

- Sensitize the performance management solution to how individuals grow in terms of skills and competencies. This means it must obtain enough input from those who work with the individual to determine when and how skills and competencies needed by the business are acquired and applied effectively.

- Let simple solutions take priority over elaborate alternatives. The temptation is great to design something so detailed that it burdens the entire process. It is better to implement and fine-tune as you go rather than to deluge the user with an administrative burden.

DEVELOPMENTAL FOCUS FOR PERFORMANCE MANAGEMENT

A debate exists over whether the performance management process can play more than one role effectively. Some argue to tie performance management to the pay increase process; others argue to separate them. The key issue is whether both effective developmental feedback and performance appraisal for pay purposes can be conducted using the same feedback instrument. The divergence of opinion will continue with good points being made on either side.[13]

It is critical in a scarce talent market to keep track of how people with critical skills and competencies progress from a career growth perspective. This should also be compatible with keeping pay competitive at a rate that matches the progress of an individual's skill and competency development. One could argue that, because companies must assume that all of their people possess some level of skill and competency the business requires, that a career growth tracking system with these features may be universally valuable. This is so because the market value of skills and competencies varies over time, and this type of performance management may protect the company's talent future. However, no matter what side of the argument someone may make about the role of performance management, the performance management system must include both features to be an effective tool for scarce skills.

The features of the performance management linkage with scarce skills and competencies acquisition are generally as follows:

- Performance management should communicate the skill or competency the individual is to acquire to add value to the business. The process must also show why the skill or competency is valuable by communicating the business reasons and how skill or competency adds value.

- The career approach must provide for people to acquire the skill or competency. This can be a shared accountability between the individual and the company, it can be the individual's sole responsibility, or the company can provide the training to acquire the skill or competency. Whatever the solution, it is necessary to provide a process for positive growth.

■ Skill and competency growth in a complex workplace cannot be readily judged by information gathered only from the manager. Therefore, some provision must be made to obtain information concerning career growth from additional sources. This may involve multisource performance management or some other solution whereby the company can get help from others in addition to the manager.

Information about the acquisition and application of market-sensitive skills and competencies must be an integral part of the pay process. This suggests that performance management that tracks skills and competencies and communicates this to the pay approach will play an increasing role in keeping pay responsive to major changes in the value of scarce talent skills.

DESIGN TO FIT

Many skill and competency pay approaches are so cumbersome and bureaucratic that they put the most laborious point-factor systems of the 1950s to shame. I see companies spending years developing elaborate skill and competency models. Once completed, they are so complex that their administrative procedures and communications materials rival *Webster's Unabridged Dictionary* in length and programming a VCR in complexity.

While solutions should be complete and thorough, some keys to designing a more agile approach could be the following:

■ Focus on a limited number of critical skills and competencies from the start. More can be added later if needed.

■ Minimize the number of levels used in skill blocks or competency descriptions. Make the defined differences meaningful, and avoid semantic differentials where possible.

■ Develop performance management and skill and competency pay at the same time so that the solutions are realistic, practical, and coordinated.

■ Get a training and communications process going early—"the earlier, the simpler."

One of the best performance solutions I have seen resulted in an *annual piece of paper,* or APOP, as the performance management instrument. It emphasizes the dialogue between parties to the feedback process and not the paperwork surrounding it. Solutions like this stress the exchange and use of feedback information rather than the elaborate forms that often characterize alternative solutions.

PERFORMANCE PAY

Perhaps the most disastrous experiment in skill and competency pay is that used in many public school systems. Teacher pay is geared toward encouraging enrollment in continuing college courses to gain the additional skills and competencies required for becoming a more effective educator. To receive the appropriate pay increase credit for the training, the teacher presents a certificate of course completion. The connection with the actual student education process is missed—there is no verification in the classroom setting that teachers are actually applying what they learned. Because teachers completed the courses, it is assumed this translates into something useful for their students. However, there is also no link made between the acquisition of new skills and the performance of the teacher's students.

This is a "pay-for-taking-classes" approach and not one that pays for acquiring and applying skills and competencies that are at the core of the objective of having children learn something of value. Results, not just getting more proficient, count. This does not encourage improvement in capability, nor does it attract top talent to the profession, as shown during teacher shortages when this system has done nothing to make teaching more attractive as a career compared to other alternatives.

Figure 41.1 suggests an alternative design for pay. It focuses on performance as well as on skills and competencies. The skill and competency elements ensure that people's critical skills are paid for as acquired and applied. However, the performance element is essential in a scarce talent market to permit a company to allocate pay dollars not only to those with needed skills and competencies but also to those who add the most value by applying skills and competencies to achieve results. In a scarce talent market, this combination makes the workplace attractive because of the obvious focus on paying for skill and competency growth.

Why is pay based only on jobs and periodic base pay adjustments not nimble? Traditional merit approaches are too inflexible to partner with skill and competency pay. They give too many confusing messages concerning a host of issues including competitive practice, internal equity, and individual performance to be able to respond to fast-changing competitive market situations. Budgets in the area of 4 to 6 percent for all workforce groups and for addressing a wide range of objectives will not serve a scarce talent market of any kind. The key is not just to spread around increases based on jobs that are not defined in terms of how people grow and learn but to make joining, staying, developing, and performing at the company attractive to the individual.

The performance pay dimension is critical to the overall scarce talent solution. As with skill and competency pay, performance pay can support a market with scarce talent if it includes some of these key features:

- Variable pay that is agile and focuses on a few key performance measures defined from the business strategy and that are also related to the application of scarce skills and competencies to achieve results

FIGURE 41.1 Rewarding a combination of skill and performance. (Adapted from Zingheim, P. K., and Schuster, J. R. "Dealing with Scarce Talent: Lessons from the Leading Edge." *Compensation & Benefits Review,* 1999, 31(2), p. 41.)

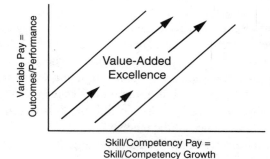

- Stock options and cash long-term variable pay that make it attractive to stay and contribute to key business goals

- Special recognition plans that enable the company to recognize high-performance individuals without disrupting a focus on a collaborative organization

- Referral awards, hiring awards, spot bonus awards, lump-sum cash retention awards, and possibly additional special-use rewards that are kept exciting and agile

- Performance solutions that are associated with communicating how "super" the company is and that are styled after what the company wants to be in the future

The main focus is to try to go, as early as possible, where competitors have not. While performance pay has remained stable and even stagnant in the past, changing and focusing on making the company an attractive place to work probably characterizes the future.

VARIABLE PAY

The word *agile* applies to how performance pay should be designed for a workforce that must continually learn and grow. Only variable pay is sufficiently agile to facilitate changing goals and measures and implementing new organization designs. Variable pay can focus on the team, individual, functional unit, business unit, or entire company. It can communicate a variety of combinations of measures and goals from finance to quality or customer satisfaction. Variable pay can reward membership in multiple projects and teams and is sufficiently flexible to strongly communicate changes in direction and support new business initiatives. Because the importance of certain goals varies, variable pay can adapt the award opportunity to the importance of what needs to be accomplished.[14]

While base pay remains the major compensation opportunity cost, variable pay permits considerable flexibility in directing at least a portion of total cash compensation toward emphasizing key messages the company wishes to deliver. Focusing base pay and lump-sum awards on skill and competency acquisition and growth permits the company to spend most of its pay dollars on ensuring workforce development and continued learning. The way performance is defined changes to match company objectives; variable pay is sufficiently agile to adapt to these changes in relatively short time periods. Using base pay for skills and competencies and variable pay for applying these skills and competencies to achieve results is a powerful and effective combination.[15]

LONG-TERM PAY

To build the core competency and talent base of a company, it is essential to keep the attention of the workforce for a sustained period of time. While stock options are the long-term incentive tool of the decade because of the inflation in the stock market, no conclusive evidence exists to suggest that scarce talent people who have options remain with an organization beyond the time they have a chance to exercise their original option grant. Most optionees cash in their options as soon as they can and seldom become long-term owners of company stock. However, options do retain people before vesting.

While most companies view options as relatively inexpensive, many discount the impact options have on dilution of shareholder equity. If they have options, scarce talent companies need something in addition. Those that do not have enough options to go around need a long-term-incentive alternative.

Long-term plans having unit, or "share," value that varies based on some key measure or measures of performance have the powerful aspect of being adaptable to the performance of an organizational unit other than the entire company or a major unit of the company. Most scarce talent people are assigned to a specific business unit of a company. These business units are often profit centers or are asked to behave like separate businesses that add to the performance of a larger organizational unit. Plans that measure performance at the business unit shorten the line of sight to the organizational unit to which people best contribute and show how this organizational unit contributes to company performance. Stock price of a large company is often far from the scarce talent individual. The goal of focusing the efforts of the individual on adding value to the organizational unit in which they work is often best accomplished with long-term pay that emphasizes business unit performance.

SPECIAL RECOGNITION

A number of books provide ideas for recognition and celebration; however, what you do is less important than the fact that you actually do it. The key to successful recognition strategies is to grant valued rewards for what you want people to do.[16] If you want talent referrals, focus rewards on this. If you want outstanding contributions, acknowledge this. The key word is *special*. Whether you say thank you or distribute parking places or jackets, what makes the difference is that what you recognize makes sense to the business and that the people being recognized feel good about the recognition.

What you acknowledge must be something people would be proud to have others know they did. Whether the recognition award is made publicly or not, the recipients must understand why they got it. Although much attention falls on such things as child care, flexible hours, home use of technology, and van service, unless these elements are woven into a work environment that also focuses on enabling career growth and performance, the novelty will wear off. Hot talent *superpay* must be more than the latest "Beanie Baby" craze to create credibility.

One company I studied used special recognition in about half of its organizational units. All the plans were different, reflecting the character of each organization and its leader. Differentiating is often very good because it creates variety and keeps attention high. However, in this particular company, one of the differences was in who provided the funding for the awards. Some managers put up their own money for special recognition; others had some money allocated for this purpose in their budget. In other instances, people took up a collection to pay for special recognition awards. These differences created confusion because they sent mixed messages about just who was giving the recognition award: the company, the manager, or the people themselves. Also, their reasons for giving the special recognition awards differed, and these differences did not relate to business challenges or opportunities. For example, one approach paid a significant award for referring new talent in an organizational unit that was reducing staff. An adjoining unit that was actively recruiting did not include referring new talent as a reason for an award. In both cases, the logic of recognition was uncertain as it related to the objectives of the business.

If there is a secret sauce for recognition awards, it is to keep things fresh and interesting and to be sincere when giving recognition. However, the business logic about the reason for recognition must be present. If the only form of special recognition a company offers is "employee of the month," how exciting or attention getting will this be year after year?

CONCLUSIONS

Total pay and other rewards that match the business strategy of a company are critical in a scarce talent market. Sometimes scarce talent is defined by how a company is enhancing itself as much as by the external competitive market. For example, early Internet companies actually created the Internet development skills and competencies before an external market existed for this talent. This need is magnified where company performance is an additional issue. If a case can be made for straightforward and focused pay, it is where advantage is on the line. Companies that are willing to break the mold of just paying more and more money and continuing to lose key talent can gain advantage by changing their pay plan strategies. Experience suggests that even though a chapter like this reaches hundreds of people in companies that are struggling for dominance, only a fraction will take positive action. Thus, the opportunity remains to do something that adds value that others will not do.

The key to a scarce talent solution, and to total pay and total rewards in general, is focusing on the message to be delivered. The most important action is "to go where no company has gone before," to paraphrase from the *Star Trek* television series. Each company is different in how they make themselves attractive to people, as you will find if you talk with successful companies such as 3M, Intel, and Monsanto. For years 3M has focused on hiring scarce talent directly out of college and helping their recruits build attractive and financially enriching careers. Intel and Monsanto have been very successful in enticing scarce talent professionals from other companies.

It is important to do what matches your company's view of how best to encourage people to add value. Whatever you do, find something special and unique to make your company attractive. No company that is fully responsive to scarce talent challenges relies solely on financial rewards. While the economics of working are important, an exciting career with a company that really cares about people counts most.

REFERENCES

1.   Anne Fisher. 1998. "The 100 Best Companies to Work for in America." *Fortune,* January 12, pp. 69–70.

2.   Patricia K. Zingheim and Jay R. Schuster. 2000. *Pay People Right! Breakthrough Reward Strategies to Create Great Companies.* San Francisco: Jossey-Bass.

3.   Patricia K. Zingheim and Jay R. Schuster. 1999. "Rewards for Scarce Information Technology Talent," *ACA Journal,* vol. 8, no. 4.

4.   Patricia K. Zingheim and Jay R. Schuster. 1995. "Exploring Three Pay Transition Tools: Readiness Assessment, Benchmarking, and Piloting." *The New Pay Tools & Strategies,* eds. Patricia K. Zingheim and Jay R. Schuster, special issue *Compensation & Benefits Review,* July/August, pp. 40–45.

5.   Patricia K. Zingheim and Jay R. Schuster. 2000. *Pay People Right! Breakthrough Reward Strategies to Create Great Companies.* San Francisco: Jossey-Bass.

6.   Edward E. Lawler III. 1990. *Strategic Pay: Aligning Organizational Strategies and Pay Systems.* San Francisco: Jossey-Bass.

7. Jeffrey Pfeffer. 1994. *Competitive Advantage through People: Unleashing the Power of the Work Force.* Boston: Harvard Business.

8. Patricia K. Zingheim and Jay R. Schuster. 1999. "Dealing with Scarce Talent: Lessons from the Leading Edge." *Compensation & Benefits Review,* March/April, pp. 36–44.

9. Patricia K. Zingheim, Gerald E. Ledford Jr., and Jay R. Schuster. 1996. "Competencies and Competency Models: Does One Size Fits All?" *ACA Journal,* Spring, pp. 56–65.

10. Gerald E. Ledford, Jr. 1995. "Designing Nimble Reward Systems." *The New Pay Tools & Strategies,* eds. Patricia K. Zingheim and Jay R. Schuster, special issue *Compensation & Benefits Review,* July/August, pp. 46–54.

11. Gary Hamel and A. Heene. 1994. *Competence-Based Competition.* New York: Wiley.

12. Jay R. Schuster and Patricia K. Zingheim. 1996. *The New Pay: Linking Employee and Organizational Performance.* San Francisco: Jossey-Bass.

13. Allan M. Mohrman, Jr., Susan M. Resnick-West, and Edward E. Lawler III. 1989. *Designing Performance Appraisal Systems: Aligning Appraisals and Organizational Realities.* San Francisco: Jossey-Bass.

14. Jay R. Schuster and Patricia K. Zingheim. 1996. *The New Pay: Linking Employee and Organizational Performance.* San Francisco: Jossey-Bass.

15. Patricia K. Zingheim and Jay R. Schuster. 1997. "Best Practices for Small-Team Pay." *ACA Journal,* vol. 6, no. 1, spring, pp. 40–49.

16. Bob Nelson. 1997. *1001 Ways to Energize Employees.* New York: Workman.

GAINING A COMPETITIVE EDGE BY IMPROVING THE RETURN ON HUMAN CAPITAL

Peter V. LeBlanc, CCP, Principal

Sibson & Company

At a time when there is a shrinking labor market and a rapidly growing demand for talent, people matter more than ever.

"**H**UMAN CAPITAL" IS THE NEXT CENTURY'S RENDITION OF "A FAIR DAY'S WAGE FOR A FAIR DAY'S WORK." But it goes beyond the notion of basic reciprocity to suggest that people can provide substantial economic returns on investments. Moreover, the idea that human beings are organization capital implies that employees are a financial investment to be optimized as opposed to a cost to be minimized. Human capital investments include on-the-job training, formal education, career-professional development, and salary and benefits. Human capital returns include company loyalty and commitment, high achievement, productivity, skills and knowledge, and creativity and innovation. Could this be the "people are our most important asset" hooey that has become a politically correct boilerplate in annual reports and vision statements? Maybe, but there is a hard enough edge to the concept of human capital to believe that this is more than corporate happy talk.

In fact, human capital—the debt plus equity of people—is rapidly becoming a relevant measuring rod of company value. However, the intangible nature of this asset makes it more difficult to calculate a human capital balance sheet. People are in fact nondurable capital, yet according to one author and leading thinker, the knowledge that people possess is the new factor of production, and managing knowledge is the most critical focus of business leaders.[1] Before we think that the private sector is going soft, let's be clear, it is the *return* on knowledge that is capturing the greatest interest. The idea that a return on human assets is both expected and to be realized is hardly new. The turn-of-the-century (the last one) industrial engineer made a living defining the standards of work pace and output—"standard allowable hours"—to derive a projected financial return. The idea was that the faster people worked, the greater the return, a reasonable assumption given the limited autonomy of yesterday's worker. People weren't asked to *think,* just to *do*—"as I say"! Consider how far most modern work has come. The adage "work smarter, not harder" has even become trite. Why "human capital"? Because thinking—knowing how to find and use information—has become at least as valuable as doing, and companies that have the best thinkers are winning.

ORIGINS OF HUMAN CAPITAL

The origins of the earliest form of human capital management go way back to the late 1800s when the NCR Company (National Cash Register Company) in Dayton, Ohio, and William Filene & Sons Company, the Boston department store, introduced the "welfare plan." Welfare plans made life more secure and comfortable for workers, addressing needs such as employee housing, community work, and, later, factory conditions. Modern benefit programs emanated from, but pale in comparison to, the paternalism of that early time. The development of company cities and towns, modern ventilated factories, an accident insurance plan and company doctors, a well-resourced school system, a library, a savings and loan association, and men's and women's social clubs were expensive debts incurred by early industrial

---

[1]Thomas A. Stewart, *Intellectual Capital: The New Wealth of Organizations* (New York: Doubleday, 1997)

and service companies. Why? First, workers were so poorly paid that they could not provide for even basic necessities. Second, workers were migratory—here today gone tomorrow. These were highly unsettled times—unmatched levels of turnover and absenteeism—and many managers and owners were feeling that they had lost touch with their employees. Though it was true that the work was designed around machines and tasks were kept routine and simple, workers were not nearly as interchangeable as managers had hoped. In fact, though this was the "stop-watch workplace," where speed and efficiency were the goals, machines sputtered without skilled machinist operators. These welfare programs tied people to companies, making it more difficult for them to walk away. The industrialists expected to profit from their investments. The idea was that a healthy, loyal, and dependable workforce would stabilize the production-service process, reducing hiring and training costs.

Growing unrest and discord at the workplace between managers and workers forced a change in strategy for improving the return on human capital in the pre-World War II era. The power of the shop foreman had gone unchecked and included hiring, firing, and setting the basic terms of employment for each worker. In too many instances the personnel decisions they made were capricious, inconsistent, and harsh. Also workplace safety and sanitation became a serious worker concern, as a growing number of employees were killed or maimed on the job. These issues had a huge negative impact on worker productivity. There was a need to protect the company from the cost of accidents, lost time, and unionization or, in cases where unions were already present, expensive grievance settlements or labor strikes. In response, the autonomy of the foreman was bounded and their power balanced. Investments were made in labor relations, workplace democracy, safety, and the work environment. The idea was that the payback on improved labor-management relations was an uninterrupted workplace where people focused on their job, not the unpleasantness of the workplace.

In the 1970s and through the early 1990s, a period of unstable markets and economic conditions, people management evolved beyond simply the care taking and protecting of employees. Previous investments had resulted in a relatively stable, secure, and fairly treated workforce, largely through the use of entitlement-based membership programs extended for continuing employment. But during these ensuing decades, global competition made it necessary to get a greater return on human capital, as work processes were reengineered, hierarchies flattened, and organizations and jobs redesigned.

These competitive pressures required companies to implement new strategies for cost control, total quality management, and customer service. In many instances people were required to become far more flexible and responsive to the demands of customers. In short, people needed to do more than just show up for work on time every day. Among other improvements, they needed to work in teams, own quality and service, solve problems, and reduce cycle time. To accomplish this, companies invested in training, work redesign, and pay redesign. Employers also rewrote the long-standing employment contract, challenging expectations for cradle-to-grave job security and automatic career and salary growth. American companies attempted to share the uncertainties of the marketplace with their employees. The return on this investment was greater employee involvement and commitment and more attention to performance. Though threatening to most members of the workforce, they also achieved a striking level of business risk sharing resulting in ongoing cuts in full-time jobs and the emergence of a contingent workforce—part-timers, temporaries, contractors, and outsourcing partners.

In summary, the types of investments made in human capital have varied significantly based on labor markets and business needs. During the 90-year period managers introduced ways to get more people to come to work, focus on work, work faster, and become more versatile and less dependent. Many companies still struggle with these basic challenges as labor shortages and cost pressures have led to cuts in human capital investments resulting in unacceptably high turnover levels, unscheduled absences, and skill deficiencies. (See Exhibit 42A, the Qualex Case Study, for one company's success story.) In addition to these ongoing workforce issues, companies must now address the increasing demands on people caused by three emerging factors: (1) new, sophisticated technology (2) the increased speed of business, and (3) the expanding role and accountability of each employee.

THE EMERGENCE OF KNOWLEDGE-BASED WORK

From a time when business and industry were dominated by the need for natural resources, through a period when the availability of financial capital often limited market access, business has evolved to the point where knowledge and its application have become the scarcest and most precious of resources. Rather than simply taking care of people's basic needs, or defending them from the adverse treatment of supervisors and inhospitable work environments, or ensuring that people were organized and motivated to care for customers, the need for more and different knowledge and capabilities has once again changed human capital management.

As the book is closed on the last century of work, it is important to understand why this new era is referred to as "knowledge-based." It isn't just that most workers need to operate a computer; it's that they need more information, sooner about a more diverse set of things than ever before, and they need to apply that information in more challenging ways. For the reason that problem solving and decision making are no longer just the domain of managers, more workers need access to data. To resolve customer complaints or inquiries, representatives at truly service-oriented companies are encouraged to avoid transferring callers to multiple desks and are asked to field a wider array of issues before referring them upward.

To ensure that those callers are not put on hold for an extended period, representatives are trained to know where to get and how to use the information they need. They are also skilled at dealing with unhappy customers. These are knowledge worker jobs because they are required to get information, retain it, think about it, and resolve problems with customers, the real asset of the company. And it isn't just service occupations that use more knowledge.

A growing number of operative jobs fit the knowledge worker category. For instance, auto mechanics need to know how to troubleshoot car performance using sophisticated computer testing devices. More often than not, they are replacing microchip modules that control much of the car's functions. Factories require operators to understand precise machine settings and diagnose the need for small adjustments when product quality is not up to increasingly demanding tolerances. Moreover, they are often members of various types of work teams that are expected to set work schedules, order materials, increase production volumes, initiate line changes, and even settle interpersonal problems without involving supervisors who manage work groups of 40 and larger.

Positions that have been traditionally thought of as knowledge worker roles are also being stretched to think differently. Not only do they have new technology to deal with but also they are expected to abandon tried-and-true approaches and embrace new methods, analyses, tools, models, and theories to help their company stay on the competitive edge. In the process, administrative bureaucracy is under increasing attack. Time to review and approve decisions is being sharply reduced. In their offices, marketing specialists, human resources representatives, information technologists, accountants, and engineers are under pressure to do it faster, better, and cheaper.

The requirements of knowledge work and the expanding service economy place far greater importance on the effectiveness of each individual. In fewer and fewer instances are people who perform tasks interchangeable. In some industries the number, quality, and type of machines still makes a big difference. It is now known that the number, quality, and type of *people* can differentiate almost all companies. Unfortunately, compared to machines, human capital is harder to manage and control. Measuring a "fair day's work" is not simply a matter of counting how many units were produced within a certain time period. In fact, the new millennium workforce is often not even expected to work in the same place or at the same time, as telecommuting, flexible work scheduling, job sharing, and part-time employment are gaining prominence.

Organizations need an approach for valuing, measuring, and optimizing investments in people in this fast-paced knowledge era, when human capital needs shift quickly. It is widely known, for instance, that much of the Year 2000 computer programming capability will instantly become outdated once programs are fixed, so what do companies do with all those Y2K skills? Many companies that have adopted a human capital mindset are already preparing to up-skill those who can and want to learn new capabilities, helping to address the service, productivity, and quality issues already felt by a growing shortage of high-tech workers. Yet, investing in people must make economic sense. After all, most companies simply won't need as many programmers once the Y2K problem is solved, and not all Cobol language programmers are going to learn new skills. This decision—how to address skill obsolescence to the economic benefit of the company—is a practical example of a critical human capital management decision.

So how do business leaders know whether investing in human capital will actually pay off? Just as would be expected when investing in any other asset, a financially driven cost-benefit analysis using assumptions and probabilities will help managers make fact-based choices about people. Yet it is rare for companies to conduct such studies on soft assets, presumably because the behavior of people is not predictable and it is difficult to measure. Nevertheless, companies like Kodak's photofinishing-imaging division Qualex are making informed, business-based people decisions using human resource accounting methodologies available to all companies in the public forum (see Exhibit 42B). Additional return-on-investment studies have been conducted on human capital in both the public and private sectors.

THE TANGIBLE RETURN ON HUMAN CAPITAL

In 1992 Gary Becker won a Nobel Prize in economics for his work in the early 1960s evaluating the impacts of human capital on economic growth and development of countries. His thesis was that investments in human capital (not just physical capital), including both formal education and on-the-job training, further the growth and development of economies. Becker proved that investments in schooling and training impact the productivity and earning level of people and that they make rational choices based on the costs and benefits of such investments. Over the past three decades, Becker's work has generated a slate of research on the efficacy of public and private education and training. Some politicians have even begun to address the state government's role in financing life-long learning.

In the private sector, return on human capital studies have reported compelling results. An award-winning study of the effects of people management practices on financial performance conducted by Mark Huselid found that companies that use "high-commitment work practices" have experienced more than an $18,000 increase in stock market value per employee. High-commitment work practices include "a broad range of practices intended to enhance employees' knowledge, skills and abilities and...provide mechanisms through which employees can use those attributes in performing their roles."[2] They also include performance man-

---

[2]Mark A. Huselid, "The Impact of Human Resource Management Practices on Turnover, Productivity, and Corporate Financial Performance," *Academy of Management Journal,* vol. 38, no. 3. June 1995, pp. 635–668.

agement, linking pay with performance, and using performance as the criterion for promotion. A more recent study found even more impressive economic impacts due to high-performance management practices—a boost in shareholder wealth of $41,000 per employee. Research focused on executive talent and conducted in the private sector indicates that those companies with more capable people at the top perform better in their respective market. This landmark study, published in 1998 by Mckinsey & Company and Sibson & Company, discovered that companies in the top quintile of shareholder return report having stronger talent and talent management practices than those in the midquintile (a group of very respectably performing companies). Most significantly, the "War for Talent" study of 77 companies and over 5,700 of their top 200 managers revealed that those companies achieve a 70 percent higher total return to shareholders.

These and other studies of public and private organizations reveal that managing people more effectively can have a positive financial impact. But how do business leaders improve the return on human capital within *their* companies in this new era—the knowledge era—of business?

EFFECTIVE STRATEGIES FOR IMPROVING THE RETURN ON PEOPLE

Optimizing the return on human capital begins with a long-term "people strategy." Such a strategy needs to explicitly acknowledge the fact that employees in the knowledge era need and want access to critical business information, can differentiate the company within its marketplace, and need to be appropriately rewarded for their contribution:

- How will the company attract, retain, and motivate highly talented individuals?

- How well does employee performance support the needs of customers and investors?

- How well are rewards linked to performance?

- How prepared is the workforce to change rapidly with the needs of the business?

Talent Management

The first step to managing successfully in the knowledge era begins with getting people who are smart enough, driven enough, and agile enough to compete in this new, demanding marketplace. Effective talent management enables companies to attract, grow, and retain the right number, type, and quality of people needed to execute a knowledge-based business strategy. There is already a shortage of talent in many occupations, and the supply of talent will shrink even more as the U.S. population ages.

There will be a 12 percent drop in the number of Americans between the ages of 25 and 34 by the year 2005.[3] The number of 35-to 44-year-olds in the United States will decline by 15 percent between the years 2000 and 2015.[4]

Unfortunately, even as labor markets tighten, most companies will grow, and numerous others will be founded, intensifying the competition for talented workers. A preview of this new environment can already be spotted, as the number of service jobs and software design jobs have way outstripped the supply. Partly because of this supply-demand imbalance, most companies accept a lower standard of talent than they would like, limiting their ability to perform and grow. Unfortunately some organizations are not aware of their inventory of talent because information about the capabilities and development needs of people often does not exist, as it routinely does for other business assets. Interestingly, the available talent is increasingly nontraditional—contingent, part-time, contractor, distant, etc.—but too few companies have a strategy or a response to this opportunity. It is not stretching the facts to predict that as talent increasingly becomes scarce, better talent will become *the* competitive weapon.

What do companies who report having better people in the recent McKinsey & Company and Sibson & Company "War for Talent" study do to build a talent bench? First, they create a distinctive value proposition—with their own unique combination of offerings, such as a preeminent company reputation, challenging jobs, and above competitive rewards. Second, they raise talent management to a burning corporate priority—instilling a talent mindset, infusing the right behaviors, and holding line managers accountable. Last, they execute against a "building great talent" aspiration, reached by using robust methods for finding good people, promoting the best people early and often, providing lots of feedback and coaching, learning more about who is leaving and why, and addressing performance issues and paying for contribution.

Traditional formulas for human resource management developed over the last 20 years are ill equipped for this knowledge-era challenge since they were developed in what has generally been a buyer's market for talent and at a time when less was needed and expected from people inside the organization.

Performance Optimization

Having a talented workforce does not ensure that a knowledge-era company will achieve a high return on its human capital. With so much information available and the need to accomplish more than just one goal, successful companies are able to focus the workforce on the critical behaviors, priorities, and results that are needed to win in the market. Human capital investments yield the greatest return when com-

---

[3]U.S. Bureau of the Census, *Statistical Abstract of the US: 1998,* 118th ed. Washington, D.C.: Government Printing Office, 1998, pp. 16, 25.
[4]Elizabeth G. Chambers, et al., "The War for Talent," *The McKinsey Quarterly,* no. 3. 1998.

panies clearly communicate priorities. This can be a complicated challenge to meet when so often companies communicate the impression that they need it all (e.g., lower costs *and* higher quality). Actually, most companies say they need the same things, but the market leaders do two things better: They balance the inherent conflicts between investors and customers, and they prioritize their list of needs. Doing so provides goal clarity to individuals, teams, and business units.

Most for-profit private-sector organizations have done a reasonably good job of impressing on the workforce the need for superior financial returns, as evidenced by the large number of profit-sharing bonus plans and executive incentive plans that are anchored on financial performance goals. But overrelying on financial measures of performance is inadequate, as they are, at best, indicators of historical performance ("rear window") and most knowledge-era companies need real-time ("front windshield") information. A more effective performance optimization model includes both leading and lagging indicators of performance (Figure 42.1). For many companies, feedback from both customers and employees is proving helpful as early warning signals of financial performance. Companies like Sears, Roebuck and Company have found linkages between employee, customer, and investor satisfaction and are now focusing attention on improving the value propositions of employees and customers as a way to improve shareholder return. According to this logic, customers are more likely to be better served by employees who are satisfied themselves.[5]

An effective process for managing investor and customer expectations requires that executives think beyond the much-publicized "truth serums" of the 1980s and early 1990s, such as economic value added (EVA) and the balanced

FIGURE 42.1   Perfromance optimization model. CEOs report that rising customer and shareholder expectations are their top two issues.

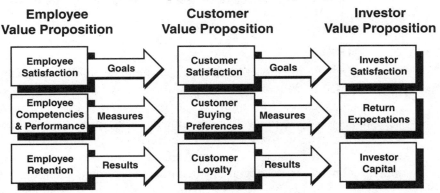

---

[5]"The Employee-Customer-Profit Chain at Sears," *Harvard Business Review,* January–February 1998, pp. 83–97.

scorecard. Knowledge-era workers need timely and effective feedback about how their performance is affecting the whole business, requiring that performance measures be linked vertically and horizontally (no performance silos) and that the traditional individual performance appraisal approach be dismantled.

It has been customary to hold individual employees responsible for meeting objectives that were activity based, making it hard to know how they were connected to the business, especially to customers. These systems have required supervisors to complete lengthy forms and assign ratings summarizing individual contributions. In too many cases honest and open discussions about performance have not taken place, even though all the boxes were checked. These practices have also focused an inordinate amount of energy and time on the "winners" and "losers," meaning those performers who stick out as exemplars or problems, at the exclusion of those who fall in the middle.

The next wave of performance management will focus on the following areas:

- Relating to business results, not just to individual activities

- Standards and observations, not ratings and forms

- Both individual and team contributions

- Holding *employees* accountable for collecting feedback on their own performance and identifying appropriate development actions, placing less burden and reliance on supervisors

- Address the needs of all performers, not just the fortunate or unfortunate few

These improvements are needed to reduce the fear and anxiety that are currently associated with typical performance appraisal systems and to better align individual contributions with the business as a whole. Performance is also more likely to be optimized if it is connected to a set of consequences—both positive and negative—especially rewards.

Linking Rewards to Performance

Companies with the most effective people strategies in the knowledge era strive to build high-commitment and high-performance work cultures that make it easier and more appealing for employees to give their very best. To accomplish this, companies must use innovative and motivating rewards, beyond base pay.

People need to know they count. The return on people is optimized when those employed by the enterprise are viewed as important stakeholders who possess individual needs and expectations that get management attention. It's obvious that shareholders matter; the world's financial markets are driven by changes in shareholder value. In the last two decades the needs of customers have become paramount as core business processes have been redesigned to better serve buyer habits and preferences.

Investing in human capital requires that employers address and align the interests of all stakeholders—customers, investors, and employees.

Work is about the search for daily meaning, as well as daily bread, for recognition as well as cash, for astonishment rather than torpor; in short, for a sort of life rather than a Monday through Friday sort of dying. Perhaps immortality, too, is part of the quest (Studs Terkel, *Working,* 1974).

Those who are both owners and employees of the organization are known to have a stronger commitment and interest in its success. Research sponsored by the National Center for Employee Ownership indicates that broad-based employee ownership can have a very positive effect on a company's bottom line. In their study of 45 companies with stock ownership plans (ESOPs) and 225 non-ESOP companies, they found that companies who combined an ESOP program with a participative management style grew 8 to 10 percent per year faster than they did prior to the establishment of such approaches.[6] These companies created a culture in which employees were trained and motivated to think as owners. It is understandably easier for chief executive officers to think as owners do, but results are also noticeably better for shareholders when stock is a significant portion of their total compensation package. Numerous studies have shown that executive equity ownership programs create meaningful gains in shareholder value, including one in 1996 that reported that when top management has above average-stock ownership, there is a 6-point improvement in shareholder return compared to below-median ownership (21 versus 15 percent).[7]

In the knowledge era, companies need to reward people effectively to ensure that customers and shareholders are well served. They can't just be paid for their time. Nor can they be rewarded using only money, as people work for a variety of reasons and cannot be motivated using a one-size-fits-all approach to rewards. Motivation research tells us that people are more willing to exert effort if performance goals are perceived as high, but achievable, and they value the rewards for goal accomplishment. In the knowledge era the employee value proposition includes both financial and nonfinancial rewards for work (Figure 42.2). For example, professionals place great value on career growth and development opportunities. "Direct financial," "indirect financial," "work content," "career opportunity," and "affiliation" are the basic elements of the knowledge era's rewards for work.

Balancing rewards among these five elements is both the challenge and the idea. For example, a company can hardly support the need for team performance without checking to ensure that the direct financial rewards are not overemphasizing individual performance. Valuing a (nonmanagement) technical career path

---

[6]The National Center for Employee Ownership, *The Stock Options Book* (Oakland, Calif., August 1977.)

[7]Ira T. Kay, 1988. *CEO Pay and Shareholder Value: Helping the U.S. Win the Global Economic War* (St. Lucie Press: Boston).

FIGURE 42.2 Employee value proposition model.

27th Annual Industry Week Magazine CEO Survey, 1998.

within a compensation structure that values only promotions into management is conflicting.

To meet customer and investor demands, employee behaviors and results must be aligned and rewarded appropriately. Financial and nonfinancial rewards are powerful signaling devices to people who are inundated with information and messages (sometimes mixed) about what is important.

Change Management

To stay ahead of competitors in the knowledge era, organizations must be responsive to market forces and be able to change quickly, even before it becomes necessary. It's not enough for company executives to change business strategy. Management needs to mobilize the workforce to implement changes, even when the transition is difficult for people. Executing large-scale changes to business strategy with a workforce that is involved and supportive differentiates companies that can see the future equally well.

Technological, legal, social, and economic pressures have forced organizations to undergo unparalleled change in this current era. Unfortunately, it is not uncommon for business leaders to turn around in the midst of change and find precious few followers. Too often people are hunkered down, fearful of losing that which they have worked so hard to earn—their job, title, status, and so on. Resistance to change can be overcome by acknowledging not just the business rationale for change but also the hopes, fears, and dreams of those affected.

Yet in the race to make change happen, companies frequently overlook the real costs of a poorly planned and managed change effort. Organizational leaders often fail to recognize the explicit and implicit cultural barriers that can impede change—or they simply neglect to tell the complete story to people, who then fill the void with their own script. The more progressive companies go to great lengths to involve people in a transformation that affects them, which sends critical messages about validation and involvement. As business leaders have learned, many the hard way, building trust and managing fear are the two most important needs when directing people through a time of change.

For change to succeed, leaders must take the following steps:

- Openly *communicate* the intent and extent of the changes.

- Actively *role model* and encourage the kinds of behaviors needed to implement the new business strategy—such as flexibility, teamwork, collaboration, and clear decision making.

- Accurately *measure* for the new outcomes and results desired.

- Generously *reward and recognize* those who achieve the desired outcomes and results.

Formula for Large-Scale Change Management

Large-scale change=f[communicating+role modeling+measuring+rewarding]

This approach will ensure that people know that the change is for real and define for them what "success" looks like in the new culture.

Maximizing Human Capital

Managing people has become a high-stakes game. In the Old World of work, when employees quit, companies lost a pair of arms and legs. When people leave organizations today, many walk out with valuable knowledge and information—about business processes, customers, competitive strategies, and research projects. Almost as destructive to a company are offices full of nonperforming assets—people who are either not able or not willing to contribute their value to customers or investors. Those who leave create space. Those who stay but aren't contributing take up space. In both cases human capital is suboptimized.

To succeed in the knowledge era, companies cannot simply rely on whiz-bang technology. They must develop people strategies that address the need for attracting top talent, focusing that talent on the right things, rewarding people for results, and creating a high tolerance of and acceptance for organizational change.

BIBLIOGRAPHY

Branch, Shelly. 1999. "100 Best Companies to Work For." *Fortune,* vol. 139, no. 1, January 11, pp. 118–144.

Chambers, Elizabeth G., et al. 1998. "The War for Talent." *The McKinsey Quarterly,* no. 3.

Huselid, Mark A. 1995. "The Impact of Human Resource Management Practices on Turnover, Productivity, and Corporate Financial Performance." *Academy of Management Journal,* vol. 38, no. 3, June, pp. 635–668.

Kay, Ira T. 1998. *CEO Pay and Shareholder Value: Helping the U.S. Win the Global Economic War.* St. Lucie Press: Boston.

Kochanski, James T., and Donald H. Ruse. 1996. "Designing a Competency-Based Human Resources Organization." *Human Resource Management,* vol. 35, no. 1, spring, pp. 19–33.

National Center for Employee Ownership. *The Stock Options Book.* August 1997, Oakland, Calif.

Nelson, Daniel. 1975. *Managers and Workers.* University of Wisconsin Press, Madison.

Leblanc, Peter V., and David C. Leonard, Ph.D. 1999. "Burying the Cost Plus Mentality—The Qualex Story," *Perspectives,* Sibson and Company, vol. ix, no. 1.

Rucci, Anthony J., Steven P. Kirn, and Richard T. Quinn. 1998. "The Employee-Customer-Profit Chain at Sears." *Harvard Business Review,* January–February.

Stevens, Tim. 1998. "Chief Among Us: 27th Annual CEO Survey." *Industry Week,* vol. 247, no. 21, November 16, pp. 24–64.

Stewart, Thomas A. 1997. *Intellectual Capital: The New Wealth of Organizations.* New York: Doubleday.

Terkel, Studs. 1974. *Working.* New York: New Press. Reprinted 1997.

U.S. Bureau of the Census. 1998. *Statistical Abstract of the US: 1998,* 118th ed. Washington, D.C.: Government Printing Office.

QUALEX CASE STUDY: BURYING THE "COST-PLUS" MENTALITY

Peter V. LeBlanc
David C. Leonard, Ph.D.

Measuring a company's return on human capital begins by treating the dollars invested in recruiting, developing, motivating, and retaining employees like investments in capital equipment and plant expansion—that they should have an expected return. Two questions must be addressed: "How much will be invested?" and "What is the expected payback?" Qualex, Inc., the overnight-photofinishing division of Eastman Kodak, abandoned the "cost-plus" approach to increasing employee pay in 1997, which had resulted in pay being managed like most other operating expenses—to the lowest possible increase. Instead, they looked at employee compensation as an investment in plant performance improvement by finding a quasi-casual relationship between pay levels, turnover and absenteeism and productivity, and quality and overtime.

Historically Qualex had followed a traditional compensation philosophy investing incrementally in compensation—4 percent one year, 5 percent the next, to match market movements. While these base wage increase costs had exceeded $7 million per year, they had yielded no payback. These cost-of-labor adjustments, not targeted specifically to any operating needs, had little impact on operational performance. Neither were they enough to stem the rash of unscheduled absences and voluntary terminations in their processing workforce that occurred in greatest numbers during the busiest production periods.

To identify opportunities for improved operational performance, Qualex examined its key people leverage points, or the places in the organization where individual employees or groups of employees had the greatest impact on operating costs and business results. These included steps in the production and service delivery process that were especially susceptible to losses in productivity and/or errors, as well as particular labs, and jobs that experienced especially high turnover or absenteeism. Understanding its key people leverage points allowed the organization to estimate the potential cost savings available from operational improvements in its process and served to build an ROI-focused business case for significant investments in compensation. After this analysis the company concluded that spending $7 million and getting no return did not look like a smart idea when compared with strategically spending $17 million and potentially gaining as much as a $14 million return, resulting in relative net savings of $4 million per year.

Qualex decided that reducing turnover and absenteeism during their critical high volume production period—summer vacation season—represented a key people leverage point and a promising investment opportunity. And with a supportable estimate of the returns to the business available from a more dependable workforce, the company's leadership was able to build an economic case for the sizeable investment of compensation dollars to improve overall business results.

Innovative attendance and retention incentives were designed for Qualex, resulting in significant reductions in turnover and absences. Across-the-board increases to base pay were also awarded to bring employee total pay closer to market average. But what did this buy the organization? After two high-volume (summer) seasons, the company reported substantially fewer work hours per unit produced, fewer errors, lower operating expenses, and significant cost savings. Additionally, an analysis of staffing, payroll, and production data indicated that the cost of turnover for this company averaged between $8,300 and $11,400 per "turn." Absences were conservatively costed at $200 per day. Based on these figures, it was determined that overall productivity, quality, and overtime savings from the plan would exceed $20 million. In total, it was estimated that Qualex's incremental compensation investment would entirely pay for itself within 1 year and that future returns would go straight to the bottom line.

Qualex's bold decision to more than double their investments in annual total compensation increases had a positive impact on both people and the business. They discovered that higher total pay increased employee commitment and loyalty, which improved operational productivity and quality—a compelling human capital business case.

ACCOUNTING FOR HUMAN CAPITAL

David C. Leonard, Ph.D.

For many, placing a value on human capital has led to a focus on intellectual-knowledge capital, or the value of what an individual or group knows—a tricky undertaking at best. On a more practical level, it can be just as helpful and somewhat less difficult to price human capital by using common measures found in human resource accounting. Using this approach, the value of human capital is determined by calculating the value, or cost, of individuals' behaviors and activities in the organization.

The Saratoga Institute, and other employer organizations, regularly publish standards for human resource accounting. A *sample* of these metrics include:

- The human resource investment factor equals the human resource management (HRM) expense divided by the number of full-time-equivalent employees (part-time workers treated as less than one full-time employee).

- The benefit cost per employee equals the total benefits costs divided by the number of employees.

- The cost per trainee equals the training expense divided by the number of trainees.

- The turnover rate equals the percentage of employees terminating during a particular time period.

- The turnover cost equals the training costs plus recruiting costs plus lost-productivity costs pus lower-quality costs plus the cost for temporary workers, and so on.

- The absence cost equals the lost-productivity costs plus the lower-quality costs plus the cost for temporary workers plus the cost for additional supervisory time, and so on.

These metrics are useful for comparing organizations in similar industries or regions, for evaluating an organization's effectiveness in recruiting, training, developing, and retaining human capital (e.g., through a year-over-year trend analysis), and for calculating the value of an organization's human capital. For example, the quality of new human capital can be assessed using the following formula:

Quality per hire = (average job performance rating for new hires + percentage of new hires promoted within 1 year + percentage of new hires retained after 1 year)/3

Similarly, the cost to hire each new employee can be calculated using another formula:

Cost per hire = (cost of ads + agent fees + referrals and/or signing bonuses + travel expenses + relocation cost + value of recruiting staff's time)/number of new hires

The quality of new employees and the cost of hiring them can be used to create a cost-benefit ratio with which an organization can evaluate its effectiveness across time in recruiting talent.

"Softer" aspects of human capital like "employee commitment" can also be valued using these metrics. If commitment for hourly personnel is defined as being at work every day on time and remaining with the organization for a minimum of 5 years, then the value of employee commitment can be calculated by adding the cost of turnover (e.g., recruiting, training, and lost-productivity costs) and absenteeism-punctuality (e.g., lost-productivity costs). This value can then be multiplied by the number of employees with at least 5 years' tenure to obtain a value for human capital.

The actual metrics included in a calculation of human capital value will vary based upon an organization's business strategy, competitive environment, and available human resource measures. For an example of one company's success in determining the value (and ROI) of their human capital, see "Burying the Cost Plus Mentality."

43

THE ROLE OF WORK-LIFE BENEFITS IN THE TOTAL PAY STRATEGY

James F. Kisela, Chief Executive Officer

Work-Life Productions, Inc.

THE IMPORTANCE OF THE TOTAL PAY STRATGY

A feast is made for laughter, and wine maketh merry: but money answereth all things.
Ecclesiastes (10:19): The Old Testament

How organizations pay employees for the services rendered by those employees is a crucial variable in the management process. Just as marketing strategy and financing strategies are important, equally as important is the human resource, or people, strategy. Within the human resources strategy, pay is the foundation upon which everything else is built. Poorly conceived and executed, all the other strategies are negated and undermined.

The total pay strategy is made up of two major segments: direct and indirect pay.

Direct Pay

Direct pay is made up of immediate forms of payment (wages and salary) and contingent types (performance-based incentives, unit-based profit sharing, etc.).

The responsibility of the employer is to be legal, competitive, fair, and fiscally responsible to meet its obligations to employees, owners, creditors, and society.

Indirect Pay

Indirect pay, usually called *benefits,* is divided into government mandated, across the board, and targeted plans.

A benefit, by definition, is not a payment in money to the employee but a payment to a third party for some goods or services on behalf of employees

Impact of Direct Pay

Direct compensation has a visceral immediacy that for better or worse is its most notable feature, especially in regard to performance-based plans,[1] whereas a benefit has a more intermittent and somewhat more distant impact for most of the participants.

Part of this impact comes from the relative size, with direct pay typically about 70 percent of the total.[2] Adding to the impact is the regular nature of the pay process, which gives it a concreteness that is reinforced on a weekly or monthly basis.

Benefits, on the other hand, are a smaller percentage of the total, and their use is very much less frequent. Out of sight, out of mind, is the main characteristic unless very aggressively addressed through active and highly visible communications programs.

Another dimension of the impact of various forms of pay has to do with flexibility. All forms of compensation can be put on a continuum of flexibility ranging from currency (money), which is very flexible, to benefits, which are relatively inflexible, all the way to bartering (very unusual in today's industrial economy), which is the least flexible of all.

In an agricultural economy the worker in the field would probably be paid in grain, the very thing they helped produce. But in today's manufacturing world, the

---

[1] For a recent review of performance-based compensation, see "Pros & Cons of Pay for Performance" by Scott Hays in the February 1999 *Workforce* magazine. Of particular interest is the discussion of the downside of performance-based compensation. Hays quotes Alfie Kohn, author of *Punished by Rewards* (Houghton Mifflin, 1993) who has been an advocate for this challenge to traditional thinking for almost 10 years.

[2] Direct pay versus indirect pay has decreased in this century from almost 100 percent to the range of 60 to 75 percent that we see today.

widget factory workers do not want to be paid in widgets, they want money. Furthermore, they need money because, to paraphrase a popular commercial, their landlord doesn't take widgets or credit cards for the rent; she takes only money.

People also prefer money for payment because it has almost unlimited usefulness to be traded for whatever they want.

It is only when they get "enough" (believe it or nor, people do seem to have enough at some point[3]) that they start to give value to payments made in any form other than money. Psychologists such as Maslow have suggested that people move toward fulfilling needs along a continuum starting with the basics and then working up to the more intellectual and emotionally satisfying.

What we see in organizations today seems to fit that pattern. People look to see if their pay is competitive for the work they do compared to others in the world around them, then they look to fairness in the distribution of pay within their organization. For most people there seems to be a level at which when competitiveness and fairness are satisfactory and each additional dollar of payment has a reduced ability to provide commensurate additional value, implying that dramatically high increases in pay are required to get people's attention in that situation.

Few organizations have the financial capacity to provide pay in these much larger amounts, particularly if the form of pay permanently increases overhead for the future. From an overall business perspective the organization should not commit to this type of overpayment in relation to the market.

This sets the stage for the introduction of contingent pay systems that pay out (1) only when overall business results support the amount of cash required, and (2) then measure and pay out proportionately to the individual on the job for his or her contributions that created the results. But even here most organizations have a limit to the amount of money they create in any given year on a sustained basis.

Impact of Indirect Pay (Benefits)

Benefits have little attractiveness or motivational power until the underlying direct pay reaches competitive levels. When underlying direct pay levels are above average, benefits gain potential competitive advantage to differentiate one organization from another.

Employees whose total direct income is below average (as they themselves perceive it) will change for relatively small increases in direct pay, regardless of benefit levels—unless the benefit levels are extraordinarily high and perceived as immediately useful.

Since virtually every organization has the standard government-mandated benefits, and most organizations of over 100 employees have medical and retirement

---

[3]"Enough" may mean that people realize that they cannot reasonably expect very much more for the job they are doing.

benefits as well, it is the benefits that most organizations do not have that become the differentiating factor.

Work-life benefits are still available to substantially fewer than half of American workers, and, in most of the situations in which they are present, they are superficial and apply to only select groups of employees.

This uniqueness provides a major positive value for work-life benefits. Combined with strong management commitment and support, a well-communicated and comprehensive array of work-life benefits as part of a better-than-average indirect and direct pay package results in an employer that will be the employer of choice in their area and industry. These are the organizations that make the lists of best companies to work for in publications such as *Fortune* and *Working Mother* magazines.

HOW WORK-LIFE BENEFITS FIT IN THE TOTAL PAY STRATEGY

...I guess Rosebud is just a piece in a jigsaw puzzle, a missing piece.
Orson Welles, Citizen Kane

There is an overwhelming consensus among the academics[4] and consultants[5] who have studied the impact of work-life benefits that these initiatives have a substantial positive impact on the organization. This is in addition to the value as a differentiator in the total pay package. It turns out that work-life benefits are also good for the bottom line. The areas in which they have the most positive impact include:

- Recruiting

- Retention

- Productivity

- Morale

- Motivation

- Satisfaction

---

[4] See *Work-Family Research: An Annotated Bibliography*, compiled by Teri Ann Lilly, Marcie Pitt-Catsouphes, and Bradley K. Googins (Westport, Conn.: Greenwood Press, 1997). Prepared under the auspices of the Center for Work & Family at Boston College, The Wallace E. Carroll School of Management. This comprehensive annotated bibliography contains 934 entries describing articles, research studies, and books.

[5] Studies by consultants usually relate the successful programs of specific companies and then draw generalized conclusions. A few of the better-known consultant's studies are the following:

a. Dana E. Friedman, Linking Work-Family issues to the Bottom Line, Report no. 962 (New York: The Conference Board, 1991).

b. Ellen Galinsky, *Child Care and Productivity,* prepared for the Child Care Action Campaign, March 1988 (New York: Bank Street College).

c. The Conference Board, *Redefining the Business Case* (New York: The Conference Board, 1993).

- Loyalty
- Commitment
- Absenteeism
- Stress reduction
- Openness to change

These are clearly financial and operational drivers of significant impact on the organization.

Beyond Direct Pay

But doesn't direct pay do the same things? And if so, why bother with the administrative overhead of creating and administering work-life benefits?

The answer seems to be that once a certain high level of direct pay is reached, and this seems to be a somewhat different absolute level for different people in different occupations, direct pay seems to lose its ability to motivate people in the same way that it did at lower absolute levels.

In top-paying organizations, employees express their desire to achieve career growth, professional advancement, work-life balance, personal involvement with their job, more understanding in their supervision of them as individuals, more training opportunities, and so on. More pay, or a feeling that pay is important, ranks low in the employees' perception of what is of value to them.

Practically speaking, this means that it takes more and more incremental cash to motivate people, all other things being equal when relative pay levels are high. People's expectations change over time, and as long as they are earning above the going rate for their job, they begin to believe that what they are paid is the correct amount for what they are producing even if their pay is above the market rate by a substantial amount.

Strategically, it is important to maintain pay levels that are competitive and if warranted, some percentage over the competition, but not out of control. Pay levels tend to be flexible upward, but sticky downward. We have seen the organization that has found itself in trouble by overpaying and then being unable to easily adjust to new market forces.

Leverage of Work-Life Benefits

It is at this point that work-life benefits take on an important role. These benefits have the characteristic of being highly valued by employees in today's tight labor market, they are relatively inexpensive to provide, and they can be modified more easily than direct pay. We call this being *highly leveraged.*

A highly leveraged benefit is one that is important to the employees and has a perception of high value relative to the actual cost of providing it.

A benefit can achieve this status in the mind of employees in a number of ways. One time-honored tradition is to use the economies of scale the employer has in its favor to buy goods or services on behalf of the employees more cheaply than they could on their own. Group medical benefits are the classic case in point.

The clear fact is that medical benefits for which a typical employee pays say $100 a month would usually cost four to five times as much on an individual basis. This is a shocking realization to employees who tend to be blasé about it when employers try to communicate it during the work year, but it hits them hard if they leave the company and have to provide them on their own.

Another response is to provide employees more control over the use of their time. Technology makes possible flexible work patterns today that were unthinkable 20 years ago. Telework, telecommuting, and flexible work schedules let the employer and the employee work together to develop an approach that shifts the time and place of work. This appeals to younger employees who have come to expect more control over their lives, as well as to those who need the flexibility to balance the demands of family and job.

DEFINING WORK-LIFE BENEFITS

Life is what happens to you while you're busy making other plans.
John Lennon, Beautiful Boy (Darling Boy)

Work-Life benefits have evolved as a topic of interest since the mid-1980s as an awareness of, and concern for, the impact of work on people's lives has become a major bottom-line business issue.

Of particular concern is the degree to which employees and employers can work together to enhance the balance between the frequently conflicting demands of job and family with what are called *work-life benefits*. These benefits are usually a part of a larger initiative that includes policies, programs, practices, and cultural changes to facilitate the balance between work demands and family needs. Effectively implemented, these benefits provide bottom-line gains to the employer and improve the quality of life for the employee.

A driving factor in the evolution of work-life benefits into the important role they play today is the movement of women, especially mothers, into the workforce. In 1900 women made up 18 percent of the workforce, but by 1997 that had risen to 46 percent and is still increasing. This has put a strain on family relations and has led to a complete rethinking of the male and female roles vis-à-vis such fundamental family duties as creating family income, child rearing, and time management.

It is no wonder that the issue raised in this changing workplace was from women about problems with child care. Subsequently, there are more programs relating to child care than any other work-life issue today. In fact, the entire topic was labeled "work-family" for a time. But as other issues, such as elder care (driven by the demographics of the baby-boomer generation), increased time off, and job flexibility as to time and place have been raised, we are seeing them be addressed, and the field now being known as work-*life* instead of work-*family* reflects a much broader perspective.

Examples of work-life benefits include:

1. Child care
   a. Flexible spending accounts (*dependent care assistance plans,* or DCAPs)
   b. Resource and referral (with or without counseling)
   c. Backup child care
   d. Near-site daycare
   e. On-site daycare
   f. After-school care
   g. Prenatal care program
   h. Lactation programs (mothers' rooms)
   i. Emergency care
   j. Sick child care
   k. Summer child care
   l. Holiday child care
   m. Employer consortiums to improve child care
   n. Discounts on child care services
   o. Company-negotiated discounts for daycare
   p. Odd-hour child care
   q. Intergenerational care

2. Paid time off
   a. Paid-time-off bank (sick days, vacation, and holidays combined into one account for any type of time off)
   b. Extended Family Medical Leave Act time

3. Family services
   a. Brown bag lunch seminars on family topics
   b. Multimedia family resource center
   c. Employee assistance program
   d. Financial counseling
   e. Work-life fairs (suppliers of services give information)

4. Flexible work arrangements
   a. Telework
   b. Telecommuting
   c. Virtual offices
   d. Hoteling
   e. Flex-time
   f. Part-time

5. Elder care
   a. Resource and referral services (with or without counseling)
   b. Long-term-care insurance
   c. Intergenerational care
6. Convenience or concierge services

   a. Dry cleaning
   b. Company convenience store
   c. Travel services
   d. Vehicle cleaning and servicing
   e. Entertainment information and ticket sales
   f. Discounts on convenience services
   g. Discount buying clubs
   h. "Grab-and-go" dinner and snack food

Organizations usually have some combination of these programs developed for the specific needs of their employees.

WHO SHOULD CONSIDER WORK-LIFE BENEFITS

Progress…is not an accident, but a necessity….
Herbert Spencer, Social Statistics

Employers Who Want to Be Recognized As the Employer of Choice

An organization that wants as a part of its business strategy to be recognized as the employer of choice in their area or industry may be motivated by human resource issues, public relations advantages, and social or political needs.

Employers Who Have Recruitment Needs

Work-life benefits are particularly effective in recruiting and retaining professional employees, so they have a special role in a tight labor market.

In the late 1990s we have the equivalent of full-employment economy; in fact, in many categories such as computer technology we have a deficit: More jobs are open than there are qualified people to fill them. As it turns out, the jobs that are viewed as key to future business are the ones that are in short supply, and this is a trend that cuts across all industries because of the ubiquitous use of computers in our information infrastructure.

This has fueled a need for highly trained people for both sides of the equation, the computer software and manufacturing industry as well as the organizations that use computers for their information infrastructure.

Add to this widespread trend the explosive growth of the Internet, which has attracted many of the most creative and entrepreneurial information technology professionals from all other segments and you have the making of a serious short-fall of talent.

Direct pay has a limited ability to motivate in this situation. Absolute pay levels have risen to the point where organizations simply cannot, and should not, allocate the magnitude of cash necessary to provide incremental motivation through pay itself. Those that are able to use stock options use them as the way to fill this gap, but many organizations cannot use options for one reason or another, while some individuals do not want to take that much risk in their pay package.

Work-life benefits have been very effective in these situations, particularly when combined with programs such as career development, extensive professional training, mentoring, and formal recognition.

Employers Who Are Cultivating Positive PR with Some Constituency

An organization that has some constituency, external or internal, that would respond to a major public relations effort has an opportunity to use work-life benefits for this purpose. Showing a sensitivity to the needs of certain demographic groups that are part of an organization's marketing efforts can be productive internally and externally.

Employers Who Want to Make a Social or Political Statement

In some cases an organization wants to make a social statement through the implementation of work-life benefits that are significantly better than average to set an example and to be seen as a leader in humanistic management practices. Sometimes this combines with a political motivation to be seen in a positive light for reasons of influence of governmental or industry groups, especially regulatory bodies.

IMPLEMENTING WORK-LIFE BENEFITS

What we've got here is a failure to communicate.
Donn Pearce, Cool Hand Luke

Plan

An organization should choose programs that will maximize the positive impact on its employee population. This starts with an audit of what programs are currently in place, followed by detailed surveys to determine the perception of the current programs and any specific needs and wants that are not being addressed. Senior management needs to avoid thinking that it knows what is "good" for the employees. They need to get the actual data and information on the real, down-to-earth wants and needs of their employees.

Remember that there is some level of cost involved to implement all of these work-life programs and to communicate about them, and to administer them effectively. Offsetting these costs are the paybacks to the bottom line from having these programs: improved recruiting and retention, higher morale, increased productivity, and lower absenteeism.

Survey

Find out what the employees really think and feel about their jobs, pay levels, benefits, and so on through a combination of focus groups and comprehensive surveys with all employees. Setting the employees' expectations in advance is important so that they don't think that everything will change overnight. You may want to point out that perhaps nothing will change; it all depends on what is discovered.

Surveying is best done as a coordinated long-term program to create data that can be tracked over time to detect trends and changes. But even as a single event, this is important to do thoroughly.

Comparing the results of the focus groups and surveys to norms from outside databases is an excellent way to understand the results from a more objective perspective as well.

Communicate

Communicate the results in detail to the employees with management's interpretations and an action plan of what happens next and who will being doing it. The best feedback to employees is the most open and honest. If nothing is going to happen in some aspect of what was surveyed, come out and say that directly. The credibility of the outcomes depends on the employees' judgment about how management handles the feedback and followup to the survey.

Followup

Rigorous followup by management at all levels becomes the key dimension to whether employees see this process as having credibility or not. Lack of credibility breeds cynicism and lowered morale. Without effective followup, the entire effort can fail

Communicate Continually

Tell employees what is happening. Keep them informed of the good, the bad, and everything in between. You cannot communicate too much or too often.

Ongoing Monitoring

The employer needs to stay alert to changes in the pattern of needs and wants in the workforce through frequent surveys, focus groups, and other sensing techniques. Rapid response to the changes is important to stay ahead of the curve of the constantly changing employee perspective.

It is important to avoid employees' taking compensation, in any form, for granted. The programs should be weighted in favor of variable systems that can either automatically or by management decision adjust to business circumstances. The automatic adjustment is better, and systems that affect everyone are better than systems that target specific employees, particularly nonmanagerial employees.

Working against the employer at all times is human nature's way of taking things for granted after a while, which leads to a cycle of periodic changes in, or the addition of new, programs with each change leading to a higher cost threshold. These programs tend to become viewed as entitlements over time, leaving reductions in benefit levels up to draconian measures at some time in the future.

Next Steps

Consider starting the process again in a year and repeating the survey. The most successful companies commit to this annual cycle as a way of life, and it is a fundamental element in their culture.

THE FUTURE OF WORK-LIFE BENEFITS

It's been a long time coming
But I know a change is going to come.
Sam Cooke, A Change is Going to Come

Work-life benefits have an important part to play in the total pay strategy. Consequently, there will be new benefits and myriad variations on current benefits developed in the future. Some trends are already evident.

Flexible Work

Flexible work arrangements, especially telecommuting and telework in general, will continue to expand. Rapid improvements in technology will support this trend, and the only barrier will continue to be the resistance of middle- and front-line management. These management groups have been uncomfortable with telework since the early experiments. The single most important reason for failures has been an inability to manage the employees effectively. Supervisory and management skills need to be upgraded to levels rarely reached before to cope with the type of flexibility as to place and time of work that is now coming into organizations.

Life Cycle

One trend that has started already is the consideration of all employees for some type of work-life benefit, not just those with families and young children. There are many single people, married couples without children, and married couples whose children have grown who are motivated by benefits that could help them better cope with the demands of the job versus their personal life—things like interest groups sponsored by the organization, discounts on recreational activities, long-term-care insurance, retirement planning, singles clubs, and activities.

Government Influence

There will be increased governmental activity in the work-life field. On the legislative side, it is clear that the Family Medical Leave Act will be expanded. It will provide longer time off and cover more employers. Long-term-care insurance will be encouraged through tax incentives to both employers and employees.

The government as an employer will take a higher-level profile in providing work-life benefits for government employees because it does not have the direct pay alternatives the private sector has to attract, motivate, and retain employees with the skills it needs. This role model will then be used by private-sector employees as leverage in their negotiations with their employers.

Labor Markets

The overall labor market will move from high employment to low employment and back again—we just don't know when or by what degree. What we do know is that change will happen quickly, and these rapid changes will create new shortages of trained employees that will have to be addressed by industry. Work-life benefits have the proven ability to appeal across all labor markets to attract, motivate, and retain employees. The organization positioned to respond to labor market changes should have work-life benefits as an integral part of its total pay strategy.

Unions

Unions are starting to take an interest in work-life.[6] Increasingly, their membership is interested in obtaining these new benefits and asking that they be negotiated. Also, as more women and college students enter the union hierarchy, there is a greater sensitivity to these issues. This will continue to grow as a trend, as unions begin to set an example with work-life initiatives for their own employees.

Child Care

More discounts will be negotiated on behalf of employees as employers agree to collect fees for outside child care vendors from employees and remit them regularly to the vendors, which will dramatically reduce collection costs for the vendors.

On- or near-site elementary and high schools, connected with charter schools sponsored by employer consortiums, will be developed in response to employees' concerns about the public school system.

---

[6]Labor Project for Working Families, Labor News for Working Families (Berkeley, Calif.: Institute for Industrial Relations, UC Berkeley, published quarterly). This newsletter reviews work-life programs involving unions around the country

Elder Care

Intergenerational care combining child care and elder care will develop as a standard practice as professional caregivers learn how to manage the economies of scale in these combined centers.

Discounts for elder care will be negotiated with vendors by individual companies or consortiums, with payment made directly to the vendor with the employer responsible for deducting the payment from the employee's pay.

Concierge Services

Traveling barbers and hairstylists will be available to visit employees at their workplace, wherever that may be.

Entire meals will be ordered from a menu that is serviced from a central commissary and delivered ready to eat at the employees' homes.

Additional Services

Additional services will be limited only by the creativity of organizations searching for a competitive edge in recruiting, retaining, and motivating the best professionals available.

SUMMARY

What we call the beginning is often the end
And to make an end is to make a beginning.
The end is where we start from.
T.S. Eliot, Little Gidding

Ultimately the role of work-life benefits is in tight labor markets or other situations in which the business strategy calls for an organization to be the employer of choice and be perceived as having a total pay strategy that is significantly above average, without actually loading up the package with cash payments that are not sustainable in the future. The work-life initiatives as noncash programs are highly leveraged in their ratio of perceived value to actual cash invested.

There is every reason to plan for the continued use of work-life benefits as long as the current economic boom continues or as long as there are labor market shortages for specific skill sets.

For the organization that has adopted as their total compensation strategy the concept of being the employer of choice or that is struggling to attract and retain scarce talent, it will be important to stay on the cutting edge of new and more attractive work-life benefits that are being developed.

WORKS CITED

The Conference Board. 1993. *Redefining the Business Case*. New York: The Conference Board.

Friedman, Dana E. 1991. *Linking Work-Family Issues to the Bottom Line,* Report No. 962. New York: The Conference Board.

Galinsky, Ellen. 1988. *Child Care and Productivity.* Prepared for the Child Care Action Campaign, March 1988. New York: Bank Street College.

Hays, Scott. 1999. "Pros & Cons of Pay for Performance." *Workforce,* February, pp. 69–72.

Heilboner, Robert. 1996. *Teachings from the Worldly Philosophy.* New York: Norton.

Labor Project for Working Families. *Labor News for Working Families,* vol. vi, Fall 1998, Berkeley, Calif.: Institute for Industrial Relations, UC Berkeley (published quarterly).

Lilly, Teri Ann, Marcie Pitt-Catsouphes, and Bradley K. Googins, compilers. 1997. *Work-Family Research: An Annotated Bibliography.* Westport, Conn.: Greenwood Press.

Zedeck, Sheldon, ed. 1992. *Work, Families, and Organizations.* San Francisco: Jossey-Bass.

International Compensation

44

ESTABLISHING GLOBAL COMPENSATION STRATEGIES

Sydney R. Robertson, Executive Vice President

Organization Resources Counselors, Inc.

S A COMPANY EVOLVES IN ITS BUSINESS from an orientation within one or more national boundaries to actually doing business across national boundaries, there is a quantum difference in human resources strategy and consequently a major impact on compensation strategy. Compensation strategy for most international firms has simply been "how do we send people overseas and how do we pay them." This represents a point-to-point compensation design strategy. As a company becomes more global and its business truly transcends international boundaries, it can no longer have the character of one national company. Therefore, it must develop a three-tier approach to compensation. The three tiers are global compensation strategy, strategy for paying people working outside their home countries, and local national compensation. Most companies have the latter two; truly global companies must deal with the first.

When developing compensation strategies, there are key elements that must be considered by the global company:

1.   The confines of its home country perspective must be avoided.
2.   Compensation strategies have to be aligned with and driven by the business strategy.
3.   Compensation must be aligned with all other human resources processes.
4.   The role of human capital must be understood.

RECOGNIZING AND DEALING WITH THE CULTURAL DOMINANCE OF HEADQUARTERS

A number of observers who have analyzed the merger of large companies have cited headquarters' cultural dominance as the biggest impediment to integrating and developing a global enterprise. Global companies at an early stage of evolution have to wrestle with this dilemma. The home or headquarters country is the "backdrop" for presumptions about the design of key business processes such as compensation programs. The company headquarters dominates the business philosophy about the way things are done. There are a number of unstated assumptions about how people relate to each other, how compensation systems are designed, how performance is evaluated, how decisions are made, and how organizations are managed that tend to be exported overseas. This is one of the greatest dangers in becoming a global company.

BALANCING GLOBAL AND LOCAL CONSIDERATIONS

Most companies start out in one country serving one national local market and evolve through a series of stages. The first stage is usually an examination of the feasibility of delivering products or services to another country. This initially may mean opening marketing, sales, or representational offices and then may evolve to exporting product into one or more offshore countries. As the volume of commerce increases, the necessity of moving key staff capability outside the home country arises, and the issue of how to pay these people appears. Generally, the issue of paying people leads to examining a balance-sheet style of compensation.

At this stage of globalization, someone is sent to set up processes and make sure things are started properly according to home country standards. Typically after a 2- or 3-year alignment, this out-and-back person returns to the home country.

What perspective should be used to balance global and local considerations? The answer starts with a quote by Percy Barnevik, former CEO of ABB: "Think global, act local." As the organization evolves and business is conducted in multiple settings, business solutions become increasingly complex. Eventually the enterprise reaches the point where it has some businesses that are truly international and some businesses that are local and regional requiring sensitivity to individual markets, customers, and cultures. It is evident in examining existing global companies that the need for some managers with transnational perspective rises as complexity increases. These companies put into place international management teams of 50 to 150 people who become responsible for managing the international global enterprise and no longer fit the out-and-back model. These employees fall into the global category—thus the inception of an international compensation strategy in companies.

DEVELOPING THE TEAM OF INTERNATIONAL MANAGERS

Truly global enterprises have fundamentally more complex management and organization processes than multinational and domestic companies. They must deal with a process organization including networks, alliances, and multicentered organizations. More importantly, they must deal with multicultural teams equipped to manage across national borders and across cultures. This results in a much less hierarchical structure, a multicentered networked organization, multiculturalism as a value of the organization, and a process orientation to conducting business.

In a truly global company, top management faces unique sets of tasks in developing the business and ultimately the compensation strategies. Top management must establish the overarching principles that will govern the enterprise and the compensation system. Management must establish the competitive positioning of the enterprise in both local and multiple local compensation markets and a growing international compensation market. They must also establish the basic structural definition of pay system design components and strategy that define each of the basic components. Management must deal with job structure relationships that are both national and transnational. For example, they frequently have to deal with positions that have to transact business with each other in separate national locations, on different national pay lines; yet the incumbents in those positions are doing essentially the same job and dealing with each other on a day-to-day basis. This interchange makes it extremely difficult to maintain separate pay strategies. Managers in a global enterprise must then balance national performance management strategy traditions against integrated global businesses that have performance objectives and business plans and transcend national boundaries. Finally, they must define the degree to which the business is international and does not pay attention to national perspectives and the degree to which the business is local and must be linked to regional pay systems.

Managers need to answer questions like the following:

- Will there be an international management team paid by a common compensation system?

- Will the pay terms and conditions for that team be the same, or similar with some differences, or be completely different?

- How essential is this team, and how leveraged are the team members in accomplishing the international business strategy?

- What multiple compensation systems must be adopted to ensure that team members are effectively aligned with the business strategy?

- Will the international management team be primarily composed of home country nationals, or will the team be an international mix of third-country nationals?

- What will be the organization and power relationship between the headquarters or parent country and other overseas locations?

- What will be the fundamental organizational and management process of the enterprise?

- How will the various centers relate to each other?

CULTURE AND COMPENSATION

For the global enterprise, dealing with differences in culture is an important consideration impacting on the design of compensation strategy. There are five cultural parameters that differ among the world's nations that have significant impact on doing business. The first, and most important, is language; second is context; third is the utilization of time; fourth is the manner in which equality and/or power are integrated into cultural processes and interrelationships; and last is the manner in which information flows. A fundamental level of understanding of the local cultures in which the enterprise operates and the subtle deviations in the key parameters form the basis for not only designing compensation practices but all human relations processes. These cultural components determine the way motivation, personal behavior, ethics, and other aspects of human activity play themselves out in the company.

It is often said that compensation is the most direct human relations lever, and it can be a blunt instrument. However, the role compensation plays in dissimilar cultures can be significantly disparate. A global enterprise must understand cultural compensation implications before designing the pay package. The compensation policy must offend no one, work within the traditions of each culture, and ultimately motivate workers to accomplish business objectives.

Probably the most difficult task for a global enterprise is to assure that key business messages get translated into the transcultural context. Misunderstandings, no matter how minor, will tend to have repercussions in meeting business objectives. Because compensation or reward is a particularly important element in any human resources program, it is important to understand the range of differences across cultures in the ways in which these programs are viewed. For example, an individualist culture can be contrasted with a consensus or collective culture. In the individualist culture, individual rewards, which distinguish personal accomplishments in comparison to others, are highly valued. This is fairly typical of reward systems in the American culture. In many Asian cultures, in contrast, consensus building and shared accomplishment of objectives is an integral part of the culture, and differential individual rewards would be perceived as disruptive and inconsistent with the way work is accomplished. Another example comparing western to eastern cultures is the ratio of the highest-paid individuals in an enterprise to the lowest-paid individuals. In a consensus culture, the ratio between the highest-paid and the lowest-paid individuals tends to be much lower than in individualist societies where few people carry both the burden and the ultimate reward for the accomplishments of the enterprise.

COMPENSATION AND COMMUNICATION

Communication in compensation is critical, and communication varies greatly across cultures. In many cultures, messages are communicated subtlety by means of context or unstated assumptions about the way things are done. Compensation management frequently requires direct, clear, black-and-white communication of requirements and accomplishments and their link to reward. The communications process in each national culture will have to be adapted to the cultural traditions, norms, and patterns while ultimately delivering the same message. There are many roads to the same end in a global company.

THE ROLE OF HUMAN CAPITAL IN DRIVING BUSINESS OBJECTIVES

In order to design the compensation strategy for a complex international enterprise, it is necessary to understand the role human capital plays in driving the businesses. An examination of the relative workforce strategies in each of the various businesses in the enterprise must be the first step. This requires an overview of the key roles individuals play in leveraging and driving the business. These roles can be separated into four categories:

1. Cutting edge
2. Critical
3. Core
4. Complimentary

Cutting-edge people are those whose skills are the source of tomorrow's competitive advantage; these people are the resources leading the enterprise forward. *Critical people* are the price of admission for today's competitive advantage. *Core workers* are those people with skills common to most companies in a particular business. *Complimentary individuals* provide supporting services that enable the company to do business with itself; complimentary jobs are prime candidates for outsourcing. The four components serve as raw material for the design of the compensation strategy based on an individual employee's strategic contribution to the business. In a global company, the four components must be examined in an international dimension across national boundaries forming essentially a three-dimensional matrix. Defining the four roles based on company requirements allows basic decisions about market pricing and positioning of the compensation structure. If core business skills, for example, are in scarce supply internationally, a company must compete in an international market and compete with a global rather than a local national pay line. If skills are in short supply in some countries and not in others, then different pay strategies are utilized because of the importing or exporting of vital human resources.

An understanding of the profiles of the employees within the four categories identifies the pay strategies that need to be adopted for the global enterprise. For example, complimentary or supporting resources may be viewed as commodities that can be hired or outsourced at the local level with pay lines set at the median for the local market. Core skills may be paid at a median industry pay line. Critical and cutting-edge skills, depending on their scarcity and their distribution on a global basis relative to the required business distribution, may be paid at premium levels in order to leverage both the current and future competitiveness of the enterprise.

OTHER FACTORS IN DEVELOPING GLOBAL PAY SYSTEMS

Emerging technology may also play a role in developing global pay systems. Technology allows resources to be increasingly more mobile and knowledgeable. Technology makes information more widely available to the workforce and may also impact on the knowledge of key resources about their vital role and scarcity in the job market. These factors may drive aggressive decision making when setting pay practices.

Cultural considerations must come into play even when pondering the mix between variable and fixed pay in designing a compensation policy. Some cultures, like the German culture, have a tradition of very high fixed pay and relatively small variable pay. This is in contrast with American culture, which has increasingly larger proportions of variable pay.

The overriding truism when designing a compensation strategy in a global firm is that one size doesn't fit all. The design of a compensation package begins with establishing a strategic framework and then adapting that strategy to the multiple cultures in which the enterprise operates so that business objectives can be reached within the cultural norms.

EXPATRIATE COMPENSATION PRACTICES

Geoffrey W. Latta, Executive Vice President

Organization Resources Counselors, Inc.

ORGANIZATIONS THAT SEND EMPLOYEES TO ANOTHER COUNTRY TO WORK face a set of decisions about how such employees should be paid. The principles that drive compensation design within one country break down in the face of the challenge of dealing with two labor markets at the same time. As a result, compensation systems for "expatriates," as such employees are often known, are complex and frequently expensive.

There might appear to be some simple answers to paying an expatriate. For those not familiar with the area, the first response might be to place the expatriate in the salary structure of the country in which the employee is working. Unfortunately, for the typical expatriate, working on a fixed-duration assignment of 2 to 5 years, this often does not work. An alternative response might be to simply pay the employee the same salary for the job as would have been paid at home and to make no other adjustments. Once again, this usually does not work.

Because neither of the obvious approaches is satisfactory, companies have over the years devised more sophisticated pay systems. While no two organizations pay their expatriates in exactly the same way, a pattern has emerged that allows us to make reasonable generalizations about expatriate pay practices.

This chapter will summarize the key issues that create the complexity in expatriate pay systems; it will explain the major pay options; and it will seek to outline the underlying factors that should be considered in choosing between alternative approaches.

WHAT ARE THE ISSUES?

The key factors that drive pay practices are the following:

1. Gross and net compensation levels for the same job vary between countries.

2. The purchasing power of any nominal salary varies from one country to another.

3. Comparisons of home and assignment location income will be affected by changes in exchange rates between the two locations.

4. Most expatriates are taken temporarily from one housing market and placed in another in conditions where they are not able to compete evenly with local nationals.

5. Many employees (and their families) may not welcome the disruption to family and social life caused by an international move.

6. Some locations to which employees may be transferred are not necessarily considered intrinsically desirable places to live.

7. There are difficulties in addressing benefit provisions, especially in relation to pensions and social security, across two countries.

8. There is a need to provide for certain special circumstances such as education for the children of expatriates and the need to assist the employee in returning to the home location periodically during the expatriate assignment.

The impact of these factors will be explained below in relation to the individual components of package design.

THE COMPENSATION OPTIONS: SALARY BASE

The key decision in compensation design is the designation of base salary. As we will see, this decision impacts most other areas of the package in a very direct manner. The choices are to retain the employee in the home country salary structure; to put the employee into the assignment country structure; or to adopt some other salary base.

Option 1. Home Salary

Most organizations retain employees in the home salary structure, especially when they are on assignment for a limited duration and they are expected to return to their home country. Retention in the home structure makes it easier to bring the employee back at the end of the assignment as they have never lost contact, in practical or psychological terms, with their home salary.

Most organizations also wish to retain employees in home benefit programs, and the home salary structure retention facilitates this.

The major drawback of retaining employees in their home structure is that by definition the expatriate will have a different income from comparable local peers and from expatriates of other nationalities working in the assignment location. A company with expatriates mostly of one nationality may not worry about this latter issue. Even when the nationality mix is greater, the degree of concern about comparability with local nationals varies by organization.

Retaining employees in the home country structure requires the company to review the base salary level while the employees are on assignment as they would have done at home. Failure to do this will mean that the employees are suffering a disadvantage from holding an international position.

Option 2. Host Salary

Fitting employees into the host salary structure is administratively straightforward and addresses the issue of comparability with other employees. The prime drawback is that in many cases, the attraction for the employees to accept the assignment disappears. A move from the United States to Nigeria on local pay is unlikely to attract employees to relocate; but a move to the United Kingdom or Australia will lead to an American's taking a pay cut in nominal pay terms. If the pay cut is accompanied by an equal reduction in living costs, it might be acceptable, but this is not necessarily the case. A move from the United States to the United Kingdom on a British salary represents a clear reduction in purchasing power. Even a move to a country with higher nominal gross salaries such as a move from the United States to Switzerland may turn out to be less attractive when the higher cost of living in Switzerland is taken into account. Thus, integration into the local salary structure works only where it involves an increase in real purchasing power. Thus a move from a low-wage country to a high-wage developed country is feasible on this basis, and many companies pay people a host salary in the case of transfers from Thailand or India, for example, to the United States. Even then, some companies keep a link to the home salary because it provides a base for benefits and it helps ensure that the employee keeps in mind the salary level to which he or she will return.

This problem of different purchasing power can be overcome if the employee is placed in the assignment salary structure but paid other allowances to compensate for the higher costs. However, this approach can become complex as it involves tracking the relationship of the home pay to the assignment pay level, and it undermines the value of equalizing expatriates with local employees.

Other Options

Some companies opt for an approach that is neither pure home nor pure host. A rare approach is to create an entirely separate pay scale for international employees. A few companies use this approach but usually only for a small group of their employees who are highly mobile and no longer have any real link to any home country. This approach is much more common in organizations like the United Nations in which almost all professional employees work outside their "home" country.

Another approach that is more common is to put all employees who are being expatriated on to the salary structure of one country, usually the country in which the company is headquartered. This approach is used by some companies that have few expatriates other than those from the headquarters country. It is also used, however, by some companies with a large multinational workforce to overcome the problem of expatriates of multiple nationalities having different compensation packages in the same assignment location.

Another variant, popular particularly in Europe, is the so-called higher-of-home-or-host approach. In this model, the company calculates a pay package based on home pay plus allowances (see below) and compares the net pay to the employee with the net of the peer position in the assignment location. The higher of the two will be paid. The precise calculation methods used vary considerably, but the perceived advantage is that there is the potential for integration in the host pay structure but with a guarantee that the employee will not suffer a reduction in living standards. In many companies using this approach, the majority of employees are actually paid based on the home calculation, and so the advantage of integration into the host pay structure may be questioned.

COMPENSATION OPTIONS: COST ALLOWANCES

In conjunction with retaining the expatriate in the home country salary structure, most companies pay the employee a set of allowances designed to deal with additional costs that the employee could incur. The most significant are in relation to goods and services (food, clothing, recreation, etc.), housing, personal taxation, and education.

Goods and Services

Where the costs of purchasing a similar range of goods and services in the assignment location are higher than costs at home, most organizations pay a cost-of-living or a goods-and-services allowance, usually based on information from external consultants. There are numerous ways of comparing such costs, which need to be monitored regularly to reflect the impact of the exchange rate between the two locations. Typically the external consultant provides an index that compares costs in the two locations, where 100 indicates that costs are the same in the two locations. The allowance is usually paid at each pay period. The purpose of the allowance may be viewed in two slightly different ways. It may be seen as a protection against higher costs, or it may be seen as part of an attempt to ensure that the employee neither gains or loses in living standards from accepting the assignment other than from changes in direct pay. The latter philosophy may be termed a *cost equalization approach*. The distinction is not just a semantic issue. A company that sees the payment in *protection terms* will not take any action when the employee moves to a country with lower costs; a company adopting the equalization approach may do so. Those who adopt the equalization approach argue that to do so avoids employees' receiving arbitrary variations in real living standards based on the location to which they are sent. Thus an employee sent to a much lower cost country will receive an additional windfall unrelated to the amount of money needed in the location; another employee sent to a higher-cost location is protected but does not enjoy any such windfall. If costs suddenly rise in the low-cost location, the employee may perceive a decline in living standards when, in reality, there has merely been a reduction in the windfall gain. Because of this, some companies that do not reduce the employee's pay in lower-costs locations choose to show the employee the windfall gain to avoid complaints if costs rise.

It should be emphasized that the approach above should be used in conjunction with retention in the home salary structure. If the employee is placed in the host structure, a comparison back to home costs is inappropriate because the local salary may reflect local living costs. If a higher (or lower) salary exactly reflects living-cost differences, no allowance would be needed. Unfortunately, the salary levels of two countries rarely precisely reflect differential living costs, hence one of the problems of a host pay approach; most commonly the cost differences are partially reflected and so a payment of a goods-and-services allowance in addition to host salary would still be overly generous.

Where a company uses a headquarters approach, the cost comparison should still be made but between the headquarters country and the assignment location. The result will be that the salary reflects the headquarters living costs, not the actual home location of the employee. It also ensures that expatriates of different nationalities receive the same pay, which is often the underlying objective of those using a headquarters approach.

Housing

Housing is affected by two considerations. Most companies prefer their expatriates to rent rather than purchase housing in the assignment location. This is felt to be administratively simpler, to protect against possible losses if the host housing market falls, and to provide greater flexibility in disposing of the home on return.

Second, consideration needs to be paid to the employee's house in the home country. The most common approach is that the company encourages the employee to retain the home if the expectation is that the employee will return to the same location. In this case the company usually provides assistance in renting out and managing the property. In the assignment location the company will assist the employee in finding a home and will pay the rental cost either directly to the landlord or as an allowance to the employee. Some companies pay an allowance equal to the actual rent of the property; others pay a defined amount but leave the employee to select the property and to keep any amount by which the housing allowance falls below the actual rent or to pay out of their own pocket any amount by which the rent exceeds the allowance. Whatever approach is adopted, companies need to decide how much they are willing to pay for the employee's housing. Many companies use external consultants to set housing allowance levels, which often vary by family size and by job level.

Most U.S. companies take a "housing deduction" to reflect the savings that the employee is realizing in home housing costs. European companies are less likely to take this deduction, largely because they do not assume that the employee will rent out the home property while on assignment. Once again, the philosophy of most companies is to equalize costs for the employee, and whether this is done by requiring a home deduction or not depends on the circumstances of the employee. Some companies will allow the policy to vary depending on individual circumstances; others choose a policy that reflects the majority of their expatriate population.

The payment of host housing costs is a policy that most companies adopt regardless of whether they use home, host, or headquarters pay as a base. Again, in one sense this undermines the logic of host pay systems because it represents a clear distinction between expatriates and local nationals. However, it is a pragmatic reflection of the need to help employees find and pay for housing when on limited-term assignments.

Personal Taxation

In the area of taxes, the equalization philosophy is firmly entrenched. Most companies use an external accounting firm to prepare expatriate tax returns. This is particularly important for U.S. citizens and U.S. permanent residents as they are taxed by the United States even when they are not resident. For most other nationalities, tax liability depends not on citizenship but on residence and the source of income. Thus, a British expatriate working in the United States is not taxed by the United Kingdom on U.S. earnings but only on residual British earnings (interest, etc.) as long as the expatriate is not in the United Kingdom for more than a certain number of days in the year. Despite this, the principle of tax equalization is usually followed for other nationalities although practice is more varied than for Americans.

For the employee, the normal approach is that the company will pay all personal taxes that arises from employment income; increasingly companies also pay all or a portion of the liability related to nonemployment income. In return, the employee pays the company through regular payroll deductions, an amount usually termed a "hypothetical tax deduction," equivalent to what would have been paid in taxes at home.

Education

For expatriates with children, an international assignment is disruptive. Where the language of the assignment country is different from the home country, most expatriates want to send their children to a school in the assignment location that provides teaching in the home country language. Such schools nearly always charge tuition and fees, and companies will generally meet tuition costs. For U.S. expatriates, this usually means the "American" schools that exist in many cities around the world; similar schools exist for French, Japanese, and British children although in smaller numbers. If no school is available in the assignment location, most companies will pay for boarding schools in the home country or in a third location. The cost impact for companies is therefore quite high if they send expatriates with children on assignment. This has led some companies to seek to persuade expatriates to send children to local schools if the language of the assignment and home countries are the same. This is sometimes acceptable for younger children, but differences in the curricula and in university entrance requirements make this difficult for older children.

As with housing, most companies pay for education, regardless of the salary base for expatriates.

COMPENSATION OPTIONS: INCENTIVES

In addition to allowances to reflect specific costs, most companies pay direct cash incentives to expatriates that are unrelated to cost. Many companies make a payment to all expatriates going on assignment. Historically the most common form of payment has been a *foreign-service premium,* usually expressed as a percentage of base pay. The most common formula has been 15 percent of pay, sometimes capped at an upper level, paid along with each regular paycheck. An alternative approach consists of providing a lump-sum incentive payment, usually termed a *mobility premium,* paid in two amounts at the beginning and end of the assignment. This has grown in popularity and is seen to have three main advantages over the traditional approach:

1. It does not become buried in the ongoing salary, a situation that leads expatriates to forget why the payment is being paid and to perceive a pay cut when it is removed at the end of the assignment.

2.   It associates the payment with the actual process of moving from one country to another. This is particularly important if the employee moves from one assignment country directly to another one. If the premium is ongoing, the employee sees no change in pay despite the need to move; if a lump sum is paid, it is triggered by the move.

3.   The payment can be made in the home country immediately prior to assignment and in the home country immediately after return. This minimizes taxes as the payments are not taxable in the assignment country.

Not all companies feel they need to pay a premium, but it remains the majority practice. Companies using a host pay approach are unlikely to pay a premium.

In addition, most companies feel they need to pay an incentive if the employee is moving to a "difficult" location. Such payments are often termed *hardship premiums,* although some companies see this terminology as vaguely insulting to local employees in the assignment country and may use more neutral language like a *location premium.* The payment is usually expressed as a percentage of salary varying by location; a common approach is to make payments that vary in 5 percent increments from 5 percent for slightly undesirable locations to 25 percent (or more) for very problematic locations. It is rarely paid in lump-sum form. Because the type of locations that attract a hardship premium are not those in which a host pay approach could be used, the issue of paying hardship along with host pay almost never arises.

EMPLOYEE BENEFITS

For expatriates going on assignment for a limited duration, the main benefit issue that companies face is in relation to both company and state pensions. Most companies sending employees for limited-duration assignments try to keep employees in the home country company pension plan. This is usually feasible, although it may raise administrative and tax problems. It is also usually possible to retain an employee in the home social security program; in addition, companies would like to exempt assignees from required payments to the host country system. This is usually possible for up to 5 or 6 years when the home and assignment countries have a bilateral social security agreement (often termed a *totalization agreement).* Retention in home benefit plans is clearly consistent with retention in home salary structures, but not with host pay approaches. Notwithstanding the apparent anomaly, most companies using a host approach for base pay continue to opt for a home approach to benefits.

Issues also arise with other benefit plans, particularly medical plans. The company needs to decide how to cover the employee when on assignment; this may involve a special international plan or a plan on a home or host country base.

OTHER PAYMENTS

Most expatriates receive a number of other payments as part of their compensation package. Companies incur significant expenses from payments for actual relocation costs such as shipping goods to the assignment location or storage at home as well as miscellaneous additional relocation expenses. These may be reimbursed against actual expenses, or they may be covered by a lump-sum payment.

The cost of providing home leave for the expatriate and family, usually once a year, is significant. In addition, in difficult locations, many companies pay for *rest-and-recreation* (R&R) *leaves* to a third location.

PAY DELIVERY

Companies must decide how much of the compensation package to deliver in home currency and how much in host currency. Some companies, especially smaller ones, may lack the capability to deliver pay in local currency, and so they pay entirely in home currency, leaving the employee to decide when and in what quantities to exchange home into host currency. Other companies find that there are advantages to delivering, in local currency, the amount required by the employee to buy goods and services (and housing if the company does not pay this directly). This protects the employee more readily against exchange-rate fluctuations and prevents delivering pay in constantly varying amounts. The rest of the pay package will then be delivered in home currency. This so-called *split-pay approach* is increasingly popular.

SUMMARY OF EXPATRIATE OPTIONS

From the preceding discussion, it should be clear that the most common approach to paying expatriates adopted by companies is the following:

1. To retain the employee in the home salary structure
2. To pay a cost-of-living allowance if costs in the assignment location are higher than at home
3. To pay the employee's housing costs in the assignment location, with or without a direct contribution from the expatriate
4. To use a system of tax equalization that ensures as nearly as possible that the employee pays no more and no less tax than if he or she had remained in the home country
5. To pay an incentive to the employee above base pay for accepting and remaining on the assignment
6. To pay a special additional incentive to employees transferring to designated "difficult" locations
7. To pay for private education in the assignment location for the children of expatriate employees

This combination of policies has become known in the compensation area as the *balance-sheet approach* to expatriate compensation, or in Europe as the *home build-up approach.* In recent years there has been much discussion as to whether this approach is the most appropriate, but it remains the dominant model.

The main alternative to a home approach in practice has been a headquarters approach. For all practical purposes, this makes the employee an "honorary citizen" of the headquarters country and then works in exactly the same way as a home approach. The host pay approach is a more fundamental change but some of its advantages are undermined by providing many of the elements that an expatriate employee paid under a home approach would receive.

The Underlying Variables

There are several variables that lead organizations to differing answers to the question of how to design an expatriate program. Some of these are factors that spring from the organizations' human resources strategy or from deeply entrenched cultural factors. Others have a more concrete origin. In designing your policy, you should look at all these factors and assess their impact.

Assignment Length.   Most expatriate assignments fall in the range of 2 to 5 years, and most compensation systems are predicated on the assumption of this length. If assignments are intended from the outset to be much longer, an attempt should be made to place the employee in the assignment country salary structure. Unfortunately, this does not work in situations where the local salary structure is much lower than the home, and so it is not uncommon to retain elements of the more typical shorter-term expatriate package. In addition, many organizations find that what was initially intended as a shorter assignment turns into a longer one during the course of the assignment. The employer then faces the challenge of converting the assignee from one type of compensation package to another. Many organizations have a policy provision that states that employees should be "localized" after 5 years on assignment in the same location. This involves the removal in phases or in one single step of the expatriate package. Despite the policy provision, many organizations do not actually put this into practice unless the decision to remain on assignment is clearly the wish of the employee.

A different situation arises with short assignments of under 1 year. Organizations increasingly have special policies for such assignments. A major factor is that many of these assignments take place without the whole family's relocating to the assignment location, and this simplifies or alters some of the elements of package design in areas like education and housing.

Assignment Patterns.   In many companies, the typical assignment pattern is for an employee to go out on assignment and return to the home country, perhaps going on another assignment at some future point in their career. The mainstream solutions to expatriate policy design are based on this pattern. If employees are on a sequential assignment pattern, moving from one location to another but not necessarily back to a home country, the compensation design may need to be different. Many companies pay these "global nomads" by placing them on the salary structure of the headquarters country. Others use an international pay scale. Benefits may be funded on an offshore basis as one of the major concerns for this group lies in the provision of pensions.

Type of Assignee. Some organizations have a strong philosophy that all assignees should be covered by one policy. Others distinguish among employees based on the type and/or level of job performed, on the business unit for which the employee works, or on the geographic pattern of movement. Thus some companies have one policy for management development assignments and another for technical transfers. Some distinguish between a European employee transferring within the region and one transferring out to another region. The advantages that derive from "multitier" policies are that they may help reduce overall costs by matching compensation elements to clear needs, and they may allow business units with different economic circumstances to reflect these in the level of compensation. The disadvantages are more complex administration and potential employee resentment if they are on a less generous package. Companies that have used such an approach find that it works best when there is little movement of employees from one expatriate policy to another, when the economic reasons for differences can be clearly explained, and when the categories of policy can be clearly defined. The last is a problem where policy is based on assignment type for which there may be room for differences of view about the classification of a particular assignment.

Assignment types also clearly influence the differences in policy from one organization to another. A company that sends only high-level executives may adopt a different strategy from one that sends primarily project engineers.

Industry. The industry in which an organization operates will have some impact on policy. The oil industry requires specialized expatriates to work in a variety of often remote locations; an investment bank is likely to send employees mainly to more developed locations.

Globalism. An organization employing and transferring employees who are predominantly of one nationality faces a different set of challenges from those that are transferring employees of multiple nationalities.

CONCLUSION

The dominance of the balance-sheet approach to expatriate compensation has been achieved in the face of frequent criticism that it is expensive and complex. The problem, however, is that the complexities are inherent in the process of transferring employees internationally, and no simple solution has been advanced that allows companies to attract employees to go on assignment and to pay them in a fair and cost-effective manner while there. Pay administration requires the company to track many more payments than it does for a domestic employee; moreover, such payments may be in two currencies, and some of them such as the goods-and-services allowance are subject to frequent change. Compensation professionals used to working with pay structures in a single country will find that expatriate compensation has unusual challenges. Addressing those challenges is, however, fundamental to those companies wishing to operate on a global basis.

BIBLIOGRAPHY

Chesters, Alan. 1995. "The Balance Sheet Approach: Problem or Solution?" *International Human Resources Journal*, Fall.

Harvey, Michael. 1993. "Designing a Global Compensation System." *Columbia Journal of World Business,* Winter.

Hodgetts, Richard M., and Luthans, Fred. 1993. "U.S. Multinationals' Expatriate Compensation Strategies," *Compensation and Benefits Review,* January–February.

Latta, Geoffrey W. 1995. "Innovative Ideas in International Compensation," *Benefits and Compensation International,* July/August.

Reynolds, Calvin. 1994. *Compensation Basics for North American* Expatriates. American Compensation Association, Scottsdale, AZ.

————1992. "Developing Global Strategies in Total Compensation." *ACA Journal,* Autumn.

Solomon, Charlene M. 1995. "Global Compensation: Learn the ABCs." *Personnel Journal,* July.

GLOBAL LOCAL NATIONAL COMPENSATION PRACTICES

Neil K. Coleman, Vice President

Organization Resources Counselors, Inc.

WITH THE INCREASING GLOBALIZATION OF BUSINESS, there has been a corresponding interest in the more effective management of local national employees and in rationalizing the ways in which they are compensated. *Local national employees* are defined as those who are employed within a given country and whose conditions of employment are established by the local organization. As such, a local national could be of any nationality as long as he or she were eligible to work in a given location. The conditions of employment for the local national employee typically reflect the local statutory requirements, local customs, and practices found in the marketplace. This is in contrast to the *expatriate,* who would be working with local nationals in a given location but whose compensation and conditions of employment are typically tied to a home location where he or she is expected to return at the end of the expatriate assignment. These assignments typically extend from 3 to 5 years, but long-term, or permanent, expatriate assignments typically have built-in processes to integrate individuals to the local national conditions of employment over a period of time. The other class of employee is defined as *international cadre* and typically represents those having a career path based on many global assignments. Employers of this type of employee typically create a special employment policy providing for employee compensation, benefits, and retirement that are necessary to facilitate frequent relocations.

The management and compensation of local nationals are a good deal more complicated than they are for employees with several geographical locations within a given country. In determining pay practices and levels of pay in the United States or in almost every country, there are considerable variations that relate to the size of the organization, the industry, and, for jobs below the executive level, the location. In addition to these items and as compared to the United States, country locations compensation practices differ in the following areas:

1. The type and number of specific pay elements
2. The absolute levels of pay that are related to supply and demand (and other cultural factors) and vary widely among country locations
3. The marketplace by type of employer such as global multinational companies and local indigenous companies
4. The local statutory requirements regarding pay and benefit practices
5. The hierarchy of jobs as determined by the marketplace
6. The administration of compensation that ranges from merit-based systems to progression (nonmerit) systems

As if all of the above differences were not enough, the situation is further complicated by converting local currencies to a common currency for comparative analysis. Foreign exchange rates in the global dynamic marketplace are volatile and are in a constant state of change. Such comparisons of compensation can be made only at specific times. The challenge for analysts is to view the relative compensation and try to understand the degree to which differences in compensation are due to the market or due to the impact of the foreign exchange rates.

The following section is an overview of the complexities associated with making intercountry comparisons using incentive compensation plans as a vehicle for describing the variations in pay elements and levels of compensation.

IDENTIFICATION OF THE NEED FOR LOCAL COMPENSATION DATA

Historically, most multinational companies delegated the establishment and maintenance of local pay systems to the management. Traditionally, expatriates filled the management jobs, and the workers were locals. As executives emerged, so did the interest in local pay systems. The globalization of the marketplace and the attraction of low-cost labor during the second half of the twentieth century has caused the compensation of local nationals to be a major focus. In an increasingly competitive marketplace, the costs of equipment, materials, *and* labor are all tightly controlled.

There are two specific needs that are identified with employees. The first relates to the cost of employees. This cost is reflected in the payroll, benefits, and in the overall costs of human capital. Of particular interest are the relative costs of local national employees—especially those in the areas of production or manufacturing or for occupations composed of unskilled or semiskilled workers. These relative costs are a major factor in selecting site locations as companies seek to lower production costs. It should be noted that absolute relative costs can be misleading because total costs must take into consideration issues of efficiency and productivity. At its most basic level, unit costs are a function of both payroll labor costs and productivity.

The second identified need is to consider the other factors that contribute to productivity but are not payroll items. For example, the wide range of statutory requirements that comprise pay for time not worked, termination indemnification, and the rising interest in incentive compensation are all factors that cannot be ignored in considering the compensation of local employees. These costs tend to be "hidden" or their existence is overlooked when making intercountry comparisons, and the impact of these items can be very substantial.

Finally, there is rising interest in and a need to manage the internal equity among executives and some levels of professionals on a global scale. This issue will be addressed next.

THE COMPLEXITY OF UTILIZING LOCAL COMPENSATION DATA

The complexity of comparing local compensation data is most evident in the area of incentive or bonus plan eligibility and the distribution of awards under such plans. Most companies find a need to maintain some level of consistency regarding eligibility to participate in such plans.

The current trend is to view performance in terms of the results from local and global operations and in many cases regional and product line results as well. If a job incumbent only participated in the results of a local plan, the issues of internal equity would not be great. However, internal equity comparisons arise when a broader organizational unit's results are identified.

The issue of eligibility would seem to be relatively easy to determine and maintain. In some cases it can be based on salary grade (if a global grading or job evaluation exists) or on the basis of reporting relationships. Eligibility can be based on management's discretion as well. This process is made much more complicated and difficult if a fixed salary hurdle is established since relative pay levels by country vary widely. For example, if such a hurdle were established, eligibility would be *expanded* in countries such as Germany, Switzerland, and the United States (where compensation is relatively high), whereas eligibility would be *contracted* or eliminated in India (where relative compensation is low).

Another complication is that the mix of salary and others forms of compensation vary widely among countries. For example, in comparison to total cash compensation, salaries are relatively low in the traditional Japanese pay system, whereas in Germany they are relatively high, and finally in some countries salary and total cash compensation are the same. In addition, many countries in Europe, Latin America, and Asia have practices of 13, 14, and up to 18 months of "extra" salary. Clearly, just salary comparisons would lead to misleading results since salaries may be defined as including some or all of the extra months' pay.

In an effort to make the comparisons more useable for analysis, compensation surveys conducted by Watson/Wyatt, ORC/ Mercer, and others report a basic salary and a guaranteed salary (including the extra months either required by statute or provided by local practice). Thus, the determination of an appropriate threshold salary for incentive eligibility is made more complicated. What salary is to be used as the basic? Is it to be guaranteed, or some combination of the two? Although not widely used, one could make comparisons using the total cash compensation to determine the mix of base and bonus and other payments and apply this concept on a global basis. If used on a global scale, such a practice might be at variance to the local practice in the mix, but it would remain competitive on a total cash compensation basis within the local marketplace.

The second complication of using a fixed-salary threshold as a basis for determining eligibility is in converting the salary to a single common currency. In terms of determining eligibility, currency fluctuations alone would increase or decrease the list of those eligible, thus requiring some discretion in keeping the list stable.

The larger issue is in determining how the actual level of payout can be rationalized on the basis of internal equity. Where a global grading system exists, the assignment of target incentive percentages ensures a degree of internal equity. In this case, the only potential problem is in comparing the actual amounts in a common currency. Comparisons will reveal the variations in markets. Some locations will appear very low (India) and others high (Germany) when compared to the country in which the headquarters is located.

In a majority of companies, no global grading system exists, and the determination of the payout of the annual incentive plan for local national executives becomes a frustrating process. In the case where a job grading system exists, the problem is in comparing the proposed incentive payout amounts in a common currency. Such comparisons are essential in order to determine the total amount of the funding pool as well as rationalizing individual amounts to plan participants. This process is further complicated by comparisons to former years where foreign exchange rates add a considerable distortion to the comparisons.

For nonincentive plan local national employees, there are also complexities associated with balancing the competitive nature of local compensation practices with specified or implied companywide values associated with compensation.

In summary, compensation analysts need to understand local competitive compensation practices and to also rationalize compensation values and pay philosophies within an organization to be able to balance the often conflicting nature of local national compensation.

VARIATIONS IN INDIVIDUAL PAY ELEMENTS

Any discussion of local national compensation would be incomplete without an exploration of the variety of individual pay elements that exist in the marketplace. There is no simple answer. What is the compensation for a given job? The only reasonable response is another question: What elements do you include in the definition of compensation? There are three initial ways in which compensation is commonly defined:

Compensation defined as cash compensation. This definition specifically includes wage rates, salary, cash bonuses, and incentives but excludes the value of employee benefits, special allowances, long-term incentives, deferred compensation, contributions to savings plans, distributions through profit-sharing plans, and noncash compensation such as equities (stock). In the United States this would typically include wage rates, salaries, and annual bonuses.

Compensation defined as gross compensation. This definition typically includes the payroll costs of all employee benefits and allowances as well as the total of cash compensation as defined above.

Compensation defined as net compensation. This definition is used when comparing the *net* (after-tax) calculation of compensation.

Obviously, the most meaningful comparisons identify each pay element so that like items can be compared. The difficulty is in making comparisons between different countries and in knowing what specific pay elements are typically included in the comparisons. The following example is based on employment in Mexico:

Method Used.   Both gross and net compensation comparisons.

Listing of Pay Elements: Salaried Employees

Salary (reported monthly and annual)
Number of extra months of salary

Christmas bonus (*Aguinaldo*)

Annual (reported in currency and in number of days' pay)

Profit sharing (*fundo de ahorro,* reported in currency and in number of days' pay)

Vacation bonus (reported in currency and in number of days' pay)

Transportation or car allowance (reported as a monthly allowance)

Social provision (reported as a monthly allowance)

Housing fund (*Infonavit*): Statutory requirement to individual accounts

Other benefits include costs associated with the following:

Medical insurance

Life insurance

Pension and retirement

Social security (*IMSS*) where the employer pays the *employee's* contribution

In some published surveys (e.g., Watson/Wyatt), salary data are reported as monthly salary and as guaranteed annual salary (which include all statutory requirements).

There is also considerable difference in the pay elements depending upon the class of employee. Hourly paid employees (craft or factory workers typically classified as "blue collar") have a range of additional allowances and benefits not applicable to salaried or executive employees. Again using Mexico as an example, the following pay elements are typically provided to this class of employee (however, variations exist depending upon the actual geographical location).

In addition to the cash compensation elements enumerated above, the following items are utilized in the local marketplace:

Transportation provisions

Clothing allowance

In-house meal provisions

Housing (in some locations for larger employers)

Punctuality bonus

Discounts on company products

Seniority payments

Cost-of-living (COL) allowance in some locations

Executive pay elements also vary from country to country. Frequently, they are the result of the tax policy for a given country. Such executive elements of compensation that have been identified in the global marketplace include the following:

Listing of Compensation Elements Unique to Executives in Mexico

Stock options

Long-term deferred compensation

Home entertainment allowances

Housing supplements

Low-cost or no-cost housing loans

Company-provided car and driver

Education allowances for dependents

In summary, the differences in pay elements among countries make comparison difficult. Great care should be taken in making these comparisons when different data sources are used. To the degree that annual total cash compensation can be compared, the individual differences in pay elements can be minimized. The greatest risk is in making limited comparisons between monthly salaries without regard to the total.

Current Compensation Issues for Local National Employees

Four key issues have been identified and included in this section:

1. The emergence of comprehensive global compensation philosophies
2. The changes occurring in traditional local marketplaces
3. The expected development of regionally identified markets
4. Issues of internal equity among various classifications of employees

The Emergence of Comprehensive Global Compensation Philosophies. For many years, international compensation specialists have sought to develop a consistent and comprehensive compensation philosophy that would be applicable on a global basis. Due to the complexity of the marketplace, such efforts have resulted in clear pay philosophies for expatriates and, to a much lesser degree, for senior executives. Local national employees below the executive level have largely been ignored. Typically, such comprehensive pay philosophies have been so vague, flexible, and generalized as to not be very useful in the day-to-day work of compensation professionals. It has been easier and more practical to establish a policy that encourages local compensation to be consistent with the local market practices and to ignore the inconsistencies between locations.

Traditionally, the key inhibitors to the development of comprehensive pay philosophies have fallen into two categories. First is in the definition of total compensation. As indicated earlier, intercountry comparisons are difficult, especially when one includes long-term incentives and employee benefits. Efforts have included establishing guidelines for minimum levels of employee benefits on a global basis. The benefits would include both statutory requirements as well as private coverage. In terms of stock options for executives, efforts to establish global guidelines have been difficult due to the very high level of option grants typically given in the United States and the relatively low level of grants provided in other countries where the local cultural values make large grants impractical or illegal. Another factor is the tax requirements that vary as well. They range from countries in which grants are not permitted to those in which taxation makes grants less attractive. In some locations tax liability may occur at the time of the grant or over time, but they are not deferred until the time of exercise. Obviously this complicates the development of a consistent global policy.

Global pay philosophies that relate to a narrower definition of compensation are emerging—namely, limiting them to salary and short-term bonuses or incentives. A recent example is a newly developed and implemented global compensation policy established by Unilever N.V. Their global policy establishes guidelines as to how the marketplace is to be defined, where in the marketplace compensation is to be targeted, and how the mix of base salary and forms of incentive is to be determined. Furthermore, the policy establishes an internal relationship of jobs classified into bands. The global policy encourages local adaptation of the overall principles to the local marketplace. One of the substantial benefits is the communication of highly regarded benchmark practices that might be considered by local units who wish to challenge the traditional local practices.

Changes Occurring in Traditional Local Markets. The concept that each country had a fixed and consistent culture related to compensation has been a myth widely circulated and assumed to be accurate. As more compensation data are gathered and analyzed, it is clear that variations exist within locations and that the most traditional cultures are changing. An example is Japan, which has had a long history of unique pay values. These traditional values relate to the high correlation between compensation and age, pay related more to the person than to a specific job, and the concept of variable pay related to individual performance. All these concepts are changing as a result of considerable experimentation by the very large Japanese trading companies.

Many multinational firms are finding that they can be innovative in local markets in a way that is nontraditional but that makes good business sense and is acceptable to local employees. Much of the data being generated on this subject is anecdotal, but it appears that best practices in compensation (especially the concept of variable pay) is being considered in locations where such practices were not considered a few years ago.

The emerging concept is that traditional local practices can be changed and that organizations need not be locked into them if alternative creative initiatives make good business sense. In most local markets there is more room for creativity than was previously believed to be the case.

The key question is whether a basic compensation approach might become more universally acceptable than it has been in the past. Clearly, many elements of the systems and innovations developed in the United States are being adapted in many locations.

The Development of Regionally Identified Markets. Over the past decade, many analysts have believed that a single compensation market would begin to emerge in Europe. It has been hoped that the concept of supply and demand would create a single market in terms of pay levels as trade barriers have declined and the workers have been able to cross country borders. This has not occurred and appears to be inhibited by two major factors. First is the difference in tax policies among country locations that impact the level of pay and the way in which pay is delivered. The second has been the differences in currencies, which make comparisons difficult. The introduction of the EURO will make comparison easier, but not all countries in Europe will be included. This consolidation is likely to take a long time, and there are many factors that impact regionalization. In addition to tax policies, the design of and benefit levels associated with social security systems are also a factor.

Interest in the development of Asian regional compensation polices has been a topic of discussion, but the variations among countries are even wider than they are in Europe. Although the desire for regional offices in the area is to develop such policies to facilitate regional relocations, to date the common ground for such policies is not apparent.

Internal Equity among All Classifications of Employees. The different levels of pay and conditions of employment among expatriates, international cadre, and local nationals residing in a single country location have been a constant concern in terms of internal equity. The differences in practices have been rationalized in terms of the different markets to which each group has been compared. Each classification had a policy designed to attract and retain the necessary talent based on business need. Although conceptually consistent, the perception has been that some classifications are treated preferentially. This is further complicated with expatriates who remain for long periods of time and expatriates who have home countries in high- and low-cost living countries. The appearance is that the expatriates and international cadre live better and have a higher level of purchasing power than do the locals.

Some approaches to minimize the inequities relate to housing where a common standard of housing for a given location is targeted for all employees and policies are designed to permit access to a similar housing market. A tougher issue is to seek to equalize the perceived level of discretionary spending by the individuals involved. Traditionally, compensation professionals have avoided any such involvement.

Differences in conditions of employment become more apparent and less acceptable with the organizational principles of teamwork, employee involvement, and shared responsibilities. The longer-term strategy for many companies is to continually reduce the number of expatriates and to limit the time of the assignment. In addition, there is an increasing interest in the processes needed to "localize" expatriates as quickly as possible in order to minimize inequities with the local employees.

No single approach appears to be emerging, but to the degree possible, more expatriates are being asked to accept local practices in areas not directly related to salary. Where practical, expatriates are put into the local host pay system in order to minimize internal inequities.

Anticipated Trends for Local National Compensation in the Future.   There is no single trend that will impact all local national locations; each location is subject to pressures unique to its history and culture. However, there appear to be some power drivers of change that can be recognized. They are summarized as follows:

1. The concept of meritocracy, and specifically the vehicle of variable pay (variable in terms of the relationship of pay to business success), is widely accepted in market-driven economies. In some locations it may be in the form of statutory profit sharing, while in others it will follow the U.S and European models of short- and long-term incentives. There is likely to be a corresponding decrease in pay systems that are related to tying pay to age, seniority, gender, and other nonperformance-related criteria.

2. Traditional systems of compensation, which have been unique to a particular country's set of values, is likely to encounter a broadening variety of nontraditional initiatives. This will be led primarily by multinational firms but will provide a broader range of acceptable pay systems than has been the case in the past.

3. Employee retirement delivery vehicles will shift gradually. Both social security and private plans will continue to move toward defined contribution plans rather than defined benefit plans.

4. The demands for market compensation data for local nationals will create additional and improved survey designs, and there will be an increased level of participation. The survey technology will make surveys easier to complete, and they will be available more quickly as all-electronic surveys become the preferred vehicle.

SOURCES OF COMPENSATION SURVEY DATA

There is not a single source of data for local national compensation that covers all country locations. The quality and validity of market data vary widely, and care must be taken in assessing individual market data. The availability of data falls into three broad categories:

Published data that can be obtained with or without cost

Annual or ongoing custom survey data available only to survey participants

Custom surveys conducted at a sponsor's request

The following is a listing of the most widely used data sources.

Published Data

> Watson/Wyatt, *Global 50 Remuneration Planning Report*
> Watson/Wyatt, local reports on various countries
> William M. Mercer, *International Benefit Guidelines*

Custom Reports

> MCS International Study (Management Compensation Services, affiliated with Hewitt Associates)
> Hay Associates, local reports on various countries
> William M. Mercer, local reports on various countries
> Towers Perrin, local reports on various countries
> The European Remuneration Network, reports on nine European countries
> Organization Resources Counselors, Inc., *Latin America Salary Survey, Eastern Europe Remuneration Survey,* and *Global Salary Increase Survey*
> Buck Consultants, Inc., local reports on various countries
> AON Consulting, local reports on various countries
> U.S. Chambers of Commerce in various country locations
> The U.S. State Department, Surveys of U.S. embassy locations

The above listing is primarily focused on gathering data from multinational companies. This reflects a bimodal market that exists in most countries. The "local" local market, which is composed of organizations that operate only within the country location, are typically smaller and represent a lower-paid market than exists for the larger multinational firms. Care should be taken to ensure that the appropriate market has been identified and that the survey data are appropriate.

In many countries the market data show a fairly wide distribution frequently without a strong central tendency in the data. This is a common situation in locations that are unstable from a compensation perspective or are experiencing high rates of inflation. Examples include Russia, China (PRC), Brazil, Venezuela, Turkey, and Indonesia. The effective data of the survey data is critically important and must be carefully "aged" to approximate current levels of compensation where the inflation rate is high.

Consulting Services Related to Local National Job Pricing. All of the above consulting organizations offer job-pricing services. These consultants can provide clients with compensation, benefits, and pay-related policies and practices for a number of country locations using various survey sources. Typically, these services use public and custom-designed surveys for the purposes of job pricing. They will also conduct specialized surveys when requested. Compensation consultants who offer job-pricing services typically have access to many local consulting organizations in various countries that conduct specialized data gathering activities.

Index

About the Editors

Lance A. Berger is CEO of Lance A. Berger & Associates, Ltd., a management consulting firm specializing in compensation and change management. A former general partner for the largest compensation practice worldwide at the Hay Group, he wrote and edited (with Milton Rock) *The Compensation Handbook, Third Edition*. He also wrote *The Change Management Handbook: A Road Map to Corporate Transformation* and *Deengineering the Corporation: Leading Growth from Within*. He has been a featured speaker at the United Nations, The Conference Board, American Management Association, and the American Compensation Association.

Dorothy R. Berger is managing director of Haverford Business Press, a firm specializing in the development of business publications. She edited *The Change Management Handbook*, *Deengineering the Corporation*, and is the editor for *The Change Newsletter*.